ICD-10-CM AND ICD-10-PCS
Coding Handbook

ICD-10-CM AND ICD-10-PCS
Coding Handbook
with Answers

2012 Revised Edition

NELLY LEON-CHISEN, RHIA

CENTRAL OFFICE ON ICD-10-CM AND ICD-10-PCS
OF THE
AMERICAN HOSPITAL ASSOCIATION

HEALTH FORUM, INC.
An American Hospital Association Company
Chicago

At press time, additional guideline and code changes were anticipated for 2012 implementation.

AHA and American Hospital Association are service marks of the American Hospital Association used under license by Health Forum, Inc.

Printed in the United States of America—08/11

PROJECT MANAGEMENT by Joyce Dunne
INTERIOR DESIGN AND TYPOGRAPHY by Fine Print, Ltd.
COVER DESIGN by Cheri Kusek
ILLUSTRATIONS new to this edition by Christoph Blumrich

ISBN: 978-1-55648-372-1
Item Number: 148050

To my husband, Penku (Jorge) Chisen,
who supported and encouraged me
with his patience and understanding
throughout the long and arduous months
it took to complete this handbook

Contents

FORMAT AND CONVENTIONS AND CURRENT CODING PRACTICES FOR ICD-10-CM AND ICD-10-PCS

CODING OF SIGNS AND SYMPTOMS

CODING OF INFECTIOUS AND PARASITIC DISEASES, ENDOCRINE DISEASES AND METABOLIC DISORDERS, AND MENTAL DISORDERS

CODING OF DISEASES OF THE BLOOD AND BLOOD-FORMING ORGANS, CERTAIN DISORDERS INVOLVING THE IMMUNE MECHANISM, AND DISEASES OF THE NERVOUS SYSTEM

CODING OF DISEASES OF THE RESPIRATORY, DIGESTIVE, AND GENITOURINARY SYSTEMS

CODING OF DISEASES OF THE SKIN AND DISEASES OF THE MUSCULOSKELETAL SYSTEM

CODING OF PREGNANCY AND CHILDBIRTH COMPLICATIONS, ABORTION, CONGENITAL ANOMALIES, AND PERINATAL CONDITIONS

CODING OF CIRCULATORY SYSTEM DISEASES AND NEOPLASTIC DISEASES

CODING OF INJURIES, BURNS, POISONING, AND COMPLICATIONS OF CARE

List of Figures and Tables

About the Author and Contributors

Nelly Leon-Chisen, RHIA, is the director of coding and classification at the American Hospital Association (AHA), where she heads the Central Office on ICD-9-CM and the Central Office on HCPCS. She represents the AHA as one of the cooperating parties responsible for the development of *AHA Coding Clinic® for ICD-9-CM* and the *ICD-9-CM Official Guidelines for Coding and Reporting.*

Ms. Leon-Chisen's ICD-10 activities include representing the AHA in the development of the *ICD-10-CM Official Guidelines for Coding and Reporting* and the *ICD-10-PCS Official Coding Guidelines,* membership in the ICD-10-PCS Technical Advisory Panel, past co-chair of the Workgroup for Electronic Data Interchange (WEDI) ICD-10 Implementation Workgroup, and numerous testimonies on ICD-10-CM and ICD-10-PCS before the ICD-9-CM Coordination and Maintenance Committee and the National Committee on Vital and Health Statistics. She was also the AHA lead project manager on the joint American Hospital Association–American Health Information Management Association (AHIMA) ICD-10-CM Field Study. She is an AHIMA-certified ICD-10 Trainer.

Ms. Leon-Chisen has lectured on ICD-9-CM, ICD-10, and POA coding, data quality, and DRGs throughout the United States, Europe, and Latin America. She is also a speaker for the popular *AHA Coding Clinic®* audioseminar series. She has broad HIM experience in hospital inpatient and outpatient management, consulting, and teaching. She has been an instructor in the HIM and Health Information Technology Programs for the University of Illinois and Truman Community College, both in Chicago. She is a past president of the Chicago Area Health Information Management Association and the recipient of its Distinguished Member Award. She is the recipient of the Professional Achievement Award from the Illinois Health Information Management Association. She is a member of the Advisory Board of the Health Information Technology Program of DeVry University in Chicago.

The Central Office on ICD-9-CM was created through a written Memorandum of Understanding between the AHA and the National Center for Health Statistics in 1963 to do the following:

- Serve as the U.S. clearinghouse for issues related to the use of ICD-9-CM
- Work with the National Center for Health Statistics and the Centers for Medicare & Medicaid Services to maintain the integrity of the classification system
- Recommend revisions and modifications to the current and future revisions of the ICD
- Develop educational material and programs on ICD-9-CM

The Central Office on ICD-9-CM is the publisher of the *AHA Coding Clinic® for ICD-9-CM.* In addition, the Central Office provides expert advice by serving as the clearinghouse for the dissemination of ICD-9-CM information. The Central Office intends to continue this long-standing tradition with ICD-10-CM and ICD-10-PCS.

Acknowledgments

Nelly Leon-Chisen gratefully acknowledges the invaluable contributions of Anita Rapier, Gretchen Young-Charles, and Denene M. Harper, members of the AHA Central Office on ICD-9-CM, who assisted in the revision and review of the manuscript for the handbook and the case summary exercises.

Anita Rapier, RHIT, CCS, is a senior coding consultant with the AHA Central Office on ICD-9-CM. She is also the managing editor of *AHA Coding Clinic® for ICD-9-CM,* for which she is responsible for developing educational material. She has more than 25 years of experience in health information management and has held several positions in HIM, including education, quality, compliance, hospital-based outpatient and acute care, and long-term care. Ms. Rapier has presented numerous educational seminars and has authored articles on coding and compliance. She is also a speaker for the popular *AHA Coding Clinic®* audioseminar series and an AHIMA-certified ICD-10 Trainer.

Gretchen Young-Charles, RHIA, is a senior coding consultant at the AHA Central Office on ICD-9-CM. In this role, she develops educational articles on official coding advice for publication in *AHA Coding Clinic® for ICD-9-CM.* She also served as the secretary to the AHA's Rehabilitation Coding Workgroup. Ms. Young-Charles has more than 20 years of experience in the HIM field. She has worked in numerous HIM roles, including education, quality, hospital-based outpatient and acute care, and rehabilitation. She also spent a number of years with the Peer Review Organization for the state of Illinois. She is also a speaker for the popular *AHA Coding Clinic®* audioseminar series and an AHIMA-certified ICD-10 Trainer.

Denene M. Harper, RHIA, is a senior coding consultant at the AHA Central Office on ICD-9-CM. She is responsible for writing articles on official coding advice for publication in *AHA Coding Clinic® for ICD-9-CM.* Ms. Harper has more than 20 years of experience in the HIM field, including hospital-based outpatient and acute care, utilization review, and quality improvement. She is also an AHIMA-certified ICD-10 Trainer.

In addition, Nelly Leon-Chisen gratefully acknowledges the significant contributions of Janatha Ashton, MS, RHIA, who authored the original case summary exercises in appendix B, and Therese (Teri) Jorwic, who revised those exercises and converted them to ICD-10.

Therese (Teri) Jorwic, MPH, RHIA, CCS, CCS-P, FAHIMA, is an assistant professor in Health Information Management at the University of Illinois at Chicago. She presents numerous workshops and develops educational material for in-class and online courses on ICD-10-CM/PCS, ICD-9-CM, and HCPCS/CPT coding as well as on reimbursement systems for hospitals, physicians, and other health care providers. She also presents workshops for associations and serves as External Faculty for the AHIMA ICD-10 Academy programs.

Thanks are due to Richard Hill, AHA Press editor, who read the author's drafts and helped me to say in plain English what I wanted to say, even without being a coding professional himself.

A sincere thanks to the representatives of the Cooperating Parties: Donna Pickett, RHIA, MPH; Pat Brooks, RHIA; and Sue Bowman, RHIA, CCS—whose collaboration and friendship have made *Coding Clinic* advice and the Official Coding Guidelines a reality. The author looks forward to continuing our collaboration as we implement ICD-10-CM and ICD-10-PCS.

Thanks are also in order to 3M for its generous permission for the author and Central Office staff to use 3M's ICD-10 Translation Tool. This tool enhanced our understanding of the implications of the code set change.

Finally, Nelly Leon-Chisen acknowledges the tradition of excellence in coding education established by Faye Brown through the *ICD-9-CM Coding Handbook.* Ms. Brown's work served as the foundation on which this handbook was built. The author humbly hopes this handbook can continue educating generations of coders as the field implements ICD-10-CM and ICD-10-PCS.

How to Use This Handbook

As with the ICD-9-CM handbooks, this ICD-10 edition is designed as a versatile resource:

- Textbook for academic programs in health information technology and administration
- Text for in-service training programs
- Self-instructional guide for individuals who would like to learn coding or refresh their skills outside a formal program
- Reference tool for general use in the workplace

The general and basic areas of information covered in chapters 1 through 11 are designed to meet the requirements of various basic courses on the use of ICD-10-CM and ICD-10-PCS. They may also be used as a foundation for moving on to the study of individual chapters of ICD-10-CM and ICD-10-PCS. Chapters 12 through 33 of the handbook include advanced material for both continuing education students and professionals in the field.

This handbook is designed to be used in conjunction with the ICD-10-CM and ICD-10-PCS coding manuals (either in book or PDF format). The coding manuals must be consulted throughout the learning process, and the material in this text cannot be mastered without using them. The official versions are available in PDF format from the National Center for Health Statistics (ICD-10-CM) and the Centers for Medicare & Medicaid Services (ICD-10-PCS). At press time, only one publisher had made available an unofficial, printed version; more publishers are expected to make printed versions available in the near future. There may be minor variations between the way material is displayed in this handbook and the way it is displayed in printed versions.

The chapters in this handbook are not arranged in the same sequence as the chapters in ICD-10-CM or ICD-10-PCS. The first two sections of the handbook (chapters 1–13) provide discussions on the format and conventions followed in ICD-10-CM and ICD-10-PCS, as well as basic coding guidelines and introductory material on the supplementary classifications (Z codes and External cause of morbidity codes). The next eight sections (chapters 14–33) progress from the less complicated ICD-10-CM/PCS chapters to the more difficult. Faculty in academic and in-service programs can rearrange this sequence to suit their particular course outlines.

Appendix A, Reporting of the Present on Admission Indicator, contains information on the reporting of the Medicare requirement associated with the hospital inpatient reporting of all ICD-10-CM diagnosis codes.

Appendix B, Case Summary Exercises, is designed for students who have learned the basic coding principles and need additional practice applying the principles to actual cases. The exercises are geared for beginning to intermediate levels of knowledge. The case summaries are based on actual health records of both inpatients and outpatients. The patients described often have multiple conditions that may or may not relate to the current episode of care. Some exercises include several episodes of care for a patient in various settings.

Students using the handbook edition without answers will need to ask their instructors for the answers. After students have completed the exercises, they can check their answers against the instructor's edition, which lists the appropriate codes for each exercise, with the codes for the principal diagnosis and principal procedure sequenced first. Explanatory comments discuss why certain codes are appropriate and others are not and why some conditions listed in the case summaries are not coded at all. The comments also indicate how the principal diagnosis and procedure codes were designated, and which symptoms are inherent to certain conditions and so are not coded separately.

The *ICD-10-CM Official Guidelines for Coding and Reporting* and the *ICD-10-PCS Official Coding Guidelines*, referenced throughout this handbook, may be downloaded from the AHA Central Office Web site: www.ahacentraloffice.org.

To use this handbook effectively, readers should work through the coding examples provided throughout the text until they fully understand the coding principles under discussion. Readers should be able to arrive at correct code assignments by following the instructions provided and reviewing the pertinent handbook material until it is fully understood. Exercises in the body of each chapter should be completed as they come up in the discussion rather than at the end of the chapter or section. Most chapters provide a review exercise with additional material that covers the entire chapter. There is also a final review exercise toward the end of the book that offers additional coding practice. Answers to all of these exercises are provided in the edition with answers.

The handbook follows three conventions:

- In some examples, a hyphen is used to indicate that additional characters are required but cannot be assigned in the example because certain information needed for assignment of these characters is not given. This is done to emphasize concepts and specific guidelines without going too deeply into specific coding situations.

- **The underlining of codes in text examples indicates correct sequencing;** that is, the underlined code must be sequenced first in that particular combination of codes. When no code is underlined, there is no implicit reason why any of the codes in the series should be sequenced first. In actual coding, of course, other information in the health record may dictate a different sequence. This underlining convention is used in the handbook solely as a teaching device. It is not an element of the ICD-10-CM/PCS coding system.

- In the edition with answers, **the underlining of words in exercise questions indicates the appropriate term to be referenced in using the alphabetic indexes. The underlining of codes in the answer column of the exercises indicates correct code sequencing,** as it does in the examples in the main text.

Changes in Code Usage

Official coding guidelines approved by the four cooperating parties responsible for administering the ICD-10-CM and ICD-10-PCS systems in the United States (American Hospital Association, American Health Information Management Association, Centers for Medicare & Medicaid Services, and National Center for Health Statistics) are published on a yearly basis. At press time, the partial code-set freeze for ICD-10-CM/PCS had not yet been implemented, and further changes were expected for the 2012 version of the guidelines as well as for the code set.

AHA Coding Clinic® for ICD-10-CM and ICD-10-PCS will be published starting in 2013 and will provide official guidance in the use of ICD-10, as it currently does for ICD-9-CM. Further information on *AHA Coding Clinic®* may be found on the next two pages.

AHA Central Office™

An American Hospital Association Service

AHA Central Office is the official clearinghouse for information on the proper use of ICD-9-CM codes, level I HCPCS codes (CPT-4 codes) for hospital providers, and certain level II HCPCS codes for hospitals, physicians, and other health care professionals.

www.ahacentraloffice.org

Order Form

	Non-Member Price	AHA Member Price	AHIMA Member	Quantity	Extended Price
AHA Coding Clinic for ICD-9-CM	$290	$196	$250		
AHA Coding Clinic for HCPCS	$135	$105	$125		

Quantity discounts apply only to quantities shipped to ONE location.
Call 800-621-6902 for bulk pricing.

Total Amount

Payment Information

☐ **Payment Enclosed**   Send this form with a check or money order payable to:
American Hospital Association
P.O. Box 92247 • Chicago, IL 60675-2247

☐ **Please Bill Me**   Purchase Order Number_____

☐ **Credit Card Payment**

Credit Card Number _____

Credit Card Type_____ Expiration Date_____

Signature _____

Send Subscription To

Name_____

Organization_____

Department _____

Address Line 1 _____

Address Line 2 _____

City, State, Zip _____

Telephone_____

Email _____

Place Your Order Today!

Mail: American Hospital Association
P.O. Box 92247
Chicago, IL 60675-2247

Phone: 1-800-621-6902 or
1-312-893-6800

Fax: 1-312-422-4799

Online: www.ahacentraloffice.org/codingclinic

Format AND Conventions AND Current Coding Practices FOR ICD-10-CM AND ICD-10-PCS

Background of the ICD-10-CM and ICD-10-PCS Classification

CHAPTER OVERVIEW

- ICD-10-CM and ICD-10-PCS have been developed to take the place of ICD-9-CM.

- The compliance date for implementation of these two classification systems in the United States is October 1, 2013.

- The change to ICD-10 is needed for a variety of reasons, including the following:

  — The ICD-9-CM classification is limited in its ability to expand to include new technology.

  — Once a category becomes full in ICD-9-CM, several types of diagnoses or procedures have to be classified within the same code to save space.

  — Many other countries in the world have already made the change. This situation makes it difficult to compare the health data of the United States with the rest of the world.

- Implementing ICD-10-CM and ICD-10-PCS could improve quality of care and patient safety and make the reimbursement claims process run more smoothly.

- Every application and database in which diagnosis or procedure codes are captured, stored, analyzed, or reported will use the new classification system.

LEARNING OUTCOMES

After studying this chapter you should be able to:

Explain the improvements that make the ICD-10 system more efficient and useful than the ICD-9 system.

Explain why a change to ICD-10-CM and ICD-10-PCS will be beneficial.

TERMS TO KNOW

ICD-10-CM
International Classification of Diseases, Tenth Revision, Clinical Modification; consists of diagnosis codes

ICD-10-PCS
International Classification of Diseases, Tenth Revision, Procedure Coding System; consists of procedure codes

REMEMBER . . .

Coders must understand the basic principles behind the classification system in order to use ICD-10-CM and ICD-10-PCS appropriately and effectively.

CHAPTER 1

*Background
of the
ICD-10-CM
and
ICD-10-PCS
Classification*

INTRODUCTION

The *International Classification of Diseases, Tenth Revision, Clinical Modification* (ICD-10-CM) and the *International Classification of Diseases, Tenth Revision, Procedure Coding System* (ICD-10-PCS) have been developed as a replacement for ICD-9-CM. ICD-10-CM consists of a clinical modification of the World Health Organization's (WHO) ICD-10. ICD-10-CM consists of diagnosis codes, while ICD-10-PCS consists of procedure codes. The clinical modification expands ICD-10 codes to facilitate more precise coding of clinical diagnoses. The ICD-10-PCS is a classification of operations and procedures developed for use in the United States; it is not a part of the WHO classification.

A classification system is an arrangement of elements into groups according to established criteria. In ICD-10-CM and ICD-10-PCS these elements are diseases, injuries, surgeries, and procedures, which are grouped into appropriate chapters and sections. Three-character categories are used in ICD-10-CM, and seven-character codes are used in ICD-10-PCS. These groups are the common basis of classification for general medical statistical use. They help to answer questions about groups of related causes and provide the capacity for the systematic tabulation, storage, and retrieval of disease-related data. Each alphanumerical code represents a counting unit, with the three-character categories forming the basis for data tabulation. In ICD-10-CM many disease and injury categories have been expanded by fourth, fifth, or sixth characters that provide additional specificity but remain collapsible to the three-character category. In addition, in ICD-10-CM some categories use a seventh-character extension to provide additional information regarding the encounter.

ICD-10-CM and ICD-10-PCS are closed classification systems—they provide one and only one place to classify each condition and procedure. Despite the large number of different conditions to be classified, the system must limit its size in order to be usable. Certain conditions that occur infrequently or are of low importance are often grouped together in residual codes labeled "other" or "not elsewhere classified." A final residual category is provided for diagnoses not stated specifically enough to permit more precise classification. Occasionally these two residual groups are combined in one code.

Medical coders must understand the basic principles behind the classification system in order to use ICD-10-CM and ICD-10-PCS appropriately and effectively. This knowledge is also the basis for understanding and applying the official coding advice provided through the *AHA Coding Clinic*®, published by the Central Office of the American Hospital Association. It is important for coders in all health care settings to keep current with the *ICD-10-CM Official Guidelines for Coding and Reporting* as well as the *Coding Clinic*. This official advice is developed through the editorial board for the *Coding Clinic* and is approved by the four cooperating parties, which include the American Hospital Association, the American Health Information Management Association, the Centers for Medicare & Medicaid Services (CMS), and the National Center for Health Statistics (NCHS). At press time, there are plans to publish a *Coding Clinic* for ICD-10-CM and ICD-10-PCS as we get closer to implementation of ICD-10.

DEVELOPMENT OF ICD-10-CM

ICD-10 was released by the WHO in 1993. In 1994 the NCHS, a federal agency under the Centers for Disease Control and Prevention, determined that a clinical modification of the ICD-10 would be a significant improvement worth implementing in the United States. It was needed to include emerging diseases and more recent medical knowledge, as well as to include new concepts and expand distinctions for ambulatory and managed care encounters. In response, the WHO authorized development of an adaptation of the ICD-10 for use in the United States. All modifications to the ICD-10 need to conform to the WHO conventions for the ICD. ICD-10 contains only diagnosis codes. ICD-10-CM was developed under the leadership of the NCHS as a replacement for volumes 1 and 2 of the ICD-9-CM (diagnosis codes).

5

CHAPTER 1

Background
of the
ICD-10-CM
and
ICD-10-PCS
Classification

The ICD-10-CM is in the public domain. However, neither the codes nor the code titles may be changed except through the Coordination and Maintenance Process overseen jointly by the NCHS and CMS. ICD-10-CM consists of 21 chapters resulting in nearly sixty-nine thousand codes. The classification of external causes of injury and poisoning and the classification of factors influencing health status and contact with health services are incorporated within ICD-10-CM.

DEVELOPMENT OF ICD-10-PCS

In 1992 the U.S. Health Care Financing Administration (HCFA, now CMS) funded a preliminary design project for a replacement for volume 3 of the ICD-9-CM. In 1995 HCFA awarded a three-year contract to 3M Health Information Systems (3M HIS) to complete the development of a procedure coding replacement system. The new system was called ICD-10 Procedure Coding System (ICD-10-PCS). The first year of the 3M HIS contract involved the completion of the first draft of the system. The second year was devoted to external review and limited informal testing, and the third year consisted of formal, independent review and testing. ICD-10-PCS was completed in 1998 and has been updated annually by 3M HIS since then. The goal of the revisions is to keep current with medical technology and coding needs. The four main objectives in the development of ICD-10-PCS were:

- Completeness: All substantially different procedures should have a unique code.
- Expandability: The structure of ICD-10-PCS should allow for the easy incorporation of unique codes as new procedures are developed.
- Multi-axial structure: The structure of ICD-10-PCS should be multi-axial, with each code character having the same meaning within a specific procedure section and across procedure sections, whenever possible.
- Standardized methodology: ICD-10-PCS should include unique definitions for the terms used, with each term having a specific meaning.

The guiding principles that were followed in the development of ICD-10-PCS are these:

- Diagnostic information is not included in the procedure description.
- Explicit "not otherwise specified" (NOS) options are not provided.
- "Not elsewhere classified" (NEC) options are provided on a limited basis.
- All possible procedures are defined regardless of the frequency of occurrence. If a procedure could be performed, a code was created.

The 16 sections in ICD-10-PCS represent nearly seventy-two thousand codes. ICD-10-PCS uses a grid structure that permits the specification of a large number of codes on a single page in the tabular division.

RATIONALE FOR CHANGE

ICD-9-CM has been in use in the United States since 1979. Many improvements in medical practice and technology have taken place since ICD-9-CM was first implemented. Although ICD-9-CM is updated on a regular basis, the classification is limited in its ability to expand enumeration because of the physical numbering constraints contained in the current system. Some categories have vague and imprecise codes. This lack of specificity creates problems such as the inability to collect accurate data on new technology, increased requirements for submission of documentation to support claims, lack of quality data to support health outcomes, and less accurate reimbursement.

CHAPTER 1

*Background
of the
ICD-10-CM
and
ICD-10-PCS
Classification*

Over the years, many of the ICD-9-CM categories have become full, making it difficult to create new codes. Once a category is full, several types of similar diagnoses or procedures are combined under one code, or a place is found in another section of the classification for a new code. Due to a lack of space in the classification, several distinct procedures performed in different parts of the body, and with widely different resource utilization, may be grouped together under the same procedure code. The structural integrity of the ICD-9-CM procedure classification has already been compromised with new code numbers being assigned to "chapter 00" and "chapter 17" when new numbers were not available within the appropriate body system chapter. More importantly, many other countries have already converted to ICD-10, making it difficult to compare United States health data with international data. Thus far, 138 countries have implemented ICD-10 for mortality, and 99 countries have implemented it for morbidity reporting. Each country has developed its own procedure coding system.

COMPLIANCE DATE

The U.S. Department of Health and Human Services (HHS) has adopted ICD-10-CM and ICD-10-PCS as medical data code sets under the Health Insurance Portability and Accountability Act, replacing the ICD-9-CM volumes 1 and 2 code sets for reporting diagnoses and the volume 3 code set for reporting procedures—including the official coding guidelines—when conducting standard transactions. Because ICD-10-PCS codes are used only by hospitals for inpatient procedures, the ICD-10-PCS codes would not be used in outpatient transactions or by physicians.

Full compliance is expected for claims submitted for encounters and discharges occurring on or after **October 1, 2013** (FY 2014). HHS believed it was in the best interests of the health care field to have a single compliance date for ICD-10-CM and ICD-10-PCS to ensure the accuracy and timeliness of claims and transaction processing. The compliance date is based on the date of discharge for inpatient claims and the date of service for outpatient claims. The date is consistent with the long-standing practice of inpatient facilities using the version of ICD codes in effect on the date of discharge. ICD-10-CM/PCS codes may not be reported before the compliance date.

A large number of provider and health plan databases and applications will be affected—every application in which diagnosis or procedure codes are captured, stored, analyzed, or reported. A successful transition to ICD-10-CM and ICD-10-PCS will require careful planning and coordination of resources. Health information coding professionals will need to become proficient in the new system. This change is welcome and long overdue because ICD-9-CM is no longer able to meet the pressing requirements for increased granularity and specificity in a hospital coding system.

EXERCISE 1.1

Without referring to the handbook material or any volume of ICD-10-CM or ICD-10-PCS, mark the following statements either true or false.

1. ICD-10-CM consists of diagnosis and procedure codes.   F

2. The compliance date for ICD-10-CM and ICD-10-PCS in the   T
   United States is October 1, 2013.

3. Three-character categories are used in ICD-10-CM, and seven-character   T
   codes are used in ICD-10-PCS.

4. Both ICD-10-CM and ICD-10-PCS were developed by the   F
   World Health Organization.

5. ICD-10-CM and ICD-10-PCS were developed because ICD-9-CM had   T
   become outdated and there were physical numbering constraints.

CHAPTER 1

*Background
of the
ICD-10-CM
and
ICD-10-PCS
Classification*

CHAPTER 2

Introduction to the ICD-10-CM Classification

CHAPTER OVERVIEW

- ICD-10-CM is a medical diagnosis classification system.
- Volume 1 is the Tabular List of Diseases and Injuries.
  - There are three-, four-, five-, six-, and seven-character codes.
  - Codes appear in numerical order.
- Volume 2 is the Alphabetic Index of Diseases and Injuries. There is a pattern to the indentions found in this volume.
  - Main terms are flush to the left-hand margin.
  - Subterms are indented. The more specific the subterm, the farther the indent.
  - Carryover lines are two indents from the indent level of the preceding line.
  - There are also strict alphabetization rules.

LEARNING OUTCOMES

After studying this chapter you should be able to:

Explain the basic principles of the medical classification system ICD-10-CM.

Demonstrate understanding of the three-, four-, five-, six-, and seven-character subdivisions.

Explain the alphabetization rules and indention patterns.

TERMS TO KNOW

ICD-10-CM
International Classification of Diseases, Tenth Revision, Clinical Modification; a medical classification system used for the collection of information regarding disease and injury

INTRODUCTION

ICD-10-CM has many similarities to ICD-9-CM, especially in regard to the classification format and conventions. The code structure has changed slightly to accommodate code expansion and improvements to the classification.

FORMAT

The ICD-10-CM is divided into the Tabular List and the Alphabetic Index. The Tabular List is a chronological list of codes divided into chapters based on body system or condition. The Index is an alphabetical list of terms and their corresponding code.

TABULAR LIST OF DISEASES AND INJURIES

The main classification of diseases and injuries in the Tabular List of Diseases and Injuries consists of 21 chapters. (See the table of contents reproduced in figure 2.1.) Approximately half of the chapters are devoted to conditions that affect a specific body system; the rest classify conditions according to etiology. Chapter 2, for example, classifies neoplasms of all body systems, whereas chapter 10 addresses diseases of the respiratory system only.

In addition, Z codes represent factors influencing health status and contact with health services that may be recorded as diagnoses. V, W, X, and Y codes are used to indicate the external circumstances responsible for injuries and certain other conditions. V, W, X, Y, and Z codes will be discussed briefly in chapter 12 of this handbook and in more detail in the chapters discussing the conditions to which they apply.

The variation in chapter titles in ICD-10-CM's table of contents represents the compromises made during the development of a statistical classification system based partially on etiology, partially on anatomical site, and partially on the circumstances of onset. The result is a classification system based on multiple axes. By contrast, a single-axis classification would be based entirely on the etiology of the disease, the anatomical site of the disease, or the nature of the disease process.

Codes in the Tabular List appear in numerical order. References from the Alphabetic Index to the Tabular List are by code number, not by page number. Code numbers and titles appear in bold type in the Tabular List. Instructional notes that apply to the section, category, or subcategory are also included in the Tabular List.

Code Structure

All ICD-10-CM codes have an alphanumeric structure with all codes starting with an alphabetic character. The basic code structure consists of three characters. A decimal point is used to separate the basic three-character category code from its subcategory and subclassifications (for example, L98.491). Most ICD-10-CM codes contain a maximum of six characters, with a few categories having a seventh-character code extension.

Each chapter in the main classification is structured to provide the following subdivisions:

- Sections (groups of three-character categories), e.g., Infections of the skin and subcutaneous tissue (L00–L08)
- Categories (three-character code numbers), e.g., L02, Cutaneous abscess, furuncle and carbuncle
- Subcategories (four-character code numbers), e.g., L02.2, Cutaneous abscess, furuncle and carbuncle of trunk
- Fifth-, sixth-, or seventh-character subclassifications (five-, six-, or seven-character code numbers), e.g., L02.211, Cutaneous abscess of abdominal wall

FIGURE 2.1   Table of Contents from ICD-10-CM

Preface

Introduction

ICD-10-CM Conventions

ICD-10-CM Official Guidelines for Coding and Reporting

ICD-10-CM Index to Diseases and Injuries

ICD-10-CM Neoplasm Table

Table of Drugs and Chemicals

ICD-10-CM Index to External Causes

ICD-10-CM Tabular List of Diseases and Injuries

CHAPTER 1—Certain infectious and parasitic diseases
CHAPTER 2—Neoplasms
CHAPTER 3—Diseases of the blood and blood-forming organs and certain
                      disorders involving the immune mechanism
CHAPTER 4—Endocrine, nutritional and metabolic diseases
CHAPTER 5—Mental and behavioral disorders
CHAPTER 6—Diseases of the nervous system
CHAPTER 7—Diseases of the eye and adnexa
CHAPTER 8—Diseases of the ear and mastoid process
CHAPTER 9—Diseases of the circulatory system
CHAPTER 10—Diseases of the respiratory system
CHAPTER 11—Diseases of the digestive system
CHAPTER 12—Diseases of the skin and subcutaneous tissue
CHAPTER 13—Diseases of the musculoskeletal and connective tissue
CHAPTER 14—Diseases of the genitourinary system
CHAPTER 15—Pregnancy, childbirth and the puerperium
CHAPTER 16—Certain conditions originating in the perinatal period
CHAPTER 17—Congenital malformations, deformations and chromosomal
                        abnormalities
CHAPTER 18—Symptoms, signs and abnormal clinical and laboratory findings
                        not elsewhere classified
CHAPTER 19—Injury, poisoning and certain other consequences of external causes
CHAPTER 20—External causes of morbidity
CHAPTER 21—Factors influencing health status and contact with health services

The ICD-10-CM Tabular List contains categories, subcategories, and codes. The basic code used to classify a particular disease or injury consists of three characters and is called a category (e.g., K29, Gastritis and duodenitis). Characters for categories, subcategories, and codes may be either a letter or a number. All categories are three characters. A three-character category that has no further subdivision is equivalent to a code. Subcategories are either four or five characters. Codes may be three, four, five, six, or seven characters. That is, each level of subdivision after a category is a subcategory. The final level of subdivision is a code.

Codes that have applicable seventh characters are still referred to as codes, not subcategories. A code that has an applicable seventh character is considered invalid without the seventh character.

For example:

- K29 Gastritis and duodenitis   *(category)*
    - K29.0   Acute gastritis   *(subcategory)*
        - K29.00   Acute gastritis without bleeding   *(code)*

- R10 Abdominal and pelvic pain   *(category)*
    - R10.8   Other abdominal pain   *(subcategory)*
        - R10.81   Abdominal tenderness   *(subcategory)*
            - R10.811   Right upper quadrant   *(code)*
                        abdominal tenderness

Placeholder Character

ICD-10-CM uses the letter "x" as the fifth character dummy placeholder for certain six-character codes. This was done to allow for future expansion without disturbing the sixth character structure for codes where the sixth character has a specific use. An example of this may be seen with the poisoning or adverse effects (T36–T50) and the toxic effects (T51–T65) codes. For these categories, the sixth character represents the intent: accidental, intentional self-harm, assault, undetermined, adverse effect, or underdosing.

For example, where the sixth character of "1" represents accidental, and "2" represents intentional self-harm:

T37.5x1   Poisoning by antiviral drugs, accidental (unintentional)
T37.5x2   Poisoning by antiviral drugs, intentional self-harm
T52.0x1   Toxic effect of petroleum products, accidental (unintentional)
T52.0x2   Toxic effect of petroleum products, intentional self-harm

Certain categories have an additional seventh-character extension. The applicable seventh-character extension is required for all codes within the category, or as the notes in the Tabular List instruct. The seventh character must always be the seventh character in the code. If a code is not a full six characters, a placeholder character "x" must be used to fill in the empty characters when a seventh character extension is required. Seventh-character extensions can be seen in chapter 19 of ICD-10-CM, Injury, Poisoning and Certain Other Consequences of External Causes (S00–T88).

An example of the use of the placeholder character "x" and the seventh-character extension is shown here with an excerpt from the Tabular List:

> **T16** **Foreign body in ear**
> Includes: foreign body in auditory canal
>
> The following seventh-character extensions are to be added to each code from category T16:
>
> > A   initial encounter
> > D   subsequent encounter
> > S   sequela
>
> **T16.1** **Foreign body in right ear**
> **T16.2** **Foreign body in left ear**
> **T16.9** **Foreign body in ear, unspecified ear**

A child presents to the emergency department with a bean in the right ear. The mother has brought the child because she was not able to remove the bean at home. This encounter would be assigned code T16.1xxA. The Tabular List shows subcategory T16.1 as the descriptor best fitting this scenario. Category T16 requires a seventh-character extension. Because the code subcategory has only four characters (T16.1), the dummy placeholder "x" is inserted twice to preserve the code structure before the seventh character "A" is added to report this as the initial encounter.

ALPHABETIC INDEX

The Alphabetic Index consists of the Index of Diseases and Injuries, the Index of External Causes of Injury, the Table of Neoplasms, and the Table of Drugs and Chemicals.

The Alphabetic Index includes entries for main terms, subterms, and more specific subterms. An indented format is used for ease of reference.

Main terms identify disease conditions or injuries. Subterms indicate site, type, or etiology for conditions or injuries. For example, acute appendicitis is listed under **Appendicitis,** acute, and stress fracture is listed under **Fracture, traumatic,** stress. Occasionally, it is necessary for the coder to think of a synonym or another alternative term in order to locate the correct entry. There are, however, exceptions to this general rule, including the following:

- Congenital conditions are often indexed under the main term **Anomaly** rather than under the name of the condition.
- Conditions that complicate pregnancy, childbirth, or the puerperium are usually found under such terms as **Delivery, Pregnancy,** and **Puerperal.** They may also appear under the main term for the condition causing the complication by referencing the subterm "complicating pregnancy." (An example of this type of entry appears under the main term **Hypertension** in the Alphabetic Index.)
- Many of the complications of medical or surgical care are indexed under the term **Complications** rather than under the name of the condition.
- Late effects of an earlier condition can be found under **Sequelae.**

A clear understanding of the format of the Alphabetic Index is a prerequisite for accurate coding. Understanding the indention pattern of the entries is a very important part of learning how to use the Index. It is expected that a variety of vendors will provide printed versions and others will have computer programs for coding, but the format may not be consistent across versions. The draft version of the Index represents each indention level by a hyphen. In general, however, the following pattern is anticipated:

- Main terms are set flush with the left-hand margin. They are printed in bold type and begin with a capital letter.

- Subterms are indented one standard indention (equivalent to about two typewriter spaces) to the right under the main term. They are printed in regular type and begin with a lower-case letter.

- More specific subterms are indented farther and farther to the right as needed, always indented by one standard indention from the preceding subterm and listed in alphabetical order.

- A dash (-) at the end of an index entry indicates that additional characters are required.

Carryover lines are indented two standard indentions from the level of the preceding line. Carryover lines are used only when the complete entry cannot fit on a single line. They are indented farther to avoid confusion with subterm entries.

In most printed versions, entries will most likely use two or three columns to a page, dictionary style.

The subterms listed under the main term **Metrorrhagia** in the following entry provide an example:

Metrorrhagia N92.1	[main term]
climacteric N92.4	[subterm]
menopausal N92.4	[subterm]
postpartum NEC (atonic) (following delivery	[subterm]
of placenta) O72.1	[carryover line]
delayed or secondary O72.2	[more specific subterm]
preclimacteric or premenopausal N92.4	[subterm]
psychogenic F45.8	[subterm]

Each of the subterms (climacteric, menopausal, postpartum, preclimacteric, and psychogenic) is indented one standard indention from the level of the main term and is listed in alphabetical order. The fifth line is a carryover line two standard indentions from the preceding line. The sixth line is a more specific entry ("delayed or secondary" under the subterm "postpartum").

EXERCISE 2.1

A reproduction of a page from the Alphabetic Index is shown below. Label the numbered lines as either main terms, subterms, or carryover lines. Each hyphen is meant to represent one level of indention.

1. **Railroad neurosis** F48.8   Main term

2. **Railway spine** F48.8   Main term

   Raised—see also Elevated
3. --antibody titer R76.0   Carryover line

   Rake teeth, tooth M26.39
   Rales R09.89
4. **Ramifying renal pelvis** Q63.8   Main term

   Ramsay-Hunt disease or syndrome—see also
5. --Hunt's disease B02.21   Carryover line

6. -meaning dyssynergia cerebellaris myoclonica G11.1   Subterm
   Ranula K11.6
   -congenital Q38.4

7. **Rape**   Main term

8. -adult   Subterm
   --confirmed T74.21
   --suspected T76.21
   -alleged, observation or examination ruled
   --out

9. --adult Z04.41   Subterm
   --child Z04.42

10. -child   Subterm
    --confirmed T74.22
    --suspected T76.22

Alphabetization Rules

In order to locate main terms and subterms quickly and efficiently, it is important to understand the alphabetization rules followed in the Alphabetic Index. Letter-by-letter alphabetization is used. The system of alphabetization ignores the following:

- Single spaces between words
- Single hyphens within words
- The final "s" in the possessive forms of words

The following list shows an example of letter-by-letter alphabetization with these modifications:

Beckwith-Wiedemann syndrome Q87.3	[ignores hyphen]
Beer drinker's heart (disease) I42.6	[ignores space between words]
Blood-forming organs, disease D75.9	[ignores hyphen]
Bloodgood's disease—see **Mastopathy**, cystic	[ignores possessive form]

Numerical Entries

Subterm entries for numerical characters and words indicating numbers appear first under the appropriate main term or subterm. These are listed in alphabetical order when listed in their spelled-out form. For example, **Paralysis,** nerve, fourth, comes before, rather than after, **Paralysis,** nerve, third.

However, when Roman numerals (such as "II") and Arabic numerals (such as "2") are used, they are listed in numerical order. For example (each hyphen below represents one level of indention):

Deficiency . . .
factor
--I (congenital) (hereditary) D68.2
--II (congenital) (hereditary) D68.2
--IX (congenital) (functional) (hereditary) (with functional defect) D67
--multiple (congenital) D68.8
---acquired D68.4
--V (congenital) (hereditary) D68.2
--VII (congenital) (hereditary) D68.2
--VIII (congenital) (functional) (hereditary) (with functional defect) D66
---with vascular defect D68.0
--X (congenital) (hereditary) D68.2
--XI (congenital) (hereditary) D68.1
--XII (congenital) (hereditary) D68.2
--XIII (congenital) (hereditary) D68.2

Connecting Words

Words such as "with," "in," "due to," and "associated with" are used to express the relationship between the main term or a subterm indicating an associated condition or etiology. Subterms preceded by "with" or "without" are not listed in alphabetical order but appear immediately below the main term or appropriate subterm entries; subterms beginning with other connecting words appear in alphabetical order. Coders who fail to remember this feature of the alphabetization rules often make coding errors by overlooking the appropriate subterm. Review the following subterm entries under the main term **Bronchitis** using the instructions at the end of this example. Note that each hyphen represents one level of indention:

Bronchitis (diffuse) (fibrinous) (hypostatic) (infective) (membranous) (with tracheitis) J40

1 -with
   --influenza, flu or grippe—see Influenza, with respiratory manifestations NEC

2 --obstruction (airway) (lung) J44.9

3 --tracheitis (15 years of age and above) J40
   ---acute or subacute J20.9
   ---chronic J42
   ---under 15 years of age J20.9

4 -acute or subacute (with bronchospasm or obstruction) J20.9

5 --with
   ---bronchiectasis J47.1
   ---chronic obstructive pulmonary disease J44.0

6 --chemical (due to gases, fumes or vapors) J68.0

7 --due to
   ---fumes or vapors J68.0
   ---*Haemophilus influenzae* J20.1
   ---*Mycoplasma pneumoniae* J20.0
   ---radiation J70.0
   ---specified organism NEC J20.8
   ---Streptococcus J20.2
   ---virus
   ----coxsackie J20.3
   ----echovirus J20.7
   ----parainfluenzae J20.4
   ----respiratory syncytial J20.5
   ----rhinovirus J20.6
   --viral NEC J20.8

8 -allergic (acute) J45.909

9 --with
   ---exacerbation (acute) J45.901
   ---status asthmaticus J45.902

10 -arachidic T17.528

Refer to sections 1, 4, 8, and 10 as indicated in the example. Note that the subterms preceded by the connecting word "with" immediately follow the main term **Bronchitis** and precede the subterms beginning with the letter "a" (sections 4, 8, and 10).

Refer to sections 5, 6, and 7 as indicated in the example. Note that the more specific subterms preceded by the connecting word "with" immediately follow the subterm "acute or subacute." In this case, the subterms beginning with the word "with" precede the subterms beginning with the letters "c" and "d" (sections 6 and 7).

Also note that the subterms indented under the connecting word "with" are listed in alphabetical order. For example, sections 1, 2, and 3 indicated in the example are in alphabetical order.

Index Tables

The main body of the Alphabetic Index uses a table for the systematic arrangement of sub-terms under the main entry **Neoplasm.** This table simplifies access to complex combinations of subterms. The use of this table will be discussed in the Neoplasm chapter. The Table of Drugs and Chemicals will be discussed later in this handbook in the chapter on poisoning and adverse effects of drugs.

The format and alphabetization rules used within the tables are the same as those followed in the rest of the Alphabetic Index. The use of these two tables will be discussed in detail later in this handbook, but it would be useful for the reader to become familiar with the location and format of the tables at this point of the discussion.

CHAPTER 3

ICD-10-CM Conventions

CHAPTER OVERVIEW

- A variety of notes appear in ICD-10-CM.

  — *General notes* commonly provide general information on usage in a specific section.

  — *Inclusion notes* and *exclusion notes* indicate when certain conditions are or are not included in a subdivision.

  — Additional instructional notes direct the coder to create a complete statement on the condition.

- Two main abbreviations (NEC and NOS) are used in ICD-10-CM.

- Cross-reference notes advise the coder to look elsewhere before assigning a code.

- Punctuation marks and relational terms have a specialized meaning in ICD-10-CM.

LEARNING OUTCOMES

After studying this chapter you should be able to:

List the different types of instructional notes.

Explain the importance of additional notes to the coding process.

Describe the difference between the abbreviations NEC and NOS.

Use your knowledge of cross-reference notes to navigate ICD-10-CM.

Define the specialized meanings of punctuation marks and relational terms in ICD-10-CM.

TERMS TO KNOW

NEC
not elsewhere classified; used in the Alphabetic Index to indicate that there is no separate code for the condition even though the diagnostic statement is specific

NOS
not otherwise specified; equivalent to the term "unspecified"

REMEMBER . . .

These conventions aren't just helpful; they're necessary to successful coding.

INTRODUCTION

ICD-10-CM follows certain conventions in order to provide large amounts of information in a succinct and consistent manner. A thorough understanding of these conventions is fundamental to accurate coding. The conventions and instructions of the classification are applicable to all health care settings, unless otherwise indicated.

ICD-10-CM conventions include the following:

- Instructional notes
- Abbreviations
- Cross-reference notes
- Punctuation marks
- Relational terms ("and," "with," "without," "due to")

INSTRUCTIONAL NOTES

A variety of notes appear as instructions to the coder. These include general notes, inclusion and exclusion notes, "code first" notes, "use additional code" notes, and "code also" notes.

General Notes

General notes in the Tabular List of Diseases and Injuries provide general information on usage in a specific section, such as the note under chapter 15 of ICD-10-CM, Pregnancy, Childbirth and the Puerperium, that explains that codes from this chapter are for use only on maternal records, never on newborn records.

Inclusion and Exclusion Notes

Codes in a classification system must be mutually exclusive, with no overlapping of content. In ICD-10-CM, therefore, it is sometimes necessary to indicate when certain conditions are or are not included in a given subdivision. This is accomplished by means of inclusion and exclusion notes.

The location of inclusion and exclusion notes is extremely important. When this type of note is located at the beginning of a chapter or a section in ICD-10-CM, that advice applies to all codes within the chapter or section and is not repeated with individual categories or specific codes. The coder must keep in mind that instructional notes affecting the code under consideration may be located on a previous page.

Inclusion Notes

Inclusion notes are introduced by the word "includes" when placed at the beginning of a chapter or section. Inclusion notes are used to further define, or give examples of, the content of the chapter, section, or category. Conditions listed in an inclusion note may be synonyms or conditions similar enough to be classified to the same code. Inclusion notes are not exhaustive; rather, they list certain conditions to reassure the coder, particularly when the title in the Tabular List may not seem to apply.

An example of an inclusion note can be found in the Tabular List, chapter 1, Certain Infectious and Parasitic diseases (A00–B99). The inclusion note states that this chapter includes diseases generally recognized as communicable or transmissible. This note applies to all codes listed from A00 through B99.

Inclusion notes may also appear immediately under a three-character code title to further define, or give examples of, the content of the category. An example of this type of inclusion note can be found in the Tabular List at category D50, Iron deficiency anemia. The inclusion note states that codes in this category include asiderotic anemia and hypochromic anemia.

Inclusion Terms

Lists of terms are included under some codes. The terms are some of the conditions that may be reported with those codes. The terms may represent terms synonymous to the code title. In the case of "other specified codes," the terms may be a list of the various conditions that are assigned to that code. As in the case of the inclusion notes, the list of inclusion terms is not meant to be exhaustive. The Index may also list additional terms classified to a code and not repeated as inclusion terms.

Exclusion Notes

Exclusion notes are introduced by the word "excludes." Excluded conditions are listed in alphabetical order, with the code number or code range shown in parentheses. Exclusion notes are the opposite of inclusion notes; they indicate that a particular condition is not assigned to the code to which the note applies. The basic message of an excludes note is "code this condition elsewhere."

There are two types of exclusion notes in ICD-10-CM—each has a different use, but both indicate that codes excluded are independent of each other.

"Excludes1"

An "excludes1" note means "NOT CODED HERE!" An "excludes1" note instructs that the code excluded should never be used at the same time as the code above the "excludes1" note. This instruction is used when two conditions cannot occur together and therefore both codes cannot be used together. For example:

> **Q03** **Congenital hydrocephalus**
> Excludes1: acquired hydrocephalus (G91.-)

In this example, the congenital form of the condition cannot be reported with the acquired form of the same condition.

"Excludes2"

An "excludes2" note means "NOT INCLUDED HERE!" An "excludes2" note instructs that the condition excluded is not part of the condition represented by the code. However, a patient may have both conditions at the same time. When an "excludes2" note appears under a code, it is acceptable to use both the code and the excluded code together. For example:

> **F90** **Attention-deficit hyperactivity disorders**
> Excludes2: anxiety disorders (F40.-, F41.-)
> mood [affective] disorders (F30–F39)

In this example, the "excludes2" note serves as a warning that if a patient has an anxiety disorder, rather than attention-deficit hyperactivity disorder, the user should go to categories F40–F41 rather than remain in category F90. However, if a patient has both attention-deficit hyperactivity and an anxiety disorder, a code from category F90 could be used along with a code from categories F40–F41.

"Code First" and "Use Additional Code"

Certain conditions have both an underlying etiology and multiple body system manifestations due to the underlying etiology. In the Tabular List, "code first" and "use additional code" instructional notes indicate the proper sequencing order of these conditions—etiology (underlying condition) followed by manifestation. The "use additional code" note is found at the etiology code as a clue to identify the manifestations commonly associated with the disease. The "code first" note is found at the manifestation code to provide instructions that the underlying condition should be sequenced first.

The manifestation codes usually have the phrase "in diseases classified elsewhere" as part of the code title. Codes with this phrase are never used as a first-listed or principal diagnosis code. They must be used with the underlying condition code sequenced first. An example of this convention is category F02, Dementia in other diseases classified elsewhere.

Other notes of this type provide a list introduced by the phrase "such as," meaning that any of the listed codes or any other appropriate code can be assigned first. Code **J99, Respiratory disorders in diseases classified elsewhere,** provides a list of conditions that may be the underlying condition.

It is not necessary to report the code identified in a "use additional code" note in the diagnosis field immediately following the primary code. There is no strict hierarchy inherent in the guidelines, nor in the ICD-10-CM classification, regarding the sequencing of secondary diagnosis codes.

"Code Also"

"Code also" notes in ICD-10-CM indicate that two codes may be required to fully describe a condition. The sequencing order will depend on the reason for the encounter and the severity of the conditions. An example of this note can be found under code **G47.01, Insomnia due to medical condition,** where the instructional note tells us to code also the associated medical condition.

ABBREVIATIONS

ICD-10-CM uses two main abbreviations:

- NEC, for not elsewhere classified
- NOS, for not otherwise specified

Although their meanings appear simple, these abbreviations are often misunderstood and misapplied by coders. It is very important to understand not only their meanings but also their differences, because they provide guidelines for correct code selection.

NEC

The abbreviation NEC is used in the Alphabetic Index and the Tabular List to indicate that there is no separate code for the condition even though the diagnostic statement may be very specific. It is used when the information in the medical record provides detail for which a specific code does not exist. It represents "other specified." In the Tabular List, such conditions are ordinarily classified to a code with a fourth or sixth character "8" (or a fifth character "9") with a title that includes the words "other specified" or "not elsewhere classified," which permits the grouping of related conditions to conserve space and limit the size of the classification system. For example, a disease of the pleura specified as hydropneumothorax is included in code **J94.8, Other specified pleural conditions.**

NOS

The abbreviation NOS is the equivalent of "unspecified" and is used in the Alphabetic Index and the Tabular List. Codes so identified are to be used only when neither the diagnostic statement nor the medical record provides information that permits classification to a more specific code. The codes in these cases are ordinarily classified to codes with a fourth or sixth character "9" and fifth character "0"; conditions listed as both "not elsewhere classified" and "unspecified" are sometimes combined in one code. Note that a main term followed by a list of subterms in the Alphabetic Index usually displays the unspecified code; the subterms must always be reviewed to determine whether a more specific code can be assigned.

For example, the main term **Cardiomyopathy** displays code 142.9. Subterms such as "alcoholic" or "congestive" are provided for more specific cardiomyopathies. Code I42.9 should be assigned only when there is no information in the medical record to identify one of these subterms.

CROSS-REFERENCE NOTES

Cross-reference notes are used in the Alphabetic Index to advise the coder to look elsewhere before assigning a code. The cross-reference instructions include "see," "see also," "see category," and "see condition."

"See"

The "see" cross-reference indicates that the coder must refer to an alternative term. This instruction is mandatory; coding cannot be completed without following this advice. For example, the entry for **Hemarthrosis,** traumatic, uses this cross-reference to advise the coder to reference the entry for "sprain" by site.

"See Also"

The "see also" cross-reference advises the coder that there is another place in the Alphabetic Index to which the coder must refer when the entries under consideration do not provide a code for the specific condition or procedure. It is not necessary to follow this cross-reference when the original entries provide all the information necessary.

For example, the cross-reference for the term **Psychoneurosis** advises the coder to "see also Neurosis" when none of the specific subterms provides a code. If a coder is attempting to locate the code for neurasthenic psychoneurosis, it would not be necessary to follow this cross-reference because there is a subterm "neurasthenic" under the term **Psychoneurosis.** If the diagnosis were psychasthenic psychoneurosis, however, the code could be located only by following the "see also" reference.

"See Category"

The "see category" variation of the "see" cross-reference provides the coder with a category number. The coder must refer to that number in the Tabular List and select a code from the options provided there. For example, a cross-reference under the index entry for **Examination,** prenatal, refers the coder to category O34.

"See Condition"

Occasionally, the Index advises the coder to refer to the main term of a condition. For example, if a coder references the main term **Arterial** for arterial thrombosis, the Index advice is to "see condition," and the coder should then go to the main term **Thrombosis.** This cross-reference ordinarily appears when the coder has referenced the adjective rather than the term (in noun form) for the condition itself.

PUNCTUATION MARKS

Several punctuation marks are used in ICD-10-CM, most of which have a specialized meaning in addition to the usual English language usage.

Parentheses

Parentheses are used in ICD-10-CM to enclose supplementary words or explanatory information that may be either present or absent in the statement of diagnosis without affecting the code to which it is assigned. Such terms are considered to be "nonessential modifiers" and are used to suggest that the terms in parentheses are included in the code but need not be stated in the diagnosis. This is a significant factor in correct code assignment. Terms enclosed in parentheses in either the Tabular List or the Alphabetic Index do not affect the code assignment in any way; they serve only as reassurance that the correct code has been located.

For example, refer to the main term **Pneumonia,** which has numerous nonessential modifiers enclosed in parentheses. Unless a more specific subterm is located, this code will be assigned for pneumonia described by any of the terms in parentheses. Diagnoses of acute pneumonia and Alpenstich pneumonia, for example, are both coded J18.9 because both terms appear in parentheses as nonessential modifiers. Pneumonia not otherwise specified is also assigned to code J18.9 because none of the terms in parentheses is required for this code assignment.

It is important to distinguish between the use of nonessential and essential modifiers. Essential modifiers are listed as subterms in the Alphabetic Index, not in parentheses, and they do affect code assignment. In contrast, words in parentheses are nonessential and do not affect the code assignment. For example, scoliosis described as acquired or postural is classified as M41.9, as the words "acquired" and "postural" are nonessential modifiers and do not affect the code; on the other hand, the term "congenital" is an essential modifier, and the code for this term is Q67.5.

EXERCISE 3.1

Referring only to the title and inclusion notes for code J40, mark an "X" next to each of the diagnostic statements listed below that is included in code J40.

1.	Catarrhal bronchitis NOS	X
2.	Chronic bronchitis	
3.	Allergic bronchitis	
4.	Tracheobronchitis NOS	X
5.	Asthmatic bronchitis	

Square Brackets

Square brackets are often used in the Tabular List to enclose synonyms, alternative wordings, abbreviations, and explanatory phrases that provide additional information—for example, human immunodeficiency virus [HIV]. They are similar to parentheses in that they are not required for the statement of diagnosis. Square brackets are also used to indicate that the number in the bracket can only be a manifestation and the other number must be assigned first for the underlying code. The code in the brackets in this situation indicates that both conditions must be used, and the code in the brackets can never be assigned as the principal diagnosis. In the following example from the Alphabetic Index, the first code represents an underlying disease, and the second code enclosed in brackets represents a manifestation:

> Nephropathy . . .
>   Sickle cell D57.- [N08]

Colons

Colons are used in the Tabular List in both inclusion notes and exclusion notes after an incomplete term that needs one or more of the modifiers following the colon in order for the term to apply. The exclusion statement under code N92.6 in the Tabular List is an example of this usage. Here, the colon following the subterms "irregular menstruation with" indicates that if it is described as irregular menstruation with lengthened intervals or scanty bleeding, or irregular menstruation with shortened intervals or excessive bleeding, code N92.6 is excluded.

> **N92.6**   **Irregular menstruation, unspecified**
>   Irregular bleeding NOS
>   Irregular periods NOS
>   Excludes1: irregular menstruation with:
>   lengthened intervals or scanty bleeding (N91.3–N91.5)
>   shortened intervals or excessive bleeding (N92.1)

EXERCISE 3.2

Referring only to the title and inclusion notes provided for the four-character code D04.5, mark an "X" next to each diagnosis listed below that is included in code D04.5.

1.	Carcinoma in situ of anal margin	X
2.	Carcinoma in situ of perianal skin	X
3.	Carcinoma in situ of skin of breast	X
4.	Carcinoma in situ of breast	
5.	Carcinoma in situ of anal skin	X

RELATIONAL TERMS

"And"

The word "and" should be interpreted to mean either "and" or "or" when it appears in a code title.

"With"

The word "with" should be interpreted to mean "associated with" or "due to" when it appears in a code title, the Alphabetic Index, or an instructional note in the Tabular List. The word "with" in the Alphabetic Index is sequenced immediately following the main term, not in alphabetical order.

"Due To"

The words "due to" in either the Alphabetic Index or the Tabular List indicate that a causal relationship between two conditions is present. ICD-10-CM occasionally makes such an assumption when both conditions are present. In other combinations, however, the diagnostic statement must indicate this relationship. For example, certain conditions affecting the mitral valve are assumed to be rheumatic in origin, regardless of whether or not the diagnostic statement makes this distinction. In other cases, the Alphabetic Index provides a subterm "due to," which must be followed when the physician's statement indicates a causal relationship. The coder should be guided by the Index entry.

CHAPTER 4

Uniform Hospital Discharge Data Set

CHAPTER OVERVIEW

- The Uniform Hospital Discharge Data Set (UHDDS) is used for reporting inpatient data.
- The following items are always found in the UHDDS:
  - General demographic information
  - Expected payer
  - Hospital identification
  - Principal diagnosis
  - Other diagnoses that have specific significance
  - All significant procedures
- The principal diagnosis is treated differently for an outpatient encounter than for an inpatient encounter.
- Following all the coding guidelines will ensure accurate and ethical coding.

LEARNING OUTCOMES

After studying this chapter you should be able to:

- Correctly identify a principal diagnosis.
- Understand the guidelines for assigning a principal diagnosis.
- Understand when other diagnoses have significance and should be reported.
- Explain the difference between a principal diagnosis and an admitting diagnosis.
- Explain the importance of accurate and ethical coding.

TERMS TO KNOW

MS-DRG system
Medicare severity-adjusted diagnosis-related groups system; a patient classification system used in hospital inpatient reimbursement

Other reportable diagnoses
conditions that coexist at the time of admission, develop subsequently, or affect patient care during the hospital stay

Principal diagnosis
the condition established after study that is chiefly responsible for admission of the patient to the hospital

UHDDS
Uniform Hospital Discharge Data Set; information used for reporting inpatient data

REMEMBER . . .

The admitting diagnosis is not an element of the UHDDS.
. . . Diagnoses that have no impact on patient care or that are related to an earlier episode are not reported on the UHDDS.

INTRODUCTION

The Uniform Hospital Discharge Data Set (UHDDS) is used for reporting inpatient data in acute care, short-term care, and long-term care hospitals. It uses a minimum set of items based on standard definitions that could provide consistent data for multiple users. Only those items that met the following criteria were included:

- Easily identified
- Readily defined
- Uniformly recorded
- Easily abstracted from the medical record

Its use is required for claims reporting for Medicare and Medicaid patients. In addition, many other health care payers use most of the UHDDS as a uniform billing system.

DATA ITEMS

The UHDDS requires the following items:

- Principal diagnosis
- Other diagnoses that have significance for the specific hospital episode
- All significant procedures

The four cooperating parties responsible for developing and maintaining ICD-10-CM (American Hospital Association, American Health Information Management Association, Centers for Medicare & Medicaid Services, and National Center for Health Statistics) have developed official guidelines for designating the principal diagnosis and for identifying other diagnoses that should be reported in certain situations. The UHDDS also contains a core of general information that pertains to the patient and to the specific episode of care, such as the age, sex, and race of the patient; the expected payer; and the hospital's identification.

The UHDDS definitions were originally developed in 1985 for hospital reporting of inpatient data elements. Since that time, the application of UHDDS definitions has been expanded to include all nonoutpatient settings. In addition to their application to acute care, short-term care, and long-term care hospitals, the definitions for principal diagnosis and other (secondary) diagnoses also apply to psychiatric hospitals, home health agencies, rehabilitation facilities, nursing homes, and other settings. Guidelines for selection of principal diagnosis and other diagnoses discussed below apply to all these settings.

Principal Diagnosis

The principal diagnosis is defined as the condition established after study to be chiefly responsible for admission of the patient to the hospital for care. It is important that the principal diagnosis be designated correctly because its establishment is significant in cost comparisons, in care analysis, and in utilization review. It is crucial for reimbursement because many third-party payers (including Medicare) base reimbursement primarily on principal diagnosis. The principal diagnosis is ordinarily listed first in the physician's diagnostic statement, but not always; the coder must review the entire medical record to determine the condition that should be designated as the principal diagnosis.

The words "after study" in the definition of principal diagnosis are important, but their meaning is sometimes confusing. It is not the admitting diagnosis but rather the diagnosis found after workup or even after surgery that proves to be the reason for admission. For example:

- A patient admitted with urinary retention may prove to have hypertrophy of the prostate, which is causing the urinary retention. In this case, the prostatic hypertrophy is the principal diagnosis unless treatment was directed only to the urinary retention.

- A patient may be admitted because of unstable angina, and a percutaneous transluminal angioplasty may be carried out to clear arteriosclerotic blockage of the coronary artery in order to abort what appears to be an impending myocardial infarction. In this case, the coronary arteriosclerosis is the principal diagnosis because, after study, it was determined to be the underlying cause of the angina and the reason for admission.

- A patient is admitted with severe abdominal pain. The white blood cell count is elevated to 16,000, with shift to the left. The patient is taken to surgery, where an acute ruptured appendix is removed. After study, the principal diagnosis is determined to be acute ruptured appendicitis.

- A patient is admitted with severe abdominal pain in the right lower quadrant, and an admitting diagnosis of probable acute appendicitis is given. The white blood cell count is slightly elevated. The patient is taken to surgery, where a normal appendix is found but an inflamed Meckel's diverticulum is removed. After study, the principal diagnosis is determined to be Meckel's diverticulum.

The circumstances of inpatient admission always govern the selection of the principal diagnosis, and the coding directives in the ICD-10-CM classification take precedence over all other guidelines. The importance of consistent, complete documentation in the medical record cannot be overemphasized. Without such documentation, the application of all coding guidelines is a difficult, if not impossible, task.

There are special instructions related to the selection of principal diagnosis when a patient is admitted as an inpatient from the hospital's observation unit or from outpatient surgery. This coding advice applies if a single bill is submitted to a payer. If separate inpatient and outpatient bills are submitted, then the advice does not apply. Hospitals should apply codes for the current encounter based on individual payer billing instructions.

For example:

- *Admission following medical observation:* A patient may be treated in a hospital's observation unit to determine whether the condition improves sufficiently for the patient to be discharged. If the condition either worsens or does not improve, the physician may decide to admit the patient as an inpatient of the same hospital for this same medical condition. The principal diagnosis reported is the medical condition that led to the hospital admission.

- *Admission following postoperative observation:* A patient undergoing outpatient surgery may require postoperative admission to an observation unit to monitor a condition (or complication) that develops postoperatively. If the patient subsequently requires inpatient admission to the same hospital, the UHDDS definition of principal diagnosis applies: "that condition established after study to be chiefly responsible for occasioning the admission of the patient to the hospital for care."

- *Admission from outpatient surgery:* A patient undergoing outpatient surgery may be subsequently admitted for continuing inpatient care at the same hospital. The following guidelines should be followed in selecting the principal diagnosis for the inpatient admission:
  —If the reason for the inpatient admission is a complication, assign the complication as the principal diagnosis.
  —If no complication or other condition is documented as the reason for the inpatient admission, assign the reason for the outpatient surgery as the principal diagnosis.
  —If the reason for the inpatient admission is another condition unrelated to the surgery, assign the unrelated condition as the principal diagnosis.

The following official guidelines for designating the principal diagnosis apply to all systems and etiologies. (Guidelines that apply only to specific body systems or etiologies are discussed in the relevant chapters of this handbook. To download a copy of the current version of the complete *ICD-10-CM Official Guidelines for Coding and Reporting,* please visit www.ahacentraloffice.org.)

1. *Two or more diagnoses that equally meet the definition for principal diagnosis:* In the unusual situation that two or more diagnoses equally meet the criteria for principal diagnosis as determined by the circumstances of the admission and the diagnostic workup and/or therapy provided, either may be sequenced first when neither the Alphabetic Index nor the Tabular List directs otherwise. However, it is not simply the fact that both conditions exist that makes this choice possible. When treatment is totally or primarily directed toward one condition, or when only one condition would have required inpatient care, that condition should be designated as the principal diagnosis. Also, if another coding guideline (general or disease specific) provides sequencing direction, that guideline must be followed.

   Example 1: A patient is admitted with unstable angina and acute congestive heart failure. The unstable angina is treated with nitrates, and intravenous Lasix is given to manage the heart failure. Both diagnoses meet the definition of principal diagnosis equally, and either may be sequenced first.

   Example 2: A patient is admitted with acute atrial fibrillation with rapid ventricular response and is also in heart failure with pulmonary edema. The patient is digitalized to reduce the ventricular rate and given intravenous Lasix to reduce the cardiogenic pulmonary edema. Both conditions meet the definition of principal diagnosis equally, and either may be sequenced first.

   Example 3: A patient is admitted with severe abdominal pain, nausea, and vomiting due to acute pyelonephritis and diverticulitis. Both underlying conditions are treated, and the physician believes both equally meet the criteria for principal diagnosis. In this instance, either condition may be listed as principal diagnosis.

2. *Two or more comparable or contrasting conditions:* In the rare instance that two or more comparable or contrasting conditions are documented as either/or (or similar terminology), both diagnoses are coded as though confirmed and the principal diagnosis is designated according to the circumstances of the admission and the diagnostic workup and/or therapy provided. When no further determination can be made as to which diagnosis more closely meets the criteria for principal diagnosis, either may be sequenced first. Note that this guideline does not apply for outpatient encounters.

   Example 1: A patient with the same complaints as those outlined in example 3 above is admitted with a final diagnosis of acute pyelonephritis versus diverticulum of the colon. The patient is treated symptomatically and discharged for further studies. In this case, both conditions meet the criteria for principal diagnosis equally, and either can be designated as the principal diagnosis.

   Example 2: The treatment of another patient with the same symptoms and the same final diagnoses is directed almost entirely toward the acute pyelonephritis, indicating that the physician considers this condition the more likely problem and that, after study, it is the condition that occasioned the admission. In this case, both conditions are coded, but the acute pyelonephritis is sequenced first because of the circumstances of the admission.

3. *A symptom followed by contrasting/comparative diagnoses:* When a symptom is followed by contrasting/comparative diagnoses, the symptom code is sequenced first. However, if the symptom code is integral to each of the conditions listed, no additional code for the symptom is reported. Codes are assigned for all listed contrasting/comparative diagnoses.

   Example 1: A patient is admitted for workup because of severe fatigue. The discharge diagnosis is recorded as fatigue, due to either depressive reaction or hypothyroidism. In this case, the symptom code for fatigue is designated the principal diagnosis, with additional codes assigned for both the depressive reaction and the hypothyroidism.

   Example 2: The discharge diagnosis is stated as gastrointestinal bleeding, due to either acute gastritis or angiodysplasia. In this case, the diagnoses are coded as contrasting/comparative diagnoses, and no separate code is assigned for the bleeding because the codes for both conditions include any associated bleeding.

4. *Original treatment plan not carried out:* In a situation in which the original treatment plan cannot be carried out due to unforeseen circumstances, the criteria for designation of the principal diagnosis do not change. The condition that occasioned the admission is designated as the principal diagnosis even though the planned treatment was not carried out.

   Example 1: A patient with benign hypertrophy of the prostate is admitted for the purpose of a transurethral resection of the prostate (TURP). Shortly after admission, but before the patient is taken to the operating suite, the patient falls and sustains a fracture of the left femur. The TURP is canceled; hip pinning is carried out the following day. The principal diagnosis remains hypertrophy of the prostate even though that condition was not treated.

   Example 2: A patient with a diagnosis of carcinoma of the breast confirmed from an outpatient biopsy is admitted for the purpose of modified radical mastectomy. Before the preoperative medications are administered the next morning, the patient indicates that she has decided against having the procedure until she is able to consider possible alternative treatment more thoroughly. No treatment is given, and she is discharged. The carcinoma of the breast remains the principal diagnosis because it is the condition that occasioned the admission even though no treatment was rendered.

Other Diagnoses

Other reportable diagnoses are defined as those conditions that coexist at the time of admission or develop subsequently or affect patient care for the current hospital episode. Diagnoses that have no impact on patient care during the hospital stay are not reported even when they are present. Diagnoses that relate to an earlier episode and have no bearing on the current hospital stay are not reported.

For UHDDS reporting purposes, the definition of "other diagnosis" includes only those conditions that affect the episode of hospital care in terms of any of the following:

- Clinical evaluation
- Therapeutic treatment
- Further evaluation by diagnostic studies, procedures, or consultation
- Extended length of hospital stay
- Increased nursing care and/or other monitoring

All these factors are self-explanatory except the first. Clinical evaluation means that the physician is aware of the problem and is evaluating it in terms of testing, consultations, or close clinical observation of the patient's condition. In most cases, a patient who is being evaluated clinically will also fit into one of the other criteria. Note that a physical examination alone does not qualify as further evaluation or clinical evaluation; the physical examination is a routine part of every hospital admission. No particular order is mandated for sequencing other diagnoses. The more significant diagnoses should be sequenced early in the list when the number of diagnoses that may be reported is limited.

Reporting Guidelines for Other Diagnoses

The following guidelines and examples should be studied carefully in order to understand the rationale for determining other diagnoses that should be reported:

1. *Previous conditions stated as diagnoses:* Physicians sometimes include in the diagnostic statement historical information or status post procedures performed on a previous admission that have no bearing on the current stay. Such conditions are not reported. However, history codes (categories Z80–Z87, subcategories Z91.4- and Z91.5-, and category Z92) may be used as secondary codes if the historical condition or family history has an impact on current care or influences treatment.

   Example: A patient is admitted with acute myocardial infarction; the physician notes in the history that the patient is status post cholecystectomy and had been hospitalized one year earlier for pneumonia. At discharge, the physician documents the final diagnoses as acute myocardial infarction, status post cholecystectomy, and history of pneumonia. Only the acute myocardial infarction is coded and reported; the other conditions included in the diagnostic statement have no bearing on the current episode of care.

2. *Other diagnosis with no documentation supporting reportability:* If the physician has included a diagnosis in the final diagnostic statement, it should ordinarily be coded. If there is no supporting documentation in the medical record, however, the physician should be consulted as to whether the diagnosis meets reporting criteria; if so, the physician should be asked to add the necessary documentation. Reporting of conditions for which there is no supporting documentation is in conflict with UHDDS criteria.

   Example 1:   A 10-year-old boy is admitted with open fracture of the tibia and fibula following a bicycle accident. On physical examination, the physician notes that there is a nevus on the leg and that the patient has a small, asymptomatic inguinal hernia. All these diagnoses are documented on the face sheet. The fracture is reduced with internal fixation, but neither the nevus nor the hernia is treated or further evaluated on this admission. The nevus and hernia are not reported because there is nothing to indicate that they had any effect on the episode of care.

   Example 2:   A patient is admitted with an acute myocardial infarction. The physician also includes in the diagnostic statement a strabismus and a bunion noted on the physical examination. Review of the medical record reveals that no further reference to these conditions was made in terms of further evaluation or treatment; therefore, no codes for either the strabismus or the bunion are assigned.

3. *Chronic conditions that are not the thrust of treatment:* The criteria for selection of chronic conditions to be reported as "other diagnoses" include the severity of the condition, the use or consideration of alternative measures or an increase in nursing care required in the treatment of the principal diagnosis due to the coexisting condition, the use of diagnostic or therapeutic services for the particular coexisting condition, the need for close monitoring of medications because of the coexisting condition, or modifications of nursing care plans because of the coexisting condition.

Chronic conditions such as (but not limited to) hypertension, Parkinson's disease, chronic obstructive pulmonary disease, and diabetes mellitus are systemic diseases that ordinarily should be coded even in the absence of documented intervention or further evaluation. Some chronic conditions affect the patient for the rest of his or her life; such conditions almost always require some form of continuous clinical evaluation or monitoring during hospitalization and therefore should be coded. This advice applies to inpatient coding.

For outpatient encounters/visits, chronic conditions that require or affect patient care treatment or management should be coded.

Example 1:   A patient is admitted following a hip fracture, and a diagnosis of Parkinson's disease is noted in the history and physical examination. Nursing notes indicate that the patient required additional care because of the Parkinsonism. Both diagnoses are reported.

Example 2:   A patient is admitted with pneumonia, and the presence of diabetes mellitus is documented in the record. Blood sugars are monitored by laboratory studies, and nursing personnel also check blood sugars before each meal. The patient is continued on his diabetic diet. Although no active treatment is provided, ongoing monitoring is required, and the condition is reported.

Example 3:   A patient is admitted with acute diverticulitis, and the physician documents in the admitting note a history of hypertension. Review of the medical record indicates that blood pressure medications were given throughout the stay. The hypertension is reportable, and the physician should be asked to add it to the diagnostic statement.

Example 4:   A patient is admitted in congestive heart failure. She has known hiatal hernia and degenerative arthritis. Neither condition is further evaluated or treated; by their nature, the conditions do not require continuing clinical evaluation. Only the code for the congestive heart failure is assigned; the other conditions are not reportable.

Example 5:   A 60-year-old diabetic patient is transferred from an extended care facility for treatment of a pressure ulcer. The physician notes in the history and physical exam that the patient is status post left below-the-knee amputation due to peripheral vascular disease. This condition requires additional nursing assistance and is reported.

4. *Conditions that are an integral part of a disease process should not be reported as additional diagnoses, unless otherwise instructed by the classification.*

Example 1:   A patient is admitted with nausea and vomiting due to infectious gastroenteritis. Nausea and vomiting are common symptoms of infectious gastroenteritis and are not reported.

Example 2:   A patient is admitted with severe joint pain and rheumatoid arthritis. Severe joint pain is a characteristic part of rheumatoid arthritis and is not reportable.

Example 3:   A patient is seen in the physician's office complaining of urinary frequency and is diagnosed with benign prostatic hypertrophy. Although urinary frequency is a common symptom of benign prostatic hypertrophy, both conditions are reported because of the instructional note in the Tabular List under code N40.1 to use additional codes to identify associated symptoms when specified.

5. *Conditions that are not an integral part of a disease process should be coded when present.*

Example 1: A patient is admitted by ambulance following a cerebrovascular accident suffered at work. The patient was in a coma but gradually recovers consciousness. Diagnosis at discharge is reported as cerebrovascular thrombosis with coma. In this case, coma is coded as an additional diagnosis because it is not implicit in a cerebrovascular accident and is not always present.

Example 2: A five-year-old boy is admitted with a 104-degree fever associated with acute pneumonia. During the first 24 hours, the patient also experiences convulsions due to the high fever. Both the pneumonia and the convulsions are reported because convulsions are not routinely associated with pneumonia. Fever is commonly associated with pneumonia, however, and no code is assigned.

6. *Abnormal findings:* Codes from sections R70–R94 for nonspecific abnormal findings (laboratory, radiology, pathology, and other diagnostic results) should be assigned only when the physician has not been able to arrive at a related diagnosis but indicates that the abnormal finding is considered to be clinically significant by listing it in the diagnostic statement. This differs from the coding practices in the outpatient setting when one is coding encounters for diagnostic tests that have been interpreted by a physician.

The coder should never assign a code on the basis of an abnormal finding alone. To make a diagnosis on the basis of a single lab value or abnormal diagnostic finding is risky and carries the possibility of error. A value reported as either lower or higher than the normal range does not necessarily indicate a disorder. Many factors influence the values in a lab sample; these include the collection device, the method used to transport the sample to the lab, the calibration of the machine that reads the values, and the condition of the patient. For example, a patient who is dehydrated may show an elevated hemoglobin due to increased viscosity of the blood. When findings are clearly outside the normal range and the physician has ordered other tests to evaluate the condition or has prescribed treatment without documenting an associated diagnosis, it is appropriate to ask the physician whether a diagnosis should be added or whether the abnormal finding should be listed in the diagnostic statement. Incidental findings on X-ray such as asymptomatic hiatal hernia or a diverticulum should not be reported unless further evaluation or treatment is carried out.

Example 1: A low potassium level treated with intravenous or oral potassium is clinically significant and should be brought to the attention of the physician if no related diagnosis has been recorded.

Example 2: A hematocrit of 28 percent, even though asymptomatic and not treated, is evaluated with serial hematocrits. Because the finding is outside the range of normal laboratory values and has been further evaluated, the physician should be asked whether an associated diagnosis should be documented.

Example 3: A routine preoperative chest X-ray on an elderly patient reveals collapse of a vertebral body. The patient is asymptomatic, and no further evaluation or treatment is carried out. This is a common finding in elderly patients and is insignificant for this episode.

Example 4: In the absence of a cardiac problem, an isolated electrocardiographic finding of bundle branch block is ordinarily not significant, whereas a finding of a Mobitz II block may have important implications for the patient's care and warrants asking the physician whether it should be reported for this admission.

Example 5: The physician lists an abnormal sedimentation rate as part of the diagnostic statement. The physician has been unable to make a definitive diagnosis during the hospitalization in spite of further evaluation and considers the abnormal finding a significant clinical problem. Code **R70.0, Elevated erythrocyte sedimentation rate,** should be assigned.

Admitting Diagnosis

Although the admitting diagnosis is not an element of the UHDDS, it must be reported for some payers and may also be useful in quality-of-care studies. Ordinarily, only one admitting diagnosis can be reported. The inpatient admitting diagnosis may be reported as one of the following:

- A significant finding (symptom or sign) representing patient distress or an abnormal finding on outpatient examination
- A possible diagnosis based on significant findings (working diagnosis)
- A diagnosis established on an ambulatory care basis or during a previous hospital admission
- An injury or a poisoning
- A reason or condition that is not actually an illness or injury, such as a follow-up examination or pregnancy in labor

If the admitting diagnosis is reported, the code should indicate the diagnosis provided by the physician at the time of admission. Although the admitting diagnosis may not agree with the principal diagnosis on discharge, the admitting diagnosis should not be changed to conform to the principal diagnosis. Examples of admitting diagnoses and subsequent principal diagnoses follow:

- *Admitting:* K92.2 Gastrointestinal bleeding
  Principal: K26.0 Acute duodenal ulcer with hemorrhage

- *Admitting:* N63 Lump in right breast
  Principal: C50.911 Carcinoma of right female breast

- *Admitting:* K81.0 Acute cholecystitis
  Principal: K80.00 Acute cholecystitis with cholelithiasis

- *Admitting:* I50.9 Congestive heart failure
  Principal: I21.09 Acute myocardial infarction, anterior wall

- *Admitting:* I21.3 Suspected myocardial infarction
  Principal: I71.01 Dissection of thoracic aorta

PROCEDURES

The UHDDS requires that all significant procedures be reported. The UHDDS definitions of significant procedures and other reporting guidelines are discussed in chapters 9 through 11 of this handbook, along with other information on coding operations and procedures.

RELATIONSHIP OF UHDDS TO OUTPATIENT REPORTING

The UHDDS definition of principal diagnosis does not apply to the coding of outpatient encounters. In contrast to inpatient coding, no "after study" element is involved because ambulatory care visits do not permit the continued evaluation ordinarily needed to meet UHDDS criteria. If the physician does not identify a definite condition or problem at the conclusion of a visit or an encounter, the coder should report the documented chief complaint as the reason for the encounter/visit.

ETHICAL CODING AND REPORTING

Whereas coded medical data are used for a variety of purposes, they have become increasingly important in determining payment for health care. Medicare reimbursement depends on the following:

- The correct designation of the principal diagnosis
- The presence or absence of additional codes that represent complications, comorbidities, or major complications or comorbidities as defined by the Medicare severity-adjusted diagnosis-related groups system
- Procedures performed

Other third-party payers may follow slightly different reimbursement methods, but the accuracy of ICD-10-CM and ICD-10-PCS coding is always vital.

Accurate and ethical ICD-10-CM and ICD-10-PCS coding depends on correctly following all instructions in the coding manuals as well as all official guidelines developed by the cooperating parties and coding advice published in the American Hospital Association's quarterly *Coding Clinic.* (At press time, it is planned that the *AHA Coding Clinic® for ICD-9-CM* will be replaced by a similar publication for ICD-10-CM/PCS by the time ICD-10 is implemented.) Accurate and ethical reporting requires the correct selection of those conditions that meet the criteria set by the UHDDS and the official guidelines mentioned above. Over-coding and over-reporting may result in higher payment, but it is unethical and may be considered fraudulent. On the other hand, it is important to be sure that all appropriate codes are reported, as failure to include all diagnoses or procedures that meet reporting criteria may result in financial loss for the health care provider.

It is important for coders to abide by the American Health Information Management Association Standards of Ethical Coding, which are available for download at http://www.ahima.org/about/ethicsstandards.aspx.

Occasionally, certain codes are identified by Medicare or another payer as being unacceptable as the principal diagnosis. This does not mean that the code should not be assigned when it is correct; it means that the third-party payer may question or deny payment. It is important to code correctly and then make whatever adjustment is required for reporting. Otherwise, the coder runs the risk of developing incorrect coding practices that will distort data used for other purposes.

Hospitals sometimes feel a need to code nonreportable diagnoses or procedures for internal use; this is acceptable if the facility has a system for maintaining this information outside the reporting system.

There are a variety of payment policies that may have an impact on coding. Many of those policies may contradict each other or may be inconsistent with ICD-10-CM/PCS rules and conventions. Therefore, it is not possible to write coding guidelines that are consistent with all existing payer guidelines.

The following advice is shared to help providers resolve coding disputes with payers:

- First, determine whether it is really a coding dispute and not a coverage issue. For example, a payer may deny code Z01.89 for encounters for radiology and laboratory examinations. This code is to be used only for routine examinations without complaint, suspected or reported diagnosis. Many payers do not provide coverage for routine tests. So, such denials are not made on the basis of incorrect coding but rather relate to non-coverage of routine tests, e.g., annual physical exams or screening tests without signs or symptoms. Therefore, always contact the payer for clarification if the reason for the denial is unclear.

- If a payer really does have a policy that clearly conflicts with official coding rules or guidelines, every effort should be made to resolve the issue with the payer. Provide the applicable coding rule/guideline to the payer. For Medicare claims, contact the fiscal intermediary (FI) or carrier contractor for clarification. If you are not satisfied with the answer you receive, follow up with the Centers for Medicare & Medicaid Services Regional Office. The FI or carrier should be able to provide you with information as to which Regional Office has jurisdiction over your area.

- If a payer refuses to change its policy, obtain the payer requirements in writing. If the payer refuses to provide its policy in writing, document all discussions with the payer, including dates and the names of individuals involved in the discussion. Confirm the existence of the policy with the payer's supervisory personnel.

- Keep a permanent file of the documentation obtained regarding payer coding policies. It may come in handy in the event of an audit.

CHAPTER 5

The Medical Record as a Source Document

CHAPTER OVERVIEW

- The medical record is the source document for coding.
- Medical records contain a variety of reports. These include the following:
  - Reason the patient came to the hospital
  - Tests performed and their findings
  - Therapies provided
  - Descriptions of surgical procedures
  - Daily records of patient progress
- The discharge summary provides a synopsis of the patient's stay.

LEARNING OUTCOMES

After studying this chapter you should be able to:

Explain what is present in a medical record.

Understand when it is appropriate to query a physician about his or her documentation.

TERMS TO KNOW

POA indicator
present on admission indicator; a data element that applies to diagnosis codes for claims involving inpatient care

Provider
a physician or any qualified health care practitioner (such as a nurse practitioner or physician assistant) who is legally accountable for establishing the patient's diagnosis

REMEMBER . . .

The coder must make sure that the medical record documentation supports the principal diagnosis.
. . . Refer to appendix A for more information on the POA indicator.

INTRODUCTION

The source document for coding and reporting diagnoses and procedures is the medical record. Although discharge diagnoses are usually recorded on the face sheet, a final progress note, or the discharge summary, further review of the medical record is needed to ensure complete and accurate coding. Operations and procedures are frequently not listed on the face sheet or are not described in sufficient detail, making a review of operative reports, pathology reports, and other special reports imperative. The entire record should be reviewed to determine the specific reason for the encounter and the conditions treated.

Physicians sometimes fail to list reportable conditions that developed during the stay but were resolved prior to discharge. Conditions such as urinary tract infection or dehydration, for example, are often not included in the diagnostic statement even though progress notes, physicians' orders, and laboratory reports make it clear that such conditions were treated. It is inappropriate for coders to assign a diagnosis based solely on a physician's orders for prescribed medications without the physician's documentation of the diagnosis being treated. If enough information is present to strongly suggest that an additional diagnosis should be reported, the physician should be consulted; no diagnosis should be added without the approval of the physician. Because diagnostic statements sometimes include diagnoses that represent past history or existing diagnoses that do not meet the Uniform Hospital Discharge Data Set (UHDDS) guidelines for reportable diagnoses, a review of the medical record is required to determine whether these diagnoses should be coded for this encounter.

It is customary to list the principal diagnosis first in the diagnostic statement. Many physicians, however, are not aware of coding and reporting guidelines, and, consequently, this custom is not consistently followed. Because the correct designation of the principal diagnosis is of critical importance in reporting diagnostic information, the coder must be sure that medical record documentation supports the designation of principal diagnosis. If it appears that another diagnosis should be designated as the principal diagnosis, or if conditions not listed should be reported, the coder should follow the health care facility's procedures for obtaining a corrected diagnostic statement.

CONTENTS OF THE MEDICAL RECORD

Medical records contain a variety of reports that document the reason the patient came to the hospital, the tests performed and their findings, the therapies provided, descriptions of any surgical procedures, and daily records of the patient's progress. Each report contains important information needed for accurate coding and reporting of the principal diagnosis, other diagnoses, and the procedures performed.

A number of standard reports can be found in almost any medical record, but other reports will appear depending on the condition for which the patient is being treated, the extent of workup and therapy provided, and the attending physician's style of documentation. For example, a physician may list final diagnoses on the admission record (face sheet), on progress notes, or on the discharge summary. Consultants occasionally record their consultation notes in the progress notes rather than on separate reports.

Review of the inpatient medical record should begin with the discharge summary, when available, because it provides a synopsis of the patient's hospital stay, including the reason for admission, significant diagnostic findings, the treatment given, the patient's course in the hospital, the follow-up plan, and the final diagnostic statement. The history section usually indicates the reason for admission (principal diagnosis), which may require confirmation by review of the history and physical examination and admitting and emergency department records.

The section of the discharge summary that describes the patient's course in the hospital usually indicates treatment that has been given and any further workup that has been done. It is particularly useful in determining whether all listed diagnoses meet the criteria for reporting and identifying other conditions that may merit reporting.

Conditions mentioned elsewhere in the body of the discharge summary do not necessarily warrant reporting but may provide clues for more specific review to make a final determination. The medical record should be reviewed further to determine whether such conditions meet the criteria for reportable diagnoses as defined in the UHDDS. The medication record is often helpful in indicating that therapeutic treatment may have been administered, but the coder must not assume a diagnosis solely on the basis of medication administration or abnormal findings in diagnostic reports. In addition, recorded diagnoses do not always contain sufficient information for providing the required specificity in coding. For example, a diagnosis of pneumonia may not indicate the organism responsible for the infection; a review of diagnostic studies of the sputum may provide this information. The physician should be asked to confirm that the organism discovered on the positive culture is the causative agent. Then the physician should indicate his or her confirmation by documenting it in the medical record; this step must be taken before a code identifying the specific type of pneumonia can be assigned. A diagnosis of fracture may indicate which bone was fractured but not the particular part of the bone, information that is necessary for accurate code assignment. The X-ray or the operative report should supply these data.

Some facilities may develop their own additional coding guidelines to provide assistance in determining when a physician query is appropriate. If the test findings are outside the normal range and the physician has ordered other tests to evaluate the condition or prescribed treatment, it is appropriate to ask the physician whether the diagnosis should be added. However, a facility's internal guidelines may not interpret abnormal findings to replace physician documentation or a physician query.

The following examples illustrate diagnoses that are often recorded with less-than-complete information but can be coded more specifically by referring to diagnostic reports within the medical record and then obtaining the appropriate physician confirmation. Note the variation in code assignment when more information is available after physician confirmation:

- *Diagnosis:*   C53.9   Cancer of cervix
  Pathology report: D06.9   Carcinoma, in situ, of cervix

- *Diagnosis:*   N39.0   Urinary tract infection
  Laboratory report: N39.0 + B96.2   *E. coli* in urine

- *Diagnosis:*   S72.90xA   Fracture of femur, initial encounter
  X-ray report: S72.21xB   Open fracture of subtrochanteric neck of the right femur, initial encounter

Code assignment is generally based on the attending physician's documentation. It is also appropriate to base code assignment on the documentation of other physicians (e.g., consultants, residents, anesthesiologists) involved in the care and treatment of the patient so long as there is no conflicting information from the attending physician. A physician query is not necessary if a physician involved in the care and treatment of the patient, including consulting physicians, has documented a diagnosis and there is no conflicting documentation from another physician. If documentation from different physicians conflicts, the attending physician should be queried for clarification because he or she is ultimately responsible for the final diagnosis.

For inpatient coding, if the attending physician does not confirm the pathological or radiological findings, query him or her regarding the clinical significance of the findings and request that appropriate documentation be provided. Although the pathologist or radiologist provides a written interpretation of a tissue biopsy or an X-ray image, this is not equivalent to the attending physician's medical diagnosis, which is based on the patient's complete clinical picture. The attending physician is responsible for, and directly involved in, the care and treatment of the patient. A pathologist's interpretation of a specimen or a radiologist's interpretation of an image is not the same as a diagnosis provided by a physician directly involved in the patient's care. For example, if the attending physician documented "breast mass" and the pathologist documented "carcinoma of the breast," this would be conflicting information requiring clarification from the attending physician.

When coding outpatient laboratory, pathology, and radiology encounters in hospital-based as well as stand-alone facilities, it is appropriate to assign codes on the basis of the written interpretation by a radiologist or pathologist.

In some institutions, midlevel providers, such as nurse practitioners and physician assistants, are involved in the care of the patient and document diagnoses in the medical record. It is appropriate to base code assignments on the documentation of midlevel providers if they are considered legally accountable for establishing a diagnosis within the regulations governing the provider and the facility. The *ICD-10-CM Official Guidelines for Coding and Reporting* use the term "provider" to mean physician or any qualified health care practitioner who is legally accountable for establishing the patient's diagnosis.

Not all reportable services or procedures during an encounter or admission are performed or documented by physicians. It is appropriate to assign a procedure code based on documentation by the nonphysician professional who provided the service. This applies only to procedure coding where there is documentation to substantiate the code. It does not apply to diagnosis coding. The documentation from the nonphysician professional who provided the service may be the only evidence that the service was provided. This is true of services such as infusions carried out by nurses and therapies provided by physical, respiratory, or occupational therapists.

Outpatient records generally contain less information than inpatient records do. Nevertheless, all available reports for the encounter should be reviewed prior to code assignment. Code assignment is dependent on the information available at the time of code assignment.

For ambulatory records, an additional data element called "patient's reason for visit" (PRV) is usually reported. The PRV is reported on unscheduled outpatient visits (e.g., emergency department or urgent care visits) to identify the main reason the patient sought treatment. The reason may differ from the physician's final diagnosis at the end of the encounter. Only one diagnosis code can be reported in this field on the electronic claim. If there are multiple conditions present, the code most likely to justify the patient encounter should be reported. This data element is now Form Locator 70a–c on the revised UB-04 paper claim. With the anticipated conversion in January 2012 to a new version (5010) for the electronic claims, both the UB-04 paper claim and the electronic claim will allow the reporting of three diagnosis codes.

The "present on admission" (POA) indicator is a data element approved by the National Uniform Billing Committee for inpatient reporting. The POA indicator applies to the diagnosis codes for claims involving inpatient admissions to general acute care hospitals or other facilities. Please refer to appendix A of this handbook for more detailed information on this topic.

CHAPTER 6

Basic ICD-10-CM Coding Steps

CHAPTER OVERVIEW

- There are three basic steps for locating codes to be assigned.
    - Locate the main term in the Alphabetic Index. Search for subterms, notes, or cross-references.
    - Verify the code number in the Tabular List.
    - Assign the verified code or codes.
- It is important to understand basic coding techniques before moving on to the harder, system-based chapters of this handbook.

LEARNING OUTCOMES

After studying this chapter you should be able to:

Locate code entries in the Alphabetic Index.

Determine the course of action when there are discrepancies between the Alphabetic Index and the Tabular List.

Perform basic coding techniques.

TERMS TO KNOW

Alphabetic Index of Diseases and Injuries and the Index to External Causes of Injury include entries for main terms (diseases, conditions, or injuries) and subterms (site, type, or etiology), the Neoplasm Table, and the Table of Drugs and Chemicals

Tabular List contains categories, subcategories, and valid codes

REMEMBER . . .

You can't begin to code unless you have determined the principal diagnosis and other reportable diagnoses from the medical record.

INTRODUCTION

Once the medical record has been reviewed to determine the principal/first-listed diagnosis and other reportable diagnoses, the following steps in locating the codes to be assigned should be undertaken:

1. Locate the main term in the Alphabetic Index.
   - Review subterms and nonessential modifiers related to the main term.
   - Follow any cross-reference instructions.
   - Refer to any notes in the Alphabetic Index.
   - A dash (-) at the end of an Index entry indicates that additional characters are required.
2. Verify the code number in the Tabular List.
   - Read the code title.
   - Read and follow any instructional notes. Refer to other codes as instructed.
   - Determine whether an additional character must be added.
   - Determine laterality (right or left) and any applicable extensions.
3. Assign the verified code or codes.

It is imperative that these steps be followed without exception; the condition to be coded must first be located in the Alphabetic Index and then verified in the Tabular List. Relying on memory or using only the Index or Tabular List may lead to incorrect code assignment.

LOCATE THE CODE ENTRY
IN THE ALPHABETIC INDEX

The first step in coding is to locate the main term in the Alphabetic Index. In the ICD-10-CM Alphabetic Index, the condition is listed as the main term, usually expressed as a noun. General terms such as "admission," "encounter," and "examination" are used to locate code entries for the Z code section. Some conditions are indexed under more than one main term. For example, anxiety reaction can be located in either of the following Index entries:

> **Anxiety** . . .
> -reaction F41.1
>
> **Reaction** . . .
> -anxiety F41.1

If a main term cannot be located, the coder should consider a synonym, an eponym, or another alternative term. Once the main term is located, a search should be made of subterms, notes, or cross-references. Subterms provide more specific information of many types and must be checked carefully, following all the rules of alphabetization. The main term code entry should not be assigned until all subterm possibilities have been exhausted. During this process, it may be necessary to refer again to the medical record to determine whether any additional information is available to permit assignment of a more specific code. If a subterm cannot be located, the non-essential modifiers following the main term should be reviewed to see whether the subterm may be included there. If not, alternative terms should be considered.

EXERCISE 6.1

Without referring to the Alphabetic Index of Diseases and Injuries, underline the word that indicates the main term for each diagnosis.

1. Acute myocardial <u>infarction</u>

2. Chronic <u>hypertrophy</u> of tonsils and adenoids

3. Acute suppurative <u>cholecystitis</u>

4. Syphilitic aortic <u>aneurysm</u>

5. Normal, spontaneous <u>delivery</u>, full-term infant

6. Drug <u>overdose</u> due to barbiturates

7. Urinary tract <u>infection</u> due to *E. coli*

8. Hemorrhagic <u>pneumonia</u>

9. <u>Admission</u> for adjustment of artificial arm

10. Bilateral inguinal <u>hernia</u>

VERIFY THE CODE NUMBER IN THE TABULAR LIST

Once a code number entry has been located in the Alphabetic Index, the coder must refer to that number in the Tabular List; a code should not be assigned without such verification. In addition to the title for the code entry, it may be necessary for coders to review the title for the chapter, section, and category in order to be sure the correct code has been identified. Although the title in the Tabular List does not always match exactly the Alphabetic Index entry, it is usually clear whether it applies. For example:

- Appendicitis (K37) has an additional modifier of "unspecified" in the Tabular List. This alerts the coder to look elsewhere when the type of appendicitis is stated in the medical record.

- Painful menstruation (N94.6) has the title **Dysmenorrhea, unspecified,** in the Tabular List. Although the title in the Tabular List is not identical to the term in the Alphabetic Index, it is clear that it is the right code for this condition.

Any significant discrepancy between the Index entry and the tabular listing should alert the coder to the need to review the Alphabetic Index for a more appropriate term.

All instructional terms and notes should be read and followed when they apply, with particular attention to exclusion notes. Ordinarily the code number listed with the main term entry in the Index is for an unspecified condition. It is important to review other codes in the related area to determine whether a more specific code can be assigned.

CODING DEMONSTRATIONS

Follow the steps outlined above to determine the correct code for each of the diagnostic statements listed below:

- **Hirsutism**

  Refer to the main term **Hirsutism** in the Alphabetic Index, which provides a code of L68.0. Note that there are no subterms. Verify this by referring to code L68.0 in the Tabular List. In this case, the Index entry and Tabular List title are identical and code L68.0 should be assigned.

- **Portal vein obstruction**

  Refer to code I81 by the main term **Obstruction** in the Alphabetic Index and the subterm for portal (circulation) (vein). An inclusion note in the Tabular List indicates "portal (vein) obstruction." If you are uncertain whether thrombosis and obstruction are the same condition for the purposes of coding, check the Index for the main term **Thrombosis.**

- **Abscess abdominal wall due to Staphylococcus**

  Look up the main term **Abscess;** and then the subterm "abdomen, abdominal"; and then subterm "wall." The code entry is L02.211. Read the "use additional note" in the Tabular List that advises you to also assign a code to identify the organism involved (B95–B96). Hint: if you have trouble locating this note, find it under the category title L02. Look up **Infection,** staphylococcal, and the subterm "as cause of disease classified elsewhere" and find code B95.8, which is assigned in the Tabular List. The code title is "Unspecified staphylococcus as the cause of diseases classified elsewhere." Review the medical record for any mention of the specific type of *Staphylococcus*. If one is mentioned, consider assigning the code B95.6 or B95.7; if not, assign code B95.8 as an additional code.

- **Aplasia of pulmonary artery**

  Refer to the main term **Aplasia.** Check the subterms, and note that there is no entry for pulmonary artery but that there is a cross-reference note to "see also Agenesis." Follow the cross-reference advice and refer to Agenesis. You immediately see a more specific subterm for "artery, pulmonary," with code entry Q25.7. The title for this code in the Tabular List is "Other congenital malformations of pulmonary artery," and it is clearly the correct code for this condition. As additional confirmation that this is the correct code, "agenesis of pulmonary artery" is listed as an inclusion term.

- **Acute bronchopneumonia due to aspiration of oil**

  Locate the main term **Bronchopneumonia** in the Alphabetic Index. Note the cross-reference instruction to "see Pneumonia, broncho." Follow the cross-reference by turning to the main term **Pneumonia** (acute) (Alpenstich) (benign). . . . Note that the term "acute" is a nonessential modifier enclosed in parentheses under the main term **Pneumonia.** This applies also to the subterm, and so this term has now been accounted for but does not directly affect code assignment. Refer to the following subterms listed under the main term:

> **Pneumonia** (acute) (Alpenstich) (benign) . . .
> -broncho-, bronchial (confluent) (croupous)
>   (diffuse) (disseminated) (hemorrhagic) . . .
> -aspiration—see Pneumonia, aspiration

Note the cross-reference to "see Pneumonia, aspiration." Refer back to the subterm "aspiration" and locate the code J69.0. Search through the main term and subterms cited above and underline the component parts of the diagnostic statement that have been located so far. Note that all component parts of the diagnostic statement except "of oil" have been located. Refer back to "Pneumonia, aspiration," and you will see that there are additional subterms here under the connecting words "due to," with a subterm for "oils and essences," that takes you to code J69.1. Refer to code J69.1 in the Tabular List, and note that the title for this code is "Pneumonitis due to inhalation of oils and essences." Although the title is not worded exactly the same as the diagnosis, there is such a close correlation that it is clear that this is the code that should be assigned. Assign code J69.1 because it covers all elements of the diagnosis and no instructional notes contradict its use.

REVIEW EXERCISE 6.2

Using the Alphabetic Index and the Tabular List, code the following diagnoses.

1.	Chronic hypertrophy of tonsils and adenoids	J35.3
2.	Fibrocystic disease of breast (female)	N60.19
3.	Acute suppurative mastoiditis with subperiosteal abscess	H70.019
4.	Recurrent direct left inguinal hernia with gangrene	K40.41
5.	Acute upper respiratory infection with influenza	J11.1
6.	Benign cyst of right breast	N60.01
7.	Bunion, right great toe	M20.11
8.	Nondisplaced abduction fracture anterior acetabulum, subsequent encounter with routine healing	S32.436D
9.	Bronchiectasis with acute bronchitis	J47.0
10.	Acute bleeding peptic ulcer	K27.0

CHAPTER 7

Basic ICD-10-CM Coding Guidelines

CHAPTER OVERVIEW

- There are basic principles that all coders must follow.
- It is important to use both the Alphabetic Index and the Tabular List during the coding process.
  - Follow all instructional notes.
  - Even if common codes have been memorized, refer to the Alphabetic Index and Tabular List.
- Always assign codes to the highest level of detail.
  - All characters must be used.
  - None can be omitted or added.
- NEC and NOS codes should be assigned only when appropriate.
- Combination codes should be used if they are available.
  - Assign multiple codes as needed to fully describe a condition.
  - Avoid coding irrelevant information.

LEARNING OUTCOMES

After studying this chapter you should be able to:

- Determine what level of detail to assign to a code.
- Understand how to use combination codes.
- Explain how to assign multiple codes to fully describe a condition.
- Determine what qualifications determine whether an unconfirmed diagnosis is coded as though it were an established diagnosis.
- Explain the difference between "rule out" and "ruled out."
- Code acute and chronic conditions.
- Code a condition labeled "impending," "threatened," or "late effect."

TERMS TO KNOW

Combination code
a single code used to classify two diagnoses, a diagnosis with a secondary condition, or a diagnosis with an associated complication

NEC
not elsewhere classified

NOS
not otherwise specified

"Rule out"
indicates that a diagnosis is still possible

"Ruled out"
indicates that a diagnosis once considered likely is no longer possible

REMEMBER . . .

For the current version of the *ICD-10-CM Official Guidelines for Coding and Reporting* visit www.ahacentraloffice.org.

INTRODUCTION

The basic coding guidelines discussed in this chapter apply throughout the ICD-10-CM classification system. Following these principles is vital to accurate code selection and correct sequencing. Guidelines that apply to specific chapters of ICD-10-CM will be discussed in the relevant chapters of this handbook. To download a copy of the current version of the complete *ICD-10-CM Official Guidelines for Coding and Reporting,* please visit www.ahacentraloffice.org. This handbook has been prepared using the 2011 version of the Official Coding Guidelines. Adherence to the guidelines when assigning ICD-10-CM diagnosis codes is required under the Health Insurance Portability and Accountability Act. The instructions and conventions of the classification take precedence over guidelines.

USE BOTH THE ALPHABETIC INDEX AND THE TABULAR LIST

Section I of the ICD-10-CM Official Coding Guidelines contains the conventions, general coding guidelines, and chapter-specific guidelines. The conventions for ICD-10-CM are the general rules for use of the classification independent of the guidelines. These conventions are incorporated within the Alphabetic Index and Tabular List of ICD-10-CM as instructional notes.

The first coding principle is that both the Alphabetic Index and the Tabular List must be used to locate and assign appropriate codes. The diagnosis, condition, or reason for visit to be coded must first be located in the Index, and the code provided there must then be verified in the Tabular List. The Index does not provide the full code. Selection of the full code, including laterality and any applicable seventh character, can only be done using the Tabular List. The coder must follow all instructional notes to ensure that more specific subterms or other instructional notes are not overlooked. Experienced coders sometimes rely on their memory for commonly used codes, but consistent reference to the Alphabetic Index and the Tabular List is imperative, no matter how experienced the coder is.

ASSIGN CODES TO THE HIGHEST LEVEL OF DETAIL

A second basic principle is that codes must be used to the highest number of characters available. This can be accomplished by following these steps:

1. Assign a three-character disease code only if it is not further divided (when there are no four-character codes within that category).

2. Assign a four-character code only when there are no five-character codes within that subcategory.

3. Assign a five-character code only when there are no six-character codes for that subcategory.

4. Assign a six-character code when a sixth-character subclassification is provided.

5. Assign a seventh-character extension when provided.

All characters must be used. None can be omitted, and none can be added. The one exception to this rule is the placeholder character "x." For codes less than six characters that require a seventh character, a placeholder "x" should be assigned for all characters less than six. The seventh character must always be the seventh character of a code. An example of this exception is at categories T36–T50 (poisoning, adverse effects, and underdosing codes).

The following examples demonstrate these basic coding principles:

- Refer to the Tabular List, category J40, Bronchitis, not specified as acute or chronic. Code J40 has no fourth-character subdivisions; therefore, the three-character code is assigned.

- Refer to Tabular List, category K35, Acute appendicitis. This category includes fourth characters that indicate the presence of generalized or localized peritonitis. Because fourth-character subdivisions are provided, code K35 cannot be assigned.

- Refer to Tabular List, category J45, Asthma. Category J45 has five fourth-character subdivisions (J45.2, J45.3, J45.4, J45.5, and J45.9). It also uses a fifth-character subclassification to specify whether there is any mention of status asthmaticus or acute exacerbation. Any code assignment from category J45 must have five characters (for subcategories J45.2–J45.5) or six characters (for subcategory J45.9) to ensure coding accuracy.

- Refer to Tabular List, category T27, Burn and corrosion of respiratory tract. Category T27 has eight four-character subdivisions to specify whether the condition is burn or corrosion and to provide detail on the part of the respiratory tract affected. The general note at category T27 also indicates that the appropriate seventh character is to be added to each code from this category. Because the codes from category T27 are only four characters long, the placeholder character "x" is used as a fifth- and sixth-character placeholder before the seventh character can be added. For example, an initial encounter for burn of the larynx and trachea would be coded to T27.0xxA.

ASSIGN RESIDUAL CODES (NEC AND NOS) AS APPROPRIATE

The main term entry in the Alphabetic Index is usually followed by the code number for the unspecified condition. This code should never be assigned without a careful review of subterms to determine whether a more specific code can be located. When the coder's review does not identify a more specific code entry in the Index, the titles and inclusion notes in the subdivisions under either the three-character, four-character, or five-character code in the Tabular List should be reviewed. The residual NOS (not otherwise specified) code should never be assigned when a more specific code is available. The following examples demonstrate this basic coding principle:

- Refer to the Alphabetic Index for nontraumatic hematoma of breast, which is classified as N64.89. This is listed as "other" specified disorders of the breast. Even though the diagnosis is very specific, no separate code is provided.

- Refer to the Alphabetic Index for phlebitis. Note that phlebitis, not otherwise specified, is assigned to code **I80.9, Phlebitis and thrombophlebitis of unspecified site.** Now suppose that review of the medical record provides even further specificity, that this is phlebitis of not only the lower extremity but the right popliteal vein. The more specific code **I80.221, Phlebitis and thrombophlebitis of right popliteal vein,** should be assigned.

ASSIGN COMBINATION CODES WHEN AVAILABLE

A single code used to classify either two diagnoses, a diagnosis with an associated secondary process (manifestation), or a diagnosis with an associated complication is called a combination code. Combination codes can be located in the Index by referring to subterm entries, with particular reference to subterms that follow connecting words such as "with," "due to," "in," and "associated with." Other combination codes can be identified by reading inclusion and exclusion notes in the Tabular List.

Only the combination code is assigned when that code fully identifies the diagnostic conditions involved or when the Alphabetic Index so directs. For example:

K80.00	Acute cholecystitis with cholelithiasis
J02.0	Acute pharyngitis due to streptococcal infection
K41.11	Bilateral recurrent femoral hernia with gangrene
H40.812	Glaucoma with increased episcleral venous pressure, left eye

---

EXERCISE 7.1

Code the following diagnoses.

1. Influenza with gastroenteritis — J11.2

2. Acute cholecystitis with cholelithiasis and choledocholithiasis — K80.62

3. Meningitis due to *Salmonella* infection — A02.21

Occasionally, a combination code lacks the necessary specificity to describe the manifestation or complication; in such cases, an additional code may be assigned. The coder should be guided by directions in the Tabular List for the use of an additional code or codes that may provide more specificity. For example, code O99.01- classifies anemia complicating pregnancy. Because it does not indicate the type of anemia, an additional code can be assigned for this purpose.

ASSIGN MULTIPLE CODES AS NEEDED

Multiple coding is the use of more than one code to fully identify the component elements of a complex diagnostic or procedural statement. A complex statement is one that involves connecting words or phrases such as "with," "due to," "incidental to," "secondary to," or similar terminology. The coder should be guided by directions in the Tabular List for the use of an additional code or codes that may provide more specificity. When no combination code is provided, multiple codes should be assigned as needed to fully describe the condition regardless of whether there is advice to that effect.

Mandatory Multiple Coding

The term "dual classification" is used to describe the required assignment of two codes to provide information about both a manifestation and the associated underlying disease or etiology. Mandatory multiple coding is identified in the Alphabetic Index by the use of a second code in brackets. The first code identifies the underlying condition, and the second identifies the manifestation. Both codes must be assigned and sequenced in the order listed.

In the Tabular List the need for dual coding is indicated by the presence of a "use additional code" note with the code for the underlying condition, and a "code first underlying condition" note with the manifestation code. In printed versions of the manuals, the manifestation code is in italics.

Manifestation codes cannot be designated as the principal diagnosis, and a code for the underlying condition must always be listed first, except for an occasional situation where other directions are provided. A code in brackets in the Alphabetic Index can be used only as a secondary code for the specific condition or procedure indexed in this way. For example:

G20 + F02.80   Dementia in Parkinson's disease
D66 + M36.2   Arthritis in hemophilia

EXERCISE 7.2

Code the following diagnoses according to the coding principles for correct sequencing of codes.

1. Amyloid heart   E85.4

                                                                           I43

2. Chorioretinitis due to histoplasmosis   B39.9

                                                                           H32

3. Combined spinal cord degeneration with anemia   D51.3
   due to dietary vitamin B12 deficiency   G32.0

4. Otomycosis, right ear   B36.9

                                                                           H62.41

5. Cataract associated with galactosemia   E74.21

                                                                           H28

Discretionary Multiple Coding

The "code first" notes appear in the Tabular List under certain codes that are not specifically manifestation codes, but codes in which the condition may be due to an underlying cause. When there is a "code first" note and an underlying condition is present, the underlying condition should be sequenced first. For example, malignant ascites (R18.0) has a note to "code first" the malignancy, such as: malignant neoplasm of ovary (C56.-). In this situation, code C56.- would be assigned first, followed by code R18.0

The "code, if applicable, any causal condition first" note indicates that multiple codes should be assigned only if the causal condition is documented as being present. For example, "Other retention of urine" (R33.8) requires that the code to identify enlarged prostate (N40.1) be assigned as the first-listed code or principal diagnosis, but only if it is documented as being the cause of the urinary retention.

The instruction to "use additional code" indicates that multiple codes should be assigned only if the condition mentioned is documented as being present. Examples include the following:

- Malignant neoplasm of base of tongue (C01) requires an additional code to identify history of tobacco use (Z87.891), but only when history of tobacco use is documented in the medical record.
- Urinary tract infection (N39.0) requires an additional code to identify the organism if it is documented, such as positive culture of *E. coli* (B96.2).

EXERCISE 7.3

Code the following diagnoses.

1.	Acute cystitis due to *E. coli* infection	N30.00
		B96.2
2.	Alcoholic gastritis due to chronic alcoholism	K29.20
		F10.20
3.	Diverticulitis of colon with intestinal hemorrhage	K57.33
4.	Diabetic neuralgia due to type 2 diabetes mellitus, patient on insulin	E11.42
		Z79.4
5.	Erythema multiforme with arthritis	L51.9
		M14.80
6.	Fulminant hepatitis, type A, with hepatic coma	B15.0

Avoid Indiscriminate Multiple Coding

Indiscriminate coding of irrelevant information should be avoided. For example, codes for symptoms or signs characteristic of the diagnosis and integral to it should not be assigned. Codes are never assigned solely on the basis of findings of diagnostic tests, such as laboratory, X-ray, or electrocardiographic tests, unless the diagnosis is confirmed by the physician. This guideline differs from the coding practices in the outpatient setting when one is coding encounters for diagnostic tests that have been interpreted by a physician. Codes should not be assigned for conditions that do not meet Uniform Hospital Discharge Data Set criteria for reporting. For example, diagnostic reports often mention such conditions as hiatal hernia, atelectasis, and right bundle branch block with no further mention to indicate any relevance to the care given. Assigning a code is inappropriate for reporting purposes unless the physician provides documentation to support the condition's significance for the episode of care.

Codes designated as unspecified are never assigned when a more specific code for the same general condition is assigned. For example, diabetes mellitus with unspecified complication (E11.8) would never be assigned when a code for diabetes with renal complication (E11.29) is assigned for the same episode of care.

Laterality

ICD-10-CM has the ability to capture information for conditions that may affect bilateral parts of the body. For bilateral sites, the final character of the code indicates which side (left or right) is affected. Character "1" is always the right side, while character "2" indicates the left side. When a bilateral code is provided, character "3" is used to denote bilateral. The classification also provides an unspecified code for when the side is not identified in the medical record. The unspecified side is either a character "0" or "9" depending on whether it is a fifth or sixth character. If no bilateral code is provided, and the condition is bilateral, assign separate codes for both the left and right side. For example:

Q70.10   Webbed fingers, unspecified hand
Q70.11   Webbed fingers, right hand
Q70.12   Webbed fingers, left hand
Q70.13   Webbed fingers, bilateral

CODE UNCONFIRMED DIAGNOSES AS IF ESTABLISHED

When a diagnosis for an inpatient admission is qualified as "possible," "probable," "suspected," "likely," "questionable," "?," or "rule out" at the time of discharge, the condition should be coded and reported as though the diagnosis were established. Other terms that fit the definition of a probable or suspected condition are "consistent with," "compatible with," "indicative of," "suggestive of," "appears to be," and "comparable with." Note that the exception to this guideline is the coding of HIV infection/illness and influenza due to certain identified influenza viruses (e.g., avian influenza or H1N1 virus). Code only cases confirmed by physician documentation. The guideline regarding unconfirmed diagnoses does not apply to coding or reporting for outpatient services. For these patients, code to the highest degree of certainty, such as symptoms, signs, or abnormalities. For example:

- A patient is admitted with severe generalized abdominal pain.
  The physician's diagnostic statement on discharge is:
  abdominal pain, probably due to acute gastritis.   K29.00
  Only the code for gastritis is assigned as the pain is implicit
  in the diagnosis.

- A patient is admitted and discharged with a final diagnosis of
  probable peptic ulcer with a recommendation for additional workup.   K27.9

- A patient is admitted as an inpatient and discharged with possible
  posttraumatic brain syndrome, nonpsychotic.   F07.81

- A patient is seen in the outpatient clinic with malaise.
  The physician's diagnostic statement is possible viral syndrome.   R53.81

Caution should be used in coding unconfirmed diagnoses of conditions such as epilepsy, HIV disease, and multiple sclerosis as if they were established. Incorrect reporting of such conditions can have serious personal consequences for the patient, such as the inability to obtain a driver's license and possible social and job discrimination. Physicians are often unaware that official coding guidelines require a diagnosis qualified as unconfirmed to be coded as if established; therefore, the coder should consult the physician before assigning codes for such unconfirmed conditions.

"Rule Out" versus "Ruled Out"

It is important to distinguish between the terms "rule out," which indicates that a diagnosis is still considered to be possible, and "ruled out," which indicates that a diagnosis originally considered as likely is no longer a possibility.

Diagnoses qualified by the term "rule out" are coded as if established for inpatient episodes of care in the same way that diagnoses described as possible or probable are coded. A diagnosis described as "ruled out" is never coded. If an alternative condition has been identified, that diagnosis should be coded; otherwise, a code for the presenting symptom or other precursor condition should be assigned. Here are some examples of codes assigned according to this coding principle:

- Rule out gastric ulcer . . .   K25.9   *[condition is coded]*
- Acute appendicitis, ruled out;
  Meckel's diverticulum found at surgery . . .   Q43.0   *[code only the diverticulum]*
- Rule out angiodysplasia of the colon . . .   K55.20 *[condition is coded]*

ACUTE AND CHRONIC CONDITIONS

When the same condition is described as both acute (or subacute) and chronic, it should be coded according to the Alphabetic Index subentries for that condition. If separate subterms for acute (or subacute) and chronic are listed at the same indention level in the Alphabetic Index, both codes are assigned, with the code for the acute condition sequenced first. (Note that a condition described as subacute is coded as acute if there is no separate subterm entry for subacute.) For example, refer to the Alphabetic Index entry for acute and chronic bronchitis:

> **Bronchitis . . .**
> -acute or subacute . . . J20.9 . . .
> -chronic . . . J42

Because both subterms appear at the same indention level, both codes are assigned, with code J20.9 sequenced first.

When only one term is listed as a subterm, with the other in parentheses as a nonessential modifier, only the code listed for the subterm is assigned. For example, for a diagnosis of acute and chronic adenoiditis, the Alphabetic Index entry is as follows:

> **Adenoiditis** (chronic) J35.02 . . .
> -acute J03.90

The only code assigned in this situation is **J03.90, Acute tonsillitis, unspecified.**

In some cases, a combination code has been provided for use when the condition is described as both acute and chronic. For example, code J96.20 includes both acute and chronic respiratory failure. When there are no subentries for acute (or subacute) or chronic, these modifiers are disregarded in coding the condition. For example, refer to **Mastopathy,** cystic. Neither acute nor chronic is listed as a subterm, and so code N60.1- is assigned.

EXERCISE 7.4

Code the following diagnoses.

1.	Acute and chronic appendicitis	K35.80
		K36
2.	Subacute and chronic pyelonephritis	N10
		N11.9
3.	Acute and chronic cervicitis	N72

IMPENDING OR THREATENED CONDITION

Selection of a code for a condition described at the time of discharge, or at the conclusion of an outpatient encounter, as impending or threatened depends first on whether the condition actually occurred. If so, the threatened/impending condition is coded as a confirmed diagnosis.

For example, a medical record shows a diagnosis of threatened premature labor at 28 weeks gestation. Review of the medical record indicates that a stillborn was delivered during the hospital stay. This is coded as **O60.14x0, Preterm labor third trimester with preterm delivery third trimester, not applicable or unspecified,** because the threatened condition did occur.

If neither the threatened/impending condition nor a related condition occurred, however, the coder must refer to the Alphabetic Index to answer the following two questions: Is the condition indexed under the main term threatened or impending? Is there a subterm for impending or threatened under the main term for the condition? If such terms appear, the coder should assign the code provided. There are several subterms under each of the main terms **Impending** and **Threatened,** as well as several main terms with such subentries. For example, if a patient is admitted with threatened abortion but the abortion is averted, the code **O20.0, Threatened abortion,** is assigned, because there is an Index entry for "threatened" under the main term **Abortion.**

When neither term is indexed, the precursor condition that actually existed is coded; a code is not assigned for the condition described as impending or threatened. For example, a patient is admitted with a diagnosis of impending gangrene of the lower extremities, but the gangrene was averted by prompt treatment. Because the gangrene did not occur and there is no index entry for impending gangrene, a code must be assigned for the presenting situation that suggested the possibility of gangrene, such as redness or swelling of the extremity.

REPORTING THE SAME DIAGNOSIS CODE MORE THAN ONCE

Each unique ICD-10-CM diagnosis code may be reported only once for an encounter. This applies both to bilateral conditions when there are no distinct codes identifying laterality and to two different conditions classified to the same ICD-10-CM diagnosis code.

LATE EFFECTS

A late effect is a residual condition that remains after the termination of the acute phase of an illness or injury. Such conditions may occur at any time after an acute injury or illness. There is no set period of time that must elapse before a condition is considered to be a late effect. Some late effects are apparent early; others may make an appearance long after the original injury or illness has been resolved. Certain conditions due to trauma, such as contractures and scarring, are inherent late effects no matter how early they occur.

Late effects include conditions reported as such or as sequela of a previous illness or injury. The fact that a condition is a late effect may be inferred when the diagnostic statement includes terms such as the following:

- Late
- Old
- Due to previous injury or illness
- Following previous injury or illness
- Traumatic, unless there is evidence of current injury

EXERCISE 7.5

Write an "X" next to each diagnostic statement given below that identifies a late effect of an injury or illness. For each such statement, underline the residual condition once and the cause of the late effect twice.

---

1. Hemiplegia due to previous cerebrovascular accident   X

2. Joint contracture of fracture, right index finger   X

3. Scoliosis due to old infantile paralysis   X

4. Laceration of tendon of finger two weeks ago; admitted now for tendon repair

5. Keloid secondary to injury nine months ago   X

6. Mental retardation due to previous viral encephalitis   X

Locating Late Effect Codes

Codes that indicate the cause of a late effect can be located by referring to the main term **Sequelae** in the Alphabetic Index of Diseases and Injuries (with the exception of late effects due to injury, poisoning, and certain other consequences of external causes). Note that ICD-10-CM provides only a limited number of codes to indicate the cause of a late effect:

B90.0–B90.9	Sequelae of tuberculosis
B91	Sequelae of poliomyelitis
B92	Sequelae of leprosy
B94.0–B94.9	Sequelae of other and unspecified infectious and parasitic diseases
E64.0–E64.9	Sequelae of malnutrition and other nutritional deficiencies

E68	Sequelae of hyperalimentation
G09	Sequelae of inflammatory diseases of central nervous system
G65.0–G65.2	Sequelae of inflammatory and toxic polyneuropathies
I69.0–I69.9	Sequelae of cerebrovascular disease
O94	Sequelae of complication of pregnancy, childbirth, and the puerperium

Two Codes Required

Complete coding of late effects requires two codes:

- The condition or nature of the late effect
- The late effect code

The condition or nature of the late effect is sequenced first, followed by the code for the cause of the late effect, except in a few instances where the Alphabetic Index or the Tabular List directs otherwise. If the late effect is due to injury, poisoning, and certain other consequences of external causes (S00–T88), a seventh-character extension for "sequelae" should be assigned to the injury code as well as the external causes code (V01–Y95). For example:

M19.111 + S42.301S	Traumatic arthritis of right shoulder due to old fracture of right humerus
G83.10 + B91	Paralysis of leg due to old poliomyelitis
B90.8 + E35	Adrenal tuberculous calcification

There are three exceptions to the coding principle that requires two codes for late effect:

- When the residual effect is not stated, the cause of the late effect code is used alone.

- When no late effect code is provided in ICD-10-CM but the condition is described as being a late effect, only the residual condition is coded. Note that conditions described as due to previous surgery are not coded as late effects but are classified as history of or complications of previous surgery, depending on the specific situation.

- When the late effect code has been expanded at the fourth-, fifth-, or sixth-character level(s) to include the manifestation condition, only the cause of the late effect code is assigned. For example, code **I69.01, Cognitive deficits following nontraumatic subarachnoid hemorrhage,** includes the cause of the late effect (nontraumatic subarachnoid hemorrhage), as well as the manifestation (cognitive deficits).

LATE EFFECT VERSUS CURRENT ILLNESS OR INJURY

A late effect code is not used with a code for a current injury or illness of the same type, with one exception. Codes from category I69, Sequelae of cerebrovascular disease, may be assigned as an additional code with codes from I60–I67, if the patient has a current cerebrovascular disease and residual deficits from an old cerebrovascular disease. For example, a patient with residual aphasia due to subdural hemorrhage two years ago who is admitted because of acute cerebral thrombosis would have the following codes assigned: **I66.9, Occlusion and stenosis of unspecified cerebral artery,** and **I69.220, Aphasia following other nontraumatic intracranial hemorrhage.**

EXERCISE 7.6

Code the following diagnoses.

---

1. Residuals of <u>poliomyelitis</u>   B91

   or <u>Sequelae</u>

---

2. <u>Sequela</u> of old crush injury to left foot   S97.82xS

---

3. Stroke two years ago with residual hemiplegia   I69.351
   of the right dominant side

---

4. <u>Contracture</u> of hip following partial hip   M24.559
   replacement one year ago   Z96.649

REVIEW EXERCISE 7.7

Code the following diagnoses.

---

1. Traumatic arthritis, right ankle, following
   fracture, right ankle

   M12.571
   S82.891S

---

2. Cicatricial contracture of left hand due to burn

   L90.5
   T23.002S

---

3. Brain damage following cerebral abscess
   seven months ago

                          Sequelae

   G93.9
   G09

---

4. Flaccid hemiplegia due to old cerebral infarction

   I69.359

---

5. Bilateral neural deafness resulting from childhood
   measles 10 years ago

   H90.3
   B94.8

---

6. Mononeuritis, median nerve, resulting
   from previous crush injury to right arm

                          Crush

   G56.11
   S47.1xxS

---

7. Posttraumatic, painful arthritis, left hand

                   Injury

   M12.542
   S69.92xS

---

8. Residuals of previous severe burn, left wrist

   T23.072S

---

9. Locked-in state (paralytic syndrome) due to old
   cerebrovascular infarction

   G83.5
   I69.369

CHAPTER 8

Introduction to the ICD-10-PCS Classification

CHAPTER OVERVIEW

- All ICD-10-PCS codes have an alphanumeric structure, no decimal points, and seven characters.
- ICD-10-PCS is divided into 16 sections relating to the general type of procedure.
- Codes in the Medical and Surgical Section specify the section, body system, root operation, body part, approach, device, and qualifier.
- ICD-10-PCS is divided into Index, Tables, and List of Codes.

LEARNING OUTCOMES

After studying this chapter you should be able to:

- Explain the structure, format, and conventions of ICD-10-PCS.

TERMS TO KNOW

Character
an axis of classification that specifies information about the procedure performed

Value
one of the 34 letters or numbers that can be selected to represent one of the characters in an ICD-10-PCS code

Approach
the fifth character in the code in the Medical and Surgical Section; the way the procedure site is reached (for example: open or percutaneous)

Qualifier
the seventh character in the code in the Medical and Surgical Section; it carries additional information for that particular procedure

Root operation
the third character in the code in the Medical and Surgical Section corresponding to the objective of the procedure; in this section alone there are 31 possible objectives

REMEMBER . . .

In the alphanumeric structure of ICD-10-PCS, don't confuse the letters "O" and "I" with the numbers "0" and "1."

INTRODUCTION

The ICD-10-PCS uses standardized terminology to provide precise and stable definitions for all procedures performed. As such, ICD-10-PCS does not include eponyms, usually the name of the surgeon (or surgeons) who developed the procedure. Instead, such procedures are coded to the operation that identifies the objective of the procedure. General information on ICD-10-PCS including conventions and definitions of the components of a code are provided in this chapter. Procedures specific to certain body systems will be covered in the relevant chapters of this handbook.

FORMAT AND ORGANIZATION

Format

The ICD-10-PCS is divided into the Alphabetic Index, Tables, and List of Codes. Codes can be located in alphabetical order within the Index. The Index will refer to a specific location within a Table, but the complete code can be obtained only by referring to the Tables. The List of Codes allows for direct lookup of each code, with the description of each code being provided.

Alphabetic Index

The Index is arranged in alphabetical order based on the type of procedure being performed. The ICD-10-PCS Index does not provide a complete code (with a few exceptions), but it points to a specific location in the Tables by specifying the first three or four characters of the code. The purpose of the Alphabetic Index is to locate the appropriate table in which you'll find the information needed to complete the other characters of the code. It is not required to consult the Index first before proceeding to the Tables to complete the code.

For example, "cholecystectomy" may be looked up by "Excision, gallbladder," or "Resection, gallbladder." The term **Cholecystectomy** has two reference notes as follows:

> **Cholecystectomy**
> —see Excision, Gallbladder [0FB4]
> —see Resection, Gallbladder [0FT4]

The Index entries "0FB4" and "0FT4" are not complete codes, but rather they point the user to the appropriate Table identified by the first three values (for example, 0FT, which is shown in figure 8.1).

Tables

The ICD-10-PCS Tables are composed of grids specifying the valid combinations of characters that make up a procedure code. Within a Table, valid codes include all combinations of choices in characters 4 through 7 contained in the same row of the Table.

FIGURE 8.1 Sample Excerpt of ICD-10-PCS Table

Section	0	Medical and Surgical
Body System	F	Hepatobiliary System and Pancreas
Operation	T	Resection: Cutting out or off, without replacement, all of a body part

Body Part	Approach	Device	Qualifier
0 Liver 1 Liver, Right Lobe 2 Liver, Left Lobe 4 Gallbladder G Pancreas	0 Open 4 Percutaneous Endoscopic	Z No Device	Z No Qualifier
5 Hepatic Duct, Right 6 Hepatic Duct, Left 8 Cystic Duct 9 Common Bile Duct C Ampulla of Vater D Pancreatic Duct F Pancreatic Duct, Accessory	0 Open 4 Percutaneous Endoscopic 7 Via Natural or Artificial Opening 8 Via Natural or Artificial Opening Endoscopic	Z No Device	Z No Qualifier

List of Codes

The ICD-10-PCS List of Codes displays all valid codes in alphanumeric order. Each entry begins with the seven-character code, followed by the full text description. The code descriptions are generated using rules that produce standardized, complete, and easy-to-read code descriptions. At press time, the published ICD-10-PCS manual did not include the List of Codes. However, the List of Codes is available from the following Web site: http://www.cms.gov/ICD10/.

Code Structure

All ICD-10-PCS codes have an alphanumeric structure, with all codes made up of seven characters and no decimal points. It is important to distinguish between "character" and "value" before we get any further. Each **character** in a code is an axis of classification that represents an aspect of the procedure. A **value** is one of the 34 letters or numbers that can be selected to represent one of the characters in an ICD-10-PCS code. These values are made up of digits 0–9, or the letters A–H, J–N, and P–Z. The letters "O" and "I" are not used so as not to be confused with the digits "0" and "1."

Refer to figure 8.2 for the structure and meaning of each character for codes within the Medical and Surgical Section.

FIGURE 8.2 Structure of Codes in the Medical and Surgical Section

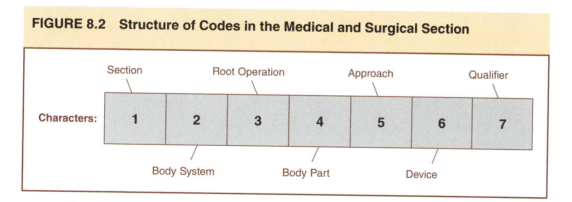

Within a defined code range, the second through seventh characters have a standard meaning—but may have different meanings across sections. Within a defined code range, a character specifies the same type of information in that axis of classification, as follows: The first character represents the axis for section, the second for body system, the third for root operation, the fourth for body part, the fifth for approach, the sixth for device, and the seventh for qualifier. These specific components of a code and their definitions will be covered in more detail later.

The number of unique values used in an axis of classification differs as needed. This means that within different axes of the classification, there may be different unique values. So, for example, the body part axis will have many more unique values than the approach axis, because there are many more body parts than surgical approaches.

As with words in their context, the meaning of any single value is a combination of its axis of classification and any preceding values on which it may be dependent. For example, the meaning of a body part value in the Medical and Surgical Section is always dependent on the body system value. The body part value "0" in the "central nervous" body system specifies "brain," and the body part value "0" in the "peripheral nervous" body system specifies "cervical plexus." (Refer to figure 8.3 for a graphic representation of this example).

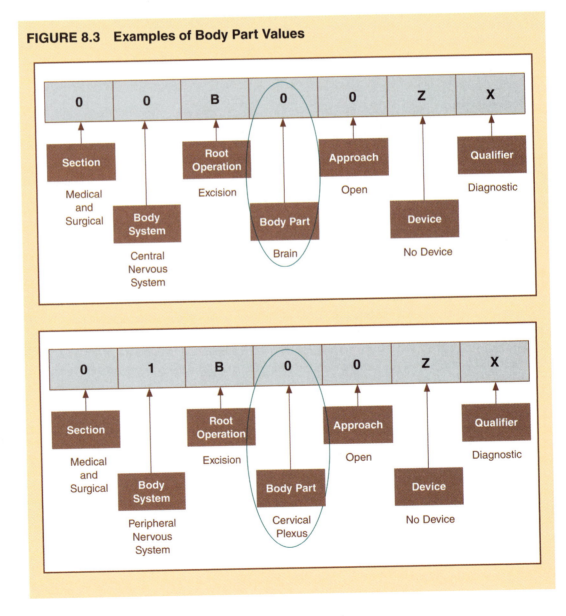

FIGURE 8.3   Examples of Body Part Values

Relational Terms

The term "and," when used in a code description, means "and/or." For example, "lower arm and wrist muscle" means lower arm and/or wrist muscle.

EXERCISE 8.1

Without referring to the handbook material or ICD-10-PCS, mark the following statements either true or false.

1. The ICD-10-PCS Index includes eponyms to identify procedures.	F
2. All ICD-10-PCS codes have an alphanumeric structure, with all codes made up of seven characters.	T
3. All complete ICD-10-PCS codes can be located within the Index.	F
4. The ICD-10-PCS Tables specify the valid combinations of characters that make up a procedure code.	T
5. The letters "O" and "I" are not used as ICD-10-PCS values so as not to be confused with the digits "0" and "1."	T

CODE CHARACTERS AND THEIR DEFINITIONS

All ICD-10-PCS codes are composed of seven characters. All seven characters must be specified for the code to be valid. If the documentation is incomplete for coding purposes, the provider must be queried for the necessary information. This section discusses each character that makes up ICD-10-PCS, and the definition of each, as well as the main values that are applicable to build a PCS code in the Medical and Surgical Section.

Character 1: Section

The first character in the code always refers to the section. A section refers to a broad procedure category or section where the code is found. ICD-10-PCS is divided into 16 sections relating to the general type of procedure. Table 8.1 displays the ICD-10-PCS sections along with the first character of each code specifying the section.

As shown in table 8.1, the number "0" represents the Medical and Surgical Section, while the other sections have a different numeric or alphabetic value. For example, Obstetrics has a first character of "1." There are also some limited ancillary diagnostic codes, such as "B" for Imaging and "C" for Nuclear Medicine. There is no section for laboratory tests, as most facilities don't code lab tests for inpatient records. The majority of the procedures that would normally be reported in an inpatient setting can be found in the Medical and Surgical Section. Therefore, the following discussion regarding the component characters of a code refers strictly to the Medical and Surgical Section. The Medical- and Surgical-Related Section and the Ancillary Section are both covered in chapter 11 of this handbook.

TABLE 8.1   ICD-10-PCS Sections and Their Corresponding Character Value

Value	Section	Value	Section
0	Medical and Surgical	8	Other Procedures
1	Obstetrics	9	Chiropractic
2	Placement	B	Imaging
3	Administration	C	Nuclear Medicine
4	Measurement and Monitoring	D	Radiation Oncology
5	Extracorporeal Assistance and Performance	F	Physical Rehabilitation and Diagnostic Audiology
6	Extracorporeal Therapies	G	Mental Health
7	Osteopathic	H	Substance Abuse Treatment

Character 2: Body System

The second character in an ICD-10-PCS code represents the body system. This character indicates the general physiological system or anatomical region involved (e.g., gastrointestinal). Within the Medical and Surgical Section, these characters will retain the same value. For example, a central nervous system procedure in this section will always have the value "0" for the second character, while a respiratory system procedure will have the value "B" for the second character.

For additional detail, some traditional body systems have been assigned multiple values. For example, the circulatory system has been subdivided into heart and great vessels, upper arteries, lower arteries, upper veins, and lower veins. Within the conventions of ICD-10-PCS, each of these areas is considered a separate body system with different values. Refer to table 8.2 for the body systems in the Medical and Surgical Section, along with their corresponding character value.

The diaphragm is used as the frame of reference for body systems classified as upper or lower (e.g., upper veins and lower veins). For example, veins located above the diaphragm are found in the Upper Veins body system, while veins located below the diaphragm are found in the "lower veins" body system.

Three body systems refer to anatomical regions, as follows:

- Anatomical regions, general
- Anatomical regions, upper extremities
- Anatomical regions, lower extremities

The "anatomical regions" body system codes should only be used when the procedure is performed on an anatomical region, rather than a specific body part. For example, they can be used when a procedure is performed on body layers that span more than one body system, such as a debridement of skin, muscle, and bone at a procedure site. "Anatomical regions" body systems can also be used on the rare occasion when no information is available to support assignment of a code to a more specific body part within a body system.

TABLE 8.2 Medical and Surgical Section Body Systems and Values

Value	Body System	Value	Body System
0	Central nervous	J	Subcutaneous tissue and fascia
1	Peripheral	K	Muscles
2	Heart and great vessels	L	Tendons—includes synovial membrane
3	Upper arteries	M	Bursae and ligaments—includes synovial membrane
4	Lower arteries		
5	Upper veins	N	Head and facial bones
6	Lower veins	P	Upper bones
7	Lymphatic and hemic—includes lymph vessels and lymph nodes	Q	Lower bones
		R	Upper joints—includes synovial membrane
8	Eye	S	Lower joints—includes synovial membrane
9	Ear, nose, sinus—includes sinus ducts	T	Urinary
B	Respiratory	U	Female reproductive
C	Mouth and throat	V	Male reproductive
D	Gastrointestinal	W	Anatomical regions, general
F	Hepatobiliary and pancreas	X	Anatomical regions, upper extremities
G	Endocrine	Y	Anatomical regions, lower extremities
H	Skin and breast—includes skin and breast glands and ducts		

EXERCISE 8.2

Referring to table 8.2, mark an "X" next to each term or phrase identifying a body system as classified by a unique value within ICD-10-PCS.

1.	Respiratory	X
2.	Heart and great vessels	X
3.	Circulatory	____
4.	Musculoskeletal	____
5.	Upper bones	X

Character 3: Root Operation

The third character refers to the root operation. Root operation is one of the most important concepts that the user needs to understand in order to identify and select the correct ICD-10-PCS code. Mastering the definitions of these root operations is the key to "building" a code in ICD-10-PCS. Root operation refers to the objective of the procedure. The distinction between the different root operations is the objective, namely, what is the procedure trying to accomplish?

In the Medical and Surgical Section, there are 31 different root operations. Each root operation is precisely defined in the classification. The definitions are easily found in the Table. For example, in the excerpt of the Table shown in figure 8.1, the root operation "Resection" is defined on the third line of the first row as "cutting out or off, without replacement, all of a body part."

Root operations include terms such as "Alteration," "Bypass," "Change," "Creation," "Dilation," "Excision," "Resection," "Fusion," "Insertion," "Occlusion," and "Repair." The complete list of root operations in the Medical and Surgical Section, along with their corresponding value, is included in table 8.3.

Some of the root operations used in ICD-10-PCS may not necessarily coincide with terminology used by physicians in their documentation. However, because many of the terms used to construct ICD-10-PCS codes are defined within the system, the physician is not expected to use the exact terms used in ICD-10-PCS code descriptions. Instead, it is the coder's responsibility to determine what the documentation in the medical record equates to in the ICD-10-PCS definitions.

The coder is not required to query the physician when the correlation between the documentation and the defined ICD-10-PCS terms is clear. For example, if the physician documents "partial resection," the coder can independently correlate "partial resection" to the root operation "Excision" without querying the physician for clarification because it meets the definition of excision within ICD-10-PCS, namely, "cutting out or off, without replacement, a portion of a body part."

Because of the large number of root operations and their importance in assigning ICD-10-PCS codes, specific root operations are covered in more detail in chapter 10 of this handbook.

TABLE 8.3   ICD-10-PCS Root Operations and Their Corresponding Value

Value	Root Operation	Value	Root Operation	Value	Root Operation	Value	Root Operation
0	Alteration	8	Division	J	Inspection	S	Reposition
1	Bypass	9	Drainage	K	Map	T	Resection
2	Change	B	Excision	L	Occlusion	V	Restriction
3	Control	C	Extirpation	M	Reattachment	W	Revision
4	Creation	D	Extraction	N	Release	U	Supplement
5	Destruction	F	Fragmentation	P	Removal	X	Transfer
6	Detachment	G	Fusion	Q	Repair	Y	Transplantation
7	Dilation	H	Insertion	R	Replacement		

Character 4: Body Part

The fourth character indicates the specific part of the body system or anatomical site where the procedure was performed (for example, appendix). Within ICD-10-PCS, body part values may refer to an entire organ (e.g., liver) or to specific portions of an organ (e.g., liver, right lobe).

If a procedure is performed on a portion of a body part that does not have a separate body part value, the value corresponding to the whole body part value should be selected. For example, a procedure that is done on the alveolar process of the mandible would get coded to the whole—the "mandible" body part.

Procedures performed on body parts identified with the prefix "peri" (meaning "around" or "near") should be coded to the body part named. For example, a procedure identified as "perirenal" would be coded to the body part "kidney."

Branches of body parts. Where ICD-10-PCS does not provide a body part value to a specific branch of a body part, the body part is coded to the closest proximal branch that has a specific body part value. For example, a procedure performed on the mandibular branch of the trigeminal nerve is coded to the "trigeminal nerve" body part value.

Bilateral body part values. ICD-10-PCS provides values for some bilateral body parts. However, not every paired organ or body part has a "bilateral" value. If the identical procedure is performed on both sides, and a bilateral body part value exists for that body part, the procedure code is assigned once using the bilateral body part value. For example, refer to figure 8.4 to code bilateral oophorectomy. The identical procedure was performed on both ovaries, and there is a body part value that includes bilateral ovaries. Because there is a value for "bilateral," we would report a single code.

FIGURE 8.4   Excerpt from Table Showing Bilateral Body Part

Section   **0**   Medical and Surgical
Body System   **U**   Female Reproductive System
Operation   **T**   Resection: Cutting out or off, without replacement, all of a body part

Body Part	Approach	Device	Qualifier
0 Ovary, Right 1 Ovary, Left 2 Ovaries, Bilateral 5 Fallopian Tube, Right 6 Fallopian Tube, Left 7 Fallopian Tubes, Bilateral 9 Uterus	0 Open 4 Percutaneous Endoscopic 7 Via Natural or Artificial Opening 8 Via Natural or Artificial Opening Endoscopic F Via Natural or Artificial Opening With Percutaneous Endoscopic Assistance	Z No Device	Z No Qualifier
4 Uterine Supporting Structure C Cervix F Cul-de-sac G Vagina K Hymen	0 Open 4 Percutaneous Endoscopic 7 Via Natural or Artificial Opening 8 Via Natural or Artificial Opening Endoscopic	Z No Device	Z No Qualifier
J Clitoris L Vestibular Gland M Vulva	O Open X External	Z No Device	Z No Qualifier

If no bilateral body part value exists, each procedure should be coded separately using the appropriate body part value. For example, consider bilateral hip replacement. There are body part values for "right hip" and for "left hip," but not for bilateral hips. If the exact same procedure was performed on both hips, two separate codes should be reported to identify that both hips were replaced.

Skin, subcutaneous tissue, and fascia overlying a joint. If a procedure is performed on the skin, subcutaneous tissue, or fascia overlying a joint, the procedure is coded to the following body part:

- Shoulder is coded to upper arm.
- Elbow is coded to lower arm.
- Wrist is coded to lower arm.
- Hip is coded to upper leg.
- Knee is coded to lower leg.
- Ankle is coded to foot.

Fingers and toes. If a body system does not contain a separate body part value for fingers, procedures performed on the fingers are coded to the body part value for the hand. If a body system does not contain a separate body part value for toes, procedures performed on the toes are coded to the body part value for the foot. For example, excision of a finger tendon is coded to one of the hand tendon body part values in the "tendons" body system.

We have now covered the majority of the body part guidelines, except for a few that are reserved for the body system. Procedures on the following body parts are covered in more detail in later chapters of this handbook.

- Tendons, ligaments, bursae, and fascia near a joint are addressed in chapter 23 of this handbook, Diseases of the Musculoskeletal System and Connective Tissue
- Coronary arteries are addressed in chapter 28, Diseases of the Circulatory System.

Character 5: Approach

The fifth character refers to the technique or approach used to reach the procedure site (e.g., open). Seven approaches are listed in the Medical and Surgical Section. Approaches can be external, through the skin or mucous membrane, or through an orifice. The following list breaks down the approaches.

- External
- Through the skin or mucous membrane
  —Open
  —Percutaneous
  —Percutaneous endoscopic
- Through an orifice
  —Via natural or artificial opening
  —Via natural or artificial opening endoscopic
  —Via natural or artificial opening with percutaneous endoscopic assistance

As with root operations, each approach is precisely defined in the classification. Refer to table 8.4 for the approaches shown in the Medical and Surgical Section, along with their corresponding value and definition, and to figure 8.5 for illustrations of surgical approaches.

TABLE 8.4   Medical and Surgical Section Approaches

Value	Approach	Definition
X	External	Procedures performed directly on the skin or mucous membrane and procedures performed indirectly by the application of external force through the skin or mucous membrane
0	Open	Cutting through the skin or mucous membrane and any other body layers necessary to expose the site of the procedure
3	Percutaneous	Entry, by puncture or minor incision, of instrumentation through the skin or mucous membrane and/or any other body layers necessary to reach the site of the procedure
4	Percutaneous endoscopic	Entry, by puncture or minor incision, of instrumentation through the skin or mucous membrane and/or any other body layers necessary to reach and visualize the site of the procedure
7	Via natural or artificial opening	Entry of instrumentation through a natural or artificial external opening to reach the site of the procedure
8	Via natural or artificial opening endoscopic	Entry of instrumentation through a natural or artificial external opening to reach and visualize the site of the procedure
F	Via natural or artificial opening with percutaneous endoscopic assistance	Entry of instrumentation through a natural or artificial external opening to reach and visualize the site of the procedure, and entry, by puncture or minor incision, of instrumentation through the skin or mucous membrane and any other body layers necessary to aid in the performance of the procedure

In addition to the approach definitions listed in table 8.4, there are a handful of guidelines related to the selection of the approach, as follows:

- *Open approach with percutaneous endoscopic assistance*: code to "open" approach. Example: laparoscopic-assisted sigmoidectomy is coded to "open."

- *External approach.* The following procedures should be coded to "external":

    —Procedures performed within an orifice on structures that are visible without the aid of any instrumentation. Example: resection of tonsils.

    —Procedures performed indirectly by the application of external force through the intervening body layers. Example: closed reduction of fracture.

- *Percutaneous procedure via device*: Code to "percutaneous." Example: fragmentation of kidney stone via percutaneous nephrostomy.

FIGURE 8.5   Illustrations of Medical and Surgical Section Approaches

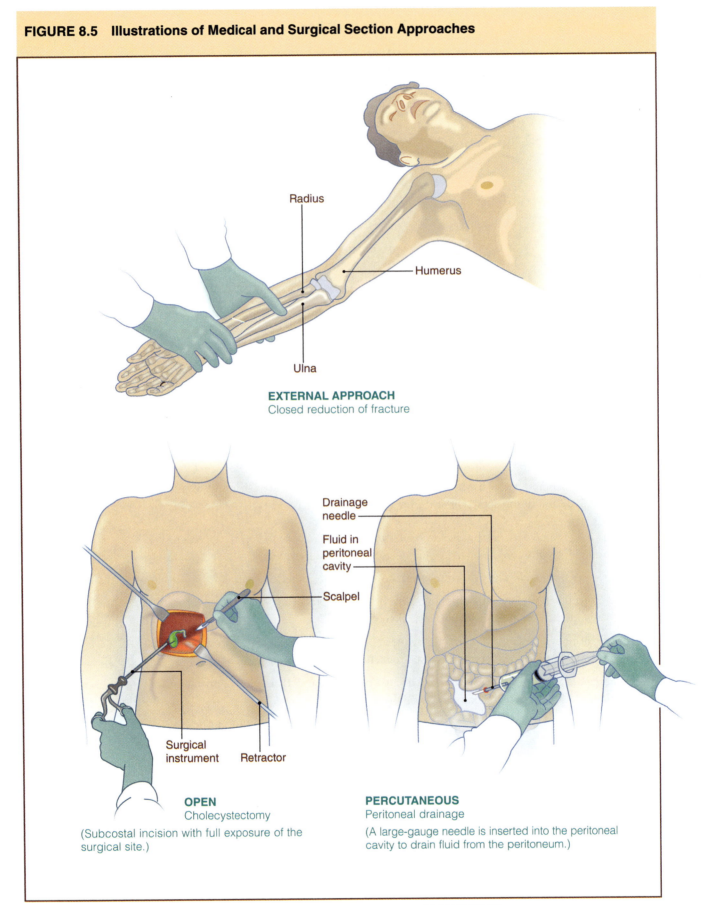

Radius

Humerus

Ulna

EXTERNAL APPROACH
Closed reduction of fracture

Drainage needle

Fluid in peritoneal cavity

Scalpel

Surgical instrument

Retractor

OPEN
Cholecystectomy
(Subcostal incision with full exposure of the surgical site.)

PERCUTANEOUS
Peritoneal drainage
(A large-gauge needle is inserted into the peritoneal cavity to drain fluid from the peritoneum.)

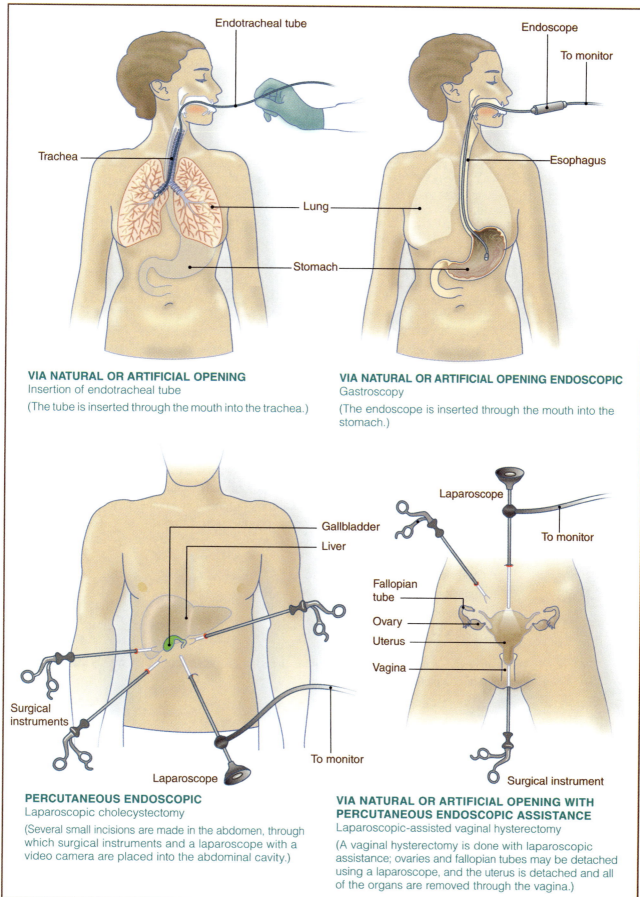

VIA NATURAL OR ARTIFICIAL OPENING
Insertion of endotracheal tube

(The tube is inserted through the mouth into the trachea.)

VIA NATURAL OR ARTIFICIAL OPENING ENDOSCOPIC
Gastroscopy

(The endoscope is inserted through the mouth into the stomach.)

PERCUTANEOUS ENDOSCOPIC
Laparoscopic cholecystectomy

(Several small incisions are made in the abdomen, through which surgical instruments and a laparoscope with a video camera are placed into the abdominal cavity.)

VIA NATURAL OR ARTIFICIAL OPENING WITH PERCUTANEOUS ENDOSCOPIC ASSISTANCE
Laparoscopic-assisted vaginal hysterectomy

(A vaginal hysterectomy is done with laparoscopic assistance; ovaries and fallopian tubes may be detached using a laparoscope, and the uterus is detached and all of the organs are removed through the vagina.)

EXERCISE 8.3

Identify the ICD-10-PCS approach value used for each of the procedures below:

Procedure	Approach Value
1. Appendectomy	0 (Open)
2. Laparoscopic cholecystectomy	4 (Percutaneous endoscopic)
3. Adenoidectomy	X (External)
4. Bronchoscopy	8 (Via natural or artificial opening endoscopic)
5. Laparoscopic-assisted hysterectomy	0 (Open)

Character 6: Device

The sixth character is used to identify whether a device was used in a procedure. Only devices that remain in or on the patient's body after the procedure is completed are coded; materials that are incidental to a procedure are not coded. Examples of incidental materials are sutures, ligatures, clips, radiological markers, and temporary postoperative wound drains.

Device values fall into four basic categories:

- Grafts and prostheses
- Implants
- Simple or mechanical appliances
- Electronic appliances

When no device is involved in the procedure, the letter "Z," representing "none," is used as the sixth character to complete the code structure.

EXERCISE 8.4

Mark an "X" next to each term or phrase that can be considered a codeable device within ICD-10-PCS.

1. Joint prosthesis   X

2. Cardiac pacemaker   X

3. Prolene sutures   _____

4. Neurostimulator   X

5. Mesh graft   X

Character 7: Qualifier

The seventh character indicates a qualifier. A qualifier has a unique meaning within individual procedures. This position within the code is used to provide additional information. Examples of qualifiers include "diagnostic" and "stereotactic." When there is no qualifier, the seventh character is the letter "Z" to complete the code structure.

CHAPTER 9

Basic ICD-10-PCS Coding Steps

CHAPTER OVERVIEW

- The Uniform Hospital Discharge Data Set (UHDDS) requires all significant procedures to be reported. Significant procedures meet any one of the following conditions:
  - The procedure is surgical in nature.
  - It carries an anesthetic risk.
  - It carries a procedural risk.
  - It requires specialized training.
- The ICD-10-PCS contains the Alphabetic Index, the Tables, and the List of Codes.

LEARNING OUTCOMES

After studying this chapter you should be able to:

Identify main terms in the Alphabetic Index.

Navigate the Tables to find the appropriate Table.

TERM TO KNOW

Principal procedure
procedure performed for definitive treatment (rather than for diagnostic or exploratory purposes)

INTRODUCTION

This chapter covers the steps to take in locating ICD-10-PCS codes. In addition, it discusses general information on reporting procedures as well as selection of the principal procedure.

The following steps should be undertaken to locate the procedure codes using ICD-10-PCS:

1. Locate the main term in the Alphabetic Index
   - Follow any cross-reference instructions.
   - Obtain the first three or four characters for the procedure.
   - In a few instances, complete seven-character codes are provided.

2. Find the applicable Table.
   - Review the section, body system, and root operation definition, and verify that the first three characters referenced by the Index are correct.

3. Continue building the ICD-10-PCS code by selecting a value from each column for the remaining four characters, as follows:
   - Select a value from the body part column for the fourth character.
   - Select a value from the approach column for the fifth character.
   - Select a value from the device column for the sixth character.
   - Select a value from the qualifier column for the seventh character.

It is important to note that valid codes can be built using all combinations of choices in characters 4 through 7 that are in the same row of the Table. Because all ICD-10-PCS codes are seven characters long, the code must specify all seven characters to be valid.

LOCATE THE MAIN TERM IN THE ALPHABETIC INDEX

The first step in coding is to locate the main term in the Alphabetic Index. The Index can be used to access the Tables. Main terms may be a common procedure term (e.g., **Appendectomy, Cholecystectomy**), a root operation value (e.g., Resection, Excision), or body parts. Subterms provide more specific information. Each indention level of the Index is represented below by a hyphen.

The following examples demonstrate the different main terms and subterms used in ICD-10-PCS.

- When the main term is a root operation value (e.g., Excision), the subterms will be body parts where the operation was performed, as shown below:

> **Excision**
> -Acetabulum
> --Left [0QB5]
> --Right [0QB4]
> -Adenoids [0CBQ]

- When the main term is a common procedure, references are provided to the corresponding ICD-10-PCS root operation and body part, as shown below:

> **Claviculectomy**
> —see Excision, Upper Bones [0PB]
> —see Resection, Upper Bones [0PT]

Condylectomy
—see Excision, Head and Facial Bones [0NB]
—see Excision, Upper Bones [0PB]
—see Excision, Lower Bones [0QB]

- When the main term is an anatomical term, helpful references are provided to identify specific ICD-10-PCS body parts, as shown below:

Adductor hallucis muscle
—use Muscle, Foot, Left
—use Muscle, Foot, Right

It is not necessary to start with the Alphabetic Index before proceeding to the Tables to complete a code. A valid code may be chosen directly from the Tables, but it will require a thorough familiarity with the body systems and root operations.

EXERCISE 9.1

Without referring to the Alphabetic Index, underline the word(s) in each item that indicate the main term for each procedure.

1. Laparoscopic cholecystectomy

2. Resection of pancreas

3. Bilateral oophorectomy

4. Incision and drainage of abscess, neck

5. Bowel resection with transverse colostomy

FIND THE APPLICABLE TABLE

Once the first three or more characters of a code have been located in the Alphabetic Index, the coder must refer to the appropriate Table. There is no need to follow the reference notes to see other terms if the Index provides the first three or four characters of a code. For example, the main term **Cholecystectomy** refers us to "0FT4" for "Resection, gallbladder." Looking up the main term "Resection" with the subterm "gallbladder" will not yield the complete seven-character code. Instead, it will reference the same Table: 0FT4.

To find the appropriate Table:

- If using the PDF version available on the Centers for Medicare & Medicaid Services Web site, the Tables can be accessed directly by clicking on the hyperlink represented by the character values provided by the Index (e.g., 0FT4).

- If using a published ICD-10-PCS book, it will be necessary to manually locate the appropriate Table. The Tables are arranged in a series, beginning with section 0, Medical and Surgical, and body system 0, Central Nervous, and proceeding in numerical order. Sections 0 through 9 are followed by sections B through D and F through H. The same convention is followed within each Table for the second through seventh characters—numeric values in order first, followed by alphabetical values in order.

EXERCISE 9.2

Without referring to ICD-10-PCS, identify the order in which the following Tables (represented by the first three characters) can be located.

1.	0JQ	4
2.	0J9	3
3.	B31	5
4.	09B	1
5.	09W	2

CODING DEMONSTRATIONS

Follow the steps outlined above to determine the correct code for each of the procedural statements listed below:

Total Laparoscopic Cholecystectomy

Refer to main term **Cholecystectomy.** Note that there are two references: "see Excision, Gallbladder [0FB4]" and "see Resection, Gallbladder [0FT4]." There is no need to find the Index entry for the main term "Excision," subterm "gallbladder," or main term "Resection," subterm "gallbladder," as they will both still refer to the same Tables. If you're not familiar with the difference between these two root operations, refer to Appendix A of ICD-10-PCS and review the definitions. Otherwise, follow the Index entries by locating both Tables (0FB) and (0FT) to determine the difference in the definitions of the root operations "Excision" and "Resection."

Review Table 0FB. Reading across the first row of the Table, the first character, "0," refers to Medical and Surgical Section; the second character, "F," refers to the body system "hepatobiliary system and pancreas"; and the third character, "B," refers to the root operation "Excision." Excision is defined on the 0FB table as "cutting out or off, without replacement, a portion of a body part." Because the procedure is total cholecystectomy, "Excision" is not the correct root operation.

Review Table 0FT. The third character, "T," refers to the root operation "Resection." Resection is defined on the 0FT table as "cutting out or off, without replacement, all of a body part." Based on this review, it becomes clear that "Excision, gallbladder" is the root operation for a partial cholecystectomy, and "Resection" is the root operation for a total cholecystectomy; therefore, 0FT is the correct Table.

Continue building the remainder of the code by selecting the remaining values among the appropriate characters from the four columns shown in figure 9.1. In the first column—body part—select the value of "4" for gallbladder. From the second column—approach—because this was a laparoscopic procedure, select the value "4" for percutaneous endoscopic. Moving across the table, select as the sixth character "Z" for device, because no device was used for this procedure, and select as the last character "Z," representing no qualifier. The ICD-10-PCS procedure code, then, is 0FT44ZZ. Figure 9.1 shows the 0FT Table used for this demonstration, with the appropriate value circled for each character of the code.

Note that within an ICD-10-PCS table, valid codes include all combinations of choices in characters 4 through 7 contained in the same row of the Table. For example, using the Table on figure 9.1, the value "8" is not valid as the fifth character for approach because it's not on the same row as the body part "4" for gallbladder.

FIGURE 9.1   Excerpt of 0FT Table from ICD-10-PCS

Section	0	Medical and Surgical
Body System	F	Hepatobiliary System and Pancreas
Operation	T	Resection: Cutting out or off, without replacement, all of a body part

Body Part	Approach	Device	Qualifier
0 Liver	0 Open	Z No Device	Z No Qualifier
1 Liver, Right Lobe	4 Percutaneous Endoscopic		
2 Liver, Left Lobe			
4 Gallbladder			
G Pancreas			
5 Hepatic Duct, Right	0 Open	Z No Device	Z No Qualifier
6 Hepatic Duct, Left	4 Percutaneous Endoscopic		
8 Cystic Duct	7 Via Natural or Artificial Opening		
9 Common Bile Duct	8 Via Natural or Artificial Opening Endoscopic		
C Ampulla of Vater			
D Pancreatic Duct			
F Pancreatic Duct, Accessory			

Below Knee Amputation, Right Leg

Look up the main term **Amputation** in the Alphabetic Index. Note the cross-reference instruction to "see detachment." Follow the cross-reference by turning to the main term "Detachment," and then the subterm "leg." Note that additional subterms specify "lower" and then "left" and "right." In this instance, the Index provides code 0Y6H0Z for the right lower leg—it is almost complete, except that it only has six characters.

Refer to Table 0Y6 (shown as figure 9.2) and locate the appropriate row for the body part character "H" for lower leg, right. Because the only acceptable values for approach and device for this body part are "0" and "Z," they have already been provided in the Index. Review the values available for the qualifier. As this particular case refers to a "below the knee" amputation, select the value "3" for "low." The ICD-10-PCS procedure code, then, is 0Y6H0Z3.

FIGURE 9.2 Excerpt of 0Y6 Table from ICD-10-PCS

Section	0	Medical and Surgical
Body System	Y	Anatomical Regions, Lower Extremities
Operation	6	Detachment: Cutting off all or a portion of the upper or lower extremities

Body Part	Approach	Device	Qualifier
2 Hindquarter, Right 3 Hindquarter, Left 4 Hindquarter, Bilateral 7 Femoral Region, Right 8 Femoral Region, Left F Knee Region, Right G Knee Region, Left	0 Open	Z No Device	Z No Qualifier
C Upper Leg, Right D Upper Leg, Left H Lower Leg, Right J Lower Leg, Left	0 Open	Z No Device	1 High 2 Mid 3 Low

UNIFORM HOSPITAL DISCHARGE DATA SET FOR REPORTING PROCEDURES

The Uniform Hospital Discharge Data Set (UHDDS) requires all significant procedures to be reported. In addition, Medicare requires the reporting of any procedure that affects payment, whether or not it meets the definition of a significant procedure. Other procedures may be reported at the hospital's discretion. Most hospitals do not code ancillary or diagnostic procedures in the inpatient setting.

A significant procedure is defined as one that meets any of the following conditions:

- Is surgical in nature
- Carries an anesthetic risk
- Carries a procedural risk
- Requires specialized training

Surgery includes incision, excision, destruction, amputation, introduction, insertion, endoscopy, repair, suturing, and manipulation. Any procedure performed under anesthesia other than topical carries an anesthetic risk. Procedural risk is more difficult to define, but any procedure that has a recognized risk of inducing functional impairment, physiologic disturbance, or possible trauma during an invasive procedure is included in this group. Procedures requiring specialized training are those that are performed by specialized professionals, qualified technicians, or clinical teams specifically trained to perform certain procedures or whose services are directed primarily to carrying them out. This definition implies training over and above that ordinarily provided in the education of physicians, nurses, or technicians.

Meeting Various Reporting Requirements

Under the Health Insurance Portability and Accountability Act of 1996, for administrative simplification purposes, standard code sets have been designated for electronic claims transactions. ICD-10-PCS is the standard for hospitals when reporting surgery and procedures for inpatients, whereas the American Medical Association's Current Procedural Terminology and the Health Care Procedure Coding System level II codes are the standards for hospital reporting of outpatient procedures and physician reporting.

A hospital may also code outpatient procedures using the ICD-10-PCS system for internal or non-claim-related purposes, if desired. In addition, hospitals may report ICD-10-PCS codes for outpatient services, for specific payers under contractual agreements, or as required by their state data-reporting requirements.

Designating the Principal Procedure

The principal procedure as described by the UHDDS is one performed for definitive treatment (rather than for diagnostic or exploratory purposes) or one that is necessary to care for a complication. If two or more procedures appear to meet this definition, the one most related to the principal diagnosis is designated the principal procedure. If both are equally related to the principal diagnosis, the most resource-intensive or complex procedure is usually designated as principal. When more than one procedure is reported, the principal procedure should be identified as that which relates to the principal diagnosis. Coders are advised to follow UHDDS definitions for reporting unless a particular payer has substantially different reporting requirements.

ICD-10-PCS
Root Operations in the Medical and Surgical Section

CHAPTER OVERVIEW

The thirty-one Medical and Surgical root operations can be divided into nine groups that share similar attributes:

- Root operations to take out some/all of a body part
- Root operations to take out solids/fluids/gases from a body part
- Root operations that involve cutting or separation only
- Root operations to put in/put back or move some/all of a body part
- Root operations to alter the diameter or route of a tubular body part
- Root operations that always involve a device
- Root operations that involve examination only
- Root operations that include other repairs
- Root operations that include other objectives

LEARNING OUTCOMES

After studying this chapter you should be able to:

Identify the objectives of each root operation.

Distinguish among the different root operations in the Medical and Surgical Section.

Discuss the general guidelines applicable to root operations.

TERM TO KNOW

Root operation
the third character in an ICD-10-PCS code, which refers to the objective of the procedure

CHAPTER 10

ICD-10-PCS
Root
Operations
in the Medical
and Surgical
Section

INTRODUCTION

The previous chapters introduce the structure of ICD-10-PCS codes and discuss the basic steps to select ICD-10-PCS codes. Character 3 in the built code, root operations, is one of the most important concepts the user needs to understand in order to identify and select the correct ICD-10-PCS code. The root operation refers to the objective of the procedure. This chapter covers in detail the 31 root operations in the Medical and Surgical Section and their corresponding definitions. In addition, applicable guidelines from the *ICD-10-PCS Official Coding Guidelines* (2011 edition) are introduced.

ROOT OPERATION GUIDELINES

The majority of the ICD-10-PCS Official Coding Guidelines relate to the third character in a code, which represents the root operation. In this section, we start with the general guidelines applicable to all root operations and then move on to overarching concepts such as coding multiple procedures and discontinued procedures. Guidelines related to specific root operations are covered under the applicable root operation.

To determine the appropriate root operation, the full definition of the root operation must be applied. The definitions for the root operations (within the ICD-10-PCS classification) are included in the classification in Appendix A as well as within each Table (see figure 10.1).

Components of a procedure specified in the root operation definition and explanation are not coded separately. The full definition of each root operation provided in the Table must be carefully considered, as that definition will guide what procedure gets coded separately and what does not. For example, resection of a joint as part of a joint replacement procedure is included in the definition for "Replacement" and is not coded separately. Procedural steps necessary to reach the operative site (such as incision or approach) and to close the operative site (such as suturing) also are not coded separately.

FIGURE 10.1   Table Excerpt Demonstrating Location of Root Operation Definition

Section	0	Medical and Surgical	
Body System	F	Hepatobiliary System and Pancreas	**Root operation definition**
Operation	T	Resection: Cutting out or off, without replacement, all of a body part	

Body Part	Approach	Device	Qualifier
0 Liver	**0** Open	**Z** No Device	**Z** No Qualifier
1 Liver, Right Lobe	**4** Percutaneous Endoscopic		
2 Liver, Left Lobe			
4 Gallbladder			
G Pancreas			
5 Hepatic Duct, Right	**0** Open	**Z** No Device	**Z** No Qualifier
6 Hepatic Duct, Left	**4** Percutaneous Endoscopic		
8 Cystic Duct	**7** Via Natural or Artificial Opening		
9 Common Bile Duct	**8** Via Natural or Artificial Opening Endoscopic		
C Ampulla of Vater			
D Pancreatic Duct			
F Pancreatic Duct, Accessory			

Coding Multiple Procedures

CHAPTER 10

*ICD-10-PCS
Root
Operations
in the Medical
and Surgical
Section*

Multiple procedures performed during the same operative episode are coded separately if they meet one of the following four conditions:

1. *The same root operation is performed on different body parts as defined by distinct values of the body part character.* One example is the diagnostic excision of the liver and pancreas. This guideline is straightforward, except that it requires knowing how "body part" is used in the context of ICD-10-PCS. Refer to the excerpt of the Table in figure 10.1. You will note that liver is an individual body part, but if you look right below it, you will see that "liver, right lobe" is considered a different body part from "liver, left lobe" because each has a distinct value. So, separate biopsies of the right and left lobes of the liver are coded separately because we have different values in the fourth character for "body part."

2. *The same root operation is repeated at different body sites that are included in the same body part value.* For example, excision of the sartorius muscle and excision of the gracilis muscle are both included in the upper leg muscle body part value, and multiple procedures are coded. This example represents two excisions performed at two muscles that are both included in the upper leg muscle body part value. If the distinct parts of the procedure are not coded separately, it will not be apparent that two excisions were performed.

3. *Multiple root operations with distinct objectives are performed on the same body part.* An example is destruction of sigmoid lesion and bypass of sigmoid colon.

4. *The intended root operation is attempted using one approach but is converted to a different approach.* For example, laparoscopic cholecystectomy converted to an open cholecystectomy is coded as percutaneous endoscopic "Inspection" and open "Resection."

Coding Discontinued Procedures

When a planned procedure is begun but cannot be completed, it is coded to the extent to which it was actually performed according to the following principles:

- If the intended procedure is discontinued, code the procedure to the root operation performed.
- If a procedure is discontinued before any other root operation is performed, code the root operation "Inspection" of the body part or anatomical region inspected.

The following examples show how to code discontinued procedures:

- A patient is admitted for transurethral removal of ureteral stone. Scope is passed as far as the bladder, but the surgeon is unable to pass it into the ureter. Code only "Inspection" of the bladder.

- A patient is admitted for cholecystectomy with exploration of common duct. When the abdominal cavity is entered, extensive metastatic malignancy involving the stomach and duodenum with probable primary neoplasm in the pancreas is found. The procedure is discontinued and the operative wound closed. Code only the exploratory laparotomy.

- A planned aortic valve replacement procedure is discontinued after the initial thoracotomy and before any incision is made in the heart muscle when the patient becomes hemodynamically unstable. This procedure is coded as an open "Inspection" of the mediastinum.

When a procedure is considered to have "failed" in that it did not achieve the hoped-for result or because every objective of the procedure could not be accomplished, the procedure is coded as performed. For example, occasionally an almost immediate reocclusion of the coronary artery occurs

CHAPTER 10

ICD-10-PCS
Root
Operations
in the Medical
and Surgical
Section

after the completion of a percutaneous coronary angioplasty, which makes it necessary to return to the operating room to perform a coronary artery bypass to correct the problem. The angioplasty might be described as a failed procedure, but, in fact, the procedure was performed and should be coded. Note that failure to achieve the therapeutic objective is not classified as a complication of the procedure.

Coding Biopsies

A biopsy is defined as the taking of tissue from a living person for the purpose of microscopic study. A biopsy code is not assigned when a lesion removed for therapeutic purposes is sent to the laboratory for examination, even though the term "biopsy" may be used in describing the procedure. Surgical specimens are routinely sent to the pathology laboratory for study; this procedure is not considered a biopsy, and assigning a biopsy code is inappropriate. Biopsies may be coded with several different root operations depending on how the biopsy was performed, keeping in mind the definitions for the different root operations. For example, biopsies may be reported with the root operations "Excision," "Extraction," or "Drainage" with the qualifier "diagnostic."

Biopsy followed by more definitive treatment. If a diagnostic "Excision," "Extraction," or "Drainage" procedure (biopsy) is followed by a more definitive procedure, such as "Destruction," "Excision," or "Resection" at the same procedure site, both the biopsy and the more definitive treatment are coded. For example, a biopsy of the breast is followed by partial mastectomy at the same procedure site; both the biopsy and the partial mastectomy procedure are coded.

Coding Procedures on Overlapping Body Layers

Occasionally, a procedure may involve overlapping body layers. In those instances, the following guideline applies: *If the root operations "Excision," "Repair," or "Inspection" are performed on overlapping layers of the musculoskeletal system, the body part specifying the deepest layer is coded.* For example, an excisional debridement that includes skin and subcutaneous tissue as well as muscle is coded to the body part "muscle."

MEDICAL AND SURGICAL ROOT OPERATIONS

The 31 Medical and Surgical root operations can be divided into nine groups that share similar attributes:

1. Root operations to remove some/all of a body part
2. Root operations to remove solids/fluids/gases from a body part
3. Root operations that involve cutting or separation only
4. Root operations that put in/put back or move some/all of a body part
5. Root operations that alter the diameter or route of a tubular body part
6. Root operations that always involve a device
7. Root operations that involve examination only
8. Root operations that include other repairs
9. Root operations that include other objectives

Root Operations to Take Out Some or All of a Body Part

CHAPTER 10

*ICD-10-PCS
Root
Operations
in the Medical
and Surgical
Section*

This group of root operations includes "Excision," "Resection," "Detachment," "Destruction," and "Extraction." Table 10.1 provides an overview of these root operations, including the objective of the procedure, the site of the procedure, and examples of each root operation.

"Excision," "Resection," and "Detachment" are similar in that they all cut out or off without replacement. The difference between these three root operations is based on the site and extent of the procedure—some ("Excision") or all ("Resection") of a body part or an extremity ("Detachment"). A breast lumpectomy is "Excision," while a total mastectomy is "Resection." When the excision is a biopsy, the qualifier "diagnostic" is used. "Excision" is defined as cutting out or off, without replacement, "a portion" of a body part, while "Resection" is cutting out or off, without replacement, "all" of a body part. This distinction is a key concept within ICD-10-PCS; "all" of a body part is uniquely defined in ICD-10-PCS, and it can vary for different organs.

Excision versus Resection

ICD-10-PCS contains values for anatomical subdivisions of a body part, such as lobes of the lungs or liver and regions of the intestine. Resection of the specific body part is coded whenever all of the body part is cut out or off; excision of a less specific body part is not coded. It is important to review the body part values within the Table to confirm whether the procedure should be coded as "Resection" or "Excision." For example, refer back to figure 10.1. The body part column shows unique values for "liver"; "liver, right lobe"; and "liver, left lobe." Removal of the entire right lobe of the liver is considered "Resection" (cutting out all of a body part) based on this Table—even though only one lobe of the liver was removed, as each lobe of the liver is considered a body part. Adjunct information about the anastomotic technique used to complete a procedure (e.g., end-to-end or side-to-end anastomosis after a colectomy) is not specified in ICD-10-PCS. Only the specific excision or resection code is assigned.

Excision for Graft

For procedures involving harvesting of graft tissue, the following guideline applies: *If an autograft is obtained from a different body part in order to complete the objective of the procedure, a separate procedure is coded.* For example, for a coronary bypass with excision of saphenous vein graft, the excision of the saphenous vein is coded separately.

TABLE 10.1 Root Operations to Take Out Some or All of a Body Part

Root Operation	Objective of Procedure	Site of Procedure	Example
Excision	Cutting out/off without replacement	Some of a body part	Breast lumpectomy
Resection	Cutting out/off without replacement	All of a body part	Total mastectomy
Detachment	Cutting out/off without replacement	Extremity only, any level	Amputation above elbow
Destruction	Eradicating without replacement	Some/all of a body part	Fulguration of endometrium
Extraction	Pulling out or off without replacement	Some/all of a body part	Suction D&C

Detachment, Destruction, and Extraction

CHAPTER 10

ICD-10-PCS
Root
Operations
in the Medical
and Surgical
Section

The root operation "Detachment" is used exclusively for extremity amputation procedures at any level. For "Detachment," the body part value is the site of the detachment, with a qualifier, if applicable, to further specify the level where the extremity was amputated.

"Destruction" and "Extraction" also share the site of procedure—some/all of a body part. But "Destruction" represents eradication without replacement, while "Extraction" represents pulling out or off without replacement. "Destruction" is defined as physical eradication of all or a portion of a body part by the direct use of energy, force, or a destructive agent. With "Destruction," none of the body part is physically taken out. Examples of the root operation "Destruction" are fulguration, ablation, cauterization, and cryoablation. "Extraction" is defined as pulling or stripping out or off all or a portion of a body part by use of force. When the extraction procedure is a biopsy, the qualifier "diagnostic" is used. Examples of the root operation "Extraction" are dilation and curettage, vein stripping, non-excisional biopsy, and dermabrasion.

EXERCISE 10.1

Code these procedures.

---

1. Laparoscopic excision of right ovarian cyst — 0UB04ZZ

---

2. Diagnostic dilatation and curettage — 0UDB7ZX

    Extraction

---

3. Below knee amputation, right leg — 0Y6H0Z3

---

4. Laparoscopic right oophorectomy — 0UT04ZZ

    Resection

---

5. Rectal polyp fulguration — 0D5P8ZZ

    Destruction

Root Operations to Take Out Solids/Fluids/Gases from a Body Part

CHAPTER 10

ICD-10-PCS
Root
Operations
in the Medical
and Surgical
Section

The next group of root operations includes "Drainage," "Extirpation," and "Fragmentation." These root operations share the same site of procedure, namely "within a body part." Table 10.2 provides an overview of these root operations, including the objective of the procedure, the site of the procedure, and examples of each root operation.

The difference between these three root operations is that "Drainage" takes or lets out fluids or gases, "Extirpation" takes or cuts out solid matter from a body part, and "Fragmentation" breaks solid matter into pieces. The root operation "Drainage" is applicable to both diagnostic and therapeutic drainage procedures. The qualifier "diagnostic" is used to identify "Extraction" or "Drainage" root operations that are biopsies. Note that a separate procedure to put in a drainage device is coded to the root operation "Drainage" with the device value "drainage device."

For "Extirpation," the solid matter may be an abnormal by-product of a biological function or a foreign body; it may be embedded in a body part or in the lumen of a tubular body part. The solid matter may or may not have been previously broken into pieces. For "Fragmentation," the physical force (e.g., manual, ultrasonic) applied directly or indirectly is used to break the solid matter into pieces. The solid matter may be an abnormal by-product of a biological function or a foreign body. While it may appear that root operations "Extirpation" and "Fragmentation" are closely related, the key difference is that for "Fragmentation" the pieces of solid matter are not taken out.

TABLE 10.2 Root Operations to Take Out Solids/Fluids/Gases from a Body Part

Root Operation	Objective of Procedure	Site of Procedure	Example
Drainage	Taking/letting out fluids/gases	Within a body part	Incision and drainage
Extirpation	Taking/cutting out solid matter	Within a body part	Thrombectomy
Fragmentation	Breaking solid matter into pieces	Within a body part	Lithotripsy

EXERCISE 10.2

Code these procedures.

1. Incision and drainage of external perianal abscess

   0D9QXZZ

2. Percutaneous mechanical thrombectomy, left brachial artery

   03C83ZZ

   Extirpation

3. Hysteroscopy with intraluminal lithotripsy of left fallopian tube calcification

   0UF68ZZ

   Fragmentation

CHAPTER 10

ICD-10-PCS
Root
Operations
in the Medical
and Surgical
Section

Root Operations Involving Cutting or Separation Only

This group of root operations is made up of two root operations: "Division" and "Release." Table 10.3 provides an overview of these root operations, including the objective and site of the procedure and examples of each root operation.

"Division" is cutting into/separating a body part. This procedure is performed *within* a body part. With "Division," all or a portion of the body part is separated into two or more portions. Examples of "Division" include neurotomy, spinal cordotomy, and osteotomy.

"Release" is freeing a body part from an abnormal physical constraint. The site of procedure is *around* a body part. With "Release," some of the restraining tissue may be taken out, but none of the body part is taken out. The body part value coded is the body part being freed, not the tissue being manipulated or cut to free the body part. An example is lysis of intestinal adhesions; the value selected should be the specific intestine body part value.

Release versus Division: If the sole objective of the procedure is to free a body part without cutting the body part, that procedure should be identified as root operation "Release." An example is freeing a nerve root from surrounding scar tissue without cutting the nerve. However, if the sole objective of the procedure is separating, or transecting, a body part, that procedure should be identified as root operation "Division," as when severing the nerve root to relieve the pain.

TABLE 10.3   Root Operations Involving Cutting or Separation Only

Root Operation	Objective of Procedure	Site of Procedure	Example
Division	Cutting into/separating a body part	Within a body part	Neurotomy
Release	Freeing a body part from constraint	Around a body part	Adhesiolysis

Root Operations That Put In/Put Back or Move Some/All of a Body Part

The next grouping of root operations includes "Transplantation," "Reattachment," "Transfer," and "Reposition." Table 10.4 provides an overview of these root operations, including the objective of the procedure, the site of the procedure, and examples of each root operation.

TABLE 10.4   Root Operations That Put In/Put Back or Move Some/All of a Body Part

Root Operation	Objective of Procedure	Site of Procedure	Example
Transplantation	Putting in a living body part from a person/animal	Some/all of a body part	Kidney transplant
Reattachment	Putting back a detached body part	Some/all of a body part	Reattach finger
Transfer	Moving a body part to function for a similar body part	Some/all of a body part	Skin transfer flap
Reposition	Moving a body part to normal or other suitable location	Some/all of a body part	Move undescended testicle

The root operation "Transplantation" refers to putting in a living body part taken from another individual or animal to physically take the place and/or function of all or a portion of a similar body part. The native body part may or may not be removed, and the transplanted body part may take over all or a portion of its function. Examples include organ transplants such as liver or kidney transplants. Please note that a procedure in which autologous or nonautologous cells are put in is coded to the Administration Section (rather than the Medical and Surgical Section), even though the procedure may be referred to as a transplantation—for example, stem cell transplantation.

Another root operation in this group is "Reattachment." This root operation involves putting back in, or on, all or a portion of a separated (detached) body part to its normal location or other suitable location. Vascular circulation and nervous system pathways may or may not be reestablished. Examples of this root operation are reattachment of fingers or hand.

The root operation "Transfer" is moving, without taking out, all or a portion of a body part to another location to take over the function of all or a portion of a body part. The body part transferred remains connected to its vascular and nervous supply. Examples include tendon transfer and skin pedicle flap transfer.

The root operation "Reposition" refers to moving a body part to normal or other suitable location. So both "Transfer" and "Reposition" involve moving a body part—but transfer is performed with the objective that the body part will take over or replace the function of a body part. Reposition, on the other hand, is moving a body part, but moving it to where it should normally be or to another appropriate position. One example is the reposition of undescended testicle and reduction of displaced fracture.

EXERCISE 10.3

Code these procedures.

1. Percutaneous right foot tenotomy — Division — 0L8V3ZZ

2. Laparotomy with lysis of large intestine adhesions — Release — 0DNE0ZZ

3. Reattachment of severed left index finger — 0XMP0ZZ

4. Liver transplant with donor matched liver — 0FY00Z0

5. Closed reduction of dislocation of the right shoulder joint — Reposition — 0RSJXZZ

CHAPTER 10 :

ICD-10-PCS
Root
Operations
in the Medical
and Surgical
Section

Root Operations to Alter the Diameter or Route of a Tubular Body Part

Four root operations are performed to alter the diameter or route of a tubular body part: "Restriction," "Occlusion," "Dilation," and "Bypass." Tubular body parts are defined in ICD-10-PCS as the hollow body parts that provide a route of passage for solids, liquids, or gases. They include the cardiovascular system and body parts in the gastrointestinal, genitourinary, biliary, and respiratory tracts. Table 10.5 provides an overview of these root operations.

The objective of the root operation "Restriction" is to *partially* close, or narrow, the diameter of an orifice or a lumen, whereas the objective of the root operation "Occlusion" is to *completely* close an orifice or a lumen. The orifice may be a natural orifice or an artificially created orifice. Both "Restriction" and "Occlusion" include intraluminal and extraluminal methods.

- An example of "Restriction" is a gastroesophageal fundoplication. In this procedure, the upper part of the stomach is wrapped around the lower esophageal sphincter to strengthen the sphincter, prevent acid reflux, and repair a hiatal hernia. It is essentially partially closing the valve between the esophagus and stomach (lower esophageal sphincter), which stops acid from backing up into the esophagus easily.

- An example of "Occlusion" is fallopian tube ligation, which is performed to completely close the fallopian tube to prevent pregnancy.

The objective of the root operation "Dilation" is to expand, or enlarge, the diameter of the orifice or lumen of a tubular body part. As with "Restriction" and "Occlusion," the orifice may be a natural orifice or an artificially created orifice and may include intraluminal or extraluminal methods. For example, a percutaneous transluminal angioplasty is performed to expand the lumen of narrow coronary vessels to improve blood circulation.

The objective of the root operation "Bypass," on the other hand, is to alter the route of passage of the contents of a tubular body part. "Bypass" may include rerouting contents of a body part to a downstream area of the normal route, to a similar route and body part, or to an abnormal route and dissimilar body part. "Bypass" includes one or more anastomoses, with or without the use of a device. "Bypass" procedures are coded by identifying the body part bypassed "from" and the body part bypassed "to." Other specific guidelines for bypass procedures are covered in the Diseases of the Circulatory System chapter and the Diseases of the Digestive System chapter. An example of a "Bypass" root operation is a coronary artery bypass graft procedure whereby blood flow is rerouted through a new artery or vein that is grafted around diseased sections of the coronary arteries to increase blood flow to the heart muscle.

TABLE 10.5 Root Operations to Alter the Diameter or Route of a Tubular Body Part

Root Operation	Objective of Procedure	Site of Procedure	Example
Restriction	Partially closing orifice/lumen	Tubular body part	Gastroesophageal fundoplication
Occlusion	Completely closing orifice/lumen	Tubular body part	Fallopian tube ligation
Dilation	Expanding orifice/lumen	Tubular body part	Percutaneous transluminal coronary angioplasty (PTCA)
Bypass	Altering route of passage	Tubular body part	Coronary artery bypass graft (CABG)

Root Operations That Always Involve a Device

CHAPTER 10

*ICD-10-PCS
Root
Operations
in the Medical
and Surgical
Section*

The next grouping involves six root operations that always involve a device: "Insertion," "Replacement," "Supplement," "Change," "Removal," and "Revision." Table 10.6 provides an overview of these root operations.

The objective of the root operation "Insertion" is to put in a nonbiological device that monitors, assists, performs, or prevents a physiological function but does not physically take the place of a body part. This root operation represents those procedures whose sole objective is to put in a device without doing anything else to the body part. Examples include insertion of radioactive implant and insertion of central venous catheter.

The objective of the root operation "Replacement" is to put in a device (biological or synthetic material) that takes the place of some, or all, of a body part. The body part may have been taken out or replaced, or may be taken out, physically eradicated, or rendered nonfunctional during the "Replacement" procedure. Examples include hip replacement, bone graft, and free skin graft.

The objective of the root operation "Supplement" is to put in a device (biological or synthetic material) that physically reinforces and/or augments the function of a body part. The biological material may be nonliving, or living, and from the same individual. The body part may have been previously replaced, and the "Supplement" procedure is performed to physically reinforce and/or augment the function of the replaced body part. Common examples include hernia repair using mesh, mitral valve ring annuloplasty, and free nerve graft.

The root operation "Change" involves procedures whereby similar devices are exchanged without cutting or puncturing the skin or mucous membrane. All procedures with the root operation "Change" are reported with an external approach. Examples of "Change" root operations include urinary catheter change and changing of gastrostomy tube.

The root operation "Removal" involves procedures for taking out, or off, a device from a body part. This root operation should be coded only when it is not an integral part of another root operation. For example, if a device is taken out and a similar device is put in without cutting or puncturing the skin or mucous membrane, the root operation is "Change," and "Removal" is not coded separately. Examples of "Removal" include drainage tube removal and removal of external fixation device.

The root operation "Revision" applies to procedures whose objective is to correct, to the extent possible, the position or function of a previously placed device without taking the entire device out and putting a whole new device in its place. This root operation may include taking out

TABLE 10.6   Root Operations That Always Involve a Device

Root Operation	Objective of Procedure	Site of Procedure	Example
Insertion	Putting in non-biological device	In/on a body part	Central line insertion
Replacement	Putting in device that replaces a body part	Some/all of a body part	Total hip replacement
Supplement	Putting in device that reinforces or augments a body part	In/on a body part	Abdominal wall herniorrhaphy using mesh
Change	Exchanging device without cutting/puncturing	In/on a body part	Drainage tube change
Removal	Taking out device	In/on a body part	Central line removal
Revision	Correcting a malfunctioning displaced device	In/on a body part	Revision of pacemaker insertion

98

CHAPTER 10

ICD-10-PCS
Root
Operations
in the Medical
and Surgical
Section

and/or putting in part of the device, so a "Removal" of the old device would not be coded separately. It is important to understand that a complete re-do of a procedure is coded to the root operation performed, rather than "Revision." Examples of "Revision" include adjustment of pacemaker leads and adjustment of hip prosthesis.

Note that for the root operations "Change," "Removal," and "Revision," general body part values are used when the specific body part value is not in the Table.

Some procedures are performed on the device only, and not on a body part. Examples include irrigation of gastrostomy tube and replacement of pulse generator. In such instances, these procedures are reported with the root operations "Change," "Irrigation," "Removal," and "Revision."

EXERCISE 10.4

Code these procedures.

---

1. Cystoscopy with intraluminal <u>dilation</u> of bladder neck stricture   0T7C8ZZ

---

2. Total right knee arthroplasty with insertion of   0SRC0JZ
   total knee prosthesis

   <u>Replacement</u>

---

3. Laparoscopic bilateral fallopian tube ligation   0UL74ZZ

   <u>Occlusion</u>

---

4. Left ventral hernia repair with Merlex mesh   0WUF0JZ

   <u>Supplement</u>

---

5. Open <u>revision</u> of right knee replacement, with removal   0SWC0JZ
   and exchange of the polyethylene patellar component

Root Operations That Involve Examination Only

CHAPTER 10

*ICD-10-PCS
Root
Operations
in the Medical
and Surgical
Section*

Two root operations involve examination of a body part: "Inspection" and "Map." Refer to table 10.7 for an overview of these root operations.

If the examination's objective is visual or manual exploration of some or all of a body part, the root operation is "Inspection." The visual exploration may be accomplished with or without optical instrumentation. Manual exploration may be performed directly or through intervening body layers. Examples of "Inspection" root operations include diagnostic arthroscopy and exploratory laparotomy.

Three important guidelines apply to the root operation "Inspection":

- *Inspection of a body part(s) performed in order to achieve the objective of a procedure is not coded separately.* For example, a fiberoptic bronchoscopy (which is the procedure to inspect the lung) is performed to irrigate the bronchus. The root operation "Inspection" is not coded because the objective of the procedure is not to visually explore the bronchus but to perform the irrigation.

- *If multiple tubular body parts are inspected, the most distal body part inspected is coded. If multiple nontubular body parts in a region are inspected, the body part that specifies the entire area inspected is coded.* For example, when endoscopies are performed, multiple areas may be inspected as in a cystourethroscopy, whereby the bladder and ureters are examined. The most distal (or farthest away) body part in this situation is the ureter, so the body part value for the ureter is selected. An example of "Inspection" of multiple nontubular body parts in a region is an exploratory laparotomy whereby the abdominal contents are inspected. In this instance, the body part value would be "peritoneal cavity" because this body part specifies the entire area inspected.

- *When both an "Inspection" procedure and another procedure are performed on the same body part during the same episode, if the "Inspection" procedure is performed using a different approach than the other procedure, the "Inspection" procedure is coded separately.* For example, if an endoscopic inspection of the duodenum and an open excision of the duodenum are performed during the same procedural episode, both procedures would be coded separately. The different approaches are endoscopic for the "Inspection" and open for the "Excision."

The root operation "Map" should be used if the examination's objective is to locate electrical impulses or functional areas in a body part. The root operation "Map" has a limited applicability to the cardiac conduction mechanism and the central nervous system. Examples include cardiac electrophysiological study, heart catheterization with cardiac mapping, percutaneous mapping of basal ganglia, or intraoperative whole brain mapping via craniotomy.

TABLE 10.7 Root Operations That Involve Examination Only

Root Operation	Objective of Procedure	Site of Procedure	Example
Inspection	Visual/manual exploration	Some/all of a body part	Diagnostic cystoscopy
Map	Location electrical impulses/ functional areas	Brain/cardiac conduction mechanism	Cardiac electrophysiological study

CHAPTER 10

*ICD-10-PCS
Root
Operations
in the Medical
and Surgical
Section*

Root Operations That Include Other Repairs

This grouping includes two root operations: "Control" and "Repair." Refer to table 10.8 for an overview of these root operations.

The root operation "Control" describes stopping or attempting to stop postprocedural bleeding. It includes irrigation or evacuation of hematoma at the operative site. The bleeding site is coded as an anatomical region and not to a specific body part. Examples of this root operation are control of post-prostatectomy hemorrhage and control of post-tonsillectomy hemorrhage. It is important to note that the root operation "Control" should not be coded if an attempt to stop the postprocedural bleeding is initially unsuccessful and a definitive root operation (such as "Bypass," "Detachment," "Excision," "Extraction," "Reposition," "Replacement," or "Resection") is required to stop the bleeding.

The root operation "Repair" represents a broad range of procedures for restoring, to the extent possible, a body part to its normal anatomical structure and function. This root operation is only used when the procedure performed does not meet the definition of one of the other root operations. Examples of "Repair" include herniorraphy and suturing of laceration.

TABLE 10.8   Root Operations That Include Other Repairs

Root Operation	Objective of Procedure	Site of Procedure	Example
Control	Stopping/attempting to stop postprocedural bleeding	Anatomical region	Post-prostatectomy bleeding control
Repair	Restoring body part to its normal structure	Some/all of a body part	Suture laceration

Root Operations That Include Other Objectives

The last group of root operations is made up of those procedures that include other objectives not included in the previous groups. This group includes the root operations "Fusion," "Alteration," and "Creation." Table 10.9 provides an overview of these root operations.

The root operation "Fusion" refers to joining together portions of an articular body part, rendering the articular body part immobile. The procedure may be accomplished by a fixation device, a bone graft, or other means. The most common example of this root operation is spinal fusion. Specific guidelines related to coding of spinal fusion are covered in detail in chapter 23 of this handbook, Diseases of the Musculoskeletal System and Connective Tissue.

The root operation "Alteration" is coded for all procedures performed solely to improve appearance. This root operation refers to modifying a body part for cosmetic purposes without affecting the function of the body part. All methods, approaches, and devices used for the objective of improving appearance are coded here. Note that coding of the root operation "Alteration" requires diagnostic confirmation that the procedure was performed to improve appearance. Examples include face lift and breast augmentation.

The last root operation, "Creation," involves a very narrow range of procedures that are performed for sex change. It involves making a new genital structure that does not physically take the place of a body part. Examples include creation of a vagina in a male patient and creation of a penis in a female patient.

In summary, ICD-10-PCS requires mastering the 31 root operations in the Medical and Surgical Section as the key to selecting the appropriate codes. These concepts are applied in future chapters in this handbook as the more common procedures for each body system are discussed.

TABLE 10.9   Root Operations That Include Other Objectives

Root Operation	Objective of Procedure	Site of Procedure	Example
Fusion	Rendering joint immobile	Joint	Spinal fusion
Alteration	Modifying body part for cosmetic purposes without affecting function	Some/all of a body part	Face lift
Creation	Making new structure for sex change operation	Perineum	Artificial vagina/penis

CHAPTER 10

ICD-10-PCS

Root

Operations

in the Medical

and Surgical

Section

EXERCISE 10.5

Code these procedures.

1. Thoracotomy with exploration of right pleural cavity

   Inspection

   0WJ90ZZ

2. Reopening of thoracotomy site with drainage and control of postoperative hemopericardium

   0W3D0ZZ

3. Open cosmetic plastic repair of deformed left ear lobe

   Alteration

   09010ZZ

4. Exploratory laparotomy peritoneal cavity

   Inspection

   0WJG0ZZ

5. Arthroscopic left subtalar arthrodesis with internal fixation device

   Fusion

   0SGJ44Z

CHAPTER 11

ICD-10-PCS Procedures in the Medical- and Surgical-Related and Ancillary Sections

CHAPTER OVERVIEW

- ICD-10-PCS provides codes for Medical- and Surgical-Related and Ancillary Procedures in addition to the Medical and Surgical Section.

- There are nine sections in the Medical- and Surgical-Related Procedures. These sections include obstetrical procedures, administration of substances, measurement and monitoring of body functions, extracorporeal therapies, osteopathic, other procedures, and chiropractic procedures.

- There are six sections in the Ancillary Procedures. These sections include imaging, nuclear medicine, radiation oncology, physical rehabilitation and diagnostic audiology, mental health, and substance abuse treatment.

LEARNING OUTCOMES

After studying this chapter you should be able to:

Identify the objectives of each root operation.

Distinguish between the different root operations in the Medical- and Surgical-Related Section.

Discuss the general guidelines applicable to root operations.

Correctly assign codes for ancillary services.

TERM TO KNOW

Root operation
the third character in an ICD-10-PCS code, which refers to the objective of the procedure

CHAPTER 11

*ICD-10-PCS
Procedures
in the
Medical- and
Surgical-
Related
and Ancillary
Sections*

INTRODUCTION

The previous chapter introduces the Medical and Surgical Section of ICD-10-PCS, where the majority of the hospital inpatient procedures are classified. In addition to the Medical and Surgical Section, ICD-10-PCS has two additional sections: Medical- and Surgical-Related and Ancillary Procedures, which are covered in this chapter.

Many hospitals do not code minor ancillary procedures for inpatient stays. However, for the sake of completeness, ICD-10-PCS includes codes for these minor procedures should a hospital wish to collect data on these services.

MEDICAL- AND SURGICAL-RELATED PROCEDURES

There are nine sections in the Medical- and Surgical-Related Procedures. These sections include obstetrical procedures, placement, administration of substances, measurement and monitoring of body functions, extracorporeal therapies, osteopathic, other procedures, and chiropractic, as shown in table 11.1. The obstetrical procedures (section 1) are covered in detail in chapter 24 of this handbook, Complications of Pregnancy, Childbirth, and the Puerperium.

TABLE 11.1   Medical- and Surgical-Related Sections

Section Value	Description
1	Obstetrics
2	Placement
3	Administration
4	Measurement and Monitoring
5	Extracorporeal Assistance and Performance
6	Extracorporeal Therapies
7	Osteopathic
8	Other Procedures
9	Chiropractic

Placement Section

Codes in the Placement Section follow the same conventions used in the Medical and Surgical Section. All seven characters retain the same meaning in both sections, as shown in figure 11.1.

The root operations in the Placement Section are different from those in the Medical and Surgical Section covered in the previous chapter. These root operations include only those procedures that are performed without making an incision or a puncture. There are two body system (character 2) values in this section: "anatomical regions" (W) and "anatomical orifices" (Y). In addition, there are two body region (character 4) values: external body regions (e.g., abdominal wall) and natural orifices (e.g., ear).

FIGURE 11.1   Structure of Codes in the Placement Section

Character 1	Character 2	Character 3	Character 4	Character 5	Character 6	Character 7
Section	Body System	Root Operation	Body Region	Approach	Device	Qualifier

CHAPTER 11

*ICD-10-PCS
Procedures
in the
Medical- and
Surgical-
Related
and Ancillary
Sections*

Table 11.2 provides an overview of the root operations (third character) in the Placement Section with the corresponding value and definition. The root operations "Change" and "Removal" are common to other sections. The remaining five root operations, unique to the Placement Section, are:

- Compression
- Dressing
- Immobilization
- Packing
- Traction

TABLE 11.2   Placement Section Root Operation Values and Definitions

Value	Description	Definition
0	Change	Taking out or off a device from a body region and putting back an identical or similar device in or on the same body region without cutting or puncturing the skin or a mucous membrane
1	Compression	Putting pressure on a body region
2	Dressing	Putting material on a body region for protection
3	Immobilization	Limiting or preventing motion of a body region
4	Packing	Putting material in a body region
5	Removal	Taking out or off a device from a body region
6	Traction	Exerting a pulling force on a body region in a distal direction

Devices in this section specify the material or device (e.g., splint, traction apparatus, bandage) and include casts for fractures and dislocations. When the placement of devices requires extensive design, fabrication, or fitting, ICD-10-PCS classifies these procedures to the Rehabilitation Section. The devices classified to the Placement Section are off-the-shelf devices.

Examples of procedures in the Placement Section are the following:

Cast change, lower right arm

Character 1 Section	Character 2 Body System	Character 3 Root Operation	Character 4 Body Region	Character 5 Approach	Character 6 Device	Character 7 Qualifier
2	W	0	C	X	2	Z
Placement	Anatomical region	Change	Lower arm, right	External	Cast	None

Application of compression dressing to abdominal wound

Character 1 Section	Character 2 Body System	Character 3 Root Operation	Character 4 Body Region	Character 5 Approach	Character 6 Device	Character 7 Qualifier
2	W	1	3	X	6	Z
Placement	Anatomical region	Compression	Abdominal wall	External	Pressure dressing	None

CHAPTER 11

ICD-10-PCS
Procedures
in the
Medical- and
Surgical-
Related
and Ancillary
Sections

Application of dressing to right hand

Character 1 Section	Character 2 Body System	Character 3 Root Operation	Character 4 Body Region	Character 5 Approach	Character 6 Device	Character 7 Qualifier
2	W	2	E	X	4	Z
Placement	Anatomical region	Dressing	Hand, right	External	Bandage	None

Placement of stereotactic head frame

Character 1 Section	Character 2 Body System	Character 3 Root Operation	Character 4 Body Region	Character 5 Approach	Character 6 Device	Character 7 Qualifier
2	W	3	0	X	8	Z
Placement	Anatomical region	Immobilization	Head	External	Stereotactic apparatus	None

Caution should be exercised with the root operation "Immobilization" to distinguish it from several similar-sounding procedures that ICD-10-PCS classifies to different sections based on the setting where the procedure is performed. When the splint and braces are placed in inpatient settings (except for the rehabilitation setting), they are coded to "Immobilization," Table 2X3 in the Placement Section. However, for the rehabilitation setting, these procedures are coded to F0DZ6EZ and F0DZ7EZ in the Physical Rehabilitation and Diagnostic Audiology Section.

Removal of stereotactic head frame

Character 1 Section	Character 2 Body System	Character 3 Root Operation	Character 4 Body Region	Character 5 Approach	Character 6 Device	Character 7 Qualifier
2	W	5	0	X	8	Z
Placement	Anatomical region	Removal	Head	External	Stereotactic apparatus	None

Cervical traction using a traction apparatus

Character 1 Section	Character 2 Body System	Character 3 Root Operation	Character 4 Body Region	Character 5 Approach	Character 6 Device	Character 7 Qualifier
2	A	6	2	X	0	Z
Placement	Anatomical region	Traction	Neck	External	Traction apparatus	None

Note that "traction" in this section includes only traction performed using a mechanical traction apparatus. When manual traction is performed by a physical therapist, it should be classified to the Manual Therapy Techniques in section F, Physical Rehabilitation and Diagnostic Audiology.

Administration Section

CHAPTER 11

*ICD-10-PCS
Procedures
in the
Medical- and
Surgical-
Related
and Ancillary
Sections*

The Administration Section includes services such as injections, infusions, and transfusions, along with related procedures such as irrigation and tattooing. The structure of codes in this section is shown in figure 11.2.

FIGURE 11.2   Structure of Codes in the Administration Section

Character 1	Character 2	Character 3	Character 4	Character 5	Character 6	Character 7
Section	Body System	Root Operation	Body System/Region	Approach	Substance	Qualifier

There are three body system (character 2) values in this section:

0   Circulatory
C   Indwelling device
E   Physiological systems and anatomical regions

There are three root operations in the Administration Section, and they are classified according to the broad category of substance administered. Blood products are classified to the root operation "Transfusion"; cleansing substances are classified to "Irrigation." All other therapeutic, diagnostic, nutritional, physiological, or prophylactic substances administered are classified to "Introduction."

Character 5 (approach) uses values defined in the Medical and Surgical Section. The percutaneous approach is used for intradermal, subcutaneous, and intramuscular injections. Catheter utilization to introduce substances into the circulatory system is classified to the percutaneous approach.

Examples of procedures for each root operation in the Administration Section are as follows:

Infusion of chemotherapy peripheral vein insertion

Character 1 Section	Character 2 Body System	Character 3 Root Operation	Character 4 Body System/ Region	Character 5 Approach	Character 6 Substance	Character 7 Qualifier
3	E	0	3	3	0	5
Administration	Physiological systems and anatomical regions	Introduction	Peripheral vein	Percutaneous	Antineoplastic	Other antineoplastic

Peritoneal dialysis via indwelling catheter

Character 1 Section	Character 2 Body System	Character 3 Root Operation	Character 4 Body System/ Region	Character 5 Approach	Character 6 Substance	Character 7 Qualifier
3	E	1	M	3	9	Z
Administration	Physiological systems and anatomical regions	Irrigation	Peritoneal cavity	Percutaneous	Dialysate	None

108

CHAPTER 11

ICD-10-PCS
Procedures
in the
Medical- and
Surgical-
Related
and Ancillary
Sections

Transfusion of embryonic stem cells into central vein

Character 1 Section	Character 2 Body System	Character 3 Root Operation	Character 4 Body System/ Region	Character 5 Approach	Character 6 Substance	Character 7 Qualifier
3	0	2	4	3	A	Z
Administration	Circulatory	Transfusion	Central vein	Percutaneous	Stem cells, embryonic	None

Measurement and Monitoring Section

The Measurement and Monitoring Section classifies procedures that determine the level of a physiological or physical function. There are two root operations in this section, and they differ in only one respect: "Measurement" describes a single level taken, at a point in time; "Monitoring" describes a series of tests performed repetitively over a period of time. The structure of the codes in this section differs from other sections in that the sixth character, instead of defining a device or substance (as in the Administration Section), defines the physiological or physical function being tested (e.g., pressure, temperature). There is a single body system value used in this section, "physiological systems." The structure of codes in this section is shown in figure 11.3.

FIGURE 11.3 Structure of Codes in the Measurement and Monitoring Section						
Character 1	Character 2	Character 3	Character 4	Character 5	Character 6	Character 7
Section	Body System	Root Operation	Body System	Approach	Function/Device	Qualifier

Examples of procedures in the Measurement and Monitoring Section are the following:

Single external EKG (electrocardiogram) reading

Character 1 Section	Character 2 Body System	Character 3 Root Operation	Character 4 Body System	Character 5 Approach	Character 6 Function/Device	Character 7 Qualifier
4	A	0	2	X	4	Z
Measurement and monitoring	Physiological systems	Measurement	Cardiac	External	Electrical activity	None

Holter monitoring

Character 1 Section	Character 2 Body System	Character 3 Root Operation	Character 4 Body System	Character 5 Approach	Character 6 Function/Device	Character 7 Qualifier
4	A	1	2	X	4	5
Measurement and monitoring	Physiological systems	Monitoring	Cardiac	External	Electrical activity	Ambulatory

CHAPTER 11

*ICD-10-PCS
Procedures
in the
Medical- and
Surgical-
Related
and Ancillary
Sections*

EXERCISE 11.1

Code the following procedures.

1. Percutaneous irrigation of pleural cavity using irrigating substance

   3E1L38Z

2. Transplant of autologous bone marrow via central vein

   Transfusion

   30243G0

3. Placement of cast on right lower arm

   Immobilization

   2W3CX2Z

4. Insertion of nasal packing

   2Y41X5Z

5. Cardiac pacemaker rate check (external)

   Measurement

   4B02XSZ

6. Application of compression dressing to the back

   2W15X6Z

Extracorporeal Assistance and Performance Section

The Extracorporeal Assistance and Performance Section includes procedures that use equipment to support a physiological function, such as breathing (e.g., mechanical ventilation), circulating the blood (e.g., hemodialysis), or restoring the natural rhythm of the heart (e.g., cardioversion). These procedures are typically performed in a critical care setting.

The structure of codes in this section is shown in figure 11.4.

FIGURE 11.4   Structure of Codes in the Extracorporeal Assistance and Performance Section

Character 1	Character 2	Character 3	Character 4	Character 5	Character 6	Character 7
Section	Body System	Root Operation	Body System	Duration	Function	Qualifier

There is a single body system (character 2) value, "physiological systems" (0). Character 5 differs from other sections in that it describes the duration of the procedure, rather than the approach. Character 5 specifies whether the procedure was a single occurrence, multiple occurrences, intermittent, or continuous. Character 6 describes the body function being acted upon (e.g., ventilation to assist with respiration).

CHAPTER 11

*ICD-10-PCS
Procedures
in the
Medical- and
Surgical-
Related
and Ancillary
Sections*

This section contains three root operations: "Assistance," "Performance," and "Restoration." "Assistance" and "Performance" vary only in the degree of control exercised over the physiological function. Assistance takes over a portion of a physiological function, while performance takes over the function completely—both by extracorporeal means. The root operation "Restoration" is defined as returning, or attempting to return, a physiological function to its original state by extracorporeal means. "Restoration" defines only external cardioversion and defibrillation procedures. Cardioversion procedures are classified to the root operation "Restoration" whether the procedure is successful or fails.

Examples of each root operation in this section are the following:

Continuous positive airway pressure for sleep apnea—eight hours

Character 1 Section	Character 2 Body System	Character 3 Root Operation	Character 4 Body System	Character 5 Duration	Character 6 Function	Character 7 Qualifier
5	A	0	9	3	5	7
Extracorporeal assistance and performance	Physiological systems	Assistance	Respiratory	Less than 24 consecutive hours	Ventilation	Continuous positive airway pressure

Continuous mechanical ventilation, over six consecutive days

Character 1 Section	Character 2 Body System	Character 3 Root Operation	Character 4 Body System	Character 5 Duration	Character 6 Function	Character 7 Qualifier
5	A	1	9	5	5	Z
Extracorporeal assistance and performance	Physiological systems	Performance	Respiratory	Greater than 96 consecutive hours	Ventilation	None

External cardioversion

Character 1 Section	Character 2 Body System	Character 3 Root Operation	Character 4 Body System	Character 5 Duration	Character 6 Function	Character 7 Qualifier
5	A	2	2	0	4	Z
Extracorporeal assistance and performance	Physiological systems	Restoration	Cardiac	Single	Rhythm	None

Extracorporeal Therapies Section

The Extracorporeal Therapies Section describes other extracorporeal procedures not defined by the root operations "Assistance" and "Performance" in section 5, Extracorporeal Assistance and Performance. The structure of codes in this section is shown in figure 11.5.

FIGURE 11.5   Structure of Codes in the Extracorporeal Therapies Section

Character 1	Character 2	Character 3	Character 4	Character 5	Character 6	Character 7
Section	Body System	Root Operation	Body System	Duration	Qualifier	Qualifier

CHAPTER 11

*ICD-10-PCS
Procedures
in the
Medical- and
Surgical-
Related
and Ancillary
Sections*

This section contains a single body system value, "physiological systems." Character 5, duration, specifies whether the procedure was single or multiple. This section is different from others in that two characters, 6 and 7, are qualifiers, but none is used for character 6. This is to comply with the overall structure of all ICD-10-PCS codes to be seven characters long. The seventh-character qualifier identifies various blood components separated out in pheresis procedures such as red blood cells, white blood cells, platelets, plasma, stem cells from cord blood, and hematopoietic stem cells.

There are 10 root operations in the Extracorporeal Therapies Section. The meaning of each root operation as used in ICD-10-PCS is consistent with the terminology used in the medical community, except for "Decompression" and "Hyperthermia," as follows:

- *Atmospheric control:* Extracorporeal control of atmospheric pressure and composition.

- *Decompression:* Extracorporeal elimination of undissolved gas from body fluids. "Decompression" describes a single type of procedure: treatment for decompression sickness (the bends) in a hyperbaric chamber.

- *Electromagnetic therapy:* Extracorporeal treatment by electromagnetic rays.

- *Hyperthermia:* Extracorporeal raising of body temperature. It is important to distinguish the objective of the hyperthermia procedure for proper code assignment. Hyperthermia may be used to treat temperature imbalance, in which case it is coded to the Extracorporeal Therapies Section. However, hyperthermia is also used as an adjunct radiation treatment for cancer, in which case ICD-10-PCS classifies it to the Radiation Oncology Section.

- *Hypothermia:* Extracorporeal lowering of body temperature.

- *Pheresis:* Extracorporeal separation of blood products. This procedure is used in medical practice for two main purposes: to treat diseases in which too much of a blood component is produced, such as leukemia, or to remove a blood product, such as platelets, from a donor for transfusion into a patient who needs it.

- *Phototherapy:* Extracorporeal treatment by light rays. Phototherapy to the circulatory system refers to exposing the blood to light rays outside the body using a machine that recirculates the blood and returns it to the body after phototherapy.

- *Ultrasound therapy:* Extracorporeal treatment by ultrasound.

- *Ultraviolet light therapy:* Extracorporeal treatment by ultraviolet light.

- *Shock wave therapy:* Extracorporeal treatment by shock waves.

Examples are the following:

Donor peripheral lymphocyte apheresis procedure, multiple

Character 1 Section	Character 2 Body System	Character 3 Root Operation	Character 4 Body System	Character 5 Duration	Character 6 Qualifier	Character 7 Qualifier
6	A	5	5	1	Z	1
Extracorporeal therapies	Physiological systems	Pheresis	Circulatory	Multiple	None	Leukocytes

Shock wave therapy for heel pain, single treatment

Character 1 Section	Character 2 Body System	Character 3 Root Operation	Character 4 Body System	Character 5 Duration	Character 6 Qualifier	Character 7 Qualifier
6	A	9	3	0	Z	Z
Extracorporeal therapies	Physiological systems	Shock wave therapy	Musculoskeletal	Single	None	None

112

CHAPTER 11

*ICD-10-PCS
Procedures
in the
Medical- and
Surgical-
Related
and Ancillary
Sections*

EXERCISE 11.2

Code the following procedures.

1. Continuous hyperbaric oxygenation   5A05221

2. Ultrasound therapy of peripheral vascular vessels, single treatment   6A750Z6

3. Hemodialysis   5A1D00Z

   Performance

4. Failed cardioversion   5A2204Z

   Restoration

5. Pheresis of hematopoietic stem cells, single episode   6A550ZV

Osteopathic Section

The Osteopathic Section is one of the smallest sections in ICD-10-PCS. There is a single body system ("anatomical regions") and a single root operation ("Treatment"). The structure of codes in this section is shown in figure 11.6.

FIGURE 11.6 Structure of Codes in the Osteopathic Section

Character 1	Character 2	Character 3	Character 4	Character 5	Character 6	Character 7
Section	Body System	Root Operation	Body Region	Approach	Method	Qualifier

Character 6, method, in this section defines the osteopathic method of the procedure. The following osteopathic methods are specified: articulatory raising, fascial release, general mobilization, high velocity–low amplitude, indirect, low velocity–high amplitude, lymphatic pump, muscle energy–isometric, muscle energy–isotonic, and other method.

One example is muscle energy isotonic osteopathic treatment of neck

Character 1 Section	Character 2 Body System	Character 3 Root Operation	Character 4 Body Region	Character 5 Approach	Character 6 Method	Character 7 Qualifier
7	W	0	1	X	8	Z
Osteopathic	Anatomical regions	Treatment	Cervical	External	Muscle energy isotonic	None

Other Procedures Section

This section contains codes for procedures not included in the other medical- and surgical-related sections. The structure of codes in this section is similar to the structure of codes in the Osteopathic Section (see figure 11.6). There is a single root operation, "Other procedures." This root operation is defined as methodologies that attempt to remediate or cure a disorder or disease. There are relatively few codes in this section, including some nontraditional, whole body therapies such as acupuncture, meditation, and yoga therapy. Character 6, method, defines the method of the procedure, such as computer-assisted procedure, robotic-assisted procedure, or acupuncture. Note that the procedure codes for robotic-assisted and computer-assisted procedures are coded in addition to the primary procedure (e.g., cholecystectomy). Another procedure included in this section is the fertilization portion of an in-vitro fertilization procedure.

Here are two examples:

Robotic-assisted laparoscopic cholecystectomy (the robotic assistance only)

Character 1 Section	Character 2 Body System	Character 3 Root Operation	Character 4 Body Region	Character 5 Approach	Character 6 Method	Character 7 Qualifier
8	E	0	W	4	C	Z
Other procedures	Physiological systems and anatomical regions	Other procedures	Trunk region	Percutaneous endoscopic	Robotic assisted procedure	None

Suture removal of left arm

Character 1 Section	Character 2 Body System	Character 3 Root Operation	Character 4 Body Region	Character 5 Approach	Character 6 Method	Character 7 Qualifier
8	E	0	X	X	Y	8
Other procedures	Physiological systems and anatomical regions	Other procedures	Upper extremity	External	Other method	Suture removal

Chiropractic Section

The last section in the Medical- and Surgical-Related Procedures is the Chiropractic Section. This section consists of a single body system, "anatomical regions," and a single root operation, "Manipulation." "Manipulation" is defined in ICD-10-PCS as a manual procedure that involves a directed thrust to move a joint past the physiological range of motion without exceeding the anatomical limit. The structure of codes in this section is similar to the structure of codes in the Osteopathic Section (see figure 11.6) and the Other Procedures Section.

An example for this section is the following:

Chiropractic mechanically assisted manipulation of right wrist

Character 1 Section	Character 2 Body System	Character 3 Root Operation	Character 4 Body Region	Character 5 Approach	Character 6 Method	Character 7 Qualifier
9	W	B	7	X	K	Z
Chiropractic	Anatomical regions	Manipulation	Upper extremity	External	Mechanically assisted	None

CHAPTER 11

*ICD-10-PCS
Procedures
in the
Medical- and
Surgical-
Related
and Ancillary
Sections*

EXERCISE 11.3

Code the following procedures.

1.	Acupuncture to the back using anesthesia	8E0H300
2.	Blood collection from indwelling vascular access device	8C02X6K
3.	Osteopathic manipulation lower back using high velocity–low amplitude	7W03X3Z
4.	Open excision of acoustic neuroma with computer-assisted magnetic resonance imaging	00BN0ZZ 8E09XBH
5.	Chiropractic manipulation of low back with high velocity, short lever arm thrust contact	9WB3XHZ

ANCILLARY PROCEDURES

There are six sections in ICD-10-PCS for ancillary procedures, as follows:

B   Imaging
C   Nuclear Medicine
D   Radiation Oncology
F   Physical Rehabilitation and Diagnostic Audiology
G   Mental Health
H   Substance Abuse Treatment

Ancillary Sections (B–H) do not include root operations. Instead, character 3 in these sections represents the root type of the procedure. Codes in these sections include characters not previously defined, such as contrast, modality qualifier, and equipment. Section G, Mental Health, and section H, Substance Abuse Treatment, are covered in chapter 16 of this handbook, Mental Disorders.

Imaging Section

The Imaging Section follows the same conventions established in the Medical and Surgical Section, except that the third and fifth characters introduce definitions not used in previous sections. The third character defines root type, rather than root operation, and the fifth character defines contrast, if used. In addition, contrast is differentiated by whether it is low or high osmolar contrast. The sixth-character qualifier in this section provides the ability to specify that an image is taken without contrast, followed by one with contrast (unenhanced and enhanced).

The structure of codes in this section is shown in figure 11.7.

CHAPTER 11

ICD-10-PCS
Procedures
in the
Medical- and
Surgical-
Related
and Ancillary
Sections

FIGURE 11.7   Structure of Codes in the Imaging Section

Character 1	Character 2	Character 3	Character 4	Character 5	Character 6	Character 7
Section	Body System	Root Type	Body Part	Contrast	Qualifier	Qualifier

The Imaging Section utilizes the following five root types:

- *Value 0—Plain radiography:* Planar display of an image developed from the capture of external ionizing radiation on photographic or photoconductive plate.

- *Value 1—Fluoroscopy:* Single plane or biplane real-time display of an image developed from the capture of external ionizing radiation on a fluorescent screen. The image may also be stored by either digital or analog means.

- *Value 2—Computed tomography (CT scan):* Computer reformatted digital display of multiplanar images developed from the capture of multiple exposures of external ionizing radiation.

- *Value 3—Magnetic resonance imaging (MRI):* Computer-reformatted digital display of multiplanar images developed from the capture of radio-frequency signals emitted by nuclei in a body site excited within a magnetic field.

- *Value 4—Ultrasonography:* Real-time display of images of anatomy or flow information developed from the capture of reflected and attenuated high-frequency sound waves.

Examples include the following:

X-ray of right upper arm

Character 1 Section	Character 2 Body System	Character 3 Root Type	Character 4 Body Part	Character 5 Contrast	Character 6 Qualifier	Character 7 Qualifier
B	P	0	E	Z	Z	Z
Imaging	Non-axial upper bones	Plain radiography	Upper arm, right	None	None	None

Retrograde pyelogram (kidneys, ureters, bladder) with low osmolar contrast

Character 1 Section	Character 2 Body System	Character 3 Root Type	Character 4 Body Part	Character 5 Contrast	Character 6 Qualifier	Character 7 Qualifier
B	T	1	4	1	Z	Z
Imaging	Urinary system	Fluoroscopy	Kidneys, ureters and bladder	Low osmolar	None	None

CT of brain without contrast, followed by high osmolar contrast

Character 1 Section	Character 2 Body System	Character 3 Root Type	Character 4 Body Part	Character 5 Contrast	Character 6 Qualifier	Character 7 Qualifier
B	0	2	0	0	0	Z
Imaging	Central nervous	Computerized tomography	Brain	High osmolar	Unenhanced and enhanced	None

CHAPTER 11

ICD-10-PCS
Procedures
in the
Medical- and
Surgical-
Related
and Ancillary
Sections

MRI of liver and spleen with contrast

Character 1 Section	Character 2 Body System	Character 3 Root Type	Character 4 Body Part	Character 5 Contrast	Character 6 Qualifier	Character 7 Qualifier
B	F	3	6	Y	Z	Z
Imaging	Hepatobiliary system and pancreas	Magnetic resonance imaging	Liver and spleen	Other contrast	None	None

Bilateral ovarian ultrasound

Character 1 Section	Character 2 Body System	Character 3 Root Type	Character 4 Body Part	Character 5 Contrast	Character 6 Qualifier	Character 7 Qualifier
B	U	4	5	Z	Z	Z
Imaging	Female reproductive system	Ultrasonography	Ovaries, bilateral	None	None	None

Nuclear Medicine Section

The Nuclear Medicine Section is organized like the Imaging Section, with the only significant difference being that the fifth character is used to define the radionuclide (radiation source) instead of the contrast material used in the procedure. Similar to the Imaging Section, the third character classifies the procedure by root type, rather than root operation. The sixth and seventh characters are qualifiers and are not used in this section.

The structure of the codes in this section is shown in figure 11.8.

FIGURE 11.8   Structure of Codes in the Nuclear Medicine Section

Character 1	Character 2	Character 3	Character 4	Character 5	Character 6	Character 7
Section	Body System	Root Type	Body Part	Radionuclide	Qualifier	Qualifier

The following seven root types are used in the Nuclear Medicine Section:

- *Value 1—Planar nuclear medicine imaging:* Introduction of radioactive materials into the body for single-plane display of images developed from the capture of radioactive emissions.

- *Value 2—Tomographic nuclear medicine imaging:* Introduction of radioactive materials into the body for three-dimensional displays of images developed from the capture of radioactive emissions.

- *Value 3—Positron emission tomography (PET):* Introduction of radioactive materials into the body for three-dimensional displays of images developed from the simultaneous capture, 180 degrees apart, of radioactive emissions.

- *Value 4—Nonimaging nuclear medicine uptake:* Introduction of radioactive materials into the body for measurements of organ function, from the detection of radioactive emissions.

117

CHAPTER 11

ICD-10-PCS
Procedures
in the
Medical- and
Surgical-
Related
and Ancillary
Sections

- *Value 5—Nonimaging nuclear medicine probe:* Introduction of radioactive materials into the body for the study of distribution and fate of certain substances by the detection of radioactive emissions; alternatively, measurement of absorption of radioactive emissions from an external source.

- *Value 6—Nonimaging nuclear medicine assay:* Introduction of radioactive materials into the body for the study of body fluids and blood elements by the detection of radioactive emissions.

- *Value 7—Systemic nuclear medicine therapy:* Introduction of unsealed radioactive materials into the body for treatment.

Examples include the following:

Brain PET scan with C-11

Character 1 Section	Character 2 Body System	Character 3 Root Type	Character 4 Body Part	Character 5 Radionuclide	Character 6 Qualifier	Character 7 Qualifier
C	0	3	0	B	Z	Z
Nuclear medicine	Central nervous system	Positron emission tomographic (PET) imaging	Brain	Carbon 11	None	None

I-131 thyroid uptake study

Character 1 Section	Character 2 Body System	Character 3 Root Type	Character 4 Body Part	Character 5 Radionuclide	Character 6 Qualifier	Character 7 Qualifier
C	G	4	2	G	Z	Z
Nuclear medicine	Endocrine system	Nonimaging nuclear medicine uptake	Thyroid gland	Iodine 131	None	None

Radiation Oncology Section

The ICD-10-PCS Radiation Oncology Section contains the radiation procedures used for cancer treatment. The structure of the codes in this section is shown in figure 11.9.

FIGURE 11.9   Structure of Codes in the Radiation Oncology Section

Character 1	Character 2	Character 3	Character 4	Character 5	Character 6	Character 7
Section	Body System	Root Type	Body Part	Modality Qualifier	Isotope	Qualifier

The differences in character meanings for this section are as follows:

- Character 3 defines root type, which is the basic radiation delivery modality used (beam radiation, brachytherapy, stereotactic radiosurgery, and other radiation).

- Character 5 specifies further the treatment modality used (photons, electrons, heavy particles, contact radiation).

- Character 6 defines the radioactive isotope used, if applicable.

- Character 7 is a qualifier and is not specified in this section.

CHAPTER 11

ICD-10-PCS
Procedures
in the
Medical- and
Surgical-
Related
and Ancillary
Sections

Examples include the following:

External beam radiation to left breast (photons 1.33 MeV)

Character 1 Section	Character 2 Body System	Character 3 Root Type	Character 4 Body Part	Character 5 Modality Qualifier	Character 6 Isotope	Character 7 Qualifier
D	M	0	0	1	Z	Z
Radiation oncology	Breast	Beam radiation	Breast, left	Photons 1–10 MeV	None	None

Prostate brachytherapy seeds, LDR, Iodine 125

Character 1 Section	Character 2 Body System	Character 3 Root Type	Character 4 Body Part	Character 5 Modality Qualifier	Character 6 Isotope	Character 7 Qualifier
D	V	1	0	B	9	Z
Radiation oncology	Male reproductive system	Brachytherapy	Prostate	Low-dose rate	Iodine 125	None

EXERCISE 11.4

Code the following procedures.

1. Intravascular ultrasound bilateral internal carotid arteries   B348ZZ3

2. MRI of the brain with contrast   B030YZZ

3. PET scan of the lungs with F-18   CB32KZZ

4. Right breast brachytherapy, LDR, Palladium 103   DM11BBZ

5. CT scan of the lungs without contrast   BB24ZZZ

Physical Rehabilitation and Diagnostic Audiology Section

The structure of the codes in the Physical Rehabilitation and Diagnostic Audiology Section is shown in figure 11.10.

FIGURE 11.10   Structure of Codes in the Physical Rehabilitation and Diagnostic Audiology Section

Character 1	Character 2	Character 3	Character 4	Character 5	Character 6	Character 7
Section	Section Qualifier	Root Type	Body System and Region	Type Qualifier	Equipment	Qualifier

This section contains character definitions unlike the other sections in ICD-10-PCS, as follows:

- Character 2 is a section qualifier that specifies whether the procedure is a rehabilitation or diagnostic audiology procedure.
- Character 3 defines the general procedure root type.
- Character 4 defines the body system and body regions combined, where applicable.
- Character 5 specifies further the procedure type.
- Character 6 specifies any equipment used.

This section contains 14 root types, which are defined in table 11.3:

TABLE 11.3   Physical Rehabilitation and Diagnostic Audiology Root Types, Values, and Definitions

Value	Description	Definition
0	Speech assessment	Measurement of speech and related functions
1	Motor and/or nerve function assessment	Measurement of motor, nerve, and related functions
2	Activites of daily living assessment	Measurement of functional level for activities of daily living
3	Hearing assessment	Measurement of hearing and related functions
4	Hearing aid assessment	Measurement of the appropriateness and/or effectiveness of a hearing device
5	Vestibular assessment	Measurement of the vestibular system and related functions
6	Speech treatment	Application of techniques to improve, augment, or compensate for speech and related functional impairment
7	Motor treatment	Exercise or activities to increase or facilitate motor function
8	Activities of daily living treatment	Exercise or activities to facilitate functional competence for activities of daily living
9	Hearing treatment	Application of techniques to improve, augment, or compensate for hearing and related functional impairment
B	Hearing aid treatment	Application of techniques to improve the communication abilities of individuals with cochlear implant
C	Vestibular treatment	Application of techniques to improve, augment, or compensate for vestibular and related functional impairment
D	Device fitting	Fitting of a device designed to facilitate or support achievement of a higher level of function
F	Caregiver training	Training in activities to support patient's optimal level of function

CHAPTER 11

ICD-10-PCS
Procedures
in the
Medical- and
Surgical-
Related
and Ancillary
Sections

The following important coding notes apply to this section:

- Treatment procedures include swallowing dysfunction exercises, bathing and showering techniques, wound management, gait training, and a host of activities typically associated with rehabilitation.

- Assessments are further classified into more than 100 different tests or methods. The majority of these assessments focus on the faculties of hearing and speech; others focus on various aspects of body function and on the patient's quality of life, such as muscle performance, neuromotor development, and reintegration skills.

- The fifth character used in device fitting describes the device being fitted rather than the method used to fit the device.

- Caregiver training is divided into 18 different broad subjects taught to help a caregiver provide proper patient care. Examples include bathing, dressing, feeding, and eating.

Examples include the following:

Pulsatile lavage of heel ulcer

Character 1 Section	Character 2 Section Qualifier	Character 3 Root Type	Character 4 Body System and Region	Character 5 Type Qualifier	Character 6 Equipment	Character 7 Qualifier
F	0	8	G	5	B	Z
Physical rehabilitation and diagnostic audiology	Rehabilitation	Activities of daily living treatment	Integumentary lower extremity	Wound management	Physical agents	None

Bedside swallowing assessment of stroke patient

Character 1 Section	Character 2 Section Qualifier	Character 3 Root Type	Character 4 Body System and Region	Character 5 Type Qualifier	Character 6 Equipment	Character 7 Qualifier
F	0	0	Z	H	Z	Z
Physical rehabilitation and diagnostic audiology	Rehabilitation	Speech assessment	None	Bedside swallowing and oral function	None	None

EXERCISE 11.5

Code the following procedures.

---

1. Aphasia <u>assessment</u> by speech therapist   F00ZCZZ

                                    <u>Speech assessment</u>

---

2. Prosthetic <u>device fitting</u>, below knee leg prosthetic   F0DZ8UZ

---

3. <u>Caregiver training</u> in keeping wound clean and dressing change   F0FZ9ZZ

CHAPTER 11

ICD-10-PCS
Procedures
in the
Medical- and
Surgical-
Related
and Ancillary
Sections

Z Codes and External Cause of Morbidity Codes

CHAPTER OVERVIEW

- Z codes and External cause of morbidity codes follow the same format and conventions as the main classification.

- Certain Z codes are used as principal diagnosis codes in specific situations.

- Aftercare management Z codes are generally listed first to explain the reason for continued care after the initial treatment of an injury or disease.

- Z codes are also useful for coding admission for observation and evaluation and admission for palliative care.

- They are also used for special investigative examinations when no problem, diagnosis, or condition is identified and for screening examinations.

- Z codes indicate personal history, family history, and genetic susceptibility to disease.

LEARNING OUTCOMES

After studying this chapter you should be able to:

Locate Z codes and External cause of morbidity codes.

Explain how and when Z codes and External cause of morbidity codes are used.

TERMS TO KNOW

Aftercare management
continued care during the healing phase or long-term care due to the consequences of a disease

External cause of morbidity codes
codes for external causes to provide information for injury research and evaluation of injury prevention strategies

Palliative care
care focused on the management of pain and other symptoms of patients who are in the terminal phase of an illness

Z codes
codes for factors influencing health status and contact with health services

REMEMBER . . .

Z and External cause of morbidity codes are used throughout the classification.

CHAPTER 12

*Z Codes
and External
Cause
of Morbidity
Codes*

INTRODUCTION

In addition to the main classification (A00.0 through T88.9), two special groups of codes are provided in ICD-10-CM:

- Factors influencing health status and contact with health service (Z codes: Z00–Z99)
- External causes of morbidity (V00–Y99)

USING Z CODES AND EXTERNAL CAUSE OF MORBIDITY CODES

Certain Z codes are designated as the principal (or first-listed) diagnosis in specific situations; others are assigned as additional codes when it is important to indicate a history, status, or problem that may affect health care. Some Z codes can be used as either the principal (or first-listed) diagnosis or as an additional code. External cause codes are assigned as additional codes to indicate how the injury or health condition happened (cause), the intent (unintentional or accidental; intentional, such as suicide or assault), the place where the event occurred, the activity of the patient at the time of the event, and the person's status (e.g., civilian, military). Because Z codes and External cause codes must be used throughout the classification, this chapter provides a general introduction before their treatment in other chapters in the handbook.

LOCATING Z CODES AND EXTERNAL CAUSE OF MORBIDITY CODES

The format and conventions used throughout the main classification are also used in the Indexes and Tabular Lists for these supplementary classifications. Index entries for Z codes are included in the main Alphabetic Index. These are the key main terms:

- Admission
- Examination
- History
- Observation
- Aftercare
- Problem
- Status

The Tabular List for Z codes follows immediately after the Injury, Poisoning and Certain Other Consequences of External Causes (S00–T98) section in the Tabular List.

External cause of morbidity codes are not used to report the intent for poisonings, toxic effects, adverse effects, or underdosing of drugs. ICD-10-CM classifies these conditions using codes in categories T36–T65, which combine the substances involved with the external cause. These situations are discussed in chapter 32, Poisoning, Toxic Effects, Adverse Effects, and Underdosing of Drugs.

Z CODES

Z codes are used as the principal (or first-listed) diagnosis in the following situations:

CHAPTER 12

*Z Codes
and External
Cause
of Morbidity
Codes*

- To indicate that a person with a resolving disease or injury or a chronic condition is being seen for specific aftercare, such as the removal of internal fixation devices such as orthopedic pins

- To indicate that the patient is seen for the sole purpose of special therapy, such as radiotherapy or chemotherapy

- To indicate that a person not currently ill is encountering the health service for a specific reason, such as to act as an organ donor, to receive prophylactic care, or to receive counseling

- To indicate the birth status of newborns

Z codes are assigned as additional diagnosis codes in the following situations:

- To indicate that a patient has a history, a health status, or another problem that is not in itself an illness or injury but may influence patient care. Note that the following Z codes can be listed first if the fact of the history itself is the reason for admission or encounter:

  Z85.-   Personal history of malignant neoplasm
  Z86.6-   Personal history of diseases of nervous system and sense organs
  Z80–Z84   Family history

- To indicate the outcome of delivery for obstetric patients

Admission or Encounter for Aftercare Management

Aftercare visit codes (Z42–Z51) are used when the initial treatment of a disease has been completed but the patient requires continued care during the healing or recovery phase or for long-term consequences of the disease. The aftercare code is not assigned when treatment is directed at a current acute disease. The diagnosis code is to be used in these cases. The exceptions to this rule are encounters for antineoplastic chemotherapy and immunotherapy (Z51.1-) or radiotherapy (Z51.0). When the encounter is for the purpose of more than one type of antineoplastic therapy (e.g., radiation and chemotherapy), both codes are assigned and either can be sequenced first. (Chapter 29 of this handbook, Neoplasms, discusses the correct use of radiation and chemotherapy codes.)

Admission for aftercare management ordinarily involves planned care, such as the fitting and adjustment of an external prosthetic device (Z44.-), attention to an artificial opening (Z43.-), breast reconstruction following mastectomy (Z42.1), or removal of an internal fixation device (Z47.2).

There are codes for encounters for attention to dressings, sutures, and drains (Z48.0-). There are also codes to report aftercare following surgery for neoplasms (Z48.3), following organ transplant (Z48.2-), and for surgery to specific body systems (Z48.810–Z48.817). These codes should be reported along with any other aftercare codes or other diagnosis codes to provide more detail regarding an aftercare visit.

Palliative care is an alternative to aggressive treatment for patients who are in the terminal phase of an illness. Care is focused on the management of pain and other symptoms of the disease, which is often more appropriate than aggressive care when a patient is dying of an incurable illness. Code **Z51.5, Encounter for palliative care,** is used to classify admissions or encounters for end-of-life care, hospice care, and terminal care. It may be used in any health care setting. It cannot be used as the principal diagnosis or reason for encounter; instead, the code for the underlying disease is sequenced first.

CHAPTER 12

Z Codes
and External
Cause
of Morbidity
Codes

The aftercare Z codes should not be used for aftercare for injuries. For aftercare of an injury, assign the acute injury code with the appropriate seventh character for subsequent encounter (e.g., "D" or "G," "K," or "P" for fractures). These codes are covered in more detail in chapter 30 of this handbook.

Aftercare codes are generally listed first to explain the specific reason for the encounter. They can be used occasionally as additional codes when aftercare is provided during an encounter for treatment of an unrelated condition but no applicable diagnosis code is available (for example, the closure of a colostomy during an admission to treat an injury sustained in an automobile accident). Aftercare codes should be used in conjunction with any other aftercare or diagnosis code(s) to provide better detail on the specifics of an aftercare visit, unless otherwise directed by the classification. The sequencing of multiple aftercare codes depends on the circumstances of the encounter. Certain aftercare Z codes need a secondary diagnosis code to describe the resolving condition or sequelae. For others, the condition is included in the code title.

When the patient is admitted because of a complication of previous care, the appropriate code from the main classification is assigned rather than the aftercare Z code. (See chapter 33 of this handbook.)

Admission for Follow-Up Examination

A code from category Z08, Z09, or Z39 is assigned as the principal diagnosis or reason for encounter when a patient is admitted for the purpose of surveillance after the initial treatment of a disease or injury has been completed. Examples include:

Z09   Encounter for follow-up examination after completed treatment for conditions other than malignant neoplasm

Z08   Encounter for follow-up examination after completed treatment for malignant neoplasm

Z39.2   Encounter for routine postpartum follow up

If a recurrence, an extension, or a related condition is identified, the code for that condition is assigned as the principal diagnosis rather than a code from categories Z08, Z09, or Z39. Examples include the following:

- An asymptomatic patient who had a resection of the descending colon a year earlier is admitted for colonoscopy to evaluate the anastomosis and determine whether there is any recurrence of malignancy. Colonoscopy proved the anastomosis to be normal, and there was no evidence of cancer recurrence. In this case, code **Z08, Encounter for follow-up examination after completed treatment for malignant neoplasm,** is coded as the principal diagnosis, with an additional code of **Z85.038, Personal history of other malignant neoplasm of large intestine,** and a code for the colonoscopy.

- An asymptomatic patient who had a resection of the descending colon a year earlier is admitted for colonoscopy to evaluate the anastomosis and determine whether there is any recurrence of malignancy. Colonoscopy showed the anastomosis to be normal, and there was no evidence of cancer recurrence. A polyp of the transverse colon was found, however, and it was removed; pathology examination showed it to be benign. Code **D12.3, Benign neoplasm of transverse colon,** is assigned as the principal diagnosis, with code **Z85.038, Personal history of other malignant neoplasm of large intestine,** assigned as an additional code. In this case, code Z08 is not assigned because a related condition was identified.

127

CHAPTER 12

*Z Codes
and External
Cause
of Morbidity
Codes*

- A patient who had a colon resection for removal of carcinoma of the descending colon one year ago is now seen for follow-up examination to evaluate the anastomosis and determine whether there is any recurrence of disease. Colonoscopy showed normal anastomosis but revealed a recurrence of cancer at the primary site. Code **C18.6, Malignant neoplasm of descending colon,** is assigned as the principal diagnosis. Code Z08 is not assigned.

- A patient who had surgical excision of a malignant neoplasm of the ovary one year ago, followed by chemotherapy, is admitted for follow-up examination. There is no evidence of recurrence or metastasis, and no other pathologic condition is identified. Code **Z08, Encounter for follow-up examination after completed treatment for malignant neoplasm,** is assigned along with a code of Z85.43 to indicate the history of ovarian cancer as the reason for the examination.

- A patient who had benign polyps of the colon removed one year ago is now complaining of pain in the left lower abdomen. A colonoscopy performed to determine whether there is any recurrence of colon polyps proved to be entirely normal. In this case, code **R10.32, Left lower quadrant pain,** is assigned rather than a Z09 code because the abdominal pain was the reason for the admission.

Code **Z09, Encounter for follow-up examination after completed treatment for conditions other than malignant neoplasm,** may be assigned as the reason for encounter only when the patient is no longer receiving treatment.

Admission for Observation and Evaluation

A code from category Z03, Encounter for medical observation for suspected diseases and conditions ruled out, or category Z04, Encounter for examination and observation for other reasons, is assigned when a person without a diagnosis is suspected of having an abnormal condition, without signs or symptoms, which requires study, but, after examination and observation, is ruled out. Categories Z03 and Z04 are also for use for administrative and legal observation status. Outpatient referral for surveillance or for further diagnostic studies does not contradict the use of a code from this category. The observation codes are not used if an injury or illness, or any signs or symptoms related to the suspected condition, are present. In those cases, the diagnosis or symptom code is used. When a related diagnosis is established, the code for that condition is assigned instead of a code from category Z03. Codes from categories P00–P04 are used for observation of a newborn suspected condition, ruled out (see chapter 27 of this handbook). For persons with feared complaint in whom no diagnosis is made, assign code Z71.1.

A code from categories Z03–Z04 can be assigned only as the principal diagnosis or reason for encounter, never as a secondary diagnosis. A code from categories Z03–Z04 is ordinarily assigned as a solo code, with two exceptions:

- When a chronic condition requires care or monitoring during the stay, a code for that condition can be assigned as an additional code. Codes for chronic conditions that do not affect the stay are not assigned.

- When admission is for the purpose of ruling out a serious injury, such as concussion, codes for minor injuries such as abrasions or contusions may be assigned as additional codes. This exception is based on the fact that such minor injuries in themselves would not require hospitalization.

128

CHAPTER 12

*Z Codes
and External
Cause
of Morbidity
Codes*

The following examples may help the coder to better understand the use of categories Z03–Z04:

- A law enforcement representative refers the patient for evaluation of a suspected mental disorder. None is found, and no other condition is identified. Code **Z04.6, Encounter for general psychiatric examination, requested by authority,** is assigned.

- An adult patient is seen in the emergency department because of alleged rape. Observation and examination reveal no physical findings, such as hemorrhage or laceration. Code **Z04.41, Encounter for examination and observation following alleged adult rape,** is assigned as the principal diagnosis. Code Z04.41 covers the collection of specimens, advice given for prophylaxis of pregnancy, and any other provision of counseling services. When physical findings suggest that a rape has occurred, code Z04.41 is not assigned; the condition identified is coded and designated as the principal diagnosis. Rape is not a medical diagnosis but a matter of jurisprudence. Confirmed adult rape is coded to **T74.21-, Adult sexual abuse, confirmed.** Suspected adult rape is coded to **T76.21-, Adult sexual abuse, suspected.**

- A patient presents with generalized complaints involving nonspecific abdominal pain, minimal weight loss, and change of bowel habits. Because of a strong family history of colon cancer, the patient is admitted for evaluation for suspected malignancy. The presence of a neoplasm is ruled out, and no alternative diagnosis is made; it seems obvious that the symptoms reported are largely subjective. Code **Z03.89, Encounter for observation for other suspected diseases and conditions ruled out,** is assigned with an additional code of **Z80.0, Family history of malignant neoplasm of digestive organs.**

Note that a code from categories Z03–Z04 is not assigned when a patient is admitted to the observation unit of the hospital immediately following same-day (outpatient) surgery, even though the medical record may suggest that the admission is for observation. Hospitals are advised to contact their individual payers to obtain billing instructions on whether a single claim should be submitted or whether separate claims should be submitted. If a single bill is submitted to a payer, code the reason for the surgery as the first reported diagnosis (reason for the encounter). If the patient develops complications during the outpatient encounter, including during the observation stay, code these complications as secondary diagnoses. Continue to report the reason for the surgery as the reason for the overall encounter. Additional codes are assigned for the procedures performed. However, if separate bills are submitted, then this advice would not apply. Hospitals should apply codes for the current encounter based on individual payer billing instructions.

Consider the following examples:

- A patient is admitted following outpatient surgery for a right direct inguinal hernia repair for "continued observation." Review of the medical record indicates that the patient was admitted to observation because he was experiencing severe nausea and vomiting.

  If a single claim is submitted: Code **K40.90, Unilateral inguinal hernia, without obstruction or gangrene, not specified as recurrent,** is assigned as the first-listed diagnosis, not a code from categories Z03–Z04. In addition, code **R11.2, Nausea with vomiting, unspecified,** is assigned as the secondary diagnosis, and code **0YQ50ZZ, Repair right inguinal region, open approach,** is assigned for the procedure.

  If separate bills are submitted: For the outpatient surgery bill, assign code **K40.90, Unilateral inguinal hernia, without obstruction or gangrene, not specified as recurrent,** as the first-listed diagnosis, along with the appropriate Healthcare Common Procedural Coding System code for the surgical procedure. For the observation bill, code **R11.2, Nausea with vomiting, unspecified,** is assigned as the first-listed diagnosis, not a code from categories Z03–Z04.

129

: CHAPTER 12
:
: *Z Codes*
: *and External*
: *Cause*
: *of Morbidity*
: *Codes*

Codes from subcategory Z03.7, Encounter for suspected maternal and fetal conditions ruled out, may either be used as a first-listed or as an additional code assignment depending on the case. Generally, this subcategory may only be reported as the principal or first-listed diagnosis, except when there are multiple encounters on the same day and the medical records for the encounters are combined. These codes should be used in very limited circumstances on a maternal record when an encounter is for a suspected maternal or fetal condition that is ruled out during that encounter. For example, a maternal or fetal condition may be suspected due to an abnormal test result, but the condition is not confirmed. If the condition is confirmed, code the condition instead of a code from subcategory Z03.7. In addition, these codes are not for use if an illness or any signs or symptoms related to the suspected condition or problem are present. In such cases the diagnosis/symptom code is used. Other codes may be used in addition to the code from subcategory Z03.7, but only if they are unrelated to the suspected condition being evaluated.

If a patient is admitted after a period in the outpatient observation unit for further evaluation unrelated to surgery, the principal diagnosis is the condition that provided the original reason for the outpatient observation. If a patient is admitted to an observation unit for a medical condition, and the medical condition worsens or does not improve, it may be necessary for the patient to be admitted to the hospital as an inpatient. In this case, the medical condition that led to the hospital admission would be the principal diagnosis.

Special Investigations and Examinations

When a patient receives only diagnostic services during an episode of care, a code for the condition or problem that was chiefly responsible for the encounter is assigned first. A code from category Z01, Encounter for other special examination without complaint, suspected or reported diagnosis, is assigned as the reason for the encounter only when no problem, diagnosis, or condition is identified as the reason for the examination. A separate procedure code is required to identify any examinations or procedures performed. Codes from category Z01 are rarely appropriate for inpatient coding and are never assigned as additional codes. For example:

- A patient is referred to the radiology department for a chest X-ray, with the reason for the examination identified as cough and fever, which may rule out pneumonia. The radiologist's report indicates that the X-ray is normal. The code for the cough (R05) or the fever (R50.9) is listed as the reason for the encounter. A code for pneumonia is not assigned; neither is a code assigned from category Z01.

- A patient is referred to the radiology department for a chest X-ray with the reason for the examination identified as cough and fever, rule out pneumonia. The radiologist's report confirms a diagnosis of bronchopneumonia. Code **J18.0, Bronchopneumonia, unspecified organism,** is listed as the reason for the visit. Codes are not assigned for the cough or fever because these symptoms are implicit in the diagnosis of bronchopneumonia. No code from category Z01 is assigned.

- A patient is referred to the clinical laboratory for blood work, with the reason for the examination identified as vertigo with possibly the need to rule out hypothyroidism. Code **R42, Dizziness and giddiness,** is assigned as the reason for the visit. A code for hypothyroidism is not assigned because hypothyroidism is not an established diagnosis. Code **Z01.89, Encounter for other specified special examination,** is not assigned.

- A patient is referred to the radiology department for a chest X-ray as part of a routine physical examination. Code **Z00.00, Encounter for general adult medical examination,** is listed as the reason for the encounter because there are no presenting symptoms and the X-ray was not performed to rule out any suspected disease.

CHAPTER 12

*Z Codes
and External
Cause
of Morbidity
Codes*

Patients are often referred to hospital ancillary services for preoperative evaluations that involve a variety of tests performed in various departments. Patients may also be referred for preoperative blood typing. Preoperative and preprocedural laboratory examination Z codes are for use only in those situations when a patient is being cleared for a procedure or surgery and no treatment is given. In this situation, one of the following codes is assigned, with additional codes for the condition for which surgery is planned and for any findings related to the preoperative evaluation:

Z01.810   Encounter for preprocedural cardiovascular examination
Z01.811   Encounter for preprocedural respiratory examination
Z01.812   Encounter for preprocedural laboratory examination
Z01.818   Encounter for other preprocedural examination
Z01.83   Encounter for blood typing

For example:

- A patient with the diagnosis of cholelithiasis is referred to the radiology department for a preoperative chest X-ray. Code **Z01.818, Encounter for other preprocedural examination,** should be listed as the reason for the encounter, with an additional code for the cholelithiasis.

Some of the codes for routine health examinations distinguish between "with" and "without" abnormal findings (for example, code Z00.00 versus code Z00.01). Code assignment depends on the information that is known at the time the encounter is being coded. For example, if no abnormal findings were identified during the examination but the encounter is being coded before test results are back, it is acceptable to assign the code for "without abnormal findings." When assigning a code for "with abnormal findings," an additional code(s) should be assigned to identify the specific abnormal finding(s).

Screening Examinations

Codes from categories Z11–Z13, Encounter for screening, are assigned to encounters for tests performed to identify a disease or disease precursors for the purpose of early detection and treatment for those who test positive. Screening is performed on apparently well individuals who present no signs or symptoms relative to the disease. A screening mammogram is an example of such a test. If a screening examination identifies pathology, the code for the reason for the test (namely, the screening code from categories Z11–Z13) is assigned as the principal diagnosis or first-listed code, followed by a code for the pathology or condition found during the screening exam. For example:

- A patient undergoes routine mammography, which reveals no pathology. Code **Z12.31, Encounter for screening mammogram for malignant neoplasm of breast,** is assigned.

- An asymptomatic patient undergoes a screening mammography. The radiologist reports the presence of microcalcifications. Assign code **Z12.31, Encounter for screening mammogram for malignant neoplasm of breast,** followed by code **R92.0, Mammographic microcalcification found on diagnostic imaging of breast.**

- A patient with a family history of breast cancer in her mother, aunt, and older sister presents for a screening mammogram because she is considered at high risk for the disease. Assign code **Z12.31, Encounter for screening mammogram for malignant neoplasm of breast,** followed by code **Z80.3, Family history of malignant neoplasm of breast.**

Codes Representing Patient History, Status, or Problems

CHAPTER 12

*Z Codes
and External
Cause
of Morbidity
Codes*

Codes from categories Z85 through Z92 are used to indicate a personal history of a previous condition. When the condition mentioned is still present or still under treatment, or if a complication is present, a code from the series Z85 through Z92 is not assigned. Categories Z80 through Z84 indicate a family history and may be assigned when the family history is the reason for examination or treatment.

Categories Z88 through Z99 indicate that the patient has a continuing condition or health status that may influence care, such as the fact that a tracheostomy (Z93.0), a colostomy (Z93.3), a cardiac pacemaker (Z95.0), or an aortocoronary bypass graft (Z95.1) is in place. Z codes indicating status are redundant when the diagnosis code itself indicates that the status exists. For example, in the case of an acute rejection crisis of a transplanted kidney, code **T86.11, Kidney transplant rejection,** is used. As the patient's transplant status is implicit in that diagnosis, an additional code Z94.0, indicating kidney transplant status, is not meaningful and should not be assigned.

A diagnostic statement expressed as "status post" most often refers to an earlier surgery, injury, or illness and usually has no significance for the episode of care. No code for the condition is assigned in this case. A personal history code can be assigned if desired. Note the important distinction between history and status codes. History codes indicate that the problem no longer exists. Status codes indicate that the condition is present.

Codes from category Z79 are assigned to indicate a patient's continuous use of a prescribed drug for the long-term treatment of a condition or for prophylactic use. Examples include situations when the patient is currently receiving long-term anticoagulant therapy (Z79.01), antithrombotics/antiplatelets (Z79.02), nonsteroidal anti-inflammatories (Z79.1), antibiotic therapy (Z79.2), hormonal contraceptives (Z79.3), insulin (Z79.4), steroids (Z79.51–Z79.52), or other long-term drug therapy (Z79.81–Z79.899). Codes from category Z79 are assigned if the patient is receiving a medication for an extended period, for example:

- As a prophylactic measure (e.g., to prevent deep venous thrombosis)
- As treatment of a chronic condition (e.g., arthritis)
- For a disease requiring a lengthy course of treatment (e.g., cancer)

An additional code is assigned for the condition for which the medication is prescribed. Do not assign a code from category Z79 when the medication is prescribed to treat an acute illness or injury and is being given for a brief period of time (e.g., antibiotics to treat bronchitis). This subcategory is not used when medications are given for detoxification or maintenance programs used to prevent withdrawal symptoms in patients with drug dependence. For example, long-term use of methadone for pain management is coded with **Z79.891, Long term (current) use of opiate analgesic,** but the use of methadone in a maintenance program to prevent withdrawal symptoms is coded using the drug dependence code.

Code Z51.81 is used to report encounters for therapeutic drug monitoring. If the drug being monitored is one that the patient has been receiving on a long-term basis, a code from category Z79 should be added. Coding guidelines do not provide a definition or time frame for long-term drug therapy. If a patient receives a drug on a regular basis and has multiple refills available for a prescription, then it is appropriate to document long-term drug use. Documentation of long-term drug use is at the discretion of the health care provider.

Codes from categories Z55 through Z65 are used to indicate certain problems that may affect the patient's care or prevent satisfactory compliance with the recommended regimen. Housing problems, social maladjustment, and economic or job concerns are examples of situations that can affect a patient's compliance.

CHAPTER 12

*Z Codes
and External
Cause
of Morbidity
Codes*

History, status, and problem codes ordinarily cannot be used as the principal diagnosis or reason for encounter, with the following exceptions:

- Codes from categories Z85–Z87 (except subcategory Z87.7)
- Code Z91.81
- Codes from categories Z80–Z84

These codes can be used when the history is the reason for admission or encounter. They can be used as additional codes for any patient regardless of the reason for the encounter, but they are ordinarily assigned only when the history, status, or problem has some significance for the episode of care. For example, a history of previously treated carcinoma or a family history of malignant neoplasm may be useful in explaining why certain tests are performed. Status subcategory Z96.6- indicates that the patient has had an orthopedic joint replacement, but this fact would probably be significant only if it limits the patient's movement to the extent that additional nursing care is required or when it prevents the patient's full participation in a rehabilitation program.

Genetic Susceptibility to Disease

Codes from category Z15 are used to report genetic susceptibility to disease. Genetic susceptibility refers to a genetic predisposition for contracting a disease. Patients with a genetic susceptibility to disease may request prophylactic removal of an organ to prevent the disease from occurring. It is important to distinguish susceptibility from carrier state. An individual who is a carrier of a disease is able to pass it on to an offspring. Subcategory Z15.0, Genetic susceptibility to malignant neoplasm, is further subdivided to identify the potential body site, such as breast (Z15.01), ovary (Z15.02), prostate (Z15.03), endometrium (Z15.04), and other (Z15.09).

Codes from category Z15 should not be used as principal or first-listed codes. Sequencing of category Z15 codes would depend on the circumstances of the encounter, as follows:

- If the patient has the condition to which he or she is susceptible, and that condition is the reason for the encounter, the code for the current condition is sequenced first, followed by the Z15.- code.

- If the patient is being seen for follow-up after completed treatment for this condition, and the condition no longer exists, a follow-up code should be sequenced first, followed by the appropriate personal history (Z85.- to Z87.-) and genetic susceptibility codes (Z15.-).

- If the purpose of the encounter is genetic counseling associated with procreative management, assign first code **Z31.5, Encounter for genetic counseling,** followed by a code from category Z15. Additional codes should be assigned for any applicable family or personal history.

Z Codes as Principal/First-Listed Diagnosis

Z codes may be assigned as the principal or first-listed diagnosis or as secondary diagnoses. The *ICD-10-CM Official Guidelines for Coding and Reporting* contain a list of Z codes that may only be a principal/first-listed diagnosis. Z codes on that list may only be reported as the principal/first-listed diagnosis except for cases in which there are multiple encounters on the same day and the medical records for the encounters are combined, or when there is more than one Z code that meets the definition of principal diagnosis (e.g., a patient is admitted to home health care for aftercare and rehabilitation, and both diagnoses equally meet the definition of principal diagnosis). These codes should not be reported if they do not meet the definition of principal or first-listed diagnosis.

CHAPTER 12

*Z Codes
and External
Cause
of Morbidity
Codes*

REVIEW EXERCISE 12.1

Code the following diagnoses.

1.	Visit to change surgical dressing	Z48.01
2.	Family history of polyps of the colon	Z83.71
3.	Status post aortocoronary bypass procedure	Z95.1
4.	Encounter for gastrostomy tube irrigation	Z43.1
5.	Adjustment of cardiac pacemaker pulse generator	Z45.010
6.	Long-term use of anticoagulant therapy	Z79.01
7.	Dependence on respirator	Z99.11
8.	Aftercare for end-of-life care	Z51.5
9.	Encounter for screening mammogram	Z12.31
10.	Encounter for radiation therapy	Z51.0

Coding of Signs and Symptoms

Symptoms, Signs, and Ill-Defined Conditions

CHAPTER OVERVIEW

- Many symptoms and signs are classified to chapter 18 of ICD-10-CM if they point to multiple diseases or systems or if they are of an unexplained etiology.

- There are few situations in which a symptom code from chapter 18 is used as a principal diagnosis.

- Conversely, for outpatients, the symptom code is often used as the reason for the encounter.

- Codes from chapter 18 are assigned as secondary only when the sign or symptom is not integral to a condition.

- The codes for nonspecific abnormal findings are rarely appropriate for use in an inpatient setting.

LEARNING OUTCOMES

After studying this chapter you should be able to:

Explain the difference between a sign and a symptom.

Determine when to properly use a code from chapter 18 of the ICD-10-CM for a principal diagnosis.

Determine when to properly use a code from chapter 18 for an additional diagnosis.

TERMS TO KNOW

Sign
objective evidence of disease observed by the examining physician

Symptom
subjective observation reported by the patient

REMEMBER . . .

In an inpatient situation, there are often more appropriate options than the codes found in chapter 18 of the ICD-10-CM.

. . . For inpatients, a diagnosis described as possible, probable, and so on is considered to be an established diagnosis.

INTRODUCTION

A sign is defined as objective evidence of disease that can be observed by the examining physician. A symptom, on the other hand, is a subjective observation reported by the patient but not confirmed objectively by the physician.

Symptoms and signs are classified in two ways in ICD-10-CM: Those that point to a specific diagnosis have been assigned to a category in other chapters of ICD-10-CM. Those that can point to more than one disease or system, or that are of unexplained etiology, are classified to chapter 18 of ICD-10-CM.

SIGNS AND SYMPTOMS AS PRINCIPAL DIAGNOSES

Codes for symptoms, signs, and ill-defined conditions from chapter 18 of ICD-10-CM cannot be used as principal diagnoses or reasons for outpatient encounters when related diagnoses have been established. Examples include:

T40.1x4A + R40.20	Coma due to poisoning by heroin, initial encounter
I44.2 + R55	Syncope due to third-degree atrioventricular block

If the patient is an inpatient, a diagnosis described as possible, probable, and so on at the time of discharge is considered to be an established diagnosis. For example, a patient is admitted with severe generalized abdominal pain. The physician's diagnostic statement is abdominal pain, probably due to acute gastritis (K29.00). Only the code for the gastritis is assigned, as the abdominal pain is integral to the probable gastritis. Words such as "possible" and "probable" are not considered to be established for outpatient visits or encounters. If there is not an established diagnosis, only symptoms or signs that are available at the highest level of certainty are assigned.

There are only a few situations in which a symptom code from chapter 18 can be correctly designated the principal diagnosis, as follows:

1. When the diagnostic statement lists the symptom first, followed by two or more contrasting/comparative conditions, a symptom code may be assigned as the principal diagnosis. More detail is offered in chapter 4 of this handbook.

2. When no related condition is identified and the symptom is the reason for the encounter, a code from chapter 18 of ICD-10-CM is assigned as the principal diagnosis even though other unrelated diagnoses may be listed. For example, a patient is admitted with tachycardia. An electrocardiogram (EKG) does not provide any conclusive evidence of the type of tachycardia or of any underlying cardiac condition. The patient is also an insulin-dependent diabetic; blood sugars are monitored daily during the hospital stay. The reason for admission is tachycardia; therefore, code **R00.0, Tachycardia, unspecified,** is the principal diagnosis. Because the diabetes was treated during the hospital stay, an additional code is assigned for the diabetes mellitus.

3. This guideline does not apply if the diagnosis is stated as a symptom due to two conditions rather than as two contrasting diagnoses. In this case, both conditions are coded, and the symptom code is assigned as an additional code only if it meets criteria for the reporting of additional diagnoses. For example, if a diagnosis is stated as chest pain due to costochondritis and possible hiatal hernia, both the costochondritis and the hiatal hernia are coded according to the guideline governing coding of contrasting/comparative conditions. No code for chest pain is assigned because it is integral to both diagnoses.

139

CHAPTER 13

Symptoms,

Signs, and

Ill-Defined

Conditions

4. Other situations in which codes from chapter 18 of the ICD-10-CM manual can be appropriately used as the principal diagnosis for an inpatient admission include the following:

- Presenting signs or symptoms are transient, and no definitive diagnosis can be made.

- The patient is referred elsewhere for further study or treatment before a diagnosis is made.

- A more precise diagnosis cannot be made for any other reason.

- The symptom is treated in an outpatient setting without the additional workup required to arrive at a more definitive diagnosis.

- Provisional diagnosis of a sign or symptom is made for a patient who fails to return for further investigation or care.

- A residual late effect is the reason for admission, and the Alphabetic Index directs the coder to an alternative sequencing.

Generally speaking, symptom codes classified to other chapters of ICD-10-CM are not designated as principal diagnoses when a related condition has been identified. The symptom can be designated as principal diagnosis, however, when the patient is admitted for the sole purpose of treating the symptom and no treatment or further evaluation of the underlying disease takes place. For example, patients with dehydration secondary to gastroenteritis are sometimes admitted for the purpose of rehydration when the gastroenteritis itself could be managed on an outpatient basis. In this case, the code for the dehydration can be designated as the principal diagnosis even though the cause of the dehydration is stated.

Note that these guidelines do not apply when coding and reporting hospital outpatient care or physician services. Outpatient encounters do not ordinarily permit the type of study that results in an established diagnosis, and treatment is often directed at relieving symptoms rather than treating the underlying condition. The highest level of certainty is reported as the reason for encounter for outpatients, which often means that a symptom code is assigned as the reason for the encounter.

SIGNS AND SYMPTOMS AS ADDITIONAL DIAGNOSES

Codes from chapter 18 are assigned as secondary codes only when the symptom or sign is not integral to the underlying condition, unless otherwise instructed by the classification, and when its presence makes a difference in the severity of the patient's condition and/or the care given. For example, many but not all patients with cirrhosis of the liver have ascites. When ascites is present, it makes a difference in the care given, and so the chapter 18 code for ascites (R18.8) should be assigned as an additional code. Codes from chapter 18 are not assigned when they are implicit in the diagnosis or when the symptom is included in the condition code. Such redundant coding is inappropriate. Examples include:

- Abdominal pain due to gastric ulcer—no symptom code is assigned to the abdominal pain because it is integral to the ulcer.

- Coma due to diabetes mellitus—the symptom code for coma is not assigned because combination codes are provided for diabetes with associated coma.

- Patient admitted with chest pain, initially thought to be angina—diagnostic studies do not support this diagnosis, and the physician's diagnosis is chest pain, probable costochondritis (M94.0). The chest pain is not coded because it is implicit in the costochondritis.

ABNORMAL FINDINGS

Although categories R70 through R97 in chapter 18 are provided for coding nonspecific abnormal findings, it is rarely appropriate to assign one of these codes for acute inpatient hospital care. They are assigned only when (1) the physician has not been able to arrive at a definitive related diagnosis and lists the abnormal finding itself as a diagnosis and (2) the condition meets the Uniform Hospital Discharge Data Set criteria for reporting of other diagnoses.

For example, if the physician lists a diagnosis of abnormal electrocardiographic findings without any mention of associated disease, assigning code **R94.31, Abnormal electrocardiogram [ECG] [EKG],** would be appropriate if there was evidence of further evaluation for a possible cardiac condition. On the other hand, a coder might note an elevated blood pressure reading in the medical record, but the physician has not listed it as a diagnosis and there is no evidence of any follow-up or treatment. In this situation, assigning a code for this abnormal finding would be inappropriate.

If the coder notes clinical findings outside the normal range but no related diagnosis is stated, the coder should review the medical record to determine whether additional tests and/or consultations were carried out related to these findings or whether specific related care was given. If such documentation is present, it is appropriate to ask the physician whether a code should be assigned.

For example, a patient with a low potassium level treated with oral or intravenous potassium has a clinically significant condition that probably should be reported; the physician should be asked whether a diagnosis should be added. On the other hand, a finding of degenerative arthritis on a routine postoperative chest X-ray of an elderly patient when no treatment or further diagnostic evaluation has been carried out does not warrant a code assignment.

GLASGOW COMA SCALE

The Glasgow coma scale is a scale for assessing the degree of consciousness, especially after a head injury. The scoring is determined by three factors: amount of eye opening, verbal responsiveness, and motor responsiveness. The test score can function as an indicator for certain diagnostic tests or treatments and for predicting the duration and ultimate outcome of coma.

Codes in subcategory R40.2, Coma, can be used in combination with traumatic brain injury or acute cerebrovascular disease codes, or sequelae of cerebrovascular disease codes. These codes are primarily for use by trauma registries but may be used in any setting where this information is collected. The coma scale codes should be sequenced after the diagnosis code(s). One code from each subcategory (amount of eye opening, verbal responsiveness, and motor responsiveness) is needed to complete the scale. The seventh character indicates when the scale was recorded (e.g., in the field, at arrival to emergency department, at hospital admission). The seventh character should match for all three codes.

At a minimum, the initial score documented upon presentation at the facility should be recorded. This may be a score from the emergency medicine technician or documented in the emergency department. A facility may choose to capture multiple Glasgow coma scale scores, if desired.

ILL-DEFINED CONDITIONS

Code **R99, Ill-defined and unknown cause of mortality,** is only for use in the very limited circumstances when a patient who has already died is brought into an emergency department or other health care facility and is pronounced dead on arrival. This code should not be used to represent the discharge disposition of death.

141

CHAPTER 13

*Symptoms,
Signs, and
Ill-Defined
Conditions*

EXERCISE 13.1

Code the following diagnoses and procedures as statements given at the time of discharge. Do not assign External cause of morbidity codes.

1. Dysuria — R30.0
   Transurethral biopsy of bladder — 0TBB7ZX

2. Acute chest pain due to influenzal pleurisy — J10.1

3. Gross, painless hematuria, cause undetermined — R31.0
   Cystoscopy with control of bladder hemorrhage by cauterization — 0T5B8ZZ

4. Pyuria, intermittent, cause undetermined — N39.0

5. Hyperplastic lymph node, left axilla — R59.9
   Open Biopsy, axillary lymph node — 07B60ZX

6. Elevated glucose tolerance test — R73.02

7. Severe vertigo, left temporal headache, and nausea — R42
   R51
   R11.0

8. Syncope, cause undetermined — R55

9. Chest pain, probably angina pectoris — I20.9

10. Psychogenic dysuria — F45.8

11. Arteriosclerotic gangrene, left foot — I70.262

12. Chronic epistaxis, severe, recurrent — R04.0
    Anterior and posterior nasal packing — 2Y41X5Z

13. Severe epistaxis due to hypertension

     I10
     R04.0

     Nasal packing

     2Y41X5Z

---

14. Hereditary epistaxis

     I78.0

---

15. Generalized abdominal pain due to pancreatitis
     versus cholecystitis

     R10.84
     K85.9
     K81.9

---

16. Chronic fatigue syndrome

     R53.82

Coding OF Infectious AND Parasitic Diseases, Endocrine Diseases AND Metabolic Disorders, AND Mental Disorders

CHAPTER 14

Infectious and Parasitic Diseases

CHAPTER OVERVIEW

- Chapter 1 of ICD-10-CM includes information on how to code infectious and parasitic diseases.

  — The primary axis of chapter 1 is the organism responsible for the disease.

  — When the main term for the condition is located, specific subterms always take precedence over general subterms.

- This chapter has information on coding specific infectious and parasitic diseases, including tuberculosis, severe acute respiratory syndrome (SARS), West Nile virus, bacteremia, septicemia, systemic inflammatory response syndrome (SIRS), sepsis, toxic shock syndrome, and gram-negative bacterial infections.

- Also included in chapter 1 of ICD-10-CM is detailed information on all aspects of HIV/AIDS coding procedures.

LEARNING OUTCOMES

After studying this chapter you should be able to:

- Code infectious and parasitic diseases.

- Explain the difference between, and be able to code properly, bacteremia, septicemia, SIRS, sepsis, and septic shock.

- Explain how to code for HIV testing, diagnosis, and treatment.

TERMS TO KNOW

Bacteremia
presence of bacteria in the bloodstream after a trauma or an infection

Sepsis
SIRS due to infection; a severe case indicates organ dysfunction

Septic shock
circulatory failure associated with severe sepsis

Septicemia
a systemic disease associated with pathological microorganisms or toxins in the bloodstream

SIRS
systemic inflammatory response syndrome; a systemic response to infection or trauma with such symptoms as fever and tachycardia

REMEMBER . . .

Codes from chapter 1 of ICD-10-CM take precedence over codes from other chapters for the same condition. . . . Coding for HIV/AIDS is not allowed unless the diagnostic statement reports the diagnosis with absolute certainty.

INTRODUCTION

Chapter 1 of ICD-10-CM classifies infectious and parasitic diseases that are easily transmissible (communicable). The primary axis for this chapter is the organism responsible for the condition. Infectious and parasitic conditions are classified in one of several ways, making careful use of the Alphabetic Index imperative. Some examples follow.

- A single code from chapter 1 is assigned to indicate the organism. For example, code B26.- is assigned for mumps. Some codes of this type use a fourth character to indicate a site or an associated condition. For example, code B37.1 is assigned for candidiasis of the lung.

- Combination codes frequently identify both the condition and the organism. For example:

  J15.21   Pneumonia due to *Staphylococcus aureus*
  B26.0   Orchitis due to mumps

Dual classification is also used extensively for chapter 1. For example:

  B49 + J99   Bronchomycosis
  B39.9 + H32   Chorioretinitis in histoplasmosis

Codes from chapter 1 take precedence over codes from other chapters for the same condition. For example, urinary tract infection due to candidiasis is classified to code **B37.49, Other urogenital candidiasis,** rather than to code **N39.0, Urinary tract infection, site not specified.** Conditions that are not considered to be easily transmissible or communicable are classified in the appropriate body system chapter, with an additional code from category B95–B97 to indicate the responsible organism. For example, codes **N41.00, Acute prostatitis without hematuria,** and **B95.0,** *Streptococcus,* **group A, as the cause of diseases classified elsewhere,** are assigned for acute prostatitis due to group A *Streptococcus.*

ORGANISM VERSUS SITE OR OTHER SUBTERM

A thorough search of the Alphabetic Index is required in coding infection. When the main term for the condition has been located, a subterm for the organism always takes precedence over a more general subterm (such as "acute" or "chronic") when both subterms occur at the same indention level in the Alphabetic Index. For example, for a diagnosis of chronic cystitis due to gonococcus, the Alphabetic Index provides subterms for both chronic and gonococcal:

> **Cystitis** (exudative) . . .
>   chronic N30.20 . . .
>   gonococcal A54.01

In this case, only code A54.01 is assigned because the subterm for the organism takes precedence over the subterm "chronic."

When the organism is specified but is not indexed under the main term for the condition, the coder should refer to the main term **Infection** or to the main term for the organism. For example, consider a diagnosis of cryptococcal cystitis. No subterm for cryptococcal is located under the main term **Cystitis,** but there is a main term entry **Infection,** followed by a subterm for *Cryptococcus neoformans,* as well as a main term **Cryptococcus.** Code B45.9 is therefore assigned for this diagnosis rather than the code for cystitis.

SEVERE ACUTE RESPIRATORY SYNDROME (SARS)

There are specific codes provided for SARS. This is a respiratory illness caused by a coronavirus. SARS begins with a fever and may include chills, headache, and malaise. In some patients, there are also mild respiratory symptoms, dry cough, and trouble breathing. The codes are as follows:

Z20.828   Contact with or exposure to SARS-associated coronavirus
B97.21   SARS-associated coronavirus infection
J12.81   Pneumonia due to SARS-associated coronavirus

WEST NILE VIRUS FEVER

Subcategory A92.3 is used to report West Nile virus infection. The virus is transmitted to humans by the bite of a mosquito that has bitten an infected bird. Most healthy people infected by the virus have few symptoms or have a mild illness consisting of fever, headache, and body aches prior to recovering. In elderly patients or those with a weakened immune system, the virus may cause encephalitis, meningitis, or permanent neurological damage and may be life threatening. Subcategory A92.3 is further subdivided to distinguish between West Nile virus infection unspecified (A92.30), with encephalitis (A92.31), with other neurologic manifestation (A92.32), and with other complications (A92.39). This expansion allows the differentiation between the milder cases of the disease and those with more serious complications and neurological manifestations.

LATE EFFECTS

Chapter 1 provides four sequelae categories for use when there is a residual condition due to previous infection or parasitic infestation:

B90   Sequelae of tuberculosis
B91   Sequelae of poliomyelitis
B92   Sequelae of leprosy
B94   Sequelae of other and unspecified infectious and parasitic diseases

As discussed earlier, the code for the residual effect is sequenced first, followed by the appropriate sequelae code, except in a few instances where the Alphabetic Index instructs otherwise. A code for the infection itself is not assigned because it is no longer present. For example:

G93.9 + B94.1   Brain damage resulting from previous viral encephalitis (three years ago)
B90.8 + E35   Tuberculous calcification of adrenal gland

TUBERCULOSIS

Tuberculosis (TB) is a bacterial disease caused by *Mycobacterium tuberculosis* and *Mycobacterium bovis*. People with weakened immune systems are at increased risk for contracting TB. It is spread through the air when a person with untreated pulmonary TB coughs or sneezes. Prolonged exposure to a person with untreated TB usually is necessary for infection to occur.

Tuberculosis is classified to categories A15 through A19 based on the general site (e.g., respiratory system) or type of tuberculosis (e.g., miliary), as follows:

A15   Respiratory tuberculosis
A17   Tuberculosis of nervous system
A18   Tuberculosis of other organs
A19   Miliary tuberculosis

Categories A15, A17, and A18 are subdivided further to specify the site. Tuberculosis usually affects the lungs (code A15.0), although other parts of the body can also be affected, for example, intrathoracic lymph nodes (code A15.4), kidneys (code A18.11), and bones and joints (subcategory A18.0). Miliary tuberculosis (category A19) is the form of TB in which the bacillus spreads through all body tissues and organs, producing many thousands of tiny tubercular lesions.

Care should be taken to differentiate between a diagnosis of tuberculosis and a positive tuberculin skin test without a diagnosis of active tuberculosis. Code R76.1 classifies the following:

- Abnormal reaction to tuberculin skin test without active tuberculosis
- Inconclusive PPD (purified protein derivative) without diagnosis
- Positive tuberculin skin test without active tuberculosis
- Positive PPD (skin test)
- Abnormal Mantoux test
- Tuberculin sensitivity without clinical or radiological symptoms
- Converter, tuberculosis (test reaction)

SEPSIS, SEVERE SEPSIS, AND SEPTIC SHOCK

For a diagnosis of sepsis, the appropriate code for the underlying systemic infection should be assigned. Streptococcal sepsis is classified to category A40 with the third character specifying sepsis due to different streptococci strains such as group A (A40.0), group B (A40.1), *Streptococcus pneumoniae* (A40.3), other (A40.8), or unspecified (A40.9). However, sepsis due to *Streptococcus* group D is assigned to code **A41.81, Sepsis due to *Enterococcus.***

Other types of sepsis are classified to other organisms, such as candidal sepsis (B37.7) or disseminated herpesviral disease (B00.7). If the type of infection or causal organism is not further specified, assign code **A41.9, Sepsis, unspecified.**

Organisms are sometimes transferred to other tissue, where they may seed infection in another site and lead to such conditions as arteritis, meningitis, and pyelonephritis. Additional codes are assigned for these manifestations when they are present.

A diagnosis of sepsis can neither be assumed nor ruled out on the basis of laboratory values alone. Negative or inconclusive blood cultures do not preclude a diagnosis of sepsis in patients with clinical evidence of the condition; however, the provider should be queried. A code for sepsis is assigned only when the physician makes such a diagnosis.

Bacteremia (R78.81) refers to the presence of bacteria in the bloodstream after trauma or mild infection. This condition is usually transient and ordinarily clears promptly through the action of the body's own immune system.

The unusual or imprecise diagnostic reference to a site-specific or organ-specific sepsis, such as urosepsis, may require further clarification for coding purposes. For example, the term "urosepsis" refers to pyuria or bacteria in the urine, not the blood. Unfortunately, urosepsis is sometimes stated as the diagnosis even though the condition has progressed from a localized urinary tract infection and has become a generalized sepsis. The term "urosepsis" is a nonspecific term and should not be considered synonymous with sepsis. It has no default code in the Alphabetic Index. When this term is documented, the coder should consult the provider for clarification.

Systemic inflammatory response syndrome (SIRS) generally refers to the systemic response to infection, trauma/burns, or other insult (such as cancer), with symptoms including fever, tachycardia, tachypnea, and leukocytosis. SIRS of noninfectious origin is coded to subcategory R65.1 depending on whether acute organ dysfunction is present (R65.11) or not (R65.10).

Severe sepsis (subcategory R65.2) generally refers to sepsis with associated acute or multiple organ dysfunction. Subcategory R65.2 is further subdivided to identify whether it is associated with septic shock (R65.21) or without septic shock (R65.20). Septic shock generally refers to circulatory failure associated with severe sepsis and therefore represents a type of acute organ dysfunction. The physician must specifically record "septic shock" in the diagnostic statement in order to code it as such. Septic shock indicates the presence of severe sepsis and code **R65.21, Severe sepsis with septic shock,** must be assigned, even if the term "severe sepsis" is not documented.

A code from subcategory R65.2, Severe sepsis, should not be assigned unless severe sepsis or an associated acute organ dysfunction is documented. When a patient has sepsis and an acute organ dysfunction, but the documentation indicates that the acute organ dysfunction is related to a medical condition other than sepsis, codes from subcategory R65.2 should not be used. If the documentation is not clear as to whether an acute organ dysfunction is related to the sepsis or another medical condition, the provider should be queried. Due to the complex nature of severe sepsis, some cases may require querying the provider prior to code assignment.

Coding and Sequencing

Coders should be guided by the following instructions when coding sepsis or severe sepsis. The coding of these conditions is dependent on the documentation available.

Severe Sepsis

The coding of severe sepsis requires a minimum of two codes:

- Sequence first a code for the underlying infection followed by a code from subcategory R65.2, Severe sepsis.
- If the causal organism is not documented, assign code **A41.9, Sepsis, unspecified,** for the infection.
- An additional code(s) should also be assigned for the associated acute organ dysfunction.

If severe sepsis is present on admission and meets the Uniform Hospital Discharge Data Set definition of principal diagnosis—that is, the condition after study that necessitated the admission—assign first the code for the underlying systemic infection (e.g., A40.-, A41.-, B37.7) followed by the appropriate code from subcategory R65.2 as required by the sequencing rules in the Tabular List. A code from subcategory R65.2 can never be assigned as a principal diagnosis.

When severe sepsis develops during an encounter (it was not present on admission), the underlying systemic infection code should be assigned first, and a code from subcategory R65.2 should be assigned as secondary diagnosis. Severe sepsis may be present on admission, but the diagnosis may not be confirmed until sometime after admission. When the documentation is not clear as to whether severe sepsis was present on admission, the provider must be queried for clarification.

Sepsis and Severe Sepsis with a Localized Infection

When the reason for admission is both sepsis, or severe sepsis, and a localized infection (e.g., pneumonia or cellulitis), a code(s) for the underlying systemic infection should be assigned first and the code for the localized infection should be assigned as a secondary diagnosis. If the patient has severe sepsis, a code from subcategory R65.2 should also be assigned as a secondary diagnosis. On the other hand, if the patient is admitted with a localized infection, such as pneumonia, and the sepsis/severe sepsis does not develop until after admission, the localized infection should be assigned first, followed by the appropriate sepsis/severe sepsis codes.

Sepsis due to a Postprocedural Infection

When sepsis results from a postprocedural infection, it is considered a complication of medical care. For such cases, the postprocedural infection code—such as **T80.2-, Infections following infusion, transfusion, and therapeutic injection; T81.4, Infection following a procedure; T88.0-, Infection following immunization;** or **O86.0, Infection of obstetric surgical wound**—should be coded first, followed by the code for the specific infection. In addition, for severe sepsis, the appropriate code from subcategory R65.2 should also be assigned along with the code(s) for any acute organ dysfunction.

Sepsis and Severe Sepsis Associated with a Noninfectious Process (Condition)

In some cases, a noninfectious process (condition), such as trauma, may lead to an infection that can result in sepsis or severe sepsis. If sepsis or severe sepsis is documented as associated with a noninfectious condition, such as a burn or serious injury, and this condition meets the definition for principal diagnosis, the code for the noninfectious condition should be sequenced first, followed by the code for the resulting infection. If severe sepsis is present, a code from subcategory R65.2 should also be assigned with any associated organ dysfunction(s) codes. It is not necessary to assign a code from subcategory R65.1, Systemic inflammatory response syndrome (SIRS) of non-infectious origin, for these cases.

If the infection meets the definition of principal diagnosis, it should be sequenced before the noninfectious condition. When both the associated noninfectious condition and the infection meet the definition of principal diagnosis, either condition may be assigned as principal diagnosis. Only one code from category R65, Symptoms and signs specifically associated with systemic inflammation and infection, should be assigned. Therefore, when a noninfectious condition leads to an infection resulting in severe sepsis, assign the appropriate code from subcategory R65.2, Severe sepsis. Do not additionally assign a code from subcategory R65.1, Systemic inflammatory response syndrome (SIRS) of non-infectious origin.

Sepsis and septic shock complicating abortion, pregnancy, childbirth, and the puerperium are discussed in chapter 24 of this handbook, Complications of Pregnancy, Childbirth, and the Puerperium. Newborn sepsis is discussed in chapter 27, Perinatal Conditions.

Note carefully in the following cases the different codes that would be assigned based on the information available:

1. Streptococcal sepsis: Assign code **A40.9, Streptococcal sepsis, unspecified.**

2. Severe sepsis: Assign first the code for the systemic infection (e.g., A40.-, A41.-, B37.7) followed by the appropriate code from subcategory R65.2 as required by the sequencing rules in the Tabular List. Additional codes are also assigned to identify the specific acute organ dysfunction (e.g., renal, respiratory, hepatic).

3. Septic shock: Assign first the code for the initiating systemic infection (e.g., A40.-, A41.-, B37.7) followed by code **R65.21, Severe sepsis with septic shock,** and codes for any associated acute organ dysfunction.

4. Patient admitted due to both pneumonia and sepsis: A41.9 + J18.9.

5. Patient admitted with pneumonia, develops sepsis after admission: J18.9 + A41.9.

6. Sepsis due to a postoperative infection: Assign code **T80.2-, Infections following infusion, transfusion, and therapeutic injection; T81.4, Infection following a procedure; T88.0-, Infection following immunization;** or **O86.0, Infection of obstetric surgical wound**—followed by the code for the specific infection (e.g., A40.-, A41.-, B37.7).

7. Bacteremia: Assign code R78.81.

TOXIC SHOCK SYNDROME

Toxic shock syndrome (A48.3) is caused by a bacterial infection. The symptoms include high fever of sudden onset, vomiting, watery diarrhea, and myalgia, followed by hypotension and sometimes shock. It was originally reported almost exclusively in menstruating women using high-absorbency tampons. The organism isolated was *Staphylococcus aureus.* A similar syndrome has been identified in children and males infected with group A *Streptococcus.* An additional code from categories B95–B96 is reported to identify the responsible organism.

GRAM-NEGATIVE BACTERIAL INFECTION

Gram-negative bacteria are a specific group of organisms with particular staining characteristics. They are clinically similar, as is the case with *Klebsiella* and *Pseudomonas,* and are thought of as a group even when the specific organism cannot be determined. Occasionally, several gram-negative organisms may be seen, but no single organism is identified as the causative agent, resulting in a diagnosis of gram-negative infection. Gram-negative infections are ordinarily more severe and require more intensive care than gram-positive infections. Again, a code is never assigned solely on the basis of gram-stain results; the assignment is based on the physician's clinical evaluation of the condition.

When the infectious organism has been identified, a specific code is often provided, such as **J15.0, Pneumonia due to *Klebsiella pneumoniae.*** Certain infections are classified in chapters other than chapter 1, and no organism is identified as part of the infection code, for example, urinary tract infection (N39.0). In these instances, an additional code from categories B95–B97 is assigned to indicate the responsible infectious agent. An instructional note will be found at the infection code advising coders to assign an additional code to identify the organism. Two examples follow:

J15.8 Pneumonia, due to anaerobic gram-negative bacteria

N11.8 + B96.89 Chronic pyelonephritis due to gram-negative bacteria

Table 14.1 provides a sampling of gram-negative and gram-positive organisms. A more complete list can be obtained from the health care organization's clinical laboratory director.

TABLE 14.1   Gram-Negative and Gram-Positive Bacteria

Gram-Negative Bacteria		Gram-Positive Bacteria
Bacteroides (anaerobic)	Hemophilus	Actinomyces
Bordetella	Klebsiella	Corynebacterium
Branhamella	Legionella	Lactobacillus
Brucella	Morganella	Listeria
Campylobacter	Neisseria	Mycobacterium
Citrobacter	Proteus	Nocardia
E. coli	Pseudomonas	Peptococcus
Enterobacter	Salmonella	Peptostreptococcus
Francisella	Shigella	Staphylococcus
Fusobacterium (anaerobic)	Trichinella vaginalis	Streptococcus
Gardnerella	Vellonella (anaerobic)	
Helicobacter	Yersinia	

NOSOCOMIAL INFECTIONS

Nosocomial infections are secondary infections that are contracted as a result of medical treatment or develop during hospitalization. They are also known as "hospital-acquired infections." ICD-10-CM provides code **Y95, Nosocomial condition,** as an additional External cause of morbidity code to identify these infections.

DRUG-RESISTANT INFECTIONS

ICD-10-CM provides code Z16 to identify infections that have become resistant to the drugs commonly used to treat them. This code may be located in the Alphabetic Index by referring to the main term **Resistance, Drug,** or **Infection.** Code **Z16, Infection with drug resistant microorganisms,** is assigned only as an additional code when the physician specifically documents an infection that has become drug resistant. Such statements as "multi-drug resistant" or "(specified drug) resistant condition" or similar terminology indicate this condition. The code for the infection should be assigned first, followed by code Z16. For example:

Z16	Resistant to penicillin
J15.20 + Z16	Staphylococcal pneumonia resistant to penicillin and bacitracin

It is important to distinguish colonization from infection. A patient may be referred to as being colonized or a carrier—meaning that an infectious organism (e.g., methicillin-resistant *Staphylococcus aureus,* or MRSA) is present on or in the body without necessarily causing illness. Colonization is not necessarily indicative of a disease process, and it may not be considered the cause of a patient's specific condition unless documented as such by the provider. A positive colonization test might be documented as "MRSA screen positive" or "MRSA nasal swab positive." ICD-10-CM provides codes under category Z22 for carrier or suspected carrier of infectious diseases and colonization status for several common infections, such as staphylococcus (Z22.32) and group B streptococcus (Z22.330).

EXERCISE 14.1

Code the following diagnoses.

---

1. Acute viral hepatitis (Australian antigen) with hepatitis
   delta and hepatic coma   B16.0

---

2. Chronic gonococcal cystitis   A54.01

---

3. Infectious gammaherpesviral mononucleosis with hepatomegaly   B27.09

---

4. Postmeasles otitis media   B05.3

---

5. Acute scarlet fever   A38.9

---

6.   Anaerobic gram-negative sepsis | A41.4

---

7.   Sepsis due to methicillin-resistant *Staphylococcus aureus* (MRSA) | A41.0
     | Z16

---

8.   Chronic moniliasis of vulva | B37.3

---

9.   Pulmonary tuberculosis, infiltrative | A15.0

---

10. Late, latent syphilis | A52.8

---

11. Herpes zoster of conjunctiva | B02.31

---

12. Pneumonia due to schistosomiasis | B65.9
     | J17

---

13. Acute empyema due to group B streptococcal infection | J86.9
     | B95.1

---

14. Encephalitis due to typhus | A75.9
     | G94

---

15. Acute respiratory distress due to sin nombre virus | J80
     | B33.4

---

16. Adenoviral pneumonia | J12.0

---

17. Chronic gonococcal urethritis | A54.01

---

18. Chronic vulvitis due to monilia with microorganisms | B37.3
     resistant to cephalosporin | Z16

---

19. Amebic abscess of brain and lung | A06.6
     Long-term use of antibiotic | Z79.2

AIDS AND OTHER HIV INFECTIONS

Because the human immunodeficiency virus (HIV) infection has become a major health care concern, the collection of accurate and complete data on conditions associated with HIV infection is important for health care resource planning. Code B20 is assigned for all types of HIV infections, which are described by a variety of terms, such as the following:

- AIDS
- Acquired immune deficiency syndrome
- Acquired immunodeficiency syndrome
- AIDS-like syndrome
- AIDS-like disease (illness)
- AIDS-related complex (ARC)
- AIDS-related conditions
- Pre-AIDS
- Prodromal-AIDS
- HIV disease

Unconfirmed Diagnosis of HIV Infection

Code B20 is not assigned when the diagnostic statement indicates that the infection is "suspected," "possible," "likely," or "?" This is an exception to the general guideline that directs the coder to assign a code for a diagnosis qualified as "suspected" or "possible" as if it were established. Confirmation in this case does not require documentation of a positive serology or culture for HIV; the provider's diagnostic statement that the patient is HIV-positive or has an HIV-related illness is sufficient. The provider should be asked to state the diagnosis in positive terms.

Serologic Testing for HIV Infection

When an asymptomatic patient with no prior diagnosis of HIV infection or positive-HIV status requests testing to determine his or her HIV status, use code **Z11.4, Encounter for screening for human immunodeficiency virus [HIV].** When the patient shows signs or symptoms of illness or has been diagnosed with a condition related to HIV infection, code the signs and symptoms or the diagnosis rather than the screening code.

When the patient makes a return visit to learn the result of the serology test, code **Z71.7, Human immunodeficiency virus [HIV] counseling,** should be assigned as the reason for the encounter when the test result is negative, inconclusive (R75), or positive. Code Z71.7 can be assigned as an additional code when counseling is provided for patients who test HIV-positive. When a patient is known to be in a high-risk group for HIV infection, code **Z72.89, Other problems related to lifestyle,** can be assigned as an additional code. When the test result is positive but the patient displays no symptoms and has no related complications and no established diagnosis of HIV infection, code **Z21, Asymptomatic human immunodeficiency virus [HIV] infection status,** is assigned. Code Z21 is not assigned when the term "AIDS" is used, when the patient is under treatment for an HIV-related illness, or when the patient is described as having any active HIV-related condition; code B20 is assigned instead.

When a patient has had contact with, or has been exposed to, the HIV virus but shows no signs or symptoms of illness and has not been diagnosed with a condition related to HIV, assign code **Z20.6, Contact with and (suspected) exposure to human immunodeficiency virus [HIV].**

Newborns with HIV-positive mothers often test positive on ELISA (enzyme-linked immuno-sorbent assay) and/or Western blot HIV tests. This finding usually indicates the antibody status of the mother rather than the status of the newborn; antibodies can cross the placenta and remain for as long as 18 months after birth without the newborn ever being infected. Such inconclusive test results are also coded R75. (See chapter 27 of this handbook for further information on coding HIV infection in the newborn.)

Sequencing of HIV-Related Diagnoses

When a patient is admitted for treatment of an HIV infection or any related complications, code **B20, Human immunodeficiency virus (HIV) disease,** is sequenced as the principal diagnosis, with additional codes for the HIV-related conditions. When a patient with an HIV infection is admitted for treatment of an entirely unrelated condition, such as an injury, that condition is designated as the principal diagnosis, with code B20 and codes for any associated conditions assigned as additional codes.

When an obstetric patient is identified as having any HIV infection, a code from subcategory O98.7, Human immunodeficiency virus [HIV] disease complicating pregnancy, childbirth and the puerperium, is assigned, with code B20 assigned as an additional code. If an obstetric patient tests positive for HIV but has no symptoms and no history of an HIV infection, codes O98.7- and **Z21, Asymptomatic human immunodeficiency virus [HIV] infection status,** are assigned rather than B20.

EXERCISE 14.2

Code the following diagnoses.

1. Candidiasis, of esophagus, opportunistic, secondary   B20
    to AIDS-like disease   B37.81

2. *Pneumocystis carinii*   B20
    AIDS   B59

3. Positive HIV test in patient who is asymptomatic, presents   Z21
    no related symptoms, and has no history of HIV infection

4. Acute lymphadenitis due to HIV infection   B20
                                                             L04.9

5. Acute appendicitis (admitted for appendectomy)   K35.80
    Kaposi's sarcoma of skin of chest, due to HIV infection B20
                                                             C46.0

6. Kaposi's sarcoma of oral cavity   B20
    AIDS   C46.7

7. Agranulocytosis due to HIV infection   B20
                                                             D70.3

8. Burkitt's tumor of inguinal region associated with AIDS B20
                                                             C83.75

9. Background retinopathy due to AIDS-like disease   B20
                                                             H35.00

10. Inconclusive HIV test   R75

Endocrine, Nutritional, and Metabolic Diseases

CHAPTER OVERVIEW

- Diabetes mellitus is the condition coders encounter most in working with chapter 4 of ICD-10-CM.

- Diabetes mellitus has two classification axes.

  — The first axis is the type of diabetes.

  — The fourth character identifies any associated complication.

- Diabetes causes many concurrent complications.

  — These complications may be either acute or chronic.

  — Assign as many codes as necessary to identify all the conditions.

- Codes from category E08, E09, and E13 are used for classification of secondary diabetes.

- Nutritional disorders classified by ICD-10-CM include deficiencies of specific vitamins and minerals and obesity.

- Specific codes for cystic fibrosis identify site of manifestation involvement.

  — There may be pulmonary, gastrointestinal, or other site involvement.

  — Use codes together if different sites are involved.

- Fluid overload is a component of congestive heart failure.

LEARNING OUTCOMES

After studying this chapter you should be able to:

Code diabetes mellitus properly.

Identify the differences when coding for diabetes during pregnancy and gestational diabetes.

Code fluid overload due to congestive heart failure.

Code nutritional disorders such as obesity.

TERMS TO KNOW

Diabetes mellitus
a chronic disorder of impaired carbohydrate, protein, and fat metabolism

Type 1 diabetes
also known as juvenile type; characterized by the body's failure to produce insulin

Type 2 diabetes
characterized by the body's production of insulin in an insufficient quantity or the body's inability to utilize such insulin

REMEMBER . . .

You can use as many codes as necessary to identify all the conditions related to diabetes that a patient is experiencing.

INTRODUCTION

This chapter covers a variety of conditions that are related in a general way. Because diabetes mellitus is a common medical problem, it is the condition coders encounter most often when working with chapter 4 of ICD-10-CM.

DIABETES MELLITUS

Diabetes mellitus, classified in categories E08 through E13, is a chronic disorder of impaired carbohydrate, protein, and fat metabolism. The disorder is caused by either an absolute decrease in the amount of insulin secreted by the pancreas or a reduction in the biologic effectiveness of the insulin secreted. Other conditions include the term "diabetes," such as bronze diabetes and diabetes insipidus, but a diagnosis of diabetes without further qualification should be interpreted as diabetes mellitus.

FIGURE 15.1   Major Organs of the Endocrine System

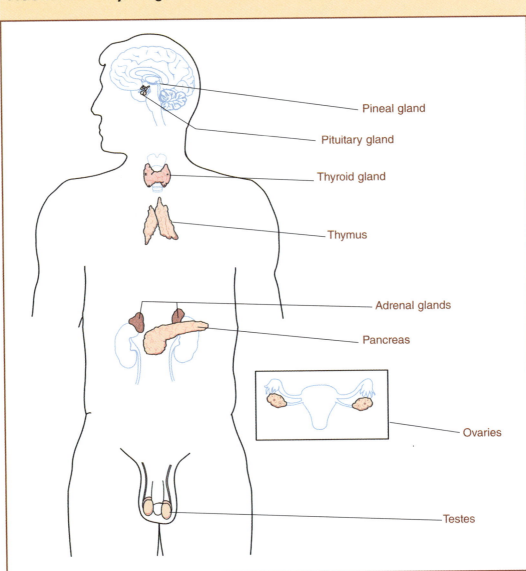

159

CHAPTER 15

Endocrine,

Nutritional,

and Metabolic

Diseases

The diabetes mellitus codes are combination codes that include the type of diabetes mellitus, the body system affected, and the complications affecting that body system. The type of diabetes (e.g., secondary, type 1, type 2) is identified at the category level, while the fourth character identifies the presence of any associated complication and the fifth-character and sixth-character subclassification provides further specificity regarding the complication. As many codes within a particular category as are necessary to describe all of the complications of the disease may be used.

Types of Diabetes Mellitus

There are three major types of diabetes mellitus: type 1 (or type I); type 2 (or type II); and secondary, such as due to an underlying condition or drug or chemical induced. The type of diabetes is the essential element in the selection of the codes in categories E08–E13, rather than whether the patient is on insulin, as follows:

E08   Diabetes mellitus due to underlying condition
E09   Drug or chemical induced diabetes mellitus
E10   Type 1 diabetes mellitus
E11   Type 2 diabetes mellitus
E13   Other specified diabetes mellitus

If the medical record documentation is not clear with regard to the type of diabetes, the default is category E11, Type 2 diabetes mellitus. When the type of diabetes is not documented but the record does indicate that the patient uses insulin, the default is still type 2. The fact that a patient is receiving insulin does not indicate that the diabetes is type 1.

Type 1 diabetes mellitus (category E10) may also be described as ketosis-prone, juvenile type, juvenile onset, or juvenile diabetes. The age of a patient is not the sole determining factor, though most type 1 diabetics develop the condition before reaching puberty. Type 1 diabetes is characterized by the body's failure to produce insulin at all or by an absolute decrease in such production. These patients require regular insulin injections to sustain life and experience significant health problems when they do not follow the prescribed regimen for medication and diet. Careful monitoring is required in order to avoid serious complications. Code **Z79.4, Long-term (current) use of insulin,** is not required for type 1 diabetics because these patients require insulin. However, this code may be assigned, if desired, to provide additional information.

Type 2 diabetes mellitus (category E11) may also be described as ketosis resistant. Insulin is produced, but either it is produced in insufficient quantity or the body is unable to utilize it adequately. Type 2 diabetic patients usually do not require insulin; they are ordinarily managed with oral hypoglycemic agents, diet, and exercise. For some patients, however, these measures are not effective, and insulin therapy may be required to control persistent hyperglycemia.

When a type 2 diabetic patient routinely uses insulin, assign code **Z79.4, Long-term (current) use of insulin.** However, code Z79.4 should not be used if insulin is given temporarily to bring the patient's blood sugar under control during the encounter.

Secondary diabetes is always caused by another condition or event. Secondary diabetes may be due to an underlying condition (E08), drug or chemically induced (E09), due to an infection, or the result of therapy such as the surgical removal of the pancreas. It can also be the result of an adverse effect of correctly administered medications, poisoning, or a late effect of using certain medications. Secondary diabetes is coded as follows:

• Secondary diabetes that is due to an underlying condition is coded to category E08, Diabetes mellitus due to underlying condition, with the underlying condition coded first. Underlying conditions include congenital rubella (P35.0), Cushing's syndrome (E24.-), cystic fibrosis (E84.-), malignant neoplasm (C00–C96), malnutrition (E40–E46), and pancreatitis and other diseases of the pancreas (K85–K86.-)

- Secondary diabetes that is drug induced or chemically induced is coded to category E09. Codes from category E10–E11 are not assigned for secondary diabetes. For example, steroid-induced diabetes mellitus due to the prolonged use of prednisone for an unrelated condition is coded as **T38.0x5-, Adverse effect of glucocorticoids and synthetic analogues,** followed by code **E09.9, Drug or chemical induced diabetes mellitus without complications.**

- The sequencing of the secondary diabetes codes is based on the Tabular List instructions for categories E08 and E09. For category E08, the underlying condition should be coded first. For category E09, the responsible drug or chemical is coded first.

- Secondary diabetes mellitus that is due to pancreatectomy is coded to **E89.1, Postprocedural hypoinsulinemia.** Assign a code from category E13 and either code **Z90.410, Acquired total absence of pancreas,** or code **Z90.411, Acquired partial absence of pancreas,** as additional diagnoses. For example, postpancreatectomy diabetes mellitus due to surgical removal of part of the pancreas is coded to E89.1, E13, and Z90.411.

- For patients with secondary diabetes who routinely use insulin, code **Z79.4, Long-term (current) use of insulin,** should be assigned. However, code Z79.4 should not be used if insulin is given temporarily to bring the patient's blood sugar under control during the encounter.

Category E13, Other specified diabetes mellitus, includes diabetes mellitus due to genetic defects of beta-cell function and diabetes mellitus due to genetic defects in insulin action.

Complications and Manifestations of Diabetes Mellitus

Type 1 and type 2 diabetes mellitus, as well as secondary diabetes mellitus, can lead to a variety of complications that involve either acute metabolic derangements (E08–E13 with .0- or .1-) or long-term complications (E08–E13 with .2- to .6-). Sequencing of the diabetes mellitus and the complication or manifestation is based on the reason for a particular encounter. Assign as many codes from categories E08–E13 as needed to identify all of the patient's associated conditions.

Acute Metabolic Complications

Acute metabolic complications include hyperosmolarity with coma (E08–E13 with .01) or without nonketotic hyperglycemic-hyperosmolar coma (E08–E13 with .00), ketoacidosis with coma (E08–E13 with .11) or without coma (E08–E13 with .10), and hypoglycemia with coma (E08–E13 with .641) or without coma (E08–E13 with .649). Typical findings for patients with diabetic ketoacidosis (DKA) are glycosuria, strong ketonuria, hyperglycemia, ketonemia (blood ketone), acidosis (low arterial blood pH), and low plasma bicarbonate. Ketoacidosis is a complication of type 1 diabetes; type 2 diabetics seldom develop ketoacidosis. A diagnosis of DKA should be classified as type 1 diabetes mellitus E10.1-. Diabetes with hyperosmolarity (E08–E13 with .01 or .00) is a condition in which there is hyperosmolarity and dehydration without significant ketosis. This condition most often occurs in patients with type 2 diabetes. Coma may or may not be present.

Diabetes with hypoglycemia may occur when an excessive amount of insulin is given, when the patient misses a meal, or when the patient is under stress. The condition may progress to coma. ICD-10-CM provides codes for diabetic hypoglycemia with coma (E08–E13 with .641) or without coma (E08–E13 with .649).

Chronic Complications

Patients with diabetes mellitus are susceptible to one or more chronic conditions that affect the renal, nervous, and peripheral vascular systems, particularly the feet and the eyes. Onset may occur early or late in the course of the diabetes and may occur in both insulin-dependent and non-insulin-dependent patients.

Diabetic patients often suffer several complications concurrently, in which case multiple codes from categories E08–E13 are assigned to identify all the associated diabetic conditions.

Renal Complications

Patients with diabetes are particularly prone to developing complications that affect the kidneys, such as nephritis, nephrosis, or chronic kidney disease. Nephritis is an inflammation of the kidney that develops slowly, over a long period of time. Nephrosis is an advanced stage of disease characterized by massive edema and marked proteinuria. Chronic kidney disease is often the ultimate progression of such conditions.

Diabetic kidney complications are coded to E08–E13 with .21 for diabetic nephropathy, .22 for chronic kidney disease, and .29 for other kidney complication. When the renal condition has progressed to chronic kidney disease, the diagnosis is sometimes stated in a way that appears to require three codes, one for the diabetes with chronic kidney disease (E08–E13 with .22), one for an interim manifestation (N08), and one for the final or current problem (N18.1–N18.6, Chronic kidney disease). It is not necessary to code the intermediate condition, but all three codes may be assigned if the hospital prefers.

Patients who have both diabetes and hypertension may develop chronic kidney disease as a result. In this case, three codes are required: one code for the diabetes with renal manifestation, E08–E13 with .22; a second code from category I12 (or I13) with a fourth character of (0) with chronic kidney disease stage 5 or end-stage renal disease or a fourth character of (9) with chronic kidney disease stage 1 through stage 4, or unspecified; and a third code from category N18 to indicate the specific stage of the chronic kidney disease. No other manifestation code is assigned. An example follows:

E10.22 + I12.0 + N18.5   Progressive type 1 diabetic nephropathy with hypertensive renal disease and chronic kidney disease stage 5

Diabetic Eye Disease

Retinopathy is a common complication of diabetes. Any disease of the retina said to be due to diabetes requires a code of E08–E13 with .3-. Diabetes with unspecified diabetic retinopathy is coded to E08–E13 with .31-. Nonproliferative diabetic retinopathy may be classified as mild (E08–E13 with .32-), moderate (E08–E13 with .33-), or severe (E08–E13 with .34-). Proliferative diabetic retinopathy is coded to E08–E13 with .35-. The sixth character provides additional information to identify the presence or absence of macular edema.

Senile cataracts develop more frequently in patients with diabetes, but they are not true diabetic cataracts and are not classified as ocular manifestations of the disease. A code from category H25, Age-related cataract, and a code from category E08–E13 should be assigned for senile cataracts in a diabetic patient, with sequencing depending on the circumstances of admission. Diabetic cataract (snowflake cataract, true diabetic cataract) is relatively rare. Assign codes for diabetic cataract only when the physician specifically describes the condition as such. For example:

E11.36   Type 2 diabetes mellitus with diabetic cataract

K86.1 + E08.9 + H25.9   Secondary diabetes mellitus due to chronic pancreatitis with mature senile cataract

162

CHAPTER 15 :
Endocrine,
Nutritional,
and Metabolic
Diseases

Diabetic Neurological Complications

Peripheral, cranial, and autonomic neuropathy are chronic manifestations of diabetes mellitus. The subclassification for diabetic neurological complications is as follows:

E08–E13 with .40	Unspecified diabetic neuropathy
E08–E13 with .41	Diabetic mononeuropathy
E08–E13 with .42	Diabetic polyneuropathy
E08–E13 with .43	Diabetic autonomic (poly)neuropathy
E08–E13 with .44	Diabetic amyotrophy
E08–E13 with .49	Other diabetic neurological complication

Do not use the code for autonomic neuropathy unless the diagnosis is stated as such by the physician. For example:

<u>E11.41</u> + H49.01	Diabetic third (cranial) nerve palsy, right eye
<u>E11.41</u> + G57.90	Mononeuropathy of the lower limb due to type 2 diabetes
<u>E10.40</u>	Diabetes type 1 with neuropathy
E10.43	Type 1 diabetes with diabetic gastroparesis

Diabetic Circulatory Complications

Peripheral vascular disease is a frequent complication of diabetes mellitus. Diabetic peripheral vascular disease without gangrene is coded as E08–E13 with .51; diabetic peripheral vascular disease with gangrene is coded as E08–E13 with .52. Diabetes with other circulatory complications is coded to E08–E13 with .59. Although arteriosclerosis occurs earlier and more extensively in diabetic patients, coronary artery disease, cardiomyopathy, and cerebrovascular disease are not complications of diabetes and are not included in subcategories E08–E13 with .5-. These conditions are coded separately unless the physician documents a causal relationship.

Other Manifestations of Diabetes Mellitus

Common chronic complications of diabetes mellitus, besides renal, ophthalmic, neurological, or circulatory, are classified to E08–E13 with .6- as follows:

E08–E13 with .61-	Diabetic arthropathy
E08–E13 with .62-	Diabetic skin complications
E08–E13 with .63-	Diabetic oral complications

Ulcers of the lower extremities, particularly the feet, are common complications of diabetes. The code for the diabetic foot ulcer complication (E08–E13 with .621) is assigned first, with an additional code of L97.4-, L97.5- indicating the specific site of the ulcer. If gangrene is present, code E08–E13 with .52 should be assigned as an additional code. It is important to recognize that not all ulcers in diabetic patients are diabetic ulcers; if there is a question as to the relationship, the physician should be consulted. Other diabetic skin ulcers are coded to E08–E13 with .622 and an additional code to identify the site of the ulcer (L97.1–L97.9, L98.41–L98.49).

Organic impotence is often the result of either diabetic peripheral neuropathy or diabetic peripheral vascular disease. It is coded first to either E08–E13 with .40 or E08–E13 with .51, with an additional code of **N52.1, Erectile dysfunction due to diseases classified elsewhere.**

Either of the preceding conditions specified as diabetic but without an indication as to whether the condition is due to neuropathy or peripheral vascular disease is coded as E08–E13 with .69 (with other specified complication), with an additional code for the complications. Codes E08–E13 with .69 are used for any other specified chronic manifestation that cannot be captured with the other codes in categories E08–E13. For example:

E10.69 + M86.171	Diabetes mellitus, type 1, with acute osteomyelitis great toe of right foot

Complications due to Insulin Pump Malfunction

Some diabetic patients require the use of an insulin pump to receive insulin therapy. An insulin pump is a small, computerized device attached to the body that delivers insulin via a catheter. The pump may provide a continuous drip of insulin all day long, or it may allow the patient to self-administer an insulin bolus by pushing a button. Failure or malfunction of the pump may result in underdosing or overdosing of insulin. Both of these situations are considered mechanical complications and are assigned a code from subcategory T85.6, Mechanical complication of other specified internal and external prosthetic devices, implants and grafts, as the principal diagnosis or first-listed code. The appropriate T85.6- code is selected depending on the type of malfunction, as follows:

T85.614   Breakdown (mechanical) of insulin pump
T85.624   Displacement of insulin pump
T85.633   Leakage of insulin pump

In addition, codes are assigned to specify underdose (T38.3x6-) or overdose (T38.3x1-), as well as the code for the type of diabetes mellitus and any associated complications.

DIABETES MELLITUS COMPLICATING PREGNANCY

Diabetes mellitus complicating pregnancy, delivery, or the puerperium is classified in chapter 15 of ICD-10-CM. Diabetes mellitus is a significant complicating factor in pregnancy. Pregnant women who are diabetic should be assigned a code from category O24, Diabetes mellitus in pregnancy, childbirth and puerperium, first, followed by the appropriate diabetes code(s) (E08–E13) from chapter 4 of ICD-10-CM to indicate the type of diabetes involved.

Because diabetes mellitus inevitably complicates the pregnant state, is aggravated by the pregnancy, or is a main reason for obstetric care, it is appropriate to assign these codes for a pregnant diabetic patient. Assign also code **Z79.4, Long-term (current) use of insulin,** if the diabetes mellitus is routinely treated with insulin.

Gestational Diabetes

A diagnosis of gestational diabetes refers to abnormal glucose tolerance that appears during pregnancy in previously nondiabetic women; it is not a true diabetes mellitus. It can occur during the second and third trimesters of pregnancy. It is thought to be due to metabolic or hormonal changes that occur during pregnancy. Patients with gestational diabetes are usually placed on a diabetic diet and sometimes require insulin therapy to maintain normal blood glucose levels during pregnancy, but the condition usually resolves during the postpartum period. Gestational diabetes can cause complications in the pregnancy similar to those of pre-existing diabetes mellitus. It also places the woman at greater risk of developing diabetes after the pregnancy. Subcategory O24.4, Gestational diabetes mellitus, is assigned for this condition. No other code from category O24 should be used with a code from O24.4.

Subcategory O24.4 is further subdivided on the basis of whether the gestational diabetes occurs in pregnancy, childbirth, or puerperium as well as whether it is diet or insulin controlled. If a patient with gestational diabetes is treated with both diet and insulin, only the code for insulin controlled is required. Code **Z79.4, Long-term (current) use of insulin,** should not be used with codes from subcategory O24.4.

An abnormal glucose tolerance in pregnancy, without a diagnosis of gestational diabetes, is assigned a code from subcategory O99.81, Abnormal glucose complicating pregnancy, childbirth, and the puerperium. Codes O24.4- (gestational diabetes) and O99.81- (abnormal glucose tolerance complicating pregnancy) should never be used together on the same record.

Neonatal Conditions Associated with Maternal Diabetes

Newborns with diabetic mothers sometimes experience either a transient decrease in blood sugar (**P70.0, Syndrome of infant of mother with gestational diabetes; P70.1, Syndrome of infant of a diabetic mother; P70.3, Iatrogenic neonatal hypoglycemia;** or **P70.4, Other neonatal hypoglycemia**) or a transient hyperglycemia (**P70.2, Neonatal diabetes mellitus**). The latter condition is sometimes referred to as pseudodiabetes and occasionally requires a short course of insulin therapy. Note, however, that these codes are assigned only when the maternal condition has actually had such an effect; the fact that the mother has diabetes in itself does not warrant the assignment of one of these codes for the newborn. When laboratory reports seem to indicate either condition, it is appropriate to check with the attending physician.

When a normal infant is born to a diabetic mother, and the infant presents no manifestations of the syndrome, assign code **Z38.00, Single liveborn, born in hospital, delivered vaginally,** as the principal diagnosis. Code **Z83.3, Family history of diabetes mellitus,** should be assigned as an additional diagnosis. In addition, assign code **P00.89, Newborn (suspected to be) affected by other maternal conditions,** as an additional diagnosis for a newborn infant who requires special surveillance after being born to a diabetic mother but who lacks manifestations of infant of a diabetic mother syndrome.

EXERCISE 15.1

Code the following diagnoses. Do not assign External cause of morbidity codes.

1. Diabetes mellitus, type 1   E10.21
   Diabetic nephrosis

2. Secondary diabetes mellitus due to pancreatic malignancy   C25.9
   Snowflake cataract   E08.36

3. Type 1 diabetes with ketoacidosis   E10.10

4. Diabetes mellitus, type 2, with   E11.01
   hyperosmolar, nonketotic coma

5. Diabetic Kimmelstiel-Wilson disease   E11.21

6. Chronic kidney disease, stage IV due to type 1   E10.22
   diabetes   N18.4

7. Impotence due to diabetic peripheral neuropathy   E11.40
   N52.1

HYPOGLYCEMIC AND INSULIN REACTIONS

Hypoglycemic reactions can occur in both diabetic and nondiabetic patients. In a diabetic patient, hypoglycemia with coma is coded as E08–E13 with .641, or E08–E13 with .649 if there is no mention of coma. Such reactions may occur when there is an imbalance between eating or exercise patterns and the dosage of insulin or oral hypoglycemic drugs. Hypoglycemia due to insulin may also occur in a newly diagnosed, type 1 diabetic during the initial phase of therapy while the dosage is being adjusted.

In a patient who does not have diabetes, code **E15, Nondiabetic hypoglycemic coma,** is assigned for hypoglycemic coma not otherwise specified. Code E15 also includes drug-induced insulin coma in a nondiabetic patient. Code **E16.2, Hypoglycemia, unspecified,** is assigned for hypoglycemia not otherwise specified.

Hypoglycemia without coma, due to a drug used as prescribed in a nondiabetic patient, requires first a code from categories T36–T50 with a sixth-character of "5" to indicate adverse effect and the responsible drug, followed by code **E16.0, Drug-induced hypoglycemia without coma.** Hypoglycemic coma or shock resulting from the incorrect use of insulin or other antidiabetic agent is coded as poisoning (T38.3x- with a sixth character of 1–4).

EXERCISE 15.2

Code the following diagnoses. Do not assign External cause of morbidity codes.

1. Neonatal hypoglycemia   P70.4

---

2. Hypoglycemic coma in patient without diabetes   E15

---

3. Patient with type 2 diabetes mellitus participated in a   E11.649
strenuous game of racquetball without adjusting his   Z79.4
insulin dosage; he is admitted with blood sugar of 35
and is diagnosed as being hypoglycemic

                     Hypoglycemia

---

4. Type 1 diabetic developed hypoglycemia even   E10.649
though she had taken only the prescribed dose of insulin
and did not alter her exercise or eating regimen

CODES FOR NUTRITIONAL DISORDERS

Nutritional disorders, such as deficiency of specific vitamins and minerals, are classified in categories E40 through E64, with the exception of nutritional anemias, which are classified in categories D50 through D53 series.

Several codes are used to identify overweight and obesity, including the following:

E66.01	Morbid (severe) obesity due to excess calories
E66.09	Other obesity due to excess calories
E66.1	Drug-induced obesity
E66.2	Morbid (severe) obesity with alveolar hypoventilation
E66.3	Overweight
E66.8	Other obesity
E66.9	Obesity, unspecified

These codes are assigned only on the basis of the physician's diagnostic statement. Category E66, Overweight and obesity, requires that an additional code (Z68.-) for the body mass index (BMI) be assigned, if known. BMI is a tool for indicating weight status in adults. It is a measure of weight for height. The BMI code assignment should be based on medical record documentation, which may be found in the notes of other clinicians involved in the care of the patient (i.e., physician or other qualified health care practitioner legally accountable for establishing the patient's diagnosis). BMI is typically documented by the dietitian or the nurse. Coding BMI is an exception to the guideline that requires that code assignment be based on the documentation by the provider. While BMI may be reported on the basis of another clinician's documentation, the codes for the associated diagnosis (such as overweight and obesity) should be based on the provider's documentation.

Code **E66.2, Morbid (severe) obesity with alveolar hypoventilation,** also known as Pickwickian syndrome, involves sleep-disordered breathing that causes a person to stop breathing for short periods of time while sleeping. It may be related to both obesity and neurological conditions.

METABOLIC DISORDERS

Metabolic disorders other than diabetes are classified to categories E70–E89. A metabolic disorder occurs when abnormal reactions in the body disrupt the metabolism. These disorders involve an alteration in the normal metabolism of carbohydrates, lipids, proteins, water, and nucleic acids.

Fluid Overload

Fluid overload (E87.7-) is the excessive accumulation of fluid in the body. It may be caused by excessive parenteral infusion or deficiencies in cardiovascular or renal fluid volume regulation. However, when fluid overload is a component of congestive heart failure, it is not coded separately.

Cystic Fibrosis

Cystic fibrosis (E84.-), also known as mucoviscidosis or cystic fibrosis of the pancreas, is a disorder of the exocrine glands that causes the accumulation of thick, tenacious mucus. It is the primary cause of pancreatic deficiency and chronic malabsorption in children. Although cystic fibrosis affects the body in a number of ways, progressive respiratory insufficiency is the major cause of illness in patients with this disease. The symptoms primarily affect the digestive and respiratory

167

CHAPTER 15

Endocrine,

Nutritional,

and Metabolic

Diseases

systems. In some glands, like the pancreas, the thick mucus may obstruct the pancreas, preventing digestive enzymes from reaching the intestines. The pulmonary manifestation results in mucus secretions that clog the airways and allow bacteria to multiply. Sometimes this state progresses to complications such as acute and chronic bronchitis, bronchiectasis, pneumonia, atelectasis, peribronchial and parenchyma scarring, pneumothorax, and hemoptysis. Intra-abdominal complications such as meconium ileus, rectal prolapse, inguinal hernia, gallstones, ileocolic intussusception, and gastroesophageal reflux also occur.

Specific codes identify the site of manifestation involvement such as pulmonary involvement (E84.0), meconium ileus (E84.11), other intestinal manifestations (E84.19), or other site involvement (E84.8). These manifestation codes may be used together if different sites are involved. Code **E84.9, Cystic fibrosis, unspecified,** should be used if the manifestation is not specified. If an infectious organism is involved with cystic fibrosis with pulmonary involvement, assign an additional code for the organism present.

Because there is no known cure for cystic fibrosis, therapy is directed toward the complications of the disease, with the major focus on the maintenance of adequate nutritional and respiratory status. Admissions due to the cystic fibrosis itself most often occur when the patient is brought in for workup to confirm the diagnosis.

Tumor Lysis Syndrome

Tumor lysis syndrome (TLS) refers to a group of serious, potentially life-threatening metabolic disturbances that can occur after antineoplastic therapy. TLS can develop spontaneously as a result of radiation therapy or corticosteroid therapy. However, it usually occurs following the administration of anticancer drugs and is often associated with leukemias and lymphomas. It is also seen in other hematologic malignancies and solid tumors. When cancer cells are destroyed, they can release intracellular ions and metabolic by-products into the circulation, leading to TLS. Code **E88.3, Tumor lysis syndrome,** is used to report spontaneous tumor lysis syndrome as well as tumor lysis syndrome following antineoplastic drug therapy. Code first T45.1- to identify the drug involved when tumor lysis syndrome is drug induced.

168

CHAPTER 15

Endocrine,
Nutritional,
and Metabolic
Diseases

EXERCISE 15.3

Code the following diagnoses and procedures. Do not assign External cause of morbidity codes.

1. Hypercholesterolemia and endogenous hyperglyceridemia — E78.2

2. Cystic fibrosis with mild mental retardation — E84.9
   F70

3. Congenital myxedema — E00.1
   Inappropriate antidiuretic hormone secretion syndrome — E22.2

4. Hypokalemia — E87.6

5. Uninodular toxic nodular goiter with thyrotoxicosis — E05.10
   Open left thyroid lobectomy — 0GTG0ZZ

6. Adenomatous goiter with thyrotoxicosis — E05.20
   Percutaneous endoscopic substernal thyroidectomy, complete — 0GTK4ZZ

7. Toxic diffuse goiter with thyrotoxic crisis — E05.01

8. Hypothyroidism, ablative, following total thyroidectomy performed three years ago — E89.0

9. Morbidly obese patient with a BMI of 39 — E66.01
   Laparoscopic gastroplasty with gastric banding — Z68.39
   Restriction — 0DV64CZ

10. Flushing and sleeplessness due to premature menopause — E28.310

CHAPTER 16

Mental Disorders

CHAPTER OVERVIEW

- Mental disorders are classified in chapter 5 of the ICD-10-CM.

- Organic anxiety disorder is a psychosis and is the direct effect of a medical condition. The medical condition should be coded first.

- Schizophrenia is classified in category F20, with a fourth character indicating the type of schizophrenia.

- Affective disorders are common mental diseases with multiple aspects, including biological, behavioral, social, and psychological factors. The most common affective disorders are the following:

  — Major depressive disorder

  — Bipolar disorders

  — Anxiety disorders

- Nonpsychotic mental disorders are also classified. These include the following:

  — Reactions to stress (both acute and chronic)

  — Psychophysiologic disorders

- Substance abuse and dependence are classified as mental disorders in ICD-10-CM.

  — Use, abuse, and dependence are different conditions and should be coded differently.

  — Alcohol dependence syndrome, drug dependence, and nondependent abuse of drugs are classified to three different categories.

LEARNING OUTCOMES

After studying this chapter you should be able to:

Code a variety of mental disorders.

Determine the difference in types of affective disorders.

Explain the difference between substance abuse and dependence and code the conditions and therapies surrounding these two distinct conditions.

TERMS TO KNOW

Abuse
problematic use of drugs or alcohol but without dependence

Dependence
increased tolerance to drugs or alcohol with a compulsion to continue taking the substance despite the cost; withdrawal symptoms often occur upon cessation

REMEMBER . . .

Although coding assignments for mental disorders are made according to ICD-10-CM, psychiatrists often state diagnoses using the different terminology found in the *Diagnostic and Statistical Manual of Mental Disorders, Fourth Edition, Text Revision*.

INTRODUCTION

Mental disorders of all types are classified in chapter 5 of ICD-10-CM.

Psychiatrists ordinarily state diagnoses in accordance with the nomenclature used in the *Diagnostic and Statistical Manual of Mental Disorders, Fourth Edition, Text Revision* (DSM-IV-TR®), published by the American Psychiatric Association. Most of these codes are the same as those used in ICD-10-CM, but the terminology may differ. Coders working with mental health records may find it useful to become familiar with this manual, but actual coding assignment is made according to the classifications in ICD-10-CM.

MENTAL DISORDERS DUE TO KNOWN PHYSIOLOGICAL CONDITIONS

Categories F01 through F09, Mental disorders due to known physiological conditions, include a range of mental disorders grouped together on the basis of having a demonstrable etiology in cerebral disease, brain injury, or other insult leading to cerebral dysfunction. The cerebral dysfunction may be primary or secondary. Primary cerebral dysfunction includes diseases, injuries, and insults affecting the brain directly and selectively. Secondary cerebral dysfunction includes systemic diseases and disorders that attack the brain only as one of the multiple organs or body systems involved.

FIGURE 16.1   Side View of the Brain

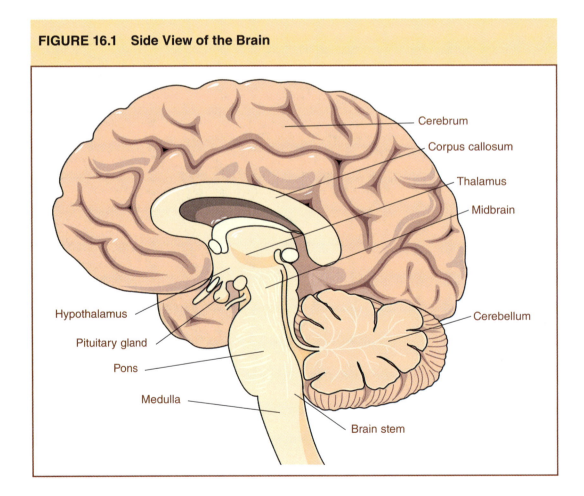

This section includes the following categories:

F01   Vascular dementia
F02   Dementia in other diseases classified elsewhere
F03   Unspecified dementia
F04   Amnestic disorder due to known physiological condition
F05   Delirium due to known physiological condition
F06   Other mental disorders due to known physiological condition
F07   Personality and behavioral disorders due to known physiological condition
F09   Unspecified mental disorder due to known physiological condition

Instructional notes to code first the underlying physiological condition are provided for categories F02 through F09, except category F03, Unspecified dementia. Category F01, Vascular dementia, has an instructional note to code first the underlying physiological condition or sequelae of cerebrovascular disease.

Organic Brain Syndrome

Organic brain syndrome is an older general term used to describe decreased mental function due to a medical disease other than a psychiatric illness. In general, organic brain syndromes cause agitation; confusion; long-term loss of brain function (dementia); and severe, short-term loss of brain function (delirium). Organic brain syndrome is common in the elderly but is not part of the normal aging process. Organic brain syndrome, not otherwise specified, is coded to **F09, Unspecified mental disorder due to known physiological condition.** The underlying physiological condition should be coded first. Posttraumatic organic brain syndrome is coded to **F07.81, Postconcussional syndrome,** with an additional code to identify any associated posttraumatic headache.

Organic Anxiety Disorder

Organic anxiety disorder is a transient organic psychosis characterized by clinically significant anxiety. It is considered to be the direct physiological effect of a general medical condition. The code for the general condition is sequenced first, with an additional code of **F06.4, Anxiety disorder due to known physiological condition.**

Dementia in Other Diseases Classified Elsewhere

Subcategory F02.8, Dementia in other diseases classified elsewhere, specifically identifies the presence or absence of behavioral disturbances such as aggressive behavior, violent behavior, wandering off, or combative behavior. The dementia classified in subcategory F02.8 is due to direct physiological effects of a general medical condition. Dementia is characterized by the development of multiple cognitive deficits such as memory impairment and cognitive disturbances including aphasia, apraxia, and agnosia. When assigning codes F02.80 and F02.81, code first the underlying physiological condition associated with the dementia, such as Alzheimer's disease (G30.-) or Parkinson's disease (G20).

ALTERED MENTAL STATE

An alteration in level of consciousness not associated with delirium or another identified condition is classified to category R40 in chapter 18 of ICD-10-CM. Category R40 is further subdivided to indicate whether it is identified as somnolence (R40.0), stupor (R40.1), coma (R40.2-), persistent vegetative state (R40.3), or transient alteration of awareness (R40.4). An altered mental status, or a change in mental status, of unknown etiology is coded to **R41.82, Altered mental status, unspecified.** If the condition causing the change in mental status is known, do not assign code R41.82; code the condition instead.

TRANSIENT GLOBAL AMNESIA

Transient global amnesia is a distinct form of amnesia of unknown etiology, characterized by a sudden loss of memory function. During an episode, the patient is unable to form memories or remember recent events and may ask the same question over and over because no memories of previous answers are formed. The episode usually lasts for a few hours, followed by total or near-total resolution of the memory loss, although the patient will remain amnesic for the event itself. Transient global amnesia is not psychotic in nature, and it is not considered to be due to ischemia; rather, it is a distinct cerebrovascular condition with its own code, G45.4.

SCHIZOPHRENIC DISORDERS

Schizophrenia is a severe mental illness characterized by a variety of symptoms including, but not limited to:

- Loss of contact with reality
- Bizarre behavior
- Disorganized thinking
- Disorganized speech
- Decreased emotional expressiveness
- Diminished or loss of contact with reality
- Diminished to total social withdrawal

Schizophrenic disorders are classified in category F20, with a fourth character indicating the type of schizophrenia as follows:

F20.0 **Paranoid schizophrenia**
Patients suffering from this type of schizophrenia are preoccupied with delusions about being punished or persecuted by others.

F20.1 **Disorganized schizophrenia**
A type of schizophrenia whereby patients are usually confused and illogical; behavior is disorganized, emotionless, and inappropriate. It may lead to the patient having a limited ability to perform normal activities of daily living.

F20.2 **Catatonic schizophrenia**
A type of schizophrenia whereby patients become unresponsive and have limited physical response.

F20.3 **Undifferentiated schizophrenia**
A form of schizophrenia characterized by a number of schizophrenic symptoms, such as delusion(s), disorganized behavior, disorganized speech, flat affect, or hallucinations, but that does not meet the criteria for any other type of schizophrenia.

F20.5   Residual schizophrenia

This type of schizophrenia is characterized by decreased severity of symptoms of schizophrenia. Delusion, hallucinations, and other symptoms may be present but are far less severe than when originally diagnosed.

F20.8   Other schizophrenia

This subcategory is further subdivided as follows:

F20.81   Schizophreniform disorder

This is a short-term type of schizophrenia that distorts the way a person thinks, acts, expresses emotions, perceives reality, and relates to others. Schizophreniform disorder generally lasts less than six months, while schizophrenia is a life-long illness.

F20.89   Other schizophrenia

This code includes cenesthopathic schizophrenia (a subgroup of schizophrenia with marked and dominating abnormal bodily sensations) and simple schizophrenia (a disorder characterized by an insidious but progressive development of oddities of conduct, inability to meet the demands of society, and decline in total performance).

F20.9   Schizophrenia, unspecified

This is not a type of schizophrenia per se, but this code is used when the type of schizophrenia is not specified.

AFFECTIVE DISORDERS

Affective disorders are common mental diseases with multiple aspects, including biological, behavioral, social, and psychological factors. Major depressive disorder, bipolar disorders, and anxiety disorders are the most common affective disorders. Affective disorders can result in symptoms ranging from the mild and inconvenient to the severe and life threatening. Affective disorders are common mental diseases characterized by mood disturbance. Mood [affective] disorders are classified under categories F30–F39 in ICD-10-CM.

Major depressive disorder (MDD) is also known as monopolar depression or unipolar affective disorder. MDD causes prolonged periods of emotional, mental, and physical exhaustion. Patients suffering from this condition have a considerable risk of self-destructive behavior, sometimes leading to suicide. MDD is classified in ICD-10-CM as:

F32.-   Major depressive disorder, single episode
F33.-   Major depressive disorder, recurrent

Categories F32 and F33 are further subdivided with fourth characters (or fifth characters) to provide information about the current severity of the disorder, as follows:

0   Mild
1   Moderate
2   Severe, without psychotic features
3   Severe with psychotic features
4   In partial remission (used for category F32 to indicate in partial remission; category F33 uses the fourth character of "4" to indicate remission and is further subdivided with fifth characters to indicate unspecified remission, partial remission, or full remission)
5   In full remission (used only for category F32)
8   Other
9   Unspecified

Fourth characters 1 through 8 are assigned only when provider documentation of severity is included in the medical record.

Bipolar affective diseases are divided into various types according to the symptoms displayed. Other names for bipolar affective disease include manic-depressive disorder, cyclothymia, manic-depressive illness, and bipolar disorder. Patients suffering from bipolar diseases experience periods of manic (hyper-excitable) episodes alternating with periods of deep depression. These disorders are chronic and recurrent with varying degrees of severity. Severe crises can lead to suicide attempts during depressive episodes or to physical violence against oneself or others during manic episodes. In many patients, however, episodes are mild and infrequent. Mixed states may also occur with elements of mania and depression simultaneously present. Some people with bipolar affective disorders show a rapid cycling between manic and depressive states.

ICD-10-CM classifies bipolar disorders under the following categories/codes:

F30.-   Manic episode (includes bipolar disorder, single manic episode, and mixed affective episode)

F31.-   Bipolar disorder (includes manic-depressive illness, manic-depressive psychosis, and manic-depressive reaction)

F34.-   Persistent mood [affective] disorders (includes cyclothymic disorder and dysthymic disorder)

F39   Unspecified mood [affective] disorder (includes affective psychosis not otherwise specified)

Category F30, Manic episode, is further subdivided to identify the severity of the current episode and to indicate that psychotic symptoms are involved. Category F31, Bipolar disorder, is further subdivided to specify the severity of the current episode; whether the current episode is hypomanic, manic, depressed, or mixed; and whether psychotic features are involved. Additionally, for patients with bipolar disorder currently in remission (F31.7-), fifth characters are available to specify whether the patient is in full or partial remission and whether the most recent episode was hypomanic, manic, depressed, mixed, or unspecified.

EXERCISE 16.1

Code the following diagnoses and procedures. Do not assign External cause of morbidity codes.

1.	Schizoaffective psychosis, depressive type	F25.1
2.	Schizophrenia, catatonic type	F20.2
3.	Schizophrenia, paranoid type	F20.0

4.	Severe depressive disorder, recurrent, current episode severe with psychotic symptoms	F33.3
5.	Reactive depressive psychosis	F32.3
6.	Bipolar disorder, in manic phase, mild	F31.11
7.	Bipolar affective disorder, most recent episode mixed, in partial remission	F31.77

NONPSYCHOTIC MENTAL DISORDERS

A variety of anxiety, dissociative, stress-related, somatoform, and other nonpsychotic mental disorders are classified in categories F40 through F48. These include such conditions as phobic anxiety disorders, reaction to stress, dissociative and conversion disorders, somatoform disorders, and other nonpsychotic mental disorders.

Anxiety Disorders

Anxiety disorders are common psychiatric disorders and are considered to be one of the most undertreated and overlooked health problems. Among their common manifestations are panic disorders, phobias, chronic generalized anxiety disorder, obsessive-compulsive disorder, and posttraumatic disorder. A phobia is a persistent and irrational fear of a particular type of object, animal, activity, or situation. Anxiety disorders are classified in ICD-10-CM under the following categories:

F40   Phobic anxiety disorders
F41   Other anxiety disorders
F42   Obsessive-compulsive disorder

Reactions to Stress

ICD-10-CM provides category F43 for coding reaction to severe stress and adjustment disorders. Code **F43.0, Acute stress reaction,** classifies acute reaction to stress, including acute crisis reaction, combat fatigue, crisis state, and psychic shock. Acute stress reaction is the result of a person experiencing or witnessing a traumatic event that causes the individual to experience extreme, disturbing, or unexpected fear, stress, or pain and that involves or threatens serious injury, perceived serious injury, or death to self or someone else.

Posttraumatic stress disorder (PTSD) is classified in ICD-10-CM to subcategory F43.1, with fifth characters for unspecified, acute, or chronic. PTSD is a severe anxiety disorder that can develop after exposure to any event resulting in psychological trauma. As an effect of psychological trauma, PTSD is less frequent and more enduring than the more commonly seen acute stress response. Symptoms of PTSD include re-experiencing the original trauma(s) through flashbacks or nightmares; avoiding stimuli associated with the trauma; and experiencing increased arousal, such as difficulty falling or staying asleep, anger, and hypervigilance. These symptoms last more than one month and cause significant impairment in social, occupational, or other important areas of functioning.

Adjustment disorders are a psychological response to an identifiable stressor or group of stressors that cause(s) significant emotional or behavioral symptoms. They differ from acute stress disorder and PTSD in that adjustment disorders are usually associated with a less intense stressor. Adjustment disorders are classified to subcategory F43.2, with the fifth-character axis being the nature of the reaction—for example, anxiety, depression, disturbance of conduct, or other symptoms. The following situations fall into this category:

F43.21   Patient depressed over death of son
F43.24   Child adopted from a foreign country, suffering from culture shock
          with conduct disturbance

Dissociative and Conversion Disorders

ICD-10-CM classifies dissociative and conversion disorders to category F44. Dissociative disorders refer to conditions that involve disruptions or breakdowns of memory, awareness, identity, and/or perception. Four codes are available for dissociative disorders, as follows:

F44.0   Dissociative amnesia
F44.1   Dissociative fugue
F44.2   Dissociative stupor
F44.81   Dissociative identity disorder

Conversion disorder is a condition whereby the patient presents with neurological symptoms but with the exclusion of neurological disease or feigning, and the determination of a psychological mechanism. The symptoms can vary from weakness/paralysis of a limb or the entire body to impaired hearing or vision, loss of sensation, impairment of speech, seizures, syncope, and other neurological findings. The following codes are used to describe conversion disorder:

F44.4   Conversion disorder with motor symptom or deficit
F44.5   Conversion disorder with seizures or convulsions
F44.6   Conversion disorder with sensory symptom or deficit
F44.7   Conversion disorder with mixed symptom presentation

In addition, two codes are available for other (F44.89) and unspecified (F44.9) dissociative and conversion disorders.

Examples of conditions that are classified in category F44 include the following:

F44.4   Psychogenic paralysis
F44.4   Abnormal hysterical gait
F44.0   Hysterical amnesia
F44.6   Emotional blindness

Somatoform Disorders

Somatoform disorders are mental disorders characterized by physical symptoms that mimic physical disease or injury for which there is no identifiable physical cause. Instead, the symptoms are caused by mental factors. A diagnosis of a somatoform disorder implies that mental factors are a large contributor to the symptoms' onset, severity, and duration. ICD-10-CM classifies somatoform disorders to category F45. Examples of conditions classified in category F45 include the following:

F45.8	Psychogenic diarrhea
F45.8	Psychogenic dysmenorrhea
F45.20	Hypochondriacal disorder

In assigning codes from categories F44 and F45 it is important to make the distinction between these conditions and similar conditions that fall under the categories for neurotic disorders, psychoses, or organic disorders.

For pain that is exclusively psychological, assign code **F45.41, Pain disorder exclusively related to psychological factors.** When the documentation reflects a psychological component for a patient with acute or chronic pain, assign a code from category G89, Pain, not elsewhere classified, followed by code F45.41.

BEHAVIORAL SYNDROMES ASSOCIATED WITH PHYSIOLOGICAL DISTURBANCES AND PHYSICAL FACTORS

Categories F50 through F59 are devoted to behavioral syndromes associated with physiological disturbances and physical factors. These codes are not assigned when the conditions are present due to a mental disorder classified elsewhere or are of organic origin. This grouping includes the following conditions:

F50.-	Eating disorders (such as anorexia nervosa and bulimia nervosa)
F51.-	Sleep disorders not due to a substance or known physiological condition
F52.-	Sexual dysfunction not due to a substance or known physiological condition
F53.-	Puerperal psychosis
F54	Psychological and behavioral factors associated with disorders or diseases classified elsewhere
F55.-	Abuse of nonpsychoactive substances
F59	Unspecified behavioral syndromes associated with physiological disturbances and physical factors

Code F54 classifies psychological and behavioral factors associated with diseases classified elsewhere. Typical conditions that are often associated with code F54 include asthma, ulcerative colitis, and dermatitis. If such a condition is considered to be psychogenic in origin, the associated physical disorder is coded first, followed by code F54. For example:

J45.20 + F54	Mild intermittent psychogenic asthma
I47.1 + F54	Psychogenic paroxysmal atrial tachycardia

EXERCISE 16.2

Code the following diagnoses.

1.	Acute delirium resulting from pneumonia	F05
	due to *Hemophilus influenzae*	J14
2.	Passive-aggressive personality	F60.89
3.	Depression anxiety	F41.8
	Conversion disorder (convulsions)	F44.5
4.	Adolescent adjustment reaction, with severe disturbance of conduct	F43.24
5.	Severe depression, recurrent	F33.2
6.	Stress reaction, psychomotor	F43.0

SUBSTANCE ABUSE DISORDERS

Substance abuse and dependence are classified as mental disorders in ICD-10-CM. These disorders are classified to categories F10 through F19. Although the terms "abuse" and "dependence" may be used interchangeably in certain treatment programs, they are different conditions and are coded differently in ICD-10-CM.

Alcohol Dependence and Abuse

Alcohol-related disorders are classified in ICD-10-CM to category F10. An additional code for blood alcohol level may be assigned, if applicable (Y90.-). Alcohol abuse refers to the recurring use of alcoholic beverages despite negative consequences. Alcohol dependence, as described in the DSM-IV, is a psychiatric diagnosis describing a condition in which an individual uses alcohol despite significant areas of dysfunction, evidence of physical dependence, and/or related hardship. Alcohol dependence is differentiated from alcohol abuse by the presence of symptoms such as tolerance and withdrawal. Both alcohol dependence and alcohol abuse are sometimes referred to by the less specific term "alcoholism."

Alcohol abuse is classified in ICD-10-CM under subcategory F10.1, Alcohol abuse, while alcohol dependence is classified under subcategory F10.2, Alcohol dependence. If alcohol use is documented without further specificity as to abuse or dependence, it is classified to subcategory F10.9, Alcohol use, unspecified. All three subcategories are further subdivided to specify the presence of intoxication or intoxication delirium. Additional characters are also provided to specify alcohol-induced mood disorder, psychotic disorder, and other alcohol-induced disorders. Codes in subclassification F10.23-, Alcohol dependence with withdrawal, provide additional detail regarding withdrawal symptoms such as delirium and perceptual disturbance.

Code **F10.129, Alcohol abuse with intoxication, unspecified,** is assigned for a diagnosis of simple drunkenness. However, acute drunkenness in alcoholism is indexed to **F10.229, Alcohol dependence with intoxication, unspecified;** chronic drunkenness is indexed to **F10.20, Alcohol dependence, uncomplicated;** and chronic drunkenness in remission is indexed to **F10.21, Alcohol dependence, in remission.** Selection of code F10.21 for "in remission" requires the provider's clinical judgment, as defined by the *ICD-10-CM Official Guidelines for Coding and Reporting*, rather than nursing or other documentation. Note that toxic effect of alcohol is not classified to category F10 but to subcategory T51.0- instead.

Drug Dependence and Abuse

ICD-10-CM classifies drug dependence and abuse in the following categories according to the class of drug:

F11   Opioid related disorders
F12   Cannabis related disorders
F13   Sedative, hypnotic or anxiolytic related disorders
F14   Cocaine related disorders
F15   Other stimulant related disorders
F16   Hallucinogen related disorders
F17   Nicotine dependence
F18   Inhalant related disorders
F19   Other psychoactive substance related disorders

In most cases, fourth characters indicate whether the disorder is nondependent abuse (1), dependence (2), or unspecified use (9). Additional characters are also provided to specify intoxication, intoxication delirium, and intoxication with perceptual disturbance. Patients with substance abuse or dependence often develop related physical complications or psychotic symptoms. These complications are classified to the specific drug abuse or dependence, with the fifth or sixth characters providing further specificity regarding any associated drug-induced mood disorder, psychotic disorder, withdrawal, and other drug-induced disorders (such as sexual dysfunction or sleep disorder).

Patients dependent on alcohol, drugs, or both frequently experience withdrawal symptoms and require detoxification. Withdrawal most commonly refers to the group of symptoms that occurs upon the abrupt discontinuation/separation or a decrease in dosage of the intake of medications, recreational drugs, and/or alcohol. Symptoms and signs of withdrawal can vary based on the substance and from individual to individual. They include tremulousness, agitation, irritability, disturbed sleep, anorexia, autonomic hyperactivity, seizures, and hallucinations. A severe form of withdrawal known as delirium tremens is characterized by fever, tachycardia, hypertension or hypotension, hallucinations, agitation, confusion, fluctuating mental states, and seizures.

ICD-10-CM provides combination codes that include both the alcohol or substance abuse/dependence and any associated complications. Examples include:

F10.231   Alcoholic withdrawal delirium due to alcohol dependence

F10.251   Alcohol-induced psychotic disorder with hallucinations due to alcohol dependence

F10.180   Alcohol-induced anxiety disorder due to alcohol abuse

F11.250   Heroin dependence with heroin-induced psychosis and delusions

Category F19, Other psychoactive substance related disorders, may be used when the specific drug class is not specified.

Similar to code **F10.21, Alcohol dependence, in remission,** the selection of codes for "in remission" for categories F11–F19 with -.21 requires the provider's clinical judgment. The appropriate codes for "in remission" are assigned only on the basis of provider documentation (as defined in the *ICD-10-CM Official Guidelines for Coding and Reporting*).

Psychoactive Substance Use

In addition to the codes for psychoactive substance abuse and dependence, ICD-10-CM provides codes for psychoactive substance use (F10.9-, F11.9-, F12.9-, F13.9-, F14.9-, F15.9-, F16.9-). As with all other diagnoses, these codes should only be assigned based on provider documentation and when they meet the definition of a reportable diagnosis per Section III, Reporting Additional Diagnoses, of the *ICD-10-CM Official Guidelines for Coding and Reporting*. The codes are to be used only when the psychoactive substance use is associated with a mental or behavioral disorder and such a relationship is documented by the provider.

Psychoactive Substance Use, Abuse, and Dependence Code Hierarchy

When the provider documentation refers to use, abuse, and dependence of the same substance (e.g., alcohol, opioid, cannabis), only one code should be assigned to identify the pattern of use, based on the following hierarchy:

- If both use and abuse are documented, assign only the code for abuse.
- If both abuse and dependence are documented, assign only the code for dependence.
- If use, abuse, and dependence are all documented, assign only the code for dependence.
- If both use and dependence are documented, assign only the code for dependence.

Selection of the Principal Diagnosis

The designation of the principal diagnosis for patients with either substance abuse or substance dependence is determined by the circumstances of the admission, as defined in the following examples:

1. When a patient is admitted for detoxification or rehabilitation for both drug and alcohol abuse or dependence, and both are treated, either condition may be designated as the principal diagnosis.

2. When a patient with a diagnosis of substance abuse or dependence is admitted for treatment or evaluation of a physical complaint related to the substance use, follow the directions in the Alphabetic Index for conditions described as alcoholic or due to drugs; sequence the physical condition first, followed by the code for abuse or dependence.

3. When a patient with a diagnosis of alcohol or drug abuse or dependence is admitted because of an unrelated condition, follow the usual guidelines for selecting a principal diagnosis.

Substance Abuse Therapy

Treatment for patients with a diagnosis of substance abuse or dependence consists of detoxification, rehabilitation, or both. The abuse or dependence is the principal diagnosis for a patient admitted for such programs.

Detoxification is the management of withdrawal symptoms for a patient who is physically dependent on alcohol or drugs. The process is more than simple observation; it involves active management. Treatment may involve evaluation, observation and monitoring, and administration of thiamine and multivitamins for nutrition as well as other medications (such as methadone, long-acting barbiturates or benzodiazepines, or carbamazepine) as needed. The detoxification program for patients with alcohol dependence is usually continued over a four- or five-day period, although it can also be provided on an outpatient basis depending on the severity of the withdrawal symptoms. Detoxification takes longer for opiates and sedatives/hypnotics, usually lasting from three weeks to a period of months, and may be carried out in either a residential or an outpatient setting. If the medical record documents detoxification as having been carried out, the code can be assigned even when no medications were actually administered.

Rehabilitation is a structured program carried out with the goal of establishing strict control of drinking and drug use. A variety of rehabilitation modalities may be utilized. These include methadone maintenance, therapeutic residential communities, and long-term outpatient drug- or alcohol-free treatments. When a patient with drug dependence is on medications for detoxification or for maintenance programs to prevent withdrawal symptoms (e.g., methadone maintenance for opiate dependence), the appropriate code for the drug dependence should be assigned, rather than code **Z79.891, Long-term (current) use of opiate analgesic,** or **Z79.899, Other long-term (current) drug therapy.**

EXERCISE 16.3

Code the following diagnoses.

---

1. Paranoid alcoholic psychosis with alcohol dependence   F10.250

---

2. Alcoholic cirrhosis of liver   K70.30

    Chronic alcoholism   F10.20

---

3. Acute alcoholic intoxication   F10.129

    Blood alcohol level of 59 mg/100 mL   Y90.2

---

4. Marijuana dependence   F12.20

---

5. Acute alcohol intoxication and dependence   F10.229

---

6. Barbiturate abuse with sleep disorder   F13.182

---

7. Cocaine dependence	F14.20
8. Amphetamine abuse	F15.10
9. Dependence on barbiturate and heroin	F13.20
	F11.20
10. Admitted because of syndrome of inappropriate secretion of antidiuretic hormone secondary to chronic alcoholism	E22.2
	F10.20

MENTAL HEALTH AND SUBSTANCE ABUSE TREATMENT PROCEDURE CODING

Mental disorders other than substance abuse disorders are commonly treated with psychodynamic ("talk") therapy, drug therapy, electroconvulsive therapy, or a combination of therapeutic modes. Because the diagnosis alone does not always explain the length of stay or the level of resource utilization for such patients, therapy codes are helpful in analyzing patterns of care.

ICD-10-PCS provides two sections for procedures related to mental health and substance abuse, as follows:

G Mental Health
H Substance Abuse Treatment

Mental Health Procedures

The Mental Health Section of ICD-10-PCS contains specific values in the third and fourth characters to describe mental health procedures. The most important character in this section is the root type (the third character), while the type qualifier (the fourth character) further specifies the procedure type as needed. The remaining characters (second, fifth, sixth, and seventh) only function as placeholders and do not represent specific information about the procedure. The value Z is used as the placeholder for these characters. The following example demonstrates the structure of ICD-10-PCS codes in the Mental Health Section.

Electroconvulsive therapy, unilateral-multiple seizure

Character 1 Section	Character 2 Body System	Character 3 Root Type	Character 4 Type Qualifier	Character 5 Qualifier	Character 6 Qualifier	Character 7 Qualifier
G	Z	B	1	Z	Z	Z
Mental health	None	Electroconvulsive therapy	Unilateral— multiple seizure	None	None	None

There are 12 values representing mental health root types, as listed in table 16.1, along with their corresponding definitions.

Examples of commonly performed mental health procedures in the inpatient setting include:

GZB1ZZZ   ECT (electroconvulsive therapy), unilateral, multiple seizure
GZ2ZZZZ   Crisis intervention
GZHZZZZ   Group psychotherapy

TABLE 16.1   Root Type Values in the Mental Health Section

Value	Description	Definition
1	Psychological tests	The administration and interpretation of standardized psychological tests and measurement instruments for the assessment of psychological function
2	Crisis intervention	Treatment of a traumatized, acutely disturbed or distressed individual for the purpose of short-term stabilization
3	Medication management	Monitoring and adjusting the use of medications for the treatment of a mental health disorder
5	Individual psychotherapy	Treatment of an individual with a mental health disorder by behavioral, cognitive, psychoanalytic, psychodynamic, or psychophysiological means to improve functioning or well-being
6	Counseling	The application of psychological methods to treat an individual with normal developmental issues and psychological problems in order to increase function, improve well-being, alleviate distress, address maladjustment, or resolve crises
7	Family psychotherapy	Treatment that includes one or more family members of an individual with a mental health disorder by behavioral, cognitive, psychoanalytic, psychodynamic, or psychophysiological means to improve functioning or well-being
B	Electroconvulsive therapy	The application of controlled electrical voltages to treat a mental health disorder
C	Biofeedback	Provision of information from the monitoring and regulating of physiological processes in conjunction with cognitive-behavioral techniques to improve patient functioning or well-being
F	Hypnosis	Induction of a state of heightened suggestibility by auditory, visual, and tactile techniques to elicit an emotional or behavioral response
G	Narcosynthesis	Administration of intravenous barbiturates in order to release suppressed or repressed thoughts
H	Group psychotherapy	Treatment of two or more individuals with a mental health disorder by behavioral, cognitive, psychoanalytic, psychodynamic, or psychophysiological means to improve functioning or well-being
J	Light therapy	Application of specialized light treatments to improve functioning or well-being

Substance Abuse Treatment

The Substance Abuse Treatment Section of ICD-10-PCS is structured as a smaller version of the Mental Health Section. Once again, the most important character in these codes is the third character, which describes the root type, while the fourth character is a qualifier that further classifies the root type. The remaining characters (second, fifth, sixth, and seventh) only function as placeholders and do not represent specific information about the procedure. The value Z is used as the placeholder for these characters. The following example demonstrates the structure of ICD-10-PCS codes in the Substance Abuse Treatment Section.

Methadone maintenance medication management

Character 1 Section	Character 2 Body System	Character 3 Root Type	Character 4 Type Qualifier	Character 5 Qualifier	Character 6 Qualifier	Character 7 Qualifier
H	Z	8	1	Z	Z	Z
Substance abuse treatment	None	Medication management	Methadone maintenance	None	None	None

Seven values represent substance abuse treatment root types, as listed in table 16.2, along with their corresponding definitions.

Examples of commonly provided substance abuse treatments in the inpatient setting include:

HZ2ZZZZ   Detoxification from alcohol and/or drugs
HZ83ZZZ   Medication management with Antabuse
HZ81ZZZ   Medication management with methadone
HZ41ZZZ   Behavioral group counseling

TABLE 16.2   Root Type Values in the Substance Abuse Treatment Section

Value	Description	Definition
2	Detoxification services	Detoxification from alcohol and/or drugs
3	Individual counseling	The application of psychological methods to treat an individual with addictive behavior
4	Group counseling	The application of psychological methods to treat two or more individuals with addictive behavior
5	Individual psychotherapy	Treatment of an individual with addictive behavior by behavioral, cognitive, psychoanalytic, psychodynamic, or psychophysiological means
6	Family counseling	The application of psychological methods that includes one or more family members to treat an individual with addictive behavior
8	Medication management	Monitoring and adjusting the use of replacement medications for the treatment of addiction
9	Pharmacotherapy	The use of replacement medications for the treatment of addiction

EXERCISE 16.4

Code the following procedures.

1. Individual supportive psychotherapy   GZ56ZZZ

2. Crisis intervention   GZ2ZZZZ

3. Substance abuse behavioral group counseling   HZ41ZZZ

4. Electroconvulsive therapy, bilateral, multiple seizures   GZB3ZZZ

5. Alcohol abuse detoxification   HZ2ZZZZ

Coding OF Diseases OF THE Blood AND Blood-Forming Organs, Certain Disorders Involving THE Immune Mechanism, AND Diseases OF THE Nervous System

CHAPTER 17

Diseases of the Blood and Blood-Forming Organs and Certain Disorders Involving the Immune Mechanism

CHAPTER OVERVIEW

- Diseases of the blood and blood-forming organs are classified in chapter 3 of ICD-10-CM.

- Anemia is the most common condition dealt with in chapter 3.

  — It can be caused by chronic or acute blood loss, chronic disease, or the use of chemotherapy. Acute blood loss anemia may occur after surgery or trauma.

  — The use of precise terminology is important in classifying anemias.

- A variety of codes are associated with sickle-cell anemia.

  — It is important to distinguish between sickle cell anemia and sickle cell trait.

  — Other conditions for sickle cell include Hb-SS disease and thalassemia.

- Coagulation defects are another type of disease of the blood.

  — They affect clotting time and ability.

  — Hypercoagulation is also a possible condition.

- Diseases may decrease or increase the production of white blood cells (leukocytes). These diseases are classified according to whether the count is low or elevated.

LEARNING OUTCOMES

After studying this chapter you should be able to:

- Code the various types of anemia.

- Understand when and when not to code a coagulation defect because certain drug therapies are being used.

- Distinguish among the various diseases of the white blood cells and the various types of white blood cells.

TERMS TO KNOW

Anemia
a condition in which blood is deficient in the amount of hemoglobin in red blood cells or in the volume of red blood cells

Aplastic anemia
a condition in which there is a deficiency of red blood cells because the bone marrow is failing to produce them

Pancytopenia
a type of aplastic anemia in which red blood cells, white blood cells, and platelets are all deficient

Sickle-cell anemia
a hereditary disease of the red blood cells passed to a child when both parents carry the genetic trait

Sickle-cell trait
a condition that occurs when a child receives the trait from only one parent

Thrombocytopenia
a deficiency in platelets, the cells that are important in blood clotting

REMEMBER . . .

A variety of conditions can be classified as an anemia. Be sure to check with the diagnosing physician if the terminology in the medical report is nonspecific or misleading.

CHAPTER 17 :

*Diseases of
the Blood and
Blood-Forming
Organs
and Certain
Disorders
Involving
the Immune
Mechanism*

INTRODUCTION

Diseases of the blood and blood-forming organs—including bone marrow, lymphatic tissue, platelets, and coagulation factors—are classified in chapter 3 of ICD-10-CM. Chapter 3 also includes certain disorders involving the immune mechanism, such as immunodeficiency disorders except human immunodeficiency virus (HIV) disease. Neoplastic diseases, such as leukemia, are classified in chapter 2 of ICD-10-CM along with other neoplastic diseases. Diseases of the blood and blood-forming organs complicating pregnancy, childbirth, or the puerperium are reclassified in chapter 15 of ICD-10-CM. Anemia of pregnancy, for example, is coded O99.01-, with an additional code from chapter 3 assigned to indicate the specific type of anemia. Hematological disorders of the fetus and newborn are classified as perinatal conditions in chapter 16 of ICD-10-CM.

ANEMIA

The condition that coders must deal with most often in chapter 3 of ICD-10-CM is anemia. Anemia refers to either a reduction in the quantity of hemoglobin or a reduction in the volume of packed red cells, a condition that occurs whenever the equilibrium between red cell loss and red cell production is disturbed. A decrease in production can result from a variety of causes, including aging, bleeding, and cell destruction.

The use of precise terminology is important in classifying anemias. When a diagnostic statement of anemia is not qualified in any way, the coder should review the medical record to determine whether more information can be located in laboratory or pathology reports or in a hematology consultation before the code for an unspecified type of anemia is assigned. Remember, however, that a code should not be assigned on the basis of a diagnostic report alone; when it appears that a more specific type of anemia is present, the coder should check with the physician for concurrence.

Deficiency Anemias

Iron-deficiency anemias are classified in category D50. This type of anemia may be due to a chronic blood loss (D50.0) from conditions such as chronic hemorrhagic gastrointestinal conditions or menorrhagia, or to inadequate intake of dietary iron (D50.8). If the cause is unspecified, code D50.9 is assigned. Note, however, that iron-deficiency anemia specified as secondary to acute blood loss is assigned to code **D62, Acute posthemorrhagic anemia,** rather than to category D50. Other deficiency anemias are coded according to the type of deficiency, such as vitamin B12 (category D51), folate (category D52), or other nutritional deficiencies (category D53), with a fourth character indicating the specific type of deficiency, such as dietary folate deficiency anemia or B12 vitamin deficiency due to intrinsic factor deficiency. In addition, code **D52.1, Drug-induced folate deficiency anemia,** requires that a code from T36–T50 be coded first to identify the drug.

CHAPTER 17

*Diseases of
the Blood and
Blood-Forming
Organs
and Certain
Disorders
Involving
the Immune
Mechanism*

EXERCISE 17.1

Code the following diagnoses and procedures. Do not assign External cause of morbidity codes.

---

1. Anemia, hypochromic, microcytic, with iron deficiency,   D50.9
   cause unknown

---

2. Macrocytic anemia secondary to selective vitamin B12   D51.1
   malabsorption with proteinuria

Anemia Due to Acute Blood Loss

It is important to distinguish between anemia due to chronic blood loss and anemia due to acute blood loss, because the two conditions have entirely different codes in ICD-10-CM. Acute blood-loss anemia results from a sudden, significant loss of blood over a brief period of time. It may occur due to trauma, such as laceration, or a rupture of the spleen or other injury of abdominal viscera, where no external blood loss is noted. A diagnosis of acute blood-loss anemia should be supported by documented evidence of the condition, such as a sustained, significant lowering of the hemoglobin level and/or hematocrit.

Acute blood-loss anemia may occur following surgery, but it is not necessarily a complication of the procedure and should not be coded as a postoperative complication unless the physician identifies it as such. Many surgical procedures, such as hip replacement, routinely involve a considerable amount of bleeding as an expected part of the operation. This may or may not result in anemia; a code for anemia should be assigned only when the anemia is documented by the physician. If, in the physician's clinical judgment, surgery results in an expected amount of blood loss and the physician does not describe the patient as having anemia or a complication of surgery, do not assign a code for the blood loss. If a postoperative blood count is low enough to suggest anemia, it is appropriate to ask the physician whether a diagnosis of anemia should be added. The coder should not assume, however, that mention of blood loss and/or transfusion during surgery is an indication that anemia is present. Blood replacement is sometimes carried out as a preventive measure. When postoperative anemia is documented without specification of acute blood loss, code **D64.9, Anemia, unspecified,** is the default. Code **D62, Acute posthemorrhagic anemia,** should be assigned when postoperative anemia is due to acute blood loss. When neither the diagnostic statement nor review of the medical record indicates whether a blood-loss anemia is acute or chronic, code **D50.0, Iron deficiency anemia secondary to blood loss (chronic),** should be assigned.

CHAPTER 17

*Diseases of
the Blood and
Blood-Forming
Organs
and Certain
Disorders
Involving
the Immune
Mechanism*

EXERCISE 17.2

Code the following diagnoses and procedures. Do not assign External cause of morbidity codes.

1. Anemia due to blood loss from chronic gastric ulcer	D50.0
	K25.4
2. Anemia, chronic, secondary to blood loss due to adenomyosis	D50.0
	N80.0
3. Posthemorrhagic anemia due to acute blood loss following perforation of chronic bleeding duodenal ulcer	D62
	K26.6

Anemia of Chronic Disease

Patients with chronic illnesses are often seen with anemia, which may be the cause of the health care admission or encounter. Treatment is often directed at the anemia, not the underlying condition. Codes for this type of anemia are classified as follows:

- Anemia in chronic kidney disease: Code first the underlying chronic kidney disease (CKD) with a code from category N18 to indicate the stage of CKD, and code D63.1.

- Anemia in neoplastic disease: Code first the neoplasm (C00–D49) responsible for the anemia and code D63.0. Code D63.0 is for anemia in, due to, or with the malignancy, and not due to the antineoplastic chemotherapy drugs, which is an adverse effect.

- Anemia of other chronic disease: Code first the underlying chronic disease, followed by code D63.8.

Anemia Due to Chemotherapy

Antineoplastic chemotherapy–induced anemia is classified to code **D64.81, Anemia due to antineoplastic chemotherapy.** This type of anemia is rarely a hemolytic process and is not truly an aplastic process. Antineoplastic chemotherapy–induced changes are generally short term and do not usually reduce the marrow cellularity to a point of aplasia. When the admission/encounter is for management of an anemia associated with an adverse effect of chemotherapy, and the only treatment is for anemia, the appropriate adverse effect code should be sequenced first, followed by the appropriate codes for the anemia and neoplasm.

Anemia due to chemotherapy should not be confused with aplastic anemia due to antineoplastic chemotherapy, which is coded to **D61.1, Drug-induced aplastic anemia.** Anemia due to a drug, where the drug is not specified, is coded to the type of anemia (or to code D64.9 if the type of anemia is not specified).

Aplastic Anemia

Aplastic anemia (D60.- and D61.-) is caused by a failure of the bone marrow to produce red blood cells. The condition may be congenital, but it is usually idiopathic or acquired. It may be due to an underlying disease such as a malignant neoplasm or an infection (for example, viral hepatitis). It may also be caused by exposure to ionizing radiation, chemicals, or drugs, and it often results from treatment for malignancy. Aplastic anemia due to drugs is coded to **D61.1, Drug-induced aplastic anemia.** Aplastic anemia due to infection, radiation, other external agents, or that is toxic is coded to D61.2. Idiopathic aplastic anemia is coded to D61.3. When the type of anemia is not specified but appears to be related to a diagnosis of malignancy or treatment for malignancy, the physician should be queried to determine whether the code for aplastic anemia may be appropriate.

Pancytopenia (D61.81) is a type of aplastic anemia that represents a deficiency of all three elements of the blood. When a patient has anemia (deficiency of red cells), neutropenia (deficiency of white cells), and thrombocytopenia (deficiency of platelets), only the code for pancytopenia (D61.81) should be assigned. Code **D61.09, Other constitutional aplastic anemia,** is assigned if the pancytopenia is congenital rather than due to chronic disease. Do not assign code D61.81 if the pancytopenia is due to, or with, aplastic anemia (D61.-), bone marrow infiltration (D61.82), congenital (pure) red cell aplasia (D61.01), drug induced (D61.1), hairy cell leukemia (C91.4-), HIV disease (B20.-), leukoerythroblastic anemia (M61.82), myelodysplastic syndromes (D46.-), or myeloproliferative disease (D47.1-).

EXERCISE 17.3

Code the following diagnoses and procedures.

---

1. Aplastic anemia due to accidental benzene exposure (subsequent encounter)

   T52.1x1D
   D61.2

---

2. Myelophthisic anemia

   D61.82

Sickle-Cell Anemia

In coding sickle-cell disorders, it is important to understand the difference between sickle-cell anemia or disease (D57.0-, D57.1-, D57.2-, D57.4-, and D57.8-) and sickle-cell trait (D57.3). Sickle-cell disease is a hereditary disease of the red blood cells; the disease is passed to a child when both parents carry the genetic trait. Sickle-cell trait occurs when a child receives the genetic trait from only one parent. Patients with sickle-cell trait do not generally develop sickle-cell disease; they are carriers of the trait. When a medical record contains both the terms "sickle-cell trait" and "sickle-cell disease," only the code for the sickle-cell disease is assigned.

A code from subcategory D57.0, Hb-SS disease with crisis, or subcategory D57.21, Sickle cell/ Hb-C disease, is assigned when vaso-occlusive crises or other crises are present. These subcategories are further subdivided to specify the type of crisis, such as acute chest syndrome (D57.01 or D57.211) or splenic sequestration (D57.02 or D57.212). If a condition such as cerebrovascular embolism occurs, a code should also be assigned to indicate its presence.

194

CHAPTER 17

*Diseases of
the Blood and
Blood-Forming
Organs
and Certain
Disorders
Involving
the Immune
Mechanism*

Another possible type of sickle-cell disease is sickle-cell thalassemia. Specific codes are available for sickle-cell thalassemia with crisis (D57.41-) or without crisis (D57.40). Codes in subcategory D57.41- have an additional sixth character to specify the type of crisis.

Other sickle-cell disorders include Hb-SD disease and Hb-SE disease, which are classified to subcategory D57.8. Codes in subcategory D57.8 have additional characters to specify whether there is crisis and the type of crisis when present.

EXERCISE 17.4

Code the following diagnoses. Do not assign External cause of morbidity codes.

1.	Classical hemophilia	D66
2.	Sickle-cell Hb-SS disease	D57.1
3.	Hereditary spherocytic, hemolytic anemia	D58.0
4.	Thalassemia	D56.9
5.	Sickle-cell crisis with acute chest syndrome	D57.01

COAGULATION DEFECTS

Coagulation defects are characterized by prolonged clotting time. Some are congenital in origin; others are acquired. **Hemorrhagic disorder due to intrinsic circulating anticoagulants,** code **D68.31,** is essentially the only condition that presents any problem to the coder. This condition results from the presence of circulating anticoagulants in the blood that interfere with normal clotting. These anticoagulants are usually inherent or intrinsic in the blood, like other coagulation defects, but occasionally may be augmented by long-term anticoagulant therapy. This condition is a relatively rare disorder, even more so when it occurs as a result of anticoagulant therapy.

Bleeding in a patient who is being treated with Coumadin, heparin, or another anticoagulant does not indicate that a hemorrhagic disorder due to intrinsic circulating anticoagulant is present. In this situation, assign code **T45.5-, Poisoning by, adverse effect of and underdosing of anticoagulants and antithrombotic drugs,** to indicate any administered anticoagulant, with code **D68.32, Hemorrhagic disorder due to extrinsic circulating anticoagulants.** Code D68.31 is not assigned unless the physician specifically documents a diagnosis of hemorrhagic disorder due to intrinsic circulating anticoagulants.

Heparin-induced thrombocytopenia (D75.82) is one of the most severe side effects of heparin therapy. Heparin therapy is widely used to prevent and treat clotting disorders. In some people, heparin triggers autoimmune conditions of severe platelet deficiency with severe thrombotic (clot-related) complications.

Hypercoagulable states refer to a group of acquired and inherited disorders caused by increased thrombin generation. There is an increased tendency for blood clotting, and there may be fibrin deposition in the small blood vessels. These disorders are divided into primary and secondary hypercoagulable states. Primary hypercoagulable states (D68.5-) are inherited disorders of specific anticoagulant factors. Secondary hypercoagulable states (D68.6-) are primarily acquired disorders that predispose to thrombosis through complex and multifactorial mechanisms involving blood flow abnormalities or defects in blood composition and of vessel walls. Examples of conditions that can cause secondary hypercoagulable states are malignancy, pregnancy, trauma, myeloproliferative disorders, and antiphospholipid antibody syndrome.

Prolonged prothrombin time or other abnormal coagulation profiles should not be coded as a coagulation defect. Code **R79.1, Abnormal coagulation profile,** is assigned for this abnormal laboratory finding. If the patient is receiving Coumadin therapy, however, a prolonged bleeding time is an expected result, and therefore code R79.1 is not assigned. Note also that Coumadin is not a circulating anticoagulant; it induces anticoagulation through other mechanisms. Examples of appropriate code assignments include the following:

T45.515A + K26.4	Duodenal ulcer with hemorrhage due to Coumadin therapy, initial encounter
T45.515D + K29.01	Acute gastritis with hemorrhage due to anticoagulant therapy, subsequent encounter

Following are case examples demonstrating code assignments:

- A 50-year-old man receiving Coumadin therapy is admitted with hematemesis secondary to acute gastritis. A prolonged prothrombin time is reported, secondary to the anticoagulant effects of the Coumadin therapy. Code **K29.01, Acute gastritis with bleeding,** is assigned; code D68.3- is not reported because no hemorrhagic disorder was identified. No code is assigned for the prolonged bleeding time because this is an expected result of Coumadin therapy. Note again that Coumadin is not a circulating anticoagulant; it induces anticoagulation through other mechanisms.

- A patient is admitted following multiple episodes of hematemesis secondary to Coumadin therapy. No significant pathology was discovered. The Coumadin is discontinued, and no recurrence of the bleeding occurs. Code **T45.515A, Adverse effect of anticoagulants, initial encounter,** is assigned to indicate Coumadin as the responsible external agent, with code **K92.0, Hematemesis.** Code D68.3- is not assigned.

DISEASES OF PLATELET CELLS

Thrombocytopenia is a deficiency in the blood cells that help the blood to clot. Post-transfusion purpura is the recipient's response to produce anti-HPA (human platelet antigen) antibodies that destroy the platelets following a transfusion of blood products from an HPA-positive donor. The alloantibody destroys the transfused platelets as well as the recipient's own platelets to produce a severe thrombocytopenia in HPA-negative women who were immunized during previous pregnancy or transfusion. Code **D69.51, Posttransfusion purpura,** is assigned for this rare condition. Code **D69.59, Other secondary thrombocytopenia,** is assigned for secondary thrombocytopenia that is due to dilutional causes, drugs, extracorporeal circulation of blood, massive blood transfusion, platelet alloimmunization, and other secondary thrombocytopenia.

CHAPTER 17

*Diseases of
the Blood and
Blood-Forming
Organs
and Certain
Disorders
Involving
the Immune
Mechanism*

DISEASES OF WHITE BLOOD CELLS

White blood cells (leukocytes) play an important role in the body's immune system by fighting off infection. Many different diseases can affect white blood cells. There are several different types of normal white blood cells (WBCs), including neutrophils, lymphocytes, monocytes, eosinophils, and basophils.

Diseases that may decrease production of WBCs include drug toxicity, vitamin deficiencies, blood diseases, infections (viral diseases, tuberculosis, typhoid), or abnormalities of the bone marrow; or the decrease could be cyclic (varying in severity, possibly due to biorhythm changes). Antibodies may attack WBCs as a result of a disease or because of medications stimulating the immune system. Pooling of WBCs occurs with some overwhelming infections, heart-lung bypass during heart surgery, and hemodialysis.

Some diseases increase the production of WBCs. If all types of WBCs are affected, leukocytosis occurs. Leukocytosis can be caused by infection, inflammation, allergic reaction, malignancy, hereditary disorders, or other miscellaneous causes—for example, medications such as cortisone-like drugs (prednisone), lithium, and nonsteroidal anti-inflammatory drugs. Other illnesses target specific types of WBCs, such as neutrophilia, lymphocytosis, and granulocytosis.

FIGURE 17.1   Four Major Types of Blood Cells

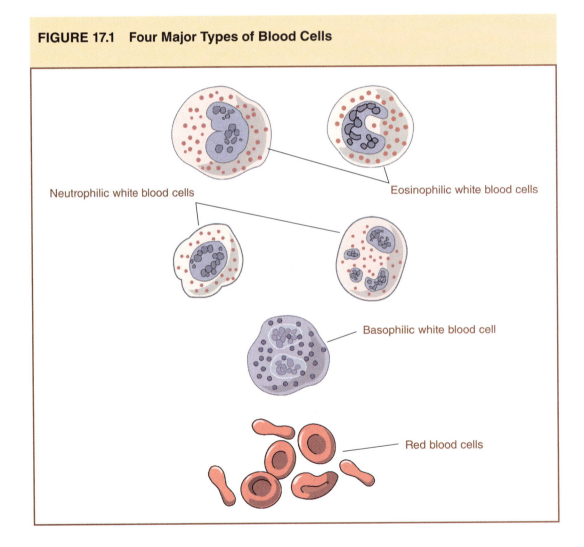

Diseases of the WBCs are primarily classified on the basis of whether the WBC count is low or elevated. In addition, more specific codes are available depending on the type of blood cell affected, as shown by the examples that follow.

CHAPTER 17

*Diseases of
the Blood and
Blood-Forming
Organs
and Certain
Disorders
Involving
the Immune
Mechanism*

- Low neutrophil count or neutropenia (category D70) is further subdivided as follows: congenital (D70.0), agranulocytosis secondary to cancer chemotherapy (D70.1), other drug-induced agranulocytosis (D70.2), neutropenia due to infection (D70.3), cyclic (D70.4), other (D70.8), and unspecified (D70.9).

- Decreased WBC counts (subcategory D72.81-) are classified as follows: decreased lymphocytes or lymphocytopenia (D72.810); other decreased WBC count including basophils, eosinophils, monocytes, or plasmacytes (D72.818); unspecified decreased WBC count (D72.819).

- Elevated WBC counts (subcategory D72.82-) are classified as follows: elevated lymphocytes or lymphocytosis (D72.820); monocytosis (D72.821); plasmacytosis (D72.822); leukemoid reaction including basophilic, lymphocytic, monocytic, myelocytic, or neutrophilic leukemoid reaction (D72.823); basophilia (D72.824); bandemia (D72.825); other elevated WBC count (D72.828); and unspecified leukocytosis (D72.829).

It is important to remember that these codes should not be assigned on the basis of laboratory findings alone. Physician concurrence regarding the significance of the laboratory results should be confirmed before assigning these codes.

DISORDERS OF THE IMMUNE SYSTEM

Categories D80 through D89 classify various disorders of the immune system, with the exception of conditions associated with or due to HIV, which are classified to code B20. The immune disorders discussed in this chapter include the following categories:

D80   Immunodeficiency with predominantly antibody defects
D81   Combined immunodeficiencies
D82   Immunodeficiency associated with other major defects
D83   Common variable immunodeficiency
D84   Other immunodeficiencies
D86   Sarcoidosis
D89   Other disorders involving the immune mechanism, not elsewhere classified

Sarcoidosis

Sarcoidosis is a disease of gradual onset in which abnormal collections of inflammatory cells (granulomas) form as nodules in many organs of the body. Sarcoidosis may be asymptomatic or chronic, and its etiology is unknown. The current working hypothesis is that in genetically susceptible individuals, sarcoidosis is caused through alteration in immune response after exposure to an environmental, occupational, or infectious agent. The granulomas most often appear in the lungs or the lymph nodes, but any organ can be affected. ICD-10-CM provides unique codes within category D86, Sarcoidosis, for the most common sites affected, such as lungs (D86.0), lymph nodes (D86.1), lung with lymph nodes (D86.2), skin (D86.3), meninges (D86.81), cranial nerves (D86.82), eye uvea (D86.83), kidney and ureters (D86.84), myocardium (D86.85), joints (D86.86), muscles (D86.87), and other sites including liver (D86.89) or unspecified (D86.9).

CHAPTER 17

*Diseases of
the Blood and
Blood-Forming
Organs
and Certain
Disorders
Involving
the Immune
Mechanism*

EXERCISE 17.5

Code the following diagnoses.

1. Pancytopenia, congenital   D61.09

2. Cyclic neutropenia   D70.4

3. Hereditary thrombocytopenia   D69.42

4. Anemia   D61.81
    Neutropenia
    Thrombocytopenia

                                    Pancytopenia

5. Autoerythrocyte sensitization purpura   D69.2

6. Cell-mediated immune deficiency with   D82.0
    thrombocytopenia and eczema

7. Sarcoidosis of lung and lymph nodes   D86.2

8. Pernicious anemia, Addison type   D51.0

9. Acute gastritis with hemorrhage, exacerbated by   T45.515A
    heparin therapy, initial encounter   K29.01

                                    Table: heparin

10. Autoimmune lymphoproliferative syndrome   D89.82

Diseases of the Nervous System and Sense Organs

CHAPTER OVERVIEW

- Nervous system diseases can be found in chapter 6 of ICD-10-CM.

- Diseases of the eye and adnexa can be found in chapter 7 of ICD-10-CM, and diseases of the ear and mastoid process are found in chapter 8.

- Dual coding is often required for infectious diseases of the central nervous system.

- Pain can be coded by recording the site of the pain.

  — Codes for pain, not elsewhere classified (G89), can be used for coding pain control or management.

  — If the cause is known but not treated during the encounter, code it as an additional diagnosis.

- Coders must be careful when coding seizures to epilepsy. Seizures may be caused by a variety of conditions and should be coded accordingly.

- Other diseases of the central nervous system covered in this chapter of the handbook are hemiplegia, Parkinson's disease, autonomic dysreflexia, and narcolepsy.

- Many problems of the peripheral nervous system are manifestations of other conditions.

  — These problems are assigned as additional codes.

  — Critical illness polyneuropathy and critical illness myopathy, for example, are complications of sepsis.

- Eye diseases are extremely complicated to code, and understanding the terminology and diagnostic statement completely is vital to proper coding.

- Eye diseases and conditions covered in this handbook include corneal injuries (from both light and wounding), conjunctivitis, cataracts, and glaucoma.

- Hearing loss may be coded as conductive, sensorineural, or a combination of the two.

LEARNING OUTCOMES

After studying this chapter you should be able to:

Explain the difference between the central and peripheral nervous systems and locate the two areas in the ICD-10-CM.

Understand how to code for pain.

Explain what is needed before a code of epilepsy is assigned.

Code for a variety of conditions of the nervous system.

Code disorders of the eye and ear.

TERMS TO KNOW

Central nervous system
the brain and spinal cord

Conductive hearing loss
hearing loss due to a problem with a part of the ear

Peripheral nervous system
all elements of the nervous system except the brain and spinal cord

Sensorineural hearing loss
hearing loss due to a problem with the sensory part of the ear or the nerves associated with hearing

REMEMBER . . .

Due to legal and personal reasons, a code of epilepsy cannot be assigned unless it is clearly diagnosed by a physician.

INTRODUCTION

Diseases of the nervous system are classified in chapter 6 of ICD-10-CM. Eye and adnexa diseases can be found in chapter 7 of ICD-10-CM, and diseases of the ear and mastoid process are found in chapter 8. Because the nervous system is complex and difficult to comprehend, thinking of it as a two-level system may help to simplify the coding process:

G00–G47; G80–G99   Central nervous system (brain and spinal cord)

G50–G73   Peripheral nervous system (all other neural elements in the rest of the body)

Cerebral degeneration, Parkinson's disease, and meningitis are conditions affecting the central nervous system. Polyneuropathy, myasthenia gravis, and muscular dystrophies affect the peripheral nerves. The peripheral nervous system includes the autonomic nervous system, which regulates the activity of the cardiac muscle, smooth muscle, and glands.

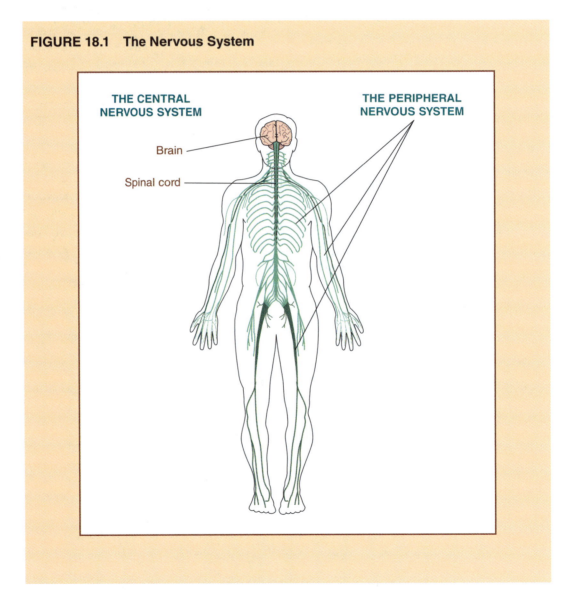

FIGURE 18.1   The Nervous System

THE CENTRAL NERVOUS SYSTEM

THE PERIPHERAL NERVOUS SYSTEM

Brain

Spinal cord

INFLAMMATORY DISEASES OF THE CENTRAL NERVOUS SYSTEM

Infectious diseases of the central nervous system are classified in several ways, and it is imperative that the coder carefully follow the directions provided by the Alphabetic Index and Tabular List. Dual coding is frequently required, with the code for the underlying condition sequenced first, followed by a manifestation code. For example, meningitis due to poliovirus is classified as **A80.9, Acute poliomyelitis, unspecified,** with a manifestation of **G02, Meningitis in other infectious and parasitic diseases classified elsewhere.** Bacterial meningitis due to certain organisms such as *Pneumococcus, Streptococcus,* and *Staphylococcus* is classified in category G00, with a fourth character indicating the responsible organism. Codes G00.2–G00.8 also require an additional code to further specify the organism. Care should be exercised to determine if the condition should be coded to the nervous system, or if there are combination codes in the Infectious Disease chapter that include the condition as well as the infectious organism. For example, candidal meningitis is coded to B37.5 and meningitis due to Lyme disease is coded to A69.21 rather than to categories G01 or G02.

EXERCISE 18.1

Code the following diagnoses and procedures.

1. Candidal meningitis — B37.5

2. Poliovirus encephalitis — A80.9 / G05.3

3. Encephalitis due to rubella — B06.01

4. Herpes zoster with meningitis — B02.1

5. *Staphylococcus aureus* meningitis — G00.3 / B95.6

PARKINSON'S DISEASE

Parkinson's disease, also known as parkinsonism, is a chronic, progressive disorder of the central nervous system characterized by a fine, slowly spreading involuntary tremor, postural instability, and muscle weakness and rigidity. Parkinson's disease is assigned to code G20 and includes primary parkinsonism. Secondary Parkinson's disease (G21.-) is often an adverse effect of the therapeutic use of medication, in which case a code from T36–T50 is assigned first to indicate the responsible drug, followed by the appropriate code from category G21 (e.g., G21.0, G21.11, G21.19). Secondary parkinsonism may also be postencephalitic (G21.3), vascular (G21.4), other (G21.8), or unspecified (G21.9). Parkinson's disease is sometimes caused by syphilis and in that case is coded to **A52.19, Other symptomatic neurosyphilis.**

ALZHEIMER'S DISEASE

Alzheimer's disease is a process of progressive atrophy involving the degeneration of nerve cells. This degeneration leads to mental changes that range from subtle intellectual impairment to dementia with loss of cognitive functions and failure of memory. Alzheimer's disease is coded to category G30 and is further subdivided to specify early onset (G30.0), late onset (G30.1), other (G30.8), or unspecified (G30.9). When associated dementia is present, code **F02.8-, Dementia in conditions classified elsewhere,** is assigned as an additional diagnosis. For example:

G30.9	Alzheimer's disease [without any mention of dementia]
G30.1 + F02.81	Dementia with behavioral disturbance due to late onset Alzheimer's disease

EPILEPSY

Epilepsy is a paroxysmal disorder of cerebral function characterized by recurrent seizures. Coders must not assume, however, that any diagnostic statement describing convulsions or seizures should be coded to epilepsy; these conditions also occur in a number of other diseases, such as brain tumor, cerebrovascular accident, alcoholism, electrolyte imbalance, and febrile conditions. Grand mal seizures, for example, can be due to causes other than epilepsy. Because a diagnosis of epilepsy can have serious legal and personal implications for the patient, such as the inability to obtain a driver's license, a code for epilepsy must not be assigned unless the physician clearly identifies the condition as such in the diagnostic statement. When the diagnosis is stated only in terms of convulsion or seizure without any further identification of the cause, code **R56.9, Unspecified convulsions,** should be assigned. When the physician mentions a history of seizure in the workup but does not include any mention of seizures in the diagnostic statement, no code should be assigned unless clear documentation indicates that the criteria for reporting the condition have been met and the physician agrees that a code should be added. Please note that the classification assigns seizure disorder and recurrent seizures to epilepsy G40.909, whereas the main term "seizure(s)" is indexed to R56.9

ICD-10-CM provides a fifth-character subclassification for category G40, Epilepsy and recurrent seizures, that permits identification of epilepsy as intractable when so described by the physician. Terms such as "pharmacoresistant (pharmacologically resistant)," "poorly controlled," "refractory (medically)," and "treatment resistant" are considered to be equivalent to intractable. The coder should not assume that the condition is intractable from general statements in the medical record. In addition, a sixth character is used to identify whether status epilepticus is present.

203

CHAPTER 18

*Diseases of
the Nervous
System and
Sense Organs*

EXERCISE 18.2

Code the following diagnoses. Do not assign External cause of morbidity codes.

1.	Parkinson's disease	G20
2.	Secondary parkinsonism due to prescribed Thorazine (neuroleptic drug), initial encounter	T43.3x5A G21.11
3.	Intractable epilepsy, grand mal type, status epilepticus	G40.311
4.	Poorly controlled generalized idiopathic epilepsy	G40.319
5.	Intractable focal epilepsy	G40.119
6.	Febrile convulsions, recurrent	R56.00
7.	Alzheimer's disease with delirium	G30.9 F05

HEADACHE AND MIGRAINE

A diagnosis of headache without any further specificity is classified to chapter 18 of ICD-10-CM and coded to **R51, Headache.** Migraines are classified to category G43, while specific headaches are classified to category G44, Other headache syndromes, in chapter 6, Diseases of the Nervous System.

Migraine is a neurological syndrome characterized by altered bodily perceptions, severe headaches, and nausea and vomiting. Approximately one-third of people who suffer from migraine headaches perceive an aura—unusual visual, olfactory, or other sensory experiences that signal the migraine will soon occur. The following terms are considered equivalent to intractable: "pharmacoresistant (pharmacologically resistant)," "treatment resistant," "refractory (medically)," and "poorly controlled." Status migrainosus generally refers to a severe migraine attack that lasts for more than 72 hours. However, the designation of status migrainosus should be confirmed by the physician.

ICD-10-CM classifies migraines to category G43 as follows:

G43.001–G43.019	Migraine without aura
G43.101–G43.119	Migraine with aura
G43.401–G43.419	Hemiplegic migraine
G43.501–G43.519	Persistent migraine aura without cerebral infarction
G43.601–G43.619	Persistent migraine aura with cerebral infarction
G43.701–G43.719	Chronic migraine without aura
G43.a01–G43.a19	Cyclical vomiting
G43.b01–G43.b19	Ophthalmoplegic migraine
G43.c01–G43.c19	Periodic headache syndromes in child or adult
G43.d01–G43.d19	Menstrual migraine
G43.801–G43.819	Other migraine
G43.901–G43.919	Migraine, unspecified

Specific headaches are classified in chapter 6 of ICD-10-CM under Other headache syndromes (category G44) as follows:

G44.001–G44.099	Cluster headaches and other trigeminal autonomic cephalgias
G44.10–G44.11	Vascular headache, not elsewhere classified
G44.201–G44.229	Tension-type headache
G44.301–G44.329	Posttraumatic headache
G44.40–G44.41	Drug-induced headache, not elsewhere classified
G44.51–G44.59	Complicated headache syndromes
G44.81–G44.89	Other specific headache syndromes

Headache following lumbar puncture is assigned to code **G97.1, Other reaction to spinal or lumbar puncture.**

NARCOLEPSY

Narcolepsy is a chronic neurological disorder characterized by the inability to regulate sleep and wakefulness normally. Symptoms are excessive daytime sleepiness, sleep paralysis (paralysis upon falling asleep or waking up), cataplexy (sudden, brief episodes of paralysis or muscle weakness), and vivid hallucinations (vivid dreamlike images that occur at sleep onset). Other possible symptoms are disturbed nighttime sleep, leg jerks, nightmares, and frequent awakenings. Irresistible sleep attacks may occur throughout the day regardless of the amount or quality of prior nighttime sleep. Affected individuals may fall asleep at work or school or while eating, talking, or driving.

ICD-10-CM distinguishes between subcategory G47.41- (narcolepsy) and G47.42- (narcolepsy in conditions classified elsewhere). Fifth characters distinguish between narcolepsy with cataplexy (G47.411, G47.421) and without cataplexy (G47.419, G47.429).

HEMIPLEGIA/HEMIPARESIS

Hemiplegia is paralysis of one side of the body. It is classified to category G81, with a fifth character to indicate the side affected and whether the affected side is dominant or nondominant.

When information is not available regarding whether the affected side is dominant or non-dominant, and when the classification does not provide a default, code selection is as follows: For ambidextrous patients, the default should also be dominant. If the left side is affected, the default is non-dominant. If the right side is affected, the default is dominant. This guideline applies to codes from category G81, Hemiplegia and hemiparesis, and subcategories G83.1, Monoplegia of lower limb; G83.2, Monoplegia of upper limb; and G83.3, Monoplegia, unspecified.

Hemiplegia occurring in connection with a cerebrovascular accident (CVA) often clears quickly and is sometimes called a transient hemiplegia. Hemiplegia is not inherent to an acute CVA; therefore, a code from category G81, Hemiplegia and hemiparesis, is assigned as an additional code when it occurs. Even if it resolves without treatment, it affects the patient's care. Any neurologic deficits caused by CVA should be reported even when they have resolved at the time of discharge. When the patient is admitted at a later time with hemiplegia and hemiparesis due to sequela of cerebrovascular disease, a code from category I69 is assigned to indicate that the condition is a late effect of a CVA. (See chapter 28 of this handbook for more discussion of cerebrovascular disease.)

Examples of appropriate coding for hemiplegia follow:

I66.9 + G81.91	Cerebral thrombosis with transient right hemiplegia that has cleared by discharge
I66.9 + G81.91	Cerebral thrombosis with hemiplegia right dominant side
I69.952	Hemiplegia of left dominant side due to previous CVA
G81.90 + S34.109S	Hemiparesis due to old lumbar spinal cord injury

PAIN

Pain may be coded by reporting the site of pain. These codes may be found in the symptom chapter (e.g., headache, R51) or in the appropriate body system chapter (e.g., pain in limb, M79.609). Codes from category G89, Pain, not elsewhere classified, may be used in conjunction with the site of pain codes if the category G89 code provides more detail about acute or chronic pain and neoplasm-related pain unless otherwise indicated below.

The determination of whether the pain is acute, chronic, or chronic pain syndrome is dependent on the provider's documentation. There is no time frame defining when pain becomes chronic. If the pain is not specified as acute or chronic, post-thoracotomy, postprocedural, or neoplasm related, do not assign codes from category G89. A code from category G89 should not be assigned if the underlying (definitive) diagnosis is known, unless the reason for the encounter is pain control/management and not management of the underlying condition.

When an admission or encounter is for a procedure aimed at treating the underlying condition, such as a spinal fusion for treatment of pain associated with a vertebral fracture, a code for the underlying condition (e.g., vertebral fracture) should be assigned as the principal diagnosis. No code from category G89 should be assigned.

Encounter/Admission for Pain Control/Management

Category G89 codes may be used as the principal diagnosis or first-listed code when pain control or pain management is the reason for the admission/encounter. These encounters are typically not for diagnostic workup or treatment of the underlying condition but for management of pain. In these situations, if the underlying cause of the pain is known, report it as an additional diagnosis. An example is a patient with displaced intervertebral disc, nerve impingement, and severe back pain who presents for injection of steroid into the spinal canal. The injection is intended to relieve the pain, but it does not treat the displaced disc.

If the admission is for control of pain related to, associated with, or due to a malignancy, code **G89.3, Neoplasm related pain (acute) (chronic),** should be assigned. The underlying neoplasm is reported as an additional diagnosis. Because the neoplasm code will provide information regarding the specific site, an additional code for the site of pain should not be assigned. When the reason for the admission/encounter is management of the neoplasm and the pain associated with the neoplasm is also documented, code G89.3 may be assigned as an additional diagnosis. It is not necessary to assign an additional code for the site of the pain.

If the admission or encounter is for a procedure to treat the underlying condition, the underlying condition should be assigned as the principal or first-listed diagnosis. For example, if a patient is admitted for a spinal fusion to treat lumbar spinal stenosis, assign code **M48.06, Spinal stenosis, lumbar region,** as the principal diagnosis. No code from category G89 should be assigned.

Patients with chronic pain whose conservative therapies have failed may undergo insertion of neurostimulators for pain control. In such cases, the appropriate pain code is assigned as the principal or first-listed diagnosis. When an admission or encounter is for a procedure aimed at treating the underlying condition, and a neurostimulator is inserted for pain control during the same admission/encounter, a code for the underlying condition should be assigned as the principal diagnosis with the pain code as a secondary diagnosis.

If the encounter is for any other reason except pain control or pain management and a related definitive diagnosis for the pain has not been established (confirmed) by the provider, the code for the specific site of pain should be assigned first, followed by the appropriate code from category G89. If the definitive diagnosis has been established, assign the code for the definitive diagnosis.

Postoperative Pain

Post-thoracotomy pain and other postoperative pain are classified to subcategories G89.1 and G89.2, depending on whether the pain is acute or chronic. The default for post-thoracotomy and other postoperative pain not specified as acute or chronic is the code for the acute form. Postoperative pain associated with a specific postoperative complication (such as painful wire sutures) or associated with devices, implants, or grafts left in a surgical site (such as a painful hip prosthesis) is assigned to the appropriate code(s) found in chapter 19 of ICD-10-CM, Injury, Poisoning, and Certain Other Consequences of External Causes. A code from category G89 is assigned as an additional code to identify acute or chronic pain (G89.18 or G89.28).

Postoperative pain may be reported as the principal or first-listed diagnosis when the reason for the encounter or admission is postoperative pain control/management. Postoperative pain may be reported as a secondary diagnosis code when a patient presents for outpatient surgery and develops an unusual or inordinate amount of postoperative pain. Please note that routine or expected postoperative pain immediately after surgery should not be coded.

AUTONOMIC DYSREFLEXIA

Autonomic dysreflexia is a syndrome characterized by an abrupt onset of excessively high blood pressure caused by an uncontrolled sympathetic nervous system discharge in persons with spinal cord injury, usually at or above the T6 level. Anything that would ordinarily cause pain below this level may trigger a parasympathetic response resulting in bradycardia, blurred vision, and sweating. True autonomic dysreflexia is potentially life threatening and is considered a medical emergency. Code **G90.4, Autonomic dysreflexia,** is used to report this condition. It is not necessary to code each manifestation or symptom separately. Unlike most dual coding, whereby the underlying condition is listed first, in this case the code for the dysreflexia is sequenced first, with an additional code for the underlying chronic condition that has precipitated this life-threatening condition (e.g., pressure ulcer, fecal impaction, urinary tract infection).

HYDROCEPHALUS

Normal pressure hydrocephalus (NPH) or secondary NPH can be caused by any condition in which the flow of cerebrospinal fluid (CSF) is blocked, such as subarachnoid hemorrhage, head trauma, cerebral infarction, infection, tumor, or complications of surgery. Assign code **G91.0, Communicating hydrocephalus,** for secondary NPH. Obstructive hydrocephalus develops secondary to a blockage in the normal circulation of CSF in the brain. In most instances, the blockage affects the third and fourth ventricles at the level of the aqueduct of Sylvius, also referred to as an aqueductal obstruction, which can result from scarring or tumor. Assign code **G91.1, Obstructive hydrocephalus,** for this acquired condition. Idiopathic normal pressure hydrocephalus (INPH) can occur without any identifiable cause. Code **G91.2, (Idiopathic) normal pressure hydrocephalus (INPH),** is assigned for this type of acquired hydrocephalus. If the medical record documentation does not specify whether the hydrocephalus is congenital or acquired, code **G91.9 Hydrocephalus, unspecified,** should be assigned.

ENCEPHALOPATHY

Encephalopathy is a general term used to describe any disorder of cerebral function. It is a very broad term and in most cases will be preceded by various terms describing the reason, cause, or special conditions leading to the brain disorder. It is important to carefully note these additional terms, as they will affect code assignment. More than 150 different terms modify or precede "encephalopathy" in the medical literature—not all of them are classified to chapter 6 of ICD-10-CM. Some of the more common encephalopathies are noted below:

- *Anoxic encephalopathy* refers to brain damage due to lack of oxygen. This type of encephalopathy is assigned to **G93.1, Anoxic brain damage, not elsewhere classified.**

- *Alcoholic encephalopathy* is a serious complication of alcoholic liver disease usually caused by excessive drinking for several years. It results in a loss of specific brain function (damage of brain tissue) caused by a thiamine deficiency. Alcoholic encephalopathy is classified to **G31.2, Degeneration of nervous system due to alcohol.**

- *Hepatic encephalopathy* is brain damage due to liver disease, and it is classified to category K72, Hepatic failure, not elsewhere classified.

- *Metabolic encephalopathy* is temporary or permanent damage to the brain due to lack of glucose, oxygen or other metabolic agent, or organ dysfunction. Symptoms include an altered state of consciousness, usually characterized as delirium, confusion, or agitation, and changes in behavior or personality. There may also be symptoms of muscle stiffness or rigidity, tremor, stupor, or coma. Symptoms can develop quickly and may resolve when the condition is reversed. Assign code **G93.41, Metabolic encephalopathy,** for this condition. Code G93.41 also includes septic encephalopathy.

- *Toxic encephalopathy* is also known as *toxic-metabolic encephalopathy*. This type of encephalopathy is a degenerative neurologic disorder caused by exposure to toxic substances. It consists of a variety of symptoms, characterized by an altered mental status, and can include memory loss, small personality changes, lack of concentration, involuntary movements, nausea, fatigue, seizures, arm strength problems, and depression. ICD-10-CM classifies this condition to code **G92, Toxic encephalopathy.** A code from categories T51–T65 is assigned first to identify the causative toxic agent.

- *Wernicke's encephalopathy* involves damage to the central nervous system and the peripheral nervous system and is caused by disorders of the liver such as cirrhosis, hepatitis, malnutrition, and conditions in which blood circulation bypasses the liver entirely. The symptoms can range from mild to severe and consist of various neurological symptoms including changes in consciousness, reflexes, and behavior. ICD-10-CM classifies this condition to **E51.2, Wernicke's encephalopathy.**

- *Unspecified encephalopathy* is assigned to code **G93.40, Encephalopathy, unspecified.**

EXERCISE 18.3

Code the following diagnoses and procedures. Do not assign External cause of morbidity codes.

1.	Chronic intractable tension-type headache	G44.211
2.	Cerebrovascular accident with left-sided hemiparesis	I63.9
		G81.92
3.	Severe hypertension and pounding headache due to autonomic dysreflexia due to fecal impaction	G90.4
		K56.41
4.	Severe chronic low back pain due to displaced lumbar disc with neuritis due to previous trauma. Epidural injection of steroid (anti-inflammatory) for pain	G89.21
		M54.5
		M51.16
		3E0S33Z
5.	Metabolic encephalopathy	G93.41
6.	Toxic metabolic encephalopathy	G92

DISORDERS OF THE PERIPHERAL NERVOUS SYSTEM

Disorders of the peripheral nervous system are classified to categories G50 through G73 according to the condition and the nerves involved. Many codes in this section are manifestations of other diseases and are assigned as additional codes, with the underlying condition listed first.

CRITICAL ILLNESS POLYNEUROPATHY

Critical illness polyneuropathy is commonly associated with complications of sepsis and multiple organ failure. It is considered to be secondary to systemic inflammatory response syndrome. Synonyms for critical illness polyneuropathy include neuropathy of critical illness, intensive care unit neuropathy, and intensive care polyneuropathy. Patients with this condition show abnormal electrophysiologic changes consistent with primary axonal degeneration of motor fibers. They also demonstrate severe weakness, making it difficult to wean them from mechanical ventilation. Assign code **G62.81, Critical illness polyneuropathy,** for this condition.

CRITICAL ILLNESS MYOPATHY

Critical illness myopathy is also associated with sepsis. It is a cause of difficulty in weaning patients from mechanical ventilation and prolonged recovery after illness. It is also associated with neuromuscular blocking agents and corticosteroids (in asthma and organ transplant patients), and neuropathy. Code **G72.81, Critical illness myopathy,** is used to report this condition.

EXERCISE 18.4

Code the following diagnoses and procedures.

---

1. Amyloid polyneuropathy — E85.1 + G63

---

2. Morton's neuroma, 3P4 and 4P5 interspaces, left foot — G57.62
   Excision of Morton's neuroma, left foot — 01BG0ZZ

---

3. Tardy palsy due to entrapment of right ulnar nerve — G56.21

---

4. Peripheral polyneuritis, severe, due to chronic alcoholism — G62.1 + F10.20

---

5. Nutritional polyneuropathy — E63.9 + G63

---

6. Tic douloureux — G50.0

DISORDERS OF THE EYE AND ADNEXAE

The classification for diseases of the eye is very detailed, and understanding the terminology used is especially important for the coder. Terms that seem similar may have entirely different meanings. The coder should be sure to fully understand the diagnostic statement in the medical record before assigning a code.

Visual impairment (H54) is classified according to severity, with the status of the lesser eye listed first and the better eye listed second in the code title. If the associated underlying cause of the blindness is known, it should be coded first. ICD-10-CM includes a table with the classification of severity of visual impairment recommended by a World Health Organization study group. The term "low vision" in category H54 comprises categories 1 and 2 of the table; the term "blindness," categories 3, 4, and 5; and the term "unqualified visual loss," category 9. The information is intended to provide the coder with "clues" to identify possible gaps in documentation where provider query may be necessary. It is not intended to replace the need for specific provider documentation to substantiate code assignment. Sample codes include the following:

H54.11   Blindness, right eye, low vision left eye
H54.41   Blindness, right eye, normal vision left eye

Occasionally, visual problems can cause tilting of the head, resulting in ocular torticollis or ocular-induced torticollis. Torticollis refers to abnormal head posture. Palsy of the superior or inferior oblique muscles causes the patient to hold the head at an angle to compensate for the visual disturbance. Ocular torticollis is coded by assigning first the appropriate code for the ocular condition causing the torticollis, e.g., nystagmus (H55.-), strabismus (H50.9), fourth nerve palsy (H49.1-), followed by code **R29.891, Ocular torticollis.**

FIGURE 18.2   The Eye

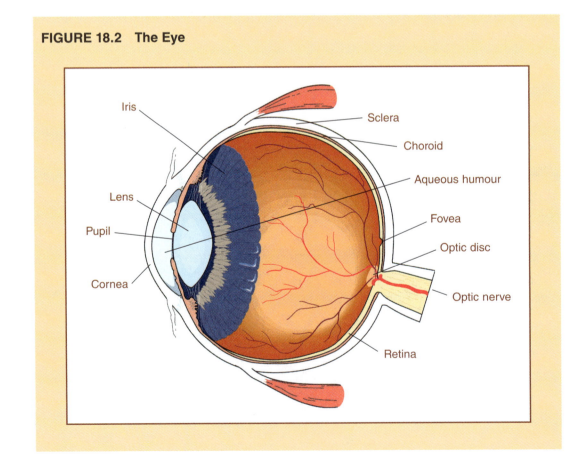

211

CHAPTER 18

*Diseases of
the Nervous
System and
Sense Organs*

Corneal Injury

Code **H16.13-, Photokeratitis,** is assigned for a corneal flash burn, generally referred to as ultraviolet keratitis. The condition typically occurs at high altitudes on highly reflective snow fields or, less often, with a solar eclipse. Artificial sources of ultraviolet light can also cause photokeratitis. These sources include sun-tanning beds, a welder's arc (flash burn, welder's flash, or arc eye), carbon arcs, photographic flood lamps, lightning, electric sparks, and halogen desk lamps. It is always an injury, and the appropriate External cause of morbidity code should be assigned as an additional code, such as codes from category W89, Exposure to man-made visible and ultraviolet light, or code **X32.-, Exposure to sunlight.**

Corneal or corneoscleral lacerations are classified in category S05, Injury of eye and orbit. The fourth characters are assigned to indicate whether there is contusion of eyeball and orbital tissues, whether there is associated prolapse or loss of intraocular tissue, whether the laceration is a penetrating injury, whether it is with or without a foreign body, whether there is avulsion of the eye, and whether the laceration is related to other conditions. The fifth characters indicate unspecified eye, right eye, or left eye. An External cause of morbidity code is assigned for the external cause. Corneal repair is classified as **08Q8XZZ, Repair right cornea, external approach,** or **08Q9XZZ, Repair left cornea, external approach.**

Conjunctivitis

Conjunctivitis (category H10) is an inflammation of the conjunctiva that may be due to infection, allergy, or other cause. When the cause of acute conjunctivitis is a chemical or toxic agent, code H10.21- is used, with a code from categories T51–T65 assigned first to identify the chemical agent and intent (e.g., accidental, assault).

Giant papillary conjunctivitis, also called contact lens–induced papillary conjunctivitis, is a common complication of contact lens wear. It is an inflammation resulting from an allergic reaction to contact lenses. Chronic giant papillary conjunctivitis is classified to subcategory H10.41-. Vernal conjunctivitis (H10.44) is due to an allergic reaction to pollen. Acute toxic conjunctivitis is classified to H10.21-, with a code from categories T51–T65 assigned first to identify the chemical and intent. Conjunctivitis due to chlamydia is classified to A74.0 or to A71.1 when designated as due to trachoma.

Disorders of conjunctivochalasis are reported using code H11.82-. This is a situation in which redundant conjunctiva lies over the lower eyelid margin and covers the lower punctum. It can create a variety of symptoms, from aggravation of a dry eye at the mild stage to disruption of the normal flow of tears at the moderate stage to exposure problems at the severe stage. Treatment consists of a simple local surgical excision to relieve the symptoms.

Code **H16.21-, Exposure keratoconjunctivitis,** is assigned for dry eye related to Bell's palsy. Code **H04.12-, Dry eye syndrome,** is provided by the Index for dry eye syndrome, a disorder of the lacrimal gland. Code H04.12-, however, is inappropriate for the dry eye associated with Bell's palsy, which does not involve the lacrimal gland but is due to exposure to the air resulting from the inability to close the eye as a result of the acute severe facial paralysis of Bell's palsy.

212

CHAPTER 18

*Diseases of
the Nervous
System and
Sense Organs*

EXERCISE 18.5

Code the following diagnoses. Do not assign External cause of morbidity codes.

1. Intermittent monocular esotropia right eye	H50.311
2. Senile entropion, left upper eyelid	H02.034
3. Blepharoptosis, congenital, bilateral	Q10.0
4. Ectropion due to cicatrix left upper eyelid	H02.114
5. Conjunctivochalasis, bilateral	H11.823

Cataracts

In coding cataracts the coder must avoid making assumptions about the type of cataract based on the patient's age or other conditions. A cataract in an older patient is not necessarily senile or mature; the coder should be alert to the terminology used in the diagnostic statement. Cataracts in patients with diabetes are most often senile; a true diabetic cataract is rare, and its code should not be assigned unless the physician clearly identifies it as such.

EXERCISE 18.6

Code the following diagnoses. Do not assign External cause of morbidity codes.

1. True diabetic cataract in type 1 diabetes mellitus	E10.36
2. Incipient senile cataract, right eye	H25.091
Diabetes mellitus, type 2	E11.9
3. Myotonic cataract with Thomsen's disease	G71.12
	H28

Glaucoma

Glaucoma is an eye disease characterized by increased intraocular pressure that causes pathological changes in the optic disk and defects in the field of vision. Category H40, Glaucoma, uses a third, fourth, or fifth character to classify glaucoma by type and to provide more specificity, and a fifth or sixth character to identify the affected eye. Category H42, Glaucoma in diseases classified elsewhere, requires that the underlying condition be coded first, for example, amyloidosis (E85.-), aniridia (Q13.1), or specified metabolic disorder (E70–E88). Glaucoma in diabetes mellitus is classified to the type of diabetes (E08–E13) with -.39. Note that glaucoma in syphilis is coded to **A52.71, Late syphilitic oculopathy,** while tuberculous glaucoma is classified to **A18.59, Other tuberculosis of eye.**

Aqueous misdirection was formerly known as malignant glaucoma. No true malignancy is associated with this type of glaucoma. Aqueous misdirection is characterized by fluid buildup in the back of the eye, pushing the lens and iris forward, blocking off the drain, and thereby increasing the intraocular pressure. This condition is extremely difficult to treat and often requires surgical intervention. Code **H40.83-, Aqueous misdirection,** is used to report this condition.

EXERCISE 18.7

Code the following diagnoses. Do not assign External cause of morbidity codes.

1. Glaucoma secondary to posterior dislocation of lens   H27.139
    due to trauma   H40.30

2. Exophthalmos secondary to thyrotoxicosis   E05.00

3. Acute narrow-angle glaucoma, right eye   H40.211
    Chronic narrow-angle glaucoma, left eye   H40.222

4. Primary open-angle glaucoma, bilateral   H40.11

DISEASES OF THE EAR AND MASTOID PROCESS

Chapter 8 of ICD-10-CM, Diseases of the Ear and Mastoid Process, includes diseases of the external ear (H60–H62), diseases of the middle ear and mastoid (H65–H75), diseases of the inner ear (H80–H83), other disorders of the ear (H90–H94), and intraoperative and postprocedural complications and disorders of the ear and mastoid process not elsewhere classified (H95).

Otitis

Otitis is a general term for infection or inflammation of the ear. Symptoms may include chills, drainage from the ear, earache, buzzing, hearing loss, malaise, irritability, itching or discomfort in the ear or ear canal, nausea, and vomiting. Otitis can affect the inner or outer parts of the ear.

ICD-10-CM classifies otitis to the following categories on the basis of whether it affects the external or middle ear and whether it occurs suddenly and for a short time (acute) or repeatedly over a long period of time (chronic):

H60	Otitis externa
H62	Diseases of external ear in diseases classified elsewhere
H65	Nonsuppurative otitis media
H66	Suppurative and unspecified otitis media
H67	Otitis media in diseases classified elsewhere

For otitis externa (category H60), additional characters provide further specificity regarding the condition, such as infective and noninfective (chemical, actinic, reactive, or eczematoid). Category H65, Nonsuppurative otitis media, is further divided to provide specificity for acute, subacute, or chronic, whether serous, allergic, or mucoid. Suppurative otitis media (H65.-) is further subdivided to identify whether the condition is acute or chronic and whether there is spontaneous rupture of the ear drum.

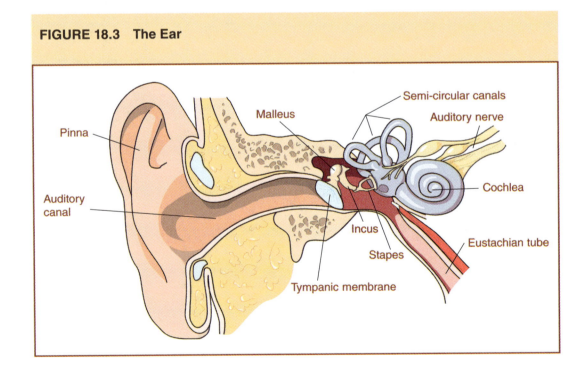

FIGURE 18.3   The Ear

Deafness and Hearing Loss

Hearing loss may be unilateral or bilateral. Most hearing loss is classified in one of three ways:

- Conductive (H90.0–H90.2), with decrease due to a defect in the conductive apparatus of the ear (also called conduction deafness)
- Sensorineural (H90.3–H90.5), with the loss due to a defect in the sensory mechanism of the ear or nerves
- Mixed conductive and sensorineural hearing loss (H90.6–H90.8)

Other classifications of hearing loss are related to the underlying cause, such as the following:

- Ototoxic hearing loss (H91.0-) caused by ingestion of toxic substances. This type of hearing loss requires that the code for the toxic agent be assigned first (T36–T65).
- Presbycusis (H91.1-), or age-related hearing loss with gradually progressing inability to hear. It is considered a sensorineural hearing loss.
- Sudden idiopathic hearing loss (H91.2-), or sudden, unexplained hearing loss.

EXERCISE 18.8

Code the following diagnoses and procedures. Do not assign External cause of morbidity codes.

1.	Congenital external canal atresia	Q16.1
2.	Bilateral otitis media due to measles	B05.3
3.	Sensory hearing loss, bilateral	H90.3
4.	Mixed conductive and sensorineural deafness, bilateral	H90.6
5.	Perforation of tympanic membrane due to chronic suppurative otitis media, right ear	H66.3x1 H72.91
6.	Acute suppurative otitis media, with spontaneous tear of ear drum, right ear	H66.011

Coding OF **Diseases**
OF THE **Respiratory, Digestive,**
AND **Genitourinary Systems**

Diseases of the Respiratory System

CHAPTER OVERVIEW

- Respiratory diseases are classified in chapter 10 of ICD-10-CM.
- Pneumonia is a common infection that is coded several ways.
  - It is coded in combination with the responsible organism.
  - It is coded as a dual classification.
- Influenza may be coded alone or in combination with other codes.
- Chronic obstructive pulmonary disease (COPD) is always caused by another condition.
- Asthma is classified with a fourth character to indicate type and a fifth character to indicate exacerbation or status asthmaticus.
- Pleural effusion is almost always integral to other diseases. Only the code for the underlying disease is assigned.
- Respiratory failure is always due to an underlying condition. Therefore, it is important to be sure that the principal diagnosis and secondary diagnosis are properly assigned.
- Acute pulmonary edema is divided into two categories.
  - Those acute pulmonary edemas of cardiogenic origin take codes that are related to heart failure.
  - Those of noncardiogenic origin take a variety of codes, such as for drowning.
- Procedures involving the respiratory system have a large section of codes. Some of these procedures include biopsies of the bronchus and lung, ablation, thoracoscopic, open, mechanical ventilation, and respiratory assistance not considered mechanical.

LEARNING OUTCOMES

After studying this chapter you should be able to:

- Classify the variety of pneumonia that you will encounter as a coder.
- Determine the correct coding of COPD based on the documented diagnosis.
- Know when to code for respiratory failure as the principal or secondary diagnosis.
- Know how to classify both cardiogenic and noncardiogenic acute pulmonary edemas.
- Code procedures commonly used to treat respiratory system diseases.

TERMS TO KNOW

Acute pulmonary edema
excessive fluid in the tissue and alveolar spaces of the lung

Atelectasis
a collapse of lung tissue; an integral part of pulmonary disease

Bronchospasm
a sudden constriction of the muscles in the walls of the bronchioles

COPD
chronic obstructive pulmonary disease; a general term describing conditions that result in an airway obstruction

Pleural effusion
accumulation of fluid within the pleural spaces

REMEMBER . . .

You should only code for avian influenza or novel H1N1 flu if the case is confirmed. Modifiers such as "suspected" are not adequate to establish a classification.

INTRODUCTION

Except for neoplastic diseases and some major infectious diseases, respiratory diseases are classified in categories J00 through J99 in chapter 10 of ICD-10-CM. Note that *Streptococcus* and *Neisseria* are normal flora for the respiratory system; therefore, their presence does not indicate an infection unless they are seriously out of control. A respiratory infection cannot be assumed from a laboratory report alone; physician concurrence and documentation are necessary. Remember also that infectious organisms are not always identified by laboratory examination, particularly when antibiotic therapy has been started; an infection code may be assigned without laboratory evidence when it is supported by clinical documentation.

PNEUMONIA

Pneumonia is a common respiratory infection that is coded in several ways in ICD-10-CM. Combination codes that account for both pneumonia and the responsible organism are included in chapters 1 and 10 of ICD-10-CM. Examples of appropriate codes for pneumonia include the following:

J15.0	Pneumonia due to *Klebsiella*
J15.21	Pneumonia due to *Staphylococcus aureus*
A02.22	Salmonella pneumonia
B05.2	Post-measles pneumonia
J10.1 + J12.9	Viral pneumonia with influenza

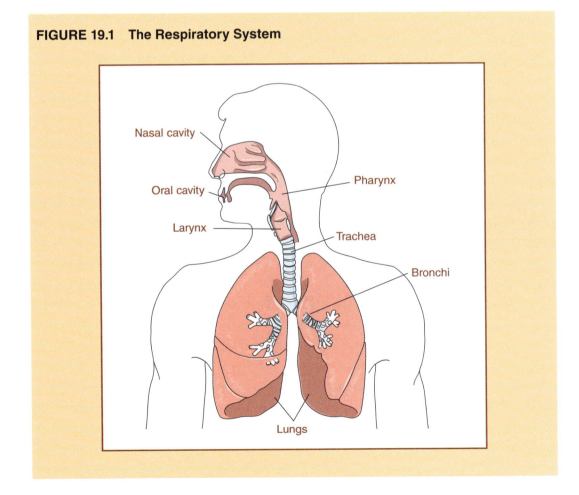

FIGURE 19.1   The Respiratory System

Nasal cavity

Oral cavity

Larynx

Pharynx

Trachea

Bronchi

Lungs

221

CHAPTER 19

*Diseases
of the
Respiratory
System*

Other pneumonias are coded as manifestations of underlying infections classified in chapter 1, and two codes are required in such cases. Examples of this dual classification coding include the following:

I00 + J17   Pneumonia in rheumatic fever
B65.9 + J17   Pneumonia due to schistosomiasis

When the diagnostic statement is pneumonia without any further specification, the coder should review laboratory reports for mention of the causative organism and check with the physician to determine whether there appears to be support for a more definitive diagnosis. When the organism is not identified, code **J18.9, Pneumonia, unspecified organism,** is assigned.

Lobar Pneumonia

A diagnosis of pneumonia that mentions the affected lobe, or "multilobar pneumonia" (pneumonia affecting more than one lobe), should be coded according to the responsible organism, if known. If the provider is unable to identify the organism causing the lobar or multilobar pneumonia, assign code **J18.1, Lobar pneumonia, unspecified organism.** Examples include:

J13   Left lobar pneumococcal pneumonia
J15.21   Multilobar staphylococcal aureus pneumonia
J18.1   Lobar pneumonia

Interstitial Pneumonia

Interstitial pneumonia is characterized by interstitial fibrosis and the shedding of mononuclear cells within the alveolar spaces. If not more specifically identified, it is classified in ICD-10-CM as **J84.9, Interstitial pulmonary disease, unspecified.** Cryptogenic organizing pneumonia, also referred to as bronchiolitis obliterans with organizing pneumonia, is an interstitial lung disease that is diagnosed by pathological examination; it is coded as **J84.8, Other specified interstitial pulmonary diseases.**

Lymphoid interstitial pneumonia (J84.2) is a rare disorder with lymphocytic infiltration of the alveolar interstitium and air spaces. It is the most common cause of pulmonary disease after *Pneumocystis* infection in human immunodeficiency virus (HIV)–positive children. It most often occurs in children with HIV infection and in people of any age with an autoimmune disorder.

Plasma cell interstitial pneumonia is an acute and highly contagious pneumonia caused by *Pneumocystis carinii.* It is coded as **B59, Pneumocystosis.** This condition is frequently seen in patients with acquired immunodeficiency syndrome (AIDS) and is a major cause of death among AIDS patients. When associated with AIDS, code B20 is sequenced first with an additional code of B59. This type of pneumonia is not limited to patients with AIDS, however; it may develop in patients with immunocompromised states due to other causes, such as cancer, severe malnutrition, and debility. It may also occur in patients treated with certain types of immunosuppressive drugs after undergoing organ transplantation or cancer treatment. Never assume that this code should be assigned because the patient's condition is severe enough to warrant admission to the hospital. Interstitial pneumonia is classified as B59 only when specifically diagnosed by the physician as plasma cell pneumonia, pneumocystosis, or pneumonia caused by *Pneumocystis carinii.*

Legionnaires' Disease

Legionnaires' disease (A48.1) is a type of pneumonia that is almost always caused by inhalation of aerosols that come from a contaminated water source. This disease usually occurs as single, isolated cases not associated with any recognized outbreak. The fatality rate of Legionnaires' disease has ranged from 5 percent to 30 percent during various outbreaks.

Gram-Negative Pneumonia

Gram-negative pneumonia not elsewhere classified is classified as **J15.6, Pneumonia due to other aerobic Gram-negative bacteria,** or **J15.8, Pneumonia due to other specified bacteria,** when it is specified as anaerobic. When the organism has been identified, the Alphabetic Index may provide a more specific code. A gram-negative organism is one that develops a particular type of stain on testing and is considered part of a group of organisms that require careful management. Gram-positive pneumonia, not otherwise qualified, is classified as **J15.9, Unspecified bacterial pneumonia.** Gram-positive pneumonia is far easier to treat, and requires the expenditure of fewer resources, than gram-negative pneumonia.

Gram-negative pneumonia most often affects people who are hospitalized, infants, the elderly, alcoholics, and patients with chronic diseases, particularly immune system disorders. These bacteria rarely infect the lungs of healthy adults. The symptoms of gram-negative bacterial pneumonia are similar to those for gram-positive pneumonia. However, patients with gram-negative pneumonia tend to be sicker, and their condition deteriorates quickly because the bacteria can rapidly destroy lung tissue. About 25 to 50 percent of patients with gram-negative pneumonia die, in spite of treatment.

Note, however, that a diagnosis of gram-negative or other bacterial pneumonia cannot be assumed on the basis of the presence of laboratory or clinical findings alone; only the physician can determine the diagnosis. Such findings can, however, help document a diagnosis or serve as the basis for a query to the doctor.

Aspergillosis

Pneumonia due to infectious aspergillosis is classified as code **B44.9, Aspergillosis, unspecified.** Allergic bronchopulmonary or pulmonary aspergillosis, however, occurs as an eosinophilic pneumonia caused by an allergic reaction to the aspergillosis fungus, commonly found on dead leaves, bird droppings, compost stacks, or other decaying vegetation. Code **B44.81, Allergic bronchopulmonary aspergillosis,** is assigned for this allergic condition.

Aspiration Pneumonia

Aspiration pneumonia is a severe type of pneumonia resulting from the inhalation of foods, liquids, oils, vomitus, or microorganisms from the upper respiratory tract or the oropharyngeal area. Pneumonitis due to inhalation of foods or vomitus is coded to J69.0, that due to inhalation of oils and essences to J69.1, and that due to inhalation of other solids or liquids to J69.8. Pneumonia due to aspiration of microorganisms is classified to bacterial or viral pneumonia in category J15 or J12. Patients transferred from a nursing home to an acute care hospital because of pneumonia are often suffering from aspiration pneumonia due to aspirated organisms, usually gram-negative bacteria.

Ventilator-Associated Pneumonia

Pneumonia associated with the use of a ventilator is assigned to code **J95.851, Ventilator associated pneumonia.** In addition, a code to identify the organism, if known (B95.-, B96.-, B97.-) should be assigned. Do not assign an additional code from categories J12 through J18 to identify the type of pneumonia. For example, ventilator-associated pneumonia (VAP) due to *Staphylococcus aureus* is coded to J95.851 and B95.6. Code J95.851 should be assigned only when the provider

223

CHAPTER 19

Diseases
of the
Respiratory
System

has documented VAP. As with all procedural or postprocedural complications, code assignment is based on the provider's documentation of the relationship between the condition and the procedure. J95.851 should not be assigned for cases where the patient has pneumonia and is on mechanical ventilation but the provider has not specifically stated that the pneumonia is VAP. The provider should be queried when the documentation is unclear.

It is clinically possible for a patient to be admitted with one type of pneumonia and to develop VAP later. The principal diagnosis is the type of pneumonia diagnosed at the time of admission (J12–J18), and code J95.851 is a secondary diagnosis.

EXERCISE 19.1

Code the following diagnoses. Do not assign External cause of morbidity codes.

1. Lobar pneumonia with influenza — J18.1
   J10.1

2. Pneumonia, left upper lobe — J18.9

3. Klebsiella pneumonia — J15.0

4. Postinfectional pneumonia — B99.9
   J17

5. Acute pneumococcal lobar pneumonia — J13

6. Perihilar viral pneumonia — J12.9

7. Pneumonia due to chlamydia — J16.0
   Intermittent positive-pressure breathing (IPPB), — 5A09358
   4 hours   Assistance

8. Aspiration pneumonia due to aspiration of vomitus — J69.0

9. Plasma cell interstitial pneumonia due to AIDS — B20
   B59

10. Pneumonia due to pulmonary coccidioidomycosis — B38.2

INFLUENZA

ICD-10-CM classifies influenza to categories J09 and J10. Category J09 is further subdivided to distinguish influenza due to identified avian influenza virus (J09.0-) and influenza due to identified novel H1N1 influenza virus (J09.1-). All other influenza viruses are classified to category J10, Influenza due to other identified influenza virus. Subcategory J09.0 is used to report avian influenza caused by the viruses that normally infect only birds and, less commonly, other animals. A strain of this virus has been transmitted to humans. Subcategory J09.1- is used to report influenza due to the novel H1N1 virus (referred to as swine flu).

Influenza in combination with any form of pneumonia or bronchopneumonia is assigned to influenza with pneumonia (J09.01-, J09.11-, or J10.0-). For codes J09.018 and J10.08, code also the specified type of pneumonia. Influenza with other types of respiratory manifestations are classifiable to J09.02, J09.12, and J10.1 and include upper respiratory infection, laryngitis, pharyngitis, and pleural effusion. Influenza may also involve body systems other than the respiratory system, such as the gastrointestinal tract (J09.03, J09.13, and J10.2), and other manifestations such as encephalopathy, myocarditis, and otitis media (J09.090, J09.13, and J10.2).

Similar to the guidelines for coding HIV infection, codes from J09.0- and J09.1- should be assigned only for confirmed cases of avian flu or novel H1N1 flu. In this context, "confirmation" does not require documentation of positive laboratory testing specific for avian influenza or novel H1N1 flu. However, it does require provider documentation of avian influenza or novel H1N1 flu.

Neither subcategory J09.0 nor J09.1 is assigned when the diagnostic statement indicates that the infection is "suspected," "possible," "likely," or "?" This advice is an exception to the general guideline that directs the coder to assign a code for a diagnosis qualified as "suspected" or "possible" as if it were established. Instead, a code from category J11, Influenza due to unidentified influenza virus, should be assigned.

LARYNGITIS AND TRACHEITIS

Category J04, Acute laryngitis and tracheitis, has unique subcategories for laryngitis, tracheitis, and laryngotracheitis; the exception of acute tracheitis, with and without obstruction, is identified at the code level.

The diagnosis of supraglottitis may represent any of the codes within category J04. It is an infection of the supraglottic structures that affects the lingual tonsillar areas, epiglottic folds, false vocal cords, and the epiglottis. Because the infection covers all the supraglottic structures, the term "supraglottitis" is nonspecific. Supraglottitis is an acute, life-threatening upper respiratory infection. It seems to occur primarily in children but can be rapidly fatal to individuals in all age groups. This fatal event appears to result from an edematous epiglottis that is obstructing the airway. Subcategory J04.3 is used for supraglottitis when the term is used and a specific site of infection is not identified; a fifth character is used to indicate the presence or absence of obstruction. The codes for the conditions affecting the supraglottic structures are as follows:

J04.0	Acute laryngitis	
J04.1	Acute tracheitis	
	J04.10	Acute tracheitis without obstruction
	J04.11	Acute tracheitis with obstruction
J04.2	Acute laryngotracheitis	
J04.3	Supraglottitis, unspecified	
	J04.30	Supraglottitis, unspecified, without obstruction
	J04.31	Supraglottitis, unspecified, with obstruction

225

CHAPTER 19

*Diseases
of the
Respiratory
System*

Acute obstructive laryngitis, or croup (J05.0), occurs in young children, usually between the ages of three and six. The manifestations are a high-pitched cough and difficulty in breathing, due to a spasm or swelling of the larynx. It can be caused by an acute infection (especially by the influenza virus or diphtheria bacterium), an allergy, a tumor of the larynx, or obstruction by a swallowed object.

Acute epiglottitis refers to a severe, rapidly progressing bacterial infection of the upper respiratory tract. Symptoms include sore throat, croupy stridor, and inflamed epiglottis, which may result in sudden respiratory obstruction and possibly death. The condition affects young children between the ages of two and seven. The infection is generally caused by *Haemophilus influenzae,* type B, although streptococci may occasionally be the causative agents. Acute epiglottitis is coded to subcategory J05.1, with a fifth character to indicate the presence or absence of obstruction. Both categories J04 and J05 use an additional code (B95–B97) to specifically identify the infectious agent.

CHRONIC OBSTRUCTIVE PULMONARY DISEASE

Chronic obstructive pulmonary disease (COPD) is a general term used to describe a variety of conditions that result in obstruction of the airway. ICD-10-CM classifies these conditions to category J44, Other chronic obstructive pulmonary disease. Category J44 includes the following conditions:

- Asthma with chronic obstructive pulmonary disease
- Chronic asthmatic (obstructive) bronchitis
- Chronic bronchitis with airways obstruction
- Chronic bronchitis with emphysema
- Chronic emphysematous bronchitis
- Chronic obstructive asthma
- Chronic obstructive bronchitis
- Chronic obstructive tracheobronchitis

Category J44 is further subdivided to specify whether there is an acute lower respiratory infection (J44.0) and whether there is an exacerbation of the condition (J44.1). If applicable, a code from category J45 is assigned to specify the type of asthma. In the case of code **J44.0, Chronic obstructive pulmonary disease with acute lower respiratory infection,** an additional code should be reported to identify the infection. The codes in category J44 distinguish between uncomplicated cases (J44.9) and those in acute exacerbation (J44.1). An acute exacerbation is a worsening or a decompensation of a chronic condition. An acute exacerbation is not equivalent to an infection superimposed on a chronic condition, though an exacerbation may be triggered by an infection. For example, COPD with acute bronchitis should be coded to J44.0, rather than J44.1.

Examples of the terms classified to **J44.1, Chronic obstructive pulmonary disease with (acute) exacerbation,** are "exacerbation," "in exacerbation," "decompensated," "acute exacerbation," "exacerbated," or "uncompensated." When the diagnosis is stated only as COPD, the coder should review the medical record to determine whether a more definitive diagnosis is documented. Code **J44.9, Chronic obstructive pulmonary disease, unspecified,** is assigned only when a more specific code cannot be assigned.

In addition to codes in category J44, codes may also be assigned to identify exposure to environmental tobacco smoke (Z77.22), history of tobacco use (Z87.891), occupational exposure to environmental tobacco smoke (Z57.31), tobacco dependence (F17.-), or tobacco use (Z72.0).

Note that emphysema without chronic bronchitis is coded to J43.-, and chronic bronchitis not otherwise specified is classified to J42.

Asthma

Asthma is a bronchial hypersensitivity characterized by mucosal edema, constriction of bronchial musculature, and excessive viscid edema. Manifestations of asthma are wheezing, dyspnea out of proportion to exertion, and cough. A diagnosis of wheezing alone is not classified as asthma; code R06.2 is assigned in such a case. Asthma is classified into category J45, with a fourth character indicating the severity (mild intermittent, mild persistent, moderate persistent, severe persistent, other, and unspecified) and a fifth character indicating whether it is uncomplicated or whether status asthmaticus or exacerbation is present.

Status asthmaticus is defined in slightly different ways by different authorities, but in general it represents a patient who continues to have extreme wheezing in spite of conventional therapy or has suffered from an acute asthmatic attack in which the degree of obstruction is not relieved by the usual therapeutic measures. Early status asthmaticus represents patients who are refractory to treatment or who fail to respond to the usual therapies; advanced status asthmaticus represents patients who show full development of an asthma attack that could result in respiratory failure, with signs and symptoms of hypercapnia (excess carbon dioxide in the blood). The fifth character of "2" is assigned for both types of status asthmaticus. Use of this fifth character usually indicates a medical emergency for treatment of acute, severe asthma. Other terms used to describe status asthmaticus include the following:

- Intractable asthma attack
- Refractory asthma
- Severe, intractable wheezing
- Airway obstruction not relieved by bronchodilators
- Severe, prolonged asthmatic attack

The coder should never assume that status asthmaticus is present without a specific statement from the provider. However, asthma described as acute, characterized by prolonged or severe intractable wheezing, or asthma being treated by the administration of adrenal corticosteroids should alert the coder that status asthmaticus may exist and that the provider should be asked whether the diagnosis is to be added.

Exacerbations of asthma are acute or subacute episodes of progressively worsening shortness of breath, cough, wheezing, and chest tightness—or some combination of these symptoms. The fifth character of "1" is used for asthma referred to as "exacerbated" or in "acute exacerbation."

Asthma characterized as obstructive or diagnosed in conjunction with COPD is classified to category J44, Other chronic obstructive pulmonary disease. An asthma code with a fifth character of "2," with acute exacerbation, may *not* be assigned with an asthma code with a fifth character of "1," with status asthmaticus. When there is documentation of both acute exacerbation and status asthmaticus, only the code with the fifth character of "1" should be assigned.

A diagnosis of asthmatic bronchitis without further specification is coded as J45.9-. If the diagnosis is stated as exacerbated or acute chronic asthmatic bronchitis, code J44.1 is assigned. A diagnosis of asthmatic bronchitis with COPD or chronic asthmatic bronchitis is coded to J44.9. Examples of coding for asthma include the following:

J45.902	Asthmatic bronchitis with status asthmaticus
J45.909	Childhood asthma
J44.9 + J45.909	Asthma with COPD
J44.1 + J45.901	Chronic asthmatic bronchitis with acute exacerbation
J45.909 + F54	Psychogenic asthma

Bronchospasm

Bronchospasm is an integral part of asthma or any other type of chronic airway obstruction, but no additional code is assigned to indicate its presence. Code **J98.01, Acute bronchospasm,** is assigned only when the underlying cause has not been identified.

EXERCISE 19.2

Code the following diagnoses. Do not assign External cause of morbidity codes.

1.	Bronchial asthma, allergic, due to house dust	J45.909
2.	Chronic bronchitis with decompensated COPD	J44.1
3.	Acute exacerbation of chronic asthmatic bronchitis	J44.1
4.	Emphysema	J43.9
5.	Chronic obstructive lung disease with acute exacerbation	J44.1
6.	Emphysema with chronic obstructive bronchitis	J44.9
7.	Mild intermittent asthma with status asthmaticus	J45.22
8.	Acute bronchitis with acute bronchiectasis	J47.1

ATELECTASIS

Atelectasis is a very common finding in chest X-rays and other radiological studies. It is a condition where the alveoli are deflated. It may be caused by normal exhalation or by several medical conditions. Atelectasis reduces the ventilatory function. Pulmonary collapse can be a severe problem, but mild atelectasis usually has little effect on the patient's condition or the therapy provided. Slight strands of atelectasis are often noted on X-ray reports, but this finding is generally of little clinical importance and is usually not further evaluated or treated. Code **J98.11, Atelectasis,** should not be assigned on the basis of an X-ray finding alone; it should be coded only when the physician identifies it as a clinical condition that meets the criteria for a reportable diagnosis.

PLEURAL EFFUSION

Pleural effusion is an abnormal accumulation of fluid within the pleural spaces. It occurs in association with pulmonary disease and certain cardiac conditions, such as congestive heart failure, or certain diseases involving other organs. It is almost always integral to the underlying disease and is usually addressed only by treatment of that condition. In this situation, only the code for the underlying disease is assigned. However, occasionally the effusion is addressed separately, with additional diagnostic studies such as decubitus X-ray or diagnostic thoracentesis. The effusion may be treated by therapeutic thoracentesis, or chest-tube drainage. When treatment is addressed only to the pleural effusion, it can be designated as the principal diagnosis; otherwise, it can be assigned as an additional code when it is further evaluated or treated. Pleural effusion noted only on an X-ray report is not reported.

Pleural effusion due to tuberculosis is classified to A15.6 unless it is due to primary progressive tuberculosis (A15.7). Pleural effusion due to systemic lupus erythematosus is coded to **M32.13, Lung involvement in systemic lupus erythematosus.** Pleural effusion in heart failure is not coded separately; only the code for the heart failure (I50.-) is assigned. Influenzal pleural effusion is coded to influenza, with respiratory manifestations (J09.02, J09.12, or J10.1), with code **J91.8, Pleural effusion in other conditions classified elsewhere,** to specify the associated pleural effusion.

Malignant pleural effusion can occur due to impaired pleural lymphatic drainage from a mediastinal tumor (especially in lymphomas) and not because of direct tumor invasion into the pleura. Malignant pleural effusion is coded to J91.0 with the underlying neoplasm assigned as the first-listed or principal diagnosis.

RESPIRATORY FAILURE

Respiratory failure is a life-threatening condition that is always due to an underlying condition. It may be the final pathway of a disease process or a combination of different processes. Respiratory failure can result from either acute or chronic diseases that cause airway obstruction, parenchymal infiltration, or pulmonary edema. It can arise from an abnormality in any of the components of the respiratory system, central nervous system, peripheral nervous system, respiratory muscles, and chest wall muscles. The diagnosis is based largely on arterial blood gas analysis findings, which vary from individual to individual, depending on several factors. The coder should never assume a diagnosis of respiratory failure without a documented diagnosis by the physician. Respiratory failure is classified as acute (J96.0-), chronic (J96.1-), acute and chronic combined (J96.2-), or unspecified (J96.9-) and a fifth character that specifies whether hypoxia or hypercapnia is present. When respiratory failure follows surgery, code **J95.82, Postprocedural respiratory failure,** is assigned.

Careful review of the medical record is required for the coding and sequencing of respiratory failure. The coder must review the circumstances of admission to determine the principal diagnosis. Code **J96.00, Acute respiratory failure, unspecified whether with hypoxia or hypercapnia,** or code **J96.20, Acute and chronic respiratory failure, unspecified whether with hypoxia or hypercapnia,** may be assigned as a principal diagnosis when it is the condition established after study to be chiefly responsible for occasioning the admission to the hospital, and the selection is supported by the Alphabetic Index and Tabular List. Respiratory failure may be listed as a secondary diagnosis if it develops after admission.

When a patient is admitted with respiratory failure and another acute condition (e.g., myocardial infarction, aspiration pneumonia, cerebrovascular accident), the principal diagnosis will depend on the individual patient's situation and what caused the admission of the patient to the hospital. This guideline applies regardless of whether the other acute condition is a respiratory or nonrespiratory condition. The physician should be queried for clarification if the documentation is unclear as to which one of the two conditions was the reason for the admission. The guideline regarding two or more diagnoses equally meeting the definition of principal diagnosis (Section II, C) may be applied in situations when both the respiratory failure and the other acute condition are equally responsible for occasioning the admission to the hospital. Examples are the following.

EXAMPLE 1: A patient with chronic myasthenia gravis goes into acute exacerbation and develops acute respiratory failure. The patient is admitted due to the respiratory failure.

Principal diagnosis:	J96.00	Acute respiratory failure, unspecified whether with hypoxia or hypercapnia
Secondary diagnosis:	G70.01	Myasthenia gravis with (acute) exacerbation

EXAMPLE 2: A patient with emphysema develops acute respiratory failure. The patient is admitted through the emergency department for treatment of the respiratory failure.

Principal diagnosis:	J96.00	Acute respiratory failure, unspecified whether with hypoxia or hypercapnia
Secondary diagnosis:	J43.9	Emphysema, unspecified

EXAMPLE 3: A patient arrived in the hospital in acute respiratory failure and hypoxia. The patient was intubated, and the physician documents that the patient is being admitted to the hospital for treatment of the acute respiratory failure with hypoxia. The patient also has congestive heart failure.

Principal diagnosis:	J96.01	Acute respiratory failure with hypoxia
Secondary diagnosis:	I50.9	Heart failure, unspecified

Some ICD-10-CM chapter-specific coding guidelines (e.g., obstetrics, poisoning, HIV, newborn) provide sequencing direction. These guidelines would take precedence over code J96.0- or J96.2- when coding respiratory failure associated with a condition from one of these chapters. Examples are the following.

EXAMPLE 1: A patient is admitted to the hospital postpartum as a result of developing pulmonary embolism leading to respiratory failure.

Principal diagnosis:	O88.23	Thromboembolism in the puerperium
Secondary diagnosis:	J96.00	Acute respiratory failure, unspecified whether with hypoxia or hypercapnia

In example 1 above, the obstetrical code is sequenced first because a chapter-specific guideline (Section I, C, 15, a, 1) provides sequencing directions specifying that chapter 15 codes have sequencing priority over codes from other chapters.

EXAMPLE 2: A patient who is diagnosed as overdosing on crack cocaine is admitted to the hospital with respiratory failure.

Principal diagnosis:	T40.5x4A	Poisoning by cocaine, undetermined, initial encounter
Secondary diagnosis:	J96.00	Acute respiratory failure, unspecified whether with hypoxia or hypercapnia
	F14.10	Cocaine abuse, uncomplicated

In example 2 above, poisoning is sequenced first because a chapter-specific guideline (Section I, C, 19, e, 5, b) provides sequencing directions specifying that the poisoning code is sequenced first,

230

CHAPTER 19

*Diseases
of the
Respiratory
System*

followed by a code for the manifestation. The acute respiratory failure is a manifestation of the poisoning.

EXAMPLE 3:   A patient is admitted with respiratory failure due to *Pneumocystis carinii* due to AIDS.

Principal diagnosis:	B20	Human immunodeficiency virus [HIV] disease
Secondary diagnosis:	J96.00	Acute respiratory failure, unspecified whether with hypoxia or hypercapnia
	B59	Pneumocystosis

In example 3, the HIV is sequenced first because a chapter-specific guideline (Section I, C, 1, a, 2, a) provides sequencing directions specifying that if a patient is admitted for an HIV-related condition (in this case the *Pneumocystis carinii*), the principal diagnosis should be B20, followed by additional diagnosis codes for all reported HIV-related conditions.

In the event that instructional notes in the Tabular List provide sequencing direction, the sequencing of respiratory failure is dependent on these notes. An example follows.

EXAMPLE: A patient is admitted to the hospital with severe *Staphylococcus aureus* sepsis and acute respiratory failure.

Principal diagnosis:	A41.0	Sepsis due to *Staphylococcus aureus*
Secondary diagnosis:	R65.20	Severe sepsis without septic shock
	J96.00	Acute respiratory failure, unspecified whether with hypoxia or hypercapnia

---

Sepsis is sequenced first in this case because an instructional note under subcategory R65.2- indicates to code first the underlying infection. In addition, subcategory R65.2- has a "use additional code" note to specify acute organ dysfunction and lists acute respiratory failure (J96.0-). Following this instruction, respiratory failure is given as a secondary diagnosis.

ACUTE RESPIRATORY DISTRESS SYNDROME

Acute respiratory distress syndrome (ARDS) is a lung condition that leads to low oxygen levels in the blood. ARDS can be life threatening because organs such as the kidneys and brain need oxygen-rich blood for proper functioning. ARDS can occur within 24 to 48 hours of an injury (trauma, burns, aspiration, massive blood transfusion, drug/alcohol abuse) or an acute illness (infectious pneumonia, sepsis, acute pancreatitis). ARDS patients usually present with shortness of breath, tachypnea, and occasionally confusion. Long-term illnesses, such as malaria, can also trigger ARDS, which may then occur sometime after the onset of a particularly acute case of the infection. ARDS is coded to **J80, Acute respiratory distress syndrome.**

ACUTE PULMONARY EDEMA

Acute pulmonary edema is a pathological state in which there is excessive, diffuse accumulation of fluid in the tissues and the alveolar spaces of the lung. It is broadly divided into two categories that reflect the origin of the condition: cardiogenic and noncardiogenic.

231

CHAPTER 19

*Diseases
of the
Respiratory
System*

Cardiogenic

Acute pulmonary edema of cardiac origin is a manifestation of heart failure and as such is included in the following code assignments:

I50.1	Left ventricular failure
I50.-	Heart failure
I11.-	Hypertensive heart disease
I01.-	Rheumatic heart disease, acute
I09.81	Rheumatic heart failure

Pulmonary edema is not included in the codes for acute myocardial infarction (I21.01–I22.9), acute ischemic heart disease (I24.0–I24.9), or chronic ischemic heart disease (I25.-). When pulmonary edema is present along with a heart condition or failure, the pulmonary edema is assumed to be associated with left ventricular failure (I50.1) unless the heart failure is described as congestive or decompensated, in which case a code for the more specific congestive heart failure (I50.2–I50.9) is assigned. Pulmonary edema is included in codes I50.-; no additional code is assigned.

Noncardiogenic

Noncardiogenic acute pulmonary edema occurs in the absence of heart failure or other heart disease. It is coded in a variety of ways depending on the cause. When the cause is not specified, code **J81.-, Pulmonary edema,** is assigned. When the cause of the pulmonary edema is known, it is coded as follows:

- Post-radiation pulmonary edema (post-radiation pneumonia) is an inflammation of the lungs due to the adverse effects of radiation. It is coded as **J70.0, Acute pulmonary manifestations due to radiation.**

- Pulmonary edema due to chemicals, gas fumes, or vapors is coded as J68.1.

- Pulmonary edema due to aspiration of water in a near-drowning is coded to **T75.1-, Unspecified effects of drowning and nonfatal submersion.**

- Pulmonary edema due to high altitude is coded as **T70.29-, Other effects of high altitude.**

- Acute pulmonary edema in cases of drug overdose is classified as poisoning, with code J81.0 assigned as an additional code. Any mention of drug dependence or abuse should also be coded.

External cause of morbidity codes should be assigned with any of these codes to indicate the external circumstances involved.

Chronic pulmonary edema or pulmonary edema not otherwise specified that is not of cardiac origin is coded as **J81.1, Chronic pulmonary edema,** unless the Alphabetic Index or the Tabular List instructs otherwise.

Pulmonary edema caused by congestive overloads, such as pulmonary fibrosis (J84.1), congenital stenosis of the pulmonary veins (Q26.8), or pulmonary venous embolism (I26.99), is noncardiogenic. Such conditions are assigned to code J81.0 when described as acute or to code J81.1 when described as chronic or not otherwise specified. Be careful not to confuse this condition with edema associated with heart disease.

SURGICAL PROCEDURES

When assigning ICD-10-PCS codes for procedures performed in the respiratory system, it is important to ensure that the documentation provides information regarding the site where the procedure was performed. Body part values include the specific lobe of the lung (when available), or at a minimum whether the site is the right or left lung, or bilateral lungs. Many of the root operations commonly performed do not provide "unspecified" body part values for when the left or right side is not stated for the lungs, pleura, or diaphragm. Examples of these root operations include "Destruction," "Drainage," "Excision," "Insertion," and "Extirpation."

It is also important to understand the surgical approaches in order to select the correct ICD-10-PCS codes. (For illustrations of such approaches, please refer to figure 8.5 on pages 74–75.) For example, thoracoscopic procedures involve the creation of small incisions into the chest wall and insertion of a thoracoscope through the incision. Thoracoscopic procedures are coded to the approach "percutaneous endoscopic." Procedures stated as "bronchoscopic" involve passing the bronchoscope through the nose (or sometimes the mouth), down the throat, and into the airway. The approach character for bronchoscopic procedures is "via natural or artificial opening endoscopic" because the procedure involves entering via a natural opening (nose or mouth) and then using an endoscope.

BIOPSIES OF BRONCHUS AND LUNG

An endoscopic biopsy of the bronchus involves passing an endoscope into the lumen of the trachea and bronchus, where a bit of tissue is removed for pathological study. ICD-10-PCS classifies biopsies to the root operation "Excision" and the qualifier "diagnostic." For example, endoscopic excisional biopsy of the right upper lobe bronchus is coded to **0BB48ZX, Excision of right upper lobe bronchus, via natural or artificial opening endoscopic, diagnostic.**

An endoscopic biopsy of the lung is performed by passing the endoscope through the main bronchus into the smaller bronchi and lung alveoli. Either type of biopsy can be performed independently, or both may be performed in the same operative episode, in which case both codes are assigned. The approach character is "via natural or artificial opening endoscopic." For example, endoscopic biopsy of the right middle lobe of the lung is coded to **0BBD8ZX, Excision of right middle lung lobe, via natural or artificial opening endoscopic, diagnostic.**

Another type of lung biopsy is the thoracoscopic biopsy. In this procedure, small incisions are made into the chest wall and a thoracoscope is inserted through them to remove specimens for pathologic examination. The approach for this type of biopsy is "percutaneous endoscopic" because it requires entering through the skin and inserting a scope. For example, thoracoscopic biopsy of the right lung is coded to **0BBK4ZX, Excision of right lung, percutaneous endoscopic approach, diagnostic.**

Bronchoalveolar lavage (BAL), also called "liquid biopsy," should not be confused with whole lung lavage. BAL is a diagnostic procedure performed via a bronchoscope under local anesthesia. It involves washing out alveoli tissue and peripheral airways to obtain a small sampling of tissue. BAL is coded to the root operation "Drainage" because it involves removing fluids. For example, bronchoalveolar lavage of the right lung is coded to **0B968ZX, Drainage of right lower lobe bronchus, via natural or artificial opening endoscopic, diagnostic.**

Whole lung lavage is a therapeutic procedure performed for pulmonary alveolar proteinosis. The procedure is performed under general anesthesia and mechanical ventilation. The lungs are lavaged by filling and emptying one lung at a time with saline solution. The second lung is usually lavaged three to seven days after the first lung has been lavaged. Report whole lung lavage using code **3E1F88Z, Irrigation of respiratory tract using irrigating substance, via natural or artificial opening endoscopic.** Assign also a code for the mechanical ventilation provided.

ABLATION OF LUNG

Tumor ablation is an alternative to surgical removal of lung lesions. Ablation can be achieved using extreme heat, freezing chemicals (cryoablation), focused ultrasound, microwaves, or radio-frequency. These procedures are typically performed by interventional radiologists using imaging guidance—such as computed tomography (CT), ultrasound, or fluoroscopy—and inserting a probe directly to the lesion.

ICD-10-PCS classifies ablation procedures under the root operation "Destruction," meaning "physical eradication of all or a portion of a body part by the direct use of energy, force, or a destructive agent." ICD-10-PCS codes for ablation do not distinguish between the different energy sources used to ablate the tumor. Examples include the following:

0B5G0ZZ	Open ablation left upper lung lobe
0B5L3ZZ	Percutaneous ablation left lung
0B5J4ZZ	Thoracoscopic ablation left lower lung lobe

Bronchoscopic ablation (or bronchial thermoplasty ablation) of airway smooth muscle of the lung is a procedure performed to reduce excess airway smooth muscle to treat asthmatic patients. The procedure is performed using a bronchoscope and a catheter to deliver radiofrequency energy into the airways to reduce the constricted airway smooth muscle. This reduction lessens the area that narrows in response to external stimuli such as dust and other allergens. For example, bronchial thermoplasty ablation of the right main bronchus is coded as **0B538ZZ, Destruction of right main bronchus, via natural or artificial opening endoscopic.**

Other examples of common lung procedures include:

0BBD4ZZ	Thoracoscopic excision of lesion right middle lobe
0BBC0ZZ	Open segmental resection of right upper lobe
0BBG0ZZ	Open lobectomy, left upper lobe
0B9N30Z	Percutaneous drainage of right pleura

MECHANICAL VENTILATION

Mechanical ventilation is a process by which the patient's own effort to breathe is augmented or replaced by the use of a mechanical device. ICD-10-PCS classifies mechanical ventilation to the extracorporeal assistance and performance section (first character = 5). Mechanical ventilation may be described as noninvasive when delivered via a noninvasive interface like a face mask, a nasal mask, a nasal pillow, an oral mouthpiece, or an oronasal mask. ICD-10-PCS classifies this type of mechanical ventilation to the root operation "Assistance" because it meets the definition of "taking over a portion of a physiological function by extracorporeal means." Character 5 in this section provides values for the duration of the ventilation, such as less than 24 consecutive hours (value = 3), 24–96 consecutive hours (value = 4), or greater than 96 consecutive hours (value = 5). Character 7, qualifier, specifies the type of ventilation with the following values:

7	Continuous positive airway pressure
8	Intermittent positive airway pressure
9	Continuous negative airway pressure
B	Intermittent negative airway pressure
Z	No qualifier

234

CHAPTER 19

Diseases
of the
Respiratory
System

Coding examples follow:

5A09357	Assistance with respiratory ventilation, less than 24 consecutive hours, continuous positive airway pressure
5A09457	Assistance with respiratory ventilation, 24–96 consecutive hours, continuous positive airway pressure
5A09458	Assistance with respiratory ventilation, 24–96 consecutive hours, intermittent positive airway pressure
5A09559	Assistance with respiratory ventilation, greater than 96 consecutive hours, continuous negative airway pressure
5A0955Z	Assistance with respiratory ventilation, greater than 96 consecutive hours

Mechanical ventilation is considered invasive when the ventilatory assistance is provided via an invasive interface such as endotracheal intubation or tracheostomy and the patient receives mechanical ventilation in an uninterrupted fashion. An endotracheal tube can be placed orally or nasally. If either intubation or tracheostomy is performed after admission or in the emergency department of the same hospital immediately before admission, it should be reported. Intubation or tracheostomy carried out elsewhere prior to admission or in an ambulance prior to arrival at the hospital cannot be reported even though the ambulance may be operated by the same facility.

Codes for invasive mechanical ventilation are classified to the root operation "Performance" because these procedures completely take over the physiological function of breathing by extracorporeal means. Similar to the root operation "Assistance," character 5 in this section provides values for the duration of the ventilation, such as less than 24 consecutive hours (value = 3), 24–96 consecutive hours (value = 4), or greater than 96 consecutive hours (value = 5).

Examples include the following codes:

5A19054	Respiratory ventilation, single, nonmechanical
5A1935Z	Respiratory ventilation, less than 24 consecutive hours
5A1945Z	Respiratory ventilation, 24–96 consecutive hours
5A1955Z	Respiratory ventilation, greater than 96 consecutive hours

Duration of Mechanical Ventilation

The starting time for calculating the duration begins with one of these events:

- Endotracheal intubation performed in the hospital or hospital emergency room, followed by initiation of mechanical ventilation

- Initiation of mechanical ventilation through tracheostomy performed in the hospital or emergency room

- Admission of a patient who is already on mechanical ventilation after previous intubation or tracheostomy

A tracheal tube is often inserted to keep the tracheostomy open for attachment to the mechanical ventilator. Start counting hours on ventilation only after mechanical ventilation has actually been initiated.

235

CHAPTER 19

Diseases
of the
Respiratory
System

It is occasionally necessary to replace an endotracheal tube because of a problem such as a leak; removal with immediate replacement is considered part of the duration and counting should continue. Patients who are started on mechanical ventilation by means of an endotracheal tube may later receive a tracheostomy through which the ventilation continues. Continue counting the number of hours the patient is on ventilation from the time the original intubation was initiated.

Once a patient's condition has stabilized and the patient no longer needs continuous ventilatory assistance, various weaning methods may be employed to allow the patient to gradually resume the work of breathing. During weaning, the patient is monitored for any evidence of cardiopulmonary instability. The period during which the weaning process takes place is counted as part of the duration time. Note that some patients do not require this weaning process.

Duration of mechanical ventilation ends with one of the following events:

- Removal of the endotracheal tube (extubation)
- Discontinuance of ventilation for patients with tracheostomy after any weaning period is completed
- Discharge or transfer while still on mechanical ventilation

Occasionally the condition of a patient who has been on ventilation earlier in the hospital stay deteriorates and a subsequent period of mechanical ventilation may be required. Use the guidelines above to calculate this additional period. In such cases, two codes should be assigned to represent the mechanical ventilation.

When mechanical ventilation is used during surgery, it is not normally coded when it is considered a normal part of surgery. However, in the event that the physician documents that the patient has a specific problem and is maintained on the mechanical ventilator longer than expected or if the patient requires mechanical ventilation for an extended period of time postoperatively, it may be coded. If the postoperative mechanical ventilation continues for more than two days, or if the physician has clearly documented an unexpected extended period of mechanical ventilation, the mechanical ventilation may be reported separately. The hours of mechanical ventilation should be counted starting from the point of intubation.

Tracheostomy Complications

Complications of a tracheostomy are classified to subcategory J95.0 in chapter 10 of ICD-10-CM. Infection of a tracheostomy is classified to code J95.02, with an additional code to identify the type of infection and/or a code from category B95–B97 to identify the organism, or sepsis, A40.-, A41.-. Hemorrhage from tracheostomy is coded to J95.01; malfunction complications are coded to J95.03; trachea-esophageal fistula following tracheostomy is assigned to J95.04; unspecified complication is classified to J95.00; other complications are coded to J95.09.

EXERCISE 19.3

The following exercise provides examples of conditions classified in chapter 10 of ICD-10-CM. Code the following diagnoses and procedures. Do not assign External cause of morbidity codes.

---

1. Chronic left maxillary sinusitis   J32.0

    Open left total maxillary sinusectomy   09TR0ZZ

---

2. Acute upper respiratory infection due to *Pneumococcus*   J06.9

    Febrile convulsions   B95.3

    R56.00

---

3. Deviated nasal septum   J34.2

    Allergic rhinitis   J30.9

    Ethmoidal sinusitis   J32.2

    Excision of nasal septum, percutaneous   09BM3ZZ

---

4. Chronic pulmonary edema   J81.1

---

5. Allergic rhinitis due to tree pollen   J30.1

---

6. Congestive heart failure with pleural effusion   I50.9

---

7. Acute respiratory failure due to intracerebral hemorrhage   I61.9

    J96.00

---

8. Acute pharyngitis due to *Staphylococcus aureus* infection   J02.8

    B95.6

---

9. Chronic chemical bronchitis due to inhalation of chlorine fumes   J68.4

    Bronchoscopy with excisional biopsy of right lower bronchus   0BB68ZX

---

10. Total tension pneumothorax, spontaneous, left   J93.0

---

11. Admitted in acute respiratory failure due to acute
    exacerbation of chronic obstructive bronchitis   J96.00
                                                                       J44.1

12. Acute tracheobronchitis due to respiratory syncytial
    virus infection   J20.5

13. Gram-negative pneumonia, anaerobic   J15.8

14. Acute pulmonary insufficiency, due to shock   J80

15. Acute respiratory distress syndrome due to
    hantavirus infection   J80
                                                                       B33.4

16. Infected tracheostomy due to staphylococcal
    abscess of the neck   J95.02
                                                                       L02.11
                                                                       B95.8

CHAPTER 20

Diseases of the Digestive System

CHAPTER OVERVIEW

- Diseases of the digestive system are found in chapter 11 of ICD-10-CM.

- Many types of gastrointestinal (GI) hemorrhage can be classified. Sometimes documentation may point to bleeding in multiple locations.

- Esophagitis is classified to the digestive system codes, but esophageal varices are coded as a disease of the circulatory system.

- Combination codes are provided for ulcers that indicate bleeding, perforation, or both. Coders should look in the medical record for any indication of site.

- Special notice should be given to conditions involving diverticula because of the similarity of the conditions and names.

- Coding diseases of the biliary system involves determining the location of the calculus.

- Other biliary system conditions revolve around removal of the gallbladder.

- Codes for adhesions include both intestinal and peritoneal. However, minor adhesions are usually not coded.

- Hernias are classified by type and site, and combination codes are used to indicate associated issues.

- Diarrhea can be related to a variety of conditions. It is important to check the Alphabetic Index carefully before coding.

- Other common digestive system issues covered in this chapter of the handbook are appendicitis and constipation.

LEARNING OUTCOMES

After studying this chapter you should be able to:

- Classify a variety of conditions that affect the GI tract.

- Explain the difference in the meaning of terms associated with diverticula.

- Classify diseases of the biliary system.

- Classify common digestive system conditions such as diarrhea, constipation, and appendicitis.

TERMS TO KNOW

Biliary system
a network including the gallbladder and bile ducts

Calculus
a stone composed of minerals that forms in an organ or duct of the body

Diverticulitis
the inflammation of existing diverticula

Diverticulosis
the presence of one or more diverticula of the designated site

Diverticulum
a small pouch or sac opening from a tubular or saccular organ; considered a medical condition; the plural term is diverticula

Esophagitis
an inflammation of the lining of the esophagus

Esophageal varices
abnormally enlarged veins in the lower part of the esophagus

GI
gastrointestinal; of the stomach and/or intestines

REMEMBER . . .

Many combination codes and exclusion notes are used in chapter 11 of ICD-10-CM.

INTRODUCTION

Diseases of the digestive system are classified in chapter 11 of ICD-10-CM. The coding principles presented in previous chapters of this handbook apply throughout chapter 11. In addition, particular attention should be given to the use of combination codes and to the many exclusion notes in chapter 11.

GASTROINTESTINAL HEMORRHAGE

Gastrointestinal (GI) bleeding manifests itself in several ways:

- Hematemesis (vomiting of blood), which indicates acute upper gastrointestinal hemorrhage
- Melena (presence of dark-colored blood in stool), which indicates upper or lower GI hemorrhage
- Occult bleeding (presence of blood in stool that can be seen only on laboratory examination), which indicates upper or lower GI bleeding
- Hematochezia (presence of bright-colored blood in stool), which indicates lower GI bleeding

The most common causes of GI bleeding are gastric and intestinal ulcers and diverticular disease of the intestine. A diverticular hemorrhage stops spontaneously in approximately 80 percent of cases, with the other 20 percent experiencing a second or third bleeding episode. ICD-10-CM provides specific codes for gastrointestinal tract ulcers, gastritis, angiodysplasia, duodenitis, gastroduodenitis, Crohn's disease, ulcerative colitis, diverticulosis, and diverticulitis to indicate whether there is associated hemorrhage or bleeding. Examples include the following:

K29.01	Acute gastritis with hemorrhage
K57.13	Diverticulitis of small intestine with hemorrhage
K31.811	Angiodysplasia of duodenum with hemorrhage

Codes **K92.0, Hematemesis; K92.1, Melena;** or **K92.2, Gastrointestinal hemorrhage, unspecified,** are not assigned when codes for bleeding of any of the sites mentioned above are available. These codes are acceptable only when the physician's diagnostic statement clearly indicates that the bleeding is due to another condition. Patients with a recent history of GI bleeding are sometimes seen for an endoscopy to determine the site of the bleeding but do not demonstrate any bleeding during the examination. If the physician documents a clinical diagnosis based on the history or other evidence, the fact that no bleeding occurs during the episode of care does not preclude the assignment of a code that includes mention of hemorrhage, or a code from K92.0 through K92.2 when the cause of bleeding could not be determined.

Occasionally, physician documentation may refer to GI bleeding and either single or multiple GI-related endoscopic findings, such as gastritis, duodenitis, esophagitis, diverticulosis (of colon), colon polyp, and so forth. If the physician does not link the GI bleeding with any specific condition or states that the GI bleeding is not due to these conditions, the physician needs to be queried to determine whether the GI bleeding was caused by any of the endoscopic findings. If the physician does not establish a causal relationship between the GI bleeding and the endoscopic findings, code **K92.2, Gastrointestinal hemorrhage, unspecified,** should be reported. In addition, codes for the GI endoscopic findings without hemorrhage should be assigned as additional diagnoses. The physician must identify the source of the bleeding and link the clinical finding from the endoscopy because the finding may be unrelated to the bleeding. The combination codes describing hemorrhage should not be assigned unless the physician identifies a causal relationship. If the documentation provides more specific information and the bleeding is linked to a specific condition, assign the appropriate combination code with bleeding.

241

CHAPTER 20

Diseases
of the
Digestive
System

Patients may present for a colonoscopy because of rectal bleeding. If the findings include internal and external hemorrhoids with no statement as to whether the rectal bleeding is due to the hemorrhoids, the physician should be queried to determine whether the rectal bleeding is secondary to the hemorrhoids or the hemorrhoids are an incidental finding. If the hemorrhoids are incidental findings and unrelated to the rectal bleeding, code **K62.5, Hemorrhage of anus and rectum,** should be assigned followed by codes for the hemorrhoids without mention of complication. If, however, the physician establishes a causal relationship between the bleeding and the hemorrhoids, assign **I84.131, Internal and external bleeding hemorrhoids.** Do not assign the combination code for hemorrhoids with bleeding unless the physician explicitly states a causal relationship.

ESOPHAGITIS

Esophagitis is classified to category code K20, with several different specific conditions. Eosinophilic esophagitis is coded to K20.0; other esophagitis is coded to K20.8, and unspecified esophagitis is coded to K20.9. Reflux esophagitis is coded to **K21.0, Gastro-esophageal reflux disease with esophagitis.** Ulcerative esophagitis without bleeding is classified to **K22.10, Ulcer of esophagus without bleeding,** whereas ulcerative esophagitis with bleeding is classified to **K22.11, Ulcer of esophagus with bleeding,** and dyskinesia of esophagus is classified to K22.4. Barrett's esophagus (codes K22.70 through K22.71-) is a precancerous condition in which the normal cells of the lining of the esophagus are replaced by columnar cells.

FIGURE 20.1   The Digestive System

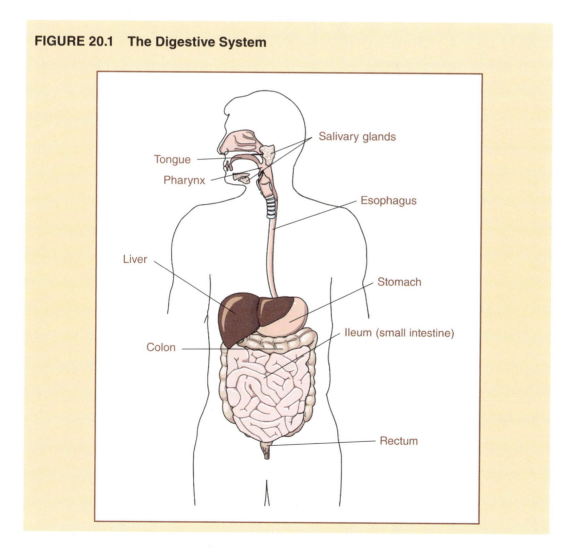

242

CHAPTER 20

*Diseases
of the
Digestive
System*

Bleeding of the esophagus is coded as **K22.8, Other specified diseases of esophagus,** unless the bleeding is due to esophageal varices. Esophageal varices are not classified as a disease of the digestive system but as a disease of the circulatory system. They are coded as follows:

I85.00   Esophageal varices without bleeding

I85.01   Esophageal varices with bleeding

When esophageal varices are associated with alcoholic liver disease, cirrhosis of the liver, schistosomiasis, toxic liver disease, or portal hypertension, dual coding is required, with the underlying condition coded first and a code for secondary esophageal varices (I85.10–I85.11). Examples include:

K74.60 + I85.11   Bleeding esophageal varices with cirrhosis of liver

K76.6 + I85.11   Bleeding esophageal varices in portal hypertension

Therapy for esophageal varices consists primarily of ligation of the esophageal vein, which ICD-10-PCS classifies to the root operation "Occlusion," meaning "completely closing an orifice or the lumen of a tubular body part." This procedure may be performed via open approach, percutaneous, or percutaneous endoscopic approach. Examples follow:

06L30ZZ   Occlusion of esophageal vein open approach

06L33ZZ   Occlusion of esophageal vein percutaneous approach

06L34ZZ   Occlusion of esophageal vein percutaneous endoscopic approach

Another treatment for esophageal varices is the endoscopic injection of a sclerosing agent or sclerotherapy, which ICD-10-PCS classifies to the root operation "Destruction." For example, endoscopic injection of sclerosing agent into varix of the lower esophagus is coded to **0D538ZZ, Destruction of lower esophagus, via natural or artificial opening endoscopic.**

ULCERS OF THE STOMACH AND SMALL INTESTINE

Combination codes are provided for gastric, gastrojejunal, and duodenal ulcers that indicate whether there is associated bleeding, associated perforation, or both. These combination codes also distinguish between acute and chronic ulcers.

Ulcers of the stomach and the small intestine are often described as peptic without any further identification of the site. The coder should review the medical record for any indication of the site involved; codes from category K27, Peptic ulcer, site unspecified, should not be used when a more specific code can be assigned. Examples of appropriate coding include the following:

K25.5   Chronic gastric ulcer with perforation

K26.3   Acute duodenal ulcer

K25.6   Gastric ulcer with hemorrhage and perforation

DIEULAFOY LESIONS

Dieulafoy lesions are a rare cause of major gastrointestinal bleeding. When gastrointestinal bleeding is present with Dieulafoy lesions, a separate code for the gastrointestinal bleeding is not assigned because it is an integral part of the disease. Assign code K31.82 for Dieulafoy lesion of the stomach and duodenum and code K63.81 for Dieulafoy lesion of the intestine.

Code K22.8 is assigned for Dieulafoy lesions of the esophagus. Dieulafoy lesions of the esophagus typically cause severe bleeding. Endoscopic adrenaline injections can be used to control the bleeding.

243

CHAPTER 20

Diseases
of the
Digestive
System

EXERCISE 20.1

Code the following diagnoses and procedures. Do not assign External cause of morbidity codes.

1.	Acute gastric ulcer with massive gastrointestinal hemorrhage	K25.0
	Exploratory laparotomy with gastric resection, pylorus, with end-to-end anastomosis	0DT70ZZ
2.	Duodenal ulcer, with perforation and hemorrhage	K26.6
3.	Penetrating gastric ulcer	K25.5
	Open resection of esophageal junction (subtotal gastrectomy) with esophageal anastomosis	0DT40ZZ
	Vagotomy	008Q0ZZ
4.	Bleeding gastric ulcer	K25.4

COMPLICATIONS OF ARTIFICIAL OPENINGS OF THE DIGESTIVE SYSTEM

Complications of a colostomy, an enterostomy, a gastrostomy, or an esophagostomy are classified to category K94, Complications of artificial openings of the digestive system, rather than complications of surgical and medical care (categories T80–T88).

Complications of Colostomy and Enterostomy

Complications of colostomy are classified to subcategory K94.0, Colostomy complications. Examples include:

K94.01	Colostomy hemorrhage
K94.03	Malfunction of colostomy
K94.12 + L03.311	Cellulitis of abdominal wall due to complication of enterostomy

244

CHAPTER 20

*Diseases
of the
Digestive
System*

Complications of Gastrostomy and Esophagostomy

Code K94.32 is assigned for an infection of the esophagostomy. An additional code is assigned to specify the infection. Code K94.33 is assigned for a malfunction of the esophagostomy, such as a mechanical complication.

The mechanical complication of a gastrostomy is assigned code K94.23. Code K94.22 is assigned for an infection of the gastrostomy. Additional codes are assigned to specify the type of infection, such as cellulitis of abdominal wall (L03.311) or sepsis (A40.-, A41.-), if that information is available in the medical record.

DIVERTICULOSIS AND DIVERTICULITIS

A diverticulum is a small pouch or sac opening from a tubular or saccular organ, such as the esophagus, intestine, or urinary bladder. Diverticulosis indicates the presence of one or more diverticula of the designated site; diverticulitis is the inflammation of existing diverticula. A diagnosis of diverticulitis assumes the presence of diverticula; only the code for diverticulitis is assigned, as indicated in the Alphabetic Index, even when both conditions are mentioned in the physician's diagnostic statement. Examples of appropriate coding include the following:

K57.10   Diverticulosis of duodenum
K57.12   Diverticulosis and diverticulitis of duodenum
K57.13   Diverticulitis of jejunum with hemorrhage
K57.20   Diverticulitis of cecum with abscess

ICD-10-CM assumes diverticulosis, not otherwise specified, to be a condition of the intestine.

Congenital versus Acquired Diverticula

Diverticula may be either acquired or congenital. For certain sites, ICD-10-CM assumes that the condition is congenital unless specified otherwise; in other sites, the presumption is that the diverticula are acquired. For example, diverticula of the colon are assumed to be acquired unless specified as congenital; but diverticula of the esophagus are assumed to be congenital unless otherwise specified. The Alphabetic Index (volume 2) lists the following entries for diverticula of the colon and the esophagus:

> **Diverticulum, diverticula** . . . K57.90 . . .
> -colon—see Diverticulosis, intestine, large . . .
> --congenital Q43.8 . . .
> -esophagus (congenital) Q39.6
> --acquired (epiphrenic) (pulsion) (traction) K22.5 . . .
> -Meckel's (displaced) (hypertrophic Q43.0

Acquired diverticula of the esophagus are often described by the type of diverticulum (pulsion or traction) or by the portion of the esophagus involved (pharyngoesophageal, midesophageal, or epiphrenic). These qualifications do not affect the code assignment; all are coded **K22.5, Diverticulum of esophagus, acquired.** For example:

K22.5   Epiphrenic diverticula of esophagus
K22.5   Midesophageal traction diverticula of esophagus

245

CHAPTER 20

*Diseases
of the
Digestive
System*

DISEASES OF THE BILIARY SYSTEM

Acute and chronic cholecystitis without associated calculus is classified into category K81, with additional characters indicating whether it is acute (K81.0), chronic (K81.1), both acute and chronic (K81.2), or unspecified (K81.9). Combination codes are assigned for cholecystitis, cholelithiasis, and choledocholithiasis to permit reporting these related conditions with a single code. These codes are presented in three groups: calculus of gallbladder (K80.0- through K80.2-), calculus of bile duct (K80.3- through K80.5-), and calculus of both gallbladder and bile ducts (K80.6- through K80.7-).

Within the K80.0-, K80.1-, K80.2-, K80.4-, K80.6- and K80.7- groups, the fourth character indicates whether there is associated cholecystitis. In subcategory K80.3, the fourth character indicates whether there is cholangitis, rather than cholecystitis, whereas the fourth character in subcategory K80.5 indicates that there is neither cholangitis nor cholecystitis. Codes K80.66 and K80.67 are combination codes that include calculus of gallbladder and bile duct with both acute and chronic cholecystitis. Fifth characters in category K80, Cholelithiasis, indicate whether there is associated obstruction.

Codes **K82.0, Obstruction of gallbladder,** and **K83.1, Obstruction of bile duct,** are assigned only when there is obstruction but no calculi are present.

Cholesterolosis

Cholesterolosis is a condition characterized by abnormal deposits of cholesterol and other lipids in the lining of the gallbladder. In its diffuse form, it is known as strawberry gallbladder. This diagnosis is usually made by the pathologist on the basis of tissue examination and is ordinarily an incidental finding without clinical significance. It should not be coded when other gallbladder pathology is present.

Postcholecystectomy Syndrome

Postcholecystectomy syndrome (K91.5) is a condition in which symptoms suggestive of biliary tract disease either persist or develop following cholecystectomy with no demonstrable cause or abnormality found on workup. A postoperative complication code from the T80–T88 series is not assigned with code K91.5.

Cholecystectomy

A cholecystectomy (excision of the gallbladder) can be total (root operation "Resection") or partial (root operation "Excision") and can be performed either as an open procedure (open approach); through a minor incision (percutaneous approach); or through a small, less-invasive laparoscopic incision (percutaneous endoscopic approach). (For illustrations of Medical and Surgical Section approaches, please refer to figure 8.5 on pages 74–75.) When coding a cholecystectomy, the coder should review the operative report to determine whether exploration or incision of the bile ducts was also performed for removal of stones or for other relief of obstruction as well as whether an intraoperative cholangiogram was performed.

Removal of Biliary Calculi

Biliary stones are removed in several ways. A cholecystectomy automatically removes any gallbladder calculus. Alternatively, a cholecystotomy can be carried out for the removal of gallbladder stones without removing the gallbladder. ICD-10-PCS classifies the removal of biliary stones to the root operation "Extirpation" with unique body part (character 4) values for the biliary ducts as shown in figure 20.2.

Stones in the biliary duct can be removed via the open approach, percutaneously, via percutaneous endoscopic approach, via natural or artificial opening, or via natural or artificial opening endoscopic.

Extracorporeal shock wave lithotripsy destroys biliary stones without invasive surgery. The advantages of lithotripsy over conventional surgery for removal of stones include a shorter hospital stay and avoidance of the potential complications associated with surgical intervention. ICD-10-PCS classifies these procedures to the root operation "Fragmentation" with the approach being "external." For example, extracorporeal lithotripsy of the left hepatic duct is coded to **0FF6XZZ, Fragmentation in left hepatic duct, external approach.**

FIGURE 20.2   Excerpt from ICD-10-PCS Table for Hepatobiliary System Extirpation

Section	0	Medical and Surgical
Body System	F	Hepatobiliary System and Pancreas
Operation	C	Extirpation: Taking or cutting out solid matter from a body part

Body Part	Approach	Device	Qualifier
0 Liver 1 Liver, Right Lobe 2 Liver, Left Lobe 4 Gallbladder G Pancreas	0 Open 3 Percutaneous 4 Percutaneous Endoscopic	Z No Device	Z No Qualifier
5 Hepatic Duct, Right 6 Hepatic Duct, Left 8 Cystic Duct 9 Common Bile Duct C Ampulla of Vater D Pancreatic Duct F Pancreatic Duct, Accessory	0 Open 3 Percutaneous 4 Percutaneous Endoscopic 7 Via Natural or Artificial Opening 8 Via Natural or Artificial Opening Endoscopic	Z No Device	Z No Qualifier

EXERCISE 20.2

Code the following diagnoses and procedures. Do not assign External cause of morbidity codes.

1. Acute cholecystitis with calculus of gallbladder
   and bile duct   K80.62

   Total laparoscopic cholecystectomy   0FT44ZZ

2. Chronic cholecystitis with calculus in common duct   K80.44
   Total open cholecystectomy   0FT40ZZ
   Open common bile duct exploration with removal of   0FC90ZZ
   common bile duct stone   BF030ZZ
   Intraoperative cholangiogram (gallbladder and   0DTJ0ZZ
   bile ducts with high osmolar contrast)
   Incidental open appendectomy

3. Biliary obstruction, extrahepatic   K83.1

4. Cholecystitis, acute and chronic, with cholesterolosis K81.2
   Total cholecystectomy   0FT40ZZ

5. Acute cholecystitis with choledocholithiasis   K80.42

6. Acute and chronic cholelithiasis with calculi in   K80.70
   gallbladder and bile duct

7. Acute and chronic cholecystitis with gallbladder   K80.67
   and bile duct calculus and obstruction

ADHESIONS

Intestinal and peritoneal adhesions are classified as code **K66.0, Peritoneal adhesions (postproce-dural) (postinfection),** or **K56.5, Intestinal adhesions [bands] with obstruction (postprocedural) (postinfection),** when obstruction is also present. These codes do not include pelvic peritoneal adhesions; such adhesions are classified as code **N73.6, Female pelvic peritoneal adhesions (post-infective).**

Usually, minor adhesions do not cause symptoms or increase the difficulty of performing an operative procedure. When minor adhesions are easily lysed as part of another procedure, coding a diagnosis of adhesions and a lysis procedure is inappropriate. For example, there are often minor adhesions around the gallbladder that can be pushed aside easily without cutting during gallbladder surgery; coding of adhesions and/or lysis is not appropriate in such situations. Sometimes, however, a strong band of adhesions prevents the surgeon from gaining access to the organ to be removed, and a surgical lysis is required before the operation can proceed. In such cases, coding both the adhesions and lysis is appropriate. If there is any question, the determination of whether the adhesions and the lysis are significant enough to merit coding must be made by the physician. Lysis of adhesions procedures are classified in ICD-10-PCS to the root operation "Release." In the root operation "Release," the body part value coded is the body part being freed and not the tissue being manipulated or cut to free the body part. For example, open lysis of small intestine adhesions are coded to the "small intestine" body part value (8) and reported as 0DN80ZZ.

HERNIAS OF THE ABDOMINAL CAVITY

Hernias are classified by type and site, with combination codes used to indicate any associated gangrene or obstruction. With inguinal and femoral hernias, the codes further subdivide the hernia as unilateral or bilateral and whether it is specified as recurrent; that is, whether it had been repaired during a previous surgery. An incisional hernia is classified as a ventral hernia. Hernias described as incarcerated or strangulated are classified as obstructed. A hernia with both gangrene and obstruction is classified to hernia with gangrene. Careful review of the medical record and attention to instructional notes are important steps in coding these conditions. Coding examples include the following:

K40.00	Bilateral inguinal hernia with obstruction (no mention of gangrene)
K40.41	Unilateral recurrent inguinal hernia with gangrene
K41.11	Gangrenous femoral hernia, recurrent, bilateral
K44.1	Diaphragmatic hernia with gangrene
K42.0	Umbilical hernia with obstruction
K41.30	Incarcerated femoral hernia

Hernia repairs can be performed with a laparoscope inserted through a small incision or through a traditional open surgical approach. When coding hernia repairs, the coder should be careful not to use a bilateral repair code when the hernia itself is described as unilateral. A unilateral repair may be performed even though bilateral hernias are present, but, obviously, it is impossible to repair bilateral hernias when only one hernia exists. Care should be taken to understand how the hernia repair is performed.

While the documentation may refer to herniorrhaphy, or hernia repair, ICD-10-PCS classifies these procedures to two different root operations. Herniorrhaphies are classified to the root operation "Repair," unless the repair is accomplished with the use of a biological or synthetic material such as a mesh or graft, in which case the root operation "Supplement" is used. In addition, herniorrhaphies are classified to the body systems "anatomical regions, lower extremities," or

249

CHAPTER 20

Diseases
of the
Digestive
System

"general" and the appropriate body part where the hernia is located. For example, an open repair of a bilateral inguinal hernia is coded to 0YQA0ZZ, while an open repair of a ventral hernia is coded to 0WQF0ZZ.

Coding examples include:

0YQ50ZZ	Open repair of right inguinal hernia
0YU54JZ	Laparoscopic repair of right inguinal hernia with mesh prosthesis
0YQA3ZZ	Percutaneous repair of bilateral inguinal hernias

EXERCISE 20.3

Code the following diagnoses and procedures. Do not assign External cause of morbidity codes.

1. Right direct inguinal hernia and left indirect sliding inguinal hernia — K40.20
   Open repair of bilateral inguinal hernias — 0YQA0ZZ

2. Incarcerated left inguinal hernia — K40.30
   Laparoscopic left inguinal herniorrhaphy with mesh prosthesis — 0YU64JZ

3. Recurrent left inguinal hernia — K40.91
   Percutaneous repair of inguinal hernia, left — 0YQ63ZZ

4. Gangrenous umbilical hernia — K42.1
   Open repair of umbilical hernia — 0WQF0ZZ

5. Strangulated umbilical hernia — K42.0
   Laparoscopic repair of umbilical hernia with mesh prosthesis — 0WUF4JZ

6. Reflux esophagitis secondary to sliding — K21.0
   esophageal hiatal hernia — K44.9
   Repair of right esophageal hiatus hernia, open abdominal — 0BQR0ZZ
   approach

7. Recurrent ventral incisional hernia with obstruction — K43.11
   and gangrene

APPENDICITIS

Category K35, Acute appendicitis, uses a fourth character to indicate the presence of either generalized peritonitis (K35.2) or localized peritonitis (K35.3). Unspecified acute appendicitis is coded to K35.80. Occasionally, an appendix ruptures during an appendectomy; this is not classified as a complication of surgery.

Category K37, Unspecified appendicitis, is a vague category that should not be used in an acute care facility. Additional information is almost always available in the medical record.

Surgical removal of the appendix is coded to the root operation "Resection." Incidental appendectomy refers to a procedure performed to remove the appendix as a routine prophylactic measure in the course of other abdominal surgery. ICD-10-PCS does not distinguish between an incidental appendectomy and an appendectomy to remove a diseased appendix.

DIARRHEA

A code from categories A00 through A09 is assigned for infectious diarrhea when the organism has been identified. Code A09 is assigned for infectious diarrhea not otherwise specified, or described only as dysenteric diarrhea, endemic diahhrea, or epidemic diarrhea. Check the Alphabetic Index carefully before coding, because diarrhea can be related to a variety of conditions. Symptom code R19.7 is assigned for diarrhea for which no appropriate subterm can be located. Examples of appropriate code assignments include the following:

A04.7	Diarrhea due to *Clostridium difficile*
R19.7	Acute diarrhea
A07.3	Coccidial diarrhea
K52.9	Chronic diarrhea
R19.7	Infantile diarrhea
K59.1	Functional diarrhea

CONSTIPATION

Unspecified constipation is coded to K59.00, but there are two distinct subtypes of constipation recognized: slow transit constipation (K59.01) and outlet dysfunction constipation (K59.02). The slow transit results from a delay in transit of fecal material throughout the colon secondary to smooth muscle. The latter type of constipation results from difficulty evacuating the rectum during attempts at defecation. Treatment for these two types of constipation is very different. The slow transit type is treated with either laxatives or surgery. Biofeedback is taught for relaxation for the outlet dysfunction constipation.

BARIATRIC SURGERY

Bariatric surgery refers to procedures performed on obese patients for the purpose of weight loss. Several types of restrictive and malabsorptive gastric procedures are performed for weight loss when other methods have failed for severely obese patients. Malabsorptive operations are the most common and restrict food intake as well as the amount of calories and nutrients the body absorbs. Restrictive operations restrict food intake but do not interfere with the normal digestive process. Restrictive operations for obesity include adjustable gastric banding and vertical banded gastroplasty. (See figure 20.3 for illustrations of these and other procedures.) The weight loss is usually achieved by reducing the size of the stomach (restrictive operations) with an implanted device, such as gastric banding, or through

FIGURE 20.3   Illustrations of Bariatric Surgery

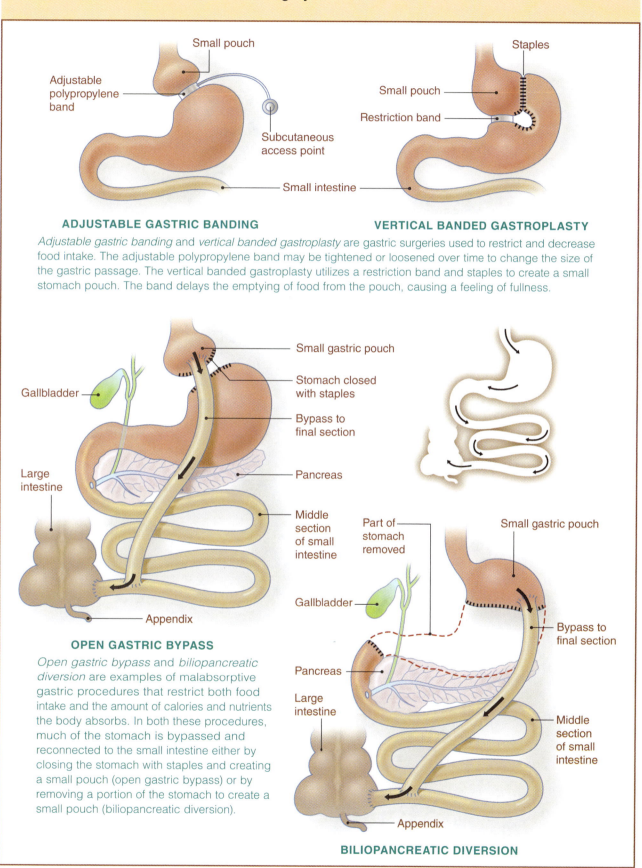

ADJUSTABLE GASTRIC BANDING

Adjustable gastric banding and *vertical banded gastroplasty* are gastric surgeries used to restrict and decrease food intake. The adjustable polypropylene band may be tightened or loosened over time to change the size of the gastric passage. The vertical banded gastroplasty utilizes a restriction band and staples to create a small stomach pouch. The band delays the emptying of food from the pouch, causing a feeling of fullness.

VERTICAL BANDED GASTROPLASTY

OPEN GASTRIC BYPASS

Open gastric bypass and *biliopancreatic diversion* are examples of malabsorptive gastric procedures that restrict both food intake and the amount of calories and nutrients the body absorbs. In both these procedures, much of the stomach is bypassed and reconnected to the small intestine either by closing the stomach with staples and creating a small pouch (open gastric bypass) or by removing a portion of the stomach to create a small pouch (biliopancreatic diversion).

BILIOPANCREATIC DIVERSION

252

CHAPTER 20

Diseases
of the
Digestive
System

removal of a portion of the stomach or by resecting and rerouting the small intestines to a small stomach pouch (malabsorptive operations), such as gastric bypass surgery. Restrictive operations such as gastric banding are classified to the root operation "Restriction." When coding bypass procedures, it is important to understand the body part bypassed from and the body part bypassed to. The ICD-10-PCS fourth character body part specifies the body part bypassed from (for example, the stomach), and the seventh character qualifier specifies the body part bypassed to (for example, the jejunum).

Coding examples include:

0DV64CZ	Laparoscopic gastric restrictive procedure
0DW64CZ	Laparoscopic revision of gastric band
0D160ZB	Open gastric bypass (stomach to ileum)

EXERCISE 20.4

Code the following diagnoses and procedures. Do not assign External cause of morbidity codes.

---

1. Acute ruptured <u>appendicitis</u> with postoperative   K35.2
   intestinal obstruction   K91.3
   Open <u>appendectomy</u>   0DTJ0ZZ

---

2. Acute <u>hepatitis</u> and early <u>cirrhosis</u> of the liver   K70.10
   due to chronic <u>alcoholism</u>   K70.30
                                                                     F10.20

---

3. Perirectal <u>abscess</u>   K61.1
   <u>Atony</u> of colon   K59.8
   Percutaneous <u>incision</u> and drainage of perirectal abscess   0D9P3ZZ

---

4. Hepatic <u>coma</u> with massive <u>ascites</u> secondary to   K72.91
   Laennec's <u>cirrhosis</u>   K70.31
   Paracentesis   0D9W3ZZ

---

5. Intestinal <u>obstruction</u> due to peritoneal adhesive band   K56.5
   Open <u>lysis</u> of adhesive band large intestine   0DNE0ZZ

---

6. Diverticulosis and diverticulitis of right colon — K57.32

    Open right hemicolectomy with end-to-end anastomosis — 0DTF0ZZ

7. Infection of gastrostomy with abscess of abdominal wall — K94.22

    due to *Streptococcus* B — L02.211

    — B95.1

8. Polyp of rectum — K62.1

    Colonoscopy with polypectomy — 0DBP8ZZ

9. Neurogenic bowel — K59.2

10. Morbid obesity — E66.01

    Laparoscopic gastric bypass to ileum — 0D164ZB

CHAPTER 21

Diseases of the Genitourinary System

CHAPTER OVERVIEW

- Diseases of the genitourinary system are classified in chapter 14 of ICD-10-CM.

  — They are not found in chapter 14 if they are classified by etiology.

  — These diseases include transmissible infections; neoplastic diseases; and conditions complicating pregnancy, childbirth, and the puerperium.

- The term "urinary tract infection" is often used by physicians when referring to conditions such as urethritis, cystitis, or pyelonephritis.

- There are different codes for urinary incontinence depending on the type of incontinence (e.g., stress, functional). When the underlying cause is known, that should be sequenced first.

- Chronic kidney disease develops in conjunction with other conditions. The instructions for sequencing of the code in conjunction with others is found in the Tabular List.

- A relationship is presumed when a patient has both hypertension and kidney disease. Codes extend to the fifth character to cover this condition.

- Renal dialysis codes vary from admission codes to codes for the insertion of catheter without the performance of dialysis. Dialysis codes cover complications such as dialysis dementia.

- Conditions involving the prostate involve a fourth and fifth character. Neoplasms of the prostate are not included within this category of codes.

- Other related codes covered in this chapter are prostatectomy, endometriosis, genital prolapse, dysplasia of the cervix and vulva, and endometrial ablation.

- Neoplasms of the breast are classified in chapter 2 of ICD-10-CM. However, not all conditions and procedures involving the breast are related to neoplasms.

LEARNING OUTCOMES

After studying this chapter you should be able to:

Distinguish among the different conditions often referred to as urinary tract infections.

Code for a variety of kidney diseases and their treatments.

Explain coding for kidney disease in conjunction with hypertension and diabetes.

Classify conditions that affect both male and female genitalia.

TERMS TO KNOW

Acute kidney failure
sudden failure of renal function following a severe insult to the kidneys

Chronic kidney disease
long-term disability of the renal function

Nephropathy
general term indicating that renal disease is present

Ureter
carries urine from the kidneys to the bladder

Urethra
carries urine from the bladder to the outside of the body

REMEMBER . . .

It is important to distinguish between chronic kidney disease, acute kidney failure, and acute kidney injury.

INTRODUCTION

Diseases of the genitourinary system are classified in chapter 14 of ICD-10-CM, except those that are classified by etiology, such as certain easily transmissible infections; neoplastic diseases; and conditions complicating pregnancy, childbirth, and the puerperium. Subterms should be checked carefully in the Alphabetic Index, and special attention should be given to the terms "urethra" and "ureter," which are often confused by coders.

INFECTIONS OF THE GENITOURINARY TRACT

Physicians often use the term "urinary tract infection (UTI)" when referring to conditions such as urethritis, cystitis, or pyelonephritis. Urethritis and cystitis are lower urinary tract infections; pyelonephritis is an infection of the upper urinary tract. The main term for the specific condition should be referred to in the Alphabetic Index before referring to the main term **Infection.** For example, under the main term **Cystitis,** subterms are located for diphtheritic (A36.85) and chlamydial (A56.01) infection. When there is no subterm for the organism, the code for the condition is assigned, with an additional code from categories B95–B97 to indicate the organism. For example, there is no subterm for *Escherichia coli* under the main term for cystitis; therefore, codes N30.90 and B96.2 are assigned for cystitis due to *E. coli.*

The following examples indicate complete coding for such infections:

A59.03	Cystitis due to trichomonas
N30.00 + B96.4	Acute cystitis due to proteus infection
N11.9 + B96.2	Chronic pyelonephritis due to *E. coli*

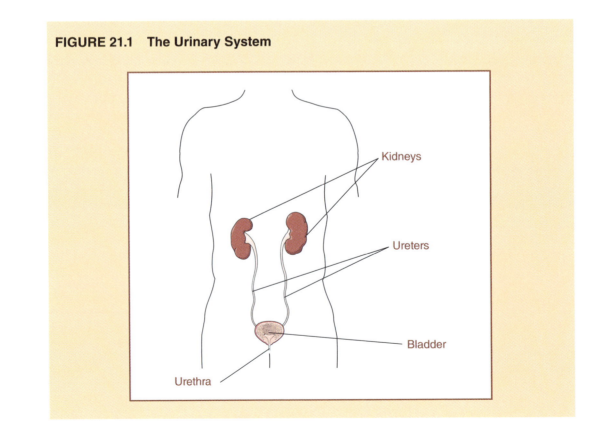

FIGURE 21.1   The Urinary System

257

CHAPTER 21

*Diseases
of the
Genitourinary
System*

Urinary tract infections that develop following surgery are rarely true postoperative infections and are not usually classified as such. When the operative procedure involves the urinary tract, however, it may be appropriate for the coder to ask the physician whether the infection is related to the procedure. When the infection is related to the presence of an implant, a graft, or a device (such as an indwelling or a suprapubic catheter), code T83.5- or T83.6 is assigned. An additional code may be included to identify the infection. As with all postprocedural complications, code assignment is based on the provider's documentation of the relationship between the infection and the procedure. In the absence of documentation indicating that the infection is due to the surgical procedure, code **N39.0, Urinary tract infection, site not specified,** should be assigned. If the provider states that the UTI is secondary to the indwelling urinary catheter, assign code **T83.51-, Infection and inflammatory reaction due to indwelling urinary catheter,** and code **N39.0, Urinary tract infection, site not specified.**

EXERCISE 21.1

Code the following diagnoses and procedures. Do not assign External cause of morbidity codes.

1. Urethral stricture due to gonorrheal infection — A54.01
   N37
   Urethral dilation via cystoscope — 0T7D8ZZ

2. Abscess of right scrotum due to group B *Streptococcus* — N49.2
   B95.1
   Percutaneous incision and drainage of scrotal abscess — 0V953ZZ

3. Acute pyelonephritis due to *Helicobacter pylori* infection — N10
   B96.81

4. Chronic cystitis with hematuria — N30.21
   Pseudomonas infection — B96.5

5. Chronic cystitis due to *Monilia* infection — B37.41

6. Urinary tract infection due to candidiasis — B37.49

HEMATURIA

Hematuria refers to blood in the urine. Gross hematuria refers to hematuria that is so plentiful that it is visible to the naked eye. Microscopic hematuria refers to blood in the urine visible only under a microscope. ICD-10-CM provides separate codes for gross hematuria (R31.0), benign essential microscopic hematuria (R31.1), other microscopic hematuria (R31.2), and unspecified hematuria (R31.9). Many genitourinary conditions have hematuria as an integral associated symptom. For example, the medical record has a diagnostic statement of hematuria due to renal calculus but only a code of **N20.0, Calculus of kidney,** is assigned. The hematuria is integral to this condition and no additional code is assigned. A certain amount of hematuria is expected following a urinary tract procedure or a prostatectomy. This is not considered a postoperative complication, and no code is assigned unless the bleeding is excessive or persistent.

Microscopic hematuria should not be confused with hemoglobinuria, which is coded as R82.3. Hemoglobinuria is an abnormal finding and refers to the presence of free hemoglobin in the urine on laboratory examination of the urine. It is reported only when the physician has indicated its clinical significance.

Codes in category N30, Cystitis, and subcategories N41.0, Acute prostatitis, and N41.1, Chronic prostatitis, provide combination codes with a fifth character identifying whether hematuria is present or not.

URINARY INCONTINENCE

Stress incontinence causes involuntary urine loss with physical strain such as coughing or sneezing. Although it occurs in both male and female patients, it occurs more frequently in women, typically as a result of physical changes brought on by earlier childbearing. Prostate surgery is the primary cause of incontinence in men. Stress incontinence is coded as **N39.3, Stress incontinence (female) (male).** Urinary incontinence due to cognitive impairment, severe physical disability, or immobility is coded to **R39.81, Functional urinary incontinence.** Urinary incontinence of nonorganic origin is coded to **F98.0, Enuresis not due to a substance or known physiological condition.**

Other types of incontinence are also classified into subcategory N39.4, Other specified urinary incontinence. When more than one type of incontinence is present, it is classified as **Mixed incontinence (male) (female),** and code **N39.46** is assigned. When the underlying cause of incontinence is known, the code for that condition should be sequenced first. Code N32.81 should also be assigned for any overactive bladder associated with conditions in codes N39.3 and N39.4-.

Treatment for incontinence depends, to a large extent, on the particular type of incontinence present. If it is due to an intrinsic sphincter deficiency, collagen injections are sometimes carried out. Code **3E0K3GC, Introduction of other therapeutic substance into genitourinary tract, percutaneous approach,** is assigned for this therapy.

Other treatments for incontinence are surgical in nature. Codes for repair of incontinence depend on the procedure performed. Typically, these procedures are classified to the root operations "Repair," "Reposition," or "Supplement." Examples of these procedure codes are:

0TSC0ZZ	Reposition bladder neck, open approach
0TSD4ZZ	Reposition urethra, percutaneous endoscopic approach
0TUC7KZ	Supplement bladder neck with nonautologous tissue substitute, via natural or artificial opening
0TQDXZZ	Repair urethra, external approach

RENAL DISEASE

Renal disease is classified into categories N00 through N29. Glomerulonephritis is a type of nephritis in which there is bilateral inflammatory change without infection. Nephrotic syndrome is a complex clinical state characterized by edema, albuminuria, and increased permeability of the glomerular capillary basement membrane. The syndrome may result from an unknown cause or from glomerulonephritis or diseases such as diabetes, systemic lupus erythematosus, hypertension, and amyloidosis. Nephropathy is a general term that indicates that renal disease is present. Infection of the kidney not otherwise specified is classified to N15.9. Kidney disease complicating pregnancy, childbirth, and the puerperium is reclassified in chapter 15 of ICD-10-CM.

Chronic Kidney Disease and End-Stage Renal Disease

Chronic kidney disease (CKD) is considered a more current and precise term than chronic renal failure or chronic renal insufficiency. CKD develops as a complication of other diseases, such as diabetes mellitus, primary hypertension, glomerulonephritis, nephrosis, interstitial nephritis, systemic lupus erythematosus, obstructive uropathy, and polycystic kidney disease. The sequencing of the CKD code in relationship to codes for other contributing conditions is based on the conventions of the Tabular List.

Patients usually live for many years with such chronic kidney disease. When kidney involvement becomes so extensive that kidney function can no longer keep up with the body's needs, dialysis is usually required.

ICD-10-CM classifies CKD on the basis of severity. Based on the glomerular filtration rate (GFR), chronic kidney disease has been categorized into five stages. Category N18, Chronic kidney disease (CKD), has been expanded to the fourth-character subcategory level for further specification of the varying stages of chronic kidney disease. The fourth-character subcategory codes are as follows:

N18.1   Chronic kidney disease, stage 1
N18.2   Chronic kidney disease, stage 2 (mild)
N18.3   Chronic kidney disease, stage 3 (moderate)
N18.4   Chronic kidney disease, stage 4 (severe)
N18.5   Chronic kidney disease, stage 5
N18.6   End stage renal disease
N18.9   Chronic kidney disease, unspecified

Chronic renal disease, chronic renal insufficiency, chronic renal failure, and unspecified kidney disease are assigned to code N18.9.

End-stage renal disease (ESRD) (N18.6) is a complex syndrome characterized by a variable and inconsistent group of biochemical and clinical changes that affect volume regulation, acid-base balance, electrolyte balance, excretion of waste products, and several endocrine functions. It is a progression of chronic kidney disease and is defined by clinicians as the point at which regular dialysis sessions or a kidney transplant is required to maintain life. For patients with end-stage renal disease, code **Z99.2**, **Dependence on renal dialysis,** should be assigned as an additional code to report dialysis status.

Chronic renal failure, not otherwise specified, and chronic renal insufficiency are both assigned code **N18.9, Chronic kidney disease, unspecified.** If both a stage of CKD and ESRD are documented for the same patient, only code N18.6 would be assigned.

Kidney transplant may be recommended for patients with severe CKD caused by severe, uncontrollable hypertension, infections, diabetes mellitus, or glomerulonephritis. Patients who have undergone kidney transplant may still have some form of CKD because the kidney transplant may not fully restore kidney function. Code Z94.0 may be assigned with the appropriate CKD code to indicate that a CKD patient is status post kidney transplant. It is incorrect to assume that mild or moderate CKD following a transplant is a transplant failure unless it is documented as such in the medical record.

260

CHAPTER 21

*Diseases
of the
Genitourinary
System*

If transplant complication such as failure or rejection, or other transplant complication is documented in patients with severe CKD or ESRD, code **T86.1-, Complications of kidney transplant,** is assigned. If a post–kidney transplant patient has CKD and the documentation is unclear whether there is transplant failure or rejection, it is necessary to query the provider.

Acute Kidney Failure

Acute kidney failure (N17.-) is very different from chronic kidney disease; it is not a phase of the same condition. Chronic kidney disease is a long-term inability of the kidneys to function adequately; acute kidney failure is the sudden cessation of renal function following severe insult to normal kidneys. Toxic agents, traumatic or surgical shock, tissue destruction due to injury or surgery, or a variety of other conditions can cause acute kidney failure.

Acute renal insufficiency (N28.9) is considered an early stage of renal impairment, evidenced by diminished creatinine clearance or mildly elevated serum creatinine or blood urea nitrogen (BUN). Clinical symptoms or other abnormal laboratory findings may or may not be present but are usually minimal. Treatment varies, depending on the underlying cause, but serious attention is given to prevent its progression to renal failure. Code **N99.89, Other postprocedural complications and disorders of genitorurinary system,** is assigned if renal insufficiency is due to a procedure.

Physicians sometimes use the terms "renal insufficiency" and "renal failure" interchangeably, but ICD-10-CM classifies these terms to different codes. ICD-10-CM classifies unspecified and acute renal insufficiency to code N28.9, whereas acute kidney failure is assigned to category N17. Unspecified renal failure is identified with code **N19, Unspecified kidney failure.** It is important for the coder to be guided by the classification. If the physician uses both terms in the medical record, the physician should be queried for clarification as to the correct diagnosis.

Acute kidney injury is a phrase used by some physicians to refer to acute kidney failure. Care should be taken to determine whether the documentation refers to a traumatic injury to the kidney (which would be assigned to a code in subcategory S37.0) or to a nontraumatic event, which is actually acute kidney failure. Nontraumatic acute kidney injury is assigned to **N17.9, Acute kidney failure, unspecified.** The default for acute kidney injury, unspecified as to traumatic or nontraumatic, is code N17.9.

Kidney Disease with Hypertension

ICD-10-CM presumes a relationship when a patient has both chronic kidney disease or renal sclerosis and hypertension, and category I12, Hypertensive chronic kidney disease, or category I13, Hypertensive heart and chronic kidney disease, should be assigned. The fourth or fifth character indicates the stage of chronic kidney disease as follows:

- Category I12
  —Fourth character of 0 is for "chronic kidney disease stage 5 or end-stage renal disease"
  —Fourth character of 1 is for "chronic kidney disease stage 1 through stage 4, or unspecified chronic kidney disease"
- Category I13
  —Fourth character of 0 is for "with heart failure and stage 1 through 4, or unspecified chronic kidney disease"
  —Fourth character of 1 is for CKD without heart failure with the fifth character indicating the CKD stage as follows:
    –Fifth character of 0 is for "chronic kidney disease stage 1 through 4, or unspecified"
    –Fifth character of 1 is for "chronic kidney disease stage 5 or end-stage renal disease"
  —Fourth character of 2 is for "with heart failure and with stage 5 or end-stage renal disease"

261

CHAPTER 21

*Diseases
of the
Genitourinary
System*

Codes from categories I12 and I13 require additional codes to identify the stage of CKD as shown on table 21.1.

Acute kidney failure is not caused by hypertension and is not included in the hypertensive kidney disease codes. When acute kidney failure and hypertension are both present, assign a code from category N17, Acute kidney failure, with an additional code for the hypertension.

The use of codes from categories I12 and I13 does not apply in the following situations:

- The renal condition is acute kidney failure.
- The hypertension is described as secondary.
- The kidney disease is specifically stated as due to a cause other than hypertension.

Examples of appropriate codes for kidney disease with hypertension include the following:

I12.9 + N18.9	Hypertensive kidney disease with chronic kidney disease
I13.10 + N18.3	Hypertensive heart and kidney disease with chronic kidney disease, stage 3
I13.2 + N18.5 + I50.9	Hypertensive heart and kidney disease with stage V chronic kidney disease and congestive heart failure
<u>N17.9</u> + I10	Acute kidney failure; hypertension

TABLE 21.1   Hypertensive Chronic Kidney Disease and Hypertensive Heart and Chronic Kidney Disease and the Applicable CKD Stages

Category I12–I13 Code	Additional CKD Stage Code Required	
	N18.1–N18.4 or N18.9	N18.5 or N18.6
I12.0		X
I12.9	X	
I13.0	X	
I13.10	X	
I13.11		X
I13.2		X

Kidney Disease with Diabetes Mellitus

Diabetic kidney complications are coded to E08–E13 with .21 for diabetic nephropathy, .22 for chronic kidney disease, and .29 for other kidney complication. Kidney disease sometimes results from both hypertension and diabetes mellitus. In this situation, the combination code from category I12 or category I13 and a code from subcategory E08–E13 with .2- are assigned. A code from category N18 is assigned to specify the stage of chronic kidney disease.

Examples of appropriate codes for kidney disease due to diabetes include the following:

E11.21	Diabetic nephrosis
I12.9 + E10.22 + N18.4	Chronic kidney disease stage IV due to hypertension and type 1 diabetes mellitus
E10.22	Chronic kidney disease, unspecified, due to type 1 diabetes

RENAL DIALYSIS

Patients with end-stage renal disease require a regular schedule of dialysis treatments to manage the symptoms arising from kidney disease. Typically, dialysis is performed as an outpatient service. However, periodically it may be necessary for care to be provided to the renal dialysis catheter, such as toilet or cleansing, or replacement of the catheter. These situations are coded to **Z49.01, Encounter for fitting and adjustment of extracorporeal dialysis catheter,** or code **Z49.02, Encounter for fitting and adjustment of peritoneal dialysis catheter.** Other encounters may be related to adequacy testing for dialysis, which are classified to codes **Z49.31, Encounter for adequacy testing for hemodialysis,** or **Z49.32, Encounter for adequacy testing for peritoneal dialysis.**

If the patient is admitted for other reasons but continues to receive dialysis therapy during the hospital stay or is known to be maintained on renal dialysis, code **Z99.2, Dependence on renal dialysis,** may be assigned as an additional code; the condition responsible for the admission is designated as the principal diagnosis. If the patient is known to be noncompliant with renal dialysis, code **Z91.15, Patient's noncompliance with renal dialysis,** may be assigned.

The performance of hemodialysis requires the insertion of a venous catheter (ICD-10-PCS code for insertion of infusion device, percutaneous approach, with the appropriate vein) or a totally implantable venous access device (requires two ICD-10-PCS codes, one for the insertion of vascular access device and another for the insertion of reservoir, with the codes being dependent on the site of insertion). The associated dialysis is coded to the Extracorporeal Assistance and Performance Section, "physiological systems" body system, and root operation "Performance" (completely taking over a physiological function by extracorporeal means). Character 5 is for duration, which distinguishes between a single encounter and multiple encounters. For example, multiple hemodialysis encounters are coded to **5A1D60Z, Performance of urinary filtration, multiple.**

Peritoneal dialysis is accomplished by instilling a prepared fluid into the peritoneal cavity and removing the uremic toxins along with the prepared fluid. Creation of a cutaneoperitoneal fistula for this purpose is coded to bypass peritoneal cavity to cutaneous with synthetic substitute. For example, if the procedure is performed using a percutaneous approach, it is coded to **0W1G3J4, Bypass peritoneal cavity to cutaneous with synthetic substitute, percutaneous approach.** Code **3E1M39Z, Irrigation of peritoneal cavity using dialysate, percutaneous approach,** is assigned for the associated dialysis.

Patients are sometimes admitted for insertion of a catheter or a vascular access device, but no dialysis is performed during the admission. When dialysis is performed during the same episode of care, procedure code 5A1D00Z (single encounter) or 5A1D60Z (multiple encounter) is assigned to specify that the dialysis was actually performed during the encounter. When the admission is for fitting or adjustment of the dialysis catheter, code Z49.01 is assigned for an extracorporeal catheter and Z49.02 for a peritoneal catheter. If concurrent dialysis is performed, procedure code 5A1D00Z (single encounter) or 5A1D60Z (multiple encounter) is assigned. Some coding examples follow:

N18.6 + 05H533Z	Patient with end-stage renal disease admitted for insertion of Hickman catheter into the right subclavian vein for renal dialysis (no dialysis performed)
Z49.01 + N18.5 + 5A1D00Z	Patient with chronic kidney disease, stage V, admitted for cleansing of hemodialysis catheter, single hemodialysis performed
N18.6 + 031C0ZF	Patient with end-stage renal disease admitted for creation of arteriovenous (AV) fistula (left radiocephalic) for renal dialysis; dialysis not performed on this admission

263

CHAPTER 21

Diseases

of the

Genitourinary

System

It normally takes two to three months for an AV fistula to mature. A nonmaturing or nondeveloping fistula is considered a mechanical complication and is coded to **T82.590-, Other mechanical complication of surgically created arteriovenous fistula.** Primary causes of a nonmaturing fistula are narrowing of a vein or multiple competing veins. Treatment may consist of performing an arteriovenostomy to create a new AV fistula. Other treatment options may be performed by interventional radiologists—such as balloon angioplasty; revision of AV fistula; and/or closing off competing veins, which can be performed using various techniques.

Other mechanical complications related to the AV fistula are breakdown (T82.510-), displacement (T82.520-), and leakage (T82.530-), while mechanical complications of the vascular dialysis catheter are coded to subcategory T82.4.

EXERCISE 21.2

Code the following diagnoses and procedures. Do not assign External cause of morbidity codes.

1.	End-stage renal disease	N18.6
	Peritoneal dialysis	3E1M39Z
2.	Chronic kidney disease, stage 5	N18.5
	Catheter insertion into the left subclavian vein for renal dialysis	05H633Z
	Single hemodialysis performed	5A1D00Z

CYSTOSCOPY AS OPERATIVE APPROACH

Cystoscopy is used as the approach for many procedures performed in diagnosing and treating urinary tract conditions and is not coded separately when it is the procedural approach. ICD-10-PCS classifies the cystoscopic approach as "via natural or artificial opening endoscopic." (For illustrations of Medical and Surgical Section approaches, please refer to figure 8.5 on pages 74–75.) Procedures described as transurethral should be coded to the approach "via natural or artificial opening," while those described as transurethral ureteroscopic are classified to the "via natural or artificial opening endoscopic" approach. When a cystoscopy is performed to visually and/or manually explore the bladder (without performing another procedure), it is coded to the root operation "Inspection" with code **0TJB8ZZ, Inspection of bladder, via natural or artificial opening endoscopic.**

REMOVAL OF URINARY CALCULUS

Urinary calculi are relatively common and often pass without surgery. Several types of surgical techniques are used when intervention is necessary. Extracorporeal shock wave lithotripsy (ESWL) of the kidney, ureter, and/or bladder (ICD-10-PCS root operation "Fragmentation," external

264

CHAPTER 21

Diseases
of the
Genitourinary
System

approach) uses shock waves to reduce the stones to a slush that can more easily pass through the urinary tract and be excreted over a short period of time. For example, ESWL of the right ureter is coded to **0TF6XZZ, Fragmentation in right ureter, external approach.**

For stones that are poor candidates for ESWL, endoscopic therapy is indicated. Ureteroscopy is the most common means of visualizing an upper urinary tract calculus. In addition, percutaneous techniques (e.g., percutaneous endourology) can be used.

Ultrasonic lithotripsy requires a rigid endoscope and is commonly performed via a percutaneous renal approach. Ultrasonic lithotriptors are used to treat large bladder stones. Because the ultrasound requires a relatively large, rigid instrument to perform, most stones treated are limited to the lower ureter or the bladder. The ICD-10-PCS root operation would still be "Fragmentation," but a separate code with the root operation "Extirpation" would be used to report the removal of the stone fragments.

Kidney stones can be removed by percutaneous nephrostomy with fragmentation (root operation "Fragmentation" with percutaneous or percutaneous endoscopic approach) or without fragmentation (root operation "Extirpation" with percutaneous or percutaneous endoscopic approach). Transurethral ureteroscopic lithotripsy with fragmentation of stones removes calculi from the ureter and renal pelvis.

EXERCISE 21.3

Code the following diagnoses and procedures. Do not assign External cause of morbidity codes.

1.	Right ureteral calculus	N20.1
	Right calyceal diverticulum	N28.89
	Left renal cyst, solitary (acquired)	N28.1
2.	Impacted renal calculus with medullary sponge kidney	N20.0
		Q61.5
	Extracorporeal shock wave lithotripsy of left kidney calculus	0TF4XZZ
3.	Calculus in bladder	N21.0
	Lithotripsy of urinary bladder with ultrasonic	0TFB4ZZ
	fragmentation and removal of fragments via	0TCB4ZZ
	percutaneous endoscopic approach	

PROSTATE DISEASE AND THERAPY

Diseases of the male genital organs are classified in categories N40 through N53, with conditions of the prostate using categories N40 through N42. Neoplasms of the prostate are classified as follows:

C61   Malignant neoplasm of the prostate
D29.1   Benign neoplasm of the prostate
D07.5   In situ neoplasm of the prostate

Hyperplasia of the prostate is classified to category N40, Enlarged prostate, with fourth characters providing additional specificity regarding the presence or absence of lower urinary tract symptoms. As indicated by the "use additional code" note under code N40.1, an additional code should be assigned to identify associated symptoms when specified, such as incomplete bladder emptying (R39.14), nocturia (R35.1), straining on urination (R39.16), urinary frequency (R35.0), urinary hesitancy (R39.11), urinary incontinence (N39.4-), urinary obstruction (N13.8), urinary retention (R33.8), urinary urgency (R39.15), or weak urinary stream (R39.12).

Category N41 classifies inflammatory disease of the prostate as follows:

N41.00   Acute prostatitis without hematuria
N41.01   Acute prostatitis with hematuria
N41.10   Chronic prostatitis without hematuria
N41.11   Chronic prostatitis with hematuria
N41.2   Abscess of prostate
N41.3   Prostatocystitis
N41.4   Granulomatous prostatitis
N41.8   Other inflammatory diseases of prostate
N41.9   Inflammatory disease of prostate, unspecified

FIGURE 21.2   The Male Reproductive System

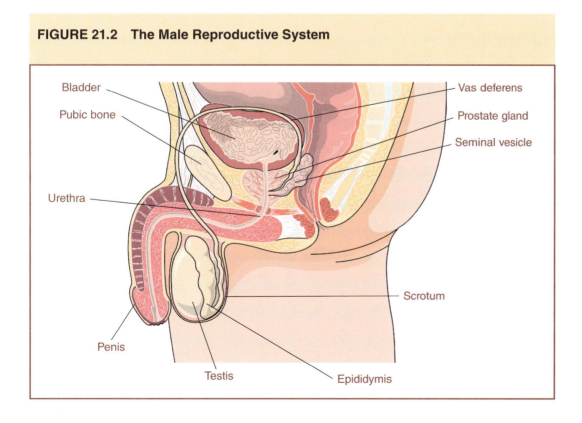

Category N42 classifies other disorders of the prostate with such conditions as follows:

N42.0   Calculus of prostate

N42.1   Congestion and hemorrhage of prostate

N42.3   Dysplasia of prostate

N42.81   Prostatodynia syndrome

N42.82   Prostatosis syndrome

N42.89   Other specified disorders of prostate

N42.9   Disorder of prostate, unspecified

In order to code a prostatectomy, it is necessary to determine whether the complete prostate was removed (root operation "Resection"), or only a portion of the prostate was removed (root operation "Excision"), as well as surgical approach (open, percutaneous endoscopic, via natural or artificial opening, or via natural or artificial opening endoscopic). (For illustrations of Medical and Surgical Section approaches, please refer to figure 8.5 on pages 74–75.) For example:

- Total transurethral prostatectomy via cystoscope: 0VT08ZZ, Resection of prostate, via natural or artificial opening endoscopic
- Suprapubic prostatectomy: 0VT00ZZ, Resection of prostate, open approach

In a radical prostatectomy, the seminal vesicles and vas ampullae are excised along with the prostate. This procedure requires two codes: one code for the prostate resection, and a separate code for the resection of bilateral seminal vessels. A prostatectomy performed with a radical cystectomy involves removal of the bladder, prostate, and seminal vessels. Thus, it requires three codes: one for the prostate resection, another for the bladder resection, and a third for the resection of bilateral seminal vessels.

Different types of energy sources may be utilized for the destruction of prostatic tissue such as microwave thermotherapy, radiofrequency thermotherapy, ablation, and cryotherapy. All these different types of energy sources are coded to the same root operation, "Destruction."

ENDOMETRIOSIS

Endometriosis is a condition in which aberrant tissue that almost perfectly resembles the mucous membrane of the uterus is found in various other sites within the pelvic cavity. A code from category N80, Endometriosis, is assigned for this condition, with a fourth character indicating the site in which the aberrant tissue is found. (See figure 21.3 for common sites of endometriosis implantation.) For example:

N80.1   Endometriosis of the ovary

N80.5   Endometriosis of the colon

N80.2   Endometriosis of fallopian tube

GENITAL PROLAPSE

Prolapse of the vagina and/or the uterus is a relatively common condition. In coding genital prolapse, it is first necessary to determine whether the condition involves the vaginal wall, the uterus, or both, and whether the prolapse is complete or incomplete. For example:

N81.2   Incomplete uterovaginal prolapse (uterus descends into introitus, and cervix protrudes slightly beyond)

N81.3   Complete uterovaginal prolapse, complete (entire cervix and uterus protrude beyond the introitus, and vagina is inverted)

FIGURE 21.3   Common Sites of Endometriosis Implantation

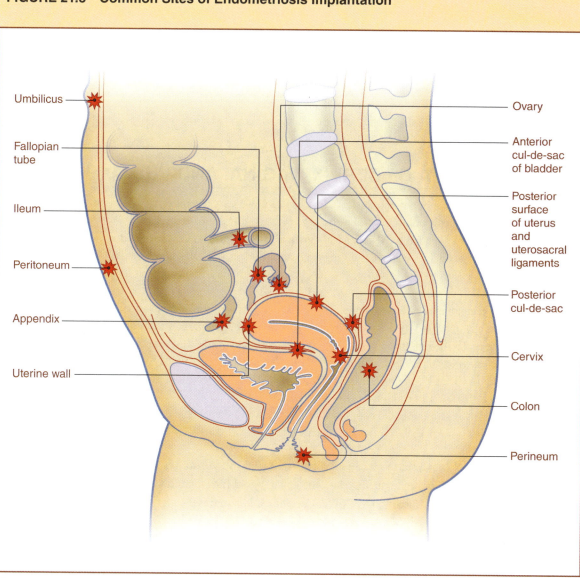

Umbilicus

Fallopian tube

Ileum

Peritoneum

Appendix

Uterine wall

Ovary

Anterior cul-de-sac of bladder

Posterior surface of uterus and uterosacral ligaments

Posterior cul-de-sac

Cervix

Colon

Perineum

Code N99.3 is assigned for prolapse of vaginal vault occurring after hysterectomy; it is not classified as a surgical complication. This condition may be due to the surgical technique or to the relaxation of supporting structures following surgery. Pelvic or vaginal enterocele, a herniation of the intestine through intact vaginal mucosa, is coded **N81.5, Vaginal enterocele,** whether it is congenital or acquired. Prolapse of the uterus in an obstetric patient is classified in chapter 15 of ICD-10-CM. Examples of appropriate coding for genital prolapse include the following:

N81.4	Prolapse of uterus (no vaginal wall involvement)
N81.5	Vaginal enterocele
N81.85	Prolapse of cervical stump
O34.522	Prolapse of gravid uterus (second trimester)
N81.11	Cystocele, midline
N81.0	Urethrocele
N81.6	Rectocele

268

CHAPTER 21

*Diseases
of the
Genitourinary
System*

ENDOMETRIAL HYPERPLASIA

Endometrial hyperplasia refers to excessive proliferation of the cells of the inner lining of the uterus. It is considered a significant risk factor for endometrial cancer and requires careful monitoring. ICD-10-CM provides the following codes for endometrial hyperplasia:

N85.00   Endometrial hyperplasia, unspecified
N85.01   Benign endometrial hyperplasia
N85.02   Endometrial intraepithelial neoplasia [EIN]

DYSPLASIA OF CERVIX, VAGINA, AND VULVA

Cervical intraepithelial neoplasia (CIN), also known as cervical dysplasia, is the potentially premalignant transformation and abnormal growth (dysplasia) of squamous cells on the surface of the cervix. CIN I is coded to **N87.0, Mild cervical dysplasia,** and CIN II is coded to **N87.1, Moderate cervical dysplasia.** Dysplasia of the cervix specified as CIN III, or severe dysplasia of cervix uteri, however, is carcinoma in situ of the cervix, and code **D06.-, Carcinoma in situ of cervix uteri,** is assigned.

Vaginal intraepithelial neoplasia (VAIN) refers to premalignant histological findings in the vagina characterized by dysplastic changes. It is a rare, generally asymptomatic disorder. Similar to CIN, it is classified in three stages: VAIN I, VAIN II, and VAIN III. Code **N89.0, Mild vaginal dysplasia,** is assigned for VAIN I, while VAIN II is classified to code **N89.1, Moderate vaginal dysplasia.** Similar to CIN III, VAIN III, or severe vaginal dysplasia, is considered to be carcinoma in situ and is coded to **D07.2, Carcinoma in situ of vagina.**

Vulvar intraepithelial neoplasia (VIN) refers to changes that can occur in the skin covering the vulva. In some cases VIN may disappear without treatment. VIN is classified as follows:

- VIN I, or mild dysplasia of vulva—N90.0, Mild vulvar dysplasia
- VIN II, or moderate dysplasia of vulva—N90.1, Moderate vulvar dysplasia
- VIN III is classified to D07.1, Carcinoma in situ of vulva

A diagnosis of CIN III, VAIN III, or VIN III can be made only on the basis of pathological examination of tissues.

Codes from **R87.61-, Abnormal cytological findings in specimens from cervix uteri,** or **R87.62-, Abnormal cytological findings in specimens from vagina,** would be assigned for abnormal results from a cervical or vaginal cytologic examination without histologic confirmation.

ENDOMETRIAL ABLATION

Endometrial ablation is used as an alternative to hysterectomy for women with dysfunctional bleeding that does not respond to hormone therapy. It can also be used to treat women with fibroid tumors or endometrial polyps. A scope equipped with either a roller ball or a u-shaped wire is inserted into the uterus. The lining of the uterus is ablated by laser, radiofrequency electromagnet energy, or electrocoagulation. Endometrial ablation is classified to the root operation "Destruction." For example, **0U5B7ZZ, Destruction of endometrium, via natural or artificial opening,** is assigned for a vaginal endometrial ablation.

269

CHAPTER 21

Diseases
of the
Genitourinary
System

FIGURE 21.4   The Female Reproductive System

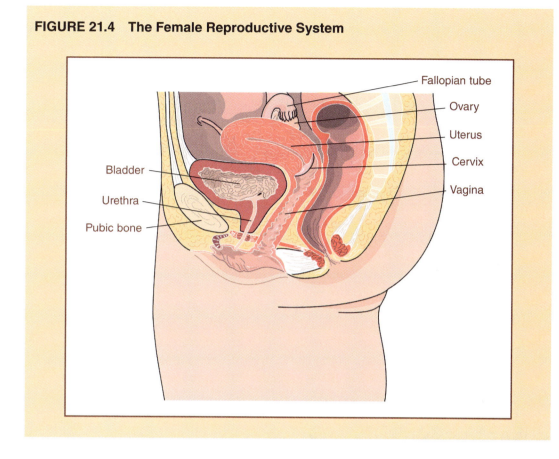

DISEASES OF THE BREAST

Neoplasms of the breast are classified in chapter 2 of ICD-10-CM. The coder should be aware, however, that terms such as "growth," "cyst," and "lump" do not necessarily refer to neoplastic disease. When surgery is performed, the pathology report provides more specific information to assist in code assignment. Examples of appropriate coding include the following:

N60.11	Fibrocystic disease of the right breast
D24.00	Benign neoplasm of female breast
D23.5	Benign neoplasm of skin of breast
N62	Gynecomastia
C50.929	Carcinoma of the male breast
C50.919	Carcinoma of the female breast

ICD-10-PCS classifies breast procedures to the body system "skin and breast" with the second character value of "H." Biopsies of the breast are classified to the root operations "Drainage" (value of "9") or "Excision" (value of "B") depending on whether the biopsy involves fluid removal ("Drainage"), as in the case of a cyst, or tissue ("Excision"), as in the case of a mass or lump. Biopsies are coded in ICD-10-PCS with a seventh character qualifier of "X" for diagnostic. When the procedure is described as an excisional biopsy, it usually refers to excision of the entire lesion rather than a simple biopsy, in which case it is coded to the root operation "Excision." The term "lumpectomy" also describes a local excision of a breast lesion.

When surgery on the breast is performed for possible neoplasm, it is customary to perform a biopsy before the definitive surgery begins. A rapid-frozen section is reviewed by a pathologist to determine whether malignancy is present. The code for the definitive procedure is sequenced

270

CHAPTER 21

*Diseases
of the
Genitourinary
System*

first, followed by the code for the biopsy. If a diagnostic excision, extraction, or drainage procedure (biopsy) is followed by a more definitive procedure, such as destruction, excision, or resection at the same procedure site, both the biopsy and the more definitive procedure are coded. For example, if a biopsy of the breast is performed first, followed by a partial mastectomy at the same procedure site during the same surgical episode, both the biopsy and the partial mastectomy procedures are coded.

With advances in cancer therapy, radical mastectomy is not performed as often as in the past because a lumpectomy or a modified radical mastectomy appears to be equally effective in most cases. The main distinction between a radical and a modified mastectomy is that all or part of the pectoralis major and all of the pectoralis minor are removed in a radical mastectomy, whereas the pectoralis major is preserved in a modified radical mastectomy. ICD-10-PCS requires separate codes for all components involved in a radical mastectomy. For example, a left radical mastectomy is coded to **0HTU0ZZ, Resection of left breast, open approach; 07T60ZZ, Resection of left axillary lymphatic, open approach;** and **0KTJ0ZZ, Resection of left thorax muscle, open approach.** On the other hand, a left modified radical mastectomy is coded as **0HTU0ZZ, Resection of left breast, open approach;** and **07T60ZZ, Resection of left axillary lymphatic, open approach.** The coder must review the operative report carefully before assigning these procedure codes.

Insertion of tissue expander is another procedure frequently carried out in conjunction with breast surgery. This tissue insertion permits a flap closure of the site, making it unnecessary for the patient to undergo a skin graft. Saline is usually injected into the breast expander at regular intervals following the expander's insertion to gradually enlarge the size of the expander. ICD-10-PCS classifies these procedures to the root operation "Insertion" with the device value of "N" for tissue expander, for example, **0HHT0NZ, Insertion of tissue expander into right breast, open approach.**

BREAST RECONSTRUCTION

Reconstructive breast surgery is performed for a variety of reasons. Prostheses are often implanted for patients who have undergone mastectomies. Breast reconstruction can be performed immediately after the surgery or delayed to a later time. When it is known that patients will undergo postoperative radiation, reconstruction is usually delayed. When a patient undergoes a mastectomy and the reconstruction is delayed, code **Z42.1, Encounter for breast reconstruction following mastectomy,** is assigned as the principal or first-listed diagnosis for the return admission for each encounter for a stage of the breast reconstruction.

If the purpose of reconstruction is to increase breast size for improved appearance, prosthetic implants are usually used. Reduction mammoplasty is sometimes performed for patients whose large breast size interferes with normal daily activities or causes significant discomfort, as well as for cosmetic reasons. When mammoplasty is performed to reduce breast size, code **N62, Hypertrophy of breast,** is assigned as the principal diagnosis. When the purpose of the mammoplasty is cosmetic, code **Z41.1, Encounter for cosmetic surgery,** is assigned as the principal diagnosis.

Coding examples for reconstruction include the following:

0HRT0JZ	Replacement of right breast with synthetic substitute, open approach
0HRU075	Replacement of left breast using latissimus dorsi myocutaneous flap, open approach
0HRUX7Z	Replacement of left breast with autologous tissue substitute, external approach
0KXH0ZZ	Transfer right thorax muscle, open approach
0HRV079	Replacement of bilateral breast using gluteal artery perforator flap, open approach
0HRW0JZ	Replacement of right nipple with synthetic substitute, open approach
0HBV0ZZ	Excision of bilateral breast, open approach

271

CHAPTER 21

*Diseases
of the
Genitourinary
System*

Problems related to deformity and disproportion post–breast reconstruction may require patients to seek further medical care. Contour irregularity, excess tissue in reconstructed breast, or misshapen reconstructed breast are assigned to code **N65.0, Deformity of reconstructed breast.** Breast asymmetry, or disproportion between native breast and reconstructed breast, and ptosis (sagging) of native breast in relation to reconstructed breast are assigned to **N65.1, Disproportion of reconstructed breast.**

Sometimes complications develop in patients who have breast implants, making removal of the implants advisable. In such cases, the code for the principal diagnosis depends on the nature of the complication. For example, if the reason for the surgery is that the implant has ruptured, the principal diagnosis is code **T85.41x-, Breakdown (mechanical) of breast prosthesis and implant.** When the reason for removal is that the patient has a capsular contracture of the right breast implant, code **T85.44x-, Capsular contracture of breast implant,** is assigned as the principal diagnosis. Other codes related to problems with breast implants include **T85.42x-, Displacement of breast prosthesis and implant,** which includes malposition of breast prosthesis and implant, and **T85.43x-, Leakage of breast prosthesis and implant.** Removal of the breast implant is classified to the root operation "Removal" and the device "synthetic substitute," for example: **0HPT0JZ, Removal of synthetic substitute from right breast, open approach.**

Patients sometimes request removal of an implant because they are concerned that a complication might occur in the future, although there is no problem at present. In this case, assign **Z45.81-, Encounter for adjustment or removal of breast implant.** For example:

- A patient experiences a ruptured breast implant on the left side and is admitted for open removal of the implant and insertion of a new implant.

Principal diagnosis:	T85.41xA	Breakdown (mechanical) of breast prosthesis and implant, initial encounter
Surgery performed:	0HPU0JZ	Removal of synthetic substitute from left breast, open approach
	0HRU0JZ	Replacement of left breast with synthetic substitute, open approach

- A patient who had undergone a previous right mastectomy with a breast implant inserted at the time of surgery suffers from a painful capsule. She is admitted for removal and reinsertion of the implant.

Principal diagnosis:	T85.84xA	Pain due to internal prosthetic devices, implants and grafts, not elsewhere classified, initial encounter
Surgery performed:	0HPT0JZ	Removal of synthetic substitute from right breast, open approach
	0HRT0JZ	Replacement of right breast with synthetic substitute, open approach

- A patient had undergone bilateral breast implantation three years ago and is now admitted for elective implant removal. She had no related problems but had become concerned because of newspaper reports describing illnesses associated with breast implants.

Principal diagnosis:	Z45.811	Encounter for adjustment or removal of right breast implant
	Z45.812	Encounter for adjustment or removal of left breast implant
Surgery performed:	0HPT0JZ	Removal of synthetic substitute from right breast, open
	0HPU0JZ	Removal of synthetic substitute from left breast, open

REVIEW EXERCISE 21.4

Code the following diagnoses and procedures. Do not assign External cause of morbidity codes.

1. Hydronephrosis with chronic pyelitis — N13.6

   Pyelonephritis, focal, chronic, left — N11.9

2. Rapidly progressive glomerulonephritis — N01.9

3. Syphilitic epididymitis — A52.76

4. Chronic prostatitis due to proteus — N41.10

   B96.4

5. Phimosis and balanoposthitis — N47.1

   N47.6

6. Encysted right hydrocele, male — N43.0

   Open excision of hydrocele of spermatic cord — 0VBF0ZZ

7. Benign prostatic hypertrophy with urinary — N40.1

   obstruction — N13.8

   Total transurethral prostatectomy via cystoscope — 0VT08ZZ

8. Acute and chronic cervicitis — N72

   Vaginal hysterectomy — 0UT97ZZ

9. Chronic pelvic inflammatory disease — N73.1

   Dysmenorrhea — N94.6

10. Menometrorrhagia   N92.1

    Endometrial polyp   N84.0

    Corpus luteum cysts of both ovaries   N83.1

    Total abdominal hysterectomy   0UT90ZZ

    Bilateral salpingo-oophorectomy   0UT20ZZ

      0UT70ZZ

---

11. Cystocele with incomplete uterine prolapse   N81.2

    and stress incontinence   N81.10

      N39.3

    Cystocele repair (open approach)   0JQC0ZZ

    Vaginal suspension of uterus (open approach)   0US90ZZ

---

12. Pelvic peritoneal endometriosis   N80.3

---

13. Dermoid cyst of left ovary   D27.1

    Laparoscopic wedge resection of ovarian cyst   0UB14ZZ

---

14. Infertility due to pelvic peritoneal adhesions   N73.6

      N97.1

    Hysterosalpingogram, radiopaque dye   BU18YZZ

                Fluoroscopy

---

15. Psychogenic dysmenorrhea   F45.8

---

16. Adhesions of ovary and fallopian tubes   N73.6

    Laparoscopic lysis of adhesions   0UN24ZZ

      0UN74ZZ

---

17. Menorrhagia   N92.0

    Dilatation and curettage with vaginal endometrial ablation   0U5B7ZZ

---

18. Submucous fibroid of uterus   D25.0

    Laparoscopically assisted vaginal hysterectomy   0UT9FZZ

Coding OF **Diseases** OF THE **Skin** AND **Diseases** OF THE **Musculoskeletal System**

CHAPTER 22

Diseases of the Skin and Subcutaneous Tissue

CHAPTER OVERVIEW

- Diseases of the skin and subcutaneous tissue can be found in chapter 12 of ICD-10-CM.

- Categories L23–L25 classify dermatitis due to plants, food, drugs, and medications in contact with skin.

- Category L27 classifies dermatitis caused by medications taken internally.

  — The coder must determine whether the condition is an adverse effect of proper administration or a poisoning due to the incorrect use of the drug.

  — Codes from categories T36 through T65 are used to classify the causation.

- Chronic ulcers of the skin are classified using the fifth character to specify the site.

- The sequencing of the code for cellulitis is dependent on the severity of the wound and the primary goal of the treatment (for cellulitis or for the wound).

- Debridement is classified as either excisional or nonexcisional (brushing, irrigating, scrubbing, or washing).

LEARNING OUTCOMES

After studying this chapter you should be able to:

Know how to classify dermatitis due to contact, food, and ingestion of drug (both correct and incorrect usage).

Code ulcers of the skin.

Explain how to classify cellulitis based on location and the primary goal of the treatment.

Code procedures done on the skin, such as excisions, debridement, and grafting.

TERMS TO KNOW

Cellulitis
an infection of the skin and soft tissues resulting from some sort of break in the skin

Debridement
removal of dead, damaged, or infected tissue

REMEMBER . . .

Chapter 12 of ICD-10-CM includes more than just conditions of the skin. It also includes conditions of the nails, sweat glands, hair, and hair follicles.

INTRODUCTION

Chapter 12 of ICD-10-CM deals with conditions affecting the skin and subcutaneous tissue. The chapter is organized around the following subdivisions:

L00–L08	Infections of skin and subcutaneous tissue
L10–L14	Bullous disorders
L20–L30	Dermatitis and eczema
L40–L45	Papulosquamous disorders
L49–L54	Urticaria and erythema
L55–L59	Radiation-related disorders of the skin and subcutaneous tissue
L60–L75	Disorders of skin appendages
L76	Intraoperative and postprocedural complications of skin and subcutaneous tissue
L80–L99	Other disorders of the skin and subcutaneous tissue

Conditions affecting the nails, sweat glands, hair, and hair follicles are included in this chapter. Congenital conditions of skin, hair, and nails are classified in categories Q80–Q84. Neoplasms of skin are classified in chapter 2 of ICD-10-CM.

DERMATITIS DUE TO DRUGS

ICD-10-CM uses the terms "dermatitis" and "eczema" synonymously and interchangeably in the L20–L30 category range. There are several types of dermatitis, such as atopic (L20.-), seborrheic (L21.-), diaper (L22), allergic contact (L23.-), irritant contact (L24.-), and exfoliative (L26).

Contact dermatitis is a localized rash or irritation of the skin caused by contact with allergens (allergic-contact dermatitis) or irritants (irritant-contact dermatitis). Category L23 is used to classify allergic-contact dermatitis due to metals, adhesive, cosmetics, drugs, dyes, chemical products, food, and plants in contact with skin. Category L24 is assigned for irritant-contact dermatitis caused by irritants in contact with skin, such as detergents, oils and greases, and solvents. Category L25, Unspecified contact dermatitis, is used when the contact dermatitis is not specified as allergic- or irritant-contact dermatitis. Category L27 is for dermatitis due to substances taken internally.

In coding dermatitis caused by medicines, the coder must first determine whether the condition represents an adverse effect due to the proper administration of a drug or poisoning due to the incorrect use of the drug. When the dermatitis is due to a medication used correctly as prescribed, it is considered an adverse effect. When the dermatitis is due to incorrect use of the drug, it is classified as a poisoning by drugs, medicaments, and biological substances.

When coding allergic-contact dermatitis, irritant-contact dermatitis, unspecified contact dermatitis, and dermatitis due to substances taken internally, a code from categories T36 through T65 should be assigned first to indicate the way in which the poisoning or adverse effect occurred (e.g., accidental, intentional self-harm) and the type of drug involved. (A more detailed discussion of the distinction between adverse effects and poisoning due to drugs and medications is provided in chapter 30 of this handbook.)

Correct coding examples include the following:

T36.0x5A + L27.0	Initial encounter for dermatitis due to allergic reaction to penicillin tablets, taken as prescribed (adverse reaction)
T36.0x1A + L27.0	Initial encounter for dermatitis due to accidental ingestion of mother's penicillin tablets (poisoning)

In the first example, which indicates an adverse reaction to a prescribed medication taken as directed, the code for the adverse effect of the penicillin is sequenced first, followed by the code for the dermatitis. In the second example, code **T36.0x1A, Poisoning by penicillin, accidental, initial encounter,** is sequenced first, with an additional code to indicate that the effect of the poisoning is dermatitis.

Palmar plantar erythrodysesthesia (PPE), also called hand foot syndrome, is an example of a specific dermatitis that occurs as an adverse reaction to antineoplastic or biologic drugs used for cancer treatment. After the administration of chemotherapy, small amounts of the drug can leak from the capillaries, damaging tissue in the palms of the hands and the soles of the feet. The leakage results in redness, tenderness, and peeling of the palms and soles. The affected area resembles sunburn and may become dry, peeled, and numb. This condition affects the hands and feet because of the increased friction and heat to which the extremities are exposed through normal use. Treatment involves reducing or stopping the drug therapy. Assign code **T45.1x5A, Adverse effect of antineoplastic and immunosuppressive drugs, initial encounter,** followed by code **L27.1, Localized skin eruption due to drugs and medicaments taken internally,** for the PPE due to antineoplastic antibiotics.

ERYTHEMA MULTIFORME

Erythema multiforme is a skin disorder resulting in symmetrical red, raised skin areas all over the body, often resembling targets because they are dark circles with purple-gray centers. In some cases, there are severe systemic symptoms. Erythema multiforme can occur in response to medications, infections, or illness. The exact cause is unknown. If the condition is drug induced, assign a code from T36–T50 first to identify the responsible drug.

FIGURE 22.1   The Skin and Subcutaneous Tissue

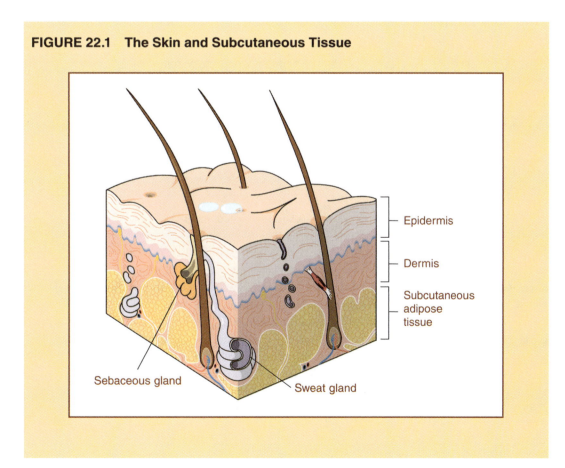

Epidermis

Dermis

Subcutaneous adipose tissue

Sebaceous gland

Sweat gland

The different types of erythema multiforme are classified as follows:

L51.0   Nonbullous erythema multiforme
L51.1   Stevens-Johnson syndrome
L51.2   Toxic epidermal necrolysis [Lyell]
L51.3   Stevens-Johnson syndrome-toxic epidermal necrolysis overlap
L51.8   Other erythema multiforme
L51.9   Erythema multiforme, unspecified

Patients with erythema multiforme may also suffer from a variety of other associated manifestations that should be coded separately. The manifestations range from arthropathy (M14.8-) to corneal ulcer (H16.0.-) to stomatitis (K12.-) and several other conditions. In addition, a code from category L49 is reported to reflect the percentage of body surface involved with skin exfoliation.

ULCERS OF THE SKIN

Most chronic ulcers of the skin are classified in categories L89, Pressure ulcer, and L97, Nonpressure chronic ulcer of lower limb, not elsewhere classified, with code I96 assigned first when gangrene is present. A code from L97 may be used as a principal or first-listed code if no underlying condition is documented as the cause of the ulcer. If one of the underlying conditions listed below is documented with a lower-extremity ulcer, a causal condition should be assumed and the underlying condition should be coded first:

I70.23-, I70.24-, I70.33-, I70.34-, I70.43-, I70.44-, I70.53-, I70.54-, I70.63-, I70.64-, I70.73-, I70.74-	Atherosclerosis of the lower extremities
I87.31-, I87.33-	Chronic venous hypertension
E08.621, E08.622, E09.621, E09.622, E10.621, E10.622, E11.621, E11.622, E13.621, E13.622	Diabetic ulcers
I87.01-, I87.03-	Postphlebitic syndrome
I87.01-, I87.03-	Postthrombotic syndrome
I83.0-, I83.2-	Varicose ulcer
I96	Any associated gangrene

Chronic ulcer of the skin, not otherwise specified, is classified to subcategory L98.4, Nonpressure chronic ulcer of skin, not elsewhere classified. Ulceration associated with arteriosclerosis of the lower extremities is classified to subcategories I70.2 through I70.7 with fifth characters 3 or 4 (with ulceration), with an additional code from category L97 with fifth character 1 or 2 to indicate the severity of ulcer, or if gangrene is present, to subcategories I70.2 to I70.7 with fifth character 6 (with gangrene), with an additional code from L98.49- to identify the severity of any ulcer, if applicable.

Codes from category L89, Pressure ulcers, are combination codes that identify the site of the pressure ulcer as well as the stage of the ulcer. Category L89 provides fifth characters to identify the specific site of the ulcer, such as elbow (L89.0-); back (L89.1-); hip (L89.2-); buttock (L89.3-); contiguous site of back, buttock, and hip (L89.4-); ankle (L89.5-); heel (L89.6-); other

281

CHAPTER 22

*Diseases of
the Skin and
Subcutaneous
Tissue*

site (L89.8-); and unspecified site (L89.9-). The sixth character for category L89 indicates the severity of the ulcer by identifying the stage of the pressure ulcers, such as unstageable, stage 1, stage 2, stage 3, stage 4, or unspecified.

The code assignment for the pressure ulcer stage may be based on nursing documentation; however, the associated diagnosis of pressure ulcer should be coded on the basis of the provider's documentation (namely, the physician or any qualified health care practitioner who is legally accountable for establishing the patient's diagnosis, as defined in the *ICD-10-CM Official Guidelines for Coding and Reporting*).

Care should be taken not to confuse a pressure ulcer in which the stage is unspecified or not documented (L89.- with a sixth character of "9") with a pressure ulcer documented as unstageable (L89.- with a sixth character of "0"). The staging of pressure ulcers takes into account the depth of tissue loss and the depth of tissue exposed. "Unstageable" refers to pressure ulcers whose stage cannot be clinically determined (e.g., the ulcer is covered by eschar or has been treated with a skin or muscle graft) as well as pressure ulcers documented as deep tissue injury but not documented as due to trauma. The assignment of the pressure ulcer stage code should be guided by clinical documentation of the stage or the terms found in the Alphabetic Index. The provider should be queried if the clinical term cannot be found in the Index or if there is no documentation of the stage.

Documentation of pressure ulcers may sometimes refer to "deep tissue injury." Care should be taken to review the provider documentation to determine whether the term refers to a traumatic injury (such as a contusion) or a pressure ulcer. The Alphabetic Index entry for "Injury, deep tissue" refers the coder to "*see Contusion, by site*"; whereas the entry for "Injury, deep tissue, meaning pressure ulcer" refers the coder to "*see Ulcer, pressure, unstageable, by site*."

If a patient is admitted with a pressure ulcer of one stage, and it progresses to a higher stage, the code for the highest stage reported for that site should be reported. For example, the condition of an individual admitted with stage 2 pressure ulcer of left heel, which advances to stage 3 during the encounter, should be coded to **L89.623, Pressure ulcer of left heel, stage 3.**

Care should be taken to distinguish between pressure ulcers documented as "healed" (no code assigned) and "healing" (assign the appropriate code for the stage documented). If the documentation does not provide information about the stage of the healing pressure ulcer, assign the appropriate code for unspecified stage.

Examples of correct coding for chronic ulcers of the skin include the following:

L89.154	Pressure ulcer, sacral area, stage 4
I96 + L89.153	Pressure ulcer, sacral area, stage 3 with gangrene
L97.909	Ulcer of lower limb, except pressure ulcer
L89.210	Unstageable pressure ulcer of the right hip
L89.149	Pressure ulcer left lower back
L98.499	Chronic ulcer of skin unspecified site

Stasis ulcers are ordinarily due to varicose veins of the lower extremities and are coded to category I83, Varicose veins of lower extremities, rather than to the categories for conditions of the skin. When the physician has used the term "stasis ulcer" but has identified a cause other than varicose veins, code the condition to **I87.2, Venous insufficiency (chronic) (peripheral).** A basic rule of coding is that further research must be done when the title of the code suggested by the Alphabetic Index clearly does not identify the condition correctly. In this case, even though the Index directs the coder to a code involving varicose veins, the code should not be used when no varicosities are present.

CELLULITIS OF THE SKIN

Cellulitis is an acute, diffuse infection of the skin and soft tissues that commonly results from a break in the skin, such as a puncture wound, a laceration, or an ulcer. Occasionally, the break is so small that it cannot be identified by either the patient or the examining physician. Clinically, cellulitis usually presents as an abrupt onset of redness, swelling, pain, or heat in the infected area. Coders should not assume, however, that a reference to redness at the edges of a wound or an ulcer represents cellulitis. The normal hyperemia associated with a wound usually extends a small distance beyond the edges of the wound rather than extending to the diffuse pattern that characterizes cellulitis.

Coding of cellulitis secondary to superficial injury, burn, or frostbite requires two codes, one for the injury and one for the cellulitis. Sequencing of codes depends on the circumstances of the admission. When the patient is seen primarily for treatment of an open wound, the appropriate code for open wound is assigned, with an additional code for the cellulitis. When the wound itself is trivial or when it was treated earlier and the patient is now being seen for treatment of the cellulitis, the code for the cellulitis may be sequenced first, with an additional code for the open wound. For example:

- A patient suffers laceration of the right lower leg while on a hiking trip two days ago and comes to the hospital on his return. By the time he is seen, cellulitis is beginning to develop. The wound is cleansed of the foreign material, nonexcisional debridement is carried out, and antibiotics are started for the cellulitis.

Principal diagnosis:	S81.821A	Laceration with foreign body, right lower leg, initial encounter
Additional diagnosis:	L03.115	Cellulitis of right lower limb
Procedure:	0HDKXZZ	Extraction of right lower leg skin, external approach

- A patient suffers a minor puncture injury to the right finger when removing a staple at the office. Five days later, he is admitted to the hospital because of cellulitis of the finger and is treated with intravenous antibiotics. The wound itself does not require treatment, and therefore no code for injury is assigned.

Principal diagnosis:	L03.011	Cellulitis of right finger

Both cellulitis and lymphangitis of skin are included in category L03. However, separate codes are available for cellulitis and lymphangitis. An additional code should be assigned to indicate the organism responsible (B95–B96), if this information is available. The responsible organism is usually *Streptococcus.*

Cellulitis may also present as a postoperative wound infection or as a result of the penetration of the skin involved in intravenous therapy. For example:

- A patient had an appendectomy six days ago and is now readmitted with evidence of staphylococcal cellulitis of the operative wound.

Principal diagnosis:	T81.4xxA	Infection following procedure
Additional diagnosis:	L03.311	Cellulitis of abdominal wall
Additional diagnosis:	B95.8	*Staphylococcus*

Cellulitis frequently develops as a complication of chronic skin ulcers, in which case it is assigned to a code from category L89 or L97, or subcategory L98.4. These codes do not include any associated cellulitis, and so two codes are required to describe these conditions. Designation of the principal diagnosis depends on the circumstances of the admission.

283

CHAPTER 22

Diseases of
the Skin and
Subcutaneous
Tissue

Cellulitis described as gangrenous is classified to code **I96, Gangrene, not elsewhere classified,** rather than in the categories L89 or L97, or subcategory L98.4, when it develops as the result of either injury or ulcer. When gangrene is present, the gangrene is coded first, with the code for the injury or ulcer assigned as an additional code. This practice follows the instructional notes in the Tabular List to code first any associated gangrene.

OTHER CELLULITIS

Although cellulitis most commonly occurs in the skin and subcutaneous tissue, it also occurs in other areas. In such cases, codes from other chapters of ICD-10-CM are assigned as appropriate.

Cellulitis of female external genital organs is classified as an inflammatory condition and assigned code N76.4. Pelvic cellulitis in women is classified as an inflammatory condition and is assigned to category N73. Occasionally, pelvic cellulitis occurs following abortion, delivery, or molar or ectopic pregnancy, in which case it is classified to chapter 15 of ICD-10-CM. In male patients, pelvic cellulitis is coded as **K65.0, Generalized (acute) peritonitis.**

EXCISION OF LESION

In order to correctly assign a procedure code for the removal of lesions, it is important to first determine whether the procedure was performed on the skin (body system "skin and breast"), or subcutaneous tissue and fascia (body system "subcutaneous tissue and fascia"). Next, determine whether the root operation performed is "Excision" (cutting out or off, without replacement, a portion of a body part) or "Destruction" (physical eradication of all or a portion of a body part by the direct use of energy, force, or a destructive agent). For most skin excisions and destructions, the approach used will be external. For example:

- A simple excision involving only the skin of the face is classified to the root operation "Excision" and coded to **0HB1XZZ, Excision of face skin, external approach.**

- Removal of lesions carried out by cauterization, cryosurgery, fulguration, or laser beam are classified to the root operation "Destruction," such as fulguration of a skin tag of the chest, which is coded to **0H55XZZ, Destruction of chest skin, external approach.**

When the removal of the lesion goes beyond the skin and involves underlying and/or adjacent tissue such as subcutaneous tissue and fascia, the procedure is classified to the "subcutaneous tissue and fascia" body system. The surgeon's description should be followed carefully when assigning these codes in order to determine whether the root operation is "Excision" or "Destruction" and whether the approach was open (cutting through the skin or mucous membrane) or percutaneous (by puncture or minor incision through the skin or mucous membrane). For example:

- Excision of Kaposi's sarcoma of the subcutaneous tissue, right thigh, is classified to the root operation "Excision" and coded to **0JBL0ZZ, Excision of right upper leg subcutaneous tissue and fascia, open approach.**

- Open fulguration of a benign subcutaneous tissue lesion of the left upper arm is classified to the root operation "Destruction" and coded to **0J5D0ZZ, Destruction of right upper arm subcutaneous tissue and fascia, open approach.**

DEBRIDEMENT

Debridement of the skin and subcutaneous tissue is a procedure by which foreign material and devitalized or contaminated tissue are removed from a traumatic or infected lesion until the surrounding healthy tissue is exposed.

Excisional debridement of the skin or subcutaneous tissue is the surgical removal or cutting away of such tissue, necrosis, or slough and is classified to the root operation "Excision." Depending on the availability of a surgical suite or the extent of the area involved, excisional debridement can be performed in the operating room, in the emergency department, or at the patient's bedside. Excisional debridement may be performed by a physician and/or another health care provider and involves an excisional, as opposed to a mechanical (brushing, scrubbing, washing), debridement. Use of a sharp instrument does not always indicate that an excisional debridement was performed. Minor removal of loose fragments with scissors or using a sharp instrument to scrape away tissue is not an excisional debridement. Excisional debridement involves the use of a scalpel to remove devitalized tissue. Documentation of excisional debridement should be specific regarding the type of debridement. If the documentation is not clear or if there is any question about the procedure, the provider should be queried for clarification.

Nonexcisional debridement of the skin is the nonoperative brushing, irrigating, scrubbing, or washing of devitalized tissue, necrosis, slough, or foreign material. Most nonexcisional debridement procedures are classified to the root operation "Extraction" (pulling or stripping out or off all or a portion of a body part by the use of force), except when it is performed by irrigating the devitalized tissue. In that case, the debridement is coded to the Administration Section, root operation "Irrigation." Nonexcisional debridement may be performed by a physician or by other health care personnel.

When coding for debridement of areas other than skin, excisional debridement is coded to the root operation "Excision" of the specific body part.

When coding multiple-layer debridements of the same site, the coder should assign a code only for the deepest layer of debridement. For example, open excision and debridement of a coccyx wound including bone is coded to **0QBS0ZZ, Excision of coccyx, open approach.** Debridement carried out in conjunction with another procedure is often included in the code for the procedure, but not always.

DERMAL REGENERATIVE GRAFT

Several new technologies that are able to permanently regenerate or replace skin layers are now being used to treat severe burns. Procedures involving the application of grafts are classified to the root operation "Replacement" (putting in or on biological or synthetic material that physically takes the place and/or function of all or a portion of a body part). The approach on all the skin replacement procedures is "external." The root operation "Replacement" identifies through the device character the use of synthetic substitutes (sixth character "J"), autologous tissue substitutes (sixth character "7"), and nonautologous tissue substitute (sixth character "K").

Examples of skin synthetic substitutes include:

- Artificial skin, not otherwise specified
- Creation of "neodermis"
- Decellularized allodermis
- Integumentary matrix implants
- Prosthetic implant of dermal layer of skin
- Regenerate dermal layer of skin

285

CHAPTER 22

*Diseases of
the Skin and
Subcutaneous
Tissue*

Code **T85.693-, Other mechanical complication of artificial skin graft and decellularized allodermis,** is assigned for failure or rejection of these systems. Codes **T86.820-, Skin graft (allograft) rejection,** and **T86.821-, Skin graft (allograft) (autograft) failure,** are assigned for complication of other skin graft. Status code Z96.81 is assigned to indicate that the patient has an artificial skin graft.

EXERCISE 22.1

The following exercise provides examples of conditions classified in chapter 12 of ICD-10-CM. Code the following diagnoses and procedures.

---

1. Varicose ulcer, lower right leg with severe inflammation — I83.219

---

2. Pilonidal fistula with abscess — L05.02

   Excision of pilonidal sinus — 0HB8XZZ

---

3. Large abscess of trunk due to *Staphylococcus aureus* — L02.219 / B95.6

   Infection

   Incision and drainage of abscess, trunk — 0H95XZZ

---

4. Hard corn deformity, right little toe — L84

   Soft corn deformities, third, fourth, and fifth toes, right

---

5. Keloid scar on left hand from previous burn — L91.0 / T23.002S

   Excision of scar left hand — 0HBGXZZ

---

6. Chronic purulent inflamed acne rosacea of lower lip — L71.9

   Wide excision of chronic acne rosacea of lower lip (external) with full-thickness autologous graft over defect, lower lip — 0CB1XZZ / 0CR1X7Z

   Replacement

---

7. Giant urticaria, initial encounter — T78.3xxA

---

8. Contact dermatitis of eyelid   H01.119

9. Seborrheic keratosis underlying the second   L82.1
    metatarsal head, right foot

10. Cellulitis of anus   K61.0

11. Acute lymphangitis, right upper arm, due to group A   L03.123
    streptococcal infection   B95.0

12. Gangrenous diabetic ulcer of right foot due to   E11.621
    peripheral circulatory disorder   E11.52

         L97.519

13. Surgical (excisional) debridement of skin and fascia   0JBQ0ZZ
    of right foot

14. Infected ingrown toenail, right great toe   L60.0

15. Cellulitis, buttock   L03.317

16. Cellulitis of left upper eyelid   H00.034

Diseases of the Musculoskeletal System and Connective Tissue

CHAPTER OVERVIEW

- Diseases of the musculoskeletal system and connective tissue are covered in chapter 13 of ICD-10-CM.

- Most of the codes within chapter 13 have site and laterality designations referring to the bone, joint, or muscle involved.

- If there is no "multiple sites" code provided and if more than one bone, joint, or muscle is involved, separate codes should be used to indicate the different sites involved.

- Coding back pain is often dependent on the distinction between degeneration and displacement and on the presence or absence of myelopathy.

- Arthritis can be coded independently or in a dual-coding situation if it is a manifestation of another condition.

- Osteoarthritis can be further classified based on whether it is primary or secondary.

- Fractures are considered either stress fractures, pathological fractures, or traumatic fractures.

  — Fractures that are spontaneous are always considered pathological.

  — A traumatic fracture should never be coded on the same bone as a pathological fracture.

- Coding joint replacements requires knowledge of the joint involved.

- Coding joint revisions requires information on the removal of any joint-replacement components.

- Coding spinal fusion requires knowing the anatomic portion (column) fused, the approach used (anterior, posterior, or lateral transverse), and whether two or more vertebrae are fused.

- Coding spinal disc prostheses requires knowledge of the type of prosthesis and the segment treated.

- Other conditions coded in chapter 13 include plica syndrome and fasciitis.

LEARNING OUTCOMES

After studying this chapter you should be able to:

Explain the different types of arthritis and what to look for when coding arthritis.

Explain the difference between pathological and traumatic fractures.

Code joint replacements and revisions.

Code back disorders and the variety of procedures for correcting spinal problems.

TERMS TO KNOW

Joint revision
procedure that adjusts, removes, or replaces a joint-replacement component

Myelopathy
damage to the myelinated fiber tracts that carry information to the brain

Osteoarthritis
the most common form of arthritis; a degenerative joint disease

Pathological fracture
fracture that occurs in a bone weakened by disease

REMEMBER . . .

A note at the start of chapter 13 of ICD-10-CM lists the site-specific fifth characters for classifying conditions of the musculoskeletal system.

CHAPTER 23

*Diseases of the
Musculoskeletal
System and
Connective
Tissue*

INTRODUCTION

Chapter 13 of ICD-10-CM is governed by the general coding guidelines already discussed in this handbook. An understanding of the following terms may be helpful to the coder in assigning codes from chapter 13:

- Arthropathy: disorder of the joint
- Arthritis: inflammation of the joint
- Dorsopathy: disorder of the back
- Myelopathy: disorder of the spinal cord
- Radiculopathy: problem in which one or more nerves are affected resulting in pain (radicular pain), weakness, numbness, or difficulty controlling specific muscles.

Most arthropathies are classified in categories M00 through M25 in ICD-10-CM, and most dorsopathies in categories M40 through M54.

Site and Laterality

Most of the codes within chapter 13 have site and laterality designations. The site refers to either the bone, joint, or muscle involved. For some conditions in which more than one bone, joint, or muscle is usually involved (e.g., osteoarthritis), a code is available for "multiple sites." If no multiple sites code is provided and if more than one bone, joint, or muscle is involved, separate codes should be used to indicate the different sites involved.

Bone versus Joint

For certain conditions, the bone may be affected at the upper or lower end (e.g., avascular necrosis of bone, M87, Osteoporosis, M80, M81). Though the portion of the bone affected may be at the joint, the site designation will be the bone, not the joint.

Acute Traumatic versus Chronic or Recurrent Musculoskeletal Conditions

Many musculoskeletal conditions are a result of previous injury or trauma to a site, or are recurrent conditions. Chapter 13 of ICD-10-CM contains bone, joint, or muscle conditions that are the result of a healed injury as well as recurrent conditions of these sites. ICD-10-CM classifies current, acute injuries to chapter 19. Chronic or recurrent conditions should generally be coded with a code from chapter 13. If it is difficult to determine from the documentation in the record which code is best to describe a condition, query the provider.

BACK DISORDERS

Back pain described as lumbago or low back pain, without further qualification, is coded **M54.5, Low back pain.** Back pain not otherwise specified is coded **M54.9, Dorsalgia, unspecified.** Psychogenic back pain is classified under M54.9 and **F45.41, Pain disorder exclusively related to psychological factors.**

Intervertebral disc disorders are classified in categories M50, Cervical disc disorders, and M51, Thoracic, thoracolumbar, and lumbosacral intervertebral disc disorders. Careful attention to the terminology is important in coding these conditions. Degeneration of the disc is not the same condition as displacement (herniation) of the disc, and each requires a different code. For cervical disc disorders (category M50), the code for the most superior level affected should be used.

FIGURE 23.1   The Human Skeleton

CHAPTER 23

Diseases of the
Musculoskeletal
System and
Connective
Tissue

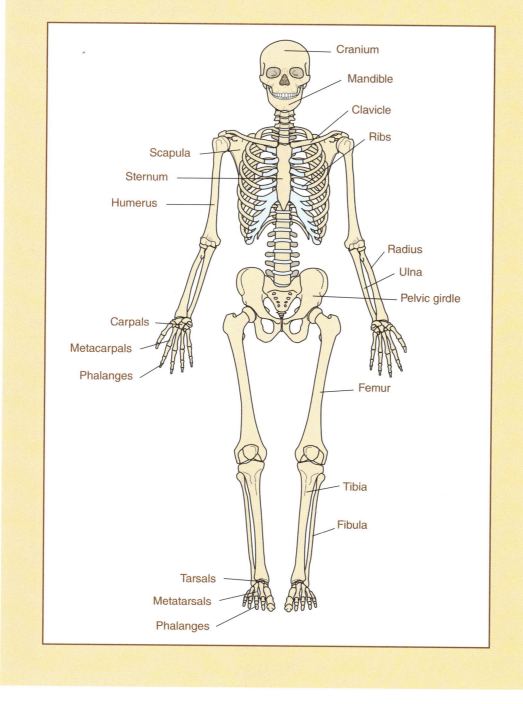

- Cranium
- Mandible
- Clavicle
- Ribs
- Scapula
- Sternum
- Humerus
- Radius
- Ulna
- Pelvic girdle
- Carpals
- Metacarpals
- Phalanges
- Femur
- Tibia
- Fibula
- Tarsals
- Metatarsals
- Phalanges

290

CHAPTER 23

*Diseases of the
Musculoskeletal
System and
Connective
Tissue*

The presence or absence of myelopathy is an important distinction to be made in assigning codes for certain back disorders. Myelopathy is a functional disorder and/or pathological change in the spinal cord that often results from compression. Codes for back disorders such as spondylosis and herniation of the intervertebral disc differentiate between conditions with and without myelopathy. Codes for a herniated disc without myelopathy include those with paresthesia but not paralysis. Terms included in intervertebral disc disorders with myelopathy are classified into subcategories M50.0- and M51.0-, with a fifth character used to indicate the site involved. Examples include the following:

M50.20   Herniated intervertebral disc, cervical, unspecified cervical region, without myelopathy

M51.06   Herniated intervertebral disc, lumbosacral, with myelopathy, lumbar region

M51.24   Herniated intervertebral disc, thoracic, without myelopathy

Categories M50 and M51 are also subclassified, according to whether radiculopathy is present, into subcategories M50.1 and M51.1, with the fifth character indicating the site involved. Radiculopathy refers to a nerve root problem resulting in weakness, numbness, or difficulty controlling specific muscles.

FIGURE 23.2   The Spinal Column

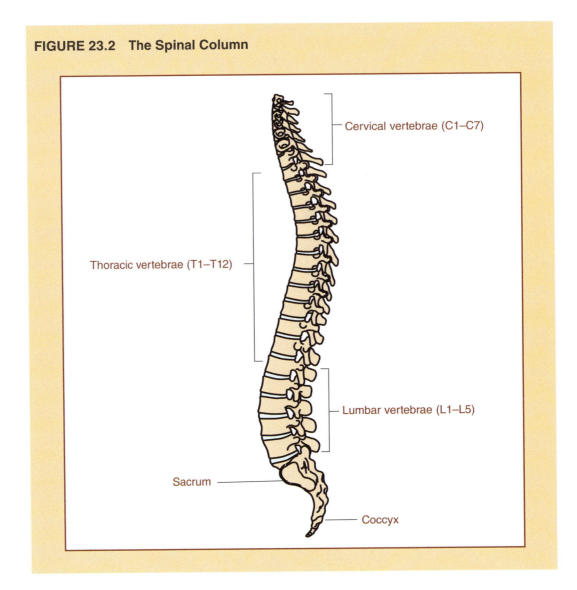

Cervical vertebrae (C1–C7)

Thoracic vertebrae (T1–T12)

Lumbar vertebrae (L1–L5)

Sacrum

Coccyx

CHAPTER 23

Diseases of the
Musculoskeletal
System and
Connective
Tissue

Back pain associated with herniation of an intervertebral disc is included in the code for the herniated disc; no additional code is assigned.

Surgery for the excision or destruction of a herniated disc is classified in ICD-10-PCS by the type of surgery performed. Examples include the following:

0SB40ZZ	Open excision of herniated lumbosacral intervertebral disc
0R5B3ZZ	Destruction of displaced thoracolumbar intervertebral disc by chemo-nucleolysis, percutaneous approach
0S523ZZ	Percutaneous destruction of lumbar vertebral disc
0RB10ZZ	Open excision of cervical vertebral joint

Code **00JU0ZZ, Inspection of spinal canal, open approach,** is assigned for a laminectomy performed for the purpose of exploration or decompression of the spinal canal. Laminectomy performed for the purpose of excision of herniated disc material, however, represents the operative approach and is not coded separately. Instead, the root operation "Excision" is coded to report the excision of the disc. Occasionally after a decompression laminotomy, Mersilene stabilization may be carried out to reconstitute the intraspinous ligament. The placement of Mersilene sutures is inherent to the total procedure and should not be coded separately.

ARTHRITIS

Arthritis is the common term for a wide variety of conditions that primarily affect the joints, muscles, and connective tissue. The associated symptoms are inflammation, swelling, pain, stiffness, and mobility problems. Arthritis may occur independently, but it is also a common manifestation of a variety of other conditions. Combination codes should be used when available, and dual-coding guidelines should be applied when combination codes are not available. Examples include the following:

M11.811	Arthritis of the right shoulder due to dicalcium phosphate crystals
E11.610	Charcot's arthritis due to type 2 diabetes
C95.90 + M36.1	Arthritis due to leukemia
D66 + M36.2	Hemophilic arthritis
A69.23	Arthritis associated with Lyme disease

Osteoarthritis is the most common form of arthritis; it is also called polyarthritis, degenerative arthritis, and hypertrophic arthritis. It is a degenerative joint disease, usually occurring in older people, with chronic degeneration of the articular cartilage and hypertrophy of the bone. It is characterized by pain and swelling. Codes from categories M15 through M19 are assigned for osteoarthritis, except when the spine is involved, in which case a code from category M47, Spondylosis, is assigned.

The primary axis for coding osteoarthritis is the site, whether it involves multiple sites (M15.-, Osteoarthritis) or single joints. Bilateral involvement of single joint is coded to categories M16 through M19. Codes further specify whether the condition is primary or secondary (for example, posttraumatic). Primary osteoarthritis, also known as polyarticular degenerative arthritis, affects joints in the spine, knee, and hip, as well as certain small joints of the hands and feet. Secondary arthritis, also called monoarticular arthritis, is confined to the joints of one area and results from some external or internal injury or disease. Osteoarthritis that involves multiple sites but is not specified as generalized is coded as **M15.9, Polyosteoarthritis, unspecified.**

CHAPTER 23

Diseases of the

Musculoskeletal

System and

Connective

Tissue

Rheumatoid arthritis (categories M05–M06), another fairly common type of arthritis, is an autoimmune disease that affects the entire body. Pyogenic arthritis (M00.-) is due to infection and is classified to the causative organism (*Staphylococcus, Pneumococcus, Streptococcus,* or other bacteria), with additional characters to indicate the joints involved. An additional code should be assigned for the responsible organism. Category M01 is used to report direct infections of joints in infectious and parasitic diseases. The underlying disease, such as leprosy, mycoses, or parathyroid fever, should be coded first. Gouty arthritis is a recurrent arthritis of the peripheral joints in which excessive uric acid in the blood is deposited in the joints. Gouty arthritis is classified to idiopathic gout. Category M10, Gout, is further subdivided to distinguish whether it is idiopathic (M10.0-), due to lead (M10.1-), drug induced (M10.2-), due to renal impairment (M10.3-), or other secondary gout (M10.4-). Unspecified gout is coded to M10.9. When the gout is specified to be chronic, it is classified to category M1A, Chronic gout.

EXERCISE 23.1

Code the following diagnoses and procedures. Do not assign External cause of morbidity codes.

1.	Acute and chronic gouty arthritis	M10.00
		M1A.00x0
2.	Chronic nodular rheumatoid arthritis with polyneuropathy	M05.50
3.	Traumatic arthritis, left ankle, due to old traumatic dislocation	M12.572
		S93.05XS
	Arthroscopic arthrodesis, left ankle	0SGG4ZZ
4.	Herniated intervertebral disc, L4-5	M51.26
	Laminectomy with excision of intervertebral disc, L4-5	0SB20ZZ
5.	Chronic lumbosacral sprain, subsequent encounter	S33.9xxD

DERANGEMENT

Derangement of the knee is classified to category M23; derangement of other sites is classified to category M24, with additional characters indicating the site. Recurrent derangement of the knee is classified to M22.0-, Recurrent dislocation of patella. Recurrent dislocation or subluxation of joints is classified to M24.4-, Recurrent dislocation of joint. Derangement of the knee due to current injury is classified to subcategory S83.2-, Tear of meniscus, current injury.

293

CHAPTER 23

*Diseases of the
Musculoskeletal
System and
Connective
Tissue*

EXERCISE 23.2

Code the following diagnoses. Do not assign External cause of morbidity codes.

1. Recurrent derangement of left ankle   M24.472

2. Recurrent derangement of knee   M22.00

3. Derangement of right knee due to a current fall, initial encounter   S83.206A

OSTEOPOROSIS

Osteoporosis is a systemic condition that affects all bones of the musculoskeletal system and leads to an increased risk of pathological fractures. In osteoporosis, the bones are thinner and weaker than normal. Osteoporosis is classified to categories M80 and M81 depending on whether a current pathological fracture is present or not. Because osteoporosis is a systemic condition, site is not a component of the codes under category M81, Osteoporosis without current pathological fracture. The codes under category M80, Osteoporosis with current pathological fracture, identify the osteoporosis and the site of the pathological fracture.

PATHOLOGICAL FRACTURES

Pathological fractures occur in bones that are weakened by disease. These fractures are usually spontaneous but sometimes occur in connection with slight trauma (such as a minor fall) that ordinarily would not result in a fracture in normal, healthy bone. There are many different underlying causes for pathological fractures, including osteoporosis, metastatic tumor of the bone, osteomyelitis, Paget's disease, disuse atrophy, hyperparathyroidism, and nutritional or congenital disorders.

Fractures described as spontaneous are always pathological fractures. When the fracture is described as a compression fracture, the record should be reviewed to determine whether any significant trauma has been experienced. A fall from a height, such as a diving board, with compression fracture of the spine is classified as an injury, but a compression fracture in an older patient resulting from a slight stumble or another minor injury is usually considered pathological, particularly when the patient also suffers from an underlying condition that frequently causes such fractures. The physician should be asked for clarification.

All pathological fractures are classified to the following categories/subcategories according to the underlying cause:

- Category M80   Osteoporosis with current pathological fracture
- Subcategory M84.4-   Pathological fracture, not elsewhere classified
- Subcategory M84.5-   Pathological fracture in neoplastic disease (code also the underlying cause)
- Subcategory M84.6-   Pathological fracture in other disease (code also the underlying condition)

CHAPTER 23

Diseases of the
Musculoskeletal
System and
Connective
Tissue

Additional characters are used to indicate the bone involved. The following seventh-character extensions are required when coding pathological fractures:

A   Initial encounter for fracture
D   Subsequent encounter for fracture with routine healing
G   Subsequent encounter for fracture with delayed healing
K   Subsequent encounter for fracture with nonunion
P   Subsequent encounter for fracture with malunion
S   Sequela

The assignment of the seventh-character extension for pathological fractures should be performed using the following guidelines:

- "A" is used when the patient is receiving active treatment for the pathological fracture. Examples of active treatment are surgical treatment, emergency department encounter, and evaluation and treatment by a new physician.
- "D" is used for encounters after the patient has completed active treatment and there is routine healing.
- "G," "K," and "P" are used for subsequent encounters for treatment of problems associated with the healing, such as delayed healing, malunions, and nonunions.
- "S" is to be used for encounters for the treatment of sequelae or the residual effect after the acute phase of the fracture has terminated.

Care for complications of surgical treatment for fracture repairs during the healing or recovery phase should be coded with the appropriate complication codes.

Sequencing of codes for pathological fractures depends on the circumstances of admission. A pathological fracture is designated as the principal diagnosis only when the patient is admitted solely for treatment of the pathological fracture. Ordinarily, the code for the underlying condition responsible for the fracture is listed first, with an additional code for the fracture. An example follows.

- Pathological fracture due to neoplasm: If the focus of treatment is the fracture, a code from subcategory M84.5, Pathological fracture in neoplastic disease, should be sequenced first, followed by the code for the neoplasm. If the focus of treatment is the neoplasm with an associated pathological fracture, the neoplasm code should be sequenced first, followed by a code from M84.5 for the pathological fracture. The "code also" note at M84.5 provides this sequencing instruction.

Never assign a code for both a traumatic fracture and a pathological fracture of the same bone; one or the other is assigned. (See chapter 33 of this handbook for a discussion of coding traumatic fractures.)

Appropriate coding examples include the following:

M80.061A + M89.761	Initial encounter for acute fracture of right tibia and major osseous defects due to senile osteoporosis
M84.559D + C79.51 + Z85.43	Subsequent encounter for healing pathological fracture of the hip due to metastatic carcinoma of bone; ovarian cancer five years ago

STRESS FRACTURES

Stress fractures are different from pathological fractures in that they are due to repetitive force applied before the bone and its supporting tissues have had enough time to provide such force, whereas pathological fractures are always due to a physiologic condition, such as cancer or osteoporosis, that

295

CHAPTER 23

*Diseases of the
Musculoskeletal
System and
Connective
Tissue*

results in damage to the bone. Stress fractures usually test negative in an X-ray display, and days or weeks may pass before the fracture line is visible on an X-ray. Stress fractures are classified to sub-category M84.3. Additional External cause of morbidity codes are used to identify the cause of the stress fracture, for example, code **Y93.01, Walking, marching and hiking.** Other terms classified to stress fractures are fatigue fracture, march fracture, and stress reaction fracture.

MUSCULOSKELETAL BODY PART GUIDELINES

Most ICD-10-PCS body part guidelines are covered in chapter 8 of this handbook, Introduction to ICD-10-PCS and ICD-10-PCS Conventions. However, there is a specific guideline that pertains more closely to this chapter, describing tendons, ligaments, bursae, and fascia near a joint.

Procedures performed on tendons, ligaments, bursae, and fascia supporting a joint are coded to the body part in the respective body system that is the focus of the procedure. Procedures performed on joint structures themselves are coded to the body part in the joint body systems. For example, repair of the anterior cruciate ligament of the knee is coded to the "knee bursae and ligament" body part in the bursae and the "ligaments" body system. Knee arthroscopy with shaving of articular cartilage is coded to the "knee joint" body part in the "lower joints" body system.

REPLACEMENT OF A JOINT

Replacement of a joint is classified in the Medical and Surgical Section to the root operation "Replacement." Code assignment depends on the joint involved. When coding hip replacements, the type of bearing surface is identified by the seventh-character qualifier using the following values:

5   Metal on polyethylene
6   Metal on metal
7   Ceramic on ceramic
8   Ceramic on polyethylene

If replacement also involves the placement of a bone-growth stimulator, it should be coded separately to the root operation "Insertion" and the device "bone-growth stimulator" (sixth character M). Other examples include the following:

0SRA0JG   Replacement of right acetabulum with ceramic prosthesis
0SRG0JZ   Total left ankle replacement with synthetic prosthesis
0SRS0JF   Replacement of left femoral head (metal)
0SRA0JH   Partial replacement (acetabular, polyethylene) of right hip
0RRL0JZ   Total right elbow replacement (synthetic)

ICD-10-PCS does not provide codes to indicate that a bilateral replacement has been carried out. The procedure code should be assigned twice when the same procedure is performed on bilateral joints.

Occasionally, a prosthesis must be removed because of infection, with a new prosthesis placed after a month or two when the infection has completely cleared. The first admission for such a problem is coded **T84.5-, Infection and inflammatory reaction due to internal joint prosthesis,** with an additional code to identify the infection and a procedure code for removal of the prosthesis (e.g., **0SP90JZ, Removal of synthetic substitute from right hip joint, open approach**). Assign code 0SH908Z if a spacer is inserted. On the follow-up admission, the principal diagnosis is acquired deformity of the site (categories M20 and M21), with a procedure code for insertion of a new device.

296

CHAPTER 23

Diseases of the
Musculoskeletal
System and
Connective
Tissue

On the other hand, if a malfunctioning device is corrected, assign a code for the root operation "Revision," for example, **0SW90JZ, Revision of synthetic substitute in right hip joint, open approach.**

Any time a joint replacement is adjusted during the same encounter, the procedure is coded as a joint revision. The definition for the root operation "Revision" is "correcting, to the extent possible, a malfunctioning or misplaced device." If a joint prosthesis is removed and replaced during the same encounter, code both the removal and replacement. However, if there is removal of a joint spacer (e.g., cement), a code with the root operation "Removal" is also assigned (e.g., **0SP908Z, Removal of spacer from right hip joint, open approach**) for the removal of the spacer.

Codes for revision of hip replacements identify the specific joint components revised (acetabular surface, femoral surface).

Any time a component of a joint has been previously replaced, the procedure is still considered a replacement even though part of the component is being replaced for the first time. For example, when a patient is admitted for conversion of a previous right hip hemiarthroplasty to a total metal-on-polyethylene right hip replacement, open approach, it should be reported with codes **0SP90JZ, Removal of synthetic substitute from right hip joint, open approach,** and **0SR90J5, Replacement of right hip joint with synthetic substitute, metal on polyethylene, open approach.**

Hip resurfacing involves grinding away the worn surfaces of the femoral head and acetabulum while retaining the femoral neck and majority of the femoral head. The procedure concludes with the placement of new bearing surfaces. Resurfacing arthroplasty is classified to the root operation "Replacement," identifying the specific joint components resurfaced (total resurfacing involves both the acetabular and femoral components; partial involves femoral surface or acetabular surface only), as follows:

0SUR0BZ + 0SUA0BZ	Resurfacing right hip, total, acetabulum and femoral
0SUR0BZ	Resurfacing right hip, partial, femoral head
0SUA0BZ	Resurfacing right hip, partial, acetabulum

Subcategory Z96.6-, Presence of orthopedic joint implants, can be assigned as an additional code when the presence of a joint replacement is significant in terms of patient care.

EXERCISE 23.3

Code the following diagnoses and procedures. Do not assign External cause of morbidity codes.

1. Primary osteoarthritis of right hip — M16.11
   Replacement, total, of hip with ceramic-on-ceramic bearing surface — 0SR90J7

2. Total right knee replacement (synthetic) — 0SRC0JZ

3. Partial replacement (synthetic) of left shoulder (humeral head) — 0PRC0JZ

SPINAL FUSION AND REFUSION

Spinal fusion is a surgical procedure whereby two or more vertebrae are fused to correct problems with the vertebrae. The vertebrae can be fused using bone grafting, genetically engineered bone substitute, and metal devices. The goal of spinal fusion surgery is pain relief after conservative treatments have failed. The procedure is indicated for spinal vertebrae injuries such as protrusion and degeneration of the cushion between vertebrae, curvature of the spine, or weak spine caused by injections or tumors.

The failure of development of solid bone between two or more levels of the spine after spinal fusion is called nonunion or pseudarthrosis. Symptoms may not occur until months or years after the original spinal fusion. Patients can often function relatively normally with pseudarthrosis unless problems develop such as sharp localized pain and tenderness over the fusion, progression of the deformity or disease, or localized motion in the fusion mass. Treatment for symptomatic pseudarthrosis consists of refusion. The procedure involves thorough removal of fibrous tissue from the intended fusion area and the addition of new bone graft.

FIGURE 23.3   Structure of the Spine Involved in Spinal Fusion

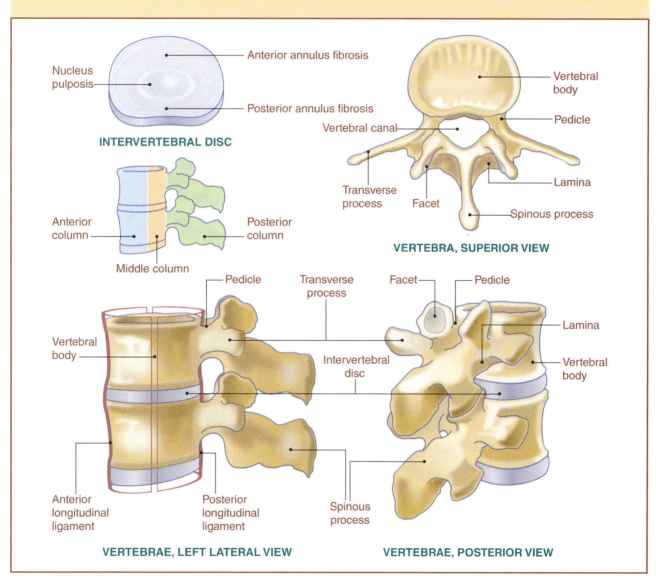

CHAPTER 23

Diseases of the
Musculoskeletal
System and
Connective
Tissue

The structure of the spine is considered to be composed of the anterior, middle, and posterior columns. The anterior column is composed of the anterior longitudinal ligament, the anterior annulus, and the anterior portion of the vertebral body. The middle column includes the posterior longitudinal ligament, the posterior annulus, and the posterior portion of the vertebral body. The posterior column includes those spinal structures that are posterior to the posterior longitudinal ligament.

During an anterior column fusion, the body (corpus) of adjacent vertebrae are fused (interbody fusion). The anterior column can be fused using an anterior, lateral, or posterior technique. For the posterior column fusion, posterior structures of adjacent vertebrae are fused (pedicle, lamina, facet, transverse process, or "gutter" fusion). A posterior column fusion can be performed using a posterior, posterolateral, or lateral transverse technique.

Traditionally, three basic approaches have been used for spinal fusion or spinal refusion: anterior, posterior, and lateral transverse. The classic anterior approach requires an incision in the neck or the abdomen, and the fusion is carried out from the front of the vertebrae through the anterior annulus. In the classic posterior approach, the incision is made in the patient's back directly over the vertebrae. Another approach is the lateral transverse, which involves an incision on the patient's side, and the vertebrae are approached through the lamina.

Spinal fusion and refusion procedures are coded to the root operation "Fusion"—joining together portions of an articular body part rendering the articular body part immobile. The body part coded for a spinal vertebral joint(s) rendered immobile by a spinal fusion procedure is classified by the level of the spine, namely, cervical, thoracic, lumbar, lumbosacral, or sacrococcygeal. There are distinct body part values for a single vertebral joint and for multiple vertebral joints at each spinal level. For example, body part values specify "lumbar vertebral joint," "lumbar vertebral joints, 2 or more," and "lumbosacral vertebral joint."

If multiple vertebral joints are fused, a separate procedure is coded for each vertebral joint that uses a different device and/or qualifier. For example, **Open fusion of lumbar vertebral joint, posterior approach, anterior column (0SG00ZJ),** and **Open fusion of lumbar vertebral joint, posterior approach, posterior column (0SG00Z1),** are coded separately because the procedures involve different portions of the column (anterior column versus posterior column).

Occasionally, instrumentation called interbody fusion devices are used to stabilize and fuse degenerative disc spaces and to provide an immediately stable segment for fusion and relief of symptoms. These devices are also known as interbody fusion cage, Bak cage, ray-threaded fusion cage, synthetic cage, spacer, or bone dowels. Combinations of devices and materials are often used on a vertebral joint to render the joint immobile. When combinations of devices are used on the same vertebral joint, the device value for the procedure is coded using the following guidelines:

- *If an interbody fusion device is used to render the joint immobile (alone or containing other material like bone graft),* the procedure is coded with the device value "interbody fusion device."

- *If internal fixation is used to render the joint immobile and an interbody fusion device is not used,* the procedure is coded with the device value "internal fixation device."

- *If bone graft is the only device used to render the joint immobile,* the procedure is coded with the device value "nonautologous tissue substitute" or "autologous tissue substitute."

- *If a mixture of autologous and nonautologous bone graft (with or without biological or synthetic extenders or binders) is used to render the joint immobile,* code the procedure with the device value "autologous tissue substitute."

299

CHAPTER 23
*Diseases of the
Musculoskeletal
System and
Connective
Tissue*

Examples include the following:

- Fusion of a vertebral joint using a cage-style interbody fusion device containing morsell-ized bone graft is coded to the device "interbody fusion device."

- Fusion of a vertebral joint using a bone dowel interbody fusion device made of cadaver bone and packed with a mixture of local morsellized bone and demineralized bone matrix is coded to the device "interbody fusion device."

- Fusion of a vertebral joint using rigid plates affixed with screws and reinforced with bone cement is coded to the device "internal fixation device."

- Fusion of a vertebral joint using both autologous bone graft and bone bank bone graft is coded to the device "autologous tissue substitute."

Synchronous excision of locally harvested bone graft is reported separately (root operation "Excision"). If recombinant bone morphogenetic protein (a genetically engineered protein) is inserted to help create a bone graft substitute, assign code **3E0V3GB, Introduction of recombinant bone morphogenetic protein into bones, percutaneous approach.**

A 360-degree spinal fusion is a fusion of both the anterior and posterior portions of the spine performed through a single incision (usually via the lateral transverse approach).

A brief explanation of common fusion and refusion procedures is listed below:

- ALIF: The anterior lumbar interbody fusion (ALIF) is an interbody fusion of the anterior and middle columns of the spine through an anterior incision, either transperitoneal or retroperitoneal. It can also be done laparoscopically.

- AxiaLIF: The axial lumbar interbody fusion (AxiaLIF®) is a percutaneous fusion of the anterior column at L5-S1. An AxiaLIF® 360° refers to the combination of an AxiaLIF® procedure of the anterior column performed along with a posterior column fusion, which may include the use of pedicle screws or facet screws. The AxiaLIF® 360° is described as providing a percutaneous 360° fusion.

- DLIF: The direct lateral lumbar interbody fusion (DLIF) is a minimally invasive alternative to conventional spinal fusion. The DLIF is performed through a lateral approach, which allows for limited soft tissue disruption. The procedure can only be performed at L4-L5 or at higher levels and requires dissection through the psoas muscle.

- PLIF: The posterior lumbar interbody fusion (PLIF) involves an anterior and middle column fusion through a posterior approach.

- TLIF: The transforaminal lumbar interbody fusion (TLIF) involves a transverse lateral interbody fusion through a posterior approach.

- XLIF: The extreme lateral interbody fusion (XLIF®) is a less invasive spinal surgery of the anterior column. The fusion may be accomplished either percutaneously or via a circular tube retractor through a lateral approach.

VERTEBROPLASTY AND KYPHOPLASTY

CHAPTER 23

*Diseases of the
Musculoskeletal
System and
Connective
Tissue*

Percutaneous vertebroplasty is a technique used to treat vertebral compression fractures. The procedure involves the insertion of cement glue–like material (polymethylmethacrylate) into the vertebral body to stabilize and strengthen collapsed or crushed bone. ICD-10-PCS classifies this procedure to the root operation "Supplement," with "synthetic substitute" for the device value. For example, percutaneous lumbar vertebroplasty is coded to **0QU03JZ, Supplement lumbar vertebra with synthetic substitute, percutaneous approach.**

The ARCUATE™ XP procedure is a variation of a percutaneous vertebroplasty in which an osteotome is used to cut arcs in the cancellous bone within the vertebral body. The arcs created with the osteotome allow for dispersion of bone cement material when it is subsequently injected into the vertebral body. No bone or bone marrow is removed from, or compacted within, the vertebral body. The ARCUATE™ XP procedure is also coded to the root operation "Supplement."

Percutaneous vertebral augmentation is a procedure using an inflatable balloon that is expanded in order to reestablish vertebral height in compression fractures. After the balloon is removed, the cavity is filled with polymethylmethacrylate, which hardens to further stabilize the bone. Coding of percutaneous vertebroplasty requires two codes, one for the root operation "Reposition" and another for the root operation "Supplement." Other similar procedures coded in the same manner include arcuplasty, kyphoplasty, skyphoplasty, and spineoplasty. For example, percutaneous kyphoplasty of the lumbar spine should be coded to **0QS03ZZ, Reposition lumbar vertebra, percutaneous approach,** and **0QU03JZ, Supplement lumbar vertebra with synthetic substitute, percutaneous approach.**

While these procedures are similar, there is no balloon involved in the vertebroplasty, and no attempt is made to restore vertebral height to reduce the compression fractures of the vertebra; therefore, only the root operation "Supplement" is coded for vertebroplasty and not "Reposition."

If a vertebral biopsy is performed during a kyphoplasty of the lumbar vertebra, assign codes **0QS03ZZ, Reposition lumbar vertebra, percutaneous approach; 0QU03JZ, Supplement lumbar vertebra with synthetic substitute, percutaneous approach;** and **0QB03ZX, Excision of lumbar vertebra, percutaneous approach, diagnostic.** The biopsy is not an inherent part of the kyphoplasty and should be coded separately if performed.

SPINAL DISC PROSTHESES

Minimally invasive arthroplasty procedures are being carried out as an alternative to spinal fusion. These procedures are performed to replace the degenerated disc nucleus and restore or maintain the normal function of the disc by inserting artificial disc prostheses. The prostheses are used to replace the entire spinal disc or replace the disc nucleus.

The insertion of spinal disc prostheses is classified to the root operation "Replacement" and the spinal segment treated, for example, cervical (0RR30JZ), thoracic (0RR90JZ), or lumbosacral (0SR40JZ). ICD-10-PCS does not differentiate between partial and total disc prostheses with unique codes.

Revision/replacement codes are used to report either the repair (root operation "Revision") or the removal of the artificial disc prosthesis with the synchronous insertion of a new prosthesis (two procedure codes, one for root operation "Removal" and another for "Replacement"). These codes specify the part of the spine treated, but they do not distinguish between partial and total prostheses.

SPINAL MOTION PRESERVATION

Patients suffering from spinal stenosis or degenerative disc disease may be treated with conservative measures, including physical therapy and pain management. When conservative care does not provide relief, surgical decompression may be an alternative treatment. Surgical decompression (root operation "Excision") involves removal of the bone and/or tissue causing pressure on the spinal cord or nerve root(s). Common surgical decompression procedures include laminotomy, laminectomy, diskectomy, foraminotomy, and medial facetectomy. The spinal segment may be deemed unstable depending on the extent of bone and tissue removed during the decompression procedure. Stabilization of the spinal segment is primarily accomplished with spinal fusion. However, new spinal motion preservation technologies have been developed to allow for spine stabilization without the motion restriction associated with fusion.

Motion preservation technologies placed in the posterior column of the spine include the following:

- Interspinous process devices (e.g., X-Stop™, Wallis®, and Coflex™ systems)
- Pedicle screw dynamic stabilization devices (e.g., Dynesys® and M-Brace™)
- Facet replacement devices (e.g., The Total Facet Arthroplasty System™ and The Artificial Facet Replacement System™)

Root operation "Insertion," "Revision," or "Replacement" is used for the insertion, revision, or replacement of posterior spinal motion preservation device(s), respectively. These codes include a dynamic stabilization device(s) and any synchronous facetectomy (partial, total) performed at the same level. If a synchronous surgical decompression (foraminotomy, laminectomy, laminotomy) is also performed, it is coded as an additional procedure.

Examples follow.

0RH6342	Insertion of interspinous process device into thoracic vertebral joint, percutaneous approach
0RW104Z	Revision of internal fixation device in cervical vertebral joint, open approach
0SH3043	Insertion of pedicle-based dynamic stabilization device into lumbosacral joint, open approach
0RW634Z	Revision of internal fixation device in thoracic vertebral joint, percutaneous approach
0SR00JZ	Replacement of lumbar vertebral joint, facet, with synthetic substitute, open approach
0SW30JZ	Revision of synthetic substitute in lumbosacral joint, open approach

PLICA SYNDROME

Although plica syndrome can occasionally be found in other areas, it almost always affects the knee. Plica syndrome occurs when the synovial bands that are present early in fetal development have not combined into one large synovial unit as they develop further. Patients with this syndrome often experience pain and swelling, weakness, and a locking and clicking sensation of the knee. The therapeutic goal is to reduce the inflammation of the synovium and the thickening of the plica. Usual treatment measures attempt to relieve symptoms within three months; if that does not occur, arthroscopic or open surgery to remove the plica may be required. Assign code **M67.5-, Plica syndrome,** for this condition and code for excision of knee joint for the surgery.

FASCIITIS

CHAPTER 23

*Diseases of the
Musculoskeletal
System and
Connective
Tissue*

Necrotizing fasciitis is a fulminating infection that begins with severe or extensive cellulitis that spreads to the superficial and deep fascia, producing thrombosis of the subcutaneous vessels and gangrene of the underlying tissue. Group A *Streptococcus* is the most common organism responsible for this condition, but any bacteria may be the cause. Code M72.6 is assigned for this condition, with an additional code for the organism when this information is known.

EXERCISE 23.4

Code the following diagnoses and procedures. Do not assign External cause of morbidity codes.

1. Acute polymyositis — M33.20
   Mild thoracogenic scoliosis — M41.30
   Percutaneous biopsy of left trunk muscle — 0KBG3ZX

2. Sclerosing tenosynovitis, left thumb — M65.842
   and middle finger

3. Osteomyelitis of left distal femur — E11.618
   due to type 2 diabetes with diabetic arthropathy — M86.152
   Sequestrectomy (percutaneous) and percutaneous — 0QCC3ZZ
   excision of sinus tract, left distal femur — 0QBC3ZZ

4. Adhesive capsulitis, left shoulder — M75.02

5. Nonunion of fracture, left femoral neck, subsequent — S72.002K
   encounter
   Inlay-type iliac bone graft to nonunion — 0QR707Z
   of left femoral neck (open approach) **Replacement**
   Left iliac crest bone excised for graft (percutaneous) — 0QB33ZZ
   Excision

6. Recurrent dislocation of patella — M24.469

CHAPTER 23

*Diseases of the
Musculoskeletal
System and
Connective
Tissue*

7. Deformity of left ring finger, due to   M20.002

old tendon laceration of left ring finger   S56.422S

Laceration

Transfer of flexor tendon from distal   0LX80ZZ

phalanx to middle phalanx (open approach)

---

8. Cervical spondylosis, C5-6, C6-7   M47.812

Anterior column cervical spinal fusion, C5-6, C6-7   0RG20H0

open, anterior approach, with interbody device

---

9. Right hallux valgus   M20.11

Resection of hallux valgus with insertion   0STP0ZZ

of prosthesis   0SRP0JZ

---

10. Dupuytren's contracture (right hand)   M72.0

Incision and division of palmar fascia (open approach)   0J8J0ZZ

---

11. Multiple compression fractures of vertebrae   M80.08xA

and major osseous defects due to senile osteoporosis   M89.78

(initial encounter)

---

12. Lumbar spinal stenosis   M48.06

Decompressive laminectomy with Dynesys stabilization

system (open approach)   0SH0043

     OSB00ZZ

Coding OF Pregnancy AND Childbirth Complications, Abortion, Congenital Anomalies, AND Perinatal Conditions

CHAPTER 24

Complications of Pregnancy, Childbirth, and the Puerperium

CHAPTER OVERVIEW

- Conditions affecting pregnancy, childbirth, and the puerperium are found in chapter 15 of ICD-10-CM.

  — Codes from chapter 15 take precedence over codes from other chapters.

  — Codes from chapter 15 are never assigned to the newborn's record.

- Assignment of the final character for trimester should be based on the provider's documentation of the trimester for the current admission/encounter.

- Z codes are used to indicate the outcome of the delivery.

- A normal delivery is contingent on a variety of criteria.

- The Tabular List must be reviewed for assignment of the final character for trimester and the correct extension for multiple gestations for all chapter 15 codes.

- Deliveries not deemed normal use as their principal diagnosis code the main circumstance or complication of the delivery.

- When assigning codes from chapter 15, it is important to assess whether a condition was pre-existing prior to pregnancy or developed during or due to the pregnancy in order to assign the correct code.

- Postpartum complications are any complications that occur throughout the six weeks following the delivery.

- There is a sequela code to use for complications that occur after the postpartum period. This code follows the codes for the condition.

- There are codes for delivery assistance procedures, such as fetal head rotation, forceps delivery, vacuum extraction, episiotomy, and cesarean delivery.

- Contraceptive management and procreative management, through both admission and outpatient encounter, are covered by a series of Z codes. These codes can be supplemented by additional codes if an underlying condition is present.

LEARNING OUTCOMES

After studying this chapter you should be able to:

Code complications of pregnancy using the proper fourth and fifth characters.

Use the proper Z codes to assign the outcome of delivery.

Code for other obstetric care besides childbirth.

Know the difference between post-partum complications and late effects of pregnancy, childbirth, and the puerperium.

Differentiate among the procedures assisting delivery.

Code for contraceptive and pro-creative management.

TERMS TO KNOW

Antepartum
the period of pregnancy from conception to childbirth

Postpartum
the period beginning right after delivery and including the next six weeks

Puerperium
the clinical term for the postpartum period

REMEMBER . . .

If the mother's record does not state the outcome of the delivery, look at the newborn's record.

307

CHAPTER 24

*Complications
of Pregnancy,
Childbirth,
and the
Puerperium*

INTRODUCTION

Conditions that affect the management of pregnancy, childbirth, and the puerperium are classified to categories O00 through O9A in chapter 15 of ICD-10-CM. Conditions from other chapters of ICD-10-CM are usually reclassified in chapter 15 when they are related to or aggravated by the pregnancy, childbirth, or the puerperium. It is the provider's responsibility to state that the condition being treated is not affecting the pregnancy.

Should the provider document that the pregnancy is incidental to the encounter, code **Z33.1, Pregnant state, incidental,** is assigned in place of any chapter 15 codes. Chapter 15 codes take precedence over codes from other chapters, but codes from other chapters may be used as additional codes when needed to provide more specificity. Codes from chapter 15 of ICD-10-CM refer to the mother only and are assigned only on the mother's record. They are never assigned on the newborn's record; other codes are provided for that purpose. (See chapter 27 of this handbook.) Codes from categories O00 through O08 are assigned for pregnancy with abortive outcome, including ectopic pregnancy, molar pregnancy, and abortion. (Code assignments for these conditions are discussed in chapter 25.)

Codes from categories O09 through O9A apply throughout the entire obstetrical experience, which begins at conception and ends six weeks (42 days) after delivery.

ICD-10-CM divides chapter 15 as follows:

O09	Supervision of high-risk pregnancy
O10–O16	Edema, proteinuria, and hypertensive disorders in pregnancy, childbirth, and the puerperium
O20–O29	Other maternal disorders predominantly related to pregnancy
O30–O48	Maternal care related to the fetus and amniotic cavity and possible delivery problems
O60–O77	Complications of labor and delivery
O80, O82	Encounter for delivery
O85–O92	Complications predominantly related to the puerperium
O94–O9A	Other obstetric conditions not elsewhere classified

The process of labor and delivery includes three stages. The first stage begins with the onset of regular uterine contractions and ends when the cervical os is completely dilated. The second stage begins with complete dilation and continues until the infant has been completely expelled. The third stage begins with the expulsion of the infant and continues until the placenta and membranes have been expelled and contraction of the uterus is complete. The puerperium begins at the end of the third stage of labor and continues for six weeks.

Occasionally, a pregnancy continues for a longer term than usual gestation and is considered to be a long pregnancy. The following two codes are used when this occurs:

O48.0	Post-term pregnancy (40 completed weeks to 42 completed weeks of gestation)
O48.1	Prolonged pregnancy (advanced beyond 42 completed weeks of gestation)

FINAL CHARACTER FOR TRIMESTER

The majority of codes in chapter 15 of ICD-10-CM have a final character indicating the trimester of pregnancy. Note that the Tabular List must be reviewed for assignment of the final character for trimester, as the codes in the Alphabetic Index of Diseases and Injuries do not include the complete

CHAPTER 24

*Complications
of Pregnancy,
Childbirth,
and the
Puerperium*

FIGURE 24.1   Primary Organs of the Female Reproductive System

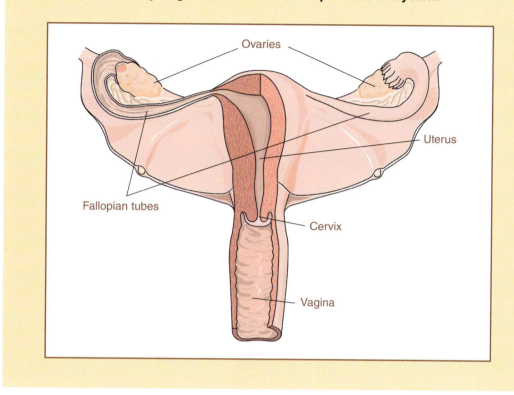

code. The time frames for the trimesters are indicated at the beginning of chapter 15 and are defined by an instructional note as follows:

- First trimester—less than 14 weeks 0 days
- Second trimester—14 weeks 0 days to less than 28 weeks 0 days
- Third trimester—28 weeks 0 days until delivery.

Assignment of the final character for trimester should be based on the provider's documentation of the trimester (or number of weeks) for the current admission/encounter. This refers to the provider as defined in the *ICD-10-CM Official Guidelines for Coding and Reporting:* "Physician or other qualified healthcare practitioner legally accountable for establishing the patient's diagnosis." This definition applies to the assignment of trimester for pre-existing conditions as well as those that develop during or are due to the pregnancy. The provider's documentation of the number of weeks may be used to assign the appropriate final character identifying the trimester. For example, if the documentation refers to the patient having completed 20 weeks, the appropriate code for second trimester may be selected; the provider does not have to explicitly document "second trimester."

Not every single code in chapter 15 has a trimester component. If trimester is not a component of a code, it is because the condition always occurs in a specific trimester or the concept of trimester of pregnancy is not applicable. For example, category O48, Late pregnancy, does not include trimester because, by definition, this category is to be used for pregnancies longer than 40 completed weeks. Certain codes have characters for only certain trimesters because the condition does not occur in all trimesters, but it may occur in more than one. For example, category O60.0, Preterm labor, is for spontaneous onset of labor before 37 completed weeks of gestation, and therefore there are no codes for first trimester, which is less than 14 weeks.

CHAPTER 24

*Complications
of Pregnancy,
Childbirth,
and the
Puerperium*

If a condition complicating the pregnancy develops prior to the current admission/encounter or represents a pre-existing condition, the trimester character for the trimester at the time of the admission/encounter should be assigned. For example, a pregnant patient with pre-existing diabetes mellitus type 1, at 16 weeks (second trimester) gestation is admitted for an emergent transvaginal cerclage for cervical shortening. Assign code **O26.872, Cervical shortening, second trimester,** as the principal diagnosis. Code **O24.012, Pre-existing diabetes mellitus, type 1, in pregnancy, second trimester,** is assigned for the diabetes along with a code from category E10 for any diabetic manifestations. Also assign code **0UVC7DZ, Restriction of cervix with intraluminal device, via natural or artificial opening,** for the placement of the cerclage.

Occasionally, an inpatient hospitalization may encompass more than one trimester, such as when a patient is admitted to a hospital for complications of pregnancy during one trimester and remains in the hospital into a subsequent trimester. In such instances, the trimester character for the antepartum complication code should be assigned on the basis of the trimester when the complication developed, not the trimester of the discharge. For example, a pregnant female is admitted to the hospital at 27 weeks completed gestation with acute appendicitis complicating her pregnancy. She requires emergency laparoscopic appendectomy, which she tolerates well. She is kept in the hospital for two weeks postoperatively, with intravenous antibiotics administered due to postoperative fever. Because the acute appendicitis developed during the second trimester, code **O99.612, Diseases of the digestive system complicating pregnancy, second trimester,** is assigned rather than O99.613.

The exception to the above guideline is when a delivery occurs during the current admission. Whenever delivery occurs during the current admission and there is an "in childbirth" option for the obstetric complication, the "in childbirth" code should be assigned. For example, a patient is admitted during the third trimester with malnutrition and stays in the hospital until she delivers. Code **O25.2, Malnutrition in childbirth,** should be assigned rather than code **O25.13, Malnutrition in pregnancy, third trimester,** for the malnutrition.

It is important to note that although each category in chapter 15 that includes codes for trimester has a code for "unspecified trimester," the "unspecified trimester" code should rarely be used, such as when the documentation in the record is insufficient to determine the trimester and it is not possible to obtain clarification.

OUTCOME OF DELIVERY

Because chapter 15 codes do not indicate the outcome of delivery, a code from category Z37 is assigned as an additional code to provide this information whenever the patient delivers in the hospital. Third characters indicate both whether the outcome was single or multiple and whether liveborn or stillborn. For multiple births with more than twins, additional characters indicate the number of outcomes (e.g., triplets, quadruplets) and whether they were all liveborn, some liveborn, or all stillborn. These codes are used only on the mother's record, not the record of the newborn, and are assigned only for the episode of care during which delivery occurred. No code from category Z37 is assigned when delivery occurs outside the hospital prior to admission. Examples of appropriate use of codes from category Z37 include the following:

O80 + Z37.0	Term pregnancy, spontaneous delivery, vertex presentation; liveborn male infant
O30.003 + Z37.3 + O36.4xx0	Term pregnancy with spontaneous delivery; twin pregnancy, with one twin liveborn and one stillborn

To locate the code assignment for outcome of delivery, the coder should refer to the main term **Outcome of delivery** in the Alphabetic Index. If the mother's record does not state the outcome, the coder should refer to the newborn's record for this information.

311

CHAPTER 24
*Complications
of Pregnancy,
Childbirth,
and the
Puerperium*

EXERCISE 24.1

For the following exercise, do not assign the delivery codes; assign only the Z codes for outcome of delivery. Remember that in actual practice the delivery code precedes the Z code.

1. Delivery of twins, both stillborn   Z37.4

   Outcome of delivery

2. Delivery of triplets, one stillborn   Z37.61

   Outcome of delivery

3. Delivery of liveborn, female infant   Z37.0

   Outcome of delivery

4. Delivery of single stillborn   Z37.1

   Outcome of delivery

FETAL EXTENSIONS

The following subcategories/codes require a seventh-character extension to identify the fetus for which the complication code applies:

O31.00–O31.8x9	Complications specific to multiple gestation
O32.0–O32.9	Maternal care for malpresentation of fetus
O33.3	Maternal care for disproportion due to outlet contraction of pelvis
O33.4	Maternal care for disproportion of mixed maternal and fetal origin
O33.5	Maternal care for disproportion due to unusually large fetus
O33.6	Maternal care for disproportion due to hydrocephalic fetus
O35.0–O35.9	Maternal care for known or suspected fetal abnormality and damage
O36.011–O36.93	Maternal care for other fetal problems
O40.1–O40.9	Polyhydramnios
O41.00–O41.93	Other disorders of amniotic fluid and membranes
O60.10–O60.14	Preterm labor with preterm delivery
O60.20–O60.23	Term delivery with preterm labor
O64.0–O64.9	Obstructed labor due to malposition and malpresentation of fetus
O69.0–O69.9	Labor and delivery complicated by umbilical cord complications

312

CHAPTER 24

*Complications
of Pregnancy,
Childbirth,
and the
Puerperium*

Seventh characters "1" through "9" are for cases of multiple gestations to identify the fetus for which the code applies. The seventh character "0," not applicable or unspecified, is used for the following situations:

- Single gestations
- When the documentation in the record is insufficient to determine the fetus affected and it is not possible to obtain clarification
- When it is not possible to clinically determine which fetus is affected

The appropriate code from category O30, Multiple gestation, must also be assigned when using a seventh character of "1" through "9." Note that the Tabular List must be reviewed for assignment of the correct extension for multiple gestations for all chapter 15 codes, because the extensions are not included in the Alphabetic Index.

Some providers prefer to refer to each fetus in multiple gestation cases by alphabetical characters, such as fetus A, fetus B, etc., rather than numbers (fetus 1, fetus 2, etc.). In such cases, fetus A should be equated to fetus 1, fetus B should be equated to fetus 2, and so on. There is no expectation that the same fetus number or alphabetical character be consistently carried over from one admission to another. Identification of the fetus, whether by number or alphabetical character, is based on the provider documentation.

SELECTION OF FIRST-LISTED AND PRINCIPAL DIAGNOSIS

The selection of first-listed diagnoses or principal diagnoses for encounters/admissions for normal deliveries and other obstetric care is based on the following guidelines.

Routine Outpatient Prenatal Visits

For routine outpatient prenatal visits when no complications are present, a code from category Z34, Encounter for supervision of normal pregnancy, should be used as the first-listed diagnosis. These codes should not be used in conjunction with chapter 15 codes.

Prenatal Outpatient Visits for High-Risk Patients

For routine prenatal outpatient visits for patients with high-risk pregnancies, a code from category O09, Supervision of high risk pregnancy, should be used as the first-listed diagnosis. Secondary chapter 15 codes may be used in conjunction with these codes if appropriate.

ICD-10-CM provides codes for the supervision of the following types of high-risk pregnancies:

O09.00–O09.03	Pregnancy with history of infertility
O09.10–O09.13	Pregnancy with history of ectopic or molar pregnancy
O09.211–O09.299	Pregnancy with other poor reproductive or obstetric history
O09.30–O09.33	Pregnancy with insufficient antenatal care
O09.40–O09.43	Pregnancy with grand multiparity
O09.511–O09.529	Elderly (pregnancy for female 35 years and older at expected date of delivery) primigravida and multigravida
O09.611–O09.629	Young (pregnancy for a female less than 16 years old at expected date of delivery) primigravida and multigravida
O09.70–O09.73	High-risk pregnancy due to social problems
O09.811–O09.899	Supervision of other high-risk pregnancies (includes pregnancy resulting from assisted reproductive technology [O09.81-] and pregnancy with history of in utero procedure during previous pregnancy [O09.82-])

CHAPTER 24

Complications
of Pregnancy,
Childbirth,
and the
Puerperium

Episodes When No Delivery Occurs

In episodes when no delivery occurs, the principal diagnosis should correspond to the principal complication of the pregnancy that necessitated the encounter. Should more than one complication exist, all of which are treated or monitored, any of the complication codes may be sequenced first.

Admission with Normal Delivery

Code **O80, Encounter for full-term uncomplicated delivery,** is used only when the delivery is entirely normal with a single liveborn outcome. There can be no postpartum complications, and any antepartum complication experienced during pregnancy must have been resolved before the time of delivery. Code O80 is always the principal diagnosis. If there is any complication, code O80 cannot be assigned. Code O80 cannot be used if any other code from chapter 15 is needed to describe a current complication of the antenatal, delivery, or perinatal period. Codes from other chapters may be used as additional codes with code O80 only when the physician has documented that the conditions are not related to, and in no way complicate, the pregnancy.

All of the following criteria must be met in order for code O80 to be used correctly:

- The delivery is entirely normal (requiring minimal or no assistance, with or without episiotomy).

- There is no fetal manipulation (e.g., rotation version) or instrumentation (forceps).

- There is a spontaneous, cephalic, vaginal delivery.

- Presentation at delivery can be only cephalic (head) or occipital. Terms such as "right occipito-anterior (ROA)," "left occipito-anterior (LOA)," "right occipito-posterior (ROP)," "left occipito-posterior (LOP)," and "vertex" describe an occipital presentation. Any other presentation, such as breech, face, or brow, disallows the use of code O80.

- Any antepartum complication experienced during pregnancy must have been resolved before the time of delivery.

- No abnormalities of either labor or delivery can have occurred.

- No postpartum complications can be present.

- No procedures other than the following can have been performed: episiotomy without forceps, episiorrhaphy, amniotomy (artificial rupture of the membranes), manually assisted delivery without forceps, administration of analgesics and/or anesthesia, fetal monitoring, induction of labor (in the absence of medical indications), and sterilization. If any other procedure is performed, code O80 cannot be assigned.

- Outcome of delivery must be single livebirth, Z37.0. When there has been a multiple birth or stillbirth, code O80 cannot be assigned.

Examples include the following:

- A patient who had a completely normal delivery suffers a postpartum hemorrhage several hours after delivery. Code **O72.1, Other immediate postpartum hemorrhage,** is assigned. Although the delivery itself was normal, complications were present during the episode of care; therefore, code O80 cannot be used.

- The prenatal history for a patient who had a completely normal delivery of a live infant indicates that she had a urinary tract infection at three months' gestation. This was treated with Bactrim on an outpatient basis. There was no recurrence of the infection during the pregnancy, and the patient had no infection at the time of delivery. In this case, code **O80, Encounter for full-term uncomplicated delivery,** is assigned.

EXERCISE 24.2

Write an "X" next to each of the following circumstances of delivery that is assigned code O80, Encounter for full-term uncomplicated delivery.

1. Liveborn, full-term, breech presentation _____

2. Liveborn, premature, cephalic presentation _____

3. Stillborn, full-term, vertex presentation _____

4. Liveborn, full-term, cephalic presentation; episiotomy with repair   X   _____

5. Liveborn, full-term, vertex presentation; elective low forceps _____

6. Liveborn, full-term, vertex presentation; postpartum breast abscess _____

7. Liveborn, full-term, breech presentation changed to vertex presentation by version prior to delivery _____

Admission with Other Delivery

When a delivery does not meet the criteria for assignment of code **O80, Encounter for full-term uncomplicated delivery,** the principal diagnosis should correspond to the main circumstance or complication of the delivery. In cases of cesarean delivery, the selection of the principal diagnosis should be the condition established after study that was responsible for the patient's admission. If the patient was admitted with a condition that resulted in the performance of a cesarean procedure, that condition should be selected as the principal diagnosis. If the reason for the admission/encounter was unrelated to the condition resulting in the cesarean delivery, the condition related to the reason for the admission/encounter should be selected as the principal diagnosis, even if a cesarean was performed. For example:

- A patient who had a previous cesarean delivery is admitted for a second cesarean delivery. She also had a pre-existing type 1 diabetes mellitus. Cesarean delivery was accomplished without complication. Code **O34.21 Maternal care for scar from previous cesarean delivery,** is assigned as the principal diagnosis, with an additional code of **O24.32 Unspecified pre-existing diabetes mellitus in childbirth.** Code **E10.9, Type 1 diabetes mellitus without complications** would also be assigned to provide more specificity.

- A patient is admitted to the hospital in obstructed labor due to a breech presentation. Version is unsuccessful, and the patient delivers by cesarean section several hours later. The principal diagnosis code is **O64.1xx0, Obstructed labor due to breech presentation.** There is no need to assign code **O32.1xx0, Maternal care for breech presentation,** as an additional code per the guidance provided with the "excludes1" note at category O32. Code O64.1xx0 already identifies the breech presentation.

Admission for Other Obstetric Care

When the admission or encounter is for obstetric care other than delivery, the principal diagnosis should correspond to the complication that necessitated the admission or encounter. If more than one complication is present, all of which are treated or monitored, any of the complication codes may be sequenced first. If no obstetric complications are present, the following guidelines govern selection of the principal diagnosis:

315

CHAPTER 24

*Complications
of Pregnancy,
Childbirth,
and the
Puerperium*

- If the reason for admission or encounter is not related to an obstetric condition but the patient is pregnant, code **Z33.1, Pregnant state, incidental,** is assigned as an additional code. This code is never assigned as the principal diagnosis, and no codes from chapter 15 can be assigned.

- When a patient delivers outside a health care facility and is then admitted for routine post-partum care with no complications present, code **Z39.0, Encounter for care and examination of mother immediately after delivery,** is assigned as the principal diagnosis. When a postpartum complication is present, the code for that condition is designated as the principal diagnosis, and code Z39.0 is not assigned.

  For example, a woman is admitted following delivery in the parking lot of the hospital. On admission, it is noted that she had sustained a first-degree perineal laceration. Code **O70.0, First degree laceration during delivery,** is assigned rather than code Z39.0.

- Occasionally, an expectant mother may visit a pediatrician to receive advice on child care or to evaluate the pediatric office. This is not a visit related to a problem with the pregnancy. Code **Z76.81, Expectant parent(s) prebirth pediatrician visit,** may be assigned for these encounters.

EXERCISE 24.3

Code the following diagnoses.

1. Antepartum supervision of pregnancy in patient
   with history of three previous stillbirths, 12 weeks gestation ... O09.291

2. Office visit for routine prenatal care, for primigravida
   patient with no complications, second trimester ... Z34.02

3. Office visit for care of 40-year-old patient who is in the
   fourth month of her third pregnancy ... O09.522

4. Hospital admission of patient in good
   condition after delivering a single liveborn
   infant in taxi on the way to the hospital ... Z39.0

   Admission for

5. Admission for intravenous antibiotic therapy of patient
   who delivered a single liveborn at home three days ago;
   patient now suffering an abscess of the breast ... O91.12

   Puerperal

CHAPTER 24

*Complications
of Pregnancy,
Childbirth,
and the
Puerperium*

FETAL CONDITIONS AFFECTING MANAGEMENT OF PREGNANCY

Codes from categories O35, Maternal care for known or suspected fetal abnormality and damage, and O36, Maternal care for other fetal problems, are assigned only when the fetal condition is actually responsible for modifying the mother's care. Such an effect may be documented by additional diagnostic studies based on the fetal problem, additional observation, special care, or termination of the pregnancy. The fact that the fetal condition exists does not in itself justify assigning a code from these categories; this applies only when the condition affects the management of the mother's care. Codes from categories O35 and O36 are used when the listed condition in the fetus is the reason for hospitalization or other obstetric care to the mother, or for termination of pregnancy.

For example, when decreased fetal movements result in a decision to perform a cesarean delivery or early induction of labor in the mother, code **O36.81-, Decreased fetal movements,** is assigned. On the other hand, if no change is made in the mother's care, code O36.81- is not assigned because the decreased fetal movement is not considered to have affected the management of the mother significantly.

Multiple Gestation

Category O30, Multiple gestation, is used to identify multiple gestation, such as twin (O30.001–O30.099), triplet (O30.101–O30.199), quadruplet (O30.201–O30.299), other specified multiple gestations (O30.801–O30.899), and unspecified (O30.90–O30.93). The risk of complications will increase, and the treatment plan will differ, depending on the number of placentas and amniotic sacs. Fifth characters under category O30 indicate the number of placentas and amniotic sacs, while sixth characters indicate the trimester.

In Utero Surgery

Surgery performed on a fetus in utero (while the fetus is still in the womb) is considered an obstetric encounter. Codes from chapter 16, perinatal codes, should not be used on the mother's record to identify fetal conditions. Instead, when surgery is performed on the fetus in utero, a diagnosis code from category O35, Maternal care for known or suspected fetal abnormality and damage, should be assigned for the fetal condition. Assign the appropriate ICD-10-PCS code for the procedure performed.

Code **O35.7-, Maternal care for (suspected) damage to fetus by other medical procedures,** describes maternal and fetal complications resulting from in utero surgery performed during the current pregnancy. Code O35.7- is used for supervision of pregnancy affected by in utero procedure during current pregnancy. If the newborn experiences any problems or complications because of in utero procedures, assign code **P96.5, Complication to newborn due to (fetal) intrauterine procedure,** on the newborn record.

Code **O09.82-, Supervision of pregnancy with history of in utero procedure during previous pregnancy,** can be used as an additional code assignment with code O35.7- if the patient also has a past history of in utero surgery during a previous pregnancy.

ICD-10-PCS classifies in utero surgeries to the Obstetrics Section, body system "pregnancy," root operation "Repair," body part "products of conception." For example, in utero surgical repair of herniated diaphragm for congenital diaphragmatic hernia is coded to **10Q00ZK, Repair respiratory system in products of conception, open approach.** The diaphragm is classified to the "respiratory" body system in the Medical and Surgical Section.

OTHER CONDITIONS COMPLICATING PREGNANCY, CHILDBIRTH, OR THE PUERPERIUM

CHAPTER 24

*Complications
of Pregnancy,
Childbirth,
and the
Puerperium*

Some conditions inevitably complicate the obstetrical experience or are themselves aggravated by pregnancy. Certain categories in chapter 15 of ICD-10-CM distinguish between conditions of the mother that existed prior to pregnancy (pre-existing) and those that are a direct result of pregnancy. When assigning codes from chapter 15, it is important to assess whether a condition was pre-existing prior to pregnancy or developed during or due to the pregnancy in order to assign the correct code. For example, hypertension complicating pregnancy, delivery, and the puerperium is classified to category O10 when it is pre-existing, to category O13 when it is gestational (pregnancy induced), and to category O16 when it is unspecified maternal hypertension.

Categories that do not distinguish between pre-existing and pregnancy-related conditions may be used for either. It is acceptable to use codes specifically for the puerperium with codes complicating pregnancy and childbirth if a condition arises postpartum during the delivery encounter.

Designated conditions, such as edema, proteinuria, and hypertensive disorders in pregnancy, childbirth, and the puerperium are classified to categories O10 through O16. Other maternal disorders, such as hemorrhage, hyperemesis gravidarum, venous complications, genitourinary infections, diabetes mellitus, malnutrition, and liver disorders, are classified to categories O20 through O29 when they complicate the obstetrical experience. Certain infectious diseases such as HIV disease, viral hepatitis, tuberculosis, and venereal disease are classified in category O98.

Some codes for such complications are very specific, and others are rather broad. When a code from chapter 15 describes the condition adequately, only that code is assigned. It is appropriate, however, to assign an additional code when it provides needed specificity. For example, a patient who has a history of vaginal herpes maintained on Valtrex is admitted to the hospital for delivery. At the time of delivery, she is symptom free with no outbreak. Code **O98.52, Other viral diseases complicating childbirth,** is assigned as the principal diagnosis. Code **A60.04, Herpesviral vulvovaginitis,** and code **Z79.899, Other long term (current) drug therapy,** should be assigned as additional diagnoses along with the Z code for the outcome of the delivery. Herpes infection during pregnancy poses a risk to the fetus and is appropriately coded as a complication of the pregnancy.

On the other hand, the code for varicose veins of the legs complicating pregnancy (O22.0-) or the puerperium (O87.4) provides complete information, and assignment of an additional code is redundant. Code **O22.3-, Deep thrombophlebitis complicating pregnancy,** requires an additional code to specify whether the deep thrombophlebitis is acute or chronic, and to specify the site.

Other examples of the appropriate use of these codes follow.

O23.12	Second-trimester pregnant patient has a chronic cystitis and has had recurrent bouts of acute cystitis during her pregnancy, with an acute episode at time of admission
<u>O26.611</u> + K76.2	Necrosis of liver, complicating first-trimester pregnancy

Hypertension

Hypertension in pregnancy is always considered a complicating factor in pregnancy, childbirth, or the puerperium. For correct code assignment, it is important to determine whether the hypertension is a pre-existing or a gestational condition. Pre-existing hypertension is classified to category O10, Pre-existing hypertension complicating pregnancy, childbirth and the puerperium, as follows:

O10.01–O10.03	Essential hypertension
O10.111–O10.13	Hypertensive heart disease
O10.211–O10.23	Hypertensive chronic kidney disease
O10.311–O10.33	Hypertensive heart and chronic kidney disease
O10.411–O10.43	Secondary hypertension
O10.911–O10.93	Unspecified

CHAPTER 24

Complications
of Pregnancy,
Childbirth,
and the
Puerperium

When assigning one of the O10 codes that includes hypertensive heart disease or hypertensive chronic kidney disease, it is necessary to add a secondary code from the appropriate hypertension category to specify the type of hypertensive heart disease (category I11), heart failure (category I50), chronic kidney disease (category I12), or hypertensive heart and chronic kidney disease (category I13).

Patients who do not have pre-existing hypertension may develop transient or gestational or pregnancy-induced hypertension during pregnancy. This condition is essentially an elevated blood pressure and clears relatively quickly once the pregnancy is over. This condition is coded to category O13, Gestational [pregnancy-induced] hypertension without significant proteinuria.

Hypertension in pregnancy sometimes leads to a pathological condition described as eclampsia or preeclampsia. Preeclampsia is a condition marked by high blood pressure accompanied with a high level of protein in the urine. Women with preeclampsia often also have swelling in the feet, legs, and hands. Eclampsia is the final and most severe phase of preeclampsia and occurs when preeclampsia is left untreated. Eclampsia usually results in seizures and causes coma and even death of the mother and baby, and it can occur before, during, or after childbirth. When eclampsia is superimposed on a pre-existing hypertension, a code from category O11 with an additional code from category O10 to identify the type of hypertension are assigned. When preeclampsia arises without any pre-existing hypertension, it is classified in category O14, Pre-eclampsia. Eclampsia, regardless of whether it is due to pre-existing hypertension, gestational hypertension, or unspecified material hypertension, is classified to category O15, Eclampsia.

Gestational hypertension associated with albuminuria (albumin in urine), edema (abnormal accumulation of fluid in body tissues), or both is generally considered to be preeclampsia or eclampsia. However, codes for eclampsia or preeclampsia are never assigned solely on the basis of an elevated blood pressure, an abnormal albumin level, or the presence of edema. The physician must specify the condition as eclampsia or preeclampsia before any of these codes may be assigned.

When gestational edema, gestational proteinuria, or both gestational edema and gestational proteinuria are present without hypertension, these conditions are classified to category O12, Gestational [pregnancy-induced] edema and proteinuria without hypertension.

Diabetes

Diabetes mellitus is a significant complicating factor in pregnancy. Pregnant women who are diabetic should be assigned code **O24, Diabetes mellitus in pregnancy, childbirth, and the puerperium,** first, followed by the appropriate diabetes code(s) (E08–E13) from chapter 4 of ICD-10-CM.

Similar to hypertension, category O24 distinguishes between pre-existing diabetes mellitus (including type 1, type 2, other, or unspecified), gestational diabetes, and unspecified diabetes as follows:

O24.011–O24.03	Pre-existing type 1 diabetes mellitus
O24.111–O24.13	Pre-existing type 2 diabetes mellitus
O24.311–O24.319	Unspecified pre-existing diabetes mellitus
O24.410–O24.439	Gestational diabetes mellitus
O24.811–O24.83	Other pre-existing diabetes mellitus
O24.911–O24.93	Unspecified diabetes mellitus

Gestational (pregnancy induced) diabetes can occur during the second and third trimester of pregnancy in women who were not diabetic prior to pregnancy. Gestational diabetes can complicate the pregnancy, and there is an increased risk in women with gestational diabetes to develop diabetes mellitus following delivery. Gestational diabetes can cause complications in the pregnancy similar

319

CHAPTER 24

*Complications
of Pregnancy,
Childbirth,
and the
Puerperium*

to those of pre-existing diabetes mellitus. Codes for gestational diabetes are in subcategory O24.4, Gestational diabetes mellitus. No other code from category O24, Diabetes mellitus in pregnancy, childbirth, and the puerperium, should be used with a code from O24.4. The codes under subcategory O24.4 include diet controlled and insulin controlled. If a patient with gestational diabetes is treated with both diet and insulin, only the code for insulin controlled is required.

Code **Z79.4, Long-term (current) use of insulin,** should also be assigned if the pre-existing or unspecified diabetes mellitus is being treated with insulin. However, code Z79.4 should not be assigned with codes from subcategory O24.4, Gestational diabetes. If a patient with gestational diabetes is insulin controlled, the appropriate insulin-controlled code O24.414, O24.424, or O24.434 should be assigned instead of Z79.4.

A pregnant patient may have an abnormal glucose tolerance and not be diagnosed with gestational diabetes. In such cases, a code from subcategory O99.81, Abnormal glucose complicating pregnancy, childbirth, and the puerperium, should be assigned instead.

Examples include the following:

O24.113 + E11.620 + Z79.4	Pre-existing type 2 diabetes mellitus, with diabetic dermatitis, on insulin, intrauterine pregnancy 29 weeks gestation
O24.012 + E10.11	Pre-existing diabetes mellitus, type 1, ketoacidosis and in coma; intrauterine pregnancy, 26 weeks
O24.414	30-weeks-pregnant female seen in physician's office with gestational diabetes. Blood sugar reveals her diabetes is under good control with both diet and insulin

HIV Infection

During pregnancy, childbirth, or the puerperium, a patient admitted because of an HIV-related illness should receive a principal diagnosis from subcategory O98.7-, Human immunodeficiency [HIV] disease complicating pregnancy, childbirth and the puerperium, followed by the code(s) for the HIV-related illness(es). Patients with asymptomatic HIV infection status admitted during pregnancy, childbirth, or the puerperium should receive codes of O98.7- and **Z21, Asymptomatic human immunodeficiency virus [HIV] infection status.** For example:

O98.711 + B20	First-trimester pregnant female with AIDS
O98.713 + Z21	30-weeks-pregnant female with complicating asymptomatic HIV status

Alcohol and Tobacco Use

The Centers for Disease Control and Prevention (CDC) urges pregnant women not to drink alcohol any time during pregnancy. According to the CDC, there is no known safe amount of alcohol to drink while pregnant. Drinking alcohol during pregnancy can cause miscarriage, stillbirth, and a range of lifelong disorders known as fetal alcohol spectrum disorders. According to the United States Surgeon General, alcohol consumed during pregnancy increases the risk of alcohol-related birth defects, including growth deficiencies, facial abnormalities, central nervous system impairment, behavioral disorders, and impaired intellectual development. For any pregnancy case in which the mother uses alcohol during the pregnancy or postpartum, codes from subcategory O99.31, Alcohol use complicating pregnancy, childbirth and the puerperium, should be assigned. A secondary code from category F10, Alcohol related disorders, should also be assigned to identify manifestations of the alcohol use.

320

CHAPTER 24

Complications

of Pregnancy,

Childbirth,

and the

Puerperium

Tobacco use also complicates pregnancy. Women who smoke prior to and during pregnancy are at risk for several adverse outcomes, such as premature rupture of membranes, placental abruption, and placenta previa during pregnancy. Babies born to women who smoke during pregnancy also have a higher risk of premature birth and low birth weight and are 1.4 to 3.0 times more likely to die of sudden infant death syndrome (SIDS). Codes from subcategory O99.33, Smoking (tobacco) complicating pregnancy, childbirth, and the puerperium, should be assigned for any pregnancy case in which a mother uses any type of tobacco product during the pregnancy or postpartum. A secondary code from category F17, Nicotine dependence, or code **Z72.0, Tobacco use,** should also be assigned to identify the type of nicotine dependence.

COMPLICATIONS OF LABOR AND DELIVERY

Complications of labor and delivery are classified to categories O60 through O77. This block of codes contains some of the most important codes for situations when code **O80, Encounter for full-term uncomplicated delivery,** cannot be used.

Category O60, Preterm labor, is defined in ICD-10-CM as "onset (spontaneous) of labor before 37 completed weeks of gestation." This category includes codes for cases with delivery as well as without delivery. Codes from category O60 should not be used with codes from subcategory O47.0- for false or threatened labor.

Failed induction of labor is classified to category O61. Fourth characters distinguish between medical (e.g., intravenous Oxytocin to stimulate contractions), instrumental (e.g., via mechanical or surgical induction, such as with transcervical Foley catheter balloon or laminaria), other, and unspecified methods of induction of labor.

Abnormalities of forces of labor are classified to category O62. Fourth characters specify primary inadequate contractions (O62.0); secondary uterine inertia (O62.1); other uterine inertia (O62.2); precipitate labor (O62.3); hypertonic, incoordinate, and prolonged uterine contractions (O62.4); other abnormalities of labor (O62.8); and unspecified abnormalities of labor (O62.9).

For patients with long labor, ICD-10-CM provides category O63, with the fourth character specifying the stages, such as prolonged first stage (O63.0); prolonged second stage (O63.1); delayed delivery of second twin, triplet, etc. (O63.2); and unspecified (O63.9).

Obstructed Labor

Obstructed labor occurs when the passage of the fetus through the pelvis is mechanically obstructed. The most common cause of obstructed labor is disproportion between the fetus's head and the mother's pelvis. Occasionally, however, obstruction is secondary to malpresentation, malposition, and fetal abnormalities. ICD-10-CM provides categories O64, O65, and O66 for obstructed labor due to different etiologies, as follows:

- Category O64, Obstructed labor due to malposition and malpresentation of fetus, is used to describe situations in which labor may be obstructed due to the position of the fetus. Fetal presentation refers to the part of the fetus that lies closest to or has entered the true pelvis at the time of delivery. Refer to figure 24.2 for examples of fetal presentations. Cephalic presentations are vertex, brow, face, and chin. Breech presentations include frank breech, complete breech, incomplete breech, and single or double footling breech. Shoulder presentations are rare and require cesarean section or turning before vaginal birth. Compound presentation involves the entry of more than one part into the true pelvis, most commonly a hand next to the head. Category O64 provides fourth characters to specify the varying fetal presentations causing the obstruction of labor, such as incomplete rotation of fetal head (O64.0), breech presentation (O64.1), face presentation (O64.2), brow presentation (O64.3), shoulder presentation (O64.4), compound presentation (O64.5), other malpresentation (O64.8), and unspecified malpresentation (O64.9).

- Category O65, Obstructed labor due to maternal pelvic abnormality, is used to report obstructed labor caused by an abnormality in the mother's pelvis, such as deformity (O65.0), generally contracted pelvis (O65.1), pelvic inlet contraction (O65.2), pelvic outlet and mid-cavity contraction (O65.3), unspecified fetopelvic disproportion (O65.4), abnormality of maternal pelvic organs (O65.5), other maternal pelvic abnormalities (O65.8), and unspecified pelvic abnormality (O65.9).

- Category O66, Other obstructed labor, is used to classify other reasons for obstructed labor, such as shoulder dystocia (when the baby's shoulder gets stuck behind the mother's pubic bone) (O66.0), locked twins (a form of malpresentation in which a breech twin and a vertex twin become locked at the chin during labor and attempted delivery) (O66.1), unusually large fetus (O66.2), other abnormalities of fetus (including dystocia due to different etiologies) (O66.3), failed trial of labor (O66.4-), attempted application of vacuum extractor and forceps (O66.5), multiple fetuses (O66.6), other specified obstructed labor (O66.8 with additional code to identify cause of obstruction), and unspecified obstructed labor (O66.9).

CHAPTER 24

*Complications
of Pregnancy,
Childbirth,
and the
Puerperium*

FIGURE 24.2   Examples of Fetal Presentations

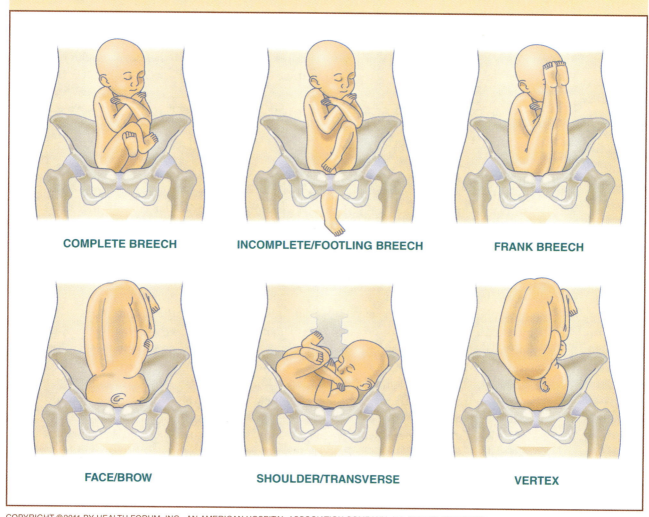

COMPLETE BREECH   INCOMPLETE/FOOTLING BREECH   FRANK BREECH

FACE/BROW   SHOULDER/TRANSVERSE   VERTEX

CHAPTER 24

Complications
of Pregnancy,
Childbirth,
and the
Puerperium

ICD-10-CM also provides the following categories for labor and delivery complications caused by different conditions:

O67.0–O67.9	Intrapartum hemorrhage
O68	Abnormality of fetal acid-base balance
O69.0–O69.9	Umbilical cord complications

Fetal Stress

Fetal stress is an uncommon complication of labor referring to the presence of signs in a pregnant woman suggesting that the fetus may not be well. It typically occurs when the fetus has not been receiving enough oxygen. Fetal stress may occur when the pregnancy lasts too long (post-maturity) or when complications of pregnancy or labor occur.

ICD-10-CM provides different codes related to fetal problems complicating labor and delivery, such as the following:

- O68, Labor and delivery complicated by abnormality of fetal acid-base balance. This code is used to describe fetal acidemia, fetal acidosis, fetal alkalosis, or fetal metabolic acidemia when these conditions complicate labor and delivery.

- O76, Abnormality in fetal heart rate and rhythm complicating labor and delivery. This code includes fetal problems such as bradycardia, heart rate decelerations, heart rate irregularity, tachycardia, and non-reassuring fetal heart rate or rhythm.

- Category O77, Other fetal stress complicating labor and delivery. This category includes codes for meconium in amniotic fluid (O77.0), fetal stress due to drug administration (O77.1), and other evidence of fetal stress (such as electrocardiographic or ultrasonic evidence) (O77.8). Unspecified fetal stress is classified to code O77.9.

It is important to remember that these codes should only be reported when the above conditions affect the management of the mother.

POSTPARTUM COMPLICATIONS

The postpartum period, clinically termed the "puerperium," begins immediately after delivery and includes the subsequent six weeks. A postpartum complication is defined as any complication that occurs during that six-week period. Postpartum complications are classified to categories O85 through O92.

One type of postpartum complication is a puerperal infection—a bacterial infection following childbirth. An estimated 2 to 4 percent of mothers who deliver vaginally may experience some form of puerperal infection. For cesarean delivery, the figure is five to 10 times higher. The genital tract is the most common site of infection (e.g., endometritis: O86.12). Other types of puerperal infections include infection of obstetrical surgical wound (O86.0), cervicitis (O86.11), vaginitis (O86.13), other infection of genital tract (O86.19), urinary tract infection (O86.20), infection of kidney (O86.21), infection of bladder (O86.22), other urinary infection (O86.29), pyrexia of unknown origin (O86.4), puerperal septic thrombophlebitis (O86.81), and other specified puerperal infections (O86.89).

Code **O85, Puerperal sepsis,** requires a secondary code to identify the causal organism. For example, for a bacterial infection, a code from categories B95 through B97 should be assigned. Codes from category A40, Streptococcal sepsis, or A41, Other sepsis, should not be used for

323

CHAPTER 24

*Complications
of Pregnancy,
Childbirth,
and the
Puerperium*

puerperal sepsis. If severe sepsis is also present, code **R65.2-, Severe sepsis,** should be assigned, along with the appropriate code for any associated acute organ dysfunction. Examples include the following:

- A patient develops endometritis two days following cesarean section delivery while still in the hospital. Code **O86.12, Endometritis following delivery,** is assigned. This condition is considered a complication of childbirth and not a complication of pregnancy. In ICD-10-CM, there is an Index entry for "endometritis, puerperal, postpartum, childbirth."

- A patient is admitted three weeks postpartum and treated for acute pyelonephritis due to *Escherichia coli* infection. Code **O86.21, Infection of kidney following delivery,** is assigned as the principal diagnosis. Code **B96.2, Escherichia coli [E. coli] as the cause of diseases classified elsewhere,** is assigned as an additional code to provide specificity regarding the infection.

- A patient who delivered via low cervical cesarean section (C-section) six days prior is readmitted with severe sepsis with acute kidney failure due to a methicillin-resistant *Staphylococcus aureus* (MRSA) of the C-section wound. Code **O86.0, Infection of obstetrical surgical wound,** is assigned for the postsurgical wound infection. Codes **O85, Puerperal sepsis; B95.6, Staphylococcus aureus as the cause of diseases classified elsewhere; Z16, Infection with drug resistant microorganisms; R65.20, Severe sepsis without septic shock;** and **N17.9, Acute kidney failure, unspecified,** are also assigned for the MRSA puerperal sepsis with acute kidney failure.

Uterine atony is a condition that can complicate delivery and refers to failure of the uterine muscle to contract adequately after the delivery. Uterine atony can occur with or without bleeding. Code **O62.2, Other uterine inertia,** is assigned for atony of the uterus without hemorrhage when it occurs immediately following delivery of the baby and placenta. Assign code **O72.1, Other immediate postpartum hemorrhage,** for postpartum uterine atony with hemorrhage when it occurs immediately following delivery of the baby and placenta. Code **O75.89, Other specified complications of labor and delivery,** is assigned for postpartum uterine atony without hemorrhage. For example:

- A patient develops postpartum hemorrhage due to uterine atony immediately after spontaneous vaginal delivery of full-term twins. The B-Lynch suture is performed to control the bleeding. The B-Lynch suture is a brace suture used to compress the uterus without compromising major vessels in cases of postpartum hemorrhage. Code **O72.1, Other immediate postpartum hemorrhage,** is assigned for postpartum uterine atony with hemorrhage. Code **O30.003, Twin pregnancy, unspecified number of placenta and unspecified number of amniotic sacs, third trimester,** and code **Z37.2, Twins, both liveborn,** are also assigned. Code **0UQ97ZZ, Repair uterus, via natural or artificial opening,** is assigned for the B-Lynch procedure.

Pregnancy associated cardiomyopathy is also referred to as peripartum cardiomyopathy because it may be diagnosed in the third trimester of pregnancy but may continue to progress months after delivery. Code **O90.3, Peripartum cardiomyopathy,** should be used only when the cardiomyopathy develops as a result of pregnancy in women who did not have pre-existing heart disease. For pre-existing heart disease complicating pregnancy and the puerperium, codes from subcategory O99.4, Diseases of the circulatory system complicating pregnancy, childbirth and the puerperium, should be used instead.

CHAPTER 24

*Complications
of Pregnancy,
Childbirth,
and the
Puerperium*

OTHER MATERNAL DISEASES

ICD-10-CM provides category O99 to describe other maternal diseases classifiable elsewhere but complicating pregnancy, childbirth, and the puerperium. This category includes conditions that complicate the pregnant state, are aggravated by the pregnancy, or are a main reason for obstetric care. Examples include:

O99.0-   Anemia

O99.1-   Other diseases of the blood and blood-forming organs and certain disorders involving the immune mechanism

O99.2-   Endocrine, nutritional, and metabolic diseases

O99.3-   Mental disorders and diseases of the nervous system

O99.4-   Diseases of the circulatory system

O99.5-   Diseases of the respiratory system

O99.6-   Diseases of the digestive system

O99.7-   Diseases of the skin and subcutaneous tissue

O99.8-   Other specified diseases and conditions

An additional code is used to identify the specific condition. For example:

- A patient is admitted five weeks postpartum with acute cholecystitis and cholelithiasis. Code **O99.63, Diseases of the digestive system complicating the puerperium,** and code **K80.00, Calculus of gallbladder with acute cholecystitis without obstruction,** are assigned.

Malignant neoplasms complicating pregnancy, childbirth, and the puerperium are classified to subcategory O9a.1, with additional code(s) to identify the specific neoplasm. This subcategory is for conditions classified to C00 through C97. Maternal care for benign tumor of corpus uteri is coded to O34.1-, while maternal care for benign tumor of cervix is classified to O34.4-.

Coding of injury, poisoning, physical abuse, sexual abuse, and psychological abuse complicating pregnancy, childbirth, and the puerperium is discussed in chapter 30 of this handbook.

SEQUELAE OF COMPLICATION OF PREGNANCY, CHILDBIRTH, OR THE PUERPERIUM

Code **O94, Sequelae of complication of pregnancy, childbirth, and the puerperium,** is assigned when an initial complication of the obstetrical experience develops a sequela that requires care or treatment at a later date. The sequelae include conditions specified as such, or as late effects, which may occur at any time after the postpartum period. Like all late-effect codes, code O94 is sequenced after the code describing the residual condition. Examples include the following:

- A patient is admitted for repair of postpartal perineum prolapse secondary to traumatic laceration sustained during childbirth two years earlier. Code **N81.89, Other female genital prolapse,** is assigned first, with code **O94, Sequelae of complication of pregnancy, childbirth, and the puerperium,** assigned as an additional code.

- A patient presents with fatigue and cold intolerance. Her history indicates that she had experienced a severe hemorrhage during delivery of a normal liveborn seven months earlier. She was diagnosed with Sheehan's syndrome and treated with replacement hormones. Code **E23.0, Hypopituitarism,** is assigned for Sheehan's syndrome, followed by code **O94, Sequelae of complication of pregnancy, childbirth, and the puerperium.**

EXERCISE 24.4

Code the following diagnoses. Do not code procedures. Assign Z codes where applicable.

CHAPTER 24

*Complications
of Pregnancy,
Childbirth,
and the
Puerperium*

1.	Intrauterine pregnancy, spontaneous delivery, single liveborn	O80 Z37.0
2.	Intrauterine pregnancy, 12 weeks gestation, undelivered, with mild hyperemesis gravidarum	O21.0
3.	Intrauterine pregnancy, 39 weeks, delivered, left occipitoanterior, single liveborn Primary uterine inertia	O62.0 Z37.0
4.	Cesarean delivery of stillborn at 38 weeks gestation owing to placental infarction	O43.813 Z37.1 O36.4xx0
5.	Intrauterine pregnancy, with pernicious anemia, second trimester	O99.012 D51.0
6.	Intrauterine pregnancy, term Spontaneous delivery, left occipitoanterior Single liveborn	O80 Z37.0
7.	Intrauterine pregnancy, twins, 33 weeks Premature rupture of membranes, onset of labor three hours later. Spontaneous delivery of premature twins, vertex presentation, both liveborn Postpartum pulmonary embolism	O60.14x0 O42.013 O30.003 O88.23 Z37.2
8.	Premature delivery, third trimester, frank breech presentation, single female liveborn First-degree tear, vaginal wall	O60.14x0 O32.1xx0 O70.0 Z37.0

326

CHAPTER 24

Complications
of Pregnancy,
Childbirth,
and the
Puerperium

9. Term pregnancy, <u>delivered</u>, single stillborn,		O45.93
left occipitoanterior		O69.1xx0
Terminal abruptio <u>placentae</u>		O36.4xx0
Cord wrapped tightly around neck with compression		Z37.1

10. Intrauterine <u>pregnancy</u>, 12 weeks;		O10.011
long-standing essential hypertension		
being monitored closely		

OBSTETRIC PROCEDURES

When coding obstetrical procedures using ICD-10-PCS, it is important to distinguish whether the procedure is performed on the fetus or on the pregnant female. Procedures performed on the fetus (products of conception) are classified to the Obstetrics Section. Procedures performed on the pregnant female, other than the products of conception, are coded to the appropriate root operation in the Medical and Surgical Section. For example, amniocentesis is coded to the "products of conception" body part in the Obstetrics Section. However, repair of obstetric urethral laceration is coded to the "urethra" body part in the Medical and Surgical Section.

The ICD-10-PCS Obstetrics Section follows the same conventions found in the Medical and Surgical Section, with all seven characters retaining the same meaning as shown in figure 24.3. The body system (character 2) in the Obstetrics Section is always "pregnancy." There are only three values used for body part in this section: "products of conception" (0); "products of conception, retained" (1); and "products of conception, ectopic" (2).

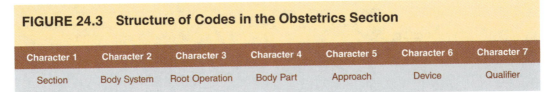

FIGURE 24.3   Structure of Codes in the Obstetrics Section

Character 1	Character 2	Character 3	Character 4	Character 5	Character 6	Character 7
Section	Body System	Root Operation	Body Part	Approach	Device	Qualifier

There are 12 root operations (as shown in figure 24.4) in the Obstetrics Section, 10 of which are also found in the Medical and Surgical Section. The two root operations unique to the Obstetrics Section are defined below:

- Abortion: Artificially terminating a pregnancy
- Delivery: Assisting the passage of the products of conception from the genital tract. This root operation applies only to manually assisted, vaginal delivery.

Cesarean deliveries are coded to the Obstetrics Section to the root operation "Extraction" rather than to the root operation "Delivery." The root operation "Extraction" is also used for vaginal deliveries requiring assistance with forceps, vacuum, or internal version.

Procedures performed following a delivery or an abortion for curettage of the endometrium or evacuation of retained products of conception are all coded in the Obstetrics Section to the root operation "Extraction" and the body part "products of conception, retained." Diagnostic or therapeutic dilation and curettage performed during times other than the postpartum or post-abortion period are all coded in the Medical and Surgical Section to the root operation "Extraction" and the body part "endometrium."

327

CHAPTER 24
*Complications
of Pregnancy,
Childbirth,
and the
Puerperium*

FIGURE 24.4 Root Operations in the Obstetrics Section

Value	Root Operation	Definition
2	Change	Taking out or off a device from a body part and putting back an identical or similar device in or on the same body part without cutting or puncturing the skin or a mucous membrane
9	Drainage	Taking or letting out fluids and/or gases from a body part
A	Abortion	Artificially terminating a pregnancy
D	Extraction	Pulling or stripping out or off all or a portion of a body part
E	Delivery	Assisting the passage of the products of conception from the genital canal
H	Insertion	Putting in a nonbiological appliance that monitors, assists, performs, or prevents a physiological function but does not physically take the place of a body part
J	Inspection	Visually and/or manually exploring a body part
P	Removal	Taking out or off a device from a body part, region, or orifice
Q	Repair	Restoring, to the extent possible, a body part to its normal anatomic structure and function
S	Reposition	Moving to its normal location or other suitable location all or a portion of a body part
T	Resection	Cutting out or off, without replacement, all of a body part
Y	Transplantation	Putting in or on all or a portion of a living body part taken from another individual or animal to physically take the place and/or function of all or a portion of a similar body part

PROCEDURES ASSISTING DELIVERY

Delivery can be assisted in a number of ways. Manually assisted vaginal delivery is coded as follows:

Character 1 Section	Character 2 Body System	Character 3 Root Operation	Character 4 Body Part	Character 5 Approach	Character 6 Device	Character 7 Qualifier
1	0	E	0	X	Z	Z
Obstetrics	Pregnancy	Delivery	Products of conception	External	None	None

Labor may be induced by artificial rupture of membranes (Medical and Surgical Section, root operation "Drainage," body part "amniotic fluid") or by other surgical induction, such as cervical dilatation (0U7C7ZZ). Artificial rupture of membranes may also be performed after labor has begun.

Amnioinfusion (Administration Section, root operation "Introduction") is typically performed during labor via a transcervical approach after rupture of the fetal membranes. An intrauterine pressure catheter is used to infuse a lactated Ringer's or normal saline solution into the amniotic cavity. Alternatively, fluid can be infused through a needle transabdominally. Amnioinfusion is performed as prophylactic treatment of oligohydramnios, for reduction of variable decelerations of the fetal heart rate because of cord compression during labor, or as treatment of preterm premature rupture of membranes.

328

CHAPTER 24

*Complications
of Pregnancy,
Childbirth,
and the
Puerperium*

For example, amnioinfusion of normal saline solution is coded as follows:

Character 1 Section	Character 2 Body System	Character 3 Root Operation	Character 4 Body System	Character 5 Approach	Character 6 Substance	Character 7 Qualifier
3	E	0	E	7	7	Z
Administration	Physiological systems and anatomical regions	Introduction	Products of conception	Via natural or artificial opening	Electrolytic and water balance substance	None

If rotation during delivery is carried out, this procedure is coded to the Obstetrics Section, root operation "Reposition," code **10S07ZZ, Reposition products of conception, via natural or artificial opening.** For a routine delivery, code **10E0XZZ, Delivery of products of conception, external approach,** may be assigned.

Forceps Delivery and Vacuum Extraction

Forceps, vacuum extraction, or internal and combined version may also assist delivery. These are coded to the Obstetrics Section, root operation "Extraction." Codes are provided for low-forceps, mid-forceps, or high-forceps delivery. In a low-forceps delivery (seventh-character qualifier value "3"), forceps are applied to a visible fetal head after it has entered the pelvic floor. Mid-forceps (seventh-character qualifier value "4") are applied to the head during its entry into the pelvic floor, and high forceps (seventh-character qualifier value "5") are applied to the head before it enters the pelvic brim. Breech presentations may require partial or total breech extraction, with or without forceps to the aftercoming head. Vacuum extraction (seventh-character qualifier value "6") uses a traction device rather than forceps applied to the fetal head for extraction of the fetus.

Episiotomy

An episiotomy is a surgical incision in the perineum made just before delivery to enlarge the vaginal opening and assist delivery. Code **0W8NXZZ, Division of female perineum, external approach,** is assigned for a routine episiotomy. When an episiotomy is performed in connection with a forceps delivery, three codes are assigned: one for the extraction, code 0W8NXZZ for the episiotomy, and code **0WQNXZZ, Repair female perineum, external approach,** for the repair of the episiotomy.

Perineal Lacerations

Perineal lacerations are classified as first, second, third, or fourth degree in category O70, Perineal laceration during delivery:

- First-degree tears (O70.0) involve damage to the fourchette and vaginal mucosa, and underlying muscles are exposed but not torn.
- Second-degree tears (O70.1) include the posterior vaginal walls and perineal muscles, but the anal sphincter is intact.
- Third-degree tears (O70.2) extend to the anal sphincter, but the rectal mucosa is intact.
- Fourth-degree tears (O70.3) involve the rectal and anal mucosa.

Code O70.4 describes an anal sphincter tear complicating delivery that is not associated with a third-degree perineal laceration. Code **O70.9, Perineal laceration during delivery, unspecified,** is used when there is no additional information on the degree of the perineal laceration.

Inclusion notes for these codes indicate what is involved in each degree. When more than one degree is mentioned, only the code for the highest degree is assigned. The appropriate surgical repair code is assigned depending on the tissue repaired (e.g., for open repair of the vaginal wall, assign code 0UQG0ZZ).

Category O71, Other obstetric trauma, is used for other obstetric trauma, including trauma from instrument for the following injuries: rupture of uterus (spontaneous) before onset of labor (O71.0-) or during labor (O71.1), postpartum inversion of uterus (O71.2), obstetric laceration of cervix (O71.3), obstetric high vaginal laceration alone (O71.4), other obstetric injury to pelvic organs (O71.5), obstetric damage to pelvic joints and ligaments (O71.6), obstetric hematoma of pelvis (O71.7), other obstetric trauma (O71.8-), and unspecified obstetric trauma (O71.9).

Occasionally, an episiotomy extends spontaneously to become a perineal laceration or tear. In this case, assign code **0W8NXZZ, Division of female perineum, external approach,** along with code **0WQNXZZ, Repair female perineum, external approach.** Both codes are needed to completely describe this situation. For the diagnosis, assign also the appropriate code from category O70, Perineal laceration during delivery, to specifically describe the laceration or tear.

Fetal Pulse Oximetry

Fetal oxygen monitoring provides the physician with a direct measure of fetal oxygen status when an irregular fetal heart rate is present. The intrapartum fetal oxygen monitor uses a single-use, disposable sensor that is inserted through the birth canal when one of the amniotic membranes has ruptured and the cervix is dilated more than 2 centimeters. The oxygen saturation is displayed on a monitor screen as a percentage. Assign code **10H073Z, Insertion of monitoring electrode into products of conception, via natural or artificial opening,** for this type of fetal monitoring.

Cesarean Delivery

Cesarean delivery is an operative delivery that is carried out when, for some reason, spontaneous delivery is not possible or does not seem advisable. Cesarean sections are classified to the root operation "Extraction," body part "products of conception," and open approach. A classical cesarean section, coded to **10D00Z0, Extraction of products of conception, classical, open approach,** removes the fetus through an incision into the upper part of the uterus using an abdominal peritoneal approach. A low cervical cesarean, coded to **10D00Z1, Extraction of products of conception, low cervical, open approach,** uses an incision into the lower portion of the uterus, with a pelvic cavity or an abdominal peritoneal incision. There is also an extraperitoneal cesarean section (seventh-character qualifier value "2").

EXERCISE 24.5

Code the following procedures.

1. Induction of labor by cervical dilation   0U7C7ZZ

2. Assisted spontaneous delivery   10E0XZZ

330

CHAPTER 24

*Complications
of Pregnancy,
Childbirth,
and the
Puerperium*

3. Vaginal delivery using low forceps	10D07Z3
Extraction	
4. Extraperitoneal C-section, low transverse incision	10D00Z2
Delivery	
5. Mid-forceps vaginal delivery with routine episiotomy	10D07Z4
	0W8NXZZ
	0WQNXZZ

SERVICES RELATED TO CONTRACEPTIVE MANAGEMENT

Category Z30, Encounter for contraceptive management, is assigned as the principal diagnosis for admissions or outpatient encounters for the purpose of contraceptive management. Codes in this category cover services such as initiation of oral contraceptive measures (Z30.011); counseling in natural family planning to avoid pregnancy (Z30.02); insertion of intrauterine contraceptive device (Z30.430); removal of intrauterine contraceptive device (Z30.432); removal and reinsertion of intrauterine contraceptive device (Z30.433); sterilization (Z30.2); and surveillance of injectable contraceptive (Z30.42). Procedure codes must also be assigned when appropriate.

EXERCISE 24.6

Code the following diagnoses and procedures.

1. Family planning counseling	Z30.09
2. Encounter for insertion of intrauterine contraceptive device	Z30.430
Insertion of intrauterine contraceptive device	0UH97HZ
3. Encounter for removal of intrauterine contraceptive device	Z30.432
Removal of intrauterine contraceptive device	0UPD7HZ

STERILIZATION

CHAPTER 24

*Complications
of Pregnancy,
Childbirth,
and the
Puerperium*

When a patient seeks health care for the purpose of contraceptive sterilization, code **Z30.2, Encounter for sterilization,** is assigned as the principal diagnosis. If there are underlying medical or psychological conditions that led to the decision to undergo sterilization, codes for these conditions may be assigned as additional diagnoses. Because sterilization may be performed as an elective procedure without any predisposing medical or psychological reasons, code Z30.2 can be used as a solo diagnosis code.

When an elective sterilization procedure is performed during a hospital episode in which an obstetrical delivery has occurred, Z30.2 is assigned as a secondary code, with a code from chapter 15 of ICD-10-CM assigned as the principal diagnosis.

Note that code Z30.2 is assigned for both female and male patients for whom a contraceptive sterilization procedure is performed. Sterilization procedures for females are sometimes referred to as "tubal ligation." Tubal ligation is a surgical procedure whereby the fallopian tubes are cut, coagulated, clipped (e.g., Filshie clip), cauterized, or blocked with an external ring (e.g., Falope ring). ICD-10-PCS classifies sterilization procedures for females to the female reproductive system, root operations "Occlusion," "Excision," or "Destruction" (depending on the technique used). Sterilization procedures for males are classified to the male reproductive system, root operations "Destruction" or "Excision." Code Z30.2 is not assigned as either a principal or a secondary diagnosis when sterilization results from other treatment or when a sterilization procedure is performed as part of the treatment for another condition. In such cases, the original condition, any complications or comorbidities, and the procedures performed are coded. For example, when a hysterectomy is performed because of injury or damage to the uterus during delivery, only the obstetrical diagnoses and procedures are coded, even though the procedure results in sterility. Code Z30.2 is used only for a sterilization performed specifically for contraception; assigning it when a sterilization is incidental to other treatment is inappropriate.

Other examples of appropriate coding of situations involving sterilization follow.

<u>Z30.2</u> + F34.1 + Z64.1 + 0UL74ZZ	A patient with multiparity (five children) with reactive depression is admitted for elective sterilization; bilateral endoscopic ligation and division of the fallopian tubes are carried out for sterilization
<u>O32.1xx0</u> + Z30.2 + Z37.0 + 10D07Z6 + 0UL74CZ	Term pregnancy, liveborn delivered; breech presentation; delivery by partial breech vacuum extraction; endoscopic bilateral partial salpingectomy with extraluminal device for sterilization

Sterilization procedures are intended to be permanent. However, there may be situations in which a patient may desire a reversal of the sterilization procedure. Admission for a tuboplasty or vasoplasty to reverse a previous sterilization procedure is coded to **Z31.0, Encounter for reversal of previous sterilization.**

332

CHAPTER 24

*Complications
of Pregnancy,
Childbirth,
and the
Puerperium*

EXERCISE 24.7

Code the following diagnostic statements and procedures.

1. Essential hypertension   Z30.2
   Admitted for sterilization   I10
   Laparoscopy with bilateral partial salpingectomy   0UB74ZZ

2. Endometriosis of uterus   Z30.2
   Admitted for sterilization   N80.0
   Bilateral laparoscopic tubal ligation   0U574ZZ
   via electrocautery for sterilization

3. Term pregnancy, with breech delivery,   O32.1xx0
   female infant, followed by sterilization   Z30.2
                                                               Z37.0

   Vacuum breech extraction   10D07Z6
   Laparoscopic occlusion of bilateral fallopian tubes   0UL74CZ
   with Falope (external) rings

4. Elective sterilization, patient request   Z30.2
   Vasectomy, bilateral (open)   0VBQ0ZZ

5. Elective reversal of previous tubal ligation   Z31.0
   Laparoscopic salpingoplasty   0UQ74ZZ

PROCREATIVE MANAGEMENT

A code from category Z31, Encounter for procreative management, is assigned when a patient who is having difficulty becoming pregnant is seen for help in correcting this problem.

Code Z31.61 is assigned as the first-listed diagnosis for an encounter/visit for procreative counseling and advice using natural family planning. Couples seeking natural methods of family planning require training/counseling by a medical professional or a qualified counselor. There are five methods of natural family planning:

- Basal body temperature method
- Ovulation/cervical mucus method

333

CHAPTER 24

Complications
of Pregnancy,
Childbirth,
and the
Puerperium

- Symptothermal method
- Calendar method
- Lactational amenorrhea

Therapy for malignant neoplasms or other serious conditions can affect reproductive health and the ability to conceive. Antineoplastic drugs (e.g., alkylating agents) and radiotherapy to the pelvic area may impair ovarian and testicular function, leading to infertility. Depending on the dosage delivered and the length of treatment, healthy sperm cells and ovarian follicles can be destroyed along with cancer cells.

Code **Z31.62, Encounter for fertility preservation counseling,** is assigned for encounters for advice and counseling on available options to conceive a child or maintain pregnancy before the start of cancer treatment or the surgical removal of gonads. The discussion may include whether to conceive before cancer treatment; banking of sperm, eggs, ovarian tissue, or embryos; and/or modification of surgery to spare the uterus.

Code **Z31.84, Encounter for fertility preservation procedure,** is assigned for the fertility preservation encounter. These codes are not limited to those seeking advice prior to cancer treatment or gonad removal. Codes Z31.62 and Z31.84 may be assigned for patients having any treatment (not only cancer treatment) that may affect fertility.

Code **Z31.83, Encounter for assisted reproductive fertility procedure cycle,** is assigned for patients undergoing in vitro fertilization. An additional code should be assigned to identify the type of infertility. Code Z31.83 is not used for encounters for diagnostic testing prior to starting in vitro fertilization. Assign the reason for the encounter when the patient presents for diagnostic testing.

Code **O09.81-, Supervision of pregnancy resulting from assisted reproductive technology,** is assigned for subsequent encounters involving antenatal supervision and/or prenatal care when in vitro fertilization has been successful.

Encounters for investigations such as sperm counts or fallopian tube insufflation are coded to **Z31.41, Encounter for fertility testing.** For encounters for sperm count following sterilization reversal, assign code **Z31.42, Aftercare following sterilization reversal,** instead of Z31.41.

ICD-10-CM provides the following codes to describe encounters for testing and counseling for genetic disease:

Z31.430	Encounter of female for testing for genetic disease carrier status for procreative management
Z31.438	Encounter for other genetic testing of female for procreative management
Z31.440	Encounter of male for testing for genetic disease carrier status for procreative management
Z31.441	Encounter for testing of male partner of patient with recurrent pregnancy loss
Z31.448	Encounter for other genetic testing of male for procreative management
Z31.5	Encounter for genetic counseling

If the encounter is for genetic screening not associated with procreative management, assign a code from subcategory Z13.7, Encounter for screening for genetic and chromosomal anomalies, rather than the Z31.4- series.

CHAPTER 24 :

Complications :
of Pregnancy, :
Childbirth, :
and the :
Puerperium :

SUSPECTED MATERNAL AND FETAL CONDITIONS NOT FOUND

Codes from subcategory Z03.7, Encounter for suspected maternal and fetal conditions ruled out, are to be used in very limited circumstances on a maternal record when an encounter is for a suspected maternal or fetal condition that is ruled out during that encounter (for example, a maternal or fetal condition may be suspected due to an abnormal test result). These codes should not be used when the condition is confirmed. In those cases, the confirmed condition should be coded. These codes should not be used if an illness or any signs or symptoms related to the suspected condition or problem are present. In those cases, the appropriate codes for the diagnosis/sign or symptom should be reported instead.

Codes from subcategory Z03.7 can be used with other codes, but only if they are unrelated to the suspected condition being evaluated. Codes from subcategory Z03.7 may not be used for encounters for antenatal screening of the mother. For encounters for suspected fetal conditions that are inconclusive following testing and evaluation, assign the appropriate code from category O35, O36, O40, or O41.

Codes in subcategory Z03.7 describe suspected fetal/maternal problems not found, as follows:

Z03.71   Encounter for suspected problem with amniotic cavity and membrane ruled out

Z03.72   Encounter for suspected placental problem ruled out

Z03.73   Encounter for suspected fetal anomaly ruled out

Z03.74   Encounter for suspected problem with fetal growth ruled out

Z03.75   Encounter for suspected cervical shortening ruled out

335

CHAPTER 24

*Complications
of Pregnancy,
Childbirth,
and the
Puerperium*

EXERCISE 24.8

Code the following diagnostic statements and procedures. Assign Z codes where applicable.

1. Elderly primigravida (37 years old); term delivery,   O09.513

   spontaneous, of living female infant   Z37.0

                              Outcome of delivery

   Manually assisted delivery   10E0XZZ

   Episiotomy and repair   0W8NXZZ

                                                                                 0WQNXZZ

2. Term pregnancy, living dichorionic twins (diamniotic sacs),   O77.9

   cesarean delivery   O30.043

   performed because fetal stress noted prior to labor   Z37.2

                              Outcome of delivery

   Low cervical cesarean delivery   10D00Z1

3. Delivery, term birth, living child,   O80

   ROA presentation   Z37.0

                              Outcome of delivery

   Fetal cardiac rhythm monitoring during labor   4A1H7FZ

   Episiotomy and episiorrhaphy   0W8NXZZ

                                                                                 0WQNXZZ

4. Uterine pregnancy, term, delivered with   O64.8xx0

   obstructed labor due to transverse lie presentation   O32.2xx0

   Pre-existing hypertension with mild preeclampsia,   O11.3

   single liveborn

                              Outcome of delivery   Z37.0

   Manually assisted delivery   10E0XZZ

5. Intrauterine pregnancy, near-term, delivered,   O30.033

   spontaneous   O72.0

   Third-stage hemorrhage with anemia   O90.81

   secondary to acute blood loss   D62

   Monochorionic twins, both liveborn, diamniotic placenta   Z37.2

                              Outcome of delivery   10E0XZZ

CHAPTER 24

*Complications
of Pregnancy,
Childbirth,
and the
Puerperium*

6. Pregnancy, delivered, frank breech   O32.1xx0
    presentation with liveborn male infant   Z37.0

             Outcome of delivery

    Partial breech extraction with mid-forceps   10D07Z4
    to aftercoming head

---

7. Term pregnancy, delivered, spontaneous   O80
    Liveborn, male infant   Z37.0

             Outcome of delivery

    Assisted spontaneous delivery   10E0XZZ
    Elective sterilization following delivery   Z30.2
    Bilateral endoscopic ligation and crushing of   0UL78ZZ
    fallopian tubes

---

8. Intrauterine pregnancy, with complicating   O34.32
    incompetent cervix, second trimester, undelivered
    Shirodkar cervical cerclage operation   0UVC7ZZ

---

9. Gestational hypertension   O13.3
    Pregnancy, third trimester, undelivered

---

10. Intrauterine pregnancy, term, delivered,   O70.1
    right occipitoanterior, liveborn male infant   Z37.0
    Episiotomy that extended to second-degree
    lacerations, perineum

             Outcome of delivery

    Amniotomy for induction of labor   10907ZC
    Low-forceps delivery with episiotomy   10D07Z3
    Repair of perineal laceration   0W8NXZZ
        0WQNXZZ

---

11. Delivery, stillborn, male infant,   O64.3xx0
    brow presentation; obstructed labor   O32.3xx0

             Outcome of delivery   O36.4xx0
        Z37.1

    Extraction with internal version   10D07Z7
    Episiotomy and repair   0W8NXZZ
        0WQNXZZ

CHAPTER 24

*Complications
of Pregnancy,
Childbirth,
and the
Puerperium*

12. Twin term pregnancy with malposition fetus 2   O32.9xx2
    One liveborn twin, one stillborn (fetus 2), two   O30.043
    placentae and two amniotic sacs   O36.4xx2
        Z37.3
    Classical cesarean section   10D00Z0

13. Postpartum uterine atony without hemorrhage   O75.89
    occurring two weeks after delivery

14. Encounter for testing of female for genetic disease   Z31.430
    carrier status (patient planning on pregnancy)

15. Encounter for in vitro fertilization (IVF);   Z31.83
    infertility due to obstructed fallopian tube   N97.1

16. Visit for procreative counseling using natural   Z31.61
    family planning

17. 32-year-old gravida 2, para 0, admitted at term   O82
    for an elective primary low cesarean section.   Z37.0
    The patient had a completely normal prenatal course,   10D00Z1
    a normal pregnancy, and an unremarkable postoperative
    course. She elected to have a cesarean section
    because of fear of vaginal delivery. She had a normal
    single liveborn without complications.

             Delivery
             Outcome of delivery

18. Woman is admitted to the hospital and delivers a healthy   O99.324
    baby. Four years ago, the woman used heroin and cocaine   F11.20
    and currently is receiving prescribed methadone as a result   Z37.0
    of past dependence. She had a normal single liveborn without   10E0XZZ
    complications. The final diagnoses are "Term gestation,
    manually assisted delivery, and methadone use."

CHAPTER 25

Abortion and Ectopic Pregnancy

CHAPTER OVERVIEW

- Codes for pregnancy with an abortive outcome are found in categories O00 through O08 in chapter 15 of ICD-10-CM.

- The primary axis for coding abortion is the type of abortion (spontaneous, induced, or failed).

- Subcategories further specify if the abortion is complete, incomplete, or unspecified and whether a complication is present.

- If the attempted termination of pregnancy results in a liveborn infant, the code for preterm labor with preterm delivery is used.

- Molar pregnancies and other abnormal products of conception are also coded to categories O02 and O07.

- Codes for ectopic pregnancies have a fourth character to indicate the location.

LEARNING OUTCOMES

After studying this chapter you should be able to:

- Classify abortive outcomes by type of abortion.

- Select the appropriate code to indicate whether the abortion is complete, incomplete, or unspecified.

- Code complications to the abortion.

- Understand how to code different types and occurrences of abortions.

- Classify abnormal products of conception (such as molar and ectopic pregnancies).

TERMS TO KNOW

Abortion
the expulsion or extraction of all or part of the placenta with or without an identifiable fetus with less than an estimated 20 weeks gestational age

Ectopic pregnancy
a pregnancy in which a fertilized ovum implants and develops outside the uterus

Molar pregnancy
a condition in which an ovum within the uterus develops into a mole or benign tumor

REMEMBER . . .

ICD-10-CM rules may be different from individual state rules when it comes to classifying abortions.

INTRODUCTION

The expulsion or extraction of all or part of the placenta or membrane with an estimated gestation of less than 20 completed weeks is considered an abortive outcome (abortion). Although requirements for fetal death reporting vary from state to state, these requirements should not be confused with ICD-10-CM rules for classifying abortions; they are entirely separate. If an expelled fetus has a period of gestation of more than 20 weeks but less than 37 weeks, it is considered an early delivery and a code from subcategory O60.1, Preterm labor with preterm delivery, is assigned.

Pregnancy with abortive outcome is classified in categories O00 through O08. Note that the term "abortion" in the disease classification of ICD-10-CM refers to a fetal death. It is important to distinguish between an encounter for the purpose of performing an elective abortion versus one for dealing with a spontaneous abortion or a complication of an abortion. Encounters for the purpose of performing an elective abortion are classified to **Z33.2, Encounter for elective termination of pregnancy.** If a procedure to terminate the pregnancy is performed in the hospital, the procedure code is also required.

TYPES OF ABORTION

The primary axis for coding abortion is the type of abortion. Abortive outcome is classified by type in ICD-10-CM as follows:

- *Spontaneous abortion (category O03):* one that occurs without any instrumentation or chemical intervention.

- *Complications following (induced) termination of pregnancy (O04):* Complications after an abortion performed for either therapeutic or elective termination of pregnancy (terms such as "elective abortion," "induced" or "artificial abortion," and "termination of pregnancy" are used when this type of abortion is performed).

- *Failed attempted termination of pregnancy (Category O07):* one in which an induction of termination of pregnancy has failed to evacuate or expel the fetus and the patient is still pregnant. It includes incomplete elective abortion.

COMPLETE VERSUS INCOMPLETE SPONTANEOUS ABORTION

Codes in subcategories O03.0 through O03.4 indicate that the abortion is incomplete, while codes in subcategories O03.5 through O03.9 indicate that the abortion is complete or unspecified. Incomplete abortion refers to retained products of conception—whether from a spontaneous abortion or an elective termination of pregnancy. When the provider documentation does not specify whether the spontaneous abortion is complete or incomplete, ICD-10-CM classifies it to "complete or unspecified." The fact that a follow-up dilatation and curettage (D & C) is performed is not evidence in itself that an abortion is incomplete; the physician makes this determination.

COMPLICATIONS ASSOCIATED WITH ABORTION

Codes in categories O03, O04, and O07 indicate whether a complication is present and the general type of complication, such as a genital or pelvic infection; delayed or excessive hemorrhage; embolism; or other complications including shock, renal failure, venous complications, cardiac arrest, sepsis, or urinary tract infection.

For subsequent encounters when there are retained products of conception following either a spontaneous abortion or an elective termination of pregnancy, assign the appropriate code from category O03, Spontaneous abortion, or codes **O07.4, Failed attempted termination of pregnancy without complication,** and **Z33.2, Encounter for elective termination of pregnancy.** This advice applies even when the patient was discharged previously with a discharge diagnosis of complete abortion.

For sepsis related to abortion, additional codes may be assigned to identify the infectious organism, and a code from R65.2- to identify severe sepsis, if applicable. Examples follow.

- A patient is admitted with incomplete spontaneous abortion, and a D & C is performed to remove any retained products of conception. There is evidence of pelvic infection. The patient is discharged on the fourth hospital day with the infection cleared. The principal diagnosis is **O03.0, Genital tract and pelvic infection following incomplete spontaneous abortion.**

- A patient is readmitted one week following discharge after a termination of pregnancy because she had developed endometritis. Code **O04.5, Genital tract and pelvic infection following (induced) termination of pregnancy,** is assigned as the principal diagnosis, with an additional code for the endometritis.

- A patient is admitted in renal failure one week after discharge following a complete spontaneous abortion. Code **O03.82, Renal failure following complete or unspecified spontaneous abortion,** is assigned as the principal diagnosis.

- A patient who underwent an elective abortion one week earlier is admitted because of continued bleeding. A D & C is performed, and the pathology report shows retained products of conception. Code **O04.6, Delayed or excessive hemorrhage following (induced) termination of pregnancy,** is assigned.

- Five days following discharge for spontaneous abortion, a patient is admitted with a diagnosis of infection due to retained fetal tissue. The retention of fetal tissue indicates that the abortion was not complete, and so code **O03.0, Genital tract and pelvic infection following incomplete spontaneous abortion,** is assigned even though the patient was hospitalized for the abortion previously.

EXERCISE 25.1

Code the following diagnoses. Consider the diagnostic statements given below as the only information available in the medical record. Do not assign procedure codes.

1. Failed attempted abortion complicated by hemorrhage — O07.1

2. Incomplete early abortion (spontaneous) — O03.4

3. Therapeutic abortion, complete, with electrolyte imbalance — O04.83

4. Electively induced abortion, complete, with amniotic fluid embolism — O04.7

5. Patient readmitted with bleeding due to retained placenta one week following previous hospital admission for spontaneous abortion — O03.1

6. Discharge #1: Electively induced abortion, complete — Z33.2
   Discharge #2 (same patient): — O04.87
   Sepsis following induced abortion during previous admission

MATERNAL CONDITION AS REASON FOR ABORTION

Codes from categories O20 through O29 and O30 through O77 can be assigned as an additional code to indicate a maternal condition that assisted in the decision to proceed with an elective abortion. Pregnancy can be terminated on a purely elective basis, however, and it is not necessary to assign a code to indicate a reason for the abortion. For example:

- A patient who is 12 completed weeks gestation is admitted for elective abortion, based on her physician's advice that her severe heart disease indicates that an abortion might be advisable to prevent cardiac complications. In this case, the principal diagnosis code is **Z33.2, Encounter for elective termination of pregnancy,** and **O99.411, Diseases of the circulatory system complicating pregnancy, first trimester,** is also assigned, along with an additional code to identify the particular heart disease.

- A patient who had rubella at six weeks gestation requests abortion because of the possibility of fetal abnormality. Code **Z33.2, Encounter for elective termination of pregnancy,** is designated as the principal diagnosis, with an additional code of **O35.3XX1, Maternal care for (suspected) damage to fetus from viral disease in mother.**

- A patient who is 26 weeks pregnant presents for elective termination of pregnancy due to fetal anomalies. Assign code **Z33.2, Encounter for elective termination of pregnancy,** as the principal diagnosis. Code **O35.9XX0, Maternal care for (suspected) fetal abnormality and damage, unspecified,** is assigned as an additional diagnosis.

- A first-trimester pregnant patient is admitted with placenta previa. She does not request abortion, but after evaluating various treatment possibilities, her physician concludes that an abortion is necessary. The patient consents, and the abortion is carried out. In this case, the code for placenta previa (O44.01) is sequenced first, followed by the abortion code.

INADVERTENT ABORTION

An inadvertent abortion sometimes occurs when a pregnant patient suffers major trauma or undergoes surgery for another condition. In this situation, the code for the condition that occasioned the admission is designated as the principal diagnosis, with an additional code for the abortion.

When abortion occurs because of surgery performed on the uterus for a condition unrelated to the pregnancy, the code for the condition that required surgery is sequenced first, with an additional code from category O03, Spontaneous abortion, or code **Z33.2, Encounter for elective termination of pregnancy,** to indicate that an abortion occurred. For example:

- A hysterectomy was performed after a diagnosis of uterine carcinoma. When the excised uterus was examined, a six-week-old fetus was found.

  Principal diagnosis: C55   Carcinoma of uterus

  Additional diagnosis: Z33.2   Termination of pregnancy

When abortion occurs as a result of major trauma or surgery other than on the uterus, a code for the traumatic injury or the condition that required the surgery is sequenced as the principal diagnosis. A code from category O03, Spontaneous abortion, is assigned as an additional code. For example:

- Appendectomy was performed because of acute appendicitis with peritonitis. On the second postoperative day, the patient experienced an inadvertent abortion (complete).

  Principal diagnosis: K35.2   Appendicitis with peritonitis

  Additional diagnosis: O03.9   Spontaneous abortion

EXERCISE 25.2

Code the following diagnoses. Do not assign procedure codes.

---

1. Therapeutic <u>abortion</u>, complete (first trimester),
   performed because of severe reactive <u>psychosis</u>

   <u>Z33.2</u>
   O99.341
   F23

---

2. Inadvertent <u>abortion</u> (complete) prompted by
   radiation treatment damage to fetus, necessitating
   termination of pregnancy (single fetus)

   <u>Z33.2</u>
   O35.6xx0
   Y84.2

---

3. Elective <u>abortion</u> (complete) performed because
   of chromosomal abnormality of fetus (single fetus)

   <u>Z33.2</u>
   O35.1xx0

ABORTION PROCEDURE RESULTING IN LIVEBORN INFANT

Occasionally, an attempt to terminate a pregnancy results in a liveborn infant. Note that a fetus that has any heartbeat, respiration, or involuntary muscle movement after expulsion is considered to be a live birth, no matter how short a time it survives. In this situation, a code from subcategory O60.1, Preterm labor with preterm delivery, and a code from category Z37, Outcome of delivery, is assigned rather than an abortion code because, by definition, an abortion cannot result in a live birth. A code for the procedure used in the attempt to terminate the pregnancy should also be assigned. For example:

- A patient delivers a liveborn infant with extreme immaturity following attempted abortion by insertion of laminaria. Code **O60.10X0, Preterm labor with preterm delivery, unspecified trimester, not applicable or unspecified,** is assigned, along with code Z37.0 (for the single liveborn) and the procedure code for the insertion of the laminaria.

LOSS OF FETUS WITH REMAINING FETUS

Occasionally, a patient with multiple gestation is admitted for what appears to be a spontaneous abortion during which one or more fetuses are expelled but one or more live fetuses remain in utero. In such cases, no code from category O00–O08 is assigned and a code from subcategories O31.1-, Continuing pregnancy after spontaneous abortion of one fetus or more, and O31.2-, Continuing pregnancy after intrauterine death of one fetus or more, is assigned instead.

MULTIPLE GESTATION FOLLOWING FETAL REDUCTION

Subcategory code O31.3 identifies continuing pregnancy after elective fetal reduction during the current pregnancy. These pregnancies are considered high risk, and there is a need to identify them, even if the pregnancy is reduced to a single fetus. For example, when the woman delivers the single newborn, these codes make it possible to document that this was originally a multiple gestation that underwent fetal reduction. Note that subcategory O31.3 refers to fetal reduction, whereas subcategories O31.1 and O31.2, described in the preceding section, are for spontaneous abortion or involuntary fetal loss.

The subcategories for multiple gestation following fetal reduction are as follows:

O31.30   Continuing pregnancy after elective fetal reduction of one fetus or more, unspecified trimester

O31.31   Continuing pregnancy after elective fetal reduction of one fetus or more, first trimester

O31.32   Continuing pregnancy after elective fetal reduction of one fetus or more, second trimester

O31.33   Continuing pregnancy after elective fetal reduction of one fetus or more, third trimester

Codes in category O31 require a seventh character. Seventh-character "0" is for single gestations and multiple gestations where the fetus is unspecified. Seventh-characters "1" through "9" are for cases of multiple gestations to identify the fetus for which the code applies. The appropriate code from category O30, Multiple gestation, must also be assigned when assigning a code from category O31 that has a seventh character of "1" through "9."

For example:

- A patient in her second trimester of pregnancy presents with monochorionic (mono-amniotic) twin gestation complicated by inter-twin vascular communication. She undergoes elective reduction of the fetus because of inter-twin vascular communication. One fetus had developed polyhydramnios. Code **O31.32X1, Continuing pregnancy after elective fetal reduction of one fetus or more, second trimester, fetus 1,** is assigned as the principal diagnosis. Code **O35.8XX1, Maternal care for other (suspected) fetal abnormality and damage, fetus 1;** code **O40.2XX1, Polyhydramnios, second trimester, fetus 1;** and code **O30.012, Twin pregnancy, monoamniotic/monochorionic, second trimester,** should be assigned as additional diagnoses.

- A patient with an initial twin pregnancy had previously undergone fetal reduction of one fetus because of suspected chromosomal anomalies. The patient is now in her third trimester and is admitted and delivers a normal single liveborn infant. Code **O31.33X2, Continuing pregnancy after elective fetal reduction of one fetus or more, third trimester,** is assigned as the principal diagnosis. Code **Z37.0, Single live birth,** is assigned to indicate the outcome of the delivery, and code **O30.003, Twin pregnancy, unspecified, third trimester,** is assigned as an additional code.

PROCEDURES FOR TERMINATION OF PREGNANCY

ICD-10-PCS classifies procedures performed on the products of conception to the Obstetrics Section. Abortion procedures are coded to the Obstetrics Section, root operation "Abortion," which is defined as "artificially terminating a pregnancy," as shown in the excerpt from the ICD-10-PCS Tables in figure 25.1.

FIGURE 25.1   Excerpt of ICD-10-PCS Table for Abortion Procedures

Section	**1**	Obstetrics
Body System	**0**	Pregnancy
Operation	**A**	Abortion: Artificially terminating a pregnancy

Body Part	Approach	Device	Qualifier
0 Products of Conception	**0** Open **2** Open Endoscopic **3** Percutaneous **4** Percutaneous Endoscopic **8** Via Natural or Artificial Opening Endoscopic	**Z** No Device	**Z** No Qualifier
0 Products of Conception	**7** Via Natural or Artificial Opening	**Z** No Device	**Z** Vacuum **W** Laminaria **X** Abortifacient **Z** No Qualifier

The root operation "Abortion" is subdivided according to whether an additional device, such as a laminaria (a medical product used to dilate the cervix and to induce labor in abortions) or an abortifacient (a substance that causes an abortion), is used, or whether the abortion was performed by mechanical means. If either a laminaria, an abortifacient, or a vacuum is used, then the approach is via natural or artificial opening. All other abortion procedures are those performed by mechanical means (the products of conception are physically removed with the aid of instrumentation), and the device value is Z, no device.

Coding examples follow.

10A07ZZ	Abortion induced by dilatation and curettage
10A07ZW	Transvaginal insertion of laminaria
10A07ZX	Abortion by insertion of prostaglandin suppository

Procedures performed following an abortion for curettage of the endometrium or evacuation of retained products of conception are all coded in the Obstetrics Section to the root operation "Extraction" and the body part "products of conception, retained." For example, dilatation and curettage for an incomplete spontaneous abortion is coded to **10D17ZZ, Extraction of products of conception, retained, via natural or artificial opening.**

ECTOPIC AND MOLAR PREGNANCIES

Ectopic and molar pregnancies and other abnormal products of conception are classified to the following categories, with an additional code from category O08 when any complication occurs:

O00	Ectopic pregnancy
O01	Hydatidiform mole
O02	Other abnormal product of conception

A molar pregnancy occurs when a blighted ovum within the uterus develops into a mole or benign tumor. The hydatidiform mole is a particular type of molar pregnancy and is classified separately (O01.-) in ICD-10-CM. All other molar pregnancies are included in code **O02.0, Blighted ovum and nonhydatidiform mole.**

Utilization of assisted technologies has resulted in an increase in multiple gestational pregnancies in which an intrauterine pregnancy may coexist with an ectopic pregnancy. An ectopic pregnancy (O00.-) occurs when a fertilized ovum is implanted and develops anywhere outside the uterus. The fourth character indicates the extrauterine location of the ectopic pregnancy. The codes are as follows:

O00.0	Abdominal pregnancy
O00.1	Tubal pregnancy
O00.2	Ovarian pregnancy
O00.8	Other ectopic pregnancy
O00.9	Ectopic pregnancy, unspecified

Tubal Pregnancy

Tubal pregnancy is the most common type of ectopic pregnancy. Surgical procedures for removing a tubal ectopic pregnancy include salpingotomy and salpingostomy; in both procedures, the ectopic pregnancy is removed from the tube by means of an incision into the fallopian tube. It can also be removed by salpingectomy (excision of the fallopian tube) with the ectopic pregnancy intact. Removal of ectopic pregnancy is classified to the Obstetrics Section, body system "pregnancy," root operation "Resection," and body part "product of conception, ectopic."

Coding examples follow.

O00.1   Tubal pregnancy
      10T24ZZ   Laparoscopy with resection of ectopic tubal pregnancy

O00.1   Tubal pregnancy
      10T20ZZ + 0UB50ZZ   Laparotomy, salpingectomy with removal of right tubal pregnancy

O00.0   Abdominal pregnancy
      10T20ZZ   Removal of abdominal pregnancy (open approach)

O00.8   Cornual pregnancy
      10T24ZZ   Laparoscopic removal of cornual pregnancy

Complications of Molar and Ectopic Pregnancy

Unlike complications of abortions, complications of ectopic and molar pregnancies are classified in category O08, whether they occur during the initial episode of care or during a later episode. When the complication occurs during an episode of care for the purpose of treating the ectopic or molar pregnancy, a code from the O00 through O02 series is sequenced first, followed by a code from category O08. When the patient is readmitted for a complication following treatment of an ectopic or molar pregnancy, assign a code from category O08 as the principal diagnosis. An additional code that describes the complication more specifically can be assigned as needed. Sample codes include the following:

O00.1 + O08.0   Pelvic peritonitis following ectopic tubal pregnancy (this admission)

O08.1   Hemorrhage following ruptured ectopic tubal pregnancy removed on previous admission

MISSED ABORTION

The term "missed abortion" refers to fetal death that occurs prior to the completion of 20 weeks of gestation, with the dead fetus retained for a period of time in the uterus. This condition may be indicated by a cessation of growth, hardening of the uterus, or actual diminution in size of the uterus. Absence of fetal heart tones after they had been previously heard is also indicative of a missed abortion. The retained fetus may be expelled spontaneously, or surgical or chemical intervention may be required. For example:

- A patient in the 19th week of gestation reports that she is no longer feeling any fetal movement. The physician cannot hear any fetal heart tones, although they were present one month ago. On examination, the uterus is hard and possibly smaller than on the last visit. Code **O02.1, Missed abortion,** is assigned.

When the period of gestation is longer than 20 weeks, retention of a dead fetus is considered a missed intrauterine death (O36.4-). A missed abortion with blighted ovum, nonhydatidiform mole or hydatidiform mole, is not coded to O02.1, but to **O02.0, Blighted ovum and nonhydatidiform mole,** or a code from category O01, Hydatidiform mole, instead.

EXERCISE 25.3

Code the following diagnoses. Do not assign procedure codes.

1.	Therapeutic abortion, complete, with embolism	O04.7
2.	Failed attempted induction of abortion	O07.4
3.	Ruptured right tubal pregnancy with peritonitis due to group A *Streptococcus*	O00.1 O08.0 B95.0
4.	Incomplete early abortion (spontaneous)	O03.4
5.	Spontaneous abortion, complete, with excessive hemorrhage	O03.6
6.	Electively induced abortion with liveborn	O60.10X0 Z37.0
7.	Electively induced abortion, complete, complicated by shock	O04.81
8.	Ectopic pregnancy, right fallopian tube	O00.1
9.	Carneous mole	O02.0
10.	Hydatidiform mole	O01.9
11.	Missed abortion, 19 weeks gestation	O02.1
12.	Electively induced abortion, complete Family problems due to multiparity	Z33.2 Z64.1

CHAPTER 26

Congenital Anomalies

CHAPTER OVERVIEW

- Congenital anomalies are classified in chapter 17 of ICD-10-CM.

- Congenital and acquired conditions are often distinguished with a parenthetical note in the main term or subterm of a condition in the Alphabetic Index.

- In a few specific cases, separate codes are provided for the congenital and acquired versions of a condition.

- Congenital anomalies are classified first by the body system involved.

- Although congenital anomalies are present at birth, they may not be recognized until later in life.

- Patient age plays no role in assigning chapter 17 codes. They can be used at any age.

- In the case of newborns, congenital conditions that may have future implications are reported even though they may not be treated during the current episode of care.

- Conditions caused by mechanical factors during gestation are coded to categories Q65–Q79, Congenital malformations and deformations of the musculoskeletal system.

- Conditions due to birth injury are considered perinatal and are not part of the congenital classifications.

LEARNING OUTCOMES

After studying this chapter you should be able to:

Distinguish between congenital and acquired conditions in the Alphabetic Index.

Code for a congenital anomaly even if the classification does not provide a specific code for it.

Explain the relationship of patient age to codes for congenital anomalies.

Explain the difference between congenital and perinatal deformities.

TERM TO KNOW

Congenital anomaly
abnormal condition present at birth, which may not be recognized until later in life

REMEMBER . . .

There are about 4,000 congenital anomalies. Not all have been classified with a specific code.

INTRODUCTION

Congenital anomalies are classified in categories Q00 through Q99 in chapter 17 of ICD-10-CM. Congenital anomalies are abnormal conditions that are present at birth, although they may be recognized later. Codes from chapter 17 may be used throughout the life of the patient. If a congenital anomaly has been corrected, a personal history code should be used to identify the history of the anomaly. Codes in subcategory Z87.7 are used for congenital malformations that may still be present but do not require additional care, as well as corrected anomalies that are no longer present. Many congenital conditions can now be repaired because of medical advances, and patients are left with no residual condition.

LOCATION OF TERMS IN THE ALPHABETIC INDEX

A distinction between acquired and congenital conditions is often noted in the Alphabetic Index by a nonessential modifier associated with the main term or a subterm. When either term appears in parentheses with the main term, the alternative term can ordinarily be located as a subterm.

Note that some conditions are congenital by definition and have no acquired version; others are always considered to be acquired. For many conditions, of course, no distinction is made. When the diagnostic statement does not describe a condition as being either acquired or congenital, ICD-10-CM often makes a presumption that it is one or the other.

The following example from the Alphabetic Index demonstrates this usage:

> **Deformity . . .**
> -breast (acquired) N64.89
> --congenital Q83.9
> --reconstructed N65.0
> -bronchus (congenital) Q32.4
> --acquired NEC J98.09

In this example, the Alphabetic Index assumes that deformity of the breast without other qualification is classified as acquired, whereas deformity of the bronchus is classified as congenital if not otherwise specified. The Tabular List may offer additional guidance by means of an exclusion note. For example, the entry under category K57, Diverticular disease of intestine, refers the coder elsewhere for congenital diverticulum of intestine, coded **Q43.8, Other specified congenital malformations of intestine.** For code Q43.8, the inclusion note indicates that congenital diverticulum of the colon is appropriately classified here.

ICD-10-CM provides separate codes for congenital hydrocephalus (Q03.-), spina bifida with hydrocephalus (Q05.-), acquired secondary normal pressure hydrocephalus (G91.0), obstructive hydrocephalus (G91.1), and acquired idiopathic normal pressure hydrocephalus (G91.2).

Congenital hydrocephalus is defined as an excessive accumulation of cerebrospinal fluid (CSF) in the brain, which is present at birth. The excessive fluid leads to increased intracranial pressure and possibly brain damage. A code from category Q03, Congenital hydrocephalus, is assigned for this birth defect. ICD-10-CM provides fourth characters to further specify malformation of aqueduct of Sylvius (Q03.0), atresia of foramina of Magendie and Luschka (Q03.1), and other congenital hydrocephalus (Q03.8); when this information is not available, the condition is coded to **Q03.9, Congenital hydrocephalus, unspecified.** If the medical record documentation does not specify whether the hydrocephalus is congenital or acquired, the classification defaults to acquired, code **G91.9, Hydrocephalus, unspecified.**

Spina bifida is a congenital anomaly involving incomplete closure of the embryonic neural tube, resulting in a spinal cord defect. Many individuals with spina bifida have an associated abnormality of the cerebellum, referred to as Chiari II malformation. In affected individuals the back portion of the brain is displaced from the skull into the upper neck. Hydrocephalus develops in approximately 90 percent of individuals with myelomeningocele/spina bifida, because the displaced cerebellum obstructs the flow of CSF. For spina bifida without hydrocephalus, assign a code from Q05.5 through Q05.8, depending on the portion of the spine affected. If spina bifida is present with hydrocephalus, assign a code from Q05.0 through Q05.4 for this type of congenital anomaly, depending on the portion of the spine affected, as follows:

Q05.0   Cervical spina bifida with hydrocephalus
Q05.1   Thoracic spina bifida with hydrocephalus
Q05.2   Lumbar spina bifida with hydrocephalus
Q05.3   Sacral spina bifida with hydrocephalus
Q05.4   Unspecified spina bifida with hydrocephalus

For a diagnostic statement of spina bifida without further specification, assign code **Q05.9, Spina bifida, unspecified.** Use an additional code for any paraplegia or paraparesis (G82.2-) associated with spina bifida.

Congenital anomalies are classified first by the body system involved. Many congenital anomalies have specific codes in ICD-10-CM; others are located under such general terms as "anomaly" and "deformity" rather than under the name of the specific condition. For example:

Q45.8   Congenital malposition of gastrointestinal tract
Q22.5   Ebstein's anomaly
Q40.1   Congenital hiatus hernia
Q82.5   Strawberry nevus
Q03.9   Congenital hydrocephalus

Because approximately 4,000 congenital anomalies have been identified, it is impossible for the classification to provide a specific code for each. When the type of anomaly is specified, but no specific code is provided, the code for other specified anomaly of that type and site should be assigned. Often, only the code for unspecified anomaly of that general type or site can be assigned. When a specific code is not available, additional codes for manifestations of the anomaly should be assigned to the extent possible. Use additional secondary codes from other chapters to specify conditions associated with the anomaly. For example:

- An eight-day-old infant is diagnosed with Finnish-type congenital nephrosis. Finnish-type congenital nephrosis is a minimal change, type I nephrotic disease of childhood, occurring during the first week of life. This condition is caused by mutations in the gene for nephrin on chromosome 19. Proteinuria, hypoalbuminemia, hypogammaglobulinemia, and hyperlipidemia are common lab findings. Codes **Q63.8, Other specified congenital malformations of kidney,** and **N04.0, Nephrotic syndrome, with minor glomerular abnormality,** are assigned for Finnish-type congenital nephrosis.

- A ten-month-old infant is diagnosed with cardiofaciocutaneous (CFC) syndrome. Assign code **Q87.89, Other specified congenital malformation syndromes, not elsewhere classified,** for CFC syndrome. Additional codes may be assigned for any manifestations of the condition as instructed by the guideline on congenital anomalies. CFC syndrome is a genetic condition associated with mutation in four known genes: BRAF, MEK1, MEK2, and KRAS.

RELATIONSHIP OF AGE TO CODES

Codes from chapter 17 can be reported for a patient of any age. Many congenital anomalies, although actually present at birth, do not manifest themselves until later in life. In addition, many cannot be corrected and persist throughout life, and these conditions may be reported for an adult patient. Patient age is not the determining factor in assigning these codes. Following are examples:

- A patient, 30 years of age, with Marfan syndrome was admitted for a heart valve replacement and repair of an abdominal aortic aneurysm. In this case, the code for **Marfan syndrome, Q87.40,** is assigned in spite of the patient's age because the condition is an inherited disorder of the connective tissue that is transmitted as an autosomal dominant trait.

- A patient, age 25, was admitted for brain surgery, which revealed a colloid cyst of the right third ventricle. In this case, code **Q04.6, Congenital cerebral cysts,** is assigned because a colloid cyst of the third ventricle is always congenital and the patient's age does not influence code assignment.

NEWBORN WITH CONGENITAL CONDITIONS

When a diagnosis of a congenital condition is made during the hospital episode in which an infant is born, the appropriate code from chapter 17 of ICD-10-CM should be assigned as an additional code, with the appropriate code from category Z38, Liveborn infants, according to place of birth and type of delivery, used as the principal diagnosis. (See chapter 27 of this handbook.) Examples follow:

Z38.00 + Q36.9	Term birth, single male, vaginal delivery; incomplete cleft lip on right side
Z38.00 + Q54.9	Term birth, single male, vaginal delivery; hypospadias

Note that this is an exception to the guidelines for reporting other conditions. Congenital conditions that may have future health care implications are reported for newborns even though they are not further evaluated or treated during the current episode of care.

CONGENITAL DEFORMITIES VERSUS PERINATAL DEFORMITIES

Certain musculoskeletal deformities that result from a mechanical factor during gestation, such as intrauterine malposition or pressure, are classified in categories Q65–Q79, Congenital malformations and deformations of the musculoskeletal system. Conditions due to birth injury are classified as perinatal conditions in categories P10–P15, Birth trauma, in chapter 16 of ICD-10-CM, with an additional code assigned to identify the specific condition whenever possible. Examples include the following:

Q65.1	Bilateral congenital dislocation of hip
Q68.2	Congenital dislocation of knee
P13.4	Fracture of clavicle due to birth trauma

NEUROFIBROMATOSIS

Neurofibromatosis (subcategory Q85.0) refers to a group of autosomal dominant genetic disorders that cause tumors to grow along the nerves. Schwannomas (Q85.03) may occur along any nerve of the body, including spinal, cranial, and peripheral nerves, except on the vestibular nerve. As the tumors grow they compress nerves and cause pain, numbness, tingling, weakness, and other neurological symptoms.

CYSTIC KIDNEY DISEASE

There are major differences in the clinical characteristics, pathophysiology, and prognosis of the various types of congenital cystic kidney disease. This fact augments the importance of being as specific as possible about the type when assigning a code. For example, symptoms and problems for polycystic kidney disease, infantile type (Q61.1), progress slowly as more and more cysts develop over the years; this disease is relatively common. Medullary cystic kidney (Q61.5) is a hereditary disorder in which cysts in the center of each kidney cause the kidneys to gradually lose their ability to work; late in the disease, symptoms of chronic kidney disease may develop. When the diagnostic statement does not indicate whether a renal cyst is congenital or acquired, ICD-10-CM presumes that the cyst is acquired.

CONGENITAL MALFORMATIONS OF GENITAL ORGANS

The development of the female reproductive tract is a complex process that involves a highly orchestrated series of events, including cellular differentiation, migration, fusion, and canalization. Failure of any part of the process results in congenital anomalies. Mullerian anomalies refer to all congenital anomalies of the uterus, cervix, and vagina. ICD-10-CM provides unique codes for the spectrum of congenital uterine, cervical, and vaginal anomalies in categories Q50 through Q52:

Q50   Congenital malformations of ovaries, fallopian tubes and broad ligaments
Q51   Congenital malformations of uterus and cervix
Q52   Other congenital malformations of female genitalia

Congenital malformations of male genital organs are classified to categories Q53 through Q55. These categories include conditions such as undescended and ectopic testes, hypospadias, and other congenital malformations of male genital organs.

Cryptorchidism refers to incomplete testicular descent; the condition may be unilateral or bilateral. The term encompasses palpable, nonpalpable, and ectopic testicles. The position of the testis can be abdominal, inguinal, prescrotal, or gliding. ICD-10-CM classifies undescended and ectopic testicle to category Q53. Code Q53.0- describes ectopic testis, and code 053.2- describes undescended testis. In addition, category Q53 specifies whether the undescended testicle is unilateral (Q53.1-) or bilateral (Q53.2-), with the fifth character indicating the location of the undescended testicle (abdominal, ectopic perineal, or unspecified).

Hypospadias is a somewhat common congenital anomaly whereby the opening of the urethra is on the underside, rather than at the end, of the penis. ICD-10-CM classifies hypospadias to category Q54, Hypospadias, with additional fourth characters to specify balanic (Q54.0), penile (Q54.1), penoscrotal (Q54.2), perineal (Q54.3), congenital chordee (ventral curvature of the penis, caused by presence of a fibrous band of tissue instead of normal skin along the corpus spongiosum) (Q54.4), other (Q54.8), or unspecified (Q54.9). Procedures to repair hypospadias are classified to the root operation "Reposition," body part "urethra."

In addition to the above female and male genital malformations, ICD-10-CM provides category Q56, Indeterminate sex and pseudohermaphroditism, which distinguishes among hermaphroditism, not elsewhere classified (Q56.0); male pseudohermaphroditism (Q56.1); female pseudohermaphroditism (Q56.2); pseudohermaphroditism, unspecified (Q56.3); and indeterminate sex, unspecified (Q56.4).

OMPHALOCELE AND GASTROSCHISIS

An omphalocele is a distinct ventral wall defect. The intestines are usually covered by a membranous sac, with the intestine being exposed only if the sac ruptures. An omphalocele is commonly associated with other structural and chromosomal anomalies. Code **Q79.2, Exomphalos,** is assigned for a congenital omphalocele.

Gastroschisis is an anomaly involving a defect of the ventral body wall to the right of the umbilical cord insertion. This anomaly is caused by failure of the developing abdominal wall to completely close, allowing the intestines to protrude from the defect. The exposed intestines are not covered by a membranous sac. Assign code **Q79.3, Gastroschisis,** for congenital gastroschisis.

EXERCISE 26.1

Code the following diagnoses and procedures. Do not assign External cause of morbidity codes.

1. Polycystic kidneys, adult type — Q61.2

2. Hypospadias with congenital chordee — Q54.4
   Repair of hypospadias and release of chordee — 0TSD0ZZ
   (open approach)   Reposition — 0VNS0ZZ

3. Congenital pyloric stenosis — Q40.0
   Endoscopic dilation of the pylorus — 0D778ZZ

4. Congenital dislocation of both hips — Q65.1
   Closed reduction of dislocation of both hips with — 0SS9XZZ
   immobilization in plaster casts   Reposition — 0SSBXZZ

5. Congestive heart failure in patient with congenital — I50.9
   interatrial septal defect — Q21.1

6. Posterior subcapsular cataract, left eye, congenital — Q12.0

7. Accessory fifth digit, right foot   Q69.2

8. Esophageal web with esophageal spasm and reflux   Q39.4
    esophagitis   K22.4
                                                                               K21.0

9. Left trigger thumb, congenital   Q74.0
    Open tenolysis of flexor sheath of left thumb   Release   0LN80ZZ

10. Urachal cyst and patent urachus   Q64.4

11. Thoracoabdominal coarctation of aorta   Q25.1

12. Hallux rigidus, left   M20.22

13. Down syndrome   Q90.9

14. Bilateral talipes equinovarus, congenital   Q66.0

15. Unilateral cleft lip and cleft palate, soft and hard   Q37.5

16. Cystic lung, congenital   Q33.0

CHAPTER 27

Perinatal Conditions

CHAPTER OVERVIEW

- Perinatal conditions other than congenital anomalies are classified in chapter 16 of ICD-10-CM.

- These conditions can be found under the main term Birth or as a subterm under the condition's main term.

- Perinatal conditions are sequenced as the principal diagnosis but behind the appropriate Z38 code for the birth episode.

- Codes for perinatal conditions can be used throughout the patient's life. There is no prohibition due to age.

- Conditions are coded if they meet the definition of reportable conditions or if they have an implication for the newborn's future care.

- Newborn immaturity and prematurity are classified by birth weight. Codes for these conditions are never assigned without a physician's clinical evaluation as indicated in the diagnostic statement.

- Newborn postmaturity is classified by length of gestation.

- The perinatal conditions in chapter 16 cover fetal distress, metabolic abnormalities, difficulties due to aspiration, and more.

- A code is assigned from P00 through P04 when a healthy infant is evaluated for a suspected condition that is not found.

- Infections specific to the perinatal period are considered congenital.

- Infections that occur after birth but within the perinatal period may or may not be classified in chapter 16.

- Z codes are used for routine newborn vaccination and health supervision.

LEARNING OUTCOMES

After studying this chapter you should be able to:

- Locate codes and follow general guidelines with regard to perinatal conditions.

- Use Z codes to classify the birth, and use them with other codes for perinatal conditions.

- Code situations involving newborn immaturity, prematurity, and postmaturity.

- Code for evaluation and observation of newborns and infants.

- Determine what chapter to use to classify a newborn or infant infection.

- Know how and when to assign codes for maternal condition on the newborn record.

TERMS TO KNOW

Newborn immaturity
implies a birth of less than 37 completed weeks gestation

Newborn postmaturity
a gestational period of more than 42 weeks

Newborn low birth weight
implies a birth weight of 1,000–2,499 grams

Newborn extremely low birth weight
implies a birth weight of less than 500–999 grams

REMEMBER . . .

Codes from chapter 16 are never found on a maternal record, and codes from chapter 15 are never found on a newborn's record.

INTRODUCTION

Conditions other than anomalies that originate in the perinatal period are classified in chapter 16 of ICD-10-CM and categories P00 through P96. The perinatal period is defined as before birth through the first 28 days after birth.

LOCATING CODES FOR PERINATAL CONDITIONS IN THE ALPHABETIC INDEX

Codes for perinatal conditions are located in the Alphabetic Index by referring to the main term **Birth** or to the main term for the condition and then to such subterms as "newborn," "neonatal," "fetal," "infants," and "infantile." If the Alphabetic Index does not provide a specific code for a perinatal condition, assign code **P96.89, Other specified conditions originating in the perinatal period,** followed by the code from another chapter that specifies the condition.

GENERAL PERINATAL GUIDELINES

Codes from chapter 16 are never used on maternal records. By the same token, codes from chapter 15, Pregnancy, Childbirth and the Puerperium, should never be reported on the newborn record.

Generally, chapter 16 codes are sequenced as the principal or first-listed diagnosis on the newborn record, except for the appropriate code from the Z38 series for the birth episode. Codes from other chapters may be assigned as secondary diagnoses to provide additional detail.

The perinatal guidelines for secondary diagnoses are the same as the general coding guidelines for "additional diagnoses" (refer to chapter 4 of this handbook). In addition, assign codes for any conditions that have been specified by the provider as having implications for future health care needs. Assign codes from chapter 16 only for definitive diagnoses established by the provider. If a definitive diagnosis has not been established, codes for signs and symptoms may be assigned.

Sometimes a newborn may have a condition that may be either due to the birth process or community acquired. If the documentation does not specify which it is, the default code selected should be due to the birth process, and a chapter 16 code should be selected. When the condition is community acquired, do not report a chapter 16 code.

RELATIONSHIP OF AGE TO CODES

Most conditions originating during the perinatal period are transitory in nature. Other conditions that originate during the perinatal period, however, persist, and some do not manifest themselves until later in life. Such conditions are classified in chapter 16, no matter how old the patient is, and may be reported throughout the life of the patient if the condition is still present. For example:

- A 53-year-old woman is admitted for treatment of vaginal carcinoma due to intrauterine exposure to DES (diethylstilbestrol) taken by her mother during pregnancy. Code **C52, Malignant neoplasm of vagina,** and code **P04.8 Newborn (suspected to be) affected by other maternal noxious substances,** are assigned because the intrauterine exposure was still an important element in the patient's condition, even though the problem did not present itself until later in the patient's life.

- An 18-year-old man was admitted for workup because he had begun experiencing respiratory problems. A diagnosis of bronchopulmonary dysplasia was made, and the patient was discharged to be seen in the physician's office in two weeks. Code **P27.1, Bronchopulmonary dysplasia originating in the perinatal period,** is assigned because bronchopulmonary dysplasia is a congenital condition even though it may not become a problem until later in the patient's life.

CLASSIFICATION OF BIRTHS

A code from category Z38 is assigned as the principal diagnosis for any newborn. The first axis for coding is whether the birth is single, twin, or multiple. The codes further specify whether the birth occurred in the hospital, outside the hospital, or unspecified as to place of birth. If the birth occurred in the hospital, additional characters indicate the type of delivery (vaginal or cesarean). The medical record will provide sufficient information regarding the type of delivery to permit selection of the code.

A code from this series is assigned only on the newborn record and is assigned only for the episode in which the birth occurred. If a newborn is discharged and readmitted or transferred to another facility, the code for the condition responsible for the transfer or readmission is designated as the principal diagnosis. For example:

- A single liveborn vaginally delivered in the hospital with an associated diagnosis of subdural hemorrhage due to birth trauma is coded as **Z38.00, Single liveborn infant, delivered vaginally,** and **P10.0, Subdural hemorrhage due to birth injury,** with the Z code sequenced first.

- If the infant is discharged and readmitted or transferred to another facility for treatment of the hemorrhage, the principal diagnosis for that admission is P10.0; no code from category Z38 is assigned.

- If the admission of an infant born outside the hospital is delayed and the newborn is admitted later because of complication, the complication code is assigned as the principal diagnosis; no code from category Z38 is assigned.

OTHER DIAGNOSES FOR NEWBORNS

A code from category Z38 indicates only that a birth occurred. Additional codes are assigned for all clinically significant conditions noted on the examination of the newborn. A newborn condition is clinically significant when it has implication for the newborn's future health care. This is an exception to the Uniform Hospital Discharge Data Set guidelines.

Insignificant or transient conditions that resolve without treatment are not coded. Medical records of newborns sometimes mention conditions such as fine rashes, molding of the scalp, and minor jaundice. Because these conditions usually resolve without treatment and require no additional workup, they are not coded. For example:

- The physician documents diagnoses of syndactyly and hydrocele on the newborn's diagnostic statement. Even though no treatment is given and no further evaluation is performed during the infant's hospital stay, both of these conditions will require treatment at some time in the future, and so they are reported.

- The physician mentions on the newborn delivery record that the infant has slight jaundice. No further evaluation is performed, and the jaundice clears by the following day. No code for jaundice is assigned.

- The pediatrician documents in the newborn medical record that the baby's heart murmur is benign and most likely due to a patent ductus arteriosus/patent foramen ovale (PDA/PFO). He orders a cardiac consult and an echocardiogram to evaluate the PDA/PFO. Assign code **Q21.1, Atrial septal defect,** for the PFO and code **Q25.0, Patent ductus arteriosus,** for the PDA. These conditions are further evaluated (e.g., cardiac consultation and echocardiogram); therefore, they can be reported.

PREMATURITY, LOW BIRTH WEIGHT, AND POSTMATURITY

Newborns delivered before full term are defined as either immature or premature by both birth weight and gestational age and are classified in category P07 as follows:

- Extreme low birth weight (P07.0-) implies a birth weight of less than 1,000 grams.
- Low birth weight (P07.1-) implies a birth weight of 1,000–2,499 grams.
- Extreme immaturity (P07.2-) implies less than 28 completed weeks gestation (less than 196 completed days of gestation).
- Preterm (P07.3-) implies 28 completed weeks or more, but less than 37 completed weeks (196 completed days, but less than 259 completed days) of gestation.

When both birth weight and gestational age of the newborn are available, both should be coded, with birth weight sequenced before gestational age. Providers use different criteria in determining prematurity. A code for prematurity should not be assigned unless it is documented.

Even when a newborn is not premature, it may be appropriate to assign a code from category P05, Disorders of newborn related to slow fetal growth and fetal malnutrition. The assigned code does not imply prematurity but indicates that the newborn is smaller than expected for the length of gestation. Occasionally, the obstetrician will document the gestational age in the mother's record, and the pediatrician will document a different gestational age in the infant's chart. For the newborn, the coder assigns the appropriate codes for gestational age based on the attending provider's (e.g., pediatrician's) documentation. Different providers (e.g., obstetrician and pediatrician) may use different criteria in determining weeks of gestation for the mother versus the gestational age of the infant.

To indicate the birth weight, fifth characters are assigned to codes for low birth weight newborns (P07.0- to P07.1-), newborn light for gestational age (P05.0-), and newborn small for gestational age (P05.1-). Note that the weight expressed by the fifth character should be reasonably consistent with the four-character code to which it is applied. For example, a diagnosis of low birth weight newborn would appear to be inconsistent with a fifth character "8" because a birth weight of 2,500 grams falls far outside the criteria for low birth weight even though there is no indication in the manual that the heavier weight is excluded. The physician should be queried when there is a significant discrepancy.

Assignment of codes in categories P05, Disorders of newborn related to slow fetal growth and fetal malnutrition, and P07, Disorders of newborn related to short gestation and low birth weight, not elsewhere classified, should be based on the recorded birth weight and estimated gestational age. For example, an infant born at hospital A at 34 weeks gestation and transferred to hospital B after 14 days for further evaluation of a congenital anomaly could still have a code for prematurity assigned as an additional diagnosis. The fifth character for these codes is always based on birth weight, not the infant's weight at the time of transfer or readmission.

For example, a 12-month-old child who was born preterm is being seen for acute bronchiolitis due to respiratory syncytial virus (RSV). The physician lists "acute bronchiolitis due to RSV, ex-26 week preemie" in the diagnostic statement. Code **J21.0, Acute bronchiolitis due to respiratory syncytial virus,** is assigned as the first-listed diagnosis. Code **P07.22, Extreme immaturity of newborn, 24-26 completed weeks,** is assigned to indicate that the child was born at 26 weeks.

As noted earlier, chapter 16 codes may be used regardless of the patient's age if the condition originated in the perinatal period and continued through the life of the patient. Moreover, codes from category P07, Disorders of newborn related to short gestation and low birth weight, not elsewhere classified, may be assigned for a child or an adult if the provider indicates the patient's prematurity and gestational age are contributing conditions affecting the patient's current health status.

Post-term is defined as a gestational period over 40 completed weeks to 42 completed weeks. Prolonged gestation or postmaturity is defined as a gestational period of more than 42 completed weeks. Category P08 classifies a long gestation and/or high birth weight as follows:

P08.0   Exceptionally large newborn baby (usually implies weight of 4,500 grams or more)

P08.1   Other heavy for gestational age newborn (heavy- or large-for-dates newborns, regardless of period of gestation)

P08.21   Post-term newborn

P08.22   Prolonged gestation of newborn

Codes **P08.21, Post-term newborn,** and **P08.22, Prolonged gestation of newborn,** may be assigned based only on the gestational age of the newborn. A specific condition or disorder does not have to be associated with the longer gestational period for these codes to be assigned.

FETAL DISTRESS AND ASPHYXIA

Fetal distress may be defined as signs that indicate a critical response to stress. It implies metabolic abnormalities such as hypoxia and acidosis that affect the functions of vital organs to the point of temporary or permanent injury or even death. ICD-10-CM provides different codes for fetal distress, depending on the specific condition, as follows:

P84   Other problems with newborn
Includes the following conditions in newborns without further specification: acidemia, acidosis, anoxia, asphyxia, hypercapnia, hypoxemia, hypoxia, and mixed metabolic and respiratory acidosis

P19.0   Metabolic acidemia in newborn first noted before onset of labor

P19.1   Metabolic acidemia in newborn first noted during labor

P19.2   Metabolic acidemia noted at birth

P19.9   Metabolic acidemia, unspecified

Asphyxia refers to a decreased level of oxygen delivered to the body or an organ with a buildup of carbon dioxide. Birth asphyxia occurs when an infant does not receive enough oxygen before, during, or just after birth, and it can cause decreased heart rate, decreased blood flow, and low blood pressure leading to cellular and organ damage. When the duration of the asphyxia is brief, the infant can recover without any long-lasting injury. If the time period is longer, it may lead to reversible damage, and when prolonged, irreversible injury. Birth asphyxia is classified to code P84.

Hypoxic-ischemic encephalopathy (HIE) is a life-threatening condition that usually results from damage to the cells of the brain and spinal cord secondary to inadequate oxygen during the birth process. HIE is evidence of acute or subacute brain injury due to asphyxia. It is the most common cause of neurologic disease during the neonatal period and is associated with significant mortality and morbidity. Infants with the mild form of HIE are hyper-alert and overreact to the slightest stimulus. This stage usually lasts 24 hours or less. Infants can recover with normal neurologic function. Moderate HIE is associated with lethargy, clinical seizures, suppressed tendon reflexes, bradycardia, and periodic breathing. This stage may last from two to 14 days. A good neurologic prognosis is seen in infants who can recover within five days. Severe HIE is characterized by stupor to coma, primitive to no reflexes, variable heart rate, and apnea. Half of infants with severe HIE die. Eighty percent of those who survive have mental retardation, epilepsy, cerebral palsy, and learning disabilities. Only 10 percent survive with no neurological disability. The codes for HIE distinguish among mild (P91.61), moderate (P91.62), severe (P91.63), and unspecified (P91.60).

Codes for fetal distress or abnormality of heart rate and rhythm are assigned to the newborn record only when the condition is specifically identified by the physician. These codes are never assigned on the basis of other information in the newborn record.

Category P28, Other respiratory conditions originating in the perinatal period, classifies respiratory problems, including atelectasis (P28.0–P28.1-), cyanotic attacks (P28.2), apnea (P28.3–P28.4), respiratory failure (P28.5), respiratory arrest (P28.81), other (P28.89), and unspecified respiratory condition (P28.9), noted after birth.

FETAL AND NEWBORN ASPIRATION

Category P24, Neonatal aspiration, describes meconium aspiration and other types of fetal aspiration in the following subcategories/codes:

P24.0-   Meconium aspiration
P24.1-   Neonatal aspiration of (clear) amniotic fluid and mucus
P24.2-   Neonatal aspiration of blood
P24.3-   Neonatal aspiration of milk and regurgitated food
P24.8-   Other neonatal aspiration
P24.9   Neonatal aspiration, unspecified

Subcategories P24.0- through P24.8- provide an additional fifth character to identify the presence or absence of respiratory symptoms. If applicable, an additional code, I27.81, should be assigned to identify any secondary pulmonary hypertension.

Meconium aspiration in newborns occurs when the fetus gasps while still in the birth canal and inhales meconium-stained amniotic, vaginal, or oropharyngeal fluids. Massive aspiration syndrome is synonymous with massive fetal aspiration. Although meconium aspiration syndrome and massive meconium aspiration are somewhat different conditions with similar clinical presentation and course, code **P24.01, Meconium aspiration with respiratory symptoms,** is assigned for both. Code P96.83 is assigned for meconium staining.

Meconium ileus and meconium plug syndrome (a transient disorder of the newborn's colon with delayed passage of meconium and intestinal dilatation) are coded to **P76.0, Meconium plug syndrome,** except when specified as meconium ileus in cystic fibrosis, which is coded to E84.11 instead. Code P03.82 is assigned for meconium passage (without aspiration) during delivery.

Tachypnea, wheezing, and apnea are sometimes present in meconium aspiration; these conditions may resolve over a short period or may take a more prolonged course. In the milder forms of this condition, dyspnea occurs soon after birth, lasts two or three days, and is followed by rapid recovery. Therapy includes bronchoscopic suction of meconium, oxygen administration, humidity control, and prophylactic antibiotics.

HEMOLYTIC DISEASE OF THE NEWBORN

Infants born to Rh-negative mothers often develop hemolytic disease owing to fetal-maternal blood group incompatibility. These conditions are classified in category P55, Hemolytic disease of newborn. Note that an indication of incompatibility on a routine cord blood test is not conclusive. Do not assign a code from category P55 on the basis of this finding alone; a diagnosis of isoimmunization or hemolytic disease requires provider confirmation.

NECROTIZING ENTEROCOLITIS

Necrotizing enterocolitis (NEC) is a severe gastrointestinal condition that involves injury to the bowel, intestinal mucosal disruption associated with enteric feedings, infectious pathogens, and immature immune response. It is a major cause of morbidity and mortality in premature infants. Although NEC commonly affects premature infants with a birth weight of less than 1,500 grams, it can also occur in infants with low risk factors. The exact etiology of NEC is unknown; however, it is thought that the intestine of the premature infant is weakened by too little oxygen and blood flow. The infant then has an increased risk of developing NEC because of difficulty with blood and oxygen circulation, digestion, and fighting infection. When feedings are started and the food moves into the weakened area of the intestinal tract, bacteria from the food can damage the intestinal tissues. These tissues can develop necrosis and perforation, leading to acute abdominal infection. ICD-10-CM classifies necrotizing enterocolitis according to the following stages:

P77.1   Stage 1 necrotizing enterocolitis in newborn
P77.2   Stage 2 necrotizing enterocolitis in newborn
P77.3   Stage 3 necrotizing enterocolitis in newborn
P77.9   Necrotizing enterocolitis in newborn, unspecified

NEONATAL CEREBRAL LEUKOMALACIA

Periventricular leukomalacia, also known as neonatal cerebral leukomalacia (P91.2), occurs with increasing frequency in infants with very low birth weight. It refers to necrosis of white matter adjacent to lateral ventricles with formation of cyst and is a major risk factor for cerebral palsy and other neurological disorders. Although the cause of this condition is still obscure, recent studies have associated it with intrauterine growth retardation, intrauterine infections, and pregnancies involving monozygotic twins. The condition is frequently associated with severe intraventricular hemorrhage, but it is not necessarily the cause of the problem. An additional code is reported when intraventricular hemorrhage (P52.0–P52.3) is associated with periventricular leukomalacia.

DISORDERS OF STOMACH FUNCTION AND FEEDING PROBLEMS

ICD-10-CM separately classifies vomiting, bilious emesis, failure to thrive, and other feeding problems in newborns. Persistent vomiting in a newborn may be a sign of a very serious condition. These codes are used for newborns experiencing feeding problems (P92.9), bilious vomiting (P92.01), other vomiting (P92.09), regurgitation and rumination (P92.1), slow feeding (P92.2), underfeeding (P92.3), overfeeding (P92.4), neonatal difficulty in feeding at breast (P92.5), failure to thrive (P92.6), and other feeding problems (P92.8) and are only assigned up to the 28th day of life. Codes in the main classification are used for infants and children older than 28 days. For example, a 10-day-old baby presents for weight recheck and feeding problems. Code **Z00.111, Health examination for newborn 8 to 28 days old,** is assigned, along with code **P92.9, Feeding problems of newborn, unspecified.**

OBSERVATION AND EVALUATION OF NEWBORNS AND INFANTS

A code from categories P00–P04, Newborn affected by maternal factors and by complications of pregnancy, labor, and delivery, is assigned when a healthy newborn is evaluated for a suspected condition that is found not to be present when study is complete.

Codes from categories P00–P04 should not be used when the patient has identified signs or symptoms of a suspected problem; in such cases, code the sign or symptom.

A code from categories P00–P04 may also be assigned as the principal diagnosis for a later readmission or encounter when a code from Z38 no longer applies. It is used only for healthy newborns and infants for whom no reportable condition is identified after study and is assigned only during the perinatal period of 28 days. When the newborn presents signs or symptoms of a suspected problem, or when a definite condition is identified, a code for the symptom or condition is assigned; a code from P00–P04 is not assigned. For example:

- The physician is concerned that a vaginally delivered newborn with a drug-dependent mother may have been adversely affected. Drug screens are carried out on the newborn, and the newborn is placed in the intensive care nursery temporarily for closer observation of potential withdrawal symptoms. Drug screens are negative. Codes **Z38.00, Single live-born infant, delivered vaginally,** and **P04.49, Newborn (suspected to be) affected by maternal use of other drugs of addiction,** are assigned.

- A newborn infant is readmitted two days after discharge because of slight cyanosis and the possibility of a perinatal respiratory problem. Complete workup discloses no problem, including no observable cyanosis, and the newborn is discharged without any diagnosis having been established. Code **P00.3, Newborn (suspected to be) affected by other maternal circulatory and respiratory diseases,** is assigned as the principal diagnosis.

- A newborn infant is readmitted two days after discharge because of cyanosis and the possibility of a perinatal respiratory problem. The infant is diagnosed as having respiratory distress syndrome. Code **P22.0, Respiratory distress syndrome,** is assigned. No code from categories P00–P04 is assigned.

Although ordinarily no additional code is assigned when a condition from categories P00–P04 is the principal diagnosis, codes can be assigned for a perinatal or congenital condition that requires continuing therapy or monitoring during the stay. Codes for congenital conditions that do not receive further evaluation or therapeutic treatment are not assigned when a newborn is admitted for observation. It is inappropriate to assign codes in subcategory Z03.7, Encounter for suspected maternal and fetal conditions ruled out, for the newborn. This code subcategory is only reported on the maternal record.

INFECTIONS ORIGINATING DURING THE PERINATAL PERIOD

Many infections specific to the perinatal period are considered to be congenital and may be classified in chapter 16 of ICD-10-CM when they are acquired before birth via the umbilicus (for example, rubella) or during birth (for example, herpes simplex). Codes are located by referring to the main term for the infection and then identifying subterms, such as "neonatal," "newborn," "congenital," "perinatal," or "maternal," affecting fetus or newborn. Certain perinatal infections (for example, congenital syphilis), however, may appear in chapter 1 of ICD-10-CM, Certain Infectious and Parasitic Diseases.

Infections that occur after birth but appear during the 28-day perinatal period may or may not be classified in chapter 16. When none of the subterms mentioned above is listed, the usual infection code is assigned. If an infection does not appear for a week or more after birth, the record should be reviewed to see whether there is any indication that it may be due to exposure to the infection rather than being congenital. Clarification should be sought from the physician when the record is not completely clear.

If a newborn has sepsis, assign a code from category P36, Bacterial sepsis of newborn. If the P36 code includes the causal organism, do not assign an additional code from category B95, Streptococcus, Staphylococcus, and Enterococcus as the cause of diseases classified elsewhere, or B96, Other bacterial agents as the cause of diseases classified elsewhere. If the P36 code does not include the causal organism, assign an additional code from category B96. If applicable, use additional codes to identify severe sepsis (R65.2-) and any associated acute organ dysfunction, such as acute respiratory failure (P28.5).

As mentioned in chapter 14 of this handbook, ELISA or Western blot tests of newborns with HIV-positive mothers are often positive. This result usually indicates the antibody status of the mother rather than that of the newborn. Code **R75, Inconclusive laboratory evidence of human immunodeficiency virus (HIV),** is assigned to the newborn chart because the HIV antibodies can cross the placenta into the newborn and may persist for as long as 18 months, producing a false positive test result in the newborn. The newborn may later lose these antibodies, which means that there was never any actual HIV infection.

MATERNAL CONDITIONS AFFECTING THE FETUS OR NEWBORN

Codes from categories P00 through P04 are assigned only on the newborn's record and only when the maternal condition is the cause of morbidity or mortality in the newborn. Unless there is an adverse effect, no code from this series is assigned. The fact that the mother has a related medical condition or has experienced a complication of pregnancy, labor, or delivery does not warrant assignment of a code from these categories on the newborn's record. Examples follow.

- A living child born to a diabetic mother in a term birth and delivered by cesarean section is coded as Z38.01. No code from the series P00 through P04 is assigned because the medical record does not document a problem affecting the newborn.

- A newborn delivered of a mother addicted to cocaine shows no sign of dependence, but a drug screen is positive. In this case, code **P04.41, Newborn (suspected to be) affected by maternal use of cocaine,** is assigned as an additional code on the newborn's record.

- A newborn is admitted following cesarean delivery and diagnosed with hypermagnesemia. The provider documents that the infant had developed hypermagnesemia due to the mother's treatment with magnesium sulfate for pregnancy-related eclampsia prior to delivery. Assign codes **P74.4, Other transitory electrolyte disturbances of newborn**, and **P04.1, Newborn (suspected to be) affected by other maternal medication.**

When a specific condition in the infant that resulted from the mother's condition is identified, a code for that condition is assigned rather than a code from categories P00 through P04. For example, infants born to diabetic mothers sometimes experience a transient abnormally low blood glucose level (hypoglycemia), classified as **P70.1, Syndrome of infant of a diabetic mother.** Others may have a transient diabetic state (hyperglycemia), sometimes referred to as pseudodiabetes, which is coded as **P70.2, Neonatal diabetes mellitus.** When fetal or newborn conditions result in hospitalization or other obstetric care of the mother, codes O35.- and O36.- are assigned on the maternal record.

SURGICAL OPERATION ON MOTHER AND FETUS

ICD-10-CM provides several codes to capture newborns affected by amniocentesis, in utero procedures, surgery performed on the mother during pregnancy, and other maternal factors unrelated to the current pregnancy (i.e., mother's history of surgery not associated with pregnancy). These codes are only assigned on the newborn's record. If the management of the pregnancy is affected because of complications of in utero surgery, assign the appropriate code from subcategory O35.-, Maternal care for (suspected) damage to fetus by other medical procedures, on the mother's record. Obstetric codes from chapter 11 of ICD-10-CM should not be used on the newborn's record.

Specific codes for newborns affected by the above factors are as follows:

P00.7   Newborn (suspected to be) affected by other medical procedures on mother, not elsewhere classified

P00.6   Newborn (suspected to be) affected by surgical procedure on mother

ENDOCRINE AND METABOLIC DISTURBANCES SPECIFIC TO THE FETUS AND NEWBORN

ICD-10-CM provides codes to describe acidosis of newborn and other neonatal endocrine and metabolic disturbances. Causes of respiratory acidosis include, but are not limited to, asphyxia, obstruction to the respiratory tract, respiratory distress syndrome, pneumonia, pulmonary edema, and/or apnea. Metabolic acidosis may be caused by renal failure, septicemia, hypoxia, hypothermia, hypotension, cardiac failure, dehydration, electrolyte disturbances, hyperglycemia, anemia, intraventricular hemorrhage, and/or metabolic disorders. The underlying cause of acidosis must be treated in order to correct the problem. ICD-10-CM classifies transitory endocrine and metabolic disorders specific to newborn to categories P70 through P74. This code range includes transitory endocrine and metabolic disturbances caused by the infant's response to maternal endocrine and metabolic factors or its adjustment to the extrauterine environment.

INFANTILE COLIC

Code **R10.83, Colic,** is assigned for infantile colic. Assign code **R10.84, Generalized abdominal pain,** for colic in an adult or child more than 12 months old. A colicky baby is a healthy, well-fed baby who cries more than three hours a day, three days a week, for more than three weeks. The crying usually occurs at about the same time every day for no apparent reason and may be intense, with the baby having clenched fists and tensed abdominal muscles. The baby may be inconsolable. There is no known cause for colic. It may last from the first few weeks of birth through four months of age.

APPARENT LIFE-THREATENING EVENT

Apparent life-threatening event (ALTE) refers to an episode that may be characterized by any of the following signs: apnea, cyanosis, changes in muscle tone, and/or choking or gagging. It was previously referred to as near-miss sudden infant death syndrome (SIDS) or aborted crib death, but these terms should not be used because they imply an association between ALTE and SIDS. Code **R68.13, Apparent life threatening event in infant,** is assigned for ALTE in a newborn or an infant.

Because of the wide variety of presentations of the ALTE episode, signs and symptoms may be coded as additional diagnoses when:

- No confirmed diagnosis or identifiable cause of the ALTE is established or
- When signs and symptoms are not associated routinely with the confirmed cause of the ALTE or
- When the reporting of signs and symptoms provides additional information about the cause of the ALTE.

ROUTINE VACCINATION OF NEWBORNS

Newborns are vaccinated shortly after birth against hepatitis B and varicella. When the need for vaccination is indicated during the newborn stay, code **Z23, Encounter for immunization,** may be assigned. If the newborn's vaccination is not administered because of parental refusal, assign code **Z28.82, Immunization not carried out because of caregiver refusal.** Procedure codes are required to identify the type of immunization given. In the inpatient setting, the following ICD-10-PCS codes are available to report vaccinations (although most hospitals generally do not code them):

3E0134Z   Introduction of serum, toxoid and vaccine into subcutaneous tissue, percutaneous approach

3E0234Z   Introduction of serum, toxoid and vaccine into muscle, percutaneous approach

HEALTH SUPERVISION OF INFANT OR CHILD

A code from subcategory Z00.1, Encounter for newborn, infant and child health examinations, is assigned for routine encounters of infants and children when no problem has been identified. Codes from subcategory Z00.11, Newborn health examination, are assigned for a routine examination or health check for children under 29 days old, with an additional code to identify any abnormal findings. Code Z00.110 is used for newborns under eight days old, and code Z00.111 is for newborns eight to 28 days old. Code Z00.111 includes newborn weight check. Codes Z00.121 (with abnormal findings) and Z00.129 (without abnormal findings) are used for routine child health examinations for children over 28 days old and include development testing. If any vaccinations are administered during any of these routine examinations, also assign code **Z23, Encounter for immunization.** Codes from subcategory Z00.1 are not assigned for a hospital admission.

EXERCISE 27.1

Code the following diagnoses and procedures as they would be assigned to a newborn's record. Presume that all births were delivered in the hospital and were vaginally delivered unless stated otherwise.

---

1. Term birth, living male, cesarean delivery,

    with hemolytic disease due to ABO isoimmunization

    Newborn

    Z38.01
    P55.1

---

2. Term birth, living child, vaginal delivery

    Physiological neonatal jaundice

    Newborn

    Z38.00
    P59.9

---

3. Normal, full-term female, spontaneous vaginal delivery

    Congenital left hip subluxation

    Newborn

    Z38.00
    Q65.32

---

4. Newborn, male, premature (33 weeks gestation, 1,400 grams)

    Hyaline membrane disease

    Z38.00
    P07.15
    P07.32
    P22.0

---

5. Term birth, living male

    Ophthalmitis of newborn due to

    maternal gonococcal infection

    Newborn

    Z38.00
    A54.31

---

6. Near-term birth, living male, delivered by

    cesarean section with neonatal hypoglycemia

    Newborn

    Z38.01
    P70.4

---

7. Term birth, living child

    Intrauterine growth retardation

    Newborn

    Z38.00
    P05.9

---

8. Premature birth, living female infant (27 weeks gestation, 1,850 grams)   Z38.00

     Withdrawal syndrome in infant due to maternal   P07.17

     heroin addiction   P07.20

     P96.1

Newborn

9. Term birth, twin, with fracture of right   Z38.30

     clavicle during birth   P13.4

Newborn

10. Five-year-old child with Erb's palsy secondary to   P14.0

     birth trauma

11. Infant with hemolytic disease due to Rh isoimmunization   P55.0

     (patient received by transfer from other facility)

     Skin phototherapy, single   6A600ZZ

12. Patient born in Community Hospital, with erythroblastosis

     fetalis due to ABO incompatibility; transferred immediately

     after birth to intensive care nursery at University Hospital

     for further care

Newborn

     a. Codes for Community Hospital stay   Z38.00

     P55.1

     b. Code for University Hospital stay   P55.1

13. Normal, male infant, delivered by cesarean   Z38.01

     when fetal acidemia was noted early in labor   P19.1

     Fetal distress due to cord compression   P02.5

Newborn

14. Newborn born on the way to hospital   Z38.1

     and admitted directly to newborn nursery   P61.3

     Anemia due to acute blood loss from umbilical stump   P51.8

15. Term birth with severe sepsis due to *E. coli* caused by
    amnionitis

    <u>Newborn</u>

    <u>Z38.00</u>
    P36.4
    P02.7
    R65.20

---

16. Term birth, delivered with meconium
    aspiration syndrome due to prolonged labor,
    first stage
    Cord around neck of infant two times

    <u>Newborn</u>

    <u>Z38.00</u>
    P24.01
    P03.89
    P02.5

---

17. Term birth, living male, with partial facial paralysis

    <u>Newborn</u>

    <u>Z38.00</u>
    P11.3

---

18. Premature infant (25 weeks, 1,300 grams) transferred
    from Community Hospital to intensive care
    nursery at University Hospital for
    supervision of weight gain

    <u>Newborn</u>

    P07.15
    P07.21

---

19. Newborn twins, #1 delivered in parking lot of
    hospital, #2 delivered after admission of mother

    <u>Newborn</u>

    #1: Z38.30
    #2: Z38.4

---

20. Term birth, living child; mother known to be a
    chronic alcoholic; newborn placed in intensive care
    nursing for observation for possible alcohol-related
    problems; none found

    <u>Observation</u>
    <u>Newborn</u>

    <u>Z38.00</u>
    P04.3

---

21. Routine visit to well-baby clinic for checkup;
    healthy 14-day-old infant

    Z00.111

Coding OF Circulatory System Diseases AND Neoplastic Diseases

CHAPTER 28

Diseases of the Circulatory System

CHAPTER OVERVIEW

- Circulatory disorders are classified in chapter 9 of ICD-10-CM.
- Rheumatic fever is classified with and without rheumatic heart disease.
- Ischemic heart disease is a general term for conditions affecting the myocardium.
  - Myocardial infarctions are classified with a fourth character to indicate the wall involved. They are also classified as to whether there is an ST-segment elevation.
  - The code for intermediate coronary syndrome includes a range of anginas.
  - Atherosclerosis is one of the conditions included in the category "other forms of heart disease."
- If a patient is admitted with stable angina (currently a rare practice), the underlying cause is the principal diagnosis.
- There are two main categories of heart failure—systolic and diastolic. It is further classified by left- and right-sided failure.
- Cardiac arrest is assigned as a principal diagnosis only when a patient is pronounced dead before the underlying cause can be identified.
- An aneurysm is diagnosed and then classified according to its location.
  - Sometimes a term is used to describe its appearance.
  - A term may also describe its etiology.
- Nontraumatic conditions affecting the cerebral arteries are coded together. These include strokes.
- Hypertension is classified by type (primary or secondary).
- Hypertension can be paired with heart disease, chronic kidney disease, or both.
- Procedures for treating circulatory disorders are varied and appear throughout this chapter of the handbook.

LEARNING OUTCOMES

After studying this chapter you should be able to:

Classify the disorders related to the heart and the rest of the circulatory system.

Distinguish between the different conditions regarded as ischemic heart disease.

Classify heart failure by category and location.

Code for a variety of procedures involving the circulatory system and the heart.

TERMS TO KNOW

Diastolic heart failure
occurs when the heart has a problem relaxing between contractions to allow enough blood into the ventricles

Systolic heart failure
occurs when the ability of the heart to contract decreases

Thrombophlebitis of a vein
a condition indicated by a clot that has become inflamed

Thrombosis of a vein
a condition indicated by the forming of a clot

REMEMBER . . .

The range of circulatory disorders is broad and complex, requiring close attention to instructional terms.

INTRODUCTION

Chapter 9 of ICD-10-CM classifies circulatory disorders except for those that have been reclassified to chapter 15 (obstetrical conditions) or to chapter 17 (congenital anomalies). This chapter covers a broad range of conditions, many of which are commonly seen for patients admitted to acute care hospitals. Because these are complex disorders and many are interrelated, it is particularly important for the coder to be alert to all instructional terms.

FIGURE 28.1   Major Vessels of the Arterial System

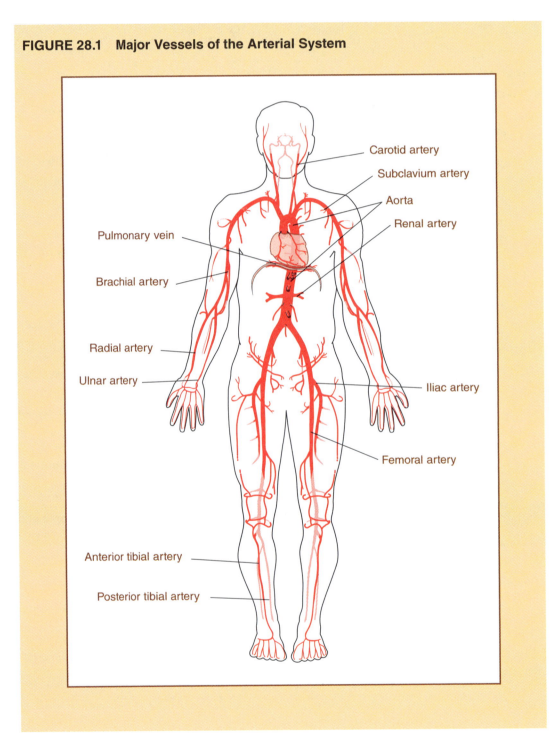

RHEUMATIC HEART DISEASE

Rheumatic heart disease occurs as the result of an infection with group A hemolytic *Streptococcus*. ICD-10-CM classifies rheumatic fever with and without rheumatic heart disease. The first axis distinguishes whether the fever is acute (I00–I02) or inactive (quiescent) (I05–I09), and the second axis determines whether there is heart involvement.

FIGURE 28.2   Major Vessels of the Venous System

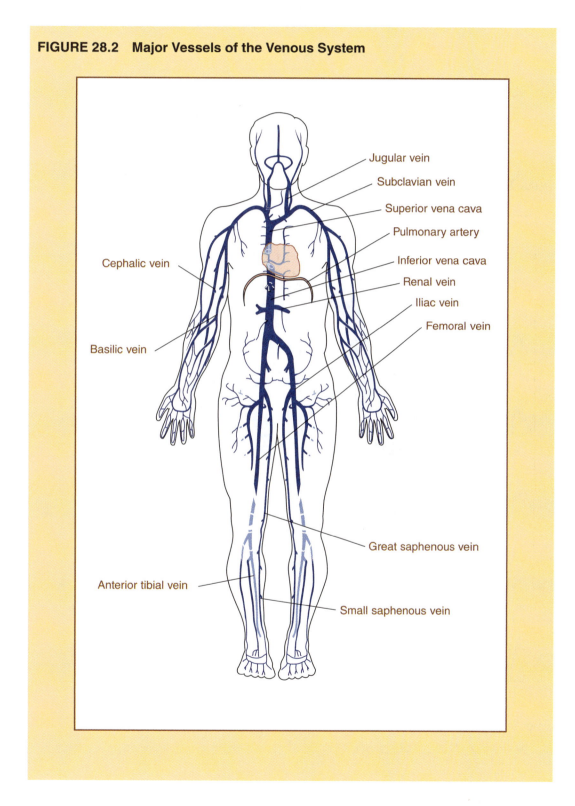

Jugular vein

Subclavian vein

Superior vena cava

Pulmonary artery

Inferior vena cava

Renal vein

Iliac vein

Femoral vein

Cephalic vein

Basilic vein

Great saphenous vein

Anterior tibial vein

Small saphenous vein

Chronic rheumatic heart disease includes heart disease that has resulted from a previously active rheumatic infection. The heart valves are most often involved. ICD-10-CM presumes that certain mitral valve disorders of unspecified etiology are rheumatic in origin. When the diagnostic statement includes more than one condition affecting the mitral valves, one of which is presumed to be rheumatic, all are classified as rheumatic. For example:

I05.0   Mitral valve stenosis

I34.0   Mitral valve insufficiency

I05.2   Mitral valve stenosis and insufficiency

In these examples the mitral valve stenosis is presumed to be of rheumatic origin, but the mitral valve insufficiency is not. In the third example, the combination code presumes both to be rheumatic because the stenosis is presumed to be rheumatic.

FIGURE 28.3   The Interior of the Heart

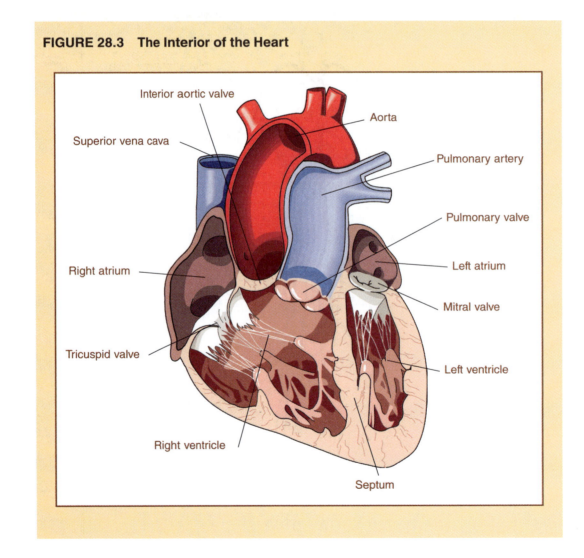

ICD-10-CM presumes that a disorder affecting both the mitral and aortic valves is rheumatic in origin. Otherwise, the aortic condition is classified as rheumatic only when specifically stated as such. Examples follow.

I35.1	Aortic valve insufficiency
I08.0	Mitral valve insufficiency with aortic valve insufficiency
I35.0	Aortic valve stenosis
I06.0	Rheumatic aortic stenosis
I08.0	Mitral stenosis and aortic stenosis

A diagnosis of heart failure in a patient who has rheumatic heart disease is classified as **I09.81, Rheumatic heart failure,** unless the physician specifies a different cause. An additional code from category I50, Heart failure, is assigned to identify the type of heart failure. However, do not make an assumption that congestive heart failure is rheumatic in nature. Unless ICD-10-CM directs the coder to assign the code for "rheumatic," it is inappropriate to assign a code for rheumatic congestive heart failure. For example:

I09.81 + I50.9 + I42.0 + I05.1	End-stage congestive heart failure due to rheumatic heart disease and dilated cardiomyopathy with mitral valve insufficiency
I50.9 + I34.0 + I07.1 + Z95.2	Congestive heart failure, severe mitral valve regurgitation, tricuspid valve regurgitation, and a history of aortic valve stenosis status post valve replacement

---

EXERCISE 28.1

Code the following diagnoses.

1.	Mitral regurgitation	I34.0
2.	Mitral valve stenosis with congestive heart failure	I05.0 I50.9
3.	Severe mitral stenosis and mild aortic insufficiency	I08.0
4.	Aortic and mitral insufficiency Atrial fibrillation	I08.0 I48.0

5. Mitral insufficiency, congenital	Q23.3
6. Mitral valve insufficiency with aortic regurgitation	I08.0
7. Chronic aortic and mitral valve insufficiency, rheumatic, with acute congestive heart failure due to rheumatic heart disease	I08.0 I09.81 I50.9

ISCHEMIC HEART DISEASE

Ischemic heart disease is the general term for a number of disorders affecting the myocardium caused by a decrease in the blood supply to the heart due to coronary insufficiency. The insufficiency is usually caused by deposits of atheromatous material in the epicardial portions of the coronary artery that progressively obstruct its branches so that the lumen of the arteries become either partially or completely occluded. Other common terms for ischemic heart disease are arteriosclerotic heart disease, coronary ischemia, coronary artery disease, and coronary arteriosclerosis (atherosclerosis).

Ischemic heart disease is classified in categories I20 through I25 as follows:

I20   Angina pectoris
I21   Acute myocardial infarction
I22   Subsequent myocardial infarction
I23   Current complications following myocardial infarction
I24   Other acute ischemic heart disease
I25   Chronic ischemic heart disease

An additional code is used to identify hypertension (I10–I15) when present.

Myocardial Infarction

Acute myocardial infarction is an acute ischemic condition that ordinarily appears following prolonged myocardial ischemia. It is usually precipitated by an occlusive coronary thrombosis at the site of an existing arteriosclerotic stenosis. Although ischemic heart disease is a progressive disorder, it is often silent for long periods with no clinical manifestations, and then it can appear suddenly in an acute form without any intervening symptoms having been experienced.

A myocardial infarction (MI) described as acute or with a duration of four weeks or less is classified in category I21, ST elevation (STEMI) and non-ST elevation (NSTEMI) myocardial infarction, with a fourth character indicating the wall involved (such as anterolateral wall or inferior wall). Codes from I21.0- through I21.2- also have a fifth character to indicate the coronary artery involved (e.g., left main coronary artery). Codes I21.0- through I21.3- identify transmural infarctions; code I21.4- identifies subendocardial infarctions that do not extend through the full thickness of the myocardial wall. Diagnostic statements do not always mention the affected wall, but this information can almost always be found in the electrocardiographic report. Code **I21.3, ST elevation (STEMI) myocardial infarction of unspecified site,** should not be assigned unless no information regarding the site is documented in the medical record. If only STEMI or transmural MI without the site is documented, query the provider as to the site, or assign code I21.3.

Myocardial infarctions can also be classified according to whether there is ST-segment elevation (codes I21.0- through I21.3) or non-ST-segment elevation (code I21.4). If there is no information regarding whether there is ST elevation or non-ST elevation, or information regarding the site of the myocardial infarction, coders should assign code I21.3. If a myocardial infarction is documented as nontransmural or subendocardial, but the site is provided, it is still coded as a subendocardial MI.

If a non-ST-elevation myocardial infarction (NSTEMI) evolves to ST-elevation myocardial infarction (STEMI), assign the code for the STEMI. If STEMI converts to NSTEMI due to thrombolytic therapy, assign the code for STEMI. Be careful to note that these codes are used for documented acute myocardial infarctions and should not be confused with abnormal findings on electrocardiograms (EKGs) of ST-segment elevation.

When the patient requires continued care for the myocardial infarction, codes from category I21 may continue to be reported for the duration of four weeks (28 days) or less from onset, regardless of the health care setting. This includes patients who are transferred from the acute care setting to the post–acute care setting within the four-week time frame. For encounters after the four-week time frame in which the patient requires continued care related to the myocardial infarction, assign the appropriate aftercare code, rather than a code from category I21. Otherwise, code **I25.2, Old myocardial infarction,** may be assigned for old or healed myocardial infarction not requiring further care.

When a patient suffers a new myocardial infarction within four weeks of an acute myocardial infarction (AMI), a code from category I22, Subsequent ST elevation (STEMI) and non-ST elevation (NSTEMI) myocardial infarction, should be used in conjunction with a code from category I21. The sequencing of these codes is dependent on the circumstances of the encounter, as follows:

- A patient is admitted to the hospital due to an AMI and has a subsequent AMI within four weeks while still in the hospital. Code I21 is sequenced first as the reason for the admission, with code I22.- sequenced as a secondary code.

- A patient suffers a subsequent AMI after discharge for care of an initial AMI. The I22.- code should be sequenced first, followed by the I21.- code. An I21.- code must accompany an I22.- code to identify the site of the initial AMI and to indicate that the patient is still within the four-week time frame of healing from the initial AMI.

- The guidelines for assigning the correct code from category I22 are the same as for the initial MI.

An associated postinfarction hypotension is sometimes experienced by patients with acute myocardial infarction. In this situation, the code for the infarction is sequenced first, with an additional code of **I95.89, Other hypotension.**

For both AMIs and subsequent MIs, additional codes may be assigned to identify risk factors, such as the following:

Z77.22	Exposure to environmental tobacco smoke
Z87.891	History of tobacco use
Z57.31	Occupational exposure to environmental tobacco smoke
F17.-	Tobacco dependence
Z72.0	Tobacco use

Evolving Infarction

An evolving myocardial infarction sometimes precipitates right ventricular failure that progresses to congestive heart failure. The patient may then be admitted because of this precursor condition, which then progresses to an acute myocardial infarction. After study, the principal diagnosis in this situation is the infarction, with an additional code assigned for the heart failure. Additional codes should also be assigned for any mention of cardiogenic shock, ventricular arrhythmia, and fibrillation. For example:

I21.09 + I50.9 + I49.01   Congestive heart failure with acute myocardial infarction of anterolateral wall with ventricular fibrillation

---

EXERCISE 28.2

Code the following diagnoses; do not code procedures.

---

1. A patient felt well until around 10:00 p.m., when he began
having severe chest pain, which continued to increase
in severity. He was brought to the emergency department
by ambulance. There was no previous history of cardiac disease,
but the EKG showed an acute posterolateral myocardial infarction,
and the patient was admitted immediately for further care.

I21.19

---

2. A patient with compensated congestive heart failure on
Lasix began to have extreme difficulty in breathing and was
brought to the emergency department, where he was found
to be in congestive failure. Because it was felt that an
impending infarction was possible, a percutaneous transluminal
coronary angioplasty (PTCA) was performed,
but the patient went on to have an acute inferolateral infarction.

I21.19
I50.9

---

3. A patient was admitted with acute myocardial infarction
involving the left main coronary artery
with no history of previous infarction or previous care
for this episode. A week later during the hospital stay,
he also experienced an acute anterolateral infarction.

I21.01
I22.0

---

4. A patient was admitted to Community Hospital with severe chest pain, which was identified as an acute anterolateral wall <u>infarction</u> (no history of earlier care). Patient was transferred to University Hospital two days later for angioplasty and returned to Community Hospital after three days at University to continue recovery.

Code for first admission to Community Hospital	I21.09
Code for transfer to University Hospital	I21.09
Code for transfer back to Community Hospital	I21.09

5. The patient in the situation described in item 4 above was readmitted to Community Hospital a week later because he was having severe chest pains and was diagnosed with a new inferior wall MI.

	I22.1
	I21.09

If the infarction is described as old or healed, the coder should review the medical record to determine whether the infarction is actually old and/or healed or whether the diagnosis refers to a more recent infarction still under care. A diagnosis of old myocardial infarction is usually made on the basis of electrocardiographic findings or some other investigation in a patient who is not experiencing symptoms. Code **I25.2, Old myocardial infarction,** is essentially a history code, even though it is not included in the Z-code chapter of ICD-10-CM. It should not be assigned when current ischemic heart disease is present and should be assigned as an additional code only when it has some significance for the current episode of care.

Current Complications Following Myocardial Infarction

ICD-10-CM provides codes within category I23 to identify current complications following acute myocardial infarctions when they occur within the 28-day period, as follows:

I23.0   Hemopericardium
I23.1   Atrial septal defect
I23.2   Ventricular septal defect
I23.3   Rupture of cardiac wall without hemopericardium
I23.4   Rupture of chordate tendineae
I23.5   Rupture of papillary muscle
I23.6   Thrombosis of atrium, auricular appendage, and ventricle
I23.7   Postinfarction angina
I23.8   Other complications

A code from category I23 must be used in conjunction with a code from category I21 or category I22. Sequencing of the code from category I23 will depend on the circumstances of admission, as follows:

- If the complication of the MI is the reason for the encounter, the I23 code should be sequenced first.
- If the complication of the MI occurs during the encounter for the MI, the I23 code should be sequenced after the I21 or I22 code.

Other Acute and Subacute Ischemic Heart Disease

Code **I20.0, Unstable angina,** includes conditions described as accelerated angina, crescendo angina, de novo effort angina, intermediate coronary syndrome, preinfarction angina, or worsening effort angina. These conditions occur after less exertion has been expended than in angina pectoris; the pain is more severe and is less easily relieved by nitroglycerin. Without treatment, unstable angina often progresses to acute myocardial infarction.

Code I20.0 is designated as the principal diagnosis only when the underlying condition is not identified and there is no surgical intervention. Patients with severe coronary arteriosclerosis and unstable angina may be admitted for cardiac bypass surgery or a percutaneous transluminal coronary angioplasty to prevent further progression to infarction. In such cases, the combination code for coronary arteriosclerosis with unstable angina (I25.110) is assigned as the principal diagnosis. Examples of appropriate coding follow.

- A patient was admitted with unstable angina and underwent right and left heart catheterization, which showed coronary arteriosclerosis. A coronary bypass procedure was recommended, but the patient felt he needed some time to think it over and to discuss it with his family. For this admission, the coronary arteriosclerosis with unstable angina (I25.110) is the principal diagnosis.

- A patient was admitted with unstable angina and a history of myocardial infarction five years ago. She was treated with IV nitroglycerin, and the angina subsided by the end of the first hospital day. No other complications were noted, and no additional diagnostic studies were carried out. In this case, the unstable angina (I20.0) is the principal diagnosis. Assign also code I25.2 to describe the old MI.

A diagnosis of acute ischemic heart disease or acute myocardial ischemia does not always indicate an infarction. It is often possible to prevent infarction by means of surgery and/or the use of thrombolytic agents if the patient is treated promptly. If there is occlusion or thrombosis of the artery without infarction, code **I24.0, Acute coronary thrombosis not resulting in myocardial infarction,** is assigned. Code **I24.8, Other forms of acute ischemic heart disease,** includes coronary insufficiency and subendocardial ischemia.

Postmyocardial Infarction Syndrome

Patients with acute myocardial infarction sometimes experience postmyocardial infarction syndrome (I24.1) or angina described as postinfarction angina (I23.7). Postmyocardial infarction, also called Dressler's syndrome, is a pericarditis characterized by fever, leukocytosis, pleurisy, pleural effusion, joint pains, and occasionally pneumonia. Except for these two conditions, no code from categories I20 or I24 should be assigned with a code from category I21 or I22.

EXERCISE 28.3

Code the following diagnoses.

1. Acute myocardial infarction,   I21.19
   inferolateral wall   I44.2
   Third-degree atrioventricular block

2. Acute myocardial infarction of   I21.11
   inferoposterior wall   I50.9
   Congestive heart failure   I10
   Hypertension

3. Impending myocardial infarction   I24.0
   (crescendo angina) resulting in
   occlusion of coronary artery

4. Acute coronary insufficiency   I24.8

5. Hemopericardium as a complication of acute   I23.0
   myocardial infarction of the inferior wall, which   I21.19
   occurred three weeks ago. Patient had been discharged
   a week before.

Chronic Ischemic Heart Disease

Category I25, Chronic ischemic heart disease, includes such conditions as coronary atherosclerosis, old myocardial infarction, coronary artery dissection, chronic coronary insufficiency, myocardial ischemia, and aneurysm of heart. Diagnoses of coronary artery disease or coronary heart disease without any further qualification are too vague to be coded accurately; the physician should be asked to provide a more specific diagnosis. Code **I25.9, Chronic ischemic heart disease, unspecified,** should rarely be assigned in an acute care hospital setting.

Code **I25.1-, Atherosclerotic heart disease of native coronary artery,** includes conditions described as atherosclerotic cardiovascular disease, coronary (artery) atheroma, coronary artery disease, and coronary artery sclerosis. A fifth-character subclassification indicates the presence or absence of angina pectoris, with a sixth-character subclassification specifying the type of angina (unstable, with documented spasm, other, or unspecified).

ICD-10-CM has combination codes for atherosclerotic heart disease with angina pectoris, which are included in subcategories I25.11 and I25.7. It is not necessary to use an additional code for angina pectoris when these combination codes are used. A causal relationship can be assumed in a patient with both atherosclerosis and angina pectoris, unless the documentation indicates that the angina is due to a condition other than atherosclerosis. If a patient with coronary artery disease is admitted due to an acute myocardial infarction, the AMI should be sequenced before the coronary artery disease.

Subcategory I25.7, Atherosclerosis of coronary artery bypass graft(s) and coronary artery of transplanted heart with angina pectoris, includes a fifth-character subclassification to provide additional information on the type of bypass graft (unspecified, autologous vein, autologous artery, nonautologous biological coronary artery bypass graft, native artery of transplanted heart, bypass graft of coronary artery of transplanted heart). A sixth-character subclassification specifies the type of angina pectoris (unstable, with documented spasm, other, or unspecified). For atherosclerosis of coronary vessels without angina pectoris, codes from I25.81-, Atherosclerosis of other coronary vessels without angina pectoris, are reported. The sixth character indicates the type of coronary artery (bypass graft, native artery of transplanted heart, or bypass graft of transplanted heart).

For example:

I25.10	Native coronary artery without angina pectoris
I25.710	Autologous vein bypass graft with unstable angina
I25.810	Nonautologous biological bypass graft without angina
I25.810	Artery bypass graft, including internal mammary artery
I25.750	Native coronary artery of transplanted heart with unstable angina
I25.812	Bypass graft (artery) (vein) of transplanted heart
I25.810	Unspecified type of bypass graft
I25.10	Unspecified type of vessel, native or graft

Physicians rarely include information regarding the type of graft in the diagnostic statement, but it is almost always available in the medical record. If the medical record makes it clear that there has been no previous bypass surgery, code **I25.1-, Atherosclerotic heart disease of native coronary artery,** can be assigned. If there is a history of previous bypass, codes I25.70- through I25.73-, I25.79-, or I25.810 should be assigned when information indicating the material used in the bypass is available. Note that arteriosclerosis of a bypass vessel is not classified as a postoperative complication.

When atherosclerosis of a native coronary artery in a transplanted heart is identified in the diagnostic statement, code I25.75- or I25.811 is assigned. Code I25.76- or **I25.812, Atherosclerosis of bypass graft of coronary artery of transplanted heart,** is assigned to identify atherosclerosis of a bypass graft in a transplanted heart.

Chronic Total Occlusion

A chronic total occlusion of coronary artery (I25.82) involves complete blockage of a coronary artery that has been present for an extended period (e.g., months or years). The chronic total occlusion develops when plaque accumulates in the artery, leading to a substantial reduction in blood flow and the development of bypass collateral blood flow. Although well-developed collaterals do not completely compensate for diminished blood flow, they help to preserve the viability of the myocardium and prevent resting ischemia. Patients with chronic total occlusion who present with a change in anginal status that is directly related to physical activity have an increased risk of myocardial infarction or death. Chronic total occlusion of a coronary artery may be treated with angioplasty (root operation "Dilation") or stent placement, usually a drug-eluting stent. These types of obstructions are more resistant to guidewire crossing and are more difficult to treat than other types of coronary stenosis. Advanced methods in treatment have been developed to specifically handle chronic total coronary occlusions.

Code I25.82 should be used as an additional code assignment if coronary atherosclerosis (code series I25.1, I25.7-, I25.81-) is present with a chronic total occlusion of a coronary artery. Code I25.82 should not be assigned if the patient is diagnosed with acute coronary occlusion with or without myocardial infarction.

Code **I25.83, Coronary atherosclerosis due to lipid rich plaque,** describes coronary atherosclerosis with the exact composition of the atherosclerotic plaque. The presence of lipid-rich atherosclerotic plaque can precipitate an acute coronary event. The identification of plaque as lipid rich or non–lipid rich is clinically significant because this information can assist interventional cardiologists in determining the correct treatment (i.e., drug-eluting stent or non-drug-eluting stent). Near infrared spectroscopy (8E023DZ) is a new intravascular diagnostic tool that can detect and differentiate lipid-rich atherosclerotic plaque. When the provider documents lipid-rich plaque, the appropriate code for the coronary atherosclerosis (I25.1-, I25.7-, I25.81-) should be sequenced first, followed by code I25.83 as an additional code assignment.

ANGINA PECTORIS

Angina pectoris (category I20) is an early manifestation of ischemic heart disease, although in rare instances it occurs as a result of congenital abnormalities of the coronary arteries or such conditions as aortic stenosis, valvular insufficiency, aortic syphilis, and Raynaud's phenomenon. It is characterized by chest pain, usually perceived by the patient as a sensation of tightness, squeezing, pressing, choking, burning; of heartburn or gas; or of an ill-defined discomfort. This type of angina can be produced by any activity or situation that increases the oxygen requirements of the myocardium, such as exercise, walking into the wind, cold weather, consumption of a large meal, emotional stress, and elevation of blood pressure. This type of pain is similar to that of unstable angina, but it is less severe; more easily controlled; and usually relieved in a predictable manner by either rest or the administration of nitroglycerin.

Angina pectoris sometimes occurs even when the patient is at rest, apparently without any stimulation, such as during the night. This condition is referred to as nocturnal or decubitus angina and is classified as I20.8. A variant type that also occurs at rest is known as Prinzmetal angina. Angina described as angiospastic, Prinzmetal, spasm induced, or variant is coded to **I20.1, Angina pectoris with documented spasm.** Code **I20.8, Other forms of angina pectoris,** includes angina equivalent, angina of effort, and stenocardia. An additional code(s) for symptoms associated with angina equivalent is assigned.

In today's health care environment, it is unlikely that a patient would be admitted to the hospital for treatment of stable angina except for the purpose of undergoing diagnostic studies to determine its underlying cause. In this case, the underlying cause, not the stable angina, is sequenced as the principal diagnosis.

EXERCISE 28.4

Code the following diagnoses and procedures.

1.	Crescendo angina due to coronary arteriosclerosis	I25.110
	Right and left cardiac catheterization, percutaneous	4A023N8
2.	Angina pectoris with essential hypertension	I20.9
		I10

HEART FAILURE

Heart failure occurs when an abnormality of cardiac function results in the inability of the heart to pump blood at a rate commensurate with the body's needs or the ability to do so only from an abnormal filling pressure. This decrease in blood supply to body tissue results in unmet needs for oxygen as well as in a failure to meet other metabolic requirements. This in turn results in pulmonary and/or systemic circulatory congestion and reduced cardiac output. Precipitating causes of heart failure include cardiac arrhythmias, pulmonary embolism, infections, anemia, thyrotoxicosis, myocarditis, endocarditis, hypertension, and myocardial infarction. All codes for heart failure include any associated pulmonary edema; therefore, no additional code is assigned. A diagnosis of acute pulmonary edema in the absence of underlying heart disease is classified with conditions affecting the respiratory system. (See chapter 19 of this handbook for more information on the respiratory system.)

There are two main categories of heart failure: systolic and diastolic. Systolic heart failure (I50.2-) occurs when the ability of the heart to contract decreases. Diastolic heart failure (I50.3-) occurs when the heart has a problem relaxing between contractions (diastole) to allow enough blood to enter the ventricles. Fifth characters further specify whether the heart failure is unspecified, acute, chronic, or acute on chronic.

When the diagnostic statement lists congestive heart failure along with either systolic or diastolic heart failure, only the code for the type of heart failure is assigned: diastolic and/or systolic. Congestive heart failure is included in the codes for systolic and diastolic heart failure. If congestive heart failure is documented without further specification, it is classified to **I50.9, Heart failure, unspecified.**

Heart dysfunction without mention of heart failure is indexed to **I51.89, Other ill-defined heart diseases.** It is not appropriate for the coder to assume that a patient is in heart failure when only "diastolic dysfunction" or "systolic dysfunction" is documented.

Heart failure is differentiated clinically by whether the right or left ventricle is primarily affected. Left-sided heart failure (left ventricular failure) is due to the accumulation of excess fluid behind the left ventricle. Code **I50.1, Left ventricular failure,** includes associated conditions such as dyspnea, orthopnea, bronchospasm, cardiac asthma, edema of lung with heart disease, edema of lung with heart failure, left heart failure, pulmonary edema with heart disease and with heart failure; therefore, no additional codes are assigned. Heart failure, unspecified, is coded to I50.9. This is a vague code, however, and an effort should be made to determine whether a code from the series I50.1 through I50.4- is more appropriate.

Right-sided failure ordinarily follows left-sided failure and is coded in ICD-10-CM as **I50.9, Heart failure, unspecified.** This code includes any left-sided failure that is present; therefore, codes I50.1 and I50.9 are not assigned for the same episode of care and code I50.9 takes precedence.

The term "congestive heart failure" is often mistakenly used interchangeably with "heart failure." Congestion—pulmonary or systemic fluid buildup—is one feature of heart failure, but it does not occur in all patients.

Hypertensive Heart Disease

Hypertensive heart disease (with or without heart failure) is classified in category I11, with a code from category I50 to identify the type of heart failure (if present) as an additional diagnosis. If chronic kidney disease (N18.-) or unspecified contracted kidney (N26.-) due to hypertension or arteriosclerosis of kidney, arteriosclerotic nephritis, hypertensive nephropathy, or nephrosclerosis is present, a code from category I12 is assigned. The appropriate code from N18.1–N18.4, N18.5, N18.6, or N18.9 is assigned as an additional diagnosis to identify the stage of chronic kidney disease. If hypertensive heart disease and hypertensive chronic kidney disease are present, a code from category I13 is used, with a code from I50.- to identify the type of heart failure (if present), and a code from N18.1–N18.4, N18.5, N18.6, or N18.9 to identify the stage of chronic kidney disease. Category I13 provides different codes to indicate with or without heart failure and/or the stage of the chronic kidney disease. Further information in classifying hypertension and other associated conditions is provided later in this chapter.

Compensated, Decompensated, and Exacerbated Heart Failure

When heart failure occurs, the heart muscle commonly develops compensatory mechanisms such as cardiac hypertrophy, raised arterial pressure, ventricular dilation, or increased force of contraction. When this occurs, the heart failure may be described as *compensated*, permitting near-normal function. When these compensatory mechanisms can no longer meet the increased workload, decompensation of the heart function results; this situation is often described as decompensated heart failure. Code assignment is not affected by the use of these terms; the code for the type of heart failure is assigned. An exacerbation is defined as an increase in the severity of a disease or any of its symptoms. The terms "exacerbated" and "decompensated" indicate that there has been a flare-up (acute phase) of a chronic condition. For example:

- A patient with a known history of congestive heart failure is admitted with an exacerbation of diastolic congestive heart failure. Code **I50.33, Acute on chronic diastolic (congestive) heart failure,** is assigned. An acute exacerbation of a chronic condition (heart failure) is coded as acute on chronic.

CARDIAC TAMPONADE

Cardiac tamponade, also referred to as pericardial tamponade or tamponade (I31.4), is the compression of the heart caused by the accumulation of fluid inside the pericardium. Cardiac tamponade is often associated with viral or bacterial pericarditis. This condition typically occurs as a result of chest trauma, heart rupture, dissecting aortic aneurysm, cancer, cardiac surgery, renal failure, and/or acute myocardial infarction. The underlying cause of the tamponade should be sequenced first, followed by code I31.4.

Cardiac tamponade can be life threatening if left untreated. The goals of therapy are to improve heart function, relieve symptoms, and treat the tamponade. This can be accomplished with pericardiocentesis (root operation "Drainage," body part "pericardial cavity") or creation of a pericardial window (root operation "Drainage," body part "pericardium").

For example, a patient develops increased pericardial effusion and undergoes pericardiocentesis (percutaneous approach) due to rapid pericardial tamponade. Assign code **I31.4, Cardiac tamponade.** For the procedure, assign code **0W9D30Z, Drainage of pericardial cavity with drainage device, percutaneous approach.**

CARDIOMYOPATHY

Cardiomyopathy (I42.-) presents a clinical picture of a dilated heart, flabby heart muscles, and normal coronary arteries. Common types of cardiomyopathy are the following:

I42.0   Dilated cardiomyopathy, which includes congestive cardiomyopathy

I42.1   Obstructive hypertrophic cardiomyopathy, including hypertrophic subaortic stenosis

I42.2   Other hypertrophic cardiomyopathy, including nonobstructive hypertrophic cardiomyopathy

I42.3   Endomyocardial (eosinophilic) disease, including endomyocardial (tropical) fibrosis and Löffler's endocarditis

I42.4   Endocardial fibroelastosis, including congenital cardiomyopathy and elastomyofibrosis

I42.5   Other restrictive cardiomyopathy, including constrictive cardiomyopathy not otherwise specified

I42.6   Alcoholic cardiomyopathy due to alcohol consumption; a code for alcoholism (F10.-) is also assigned if present

I42.7   Cardiomyopathy due to drug and external agent; the code for the cause (T36–T65) is assigned first

I42.8   Other cardiomyopathies

I42.9   Unspecified

The symptoms of congestive cardiomyopathy (I42.0) are essentially the same as those of congestive heart failure, and the condition is often associated with congestive heart failure. Treatment ordinarily revolves around management of the congestive heart failure, and so the heart failure (I50.-) is designated as the principal diagnosis, with an additional code assigned for the cardiomyopathy.

Two codes may be required for cardiomyopathy due to other underlying conditions; for example, cardiomyopathy due to amyloidosis is coded **E85.9, Amyloidosis, unspecified,** and **I43, Cardiomyopathy in diseases classified elsewhere.** The underlying disease, amyloidosis, is sequenced first. Hypertensive cardiomyopathy should be coded to category I11, Hypertensive heart disease, with an additional code of I43. Assign first code **G71.11, Myotonic muscular dystrophy,** with I43 as an additional code assignment for cardiomyopathy due to myotonia atrophica.

The term "ischemic cardiomyopathy" is sometimes used to designate a condition in which ischemic heart disease causes diffuse fibrosis or multiple infarction, leading to heart failure with left ventricular dilation. This is not a true cardiomyopathy and is coded to **I25.5, Ischemic cardiomyopathy,** when no further clarification is provided by the attending physician. A diagnostic statement of ischemic alcoholic cardiomyopathy is assigned to both code I25.5 and code **I42.6, Alcoholic cardiomyopathy,** because these conditions are not related.

TAKOTSUBO SYNDROME

Takotsubo syndrome (I51.81) is a newly recognized reversible form of left ventricular dysfunction, seen in patients without coronary disease. This syndrome is usually precipitated by emotional or physiological stress with sudden onset of chest symptoms, electrocardiographic changes characteristic of myocardial ischemia, transient left ventricular dysfunction, low-grade troponin elevation, and insignificant coronary stenosis by ventriculography. Patients presenting with Takotsubo syndrome are usually monitored and treated for left heart failure, intraventricular obstruction, and/or cardiac arrhythmias if they develop. Other conditions included in code I51.81 are reversible left ventricular dysfunction following sudden emotional stress, stress-induced cardiomyopathy, Takotsubo cardiomyopathy, and transient left ventricular apical ballooning syndrome.

CARDIAC ARREST

Code **I46.9, Cardiac arrest, cause unspecified,** may be assigned as a principal diagnosis only when a patient arrives at the hospital in a state of cardiac arrest and cannot be resuscitated or is resuscitated briefly and pronounced dead before the underlying cause of the arrest is identified. It may be assigned as a secondary code when cardiac arrest occurs during the hospital episode and the patient is resuscitated (or resuscitation is attempted). In this case, the code for the underlying cause is designated the principal diagnosis, with code **I46.2, Cardiac arrest due to underlying cardiac condition,** or code **I46.8, Cardiac arrest due to other underlying condition,** assigned as an additional code. Note that codes are not assigned for symptoms integral to the condition, such as bradycardia and hypotension. Cardiac arrest that occurs as a complication of surgery is coded as **I97.710, Intraoperative cardiac arrest during cardiac surgery,** or **I97.711, Intraoperative cardiac arrest during other surgery,** depending on the type of surgery. Code **O75.4, Other complications of obstetric surgery and procedures,** is assigned for cardiac arrest complicating obstetric surgery or procedures. None of these codes is assigned to indicate that a patient has died; in other words, do not code cardiac arrest to indicate the patient's death.

ANEURYSM

An aneurysm is a localized abnormal dilation of blood vessels. A dissecting aneurysm is one in which blood enters the wall of the artery and separates the layers of the vessel wall. As the aneurysm progresses, tension increases and the aneurysm is likely to rupture, which usually results in death.

Aneurysms are diagnosed primarily according to their location, such as the following:

I25.41	Coronary artery aneurysm
I71.02	Dissecting aneurysm of abdominal aorta
I71.3	Aneurysm of abdominal aorta with rupture
I71.2	Aneurysm of thoracic artery
I71.1	Ruptured aneurysm of thoracic artery
I71.6	Thoracoabdominal aneurysm

Occasionally, a term describing the aneurysm's appearance is used, such as "berry aneurysm" (I67.1), or a term may describe its etiology, such as "syphilitic aneurysm of aorta" (A52.01) or "traumatic aneurysm" (S25.00-, S25.20-).

AORTIC ECTASIA

Aortic ectasia refers to mild dilation of the aorta—usually less than 3 centimeters in diameter—that is not defined as an aneurysm. In ICD-10-CM, aortic ectasia is classified as follows:

I77.810   Thoracic aortic ectasia

I77.811   Abdominal aortic ectasia

I77.812   Thoracoabdominal aortic ectasia

I77.819   Aortic ectasia, unspecified site

CEREBROVASCULAR DISORDERS

Acute organic (nontraumatic) conditions affecting the cerebral arteries include hemorrhage, occlusion, and thrombosis and are coded in the I60–I68 series. Category I63, Cerebral infarction, is used to describe occlusion and stenosis of cerebral and precerebral arteries resulting in cerebral infarction. Please refer to figure 28.4 for an illustration of the types of cerebral infarction. Category I63 is subdivided on the basis of whether the cerebral infarction is due to thrombosis, embolism, occlusion, or stenosis and whether it is a precerebral or cerebral artery, with sixth characters identifying the artery (e.g., right carotid artery, right middle cerebral artery.) These codes should not be assigned unless cerebral infarction is clearly documented in the medical record and the physician has indicated a relationship between the cerebral artery thrombosis, embolism, occlusion, or stenosis and the infarction. The coder should never assume that infarction has occurred. These codes

FIGURE 28.4   Types of Cerebral Infarction

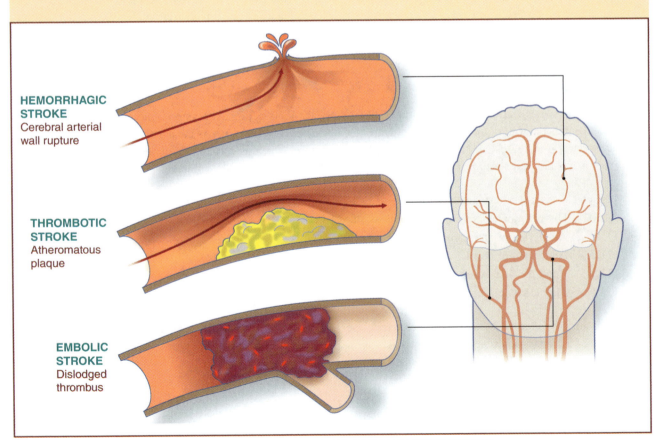

HEMORRHAGIC STROKE
Cerebral arterial wall rupture

THROMBOTIC STROKE
Atheromatous plaque

EMBOLIC STROKE
Dislodged thrombus

apply to the current episode of care only; they do not indicate that the patient has had a cerebral infarction in the past.

When there is occlusion and stenosis of precerebral or cerebral arteries without mention of cerebral infarction, codes from category I65, Occlusion and stenosis of precerebral arteries, not resulting in cerebral infarction, or category I66, Occlusion and stenosis of cerebral arteries, not resulting in cerebral infarction, should be used. Other terms classified to these categories are "embolism," "narrowing," "obstruction" (complete) (partial), and "thrombosis." Fifth characters are provided in subcategories I65.0, I65.2, I66.0, I66.1, and I66.2 to indicate whether the condition is present on the right, left, bilateral, or unspecified arteries.

Diagnostic statements often are not specific regarding the site or type of the cerebrovascular condition. When the diagnosis is stated as cerebrovascular accident (CVA) or stroke without any further qualification, it is important for the coder to review the medical record for more definitive information or to consult with the physician. When no further information is available, code **I63.9, Cerebral infarction, unspecified,** is assigned for the diagnosis of stroke or CVA to allow for improved uniformity in coding and statistical data.

Code I63.9 is assigned for an aborted CVA when there is no further specification as to the type of CVA. Patients who present with symptoms of an acute cerebrovascular infarction and are treated with tissue plasminogen activator (tPA) have actually suffered a cerebral infarction. Although brain damage may not be demonstrated by CT (computed tomography) scan, brain damage would be visible microscopically. The administration of tPA is coded to **3E03317, Introduction of other thrombolytic into peripheral vein, percutaneous approach.** It is effective in treating ischemic stroke caused by blood clots that are blocking blood flow to the brain. It is also effective in treating myocardial infarctions.

Code Z92.82 is assigned as an additional code along with category I63, Cerebral infarction, or I21, ST elevation (STEMI) and non-ST elevation (NSTEMI) myocardial infarction, or I22, Subsequent ST elevation (STEMI) and non-ST elevation (NSTEMI) myocardial infarction, to capture the information that the patient is status post administration of tPA at a different facility within the past 24 hours prior to admission to the current facility.

Each component of a diagnostic statement identifying cerebrovascular disease should be coded unless the Alphabetic Index or the Tabular List instructs otherwise. For example:

I60.7 + I67.2	Cerebrovascular arteriosclerosis with subarachnoid hemorrhage due to ruptured berry aneurysm
I61.9 + G93.6	Intracerebral hemorrhage with vasogenic edema
E85.4 + I68.0	Cerebral amyloid angiopathy

ICD-10-CM provides codes to report a postoperative stroke. However, medical record documentation should clearly specify the cause-and-effect relationship between the medical intervention and the cerebrovascular accident in order to assign a code for intraoperative or postprocedural cerebrovascular accident. Proper code assignment depends on whether it was an infarction or a hemorrhage and whether it occurred intraoperatively or postoperatively. If it was a cerebral hemorrhage, code assignment depends on the type of procedure performed. For example:

G97.31	Intraoperative hemorrhage and hematoma of a nervous system organ or structure complicating a nervous system procedure
G97.32	Intraoperative hemorrhage and hematoma of a nervous system organ or structure complicating other procedure
I97.810	Intraoperative cerebrovascular infarction during cardiac surgery
I97.811	Intraoperative cerebrovascular infarction during other surgery
I97.820	Postprocedural cerebrovascular infarction during cardiac surgery
I97.821	Postprocedural cerebrovascular infarction during other surgery

For codes from subcategory I97.8, assign an additional code to identify the specific type of stroke/cerebrovascular accident. The general coding rule for postoperative complications is that when the complication code does not specifically identify the condition, an additional code should be assigned to more fully explain it.

Conditions classifiable in categories I00 through I99 are reclassified in subcategory O99.4, Diseases of the circulatory system complicating pregnancy, childbirth and the puerperium, when they occur during pregnancy, childbirth, or the puerperium. Because code O99.4- does not indicate the nature of the circulatory system condition, it is appropriate to assign an additional code from chapter 9 of ICD-10-CM for greater specificity.

Sequelae of Cerebrovascular Disease

Codes from category I69, Sequelae of cerebrovascular disease, allow for greater specificity in reporting the residual effects of cerebrovascular diseases. These "late effects" include neurologic deficits that persist after initial onset of cerebrovascular conditions classifiable to categories I60 through I67. The neurologic deficits caused by cerebrovascular disease may be present from the onset or may arise at any time after the onset of the condition classifiable to categories I60 through I67. Fourth-character subclassifications indicate the causal condition (e.g., nontraumatic subarachnoid hemorrhage, cerebral infarction), as follows:

I69.0-	Sequelae of nontraumatic subarachnoid hemorrhage
I69.1-	Sequelae of nontraumatic intracerebral hemorrhage
I69.2-	Sequelae of other nontraumatic intracranial hemorrhage
I69.3-	Sequelae of cerebral infarction
I69.8-	Sequelae of other cerebrovascular diseases
I69.9-	Sequelae of unspecified cerebrovascular diseases

Fifth characters provide information regarding the neurological deficits (with some codes having sixth characters for additional specificity). The fifth characters and the corresponding neurological deficits are as follows:

0	Unspecified sequelae
1	Cognitive deficits
2	Speech and language deficits
3	Monoplegia of upper limb
4	Monoplegia of lower limb
5	Hemiplegia/hemiparesis
6	Other paralytic syndrome
9	Other sequelae (includes apraxia, dysphagia, facial weakness, ataxias, and other sequelae)

Codes for other paralytic syndrome following cerebrovascular disease (I69.06, I69.16-, I69.26-, I69.36-, I69.86-, and I69.96-) provide an instructional note to assign additional codes to indicate the type of paralytic syndrome, such as locked in state (G83.5) or quadriplegia (G82.5-). Also, an additional code should be added to codes I69.091, I69.191, I69.291, I69.391, I69.891, and I69.991 to identify the type of dysphagia, if known. For "other sequelae of cerebrovascular disease" (codes I69.098, I69.198, I69.298, I69.398, I69.898, and I69.998), assign additional codes to identify the specific sequelae.

Codes from category I69 are assigned for any remaining deficits when the patient is admitted at a later date. Like other late effect codes, category I69 is assigned only when it is significant for the current episode of care. Code **Z86.73, Personal history of transient ischemic attack (TIA), and cerebral infarction without residual deficits,** should be assigned rather than a code from category I69 when the patient has a history of a cerebrovascular infarction or CVA with no residual conditions, a history of TIA, a history of prolonged reversible ischemic neurological deficit (PRIND), or a history of reversible ischemic neurological deficit (RIND). Codes from category I69 differ from other late effect codes in two ways:

- These codes can be assigned as the principal diagnosis when the purpose of the admission is to deal with the late effect.
- These codes can be assigned as additional codes when a new CVA is present and deficits from an earlier episode remain. This distinction permits the identification of those deficits due to the current CVA and those remaining from an earlier episode.

Unlike other late effects, neurological deficits such as hemiplegia and aphasia due to cerebrovascular accidents are often present from the onset of the disease rather than arising after the original condition itself has cleared. Report any neurological deficits caused by a CVA even if they have resolved at the time of discharge from the hospital. For example, a patient is admitted because of subarachnoid hemorrhage with associated aphasia and hemiplegia that has cleared by the time of discharge. Even though these deficits have cleared at discharge, the following codes are assigned:

I60.9   Nontraumatic subarachnoid hemorrhage, unspecified
R47.01 Aphasia
G81.90 Hemiplegia

Note that codes from category I69 are not assigned for sequelae of traumatic intracranial injuries. Instead, assign codes from category S06, Intracranial injury, with the seventh-character extension "S" for sequelae.

EXERCISE 28.5

Code the following diagnoses.

---

1. Occlusion of right internal carotid artery   I63.231
    with cerebral infarction with mild hemiplegia   G81.90
    resolved before discharge

---

2. Hemiplegia on right (dominant) side   I69.351
    due to old cerebral thrombosis

---

3. Admission for treatment of new cerebral   I63.40
    embolism with cerebral infarction and   R47.01
    with aphasia remaining at discharge   I69.390
    (patient suffered cerebral embolism one   I69.391
    year ago, with residual apraxia and dysphagia)
                                    Sequelae

---

4. Cerebral infarction due to thrombosis   I63.30
    with right hemiparesis (dominant) and aphasia   G81.91
                                                             R47.01

---

5. Cerebral embolism right anterior cerebral artery   I66.11

---

6. Insufficiency of vertebrobasilar arteries   G45.0

---

7. Admission for rehabilitation because of monoplegia   I69.931
    of the right arm and right leg, each affecting dominant I69.941
    side (patient suffered a nontraumatic extradural
    hemorrhage one month ago)
                                    Sequelae

---

8. Quadriplegia due to ruptured berry aneurysm   I69.265
    five years ago   G82.50

HYPERTENSION

ICD-10-CM classifies hypertension by type as essential or primary (code I10) and secondary (category I15). Categories I10 through I13 classify primary hypertension according to a hierarchy of the disease from its vascular origin (I10) to the end-organ involvement of the heart (I11), chronic kidney disease (I12), or heart and chronic kidney disease combined (I13). Essential hypertension is also described as high blood pressure, primary hypertension, hypertensive vascular disease, or systemic hypertension.

Primary, Transient, and Secondary Hypertension

Malignant hypertension is a sudden and rapid development of extremely high blood pressure. The lower (diastolic) blood pressure reading, which is normally around 80 mm Hg, is often above 130 mm Hg. Without effective treatment, malignant hypertension can lead to congestive heart failure, hypertensive encephalopathy, intracerebral hemorrhage, uremia, and even death.

The term "benign hypertension" refers to a relatively mild degree of hypertension of prolonged or chronic duration. Although malignant hypertension is almost always identified in the diagnostic statement, benign hypertension is rarely specified as a diagnosis. From an ICD-10-CM coding perspective, hypertension described as accelerated, benign, essential, idiopathic, malignant, or systemic is assigned to code **I10, Essential (primary) hypertension.**

Occasionally, the hypertension may be described as controlled or uncontrolled. Uncontrolled hypertension usually refers to an existing state of hypertension that is under control by therapy. Uncontrolled hypertension may refer to untreated hypertension or hypertension that does not respond to current therapeutic regimen. However, whether the hypertension is controlled or not does not affect code selection. Assign the appropriate code from categories I10 through I15, Hypertensive disease.

When the hypertension is described as transient, assign code **R03.0, Elevated blood pressure reading without diagnosis of hypertension,** unless the patient has an established diagnosis of hypertension. For transient hypertension of pregnancy, assign code **O13.-, Gestational [pregnancy-induced] hypertension without significant proteinuria** or **O14.-, Pre-eclampsia.**

Secondary hypertension (category I15) is the result of some other primary disease or underlying condition. When the condition causing the hypertension can be cured or brought under reasonable control, the secondary hypertension may stabilize or disappear entirely. Two codes are required to report secondary hypertension: one for the underlying cause and one from category I15 to identify the secondary hypertension. The sequencing of these codes is dependent on the circumstances of admission or encounter. For example:

M32.10 + I15.8	Hypertension due to systemic lupus erythematosus
I15.2 + E22.0	Acromegaly with secondary hypertension seen for hypertension management

Hypertension described as "controlled" or with "history of" usually refers to an existing hypertension that is under control by means of continuing therapy. The coder should review the medical record to determine whether the hypertension is still under treatment; if so, the appropriate code from categories I10 through I15 should be assigned.

Some providers may document hypertensive urgency without further specification. When only hypertensive urgency is documented, query the provider regarding the specific type of hypertension. If, however, upon clarification the hypertension is still not further specified (e.g., essential or secondary), assign code **I10, Essential hypertension.** The coder is directed to "*See* hypertension" when "urgency, hypertensive" is referenced in the Index.

HYPERTENSIVE HEART DISEASE

Certain heart conditions are assigned to category I11, Hypertensive heart disease, when a causal relationship is stated (due to hypertension) or implied (hypertensive). Hypertensive heart disease includes heart failure, myocarditis, cardiomegaly, cardiovascular disease, and degeneration of the myocardium. Category I11 includes a fifth-character subclassification that indicates whether heart failure is present. However, an additional code from category I50 is still required to specify the type of heart failure, if known.

A cause-and-effect relationship between hypertension and heart disease cannot be assumed, however, and careful attention must be given to the exact wording of the diagnostic statement. When the diagnostic statement mentions both conditions but does not indicate a causal relationship between them, separate codes are assigned, with sequencing being dependent on the circumstances of the admission/encounter. For example:

I11.0 + I50.9	Congestive heart failure due to hypertension
I11.0 + I50.9	Hypertensive heart disease with congestive heart failure
I50.9 + I10	Congestive heart failure with hypertension

A causal relationship is presumed to exist for a cardiac condition when it is associated with another condition classified as hypertensive heart disease. For example:

I11.0 + I50.9	Hypertensive myocarditis with congestive heart failure
I11.0 + I50.9	Hypertensive cardiovascular disease with congestive heart failure

The coder should review the medical record for any reference to the presence of conditions such as coronary arteriosclerosis or chronic coronary insufficiency that could merit additional code assignments.

HYPERTENSION AND CHRONIC KIDNEY DISEASE

When the diagnostic statement includes both hypertension and chronic kidney disease or renal sclerosis (in contrast to hypertension and heart disease), ICD-10-CM usually assumes that there is a cause-and-effect relationship and a code from category I12, Hypertensive chronic kidney disease, is assigned. A causal relationship need not be indicated in the diagnostic statement. A fourth character is used with category I12 to indicate the stage of the chronic kidney disease. The appropriate code from category N18 should be used as a secondary code to identify the stage of chronic kidney disease.

Note that category I12 does not include acute kidney failure, which is an entirely different condition from chronic kidney disease and is not caused by hypertension. Kidney conditions that are not indexed to hypertensive chronic kidney disease may or may not be hypertensive; if the physician indicates a causal relationship, only the code for hypertensive chronic kidney disease is assigned. Sample codes for cases of hypertensive chronic kidney disease include the following:

I12.9	Hypertensive nephropathy, benign
I12.9	Hypertensive nephrosclerosis
I12.9 + N18.3	Accelerated hypertension with chronic kidney disease stage 3
N17.2 + I10	Acute kidney failure with renal papillary necrosis and hypertension

HYPERTENSIVE HEART AND CHRONIC KIDNEY DISEASE

The codes in category I13, Hypertensive heart and chronic kidney disease, are combination codes that include hypertension, heart disease, and chronic kidney disease. The inclusion note at category I13 specifies that the conditions classified to categories I11 and I12 are included together in I13. Therefore, if a patient has hypertension, heart disease, and chronic kidney disease, then a code from I13 should be used rather than individual codes for hypertension, heart disease, and chronic kidney disease, or codes from I11 or I12.

Fourth and fifth characters indicate with or without heart failure, as well as the stage of the chronic kidney disease. Assume a relationship between the hypertension and the chronic kidney disease, whether or not the condition is so designated. If heart failure is present, assign an additional code from category I50 to identify the type of heart failure. The appropriate code from category N18, Chronic kidney disease, should be used as a secondary code, with a code from category I13 to identify the stage of chronic kidney disease. For patients with both acute renal failure and chronic kidney disease an additional code for acute renal failure is required.

When the diagnostic statement indicates hypertension and diabetes mellitus are both responsible for chronic kidney disease, assign the appropriate code from category I12 along with a code from categories E08 through E13, with fifth character of 2, from the subcategory for diabetes with kidney complications. Sequencing is optional. An additional code is assigned for the stage of chronic kidney disease (N18.-), if known.

HYPERTENSION WITH OTHER CONDITIONS

Although hypertension is often associated with other conditions and may accelerate their development, ICD-10-CM does not provide combination codes. Codes for each condition must be assigned to fully describe the condition. For example:

I70.0 + I10	Atherosclerosis of aorta with essential hypertension
I25.10 + I10	Coronary atherosclerosis and systemic hypertension
I25.10	Arteriosclerotic heart disease
I25.10 + I10	Arteriosclerotic heart disease with essential hypertension

Hypertensive Cerebrovascular Disease

For hypertensive cerebrovascular disease, first assign the appropriate code from categories I60 through I69, followed by the appropriate hypertension code (I10–I15).

Hypertensive Retinopathy

Subcategory H35.0, Background retinopathy and retinal vascular changes, should be used with code **I10, Essential (primary) hypertension,** to include the systemic hypertension. The sequencing is based on the reason for the encounter.

EXERCISE 28.6

Code the following diagnoses.

1. Left heart failure with hypertension — I50.9 / I10

2. Hypertensive cardiomegaly — I11.9

3. Congestive heart failure — I50.9
   Cardiomegaly — I51.7
   Hypertension — I10

4. Acute congestive diastolic heart failure due to hypertension — I11.0 / I50.30

5. Hypertensive heart disease — I11.9
   Myocardial degeneration

6. Acute cerebrovascular insufficiency — I67.8

7. Cerebral thrombosis — I66.9
   Moderate arterial hypertension — I10

8. Arteriosclerotic cerebrovascular disease — I67.2
   Hypertension, primary — I10

9. Chronic coronary insufficiency — I25.89
   Essential hypertension — I10

10. Acute coronary insufficiency — I24.8
    Hypertensive heart disease — I11.9

HYPERTENSION COMPLICATING PREGNANCY, CHILDBIRTH, AND THE PUERPERIUM

Hypertension associated with pregnancy, childbirth, or the puerperium is considered to be a complication unless the physician specifically indicates that it is not. This condition includes pre-existing hypertension as well as transient hypertension of pregnancy or hypertension arising during pregnancy. Hypertension complicating pregnancy, childbirth, and the puerperium is reclassified in categories O10 through O11 and O13 through O16. (See chapter 24 of this handbook.)

ELEVATED BLOOD PRESSURE VERSUS HYPERTENSION

Blood pressure readings vary from time to time and tend to increase with age. Because of these variables, a diagnosis of hypertension must be made on the basis of a series of blood pressure readings rather than a single reading. A diagnosis of elevated blood pressure reading, without a diagnosis of hypertension, is assigned code R03.0. This code is never assigned on the basis of a blood pressure reading documented in the medical record; the physician must have specifically documented a diagnosis of elevated blood pressure.

True postoperative hypertension is classified as a complication of surgery, and code **I97.3, Postprocedural hypertension,** is assigned. However, a diagnosis of postoperative hypertension often refers only to an elevated blood pressure that reflects the patient's agitation or inadequate pain control and would be coded to R03.0.

When the patient has a pre-existing hypertension, only a code from categories I10 through I13 is assigned; neither pre-existing hypertension nor simple elevated blood pressure is classified as a postoperative complication. Any other diagnosis of transient hypertension, except that occurring in pregnancy, or a diagnosis of postoperative hypertension not clearly documented in the medical record should be discussed with the physician to determine whether it represents an elevated blood pressure reading or a true hypertension.

ATHEROSCLEROSIS OF EXTREMITIES

Atherosclerosis of the native arteries of the extremities is classified into subcategory I70.2. Fifth characters used with subcategory I70.2, Atherosclerosis of native arteries of the extremities, indicate the progression of the disease as follows:

- Code I70.21- indicates atherosclerosis of the extremities with intermittent claudication.
- Code I70.22- indicates the presence of rest pain; it includes any intermittent claudication.
- Codes I70.23-, I70.24-, and I70.25- indicate a condition that has progressed to ulceration; it includes any rest pain and/or intermittent claudication.
- Code I70.26- indicates the presence of gangrene; it includes any or all of the preceding conditions. Code L98.49- is assigned as an additional code to identify the severity of any ulcer, if applicable.

Atherosclerosis of extremities involving a graft is coded to I70.3- through I70.7-, as follows:

I70.3-	Unspecified graft
I70.4-	Autologous vein bypass graft
I70.5-	Nonautologous biological bypass graft
I70.6-	Nonbiological bypass graft
I70.7-	Other type of bypass graft

Codes from I70.3- through I70.7- provide additional characters to indicate the same progression of disease discussed above under subcategory I70.2, Atherosclerosis of native arteries of the extremities, namely, intermittent claudication, rest pain, ulceration, and gangrene.

A chronic total occlusion of an artery of the extremities (I70.92) develops when hard, calcified plaque accumulates in an artery over an extended period of time, resulting in a clinically significant decrease in blood flow. Approximately 40 percent of patients with peripheral vascular disease present initially with partial occlusion, which progresses to a chronic total occlusion. Intervention with angioplasty and stenting is more complex because passing a guidewire through a total occlusion is extremely difficult.

Code I70.92 should be used as an additional code assignment with subcategories I70.2 through I70.7 when a chronic total occlusion is present with arteriosclerosis of the extremities. An acute total occlusion of a peripheral artery is assigned to code series I74.2-, I74.3-, and I74.4-.

PULMONARY EMBOLISM

An embolus is a blood clot that usually occurs in the veins of the legs (deep vein thrombosis, or DVT). Emboli can dislodge and travel to other organs in the body. A pulmonary embolism is a clot that lodges in the lungs, blocking the pulmonary arteries and reducing blood flow to the lungs and heart. Pulmonary embolic disease may be acute or chronic (long-standing, having occurred over many weeks, months, or years). In the majority of cases, acute pulmonary emboli do not cause chronic disease because the body's mechanisms will generally break down the blood clot.

An acute embolus is usually treated with anticoagulants (e.g., intravenous heparin and warfarin or oral Coumadin) to dissolve the clot and prevent new ones. For acute pulmonary embolism, anticoagulant therapy may be carried out for three to six months. Therapy is discontinued when the embolus dissolves. A filter to interrupt the vena cava is another treatment option. The device filters the blood returning to the heart and lungs until the pulmonary embolism dissolves.

The tulip filter device is indicated in cases of recent pulmonary embolism and proximal DVT with a contraindication to anticoagulation, and as prophylaxis following trauma. When the tulip filter is used on a temporary basis, complications of permanent filters (i.e., thrombosis, migration, inferior vena cava occlusion or perforation, filter fragmentation, and increased risk for DVT) can be avoided. The tulip filter device consists of four legs that form the shape of a cone. A small hook at the base of each leg is used for fixation of the device. Filter wires form the shape of tulip petals, giving the device its name. A hook at the apex of the cone allows the filter to be retrieved, although it may be used as a permanent fixture to manage thromboembolic disease. For example:

- A patient with pulmonary embolism (I26.99) undergoes placement of bilateral common femoral vein tulip filters. Code **06H03DZ, Insertion of intraluminal device into inferior vena cava, percutaneous approach,** is assigned for insertion of the femoral tulip filter.

Acute pulmonary embolisms are classified to category I26, Pulmonary embolism, with fourth characters to indicate whether there is acute cor pulmonale, and fifth characters to indicate septic pulmonary embolism. Code **I26.99, Other pulmonary embolism without acute cor pulmonale,** is used for an acute pulmonary embolism not otherwise specified. Code **I27.82, Chronic pulmonary embolism,** is assigned for a chronic or recurrent pulmonary embolism. In addition, assign code **Z79.01, Long-term (current) use of anticoagulants,** along with code I27.82 to describe any associated long-term use of anticoagulant therapy.

THROMBOSIS AND THROMBOPHLEBITIS OF VEINS OF EXTREMITIES

Deep vein thrombosis and thrombophlebitis are two distinct processes that can coexist. A patient can develop a thrombus with or without inflammation. A diagnosis of thrombosis of a vein indicates that a clot has formed; a diagnosis of thrombophlebitis indicates that the clot has become inflamed. When both thrombosis and thrombophlebitis of the lower extremities are documented, assign only the code from subcategories I82.4-, Acute embolism and thrombosis of deep veins of lower extremity; I82.5-, Chronic embolism and thrombosis of deep veins of lower extremity; and I82.81-, Embolism and thrombosis of superficial veins of lower extremities.

Thrombophlebitis of the extremities is classified according to the veins involved, as follows:

I80.0-	Superficial vessels of lower extremities
I80.1-	Femoral vein
I80.20-	Unspecified deep vessels of lower extremities
I80.21-	Iliac vein
I80.22-	Popliteal vein
I80.23-	Tibial vein
I80.29-	Other deep vessels of lower extremities
I80.3-	Lower extremities, unspecified
I80.8	Other
I80.9	Unspecified site

Deep vein thrombosis, also referred to as venous thromboembolism, is a blood clot in a major vein. DVT generally involves the veins of the lower extremity, but it can also occur in the veins of the upper extremity. With the use of catheters for venous access and cardiac devices, there is increased risk of developing DVT in the upper extremities, such as the axillary, subclavian, or brachiocephalic veins. DVT can occur following orthopedic surgery, pelvic/abdominal surgery, or prolonged inactivity (e.g., long-distance travel, bed rest due to injury or illness, paralysis). Some individuals have a predisposition for developing blood clots due to an abnormality in their blood clotting system (e.g., factor V mutation, protein C or S deficiency, lupus).

Treatment involves anticoagulants to inhibit further development of blood clots or clot-dissolving drugs. In the hospital, heparin is usually administered intravenously. In some cases, a filter is placed in the vena cava to prevent emboli or clots from traveling to the heart and lungs. Following discharge, anticoagulant therapy is recommended for three to six months (or longer). High-risk patients may be maintained on anticoagulant therapy for an indefinite period.

Venous embolism and thrombosis can be of deep vessels or superficial vessels, and it can be acute or chronic, with recurrent episodes. Recurrent deep vein thrombosis can be prevented through prophylactic anticoagulant therapy, venous stasis prevention with gradient elastic stockings, and intermittent pneumatic compression of the legs.

ICD-10-CM classifies venous embolism and thrombosis to category I82, Other venous embolism and thrombosis, according to the veins involved, with the codes for veins of the extremities being further specified as acute or chronic, as follows:

I82.0	Budd-Chiari syndrome
I82.1	Thrombophlebitis migrans
I82.2-	Vena cava and other thoracic veins
I82.3	Renal vein
I82.4-	Deep veins of lower extremity (acute)
I82.5-	Deep veins of lower extremity (chronic)
I82.6-	Veins of upper extremity (acute)
I82.7-	Veins of upper extremity (chronic)
I82.a-	Axillary vein (acute and chronic)
I82.b-	Subclavian vein (acute and chronic)
I82.c-	Internal jugular vein (acute and chronic)
I82.81-	Superficial veins of lower extremities
I82.89-	Other specified veins (acute and chronic)
I82.9-	Unspecified veins

Code **Z79.01, Long-term (current) use of anticoagulants,** is reported along with codes in subcategories I82.5 and I82.7 to describe any associated long-term use of anticoagulant therapy.

Atheroembolism is separate and distinct from atherosclerosis, thrombosis, or embolism. Thrombosis and embolism involve true clots, whereas atheroembolism involves cholesterol crystals from atheromatous plaques from vessels like the aorta or the renal artery. Atheroembolism is most commonly associated with the extremities. Category I75 is used to report atheroembolism.

OTHER CIRCULATORY CONDITIONS

In general, the coding principles applicable throughout ICD-10-CM apply to other sections of the ICD-10-CM chapter on circulatory diseases, which are not discussed specifically in this handbook.

EXERCISE 28.7

Code the following diagnoses and procedures.

1.	Bleeding internal and external hemorrhoids	I84.111
	Stasis ulcer, left lower extremity	I84.121
		I83.029
	Hemorrhoidectomy	0DBQXZZ
		0DBQ7ZZ

2.	Chronic venous embolism and thrombosis	I82.B23
	of subclavian veins on long-term Coumadin therapy	Z79.01
	Chronic orthostatic hypotension	I95.1

---

3. Arteriosclerosis of legs with intermittent
   claudication

   I70.213

---

4. Septic embolism pulmonary artery due to *Staphylococcus*
   Aureus sepsis
   Saphenous phlebitis, right leg

   A41.0
   I26.90
   I80.01

---

5. Pulmonary hypertension

   I27.0

---

6. Raynaud's syndrome with gangrene

   I73.01

---

7. Esophageal varices, hemorrhagic

   I85.01

---

8. Bleeding esophageal varices due to portal hypertension

   Ligation of esophageal varices (endoscopic)

   K76.6
   I85.11
   06L34ZZ

---

9. Arteriosclerotic ulcer and gangrene of left
   lower leg

   I70.262
   L98.499

---

10. Patient was admitted with acute headache and
    problems with vision; condition deteriorated rapidly,
    and patient died within four hours of admission;
    final diagnosis: ruptured berry aneurysm

    I60.7

---

11. Dissecting aneurysm of thoracic aorta
    Excision of the aneurysm with anastomosis
    (open approach)

    I71.01
    02BW0ZZ

STATUS Z CODES

ICD-10-CM provides several Z codes to indicate that the patient has a health status related to the circulatory system, such as the following:

Z94.1	Heart transplant status
Z95.0	Presence of cardiac pacemaker
Z95.1	Presence of aortocoronary bypass graft
Z95.2	Presence of prosthetic heart valve
Z95.3	Presence of xenogenic heart valve
Z95.4	Presence of other heart-valve replacement
Z95.5	Presence of coronary angioplasty implant and graft
Z95.8	Presence of other cardiac and vascular implants and grafts
Z95.810	Presence of automatic (implantable) cardiac defibrillator
Z95.811	Presence of heart assist device
Z95.812	Presence of fully implantable artificial heart
Z95.818	Presence of other cardiac implants and grafts
Z95.82	Presence of other vascular implants and grafts
Z95.820	Peripheral vascular angioplasty status with implants and grafts
Z95.828	Presence of other vascular implants and grafts

These codes are assigned only as additional codes and are reportable only when the status affects the patient's care for a given episode.

PROCEDURES INVOLVING THE CIRCULATORY SYSTEM

Several complex diagnostic tests have been developed for evaluating a patient's circulatory status, and several intensive procedures are currently in use for treating diseases of the circulatory system. The coronary artery bypass, used for patients with severe blockage in the coronary arteries, has been augmented by less invasive procedures, such as angioplasty. Some of these tests and procedures are described briefly in this section.

Intravascular Imaging Procedures

A new imaging technique for diagnosing intravascular vessels is known as intravascular vessel imaging. This procedure utilizes a catheter-based ultrasound imaging method that allows viewing of the vessels from within. The codes for the intravascular imaging procedures are found in the Imaging Section; body system "upper arteries," "lower arteries," or "veins"; root type "Ultrasonography" and qualifier "intravascular," as shown in the example below:

Character 1 Section	Character 2 Body System	Character 3 Root Type	Character 4 Body Part	Character 5 Contrast	Character 6 Qualifier	Character 7 Qualifier
B	4	4	0	Z	Z	3
Imaging	Lower arteries	Ultrasonography	Abdominal aorta	None	None	Intravascular

Other examples of codes for intravascular imaging procedures follow.

B343ZZ3	Ultrasonography of right common carotid artery, intravascular
B344ZZ3	Ultrasonography of left common carotid artery, intravascular
B345ZZ3	Ultrasonography of bilateral common carotid arteries, intravascular

B340ZZ3   Ultrasonography of thoracic aorta, intravascular

B341ZZ3   Ultrasonography of right brachiocephalic-subclavian artery, intravascular

B34JZZ3   Ultrasonography of left upper extremity arteries, intravascular

B240ZZ3   Ultrasonography of single coronary artery, intravascular

Diagnostic Cardiac Catheterization

Cardiac catheterization is an invasive diagnostic procedure performed for diagnosing and assessing the severity of cardiovascular disease. The procedure includes recording intracardiac and intravascular pressures, recording tracings, obtaining blood for blood-gas testing, and measuring cardiac output. A number of other tests involve the insertion of cardiac catheters, but they are not classified as diagnostic catheterization unless a separate procedure with a report including the measurements listed in the preceding sentence has been documented.

ICD-10-PCS classifies cardiac catheterizations to the Measurement and Monitoring Section; "physiological systems" body system; function/device (character 6) "sampling and pressure"; and qualifier specifying whether it was a left heart, right heart, or bilateral catheterization, as shown below.

Character 1 Section	Character 2 Body System	Character 3 Root Type	Character 4 Body Part	Character 5 Approach	Character 6 Function/Device	Character 7 Qualifier
4	A	0	2	3	N	7
Measurement and monitoring	Physiological systems	Measurement	Cardiac	Percutaneous	Sampling and pressure	Left heart

Other examples of cardiac catheterization codes include:

4A023N8   Measurement of cardiac sampling and pressure, bilateral, percutaneous approach

4A023N6   Measurement of cardiac sampling and pressure, right heart, percutaneous approach

4A020N7   Measurement of cardiac sampling and pressure, left heart, open approach

Angiocardiography

Cardiac angiography is a diagnostic test ordinarily performed in conjunction with diagnostic cardiac catheterization. Ergovine provocation testing is often performed in association with coronary arteriograms to diagnose coronary spasm and is included in the code for the coronary arteriogram. Angiographies and arteriographies are classified in ICD-10-PCS in the Imaging Section; root type "Plain radiography" or "Fluoroscopy," depending on the imaging modality used; with the body part character identifying the vessel imaged and whether the contrast material used was high osmolar, low osmolar, or other contrast. For cardiac angiographies, ICD-10-PCS distinguishes in the body part character whether it is single or multiple coronary arteries and whether the procedure was performed on a bypass graft. For example:

B2120ZZ   Fluoroscopy of single coronary artery bypass graft using high osmolar contrast

B211YZZ   Fluoroscopy of multiple coronary arteries using other contrast

B2061ZZ   Plain radiography of right and left heart using low osmolar contrast

Intraoperative Fluorescence Vascular Angiography

Intraoperative fluorescence vascular angiography is a new imaging technology that allows real-time evaluation of the coronary vasculature and cardiac chambers during coronary artery bypass graft (CABG) procedures. It is used to assess the quality of the vascular anastomoses and patency of the graft, with results that are similar to selective coronary arteriography and cardiac catheterization. This new imaging technique is accomplished in less time and without the use of potentially harmful contrast material. This procedure is classified in ICD-10-PCS similar to conventional angiographies with fluoroscopy but distinguished by the use of the qualifier "laser" in character 6 and the qualifier "intraoperative" in character 7. For example, compare these codes with the two fluoroscopy examples listed above under angiocardiography:

B212010   Fluoroscopy of single coronary artery bypass graft using high osmolar contrast, laser intraoperative

B211Y10   Fluoroscopy of multiple coronary arteries using other contrast, laser intraoperative

Intraoperative fluorescence vascular angiography (IFVA) can also be used in noncoronary applications, such as breast cancer surgery, pediatric micro and reconstructive surgery, and other types of tissue reconstruction. In addition, IFVA not only visualizes the coronary vasculature but also enables intraoperative visualization of blood perfusion to the heart muscle, allowing surgeons to successfully perform transmyocardial revascularization (TMR).

Electrophysiologic Stimulation and Recording Studies

Electrophysiologic stimulation and recording studies, commonly referred to as EP studies, are performed as part of the diagnosis and therapeutic management of patients with ventricular tachycardia or ventricular fibrillation, both forms of cardiac arrhythmia that carry a high risk of sudden death. Sometimes a bundle of His electrocardiography will be done as part of an EP study. The bundle of His electrocardiography is a test that measures electrical activity in a part of the heart that carries the signals that control the time between heartbeats (contractions).

EP studies are also performed for patients who have unexplained syncope and palpitation or supraventricular tachycardia. The procedure involves inserting a catheter—a narrow, flexible tube—attached to electricity monitoring electrodes, into a blood vessel, often through a site in the groin or neck, and winding the catheter wire up into the heart. After cardiac access is obtained either percutaneously or via cutdown, specialized electrophysiologic catheter electrodes are inserted and guided into position under fluoroscopy. Once the catheter reaches the heart, electrodes at its tip gather data and a variety of electrical measurements are made. These data pinpoint the location of the faulty electrical site. During this "electrical mapping," the cardiac arrhythmia specialist, an electrophysiologist, may instigate, through pacing (the use of tiny electrical impulses), arrhythmias that are the crux of the problem.

Coding of invasive EP studies requires two codes: **4A023FZ, Measurement of cardiac rhythm, percutaneous approach,** and **3E063KZ, Introduction of other diagnostic substance into central artery, percutaneous approach.**

For noninvasive programmed electrical stimulation, assign code **4A02X4Z, Measurement of cardiac electrical activity, external approach.**

Implant of Automatic Defibrillator/Cardioverter

The automatic implantable cardioverter defibrillator (AICD) is an electronic device designed to detect and treat life-threatening tachyarrhythmias by means of countershocks. Patients receiving this therapy have usually had one or more episodes of life-threatening arrhythmias that cannot be controlled by other therapy.

A total cardioverter defibrillator system implant is usually performed as a single procedure. It includes the formation of a subcutaneous tissue pocket or an abdominal fascia pocket, implantation or replacement of the defibrillator with epicardial patches and any transvenous leads, intraoperative procedures for evaluation of the lead signal, defibrillator threshold measurements, and tests of the implanted device with induction of arrhythmia. During the surgery to implant the AICD, the device is tested by inducing ventricular fibrillation (VF). Shocks are delivered and normal sinus rhythm is restored. A diagnosis of ventricular fibrillation is not coded when it is induced by the use of a defibrillator (shocking) to make sure the AICD recognizes the VF because the arrhythmia is being induced to check the functioning of the device.

The implant is sometimes performed in two stages, however, with the leads implanted first and the generator implanted on a subsequent day during the same hospital admission.

Coding of the insertion of an AICD requires multiple codes, as follows:

1. A code for the insertion of the defibrillator generator into the subcutaneous pocket either into the chest or the abdomen, using either an open approach or a percutaneous approach. Examples of codes:

0JH60P4	Insertion of defibrillator generator into chest subcutaneous tissue and fascia, open approach
0JH63P4	Insertion of defibrillator generator into chest subcutaneous tissue and fascia, percutaneous approach
0JH80P4	Insertion of defibrillator generator into abdomen subcutaneous tissue and fascia, open approach
0JH83P4	Insertion of defibrillator generator into abdomen subcutaneous tissue and fascia, percutaneous approach

2. A code for the insertion of the defibrillator lead(s). There are multiple possible codes depending on whether the lead is inserted into the right atrium, left atrium, right ventricle, or left ventricle. There are also different codes based on whether the leads were inserted using the open or percutaneous approach. Examples of codes follow.

02H60ME	Insertion of defibrillator lead into right atrium, open approach
02H63ME	Insertion of defibrillator lead into right atrium, percutaneous approach
02H64ME	Insertion of defibrillator lead into right atrium, percutaneous endoscopic approach
02H70ME	Insertion of defibrillator lead into left atrium, open approach
02H73ME	Insertion of defibrillator lead into left atrium, percutaneous approach
02H74ME	Insertion of defibrillator lead into left atrium, percutaneous endoscopic approach
02HK0ME	Insertion of defibrillator lead into right ventricle, open approach
02HK3ME	Insertion of defibrillator lead into right ventricle, percutaneous approach
02HK4ME	Insertion of defibrillator lead into right ventricle, percutaneous endoscopic approach
02HL0ME	Insertion of defibrillator lead into left ventricle, open approach
02HL3ME	Insertion of defibrillator lead into left ventricle, percutaneous approach
02HL4ME	Insertion of defibrillator lead into left ventricle, percutaneous endoscopic approach

3. Any extracorporeal circulation (continuous cardiac output) (5A1221Z) or any other con-comitant surgical procedure should also be coded.

There are two codes for the revision or relocation of a cardiac device pocket depending on whether an open or percutaneous approach is used:

0JWT0PZ   Revision of cardiac rhythm related device in trunk subcutaneous tissue and fascia, open approach, or

0JWT3PZ   Revision of cardiac rhythm related device in trunk subcutaneous tissue and fascia, percutaneous approach

These codes may be used for the creation of a pocket for a loop recorder or pocket for an implantable, patient-activated cardiac event recorder. Insertion and relocation of both devices are included in these codes.

When a patient is admitted for replacement or adjustment of an automatic cardioverter/defibrillator, code **Z45.02, Encounter for adjustment and management of automatic implantable cardiac defibrillator,** is assigned as the principal diagnosis unless the procedure is being performed because of a mechanical complication, in which case a code from subcategory T82.1, Mechanical complication of cardiac electronic device, is assigned. When only the leads are replaced, code the removal of the old lead, and then the insertion of the new lead. When only the pulse generator is replaced, code the removal of the old generator as well as the insertion of the new generator. For example, if the pulse generator is removed from the chest and replaced with a new one, code both procedures using the open approach:

0JPT0PZ   Removal of cardiac rhythm related device from trunk subcutaneous tissue and fascia, open approach, and

0JH60P4   Insertion of defibrillator generator into chest subcutaneous tissue and fascia, open approach

Automatic implantable cardioverter/defibrillators sometimes require checking of the pacing thresholds or interrogation without arrythmia induction. This procedure is coded to **4B02XTZ, Measurement of cardiac defibrillator, external approach.** For example, a bedside check or interrogation of an AICD device is assigned to code 4B02XTZ.

Cardiac Pacemaker Therapy

Cardiac pacemaker therapy (figure 28.5) involves electrical control of the heart rate. ICD-10-CM codes differentiate between the insertion of temporary pacemakers and the insertion of permanent pacemakers. In a temporary pacemaker insertion, leads are inserted via a catheter and attached to an external pulse generator. This type of pacemaker is generally used for an acutely ill patient until a permanent pacemaker can be inserted. Another type of temporary pacemaker is used intraoperatively or immediately following surgery, with the leads inserted into the myocardium in an already-opened chest. These procedures are classified to **5A1213Z, Performance of cardiac pacing, intermittent,** or **5A1223Z, Performance of cardiac pacing, continuous,** plus the appropriate code for the lead insertion.

A temporary transmyocardial pacemaker, in which a needle is inserted into the chest and into the myocardium with leads fed through the needle directly into the heart muscle and attached to an external pacing device, is sometimes used in an effort at cardiopulmonary resuscitation. This procedure is considered an integral part of cardiopulmonary resuscitation (5A2204Z), and no additional code is assigned.

At least two codes are required for the initial insertion of a permanent pacemaker. One code indicates the type of device, commonly called a pulse generator, which is coded to the Medical and Surgical Section; "subcutaneous tissue and fascia" body system; root operation "Insertion"; device "cardiac rhythm related device," with the character 7, qualifier, providing information regarding the type of pacemaker (single chamber, single chamber rate responsive, or dual chamber). Separate codes are used to report the insertion of the leads.

Pacemaker leads (electrodes) can be placed either transvenously into the inside of the heart or epicardially onto the outside of the heart. In order to insert a transvenous lead into the ventricle, an incision is made in the skin and the lead is passed into the subclavian vein, down the superior vena cava, across the right atrium, and into the right ventricle. When transvenous leads are used, the pacemaker device is ordinarily placed in a subcutaneous pocket in the upper chest wall. Code 0JWT0PZ or 0JWT3PZ is assigned for the revision or relocation of a pocket for a pacemaker, defibrillator, or other implanted cardiac device.

No incision into the chest cavity is needed for the insertion of an epicardial lead. The most common site for the pacemaker pocket when epicardial leads are used is the abdominal wall.

There are three types of pacemaker devices on the market—single chamber, single chamber rate responsive, and dual chamber—each of which has a unique ICD-10-CM seventh-character value for its insertion. For example, for a single-chamber pacemaker inserted into a chest pocket using an open approach, code **0JH60P0, Insertion of single chamber pacemaker into chest subcutaneous tissue and fascia, open approach,** is assigned.

FIGURE 28.5   Pacemaker Insertion

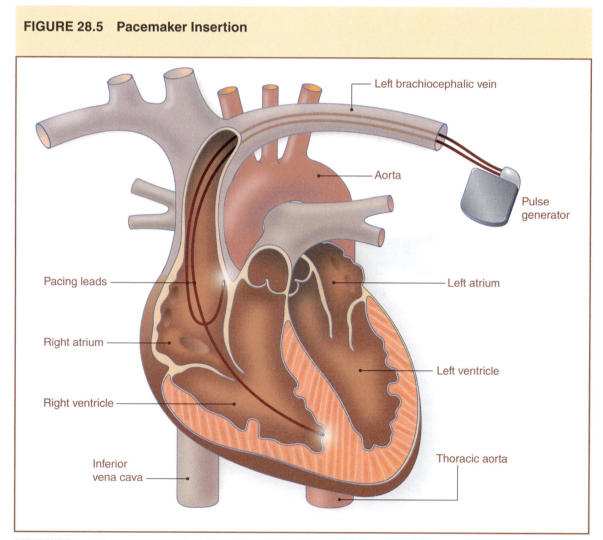

A single-chamber device uses a single lead; a dual-chamber device requires two leads, one in the atrium and one in the ventricle. It is important to be sure that the code for the lead insertion and the code for the pacemaker device are compatible. A rate-responsive device is one in which the pacing rate is determined by physiological variables other than the atrial rate. This type of pacemaker permits patients to lead a more normal life and is strongly preferred for a potentially active patient. Physicians use various terms for this ability to respond and in many cases mention only the device number in documenting an insertion. The coding department should work with the hospital operating room staff and/or physicians to identify the devices commonly used in the facility and how they might be consistently identified in the operative report.

For example, insertion of a dual-chamber permanent pacemaker with electrodes into the right atrium and right ventricle is coded to:

0JH60P2   Insertion of dual chamber pacemaker into chest subcutaneous tissue and fascia, open approach

02H63MA   Insertion of pacemaker lead into right atrium, percutaneous approach

02HK3MA   Insertion of pacemaker lead into right ventricle, percutaneous approach

Sometimes pacemakers require replacement of the pulse generator, or there may be a need to upgrade from a single-chamber pacemaker to a dual-chamber pacemaker. ICD-10-PCS provides individual codes for each component of the procedure. For example, a replacement of the pulse generator alone requires codes for the removal of the old generator and insertion of the new generator. Similarly, if replacement of the existing leads is required, codes will be required for the removal of the old leads, as well as codes for the insertion of the new leads.

For example, if a single-chamber pacemaker is removed from the chest and replaced with a new one, code both procedures using the open approach:

0JPT0PZ   Removal of cardiac rhythm related device from trunk subcutaneous tissue and fascia, open approach, and

0JH60P0   Insertion of single chamber pacemaker into chest subcutaneous tissue and fascia, open approach

When an existing pacemaker device is replaced with a new device, the type of device removed does not affect the removal code. ICD-10-PCS provides a single code (0JPT0PZ) for removal of cardiac rhythm–related device from the chest or abdomen—whether pacemaker or cardiac defibrillator. However, the codes for device insertion do provide information regarding the type of cardiac rhythm device.

When a patient is admitted for routine removal, replacement, or reprogramming of a cardiac pacemaker, code **Z45.010, Encounter for checking and testing of cardiac pacemaker pulse generator [battery],** or code **Z45.018, Encounter for adjustment and management of other part of cardiac pacemaker,** is assigned as the principal diagnosis. Reprogramming is a simple nonoperative procedure that does not require a procedure code. Physicians sometimes indicate that a patient is being admitted for battery replacement. This is something of a misnomer because pacemakers no longer use batteries and the whole device is actually replaced. When the pacemaker device is being replaced only because it is nearing the end of its expected life, code Z45.010 or Z45.018 is assigned as the principal diagnosis. When it is being replaced because of a mechanical complication of the device, a code from subcategory T82.1, Mechanical complication of cardiac electronic device, is assigned.

Cardiac Resynchronization Therapy

Cardiac resynchronization therapy (CRT) is a newer technology similar to conventional pacemaker therapy and implantable cardioverter defibrillators. CRT is different because it requires the implantation of a special electrode within the coronary vein to attach the device to the exterior wall of the left ventricle. CRT treats heart failure by providing strategic electrical stimulation to the right atrium, right ventricle, and left ventricle of the heart to recoordinate ventricular contractions and improve cardiac output. CRT is also sometimes referred to as biventricular pacing.

ICD-10-PCS codes distinguish between the insertion of cardiac resynchronization pacemaker without internal cardiac defibrillator (CRT-P) and the insertion of cardiac resynchronization defibrillator (CRT-D). The codes differ in the values for the seventh-character qualifier, which distinguish between "cardiac resynchronization pacemaker pulse generator" and "cardiac resynchronization defibrillator pulse generator," as shown in the examples below, when these pulse generators are inserted using a percutaneous approach:

0JH63P3   Insertion of cardiac resynchronization pacemaker pulse generator into chest subcutaneous tissue and fascia, percutaneous approach

0JH63P5   Insertion of cardiac resynchronization defibrillator pulse generator into chest subcutaneous tissue and fascia, percutaneous approach

No additional codes are assigned for the creation of the pocket to hold the device, implantation of the device, or intraoperative procedures to evaluate lead signals. However, separate codes are required for the insertion of the transvenous leads.

For the CRT-P, codes are needed for the insertion of pacemaker leads into the right or left ventricle (e.g., **02HK3MA, Insertion of pacemaker lead into right ventricle, percutaneous approach**). For the CRT-D, codes are needed for the insertion of defibrillator leads (e.g., **02HK3ME, Insertion of defibrillator lead into right ventricle, percutaneous approach; 02HL3ME, Insertion of defibrillator lead into left ventricle, percutaneous approach; 02H43ME, Insertion of defibrillator lead into coronary vein, percutaneous approach**).

Over time, there may be a need to replace the lead into the left ventricular coronary venous system, replace the pacemaker pulse generator on a CRT-P, or replace the defibrillator pulse generator on a CRT-D. In all of these situations, code the removal and insertion of the replacement device separately. When the leads are repositioned only (not replaced), the code for the root operation "Revision" is assigned. For example, code **02WA3MZ, Revision of cardiac lead in heart, percutaneous approach,** is assigned for repositioning of the CRT-D or CRT-P lead only via a percutaneous approach.

Cardiac Contractility Modulation

The cardiac contractility modulation (CCM) system is a new treatment modality for patients with moderate to severe heart failure resulting from either ischemic or nonischemic cardiomyopathy. In cardiac contractility modulation, nonstimulatory impulses are delivered during the absolute refractory period to enhance cardiac function and contractility. The CCM system is dissimilar to a cardiac pacemaker because the signals do not initiate a new heartbeat; instead, they are intended to improve the strength of the heart.

The implantable pulse generator produces signals delivered to the heart via the pacemaker leads. Three leads are implanted in the heart: two leads are placed in the right ventricular septum, and a third lead is placed in the right atrium. The leads are connected to a pulse generator, and the generator is placed in a subcutaneous pectoral pocket. An external programmer allows medical personnel to customize the signal parameters according to the patient's specific needs. The charger allows the patient to recharge the battery of the pulse generator in the comfort of his or her home.

The implantation of the CCM system can occur alone, in the presence of an AICD, or in combination with implantation of both a CCM system and an AICD. Coding for the insertion of the CCM device is similar to the coding of pacemakers and cardiac resynchronization devices. A code is required for the insertion of the device, similar to the pacemaker, CRT-D, and CRT-P, but with a different seventh-character qualifier value for "contractility modulation device" and separate codes for the insertion of the leads. For example:

0JH63PA	Insertion of contractility modulation device into chest subcutaneous tissue and fascia, percutaneous approach
02HK3MZ	Insertion of cardiac lead into right ventricle, percutaneous approach; assigned only once, even though two leads are inserted into the ventricle, because it does not meet the ICD-10-PCS guideline for reporting of multiple procedures
02H63MZ	Insertion of cardiac lead into right atrium, percutaneous approach

Percutaneous Mitral Valve Repair

The MitraClip® implant is a minimally invasive, closed chest, catheter-based approach for intracardiac repair of mitral regurgitation caused by valve pathology and/or left ventricular dysfunction. The procedure is performed on a beating heart and is an alternative to the open heart surgical approach. Interventional cardiologists can perform the procedure in the cardiac catheterization laboratory or in a hybrid operating suite under general anesthesia. The procedure does not require cardiopulmonary bypass. Insertion of the MitraClip® implant is coded to **02UG3JZ, Supplement mitral valve with synthetic substitute, percutaneous approach.**

Percutaneous Balloon Valvuloplasty

Percutaneous balloon valvuloplasty (027H3ZZ) is a noninvasive treatment for pulmonary valve stenosis. It involves a balloon wedge catheter that is advanced via the femoral vein into the heart and across the stenotic valve. The balloon is then inflated by hand pressure. There is no need for general anesthesia, the hospital stay is short, and no scarring results from the procedure.

Percutaneous Transluminal Coronary Angioplasty

Percutaneous transluminal coronary angioplasty (PTCA) procedures are classified in the Medical and Surgical Section to the root operation "Dilation," percutaneous approach. Code selection is based on the number of coronary artery sites treated using the fourth-character, body part value to indicate coronary artery at one site, two sites, three sites, or four or more sites. Coronary arteries are classified by the number of distinct sites treated rather than the number of coronary arteries or the anatomic name of a coronary artery (e.g., left anterior descending).

When a thrombolytic agent is also administered, assign a separate code, for example, code **3E03317, Introduction of other thrombolytic into peripheral vein, percutaneous approach.**

Because reclosure often occurs following angioplasty, a stent is frequently inserted to prevent reclosure. Please refer to figure 28.6 for an illustration of angioplasty with stent insertion. In this procedure, a small, stainless steel mesh stent is inserted during angioplasty to prop open the blocked coronary arteries. After the balloon has been threaded into the coronary artery and inflated to squash plaque deposits against the vessel wall, the process is repeated with a second balloon carrying the stent. Expansion of the balloon pushes the stent against the artery wall, where it remains to maintain patency.

ICD-10-PCS provides different values for character 6, device, to identify whether a "drug-eluting intraluminal device (stent)," "intraluminal device (stent)," "radioactive intraluminal device," or no device was used. Note that a separate procedure code is coded for each artery dilated when the device value differs for each artery. For example, when PTCA of two coronary artery sites is performed, one with a drug-eluting stent and the other with a non-drug-eluting stent, code **027034Z, Dilation of coronary artery, one site with drug-eluting intraluminal device, percutaneous approach,** and **02703DZ, Dilation of coronary artery, one site with intraluminal device, percutaneous approach.**

ICD-10-PCS coronary dilation root operations provide a seventh-character qualifier to report when the procedure is performed at a vessel bifurcation. Use of this qualifier captures data regarding the procedural differences between interventional procedures on a straight vessel and a vessel bifurcation. Bifurcation lesions usually involve blockages of a main coronary vessel and an adjacent side vessel, resulting in a lesion that is more complex to treat.

Minor intimal tears often occur during angioplasty or the newer rotational atherectomy procedures; these are considered to be an unavoidable part of the procedure and are not classified as complications.

FIGURE 28.6   Angioplasty with Stent Insertion

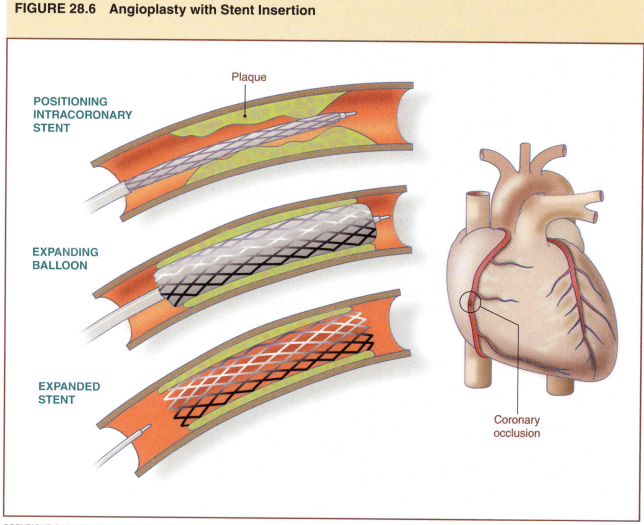

Angioplasty of Noncoronary Vessels

ICD-10-PCS provides myriad unique codes to report angioplasty of noncoronary vessels. Because of the level of detail available, the circulatory system is divided into several body systems, such as "heart and great vessels," "upper arteries," "lower arteries," "upper veins," and "lower veins." The diaphragm is the dividing line for determining where the code is classified. For example, the subclavian vein is located above the diaphragm and is found in the "upper veins" body system, while the femoral vein is located below the diaphragm and is found in the "lower veins" body system. Angioplasty procedures are classified to the root operation "Dilation" and include different values for the device character 6 to distinguish "drug-eluting intraluminal device," "intraluminal device (non-drug eluting)," or no device.

Examples of codes for noncoronary vessel angioplasty procedures include:

027V3ZZ   Dilation of superior vena cava, percutaneous approach

047H3DZ   Dilation of right external iliac artery with intraluminal device, percutaneous approach

047P34Z   Dilation of right anterior tibial artery with drug-eluting intraluminal device, percutaneous approach

037J34Z   Dilation of left common carotid artery with drug-eluting intraluminal device, percutaneous approach

037G3ZZ   Dilation of intracranial artery, percutaneous approach

If a thrombolytic agent is used, it should be assigned as an additional code, with the appropriate code from the Administration Section, root type "Introduction." For example:

3E03317   Introduction of other thrombolytic into peripheral vein, percutaneous approach

3E04317   Introduction of other thrombolytic into central vein, percutaneous approach

3E05317   Introduction of other thrombolytic into peripheral artery, percutaneous approach

Coronary Artery Bypass Graft

CABGs are performed to revascularize the myocardium when a blockage in a coronary artery limits the blood supply to the heart. The grafts bypass the obstructions in the coronary arteries. (See figure 28.7.)

Coronary circulation consists of two main arteries, right and left, each with several branches:

- Right coronary artery (RCA)
  —Right marginal
  —Right posterior descending (PDA)
- Left main coronary artery (LMCA)
  —Left anterior descending branch (LAD)
  —Diagonal
  —Septal
  —Circumflex (LCX)
  —Obtuse marginal (OM)
  —Posterior descending
  —Posterolateral

The aortocoronary artery bypass is the one most commonly used. It brings blood from the aorta into the obstructed coronary artery, bypassing the obstruction by means of a segment of the patient's own saphenous vein, nonautologous biological material, or occasionally a segment of the internal mammary artery.

Coronary artery procedures are classified by the number of distinct sites treated rather than the number of coronary arteries or the anatomic name of a coronary artery (e.g., left anterior descending). Coronary artery bypass procedures are coded differently from other bypass procedures. Rather than identifying the body part bypassed from, the body part identifies the number of coronary artery sites bypassed to, and the qualifier specifies the vessel bypassed from. For example, aortocoronary artery bypass of one site on the left anterior descending coronary artery and one site on the obtuse marginal coronary artery is classified in the body part axis of classification as two coronary artery sites, and the qualifier specifies the aorta as the body part bypassed from.

ICD-10-PCS also identifies the type of tissue used in the device character 6 as "autologous venous tissue," "autologous arterial tissue," "synthetic substitute," or "nonautologous tissue substitute."

Examples of aortocoronary bypass procedure codes follow.

021009W	Bypass coronary artery, one site to aorta with autologous venous tissue, open approach
02100JW	Bypass coronary artery, one site to aorta with synthetic substitute, open approach
02110KW	Bypass coronary artery, two sites to aorta with nonautologous tissue substitute, open approach

FIGURE 28.7 Coronary Artery Bypass Graft

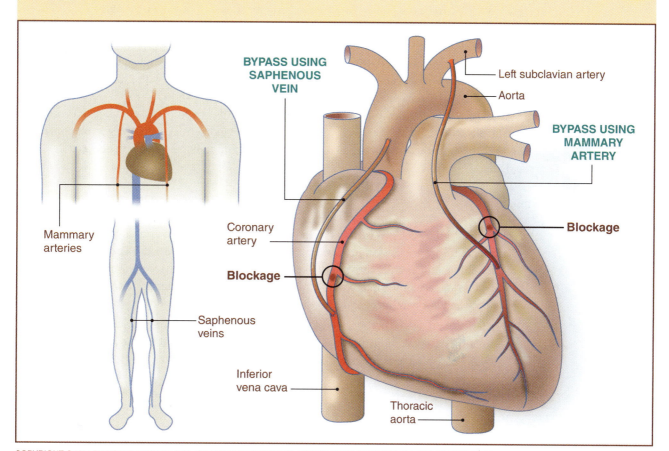

All coronary bypass procedures do not involve the aorta. The internal mammary-coronary artery bypass graft is accomplished by loosening the internal mammary artery from its normal position and using it as a conduit to bring blood from the subclavian artery to the occluded coronary artery. When coding internal mammary-coronary artery bypass grafts, the body part identifies the number of coronary artery sites bypassed to, and the qualifier specifies the vessel bypassed from— namely, the internal mammary artery. ICD-10-PCS also identifies the type of tissue used in the device character 6 as "autologous venous tissue," "autologous arterial tissue," "synthetic substitute," or "nonautologous tissue substitute."

Examples of internal mammary-coronary artery bypass procedure codes follow.

02100Z8   Bypass coronary artery, one site to right internal mammary, open approach

02110J9   Bypass coronary artery, two sites to left internal mammary with synthetic substitute, open approach

It is rare for only one coronary artery to be bypassed, and it is also fairly common to perform both an internal mammary-coronary artery bypass and an aortocoronary bypass at the same operative episode. The surgeon's brief statement of the operation performed does not always distinguish the types of bypasses involved, which makes it necessary for the coder to refer to the body of the operative report when the statement is not clear.

When multiple coronary artery sites are bypassed, a separate procedure is coded for each coronary artery site that uses a different device and/or qualifier. For example, aortocoronary artery bypass and internal mammary coronary artery bypass are coded separately.

Other arteries are also used to bypass an obstruction in the coronary artery. ICD-10-PCS distinguishes these procedures by the use of different values for character 7, qualifier, such as thoracic artery and abdominal artery. For example:

02130ZC   Bypass coronary artery, four or more sites to thoracic artery, open approach

02130ZF   Bypass coronary artery, four or more sites to abdominal artery, open approach

If an autograft is obtained from a different body part in order to complete the objective of the procedure, a separate procedure is coded. For example, coronary bypass with excision of saphenous vein graft, excision of saphenous vein, is coded separately.

An additional code should also be assigned for any use of extracorporeal circulation (continuous cardiac output) (5A1221Z). However, procedures such as hypothermia, cardioplegia, intraoperative pacing, and chest tube insertions are considered to be integral to bypass surgery; no separate codes are assigned.

In coding coronary artery bypass procedures, it is important to keep the following points in mind:

- The fact that a detached segment of the internal mammary artery is used as graft material instead of saphenous vein in performing an aortocoronary bypass does not make it an internal mammary-coronary artery bypass. The internal mammary-coronary artery bypass involves the use of the internal mammary itself as a still vascularized conduit for the blood supply and does not involve the aorta.

- When more than one coronary artery is involved in either type of graft, the anastomosis is sometimes carried out in a sequential manner, bypassing more than one artery. The mention of sequential anastomoses does not affect the code in any way.

The following examples may provide further assistance in coding coronary bypass grafts:

1. Coronary artery vascularization (via thoracotomy) is carried out with four grafts: the aorta to the diagonal branch of the left coronary and in sequential fashion to the obtuse marginal branch of the circumflex, the right coronary artery, and the left anterior descending coronary artery. This procedure involves only the aorta and the coronary arteries. Because four coronary arteries were bypassed, code **02130AW, Bypass coronary artery, four or more sites to aorta with autologous arterial tissue, open approach,** is assigned.

2. During an open procedure, grafts from the aorta to the coronary arteries are carried out by grafting the bifurcated left anterior descending system with a 1.5-millimeter section of the left internal mammary artery. The first diagonal was then grafted side-to-side with a 4-millimeter section of the saphenous vein. The obtuse marginal was then grafted with a 4-millimeter section of the saphenous vein. The posterior descending was diffusely diseased and was grafted with a 4-millimeter section of the right greater saphenous vein. All four grafts bring blood from the aorta to the coronary arteries. Sections of both the saphenous vein and the internal mammary artery are used for this purpose. Because four arteries (LAD, diagonal, obtuse marginal, and posterior descending) were bypassed, code **021309W, Bypass coronary artery, four or more sites to aorta with autologous venous tissue, open approach,** and code **06BP0ZZ, Excision of right greater saphenous vein, open approach,** are assigned.

3. Bypass grafts are performed (via thoracotomy) by bringing the left internal mammary artery to the left anterior ascending; a right greater saphenous vein graft is then used to bring blood from the aorta to the obtuse marginal branch of the circumflex artery, to the diagonal artery, and to the proximal PDA. In this case, a single internal mammary-coronary artery bypass and three aortocoronary bypass grafts are placed (OM, diagonal, PDA). The codes assigned are **02100Z9, Bypass coronary artery, one site to left internal mammary, open approach; 06BP0ZZ, Excision of right greater saphenous vein, open approach;** and **021209W, Bypass coronary artery, three sites to aorta with autologous venous tissue, open approach.** The sequence of the codes is optional.

4. The left internal mammary artery is loosened and used to bypass the left anterior descending artery; grafts of the right great saphenous vein are bypassed to the posterior descending artery and to the obtuse marginal branch of the circumflex. In this case, three coronary arteries are bypassed, one by an internal mammary-coronary artery bypass and two by aortocoronary bypasses. The codes assigned are **02100Z9, Bypass coronary artery, one site to left internal mammary, open approach; 06BP0ZZ, Excision of right greater saphenous vein, open approach;** and **021109W, Bypass coronary artery, two sites to aorta with autologous venous tissue, open approach.**

Heart revascularization is also performed by other techniques. Transmyocardial revascularization is a procedure that uses a laser to bore holes through the myocardium to restore perfusion to areas of the heart where blood flow may be impaired due to diseased or clogged arteries. TMR is coded to the root operation "Repair" (restoring, to the extent possible, a body part to its normal anatomic structure and function). Although TMR does not restore the heart's anatomic structure, the procedure is performed to restore function to the heart. The procedure can be performed by open approach (02QA0ZZ, 02QB0ZZ, or 02QC0ZZ), percutaneous endoscopic approach (02QA4ZZ, 02QB4ZZ, or 02QC4ZZ), and percutaneous or endovascular procedures (02QA3ZZ, 02QB3ZZ, or 02QC3ZZ).

EXERCISE 28.8

Code the following diagnoses and procedures.

1. A patient was admitted through the
   emergency department complaining of chest
   pain with radiation down the left arm increasing
   in severity over the past three hours. Initial
   impression was impending myocardial infarction,
   and the patient was taken directly to the surgical suite,
   where percutaneous transluminal angioplasty with
   insertion of coronary stent was carried out on the right
   coronary artery. Infarction was aborted, and the
   diagnosis was listed as acute coronary insufficiency.

   I24.8
   02703DZ

2. Right greater saphenous vein graft was used to bring
   blood from the aorta to the right coronary artery,
   the left coronary artery, and the left anterior descending
   artery. Intraoperative pacemaker was used
   during the procedure as well as extracorporeal
   circulatory assistance.

   Bypass

   021209W
   06BP0ZZ
   5A1221Z

3. Right and left diagnostic cardiac
   catheterization

   4A023N8

4. Balloon angioplasty carried out on three
   coronary arteries with vessel bifurcation

   Insertion of two stents
   Extracorporeal circulation (continuous cardiac output)

   Performance

   02723D6
   5A1221Z

5. Initial insertion of dual-chamber
   pacemaker device into chest, percutaneous approach
   Leads right ventricle and right atrium

   0JH63P2
   02HK3MA
   02H63MA

6. Patient was <u>admitted</u> for replacement of   Z45.010
   single-chamber pacemaker device because   0JH63P1
   the battery was expected to fail within a   0JPT3PZ
   short time; device was <u>replaced</u> with
   single-chamber, rate-responsive pacemaker device.
   No leads needed to be replaced.

7. Patient was admitted for <u>replacement</u> of   T82.121A
   displaced and protruding pacemaker device   0JH63P1
   with single-chamber, rate-responsive device.

   <u>Complication, mechanical</u>

8. Catheter-based invasive electrophysiological cardiac study   4A023FZ
   (via femoral artery)   3E053KZ

Exclusion or Excision of the Left Atrial Appendage

Exclusion or excision of the left atrial appendage (LAA) is a component of most operations to treat atrial fibrillation (AF) and reduces late thromboemboli in patients with AF undergoing mitral valve surgery. LAA aneurysm is a rare anomaly, which usually presents with arrhythmia or cerebral embolism. Coding of this procedure depends on the technique used, such as "Excision," "Destruction," or "Repair." For example:

02Q74ZZ   Left-sided thoracoscopic stapling of the left atrial appendage

Surgical Ventricular Restoration

Surgical ventricular restoration (SVR) is a surgical technique that reshapes the heart and includes operative methods that reduce left ventricular volumes and restore elliptical shape to the left ventricle. With SVR, the ventricle is not excised. For example:

- A patient develops a ventricular aneurysm and undergoes surgical ventricular restoration and cardiopulmonary bypass. Code **I25.3, Aneurysm of heart,** is assigned as the principal diagnosis. Code **02QA0ZZ, Repair of heart, open,** is assigned for the SVR, and code **5A1221Z, Performance of cardiac output, continuous,** is assigned for the cardiopulmonary bypass.

Thoracoscopic and Thoracoscopically Assisted Ablation of Heart Tissue (Maze Procedure)

The maze procedure is a surgical treatment used for atrial fibrillation by creating lines of conduction block in the heart itself. The classic maze procedure is performed through an open chest approach, creating the lines with a scalpel by a carefully placed pattern of incisions in the heart tissue. Scar tissue (lesions) forms as the incisions heal, which creates the conduction block. There are variations called maze 1, maze 2, and maze 3, which represent different patterns of incisions. Through the years, various approaches for the maze procedure have been developed.

The open approach (02560ZZ, 02570ZZ) is the traditional method of surgery and is performed via a median sternotomy or thoracotomy. "Cut-and-sew" was the original open technique, involving incisions into the atrial tissue followed by reconstruction of the atria. Because of the difficulties and risks associated with multiple atrial incisions, more recently a series of linear ablations are being performed. There is a variety of energy sources used for ablation (e.g., radiofrequency, cryothermy, microwave, laser, ultrasound). The energy source is delivered via a probe or a clamp instrument and can be applied at strategic locations within the heart or on the heart's surface. The creation of the incisions/ablation lines can be directly visualized with the open approach.

Endovascular (percutaneous) approaches (02563ZZ, 02573ZZ) through peripherally inserted cardiac catheters have also been developed. Endovascular ablations have been very effective in the treatment of arrhythmias, including atrial fibrillation and atrial flutter, resulting from a single abnormal source (i.e., ectopic focus) of electrical stimulation on the right side of the heart.

The thoracoscopic approach (02564ZZ, 02574ZZ) is the newest technique. However, what is commonly referred to as the thoracoscopic approach should more accurately be referred to as "thoracoscopically assisted." The thoracoscope is used for illumination and visualization only, as the actual surgical ablation instruments are inserted via a (mini) thoracotomy or a subxiphoid incision rather than through the scope itself. Just recently, a total thoracoscopic approach has been established. As with the open approach, the thoracoscopically assisted and total thoracoscopic techniques require opening up the pericardium. Significant dissection of the pericardial sinuses and other vital structures is required in order to gain access to target areas of the heart. Additionally, as with the open technique, incisions can be made into the atria thoracoscopically, but most often linear ablations are done.

Heart Assist Devices

Heart circulatory support systems can provide temporary left, right, or biventricular support for patients whose hearts have failed but have the potential for recovery. The device can also be used as a bridge for patients who are awaiting a heart transplant. It involves an electromechanically driven pump the size of a human heart implanted within the abdominal wall. This system provides circulatory support by taking over most of the workload of the left ventricle. Blood enters the pump through an inflow conduit connected to the left ventricle and is ejected through an outflow conduit into the body's arterial system.

The system is monitored by an electronic controller and powered by primary and reserve battery packs worn on a belt around the waist or carried in a shoulder bag. There is also a stationary system that consists of a small bedside monitor. The controller is connected to the implanted pump by a percutaneous lead (a small tube containing control and power wires) through the patient's skin.

The implantation of a total internal biventricular heart replacement system (02RK0JZ and 02RL0JZ) involves substantial removal of part or all of the biological heart. Both ventricles are resected, and the native heart is no longer intact. A ventriculectomy is included in this procedure, so it should not be coded separately. However, any associated procedures performed in conjunction with the placement of the total internal biventricular system, such as combined heart-lung transplantation or heart transplantation, should be reported.

ICD-10-PCS provides the following codes for the implantation, repair, and removal of implantable and nonimplantable single or biventricular external heart assist systems:

Synthetic substitute heart/ventricle

02RK0JZ   Replacement of right ventricle with synthetic substitute, open approach

02RL0JZ   Replacement of left ventricle with synthetic substitute, open approach

02WA0JZ   Revision of synthetic substitute in heart, open approach

Implantable heart assist system

02HA0QZ   Insertion of implantable heart assist system into heart, open approach

02HA3QZ   Insertion of implantable heart assist system into heart, percutaneous approach

02HA4QZ   Insertion of implantable heart assist system into heart, percutaneous endoscopic approach

02WA0QZ   Revision of implantable heart assist system in heart, open approach

02WA3QZ   Revision of implantable heart assist system in heart, percutaneous approach

02WA4QZ   Revision of implantable heart assist system in heart, percutaneous endoscopic approach

02PA0QZ   Removal of implantable heart assist system from heart, open approach

02PA3QZ   Removal of implantable heart assist system from heart, percutaneous approach

02PA4QZ   Removal of implantable heart assist system from heart, percutaneous endoscopic approach

External heart assist system into heart

02HA0RS   Insertion of external heart assist system into heart, open approach

02HA3RS   Insertion of external heart assist system into heart, percutaneous approach

02HA4RS   Insertion of external heart assist system into heart, percutaneous endoscopic approach

02WA0RZ   Revision of external heart assist system in heart, open approach

02WA3RZ   Revision of external heart assist system in heart, percutaneous approach

02WA4RZ   Revision of external heart assist system in heart, percutaneous endoscopic approach

02PA0RZ   Removal of external heart assist system from heart, open approach

02PA3RZ   Removal of external heart assist system from heart, percutaneous approach

02PA4RZ   Removal of external heart assist system from heart, percutaneous endoscopic approach

Implantable Infusion Pump and Vascular Access Devices

Implantable vascular access devices (VADs) and implantable infusion pumps are two distinct catheter systems, each of which can be used to deliver drug therapy. The main difference between them is that the implantable infusion pump is self-contained and completely implanted in the body, whereas the implantable vascular access device is not a pump but a port implanted in the body to provide easy access to the vascular system. These procedures are classified in ICD-10-PCS to the Medical and Surgical Section, "subcutaneous tissue and fascia" body system, root operation "Insertion," and the appropriate body part where the device is inserted. The difference in the code assignment is reflected in the selection of the device (character 6) for "infusion pump" (V) or "vascular access device" (X). For example:

0JHG0VZ   Insertion of infusion pump into right lower arm subcutaneous tissue and fascia, open approach

0JHG0XZ   Insertion of vascular access device into right lower arm subcutaneous tissue and fascia, open approach

The implantable infusion pump is surgically placed in the body, usually under general anesthesia. In certain instances, a catheter is attached to the pump and inserted into an artery for direct infusion of a drug; in such cases, the code for the insertion of the infusion device into the artery (e.g., code **03HY03Z, Insertion of infusion device into upper artery, open approach**) is also assigned. The pump is used to deliver intra-arterial drugs such as chemotherapeutic agents for patients with primary hepatomas or colon cancer with metastasis to the liver, as well as to deliver pain medication for terminal cancer patients. The pump allows the patient greater flexibility and freedom of movement while receiving treatment and also permits treatment on an outpatient basis once the pump has been inserted.

The use of an infusion pump that remains outside the body and infuses medication through a subcutaneous or venous needle is not coded. Only the procedure for placing a venous needle or catheter is coded. The application of this device includes the insertion of a permanent catheter.

An implantable VAD is a sterile catheter system implanted subcutaneously under local anesthesia and used for multiple purposes, such as infusion of total parenteral nutrition and bolus injections of medication. The device is placed in central veins, such as the subclavian, rather than a peripheral vein. VADs are designed to provide repeated access to the vascular system without the trauma or complications of multiple venipunctures. The devices can be left in place for weeks or months, as opposed to days, and are generally placed in patients who require long-term access for chemotherapy, nutrition, or blood withdrawal.

Simple venous catheters are sterile catheter systems that provide repeated access to the vascular system for procedures such as blood withdrawal and medication or fluid administration. The catheter is inserted into a peripheral vein, such as the cephalic vein, by puncturing the skin and then taping the catheter in place. These catheters remain in place for a much shorter period of time than do VADs. Examples of simple venous catheters (also called heparin locks) include Angiocaths, Abbott catheters, and Jelco catheters. For example, code **05HB03Z, Insertion of infusion device into right basilic vein, open approach,** is assigned for insertion of a simple catheter system into the basilic vein in the right arm. Code **0JPVX3Z, Removal of infusion device from upper extremity subcutaneous tissue and fascia, external approach,** is assigned for the removal of an infusion device from the upper extremity, while code **0JPVXXZ, Removal of vascular access device from upper extremity subcutaneous tissue and fascia, external approach,** is assigned for removal of a vascular access device from the upper extremity.

Implantable Hemodynamic Monitor

The implantable hemodynamic monitoring system allows clinicians to identify early signs of volume overload before signs and symptoms of heart failure become apparent. Clinicians can then adjust treatment to prevent acute decompensated heart failure and the need for hospital admission. The device consists of two key components. A lead with a pressure sensor is placed within the right ventricle at the right ventricular outflow tract. The other component is the monitoring device, which includes pressure-sensing circuitry with memory to process and collect the data obtained by the sensor. ICD-10-PCS provides the following codes for these procedures:

02HK02G   Insertion of pressure sensor in right ventricle, open approach

02HK02Z   Insertion of monitoring device in right ventricle, open approach

02HK32G   Insertion of pressure sensor in right ventricle, percutaneous approach

02HK32Z   Insertion of monitoring device in right ventricle, percutaneous approach

02HK42G   Insertion of pressure sensor in right ventricle, percutaneous endoscopic approach

0JH602D   Insertion of hemodynamic monitoring device in chest subcutaneous tissue and fascia, open approach

0JH632D   Insertion of hemodynamic monitoring device in chest subcutaneous tissue and fascia, percutaneous approach

0JH802D   Insertion of hemodynamic monitoring device in abdomen subcutaneous tissue and fascia, open approach

0JH832D   Insertion of hemodynamic monitoring device in abdomen subcutaneous tissue and fascia, percutaneous approach

Intravascular and Intra-Aneurysm Pressure Measurement

Measurement of intra-aneurysm sac pressure during endovascular repair of an abdominal or thoracic aortic aneurysm can help to detect and treat endoleaks during endoluminal grafting. This procedure is classified by ICD-10-PCS to the Medical and Surgical Section, root operation "Insertion," body part either "abdominal aorta" or "thoracic aorta," and device either "pressure sensor" or "monitoring device." One code example is **02HW32G, Insertion of pressure sensor into thoracic aorta, percutaneous approach:**

Character 1 Section	Character 2 Body System	Character 3 Root Operation	Character 4 Body Part	Character 5 Approach	Character 6 Device	Character 7 Qualifier
0	2	H	W	3	2	G
Medical and surgical	Heart and great vessels	Insertion	Thoracic aorta	Percutaneous	Monitoring device	Pressure sensor

Intravascular pressure measurement of coronary arteries provides physiological assessment of intravascular lesions. The specialized guidewire-mounted pressure sensor measures pressure and flow and can be used during diagnostic cardiac catheterization to determine the significance of a blockage in a coronary artery. Pressure wire measurement can confirm therapeutic results in coronary vessel stenting, identify culprit vessels, assist in developing an individual therapeutic strategy, and provide step-by-step guidance during complex interventional procedures. This procedure is classified to the Measurement and Monitoring Section, "physiological systems" body system, root operation "Measurement," pressure function, coronary qualifier. A code example is **4A033BC, Measurement of arterial pressure, coronary, percutaneous approach:**

Character 1 Section	Character 2 Body System	Character 3 Operation	Character 4 Body System	Character 5 Approach	Character 6 Function/Device	Character 7 Qualifier
4	A	0	3	3	B	C
Measurement and monitoring	Physiological systems	Measurement	Arterial	Percutaneous	Pressure	Coronary

Any other diagnostic or therapeutic procedures performed in conjunction with intravascular pressure measurement of coronary arteries are coded separately.

Intravascular pressure measurement can be performed on other vessels, such as intrathoracic arteries (i.e., assessment of the aorta, aortic arch, and carotid arteries), pulmonary arteries, and peripheral arteries, including assessment of vessels of the arms and legs. Assign additional codes for any synchronous diagnostic or therapeutic procedures performed.

Implantation of Carotid Sinus Stimulation System

The baroreflex system helps to regulate function of the heart, kidneys, and peripheral vasculature to maintain an appropriate blood pressure. The carotid sinus baroreflex activation device is currently the only medical device used to treat refractory hypertension. It consists of an implantable pulse generator, bilateral carotid sinus leads, and a computer programming system. The pulse generator is placed in a subcutaneous pocket in the pectoral region below the collar bone. Electrodes are placed bilaterally on the carotid arteries, two main blood pressure control points, and the leads run under the skin and connect to the pulse generator. Placement of the leads is determined by intraoperative blood pressure responses to test activations. The programming system regulates the activation energy from the device to the leads and can be adjusted based on the needs of the patient.

When the device is activated, the programming system delivers activation energy through the leads to the carotid sinus. The baroreceptors of the carotid arteries send signals through neural pathways to the brain that there is a rise in blood pressure that needs to be corrected. The brain sends signals to other parts of the body to counteract the rise in blood pressure by modulating the nervous system and hormones to dilate blood vessels and allow blood to flow more freely, reduce the heart rate, and influence fluid handling by the kidneys. This results in reduced blood pressure and workload by the heart, improved circulation, and a more optimal neurohormonal balance.

Insertion of a complete system is coded by assigning separate codes for each of the following components of the surgery:

0JH60MZ	Insertion of the stimulator generator into a subcutaneous pocket in the chest
03HK3MZ	Insertion of stimulator lead into right internal carotid artery via percutaneous approach
03HL3MZ	Insertion of stimulator lead into left internal carotid artery via percutaneous approach

In the event that it becomes necessary to revise the leads or the pulse generator, ICD-10-PCS provides separate codes for these procedures as well.

For example:

- A patient who is status post implantation of a carotid sinus baroreflex activation device due to refractory hypertension is admitted to have the lead adjusted and repositioned (via percutaneous approach) within the left carotid sinus for better signal activation. Assign code **Z45.09, Encounter for adjustment and management of other cardiac device,** as the principal diagnosis. Assign code **I10, Essential (primary) hypertension,** as an additional diagnosis. Assign code **03WY3MZ, Revision of stimulator lead in upper artery, percutaneous approach,** for repositioning of the lead.

Implantation of Cardiomyostimulation System

Dynamic cardiomyoplasty is a fairly complicated new surgical technique performed using a two-step open procedure that involves elevating the latissimus dorsi muscle, then wrapping it around the heart. A stimulator similar to a pacemaker is implanted and connected to both the heart and the wrapped muscle. There are a number of components to the procedure, which are all coded separately, as follows:

- Transfer of the trunk muscle either left (0KXG0ZZ) or right (0KXF0ZZ)
- Resection of the rib, either left (0PT20ZZ) or right (0PT10ZZ)
- Insertion of cardiac lead into pericardium, open approach (02HN0MZ)

Heart Transplantation

Heart transplantation is carried out when the heart is failing and does not respond to therapies. The main reasons for heart transplants are cardiomyopathy, severe coronary artery disease, and congenital defects of the heart. Code **02YA0Z0, Transplantation of heart, allogeneic, open approach,** or **02YA0Z1, Transplantation of heart, syngeneic, open approach,** is used to report the transplantation of a heart from a donor. "Allogeneic" refers to transplant from a genetically similar, but not identical, donor; "syngeneic" refers to a transplant from a genetically identical or closely related donor. An insufficient number of organs is available for transplantation to meet the need. A patient may wait months for a transplant, and many patients do not live long enough to receive the organ.

Procedures on Aneurysms

An aneurysm of a vessel may be treated by resection with anastomosis (root operation "Excision") or replacement (root operation "Replacement"), with the body part character indicating the vessel involved. Repair is achieved by clipping or a variety of other procedures such as electrocoagulation, suture, or wiring—all of these are classified to the root operation "Restriction," with the body part character indicating the vessel where the procedure was performed. Several new procedures are now being used for aneurysm repair. Endoluminal endovascular prosthesis is a new technique for transfemoral graft placement and aneurysm exclusion in patients with abdominal aortic aneurysm. This is an alternative to open surgery, is minimally invasive, and avoids laparotomy. Hospital stays are shorter and postoperative management is less intensive.

Another technique is the use of endovascular grafts for abdominal aortic aneurysm and common iliac aneurysm. Assignment of the ICD-10-PCS codes for aneurysm repair with these techniques largely depend on whether the procedure performed is inserting a biological or synthetic graft to reinforce or augment the vessel (root operation "Supplement) or a device such as a stent is being inserted in order to partially close the orifice or lumen of the vessel (root operation "Restriction").

The following codes are examples of procedures for endovascular repair of aneurysms:

04U04JZ	Supplement abdominal aorta with synthetic substitute, percutaneous endoscopic approach
04V04DZ	Restriction of abdominal aorta with intraluminal device, percutaneous endoscopic approach
03VG0DZ	Restriction of intracranial artery with intraluminal device, open approach
02UW4JZ	Supplement thoracic aorta with synthetic substitute, percutaneous endoscopic approach

At times, an intraoperative intra-aneurysm sac pressure monitoring procedure may be performed in conjunction with an endovascular repair, which may be separately coded along with the endovascular repair. For example:

02UW3JZ	Supplement thoracic aorta with synthetic substitute, percutaneous approach
02HW32G	Insertion of pressure sensor monitoring device into thoracic aorta, percutaneous approach

Endovascular embolization uses particulate agents, such as gelfoam, polyvinyl alcohol and spherical embolics, coils, liquid sclerosing agents (such as alcohol and tissue adhesives), and other types of embolic materials. It is important to distinguish between the root operations "Restriction" and "Occlusion" when the documentation refers to embolization. If the objective of an embolization procedure is to completely close off a vessel, the root operation "Occlusion" is coded. If the objective of an embolization procedure is to narrow the lumen of a vessel, the root operation "Restriction" is coded. When referring to embolizations of aneurysms, the root operation "Restriction" should be selected because the objective of the procedure is not to close off the vessel completely, but to narrow the lumen of the vessel at the site of the aneurysm where it is abnormally wide.

For example:

- A patient has a percutaneous coil embolization of the right vertebral artery; code **03VP3DZ, Restriction of right vertebral artery with intraluminal device, percutaneous approach,** is assigned.

EXERCISE 28.9

Code the following diagnoses and procedures.

1.	Internal and external thrombosed hemorrhoids	I84.03
	Internal and external hemorrhoidectomy by cryosurgery	0D5Q7ZZ
2.	Painful varicose veins, right lower leg	I83811
	Right greater saphenous ligation and stripping for varicosities, open	06DP0ZZ
3.	Mitral stenosis and aortic insufficiency	I08.0
	Atrial fibrillation	I48.0
	Hypertension	I10
4.	Abdominal aortic aneurysm	I71.4
	Hypertensive cardiovascular disease essential	I11.9
	Resection of abdominal aortic aneurysm with synthetic graft replacement, percutaneous endoscopic approach	04R04JZ
5.	Acute myocardial infarction, anterior wall	I21.09

6. Renovascular hypertension secondary to   I77.89
   fibromuscular hyperplasia, right renal artery   I15.0
   Nuclear renal scan with Tc-99m   CT131ZZ

7. Congestive heart failure due to   I11.0
   hypertensive heart disease   I50.9

8. Acute systolic congestive heart failure   I50.21
   End-stage dilated cardiomyopathy   I42.0
   Permanent cardiac pacemaker in place   T82.598A

   Status

   Percutaneous revision of external heart   02WA3RZ
   assist device due to exposed wire and
   device malfunction

9. Cerebral occlusion, thrombotic with   I63.30
   cerebral infarction   I11.9
   Hypertensive cardiovascular disease

10. Hypertension   I12.9
    Chronic kidney disease   N18.9

11. Postoperative pulmonary artery infarction,   T81.718A
    initial encounter

12. Hypertensive encephalopathy due to   I67.4
    accelerated hypertension   I10

13. Percutaneous insertion of pacemaker leads (right   02HK3MA
    ventricle and right atrium), insertion of   02H63MA
    dual-chamber pacemaker device (open)   0JH60P2

14. Arteriosclerosis of autologous vein bypass graft   I25.810
    (four-vessel bypass graft with saphenous   Z95.1
    vein carried out two years ago)

15. Acute pulmonary edema with left   I50.1
    ventricular failure

16. Cerebral infarction, acute, with thrombosis   I63.30
    Residual hemiplegia, right, dominant side,   G81.91
    and aphasia (at discharge)   R47.01
    Essential hypertension   I10

17. Severe stenosis of left main coronary   I25.10
    arteries in patient with no previous
    history of bypass surgery
    Aortocoronary bypass, left diagonal and   021109W
    left circumflex arteries with saphenous   06BP0ZZ
    vein graft, open   5A1221Z
    Cardiopulmonary bypass (extracorporeal cardiac)
                                    Performance

CHAPTER 29

Neoplasms

CHAPTER OVERVIEW

- Neoplastic diseases are classified in chapter 2 of ICD-10-CM.
- Neoplasms are categorized by two axes.
  - The first axis for coding is by behavior (malignant, benign, carcinoma in situ, uncertain behavior, and unspecified behavior).
  - The second axis for coding is by anatomical site.
- The morphology of tumor cells is studied for classifying a neoplasm by its tissue origin.
- Neoplastic diseases are indexed by morphological type and common terms.
- The Neoplasm Table lists anatomical sites alphabetically. It uses behavior type to indicate the correct code.
- There are two types of malignant neoplasms.
  - Solid neoplasms have a localized point of origin and are considered to be the primary neoplasm of the site. They often metastasize to secondary sites.
    - The statement "metastatic to" indicates that the site of a metastatic tumor is secondary, while "metastatic from" indicates a primary site.
    - When coding, refer to the morphology type in the Alphabetic Index.
  - Lymphatic and hematopoietic tumors often circulate through the bloodstream and lymphatic system.
    - These tumors do not spread to secondary sites. All sites to which they spread through circulation are considered primary.
    - Special coding requirements are in place for Hodgkin's disease and non-Hodgkin's lymphomas.
- Sometimes treatment can be a guide when selecting a principal diagnosis.
  - When the treatment is directed at the primary site, the malignancy of that site is often the principal diagnosis.
  - When it is directed at a secondary site, the malignancy of the primary site is an additional code.
  - Admission solely for chemotherapy treatment requires a Z code as the principal diagnosis.

LEARNING OUTCOMES

After studying this chapter you should be able to:

Explain the various classifications of neoplasms.

Locate codes for neoplastic diseases.

Code for malignant neoplasms (both solid and hematopoietic or lymphatic).

Code for the treatment of neoplastic diseases.

TERMS TO KNOW

Direct extension
the invasion of adjacent sites by a malignant neoplasm

Invasive
the extension of tumor cells to other adjacent sites

Metastasis
the resulting spread of invasive tumor cells

Neoplasm
a new or abnormal growth

REMEMBER . . .

Morphology codes are optional but are used in tumor registries and pathology indexes.

INTRODUCTION

A neoplasm is a new or abnormal growth. In the ICD-10-CM classification system, neoplastic disease is classified in categories C00 through D49. Certain benign neoplasms, such as prostatic adenomas, may be found in the specific body system chapters.

BEHAVIOR CLASSIFICATION

The first axis for coding neoplasms is behavior; the second axis is the anatomical site. ICD-10-CM classifies neoplasms into five behavior groups and a sixth for unspecified behavior:

C00–C75, C76–C96	Malignant
C7a–C7b, D3a	Neuroendocrine
D00–D09	Carcinoma in situ
D10–D36	Benign
D37–D48	Uncertain behavior
D49	Unspecified behavior

Malignant Neoplasms

Malignant neoplasms are tumor cells that extend beyond the primary site, attaching themselves to adjacent structures or spreading to distant sites. They are characterized by relentless growth and are difficult to cure. The term "invasive" is often used to describe the extension of the tumor cells to other adjacent sites. The resulting spread is called "metastasis."

Certain types of malignant neoplasms are noted for their invasive properties (for example, malignant melanoma of the skin) and usually require excision beyond the primary site because of their potential microinvasiveness. In such cases, a biopsy finding of malignancy on tissue removed during outpatient surgery may indicate the need for more extensive surgery on an inpatient basis. When such further surgery is performed, however, the pathology report may or may not indicate further malignancy. When no further malignancy is found, the physician ordinarily documents the diagnosis as a malignancy in accordance with the findings of the initial biopsy, because that condition is the reason for admission and the primary neoplasm may, in fact, require further treatment. In this situation, the diagnosis provided by the physician should be coded even though the current pathology report does not confirm the diagnosis. A copy of the original pathology report should be obtained and filed with the current medical record if at all possible.

Neuroendocrine Tumors

Neuroendocrine tumors (categories C7a–C7b, D3a) arise from endocrine or neuroendocrine cells scattered throughout the body. The most common sites are the bronchi, stomach, small intestine, appendix, and rectum. These tumors are commonly classified according to the presumed embryonic site of origin, such as the foregut (bronchi and stomach), midgut (small intestine and appendix), and hindgut (colon and rectum).

A carcinoid tumor is a tumor that develops from enterochromaffin cells. These cells produce hormones that normally are found in the small intestine, appendix, colon, rectum, bronchi, pancreas, ovaries, testes, bile ducts, liver, and other organs. Carcinoid tumors are capable of producing these same hormones, often in large quantities, and can cause carcinoid syndrome (E34.0). Carcinoid tumors can be found throughout the body, but the majority are found in the gastrointestinal tract. Approximately 25 percent of carcinoid tumors are found in the bronchial airways and the lung. In some cases, it may not be possible to locate the site of origin of the carcinoid tumors, although symptoms of carcinoid syndrome may be present. Carcinoid tumors can present as a primary malignancy (category C7a), as a secondary or metastatic tumor (category C7b), or as a benign tumor (category D3a). Codes Z85.020, Z85.030, Z85.040, Z85.060, Z85.110, Z85.230, and Z85.520 are used to describe the history of a malignant neuroendocrine tumor that has been previously excised or eradicated with no further treatment.

When multiple endocrine neoplasia (MEN) syndrome is associated with malignant or benign neuroendocrine tumors, code also the MEN syndrome (E31.2-). However, this code is not assigned when the health record documentation does not support the condition. If there is an associated endocrine syndrome, assign the appropriate additional code, such as carcinoid syndrome (E34.0). For example:

C7a.092 + E31.21 + E34.0   Malignant carcinoid tumor of the stomach, Werner's syndrome, and carcinoid syndrome

Merkel Cell Carcinoma

Merkel cell carcinoma, also called neuroendocrine carcinoma of the skin, arises from the uncontrolled growth of Merkel cells in the skin. It is a rare skin cancer and potentially life threatening; aggressive therapy may be needed. Merkel cell carcinoma does not have a distinctive appearance and usually develops on sun-exposed skin (e.g., head, neck, arms) as a painless, firm, flesh-colored to red or blue bump. It is diagnosed via skin biopsy. The following subcategories and codes are assigned for Merkel cell carcinoma:

C4a.0   Merkel cell carcinoma of lip
C4a.1-   Merkel cell carcinoma of eyelid, including canthus
C4a.2-   Merkel cell carcinoma of ear and external auricular canal
C4a.3-   Merkel cell carcinoma of other and unspecified parts of face
C4a.4   Merkel cell carcinoma of scalp and neck
C4a.5-   Merkel cell carcinoma of trunk
C4a.6-   Merkel cell carcinoma of upper limb, including shoulder
C4a.7-   Merkel cell carcinoma of lower limb, including hip
C4a.8   Merkel cell carcinoma of overlapping sites
C4a.9   Merkel cell carcinoma, unspecified

Benign Neoplasms

Benign neoplasms are not invasive and do not spread to either adjacent or distant sites. They may, however, cause local effects such as displacement, pressure on an adjacent structure, impingement on a nerve, or compression of a vessel and therefore require surgery. Uterine myomas, for example, may cause pressure on the urinary bladder, which results in urinary symptoms. Most benign tumors can be cured by total excision.

Carcinoma in Situ

Tumor cells in carcinoma described as in situ are undergoing malignant changes but are still confined to the point of origin without invasion of the surrounding normal tissue. Other terms that describe carcinoma in situ include "intraepithelial," "noninfiltrating," "noninvasive," and "preinvasive" carcinoma. Severe cervical and vulvar dysplasia described as CIN III or VIN III are classified as carcinoma in situ. (See chapter 21 of this handbook for more information.)

Neoplasms of Uncertain Behavior

The ultimate behavior of certain neoplasms cannot be determined at the time they are discovered, and a firm distinction between benign and malignant tumor cells cannot be made. Certain benign tumors, for example, may be undergoing malignant transformation; as a result, continued study is necessary to arrive at a conclusive diagnosis.

Neurofibromatosis refers to a group of autosomal dominant genetic disorders that cause tumors to grow along the nerves. Code **Q85.00, Neurofibromatosis, unspecified,** is assigned for neurofibromatosis.

Schwannomas may occur along any nerve of the body, including spinal, cranial, and peripheral nerves, except on the vestibular nerve. As the tumors grow, they compress nerves and cause pain, numbness, tingling, weakness, and other neurological symptoms. Code **Q85.03, Schwannomatosis,** is assigned for this condition.

Neoplasms of Unspecified Behavior

Category D49 is provided for those situations in which neither the behavior nor the morphology of the neoplasm is specified in the diagnostic statement or elsewhere in the medical record. This usually occurs when a patient is transferred to another medical care facility for further diagnosis and possible treatment before diagnostic studies are completed, or when a patient is given a working diagnosis in an outpatient setting pending further study. Category D49 includes terms such as "growth," "neoplasm," "new growth," and "tumor" when the neoplasms are not otherwise specified. A code from category D49 would not be used for a neoplasm treated in an acute care facility because more definitive information should always be available.

It is important not to confuse neoplasms of unspecified behavior with those of uncertain behavior. The exception for coding neoplasm of unspecified behavior is when coding dark areas or spots of the retina, which are referred to as neoplasms or suspected melanoma. These spots are often difficult to biopsy and must be continually evaluated. Code **D49.81, Neoplasm of unspecified behavior, retina and choroid,** is assigned for this condition. Because a biopsy of the retina poses a risk to the eye and is only performed if the lesion extends, there is usually no tissue biopsy taken to confirm the diagnosis. Therefore, code D49.81 is appropriately assigned for this condition.

Unspecified Mass or Lesion

It is incorrect to select a code from category D49, Neoplasms of unspecified behavior, when only the terms "mass" or "lesion" are used. When coding diagnoses documented as mass or lesion of a particular site, and when that site is not listed under the main terms **Mass** or **Lesion,** the coder should follow the cross-references under the main term representing the documented diagnosis. If a final diagnosis is documented as "lump," and there is no Index entry for the affected organ or site under "lump," look up the main term **Mass** as directed by the "see" note under the main term **Lump.** If there is no Index entry for the specific site under **Mass,** look up the main term **Disease.** The Index directs the coder to see Disease of specified organ or site for **Mass,** specified organ NEC.

If a final diagnosis is documented as "lesion," and there is no Index entry for the specified organ or site under the main term **Lesion,** look up the main term **Disease.** The Index directs you to see Disease by site for **Lesion,** organ or site NEC.

EXERCISE 29.1

By referring to the following subcategories in the Tabular List, match the codes in the left column with the descriptions listed in the right column.

1.	C18.4	Transverse colon	c	a.	Benign
2.	D44.10	Adrenal gland	d	b.	Carcinoma in situ
3.	C43.0	Lip	c	c.	Malignant
4.	D02.1	Trachea	b	d.	Uncertain behavior
5.	D49.4	Bladder	e	e.	Unspecified behavior
6.	D10.6	Nasopharynx	a		
7.	C7a.025	Sigmoid colon	c		

MORPHOLOGY CLASSIFICATION

Morphology of neoplasms refers to the form and structure of tumor cells and is studied in order to classify a neoplasm by its tissue of origin. The tissue of origin and the type of cells that make up a malignant neoplasm often determine the expected rate of growth, the severity of illness, and the type of treatment given. Metastatic neoplasms are identified at the metastatic site by their morphology, which is different from the normal tissue at that site but the same as that at the primary site.

A tumor registry is a cancer data system that provides follow-up on all cancer patients. A tumor registry documents and stores all major aspects of a patient's cancer history and treatment. The registry database includes demographics, medical history, diagnostic findings, primary site, metastasis, histology, stage of disease, treatments, recurrence, subsequent treatment, and end results. Coders may use the completed cancer staging form for coding purposes when it is authenticated by the attending physician.

EXERCISE 29.2

Mark the following statements either true or false.

1. Morphology of neoplasms refers to the study of the form and structure   T
   of the tissue and cells from which the neoplasm arises.

2. Metastatic neoplasms can be identified by their morphology, which is   F
   identical to the morphology of the surrounding normal tissue and
   cells at the metastatic site.

3. Coders may use the completed cancer staging form for coding purposes   T
   when it is authenticated by the attending physician.

LOCATING CODES FOR NEOPLASTIC DISEASE

The first step in locating the code for a neoplasm is to refer to the main term for the morphological type in the Alphabetic Index of Diseases and Injuries and then to review the subentries. For some types, a specific diagnosis code is provided. For example, for a diagnosis of renal cell carcinoma, the Alphabetic Index lists the main term **Carcinoma** and the subterm "renal cell" as follows:

> **Carcinoma . . .**
> -renal cell C64.-

When the site is not listed as a subterm or when a specific code is not given in the Alphabetic Index, a cross-reference to the Neoplasm Table in volume 2 of the Index appears. Cross-references should be followed closely; the following entries indicate the help the coder can receive when the type of neoplasm is referenced in the Alphabetic Index:

> **Sarcoma . . .**
> -cerebellar C71.6
> -embryonal—*see* Neoplasm, connective tissue, malignant
> -Ewing's—*see* Neoplasm, bone, malignant

The Neoplasm Table (part of which is reproduced as table 29.1) lists anatomical sites alphabetically on the far left. (The indention levels have the same significance as those used elsewhere in the Alphabetic Index.) Columns to the right indicate the code for each behavior type for that site.

To use the Table, coders must first locate the anatomical site in the list, move across the page to the behavior type, and then select the appropriate code. For each site there are six possible code numbers according to whether the neoplasm in question is malignant, benign, in situ, of uncertain behavior, or of unspecified nature. The description of the neoplasm will often indicate which of the six columns is appropriate (e.g., malignant melanoma of skin, benign fibroadenoma of breast, carcinoma in situ of cervix uteri). Where such descriptors are not present, the remainder of the Index should be consulted, where guidance is given to the appropriate column for each morphological (histological) variety listed, such as Mesonephroma—*see* Neoplasm, malignant; Embryoma—*see also* Neoplasm, uncertain behavior; Bowen's disease—*see* Neoplasm, skin, in situ. However, the guidance in the Index can be overridden if one of the descriptors mentioned above is present; for example, malignant adenoma of colon is coded to C18.9 and not to D12.6, as the adjective "malignant" overrides the Index entry "Adenoma—*see also* Neoplasm, benign." Codes listed with a dash (-) following the code have a required fifth character for laterality. Codes from the Neoplasm Table should be verified in the Tabular List.

TABLE 29.1   Section of the Neoplasm Table in the Alphabetic Index of Diseases and Injuries

	Malignant Primary	Malignant Secondary	Ca in Situ	Benign	Uncertain Behavior	Unspecified Behavior
Neoplasm, neoplastic—continued						
-nostril	C30.0	C78.39	D02.3	D14.0	D38.5	D49.1
-nucleus pulposus	C41.2	C79.51	—	D16.6	D48.0	D49.2
-occipital						
--bone	C41.0	C79.51	—	D16.4-	D48.0	D49.2
--lobe or pole, brain	C71.4	C79.31	—	D33.0	D43.0	D49.6
-odontogenic—see Neoplasm, jaw bone						
-olfactory nerve or bulb	C72.2-	C79.49	—	D33.3	D43.3	D49.7
-olive (brain)	C71.7	C79.31	—	D33.1	D43.1	D49.6
-omentum	C48.1	C78.6	—	D20.1	D48.4	D49.0

EXERCISE 29.3

Assign diagnosis codes to the following diagnoses.

1. Bronchial adenoma   D38.1

2. Burkitt's lymphoma of intrapelvic lymph
   nodes   C83.76

3. Lipoma of head   D17.0

4. Hairy cell leukemia in remission   C91.41

5. Endometrial sarcoma   C54.1

6. Hodgkin's sarcoma   C81.9

BASIC TYPES OF MALIGNANT NEOPLASMS

There are two basic types of malignant neoplasms:

C00–C75, C76–C80	Solid
C81–C96	Hematopoietic and lymphatic

Solid tumors have a single, localized point of origin and are considered to be primary neoplasms of that site. Solid tumors tend to spread to adjacent or remote sites, with such sites classified as secondary or metastatic neoplasms. For example, a diagnosis of carcinoma of the lung with metastasis to the brain indicates that a primary neoplasm of the lung has metastasized to a secondary site in the brain.

Lymphatic and hematopoietic neoplasms arise in the reticuloendothelial and lymphatic systems and the blood-forming tissues. These neoplasms differ from solid malignant neoplasms in several ways, including the following:

- They may arise in a single site or in several sites simultaneously.
- Tumor cells often circulate in large numbers in the bloodstream and the lymphatic system rather than remaining confined to a single site.
- Spreading to other sites in the hematopoietic and lymphatic system is not considered to be secondary but is also classified as primary neoplasm.

Because of the differences between solid and hematopoietic-lymphatic diseases, this handbook deals with the two types of malignant neoplasms separately. Solid tumors are covered first, and then the discussion moves on to tumors that arise in the hematopoietic and lymphatic systems.

CODING OF SOLID MALIGNANT NEOPLASMS

A solid malignant neoplasm may spread from its site of origin by either direct extension or metastasis. Direct extension is the invasion of adjacent sites; "metastasis" refers to the spread to distant sites and the establishment of a new center of malignancy. ICD-10-CM does not make a distinction between these two types of extension. The terms "metastatic" and "secondary" are generally used interchangeably.

Overlapping Sites

When a primary malignant neoplasm overlaps two or more contiguous (next to each other) sites, it is classified to the subcategory/code ".8," signifying "overlapping lesion," unless the combination is specifically indexed elsewhere. For example, ICD-10-CM provides the following codes for certain malignant neoplasms whose stated sites overlap two or more boundaries:

C00.8	Neoplasm of overlapping sites of the lip whose point of origin cannot be assigned to any other code within category C00
C16.8	Neoplasm of stomach whose point of origin cannot be assigned to any other code within category C16
C34.80	Neoplasm of overlapping sites of lung, bronchus, and trachea whose point of origin cannot be assigned to any other code within category C34

EXERCISE 29.4

Code the following diagnoses.

1.	Carcinoma of upper and middle third of esophagus	C15.8
2.	Carcinoma of oral cavity and pharynx	C14.8
3.	Adenocarcinoma of rectum and anus	C21.8

Malignancy in Two or More Noncontiguous Sites

A patient may have more than one malignant tumor in the same organ. These tumors may represent different primary cancers or metastatic disease, depending on the site. When the documentation is unclear, the provider should be queried regarding the status of each tumor in order to select the correct codes.

When more than one primary cancer occurs in the same organ system, these are called synchronous primary cancers. This condition can occur in the lungs where the target organ, in this case the respiratory epithelium, is attacked/altered by the inciting agent (e.g., tobacco smoke). However, the physician must make that designation as to whether one of the tumors represents a second primary cancer or a metastasis. For example:

- A patient with stage IV non–small cell lung cancer of the left lower lobe is admitted with extensive peritoneal metastasis and liver metastasis. A CT scan of the lung shows a large tumor in the left lung base with diffuse extension to the right lung. When queried, the provider documents that the tumor had started in the left lung and metastasized to the right lung. Because the provider has clearly documented that the primary malignancy of the left lung had extended to the right lung, assign code **C34.32, Malignant neoplasm of lower lobe, left bronchus or lung,** as the principal diagnosis and code **C78.01, Secondary malignant neoplasm of right lung,** as a secondary diagnosis. In addition, assign codes **C78.6, Secondary malignant neoplasm of retroperitoneum and peritoneum,** and **C78.7, Secondary malignant neoplasm of liver and intrahepatic bile duct.**

Neoplasms Described as Metastatic

The terms "metastatic" and "metastasis" are often used ambiguously in describing neoplastic disease, sometimes meaning that the site named is primary and sometimes meaning that it is secondary. When the diagnostic statement is not clear in this regard, the coder should review the medical record for further information. When none is available, however, the following guidelines apply.

"Metastatic To"

The statement "metastatic to" indicates that the site mentioned is secondary. For example, a diagnosis of metastatic carcinoma to the lung is coded as secondary malignant neoplasm of the lung (C78.0-). A code for the primary neoplastic site should also be assigned when the primary neoplasm is still present; a history code from category Z85, Personal history of malignant neoplasm, should be assigned when the primary neoplasm has been excised or eradicated. The fourth character of category Z85 indicates the body system where the prior neoplasm occurred, and the fifth and sixth characters indicate the specific organ or site involved.

Ordinarily, no history code is assigned when the patient has had a prior benign or in-situ neoplasm or neoplasm of uncertain behavior. The exceptions are a few neoplasms that are included in subcategory Z86.0, as follows:

Z86.000	Personal history of in-situ neoplasm of breast
Z86.001	Personal history of in-situ neoplasm of cervix uteri
Z86.008	Personal history of in-situ neoplasm of other site
Z86.010	Personal history of colonic polyps
Z86.011	Personal history of benign neoplasm of the brain
Z86.012	Personal history of benign carcinoid tumor
Z86.018	Personal history of other benign neoplasm
Z86.03	Personal history of neoplasm of uncertain behavior

"Metastatic From"

The statement "metastatic from" indicates that the site mentioned is the primary site. For example, a diagnosis of metastatic carcinoma from the breast indicates that the breast is the primary site (C50.9-). A code for the metastatic site should also be assigned.

Multiple Metastatic Sites

When two or more sites are described as "metastatic" in the diagnostic statement, each of the stated sites should be coded as secondary or metastatic. A code should also be assigned for the primary site when this information is available; it should be coded C80.1 when it is not.

Single Metastatic Site

When only one site is described as metastatic without any further qualification and no more definitive information can be obtained by reviewing the medical record, the following steps should be followed:

1. Refer first to the morphology type in the Alphabetic Index and code to the primary condition of that site. For example, a diagnosis of metastatic renal cell carcinoma of the lung indicates that the primary site is the kidney and the secondary site is the lung. The correct coding for this is **C64.9, Malignant neoplasm of kidney, except renal pelvis, unspecified side,** and **C78.00, Secondary malignant neoplasm of lung, unspecified side.** When a specific site for the morphology type is not indicated in a code entry or is not indexed, assign the code for unspecified site within that anatomical site. For example, oat cell carcinoma is indexed to **C34.90, Malignant neoplasm of bronchus or lung, unspecified, unspecified side,** when no more specific site is stated.

2. When the morphology type is not stated or the only code that can be obtained is either C80.0 or C80.1, code as a primary malignant neoplasm unless the site is one of the following:

- Bone
- Brain
- Diaphragm
- Heart
- Liver
- Lymph nodes
- Mediastinum
- Meninges
- Peritoneum
- Pleura
- Retroperitoneum
- Spinal cord
- Sites classifiable to C76

Malignant neoplasms of these sites are classified as secondary when not otherwise specified, except for neoplasm of the liver. ICD-10-CM provides code **C22.9, Malignant neoplasm of liver, not specified as primary or secondary,** for use in this situation.

Examples of coding by this two-step procedure include the following:

C34.90 + C80.1   Metastatic carcinoma of the lung, coded by step 2, with the primary site assigned to the lung: carcinoma of lung; secondary site not specified

C79.51 + C80.1   Metastatic carcinoma of bone, coded by step 2, with the primary site unknown and the bone as the secondary site: carcinoma, site unknown; secondary site bone

No Site Stated

Code **C80.0, Disseminated malignant neoplasm, unspecified,** is for use only in those cases where the patient has advanced metastatic disease and no known primary or secondary sites are specified. It should not be used in place of assigning codes for the primary site and all known secondary sites. Code **C80.1, Malignant (primary) neoplasm, unspecified,** equates to Cancer, unspecified. This code should only be used when no determination can be made as to the primary site of a malignancy. This code should rarely be used in the inpatient setting.

When no site is indicated in the diagnostic statement but the morphology type is qualified as metastatic, the code provided for that morphological type is assigned for the primary diagnosis along with an additional code for secondary neoplasm of unspecified site. For example, a diagnosis of metastatic apocrine adenocarcinoma with no site specified is coded as a primary malignant neoplasm of the skin, site unspecified (C44.9). An additional code of C80.1 is assigned for the secondary neoplasm. Code C44.9 is obtained by referring to the following main term and subterms in volume 2:

Adenocarcinoma . . .
-apocrine . . .
--unspecified site C44.9

EXERCISE 29.5

Code the following diagnoses.

---

1. Metastatic <u>carcinoma</u> from right lung

<u>C34.91</u>
C80.1

---

2. Metastatic <u>carcinoma</u> to brain

<u>C79.31</u>
C80.1

---

3. Metastatic <u>carcinoma</u> from prostate to
pelvic bone
Previous prostatectomy

<u>History</u>

<u>C79.51</u>
Z85.46

---

4. Metastatic <u>carcinoma</u> to brain from lung
Previous resection of lung with no
recurrence at primary site

<u>History</u>

<u>C79.31</u>
Z85.118

---

5. Metastatic <u>carcinoma</u> from prostate to
pelvic bone

C61
C79.51

---

6. Metastatic <u>carcinoma</u> of brain and lung

<u>C79.31</u>
C78.00
C80.1

---

7. Metastatic <u>carcinoma</u> of pancreas and
omentum

C78.89
C78.6
C80.1

---

8. Metastatic <u>adenocarcinoma</u> of transverse
    colon

    <u>C18.4</u>
    C80.1

9. Metastatic <u>carcinoma</u> of bronchus

    <u>C34.90</u>
    C80.1

10. Metastatic <u>carcinoma</u> of spinal cord

    <u>C79.49</u>
    C80.1

11. Metastatic <u>carcinoma</u> of femur

    <u>C79.51</u>
    C80.1

12. Metastatic <u>carcinoma</u> of brain

    <u>C79.31</u>
    C80.1

13. Metastatic serous papillary <u>adenocarcinoma</u>
    of bone

    <u>C56.9</u>
    C79.51

14. Metastatic infiltrating duct cell <u>carcinoma</u>, female

    <u>C50.919</u>
    <u>C80.1</u>

15. Metastatic odontogenic <u>fibrosarcoma</u>

    <u>C41.1</u>
    <u>C80.1</u>

16. Chondroblastic <u>osteosarcoma</u> of limb with metastasis

    <u>C41.9</u>
    <u>C80.1</u>

CODING OF MALIGNANCIES OF HEMATOPOIETIC AND LYMPHATIC SYSTEMS

Unlike solid tumors, neoplasms that arise in lymphatic and hematopoietic tissues do not spread to secondary sites. Instead, malignant cells circulate and may occur in other sites within these tissues. These sites are considered to be primary neoplasms rather than secondary. Figure 29.1 shows the location of the lymph nodes in the body.

Neoplasms of Lymph Nodes or Glands

Primary malignant neoplasms of lymph nodes or glands are classified in categories C81 through C88, with a fourth character providing more specificity about the particular type of neoplasm and a fifth character indicating the nodes involved (except for categories C86 and C88, which do not specify site). If the neoplasm involves lymph nodes or glands of additional sites, the fifth character "8" is assigned to indicate that the malignancy now involves multiple sites. For example, code **C83.38, Diffuse large B-cell lymphoma, lymph nodes of multiple sites,** is assigned for a diagnosis of diffuse large B-cell lymphoma of intra-abdominal and intrathoracic lymph nodes; individual codes are not assigned.

When a solid tumor has spread to the lymph nodes, a code from category C77 is assigned. For example, adenocarcinoma of right female breast with metastasis to lymph nodes of the axilla is coded to **C50.911, Malignant neoplasm of unspecified site of right female breast,** and **C77.3, Secondary and unspecified malignant neoplasm of axilla and upper limb lymph nodes.** No code from categories C81 through C88 is assigned.

Lymphomas can be malignant or benign. Benign lymphomas are classified to code **D36.0, Benign neoplasm of lymph nodes.** Malignant lymphomas are located by referencing the subterms for the site under the main term **Lymphoma.** When a diagnostic statement of lymphoma does not match any subentry under **Lymphoma** in the Index, the coder may find that the pathology report indicates the neoplasm's behavior. However, the physician should be queried for confirmation before code selection.

Hodgkin's Lymphoma

Hodgkin's lymphoma (category C81) is a type of cancer originating from lymphocytes. Hodgkin's lymphoma is characterized by the orderly spread of disease from one lymph node group to another and by the development of systemic symptoms with advanced disease. Hodgkin's lymphoma may be treated with radiation therapy, chemotherapy, or hematopoietic stem cell transplantation. The choice of treatment depends on the age and sex of the patient and the stage, bulk, and histological subtype of the disease.

Category C81 provides a fourth-character subclassification to identify the pathologic subtype of Hodgkin's lymphoma and fifth characters to identify the lymph nodes affected (e.g., unspecified site; head, face, and neck; intrathoracic; intra-abdominal; axilla and upper limb; inguinal region and lower limb; intrapelvic; spleen; multiple sites; extranodal and solid organ sites). The pathologic subtype is identified in the following subcategories:

C81.0   Nodular lymphocyte predominant Hodgkin's lymphoma (a rare subtype)

C81.1   Nodular sclerosis classical Hodgkin's lymphoma (the most common subtype)

C81.2   Mixed cellularity classical Hodgkin's lymphoma (a common subtype, most often associated with Epstein-Barr virus infection)

C81.3   Lymphocytic depletion classical Hodgkin's lymphoma (a rare subtype)

C81.4   Lymphocyte-rich classical Hodgkin's lymphoma

C81.7   Other classical Hodgkin's lymphoma

C81.9   Hodgkin's lymphoma, unspecified

FIGURE 29.1   Lymphatic System

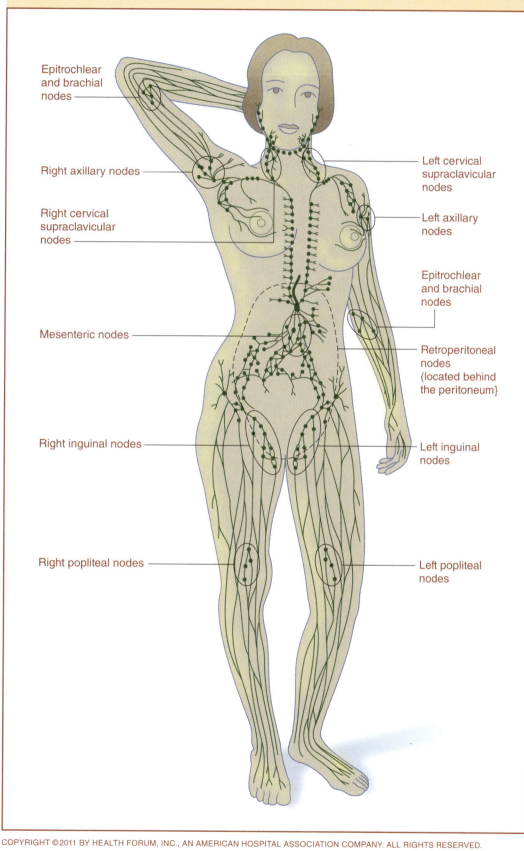

Epitrochlear and brachial nodes

Right axillary nodes

Right cervical supraclavicular nodes

Mesenteric nodes

Right inguinal nodes

Right popliteal nodes

Left cervical supraclavicular nodes

Left axillary nodes

Epitrochlear and brachial nodes

Retroperitoneal nodes (located behind the peritoneum}

Left inguinal nodes

Left popliteal nodes

Non-Hodgkin's Lymphomas

Non-Hodgkin's lymphomas are a heterogeneous group of malignant lymphomas that present a clinical picture that is broadly similar to Hodgkin's disease but with the absence of the giant Reed-Sternberg cells that are characteristic of Hodgkin's lymphoma. Lymphomas develop from the lymphoid components of the immune system. The main cell found in lymphoid tissue is the lymphocyte, an infection-fighting white blood cell, of which there are two main types: B lymphocytes (B-cells) and T lymphocytes (T-cells). Non-Hodgkin's lymphomas can occur at any age and are often marked by lymph nodes that are larger than normal and by fever and weight loss. There are many different types of non-Hodgkin's lymphoma. These types can be divided into aggressive (fast-growing) and indolent (slow-growing) types, and they can be formed from either B-cells or T-cells.

Throughout the past 40 years, the classification of lymphoma has changed considerably based on new insights provided by technological advances, as well as advances in the understanding of the clinical behavior of lymphoma. ICD-10-CM provides the following categories for non-Hodgkin's lymphomas:

C82   Follicular lymphoma
C83   Non-follicular lymphoma
C84   MatureT/NK-cell lymphomas
C85   Other and unspecified types of non-Hodgkin's lymphoma
C86   Other specified types of T/NK-cell lymphomas
C88   Malignant immunoproliferative diseases and certain other B-cell lymphomas

Follicular lymphoma (category C82) is the most common of the indolent non-Hodgkin's lymphomas, and the second most common form of non-Hodgkin's lymphomas overall. It is defined as a lymphoma of follicle center B-cells (centrocytes and centroblasts), which has at least a partially follicular pattern. Category C82 utilizes a dual-axis classification to allow the classification to accommodate the differences in terminology often encountered in medical records. Category C82 allows the classification of follicular lymphoma according to morphological grades (e.g., grade I) or the description of the follicle (e.g., diffuse follicle center), as follows:

C82.0-   Follicular lymphoma grade I
C82.1-   Follicular lymphoma grade II
C82.2-   Follicular lymphoma grade III, unspecified
C82.3-   Follicular lymphoma grade IIIa
C82.4-   Follicular lymphoma grade IIIb
C82.5-   Diffuse follicle center lymphoma
C82.6-   Cutaneous follicle center lymphoma
C82.8-   Other types of follicular lymphoma
C82.9-   Follicular lymphoma, unspecified

ICD-10-CM classifies non-follicular lymphoma to category C83, as follows:

C83.0   Small cell B-cell lymphoma
C83.1   Mantle cell lymphoma
C83.3   Diffuse large B-cell lymphoma
C83.5   Lymphoblastic (diffuse) lymphoma
C83.7   Burkitt lymphoma
C83.8   Other non-follicular lymphoma
C83.9   Non-follicular lymphoma, unspecified

Similar to category C81, Hodgkin's lymphoma, categories C82 through C85 provide fifth characters to identify the lymph nodes affected (e.g., unspecified site; head, face, and neck; intra-thoracic; intra-abdominal; axilla and upper limb; inguinal region and lower limb; intrapelvic; spleen; multiple sites; extranodal and solid organ sites).

Multiple Myeloma, Other Immunoproliferative Neoplasms, and Leukemias

Multiple myeloma and malignant plasma cell neoplasms are classified in category C90, with a fourth character indicating the particular type of neoplasm. Leukemias are classified in categories C91 through C95, with the fourth character indicating either the stage of the disease (acute or chronic) or the type of leukemia (e.g., adult T-cell, prolymophocytic leukemia of T-cell type). For all codes in categories C90 through C95, a fifth character is used to indicate the status of the patient, as follows:

0   Not having achieved remission (failed remission)
1   In remission
2   In relapse

Fifth character "0" is assigned if the health record documentation does not indicate that the patient has achieved remission. When the provider documents that the malignancy is in remission, assign fifth character "1." This character is only assigned when the physician specifically describes the neoplasm as being in remission. If the patient experiences a recurrence and the provider documents "relapse," assign fifth character "2." A relapse or recurrence can occur any time during therapy or after completion of treatment, even months or years after remission.

It is important not to confuse "in remission" with personal history. The categories for leuke-mia, and category C90, Multiple myeloma, have codes for "in remission." Relevant personal history codes are **Z85.6, Personal history of leukemia,** and **Z85.79, Personal history of other malig-nant neoplasms of lymphoid, hematopoietic and related tissues.** Personal history codes explain a patient's past medical condition that no longer exists and is not receiving treatment but has the potential for recurrence, and therefore may require continued monitoring. If the documentation is unclear as to whether the patient is in remission, the provider should be queried.

EXERCISE 29.6

Code the following diagnoses.

---

1. Aleukemic myeloid leukemia,   C92.Z1
    in remission

---

2. Reticulum cell sarcoma of the spleen   C83.37

---

3. Sarcoma, reticulum cell, intrathoracic   C83.32

4.	Intrapelvic Hodgkin's granuloma	C81.96
5.	Chronic myeloid leukemia	C92.10
6.	Plasma cell leukemia	C90.10
7.	Carcinoma of lung with metastatic carcinoma of intrathoracic lymph nodes	C34.90 C77.1
8.	Mycosis fungoides of intrathoracic and intra-abdominal lymph nodes	C84.08
9.	Chlamydial lymphogranuloma	A55
10.	Adenolymphoma of left female breast	D24.02
11.	Diffuse large B-cell lymphoma intra-abdominal	C83.33
12.	Peripheral T-cell lymphoma neck	C84.41

SEQUENCING OF CODES FOR NEOPLASTIC DISEASES

The basic rule for designating principal diagnoses is the same for neoplasms as for any other condition; that is, the principal diagnosis is the condition found after study to have occasioned the current admission or encounter. There is no guideline that indicates a code for malignancy takes precedence. Because the principal diagnosis is sometimes difficult to determine in a patient with a malignant neoplasm, however, the thrust of treatment can often be used as a guide to selecting the principal diagnosis.

Some neoplasms are functionally active in that they may affect the activity of endocrine glands. All neoplasms are classified in chapter 2 of ICD-10-CM, whether they are functionally active or not. The code for these primary neoplasms is assigned first, followed by a code from chapter 4 to identify the endocrine dysfunction associated with any neoplasm. For example:

C56.0 + E28.0   Hyperestrogenism due to carcinoma of right ovary
C56.0 + L68.0   Carcinoma of right ovary with hirsutism

Treatment Directed at Primary Site

When treatment is directed toward the primary site, the malignancy of that site is designated as the principal diagnosis, in which case the primary malignancy is coded as the principal diagnosis, followed by any metastatic sites. The only exception to this guideline is if a patient admission/encounter is solely for the administration of chemotherapy, immunotherapy, or radiation therapy, in which case the appropriate Z51.- code is assigned as the first-listed or principal diagnosis, and the diagnosis or problem for which the service is being performed is assigned as a secondary diagnosis. For example:

C18.7 + C78.7   Carcinoma of sigmoid colon with small metastatic nodules on the liver; sigmoid resection of the colon carried out

Z51.11 + C18.7   Carcinoma of sigmoid colon with prior resection; admitted for chemotherapy

Sometimes two primary sites are present; in this case, each is coded as a primary neoplasm. When treatment is directed primarily toward one site, the neoplasm of that site should be designated as the principal diagnosis. When treatment is directed equally toward both, either may be designated as the principal diagnosis.

Occasionally, a patient admitted for surgery to correct a nonneoplastic condition has a pathology report indicating that a microscopic focus of malignancy is also present. In this situation, the condition that occasioned the admission remains the principal diagnosis, with an additional code assigned for the malignancy. For example:

- A patient with severe urinary retention due to hypertrophy of the prostate is admitted for prostatectomy. Transurethral resection of the prostate is carried out, and the patient is discharged with a diagnosis of benign hypertrophy of the prostate. When the pathology report is received, this diagnosis is confirmed, but a microscopic focus of adenocarcinoma is also identified. Code **N40.1, Enlarged prostate with lower urinary tract symptoms (LUTS),** is assigned as the principal diagnosis, with codes **C61, Malignant neoplasm of prostate,** and **R33.8, Other retention of urine,** as additional diagnoses.

- A patient is admitted for treatment of endometriosis of the uterus, and a total abdominal hysterectomy is carried out. The pathology report confirms the endometriosis but indicates that carcinoma in situ of the cervix is also present. In this case, the endometriosis is the reason for admission and remains the principal diagnosis. An additional code is assigned for the cervical neoplasm.

Treatment Directed at Secondary Site

When a patient is admitted because of a primary neoplasm with metastasis and treatment is directed solely toward the secondary site, the secondary site is designated as the principal diagnosis even though the primary malignancy is still present. A code for the primary malignancy is assigned as an additional diagnosis.

When a patient is admitted because of a primary neoplasm with metastasis and treatment is directed equally toward the primary and secondary sites, the primary malignancy should be designated the principal diagnosis, with an additional code assigned to the secondary neoplasm.

Admission for Complications Associated with a Malignant Neoplasm

Patients with malignant neoplasms often develop complications due to either the malignancy itself or the therapy that they have received. When admission is primarily for treatment of the complication, the complication is coded first, followed by the appropriate code(s) for the neoplasm.

The exception to this guideline is anemia. When the admission/encounter is for management of an anemia associated with the malignancy, and the treatment is only for anemia, the appropriate code for the malignancy is sequenced as the principal or first-listed diagnosis, followed by code **D63.0, Anemia in neoplastic disease.** When the admission/encounter is for management of an anemia associated with an adverse effect of chemotherapy or immunotherapy, and the only treatment is for the anemia, the appropriate adverse effect code should be sequenced first, followed by the appropriate codes for the anemia and neoplasm. For example:

- A patient with metastatic, non–small cell lung cancer of the right upper lobe develops anemia following chemotherapy. The patient presents to the oncologist for treatment of anemia of chemotherapy. Codes **C34.11, Malignant neoplasm of upper lobe, right bronchus or lung,** and **D64.81, Anemia due to antineoplastic chemotherapy,** are assigned.

When the admission/encounter is for management of an anemia associated with an adverse effect of radiotherapy, the anemia code should be sequenced first, followed by the appropriate neoplasm code and code **Y84.2, Radiological procedure and radiotherapy as the cause of abnormal reaction of the patient, or of later complication, without mention of misadventure at the time of the procedure.** For example:

- A female patient with cancer of the right breast is seen for treatment of anemia due to radiation therapy. Code **D64.9, Anemia, unspecified,** is assigned first, followed by codes **C50.911, Malignant neoplasm of unspecified site of right female breast,** and **Y84.2, Radiological procedure and radiotherapy as the cause of abnormal reaction of the patient, or of later complication, without mention of misadventure at the time of the procedure.**

When the admission/encounter is for management of dehydration due to the malignancy or the therapy or a combination of both, and only the dehydration is being treated (intravenous rehydration), the dehydration is sequenced first, followed by the code(s) for the malignancy.

Because the principal diagnosis may be difficult to determine, the focus of treatment can often be used as a guide. For example:

- A patient under treatment for prostate cancer is admitted for gross hematuria. The patient receives 15 units of blood, and bladder irrigation is started and continues until the urine is clear. Code **R31.0, Gross hematuria,** is assigned as principal diagnosis. Assign code **C61, Malignant neoplasm of prostate,** as an additional diagnosis. In this case, the patient was admitted and treated for gross hematuria. Treatment was not directed at the malignancy.

When the admission/encounter is for treatment of a complication resulting from a surgical procedure, designate the complication as the principal or first-listed diagnosis if treatment is directed at resolving the complication. For example:

- A male patient with known adenocarcinoma of the prostate has an outpatient orchiectomy. The physician states that the patient was admitted due to a postoperative complication of postprocedural urethral stricture. Assign code **N99.114, Postprocedural urethral stricture, male, unspecified,** as the principal diagnosis. Assign code **C61, Malignant neoplasm of prostate,** as an additional diagnosis.

Admission or Encounter Involving Administration of Radiotherapy, Immunotherapy, or Chemotherapy

When an episode of care involves the surgical removal of a neoplasm, primary or secondary site, followed by adjunct chemotherapy or radiation treatment during the same episode of care, the code for the neoplasm should be assigned as the first-listed or principal diagnosis.

When a patient admission/encounter is solely for the administration of chemotherapy, immunotherapy, or radiation therapy, assign code **Z51.0, Encounter for antineoplastic radiation therapy,** or **Z51.11, Encounter for antineoplastic chemotherapy,** or **Z51.12, Encounter for antineoplastic immunotherapy,** as the first-listed or principal diagnosis. When the patient receives more than one of these therapies during the same admission, more than one of these codes may be assigned, in any sequence. Because the patient is still under treatment for the malignancy, even though it may have been removed surgically, an additional code for the malignancy is assigned rather than a code from category Z85.

When a patient is admitted for the purpose of radiotherapy, immunotherapy, or chemotherapy and develops complications such as uncontrolled nausea and vomiting or dehydration, the principal or first-listed diagnosis code is **Z51.0, Encounter for antineoplastic radiation therapy,** or **Z51.11, Encounter for antineoplastic chemotherapy,** or **Z51.12, Encounter for antineoplastic immunotherapy,** followed by any codes for the complications.

Tumor lysis syndrome (TLS) is a group of serious, potentially life-threatening metabolic disturbances that can occur after antineoplastic therapy or as a result of radiation or corticosteroid therapy. It is often associated with leukemias and lymphomas but is also seen in other hematologic malignancies and solid tumors. Code **E88.3, Tumor lysis syndrome,** is assigned following code T45.1- to identify the cause when TLS is drug induced. For example:

- A child is diagnosed with acute myeloblastic leukemia and admitted for chemotherapy. Chemotherapy is administered into a peripheral vein and the provider diagnoses tumor lysis syndrome secondary to antineoplastic therapy. Code **Z51.11, Encounter for antineoplastic chemotherapy,** is assigned as the principal diagnosis. Codes **C92.00, Acute myeloblastic leukemia, not having achieved remission; T45.1x5A, Adverse effect of antineoplastic and immunosuppressive drugs, initial encounter;** and **E88.3, Tumor lysis syndrome,** are also assigned. Code **3E03305, Introduction of other antineoplastic into peripheral vein, percutaneous approach,** is assigned for the administration of chemotherapy.

When a patient is admitted for the purpose of inserting a port for later administration of chemotherapy but no chemotherapy is given during the same episode of care, the malignancy is designated as the principal diagnosis and code **Z51.11, Encounter for antineoplastic chemotherapy,** is not assigned. When insertion of the port is followed by chemotherapy during the same episode of care, code Z51.11 is assigned as the principal diagnosis. If an intraperitoneal catheter is inserted for the chemotherapy and chemotherapy is administered during the episode of care, assign code **3E0M305, Introduction of other antineoplastic into peritoneal cavity, percutaneous approach.**

An admission for radium implant insertion or for treatment by radioactive iodine (I-131) is not considered an admission solely for a radiotherapy session. The code for the malignant neoplasm is designated the principal diagnosis; code Z51.0 is not assigned.

Encounter to Determine Extent of Malignancy

When the reason for the admission/encounter is to determine the extent of the malignancy or for a procedure such as paracentesis or thoracentesis, the primary malignancy or appropriate metastatic site is designated as the principal or first-listed diagnosis, even though chemotherapy or radiotherapy is administered.

Current Malignancy versus Personal History of Malignancy

When a primary malignancy has been excised but further treatment, such as an additional surgery for the malignancy, radiation therapy, or chemotherapy is directed to that site, the primary malignancy code should be used until treatment is completed.

Codes from category Z85, Personal history of malignant neoplasm, are assigned only when the primary neoplasm has been previously excised or totally eradicated from its site and is no longer under any type of treatment, and there is no evidence of any existing primary malignancy. This guideline applies to both solid and hematopoietic or lymphatic neoplasms, including leukemia. Note, however, that patients with leukemia are often admitted for a variety of tests or other treatment in addition to chemotherapy. If there is any question about whether the admission is for the sole purpose of chemotherapy, immunotherapy, or radiotherapy, the physician should be consulted.

Malignant Neoplasm Associated with Transplanted Organ

A malignant neoplasm of a transplanted organ should be coded as a transplant complication. A code from category T86.-, Complications of transplanted organs and tissue, is assigned as the principal diagnosis, followed by code **C80.2, Malignant neoplasm associated with transplanted organ.** An additional code is assigned for the specific malignancy.

Malignant Neoplasm in a Pregnant Patient

Codes from chapter 15 of ICD-10-CM, Pregnancy, Childbirth, and the Puerperium, are always sequenced first on a medical record. A code from subcategory O9A.1-, Malignant neoplasm complicating pregnancy, childbirth, and the puerperium, should be used first, followed by the appropriate code from chapter 2 to indicate the type of neoplasm.

Pathologic Fracture Due to a Neoplasm

The sequencing of pathological fractures due to neoplasm is dependent on the focus of treatment, as follows:

- If the focus of treatment is the fracture, a code from subcategory M84.5, Pathological fracture in neoplastic disease, should be sequenced first, followed by the code for the neoplasm.

- If the focus of treatment is the neoplasm with an associated pathological fracture, the neoplasm code should be sequenced first, followed by a code from M84.5 for the pathological fracture. The "code also" note at M84.5 provides this sequencing instruction.

Malignant Ascites

Malignant ascites (R18.0) is the abnormal buildup of fluid in the abdomen caused by malignancy. Diagnostic tests to determine the underlying cause may involve blood tests, ultrasound of the abdomen, and paracentesis. Treatment may include diuretics, therapeutic paracentesis (needle aspiration of the peritoneal cavity), or other therapies directed at the underlying cause. For example:

• A patient is admitted with pancreatic cancer with massive widespread malignant ascites. The final diagnosis is pancreatic cancer with malignant ascites and metastasis to the retroperitoneum. Therapeutic paracentesis is performed. Assign code **C25.9, Malignant neoplasm of pancreas, unspecified,** as the principal diagnosis. Codes **R18.0, Malignant ascites,** and **C78.6, Secondary malignant neoplasm of retroperitoneum and peritoneum,** should be assigned as secondary diagnoses. Assign code **0W9G3ZZ, Drainage of peritoneal cavity, percutaneous approach,** for the paracentesis.

Malignant Pleural Effusion

Malignant pleural effusions (J91.0) can occur due to impaired pleural lymphatic drainage from a mediastinal tumor (especially in lymphomas) and not because of direct tumor invasion into the pleura. The lymphoma is obstructing the drainage system, which is usually caused by disturbance of the normal Starling forces regulating reabsorption of fluid in the pleural space. The code for the malignancy is assigned first, and the code for the malignant pleural effusion is assigned as an additional diagnosis.

Encounter for Prophylactic Organ Removal

For encounters specifically for prophylactic removal of breasts, ovaries, or another organ due to a genetic susceptibility to cancer or a family history of cancer, the principal or first-listed diagnosis should be a code from category Z40, Encounter for prophylactic surgery. The appropriate codes to identify the associated risk factor (such as genetic susceptibility or family history) should be assigned as additional diagnoses.

If the patient has a malignancy of one site and is having prophylactic removal of another site to prevent either a new primary malignancy or metastatic disease, a code for the malignancy should also be assigned in addition to a code from subcategory Z40.0, Encounter for prophylactic surgery for risk factors related to malignant neoplasms. A Z40.0- code should not be assigned if the patient is having organ removal for treatment of a malignancy, such as the removal of testes for the treatment of prostate cancer.

Coding of Admissions or Encounters for Follow-Up Examinations

Once a malignant neoplasm has been excised or eradicated, periodic follow-up examinations are carried out to determine whether there is recurrence of the primary malignancy or any spread to a secondary site. When there is no evidence of recurrence at either a primary site or a metastatic site, code **Z08, Encounter for follow-up examination after completed treatment for malignant neoplasm,** is assigned as the principal diagnosis. Use an additional code to identify the personal history of malignant neoplasm (Z85.-). Use an additional code to identify any acquired absence of organs (Z90.-). Codes should also be assigned for any diagnostic procedures (such as endoscopy and biopsy) that are carried out.

When there is evidence of recurrence at the primary site, the code for the malignancy is designated as the principal diagnosis. For example, a primary carcinoma of the anterior wall of the urinary bladder that was previously excised but has recurred in the lateral wall is coded to **C67.2, Malignant neoplasm of lateral wall of bladder.**

When there is no recurrence at the primary site but there is evidence of metastasis to a secondary site, a code for secondary neoplasm of that site is assigned along with a code from category Z85. Code Z08 is not assigned.

EXERCISE 29.7

Mark the following statements either true or false.

1.	The recurrence of an original primary malignant neoplasm that was previously removed is classified to category Z85, Personal history of malignant neoplasm.	F
2.	If a primary malignant neoplasm was excised previously and the original primary site has not recurred, assign the code for the previous primary malignant neoplasm, using the appropriate code from categories C00 through D49	F
3.	Whenever secondary neoplasms are present, the Z code for identifying personal history of malignant neoplasm can never be sequenced as the principal diagnosis code for Uniform Hospital Discharge Data Set purposes.	T

TREATMENT OF NEOPLASMS

Treatment of neoplasms consists of surgery, chemotherapy, radiation therapy, and other cancer treatment methods. Surgery generally involves removal of the neoplasm. ICD-10-PCS classifies these procedures to the Medical and Surgical Section, with the most common root operations for these being "Excision," "Resection," "Destruction," and "Extirpation."

Thermal Ablation

New advancements in radiofrequency thermal ablation have expanded treatment options for some cancer patients. Thermal ablative procedures utilize heat to destroy lung, liver, or renal malignancies. Minimally invasive, image-guided thermal ablation provides effective treatment of localized neoplastic disease and can also be used as an adjunct to traditional surgery, chemotherapy, and/or radiation treatment. Under radiological imaging, a needle-electrode is inserted at the site of the tumor; radiofrequency energy is then applied to destroy the tumor. Thermal ablation can be performed by three different methods: open, laparoscopic, and percutaneous. ICD-10-PCS classifies thermal ablative procedures to the Medical and Surgical Section, root operation "Destruction." For example, code **0B5M4ZZ, Destruction of bilateral lungs, percutaneous endoscopic approach,** is assigned for thoracoscopic thermal ablation of both lungs.

Chemotherapy and Immunotherapy

Chemotherapy and immunotherapy are coded to the Administration Section, root operation "Introduction," and to the appropriate body system/region where the chemotherapy or immunotherapy agent is administered (e.g., "central vein," "peripheral vein," "peritoneal cavity"), while character 6, substance, identifies whether an antineoplastic or immunotherapeutic substance was administered. Character 7, qualifier, also provides additional information such as whether high-dose interleukin-2 (IL-2), low-dose IL-2, Clofarabine, or monoclonal antibody was administered. For example, the structure of code **3E03305, Infusion of antineoplastic chemotherapy into peripheral vein,** is shown below:

Character 1 Section	Character 2 Body System	Character 3 Root Operation	Character 4 Body System/ Region	Character 5 Approach	Character 6 Substance	Character 7 Qualifier
3	E	0	3	3	0	5
Administration	Physiological systems and anatomical regions	Introduction	Peripheral vein	Percutaneous	Antineoplastic	Other antineoplastic

Bacille Calmette-Guerin is a nonspecific immunotherapy agent used in the treatment of melanoma, cancer of the lung, soft-tissue sarcoma, carcinoma of the colon, and carcinoma of the breast. Interferon is another nonspecific immunotherapy agent used in treating malignancy. Another type of immunotherapy is IL-2, which is used to treat patients with advanced renal cell carcinoma and advanced melanoma. There is a high-dose IL-2 and a low-dose IL-2 therapy. High-dose IL-2 therapy is a hospital inpatient–based regimen usually performed in specialized treatment settings such as the intensive care unit or bone marrow transplant unit. The high-dose IL-2 therapy requires highly specialized oncology professionals to carry out because of the severity of the predictable toxicities, which need extensive monitoring.

Blood brain barrier disruption (BBBD) chemotherapy is a unique option for the delivery of drugs for the treatment of brain tumors and brain metastases. The blood brain barrier (BBB) is an impediment to the delivery of chemotherapy for central nervous system (CNS) malignancies. The BBB is the lining of the small blood vessels in the brain that prevents substances such as toxins or drugs from entering the brain. Patients receiving chemotherapy for brain tumors do not receive adequate doses because antineoplastic drugs cannot cross the BBB through conventional methods of drug delivery. An improved method for drug delivery to the CNS is the infusion of chemotherapy directly into brain arteries through disruption of the BBB. BBBD therapy delivers key drugs and other substances to the brain (i.e., rituximab, trastuzumab, antibodies, or genes), avoiding the long-term cognitive effects of radiotherapy. This technique can deliver five to 10 times the concentration of the drug into the brain without the risks of neurotoxicity. Assign code **Z51.11, Encounter for antineoplastic chemotherapy,** as the principal diagnosis when the admission is for chemotherapy with infusion of a substance to disrupt the blood brain barrier. This procedure is classified by ICD-10-PCS to the Administration Section, root operation "Introduction," and the blood brain barrier disruption is identified by character 7, qualifier. The structure of the code **3E043GN, Introduction of blood brain barrier disruption substance into central vein, percutaneous approach,** is shown below:

Character 1 Section	Character 2 Body System	Character 3 Root Operation	Character 4 Body System/ Region	Character 5 Approach	Character 6 Substance	Character 7 Qualifier
3	E	0	4	3	G	N
Administration	Physiological systems and anatomical regions	Introduction	Central vein	Percutaneous	Other therapeutic substance	Blood brain barrier disruption

The Viadur (leuprolide acetate) implant is used as palliative treatment for advanced prostate cancer. The device is implanted subcutaneously in the arm and delivers leuprolide acetate continuously over a period of 12 months. Leuprolide acetate lowers testosterone, a hormone that is needed by prostate cancer cells. Assign code **3E013VJ, Introduction of other hormone into subcutaneous tissue, percutaneous approach,** for the insertion of the Viadur implant. The code for the prostate malignancy is designated as the principal diagnosis.

Radiation Oncology

Radiation oncology refers to the radiation procedures performed for cancer treatment. ICD-10-PCS classifies these procedures in a special section strictly for radiology oncology procedures. In this section, the characters have the following meanings:

1 Section
2 Body system
3 Modality, which is the basic manner of treatment. Four different modalities are used in this section: "Beam radiation," "Brachytherapy," "Stereotactic radiosurgery," and "Other radiation."
4 Treatment site
5 Modality qualifier, which further specifies the treatment modality. For example, for "Brachytherapy," additional modality qualifiers specify high dose rate or low dose rate.
6 Isotope, which defines the isotope used, if applicable. For example, isotopes used for "Brachytherapy" include cesium-137, iridium-192, iodine-125, palladium-103, and californium-252.
7 Qualifier

The structure of the code **DM1198Z, High dose rate (hdr) brachytherapy of right breast using iridium-192 (Ir-192),** is shown below:

Character 1 Section	Character 2 Body System	Character 3 Modality	Character 4 Treatment Site	Character 5 Modality Qualifier	Character 6 Isotope	Character 7 Qualifier
D	M	1	1	9	8	Z
Radiation oncology	Breast	Brachytherapy	Breast, right	High dose rate	Iridium 192	None

Laser Interstitial Thermal Therapy

Thermal therapy can be used to destroy malignancies involving the brain, breast, liver, prostate, and other organs. The energy sources come in many forms, such as laser, microwave, and radiofrequency. The heat source may be extracorporeal (outside the body), extrastitial (outside the tumor), or interstitial (inside the tumor).

Laser interstitial thermal therapy (LITT) is a surgical procedure in which obliteration of soft tissues in the body is performed through elevated temperatures caused by the local absorption of laser energy under magnetic resonance imaging guidance. With this type of therapy, the energy is applied directly to the tumor rather than passing through surrounding normal tissue. The therapy encompasses the whole target but does not extend to surrounding critical structures. LITT may also be performed to remove cancerous lesions from other sites, such as head and neck, liver, breast, prostate, and lung. ICD-10-PCS classifies LITT to the Radiation Oncology Section, root type "Other radiation," with the character 5, modality qualifier, of "laser interstitial thermal therapy." The structure of the code **D0Y1KZZ, Laser interstitial thermal therapy of brain stem,** is shown below:

Character 1 Section	Character 2 Body System	Character 3 Modality	Character 4 Treatment Site	Character 5 Modality Qualifier	Character 6 Isotope	Character 7 Qualifier
D	0	Y	1	K	Z	Z
Radiation oncology	Central and peripheral nervous system	Other radiation	Brain stem	Laser interstitial thermal therapy	None	None

Intra-Operative Electron Radiation Therapy

Intra-operative electron radiation therapy is a specialized, intensive radiation treatment administered during surgery directly to the cancer tumor or tumor bed. Normal tissue is protected, thereby substantially increasing the effectiveness of the treatment. The code for the malignant neoplasm is designated as the principal diagnosis; code Z51.11 is not assigned. Assign the appropriate code for the radiation provided using a code from the Radiation Oncology Section, root operation "Beam radiation," modality "electrons," and selecting the "intraoperative" value for character 7, qualifier. The structure of the code **DW013Z0, Beam radiation of head and neck using electrons, intraoperative,** is shown below:

Character 1 Section	Character 2 Body System	Character 3 Modality	Character 4 Treatment Site	Character 5 Modality Qualifier	Character 6 Isotope	Character 7 Qualifier
D	W	0	1	3	Z	0
Radiation oncology	Anatomical regions	Beam radiation	Head and neck	Electrons	None	Intraoperative

EXERCISE 29.8

The following exercise provides a review of the material on neoplasms presented in this handbook. For this exercise, assign procedure codes where applicable.

1. Infiltrating papillary transitional cell   C67.5
   carcinoma of urinary bladder (neck)
   Percutaneous excision of bladder neck tumor   0TBC3ZZ

2. Carcinoma of midesophagus with spread   C15.4
   to celiac lymph nodes   C77.2
   Permanent gastrostomy procedure, percutaneous   0D163J4
   approach with synthetic substitute
   Radiotherapy to esophagus using photons 1-10 MeV   DD001ZZ

3. Malignant carcinoid tumor of small intestine   C7A.019

4. Carcinoma, scirrhous, female left breast, outer portion   C50.812
   Open biopsy with frozen section followed   0HTU0ZZ
   immediately by left radical mastectomy   07T60ZZ
   (resection of left breast, left axillary lymph nodes   0KTJ0ZZ
   and pectoral muscle)   0HBU0ZX

5. Intramural leiomyoma of uterus   D25.1

6. Multiple myeloma   C90.00

7. Carcinoma of gallbladder with metastasis   C23

     to abdominal lymph nodes and liver   C77.2

     and peritoneal implants   C78.7

                                         C78.6

     Exploratory laparotomy with   0FT40ZZ

     cholecystectomy, needle   0DBW3ZX

     biopsy of peritoneal implant, and intra-operative   D7063Z0

     electron radiation therapy abdominal lymph nodes

8. Squamous cell carcinoma in situ, floor of mouth   D00.06

     Resection of lesion, floor of mouth (mucosa)   0CB4XZZ

9. Metastatic malignant melanoma from left   C43.59

     lateral chest wall to axillary lymph node   C77.3

                                  Neoplasm

     Excision of malignant melanoma   0WB80ZZ

     of chest wall (open approach) with radical left   07T60ZZ

     axillary lymphadenectomy (open approach)

10. Metastatic adenocarcinoma of sacrum,   C79.51

     prostatic in origin   Z85.46

     Previous prostatectomy

                                  History

11. A 33-year-old female admitted for prophylactic   Z40.01

     removal of both breasts, with documented genetic

     susceptibility to breast cancer due to extensive family   Z15.01

     history of breast carcinoma   Z80.3

     Bilateral mastectomy   0HTV0ZZ

12. Seminoma, left testis   C62.92
    Bilateral radical orchiectomy (open approach)   0VTC0ZZ

---

13. Lipoma, right kidney   D17.5

---

14. Chronic lymphocytic leukemia (B-cell), in remission   C91.11

---

15. Admitted for chemotherapy (peripheral vein) following   Z51.11
    oophorectomy on previous admission for   C56.1
    carcinoma of left ovary   3E03305

---

16. Brain metastasis, admitted for chemotherapy   Z51.11
    and infusion of substance to disrupt blood brain   C79.31
    barrier (peripheral vein, percutaneous)   3E033GN
                                                                   3E03305

---

17. Ovarian carcinoma with malignant ascites   C56.9
    and metastasis to the peritoneal cavity   R18.0
                                                                   C78.6

Coding OF Injuries, Burns, Poisoning, AND Complications OF Care

CHAPTER 30

Injuries

CHAPTER OVERVIEW

- Injuries, poisoning, and certain other consequences of external causes are found in chapter 19 of ICD-10-CM.

- The primary axis for classifying injuries is the anatomical site.

- The secondary axis is the type of injury.

- The most severe cause of injury is used as the principal diagnosis.

- External cause of morbidity codes indicate how the injury occurred, the intent (accident or intentional), the place where the injury occurred, the status of the patient at the time the injury occurred, and any activity that may have caused or contributed to the injury.

- An External cause code is never a principal diagnosis.

- Multiple External cause codes can be used. The first corresponds to the most serious diagnosis.

- Code child and adult abuse before the associated injuries or conditions resulting from the abuse.

- Fractures make an extensive use of the seventh-character extension, which is more detailed than for other injuries.

- Any fracture not specified as open or closed is classified as closed in ICD-10-CM.

- A fracture not indicated whether displaced or not displaced should be coded to displaced.

- Reduction is the most common treatment for fractures.

- If dislocations accompany fractures, they are included in the fracture code.

- Internal injuries, blood vessel and nerve injuries, open wounds, and amputations are also covered in this chapter.

- An amputation not identified as partial or complete should be coded to complete.

LEARNING OUTCOMES

After studying this chapter you should be able to:

Use External cause codes to assist in the classification of an injury.

Select the correct seventh-character extension.

Code for procedures related to fractures.

Code for open wounds and other varieties of injuries.

TERMS TO KNOW

External cause codes
indicate external cause of morbidity; used with injury and poisoning codes

Pathological fracture
a fracture caused by bone weakening associated with conditions such as osteoporosis or neoplastic diseases

REMEMBER . . .

This chapter of ICD-10-CM utilizes extensive inclusion and exclusion notes, which make for some long and complicated codes.

INTRODUCTION

Chapter 19 of ICD-10-CM classifies injuries, poisoning, certain early complications of trauma, complications of surgical and medical care, and certain other consequences of external causes. Because this chapter covers such a broad range of conditions, guidelines for the coding of burns, poisoning, adverse effects, and complications of medical and surgical care will be discussed in subsequent chapters of this handbook.

Injuries are classified in the following sections:

S00–S09	Injuries to the head
S10–S19	Injuries to the neck
S20–S29	Injuries to the thorax
S30–S39	Injuries to the abdomen, lower back, lumbar spine, pelvis, and external genitals
S40–S49	Injuries to the shoulder and upper arm
S50–S59	Injuries to the elbow and forearm
S60–S69	Injuries to the wrist, hand, and fingers
S70–S79	Injuries to the hip and thigh
S80–S89	Injuries to the knee and lower leg
S90–S99	Injuries to the ankle and foot
T07	Unspecified multiple injuries
T14	Injury of unspecified body region
T15–T19	Effects of foreign body entering through natural orifice
T20–T32	Burns and corrosions
T33–T34	Frostbite
T66–T78	Other and unspecified effects of external causes
T79	Certain early complications of trauma

The primary axis for classifying injuries is the anatomical site as indicated in the preceding list; the second axis is determined by type of injury. Chapter 19 of ICD-10-CM uses the S section for coding different types of injuries related to single body regions, and it uses the T section to cover injuries to unspecified body regions as well as poisoning and certain other consequences of external causes. Inclusion and exclusion notes are used extensively in this chapter, some of them long and complex, and it is important to give careful attention to these if correct code assignments are to be made.

Codes from S00 through T14.9 are for traumatic injuries and should not be used for normal, healing surgical wounds or to identify complications of surgical wounds.

CODE EXTENSIONS

Most categories in chapter 19 have seventh-character extensions that are required for each applicable code. The seventh character must always be the seventh character in the code. For codes that require a seventh character but are not six characters long, a placeholder "x" must be used to fill in the empty characters. Most categories in this chapter have three extensions (with the exception of fractures, which are covered later in this chapter): "A," initial encounter; "D," subsequent encounter; and "S," sequela.

Extension "A"

The seventh-character extension "A," initial encounter, should be used while the patient is receiving active treatment for the injury. Examples of active treatment are surgical treatment, emergency department encounter, and evaluation and treatment by a new physician.

Extension "D"

The seventh-character extension "D," subsequent encounter, is used for encounters after the patient has received active treatment of the injury and is receiving routine care for the injury during the healing or recovery phase. For aftercare of an injury, assign the acute injury code with the seventh character "D" (subsequent encounter). Examples of subsequent care are cast change or removal, removal of external or internal fixation device, medication adjustment, other aftercare, and follow-up visits following injury treatment.

Extension "S"

The seventh-character extension "S," sequela, is used for complications or conditions that arise as a direct result of an injury, such as scar formation after a burn; the scars are sequelae of the burn. When using extension "S," it is necessary to use both the injury code that precipitated the sequela and the code for the sequela itself. The "S" is added only to the injury code, not the sequela code. The "S" extension identifies the injury responsible for the sequela. The specific type of sequela (e.g., scar) is sequenced first, followed by the injury code.

MULTIPLE CODING OF INJURIES

When coding multiple injuries, each injury should be coded separately unless a combination code is provided, in which case the combination code is assigned. General codes for multiple injuries are provided for use when there is insufficient detail in the medical record (such as trauma cases transferred promptly to another facility) to assign a more specific code. Code **T07, Unspecified multiple injuries,** should not be assigned unless information for a more specific code is not available.

As discussed in chapter 2 of this handbook, the word "with" and the word "and" are used in a specific way in ICD-10-CM, and they are used a great deal in chapter 19 of ICD-10-CM. The word "with" means that both sites mentioned in the diagnostic statement are involved in the injury.

The word "and," when it appears in a code title, is interpreted as meaning "and/or"—that is, that either or both sites are involved. In coding injuries, mention of fingers usually takes into account the thumb, but there are a few separate codes for injuries of the thumb. Terms such as "condyle," "coronoid process," "ramus," and "symphysis" refer to the portion of the bone involved in an injury, not to the bone itself.

SEQUENCING OF INJURY CODES

If admission is due to injury and several injuries are present, the code for the most severe injury, as determined by the provider and the focus of treatment, is designated as the principal diagnosis. If the diagnostic statement is not clear on this point, the physician should be asked to make this determination.

Superficial injuries such as abrasions or contusions are not coded when associated with more severe injuries of the same site—only the severe injury should be coded.

When a primary injury results in minor damage to peripheral nerves or blood vessels, the primary injury is sequenced first, with an additional code(s) for injuries to nerves and spinal cord (such as category S04) and/or injury to blood vessels (such as category S15). When the primary injury is to the blood vessels or nerves, that injury should be sequenced first.

EXTERNAL CAUSE OF MORBIDITY

As mentioned in chapter 12 of this handbook, External cause of morbidity codes (categories V01–Y99) are used with injury codes to provide information about how an injury occurred (cause), the intent (accidental or intentional), the place where the injury occurred, and the status (e.g., military, civilian) of the patient at the time the injury occurred. In the case of a person who seeks care for an injury or other health condition that resulted from an activity, or when an activity contributed to the injury or health condition, activity codes (category Y93) are used to describe the activity.

The codes for poisoning, adverse effect, and underdosing (categories T36–T50) and for toxic effects of substances chiefly nonmedicinal as to source (categories T51–T65) include information on the cause (e.g., the responsible substance) as well as the intent (accidental or intentional). No External cause code from chapter 20 of ICD-10-CM is needed for cause or intent for these codes.

Injuries are a major cause of mortality, morbidity, and disability, and the cost of care related to these conditions contributes significantly to the increased cost of health care. Reporting External cause codes provides data for injury research and evaluation of injury prevention strategies. Although reporting external cause is optional unless mandated by state or insurance carrier regulation, health care providers are strongly encouraged to report External cause codes for all initial treatment of injuries. Guidelines for reporting have been developed, and providers are urged to follow these guidelines so that there is consistency in the data.

Major categories of External cause codes include:

V00–V99	Transport accidents
W00–X58	Other external causes of accidental injury
X71–X83	Intentional self-harm
X92–Y08	Assault
Y21–Y33	Event of undetermined intent
Y35–Y38	Legal intervention, operations of war, military operations, and terrorism
Y62–Y84	Complications of medical and surgical care
Y90–Y99	Supplementary factors related to causes of morbidity classified elsewhere

The selection of appropriate External cause codes for injuries is guided by the Index to External Causes of Injury and by inclusion and exclusion notes in the Tabular List. The codes are found in the Tabular List in alphabetical order.

External Cause Status

A code from category Y99, External cause status, is assigned to indicate the work status of the person at the time the injury occurred. The status code indicates whether the injury occurred during military activity, whether a nonmilitary person was at work, or whether a student or volunteer was involved in a nonwork activity at the time of the causal event. A code from Y99 should be assigned, when applicable, with other External cause codes, such as transport accidents and falls. Category Y99 codes include status codes for activities done as a hobby, for leisure, and for recreation as well as volunteer activity and activity of off-duty military personnel.

The external cause status codes are not applicable to poisonings, adverse effects, misadventures, or late effects. Do not assign a code from category Y99 if no other External cause codes (cause, activity) are applicable for the encounter. Do not assign code **Y99.9, Unspecified external cause status,** if the status is not stated.

Activity Codes

Assign a code from category Y93, Activity codes, to describe the activity of the patient at the time the injury or other health condition occurred. Codes from category Y93 are used only once, at the initial encounter for treatment. Only one code from Y93 should be recorded on a medical record. An activity code should be used in conjunction with a place of occurrence code, Y92.

If a patient is a student but is injured while performing an activity for income, use seventh character "2," work-related activity. A work-related activity is any activity for which payment or income is received.

The activity codes are not applicable to poisonings, adverse effects, misadventures, or late effects. Coders should not assign code **Y93.9, Activity, unspecified,** if the activity is not stated.

Sequencing of External Cause Codes

An External cause code is never used as the principal diagnosis. If the reporting format limits the number of External cause codes that can be used in reporting clinical data, report the code for the cause/intent most related to the principal diagnosis. If the format permits capture of additional External cause codes, the cause/intent, including medical misadventures, of the additional events should be reported rather than the codes for place, activity, or external status.

If two or more events cause separate injuries, an External cause code should be assigned for each. The first-listed External cause code will be selected using the following sequencing hierarchy:

- External cause codes for child and adult abuse take precedence over all other External cause codes.

- External cause codes for terrorism events take priority over all other External cause codes except child and adult abuse.

- External cause codes for cataclysmic events take priority over all External cause codes except those for child and adult abuse and terrorism. Cataclysmic events include storms, floods, hurricanes, tornadoes, blizzards, volcanic eruptions, and earth surface movements and eruptions.

- Transport accidents take priority over all other External cause codes except those for cataclysmic events, child and adult abuse, and terrorism.

- Activity and external cause status are assigned following all causal (intent) External cause codes.

- The first-listed External cause code should correspond to the cause of the most serious diagnosis due to an assault, an accident, or self-harm, following the order of hierarchy listed above.

Transport and Vehicle Accidents

A transport accident (V00–V99) is one in which the vehicle involved must be moving or running or in use for transport purposes at the time of the accident. A long note at the beginning of this section defines in detail just what is meant by each type of transportation and what vehicles are included.

This section is structured in 12 groups. Those relating to land transport accidents (V01–V89) reflect the victim's mode of transport and are subdivided to identify the victim's "counterpart" or the type of event. The vehicle of which the injured person is an occupant is identified in the first two characters because it is seen as the most important factor to identify for prevention purposes.

For example, the injured person in a motor vehicle accident may be a passenger in the vehicle, a bicyclist, or a pedestrian. Definitions of these roles are provided at the beginning of this section. For example:

> $\underline{\text{S72.309B}}$ + V03.10xA + Y93.01 + Y99.8   Open fracture, shaft of femur (pedestrian during recreational walk struck by automobile)

Accidents caused by machines such as agricultural or earth-moving equipment are classified as transport accidents if the pieces of equipment were in operation as transport vehicles when the accidents occurred. Otherwise, they are classified in category W30, Contact with agricultural machinery, or category W31, Contact with other and unspecified machinery, with a fourth character indicating the specific type of equipment.

External Cause of Injury Classified by Intent

Separate External cause codes are provided to classify the external cause of injuries resulting from accident, self-harm, or assault. If the intent is unknown or unspecified, code the intent as accidental intent. All transport accident categories (V00–V99) assume accidental intent. External cause codes for events of undetermined intent should only be used if the record documentation specifies that the intent cannot be determined.

Category Y38, Terrorism, is used to identify injuries and illnesses acquired as a result of terrorism. These codes (Y38.0- through Y38.9-) follow the definition of terrorism established by the U.S. Federal Bureau of Investigation (FBI). Coders are not to classify a death or an injury as terrorist related unless the federal government has designated the incident as terrorism. The definition of terrorism employed by the FBI is found at the inclusion note at the beginning of category Y38: "These codes are for use to identify injuries resulting from the unlawful use of force or violence against persons or property to intimidate or coerce a Government, the civilian population, or any segment thereof, in furtherance of political or social objective." More than one Y38 code may be assigned if the injury is the result of more than one mechanism of terrorism (e.g., destruction of aircraft and firearms). A code from category Y92, Place of occurrence of the external cause, is assigned as an additional code to identify the place of occurrence.

Place of Occurrence

ICD-10-CM provides external cause category Y92, Place of occurrence of the external cause, for use as an additional code to indicate the location of the patient at the time of injury or other condition. A place of occurrence code is used only once, at the initial encounter for treatment. No seventh-character extensions are used for category Y92.

Only one code from Y92 should be recorded on a medical record. When the place of occurrence is not specified or is not applicable, code **Y92.9, Unspecified place or not applicable,** is not assigned. Note that codes from category Y92 refer only to the location, not to the activity of the injured person. Separate codes are provided for the activity and status. For example:

W10.0xxA + Y92.520	Fall on escalator in airport building
X03.0xxA + Y92.096 + Y93.E9 + Y99.8	Clothing caught fire while burning household trash in backyard of home, causing burn

LATE EFFECTS OF EXTERNAL CAUSES

When the condition code from the main classification is a late effect of injury, the associated External cause code must also indicate a late effect. Late effects are reported using the External cause code with the seventh-character extension of "S" for sequela. These codes should be used with any report of a late effect or sequela resulting from a previous injury. A late effect External cause code should never be used with a related current nature of injury code. Late effect External cause codes are used for subsequent visits when a late effect of the initial injury is being treated, and not for subsequent visits for follow-up care (e.g., to assess healing, to receive rehabilitative therapy) when no late effect of the injury has been documented.

For example, a diagnosis of extensive scarring of the face due to an old burn is coded as **T20.00xS, Burn of unspecified degree of head, face, and neck, unspecified site, sequela,** and **X08.8xxS, Exposure to other specified smoke, fire and flames, sequela.** In this example, code T20.00xS indicates that the condition is a late effect of burn of eye, face, head, and neck, and code X08.8xxS indicates that it is a late effect of an accident caused by fire. Note that both codes have the same seventh-character "S" for sequela.

EXERCISE 30.1

Assign only the External cause codes in the following exercises. Assume initial encounter unless stated otherwise.

---

1. Closed fracture, right tibia and fibula,   V18.0xxA

   due to fall from bicycle while patient was   Y93.55

   working as a messenger for a delivery service   Y99.0

---

2. Injury to deliveryman who got off of a   V58.4xxA

   moving truck not on a public highway   Y99.0

   because he thought the driver was stopping

   Accident

---

3. Multiple facial lacerations to military police officer   V43.52xA

   driving an automobile while on duty that was in a collision   Y99.1

   with another automobile on expressway   Y92.411

---

4. Anoxic brain damage due to previous   V03.90xS

   head injury, three years ago, when

   patient was accidentally struck by car

   while walking along highway

   Accident

---

5. Injury received by crew member of
    commercial airline when he fell
    at takeoff

    <u>Fall</u>

    V97.0xxA
    Y99.0

---

6. Injury received by guest passenger in
    hot-air balloon when balloon made
    unexpected descent

    <u>Accident</u>

    V96.02xA
    Y93.89
    Y99.8

---

7. Passenger injured when he accidentally
    collided with another passenger while
    getting off a streetcar

    <u>Accident</u>

    V82.4xxA
    Y92.410

---

8. Railway employee injured by <u>accident</u>
    involving collision with rolling stock

    V81.2xxA
    Y99.0

---

9. Railway employee injured when hit by
    rolling stock while unloading material

    <u>Accident</u>

    V81.2xxA
    Y99.0

---

10. Passenger injured in accidental
    derailment of train

    <u>Accident</u>

    V81.7xxA

---

11. Motorcyclist injured in accidental
    <u>collision</u> with train

    V25.4xxA

CHILD AND ADULT ABUSE

Expanded codes for child and adult abuse facilitate the gathering of more specific data. Child abuse has become a major concern in the United States. All 50 states, the District of Columbia, and the U.S. territories have mandatory child abuse and neglect reporting laws that require certain professionals and institutions to report suspected maltreatment to a child protective services agency. Each state has its own definitions of child abuse and neglect based on minimum standards set by federal law. Federal legislation provides a foundation for states by identifying a minimum set of acts or behaviors that define child abuse and neglect. Adult abuse is considered to be both underreported and underdiagnosed.

Keep in mind that codes for child and adult abuse are assigned only when the physician documents abuse; coders should not interpret narrative descriptions as abuse without the physician's confirmation.

ICD-10-CM provides two categories for reporting adult and child abuse, neglect, and other maltreatment. The first axis of classification is whether the abuse is confirmed (category T74) or suspected (T76). The exception to this is code **T74.4, Shaken infant syndrome,** which ICD-10-CM defaults to confirmed abuse. The fourth character for categories T74 and T76 indicates the type of abuse (neglect or abandonment, physical abuse, sexual abuse, emotional abuse, or unspecified maltreatment), while the fifth character specifies whether child or adult abuse is involved. The selection of the code for confirmed or suspected abuse is based on medical record documentation.

Abuse often results in physical injuries and other medical conditions. When this is the case, sequence first the appropriate code from categories T74 or T76, followed by any accompanying mental health or injury code. Use an additional External cause code to identify perpetrator, if known (Y07.-).

ICD-10-CM classifies confirmed adult and child abuse, neglect, and maltreatment as assault. Any of the assault codes (X92–Y08) may be used to indicate the external cause of any physical injury resulting from the confirmed abuse.

For suspected cases of abuse or neglect, do not report External cause or perpetrator codes. If a suspected case of abuse, neglect, or mistreatment is ruled out during an encounter, code **Z04.71, Encounter for examination and observation following alleged adult physical abuse, ruled out,** or code **Z04.72, Encounter for examination and observation following alleged child physical abuse, ruled out,** should be used, not a code from category T76.

Incidents of documented adult abuse complicating pregnancy, childbirth, and the puerperium, whether suspected or confirmed, are classified to chapter 15 of ICD-10-CM (rather than to T74.- or T76.-), as follows:

O9a.3-   Physical abuse
O9a.4-   Sexual abuse
O9a.5-   Psychological abuse

Codes from O9a.3-, O9a.4-, and O9a.5 should be sequenced first, followed by the appropriate codes (if applicable) to identify any associated current injury due to physical or sexual abuse, as well as a code to identify the perpetrator of the abuse.

Examples of child and adult abuse include the following:

- A patient is seen in the emergency department with a diagnosis of confirmed battered spouse syndrome and with a laceration of the right forehead. She reports that her husband hit her in the face because he was angry when she was late getting ready to go out to dinner. The following codes should be assigned: **T74.11xA, Adult physical abuse, confirmed, initial encounter; S01.81xA, Laceration without foreign body of other part of head, initial encounter; Y04.0xxA, Assault by unarmed fight or brawl, initial encounter; Y07.01, Husband as perpetrator of maltreatment and neglect,** and **Y99.8, Other external cause status.**

- A four-month-old infant is seen in the emergency department with a diagnosis of shaken infant syndrome. The baby had been unconscious for approximately two hours after being shaken vigorously by the father when he was unable to make the infant stop crying. The diagnostic statement also includes diagnoses of subdural hematoma and bilateral retinal hemorrhage. The following codes should be assigned: **T74.4xxA, Shaken infant syndrome, initial encounter; S06.5x3A, Traumatic subdural hemorrhage with loss of consciousness of 1 hour to 5 hours 59 minutes, initial encounter; H35.63, Retinal hemorrhage, bilateral; Y07.11, Biological father as perpetrator of maltreatment and neglect; and Y99.8, Other external cause status.**

- An elderly woman is brought to the hospital in a state of severe malnutrition. She had been living in an unlicensed care home, where it was suspected she was fed only one meal per day for several months. In the hospital, a gastric feeding tube is placed and high-protein supplements are given for severe caloric deficiency malnutrition. The following codes should be assigned: **T76.01xA, Adult neglect or abandonment, suspected, initial encounter; E41, Nutritional marasmus; Z59.4, Lack of adequate food and safe drinking water; and 3E0G76Z, Introduction of nutritional substance into upper G.I., via natural or artificial opening.**

- A six-month-old infant with heat prostration is brought to the hospital by her parents, who had left her alone in their car while they did their grocery shopping. The parents stated that the child was asleep and they had felt that she would be all right for the short time they would be gone. The physician documents suspected child abandonment. The following codes should be assigned: **T76.02xA, Child neglect or abandonment, suspected, initial encounter; T67.5xxA, Heat exhaustion, unspecified, initial encounter.**

Subcategory Z62.81, Personal history of abuse in childhood, provides codes to indicate that a patient has a past personal history of abuse in childhood:

Z62.810	History of physical and sexual abuse in childhood
Z62.811	History of psychological abuse in childhood
Z62.812	History of neglect in childhood
Z62.819	History of unspecified abuse in childhood

Codes from category Z91 are also available to indicate that a patient has a past personal history of adult psychological trauma:

Z91.410	History of adult physical and sexual abuse
Z91.411	History of adult psychological abuse
Z91.412	History of adult neglect
Z91.419	History of unspecified adult abuse
Z91.49	History of psychological trauma NEC

There are also counseling codes (category Z69) to provide information regarding encounters for mental health services for the victim or perpetrator of abuse. These codes include counseling for child abuse problems, spousal or partner abuse problems, and other abuse.

FRACTURES

Fractures are classified in different categories according to their anatomical locations, as follows:

S02	Fractures of skull and facial bones
S12	Fractures of cervical vertebra and other parts of neck
S22	Fractures of rib(s), sternum, and thoracic spine
S32	Fractures of lumbar spine and pelvis
S42	Fractures of shoulder and upper arm
S49	Physeal fractures of shoulder and upper arm
S52	Fracture of forearm
S59	Physeal fractures of elbow and forearm
S62	Fracture of wrist and hand level
S72	Fracture of femur
S79	Physeal fractures of hip and thigh
S82	Fractures of lower leg, including ankle
S89	Physeal fractures of lower leg
S92	Fracture of foot and toe, except ankle

Three-character categories indicate more specific sites within these broad groupings, fourth characters usually indicate the bone (e.g., mandible), and fifth characters usually indicate a more specific portion of the bone (e.g., condylar process of mandible). For fractures of the extremities, fourth characters usually indicate a general part of the bone (e.g., upper end of ulna), fifth characters indicate a more specific part of the bone (e.g., olecranon process with intra-articular extension of ulna), and the sixth characters provide information on laterality (e.g., right, left, or unspecified) as well as whether the fracture is displaced or nondisplaced.

In an open fracture, an open wound that communicates with the bone is present. Terms that indicate open fracture include the following: "compound," "infected," "missile," "puncture," and "with foreign body."

Closed fractures do not produce an open wound. They are described by terms such as "comminuted," "depressed," "elevated," "greenstick," "spiral," "simple," and "transverse." Any fracture not specified as open or closed is classified as closed in ICD-10-CM. A comminuted fracture refers to a fracture in which bone is broken, splintered, or crushed into a number of pieces. A "comminuted fracture" is distinguished from a "compound fracture," an open fracture in which the bone is sticking through the skin. (See figure 30.1 for examples of open and closed fractures.)

A fracture not indicated as either displaced or not displaced should be coded to displaced. Occasionally, a diagnostic statement contains terms that relate to both open and closed fractures. In this case, the code for the open fracture always takes precedence. For example, a diagnosis of compound comminuted fracture uses terms that can indicate both open and closed fractures. However, such a fracture would be coded as open because the term "compound" always carries this meaning, even though the term "comminuted" by itself refers to a closed fracture.

The principles of multiple coding of injuries should be followed in coding fractures. Fractures of specified sites are coded individually by site in accordance with both the provisions within categories S02, S12, S22, S32, S42, S49, S52, S59, S62, S72, S79, S82, S89, S92 and the level of detail furnished by medical record content. Multiple fractures are sequenced in accordance with the severity of the fracture.

Note that a code from category M80, Osteoporosis with current pathological fracture, not a traumatic fracture code, should be used for any patient with known osteoporosis who suffers a fracture—even if the patient had a minor fall or trauma, if that fall or trauma would not usually break a normal, healthy bone.

Seventh-Character Extensions for Fractures

ICD-10-CM makes extensive use of seventh-character extensions for fractures. While most categories in chapter 19 have three extensions—"A," initial encounter; "D," subsequent encounter; and "S," sequela—the seventh-character extensions for fractures are significantly different. More importantly, the actual seventh-character codes vary depending on the bones affected, and therefore it is imperative to review the Tabular List at each category level to determine the appropriate code extension. For example, codes in category S02, Fracture of skull and facial bones, have six available seventh-character extensions. However, category S52, Fracture of forearm, has sixteen different seventh-character extensions (see figure 30.2).

The greater number of seventh-character extensions doesn't mean that the concepts of initial encounter, subsequent encounter, and sequela no longer apply. Rather, there are additional axes of classification included in these extensions. For example, the code extensions for initial encounter (A, B, C) and subsequent encounter (D–H, J–R) applicable to category S52, Fracture of forearm (figure 30.1), also distinguish between open (B–C, E–F, H–J, M–N, Q–R) and closed (A, D, G, K, P)

FIGURE 30.1 Examples of Open and Closed Fractures

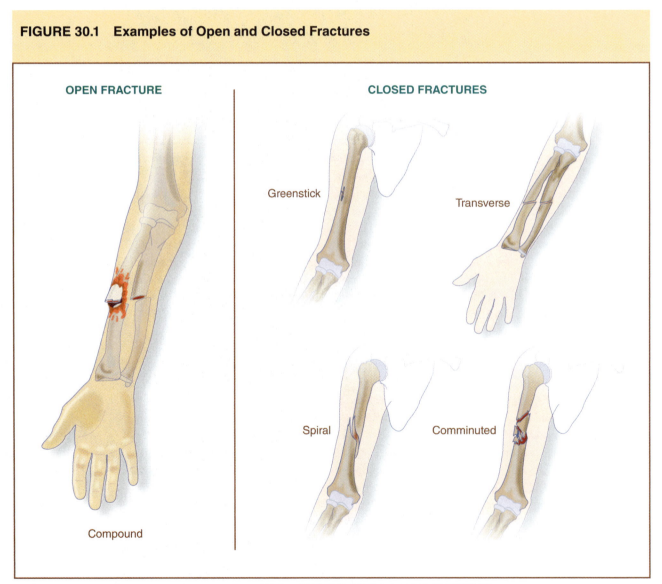

OPEN FRACTURE

CLOSED FRACTURES

Greenstick

Transverse

Spiral

Comminuted

Compound

Figure 30.2   Sample Tabular List Seventh-Character Extensions

S52   Fracture of forearm

Note: A fracture not indicated as displaced or nondisplaced should be coded to displaced

A fracture not indicated as open or closed should be coded to closed

The open fracture designations are based on the Gustilo open fracture classification

Excludes1: traumatic amputation of forearm (S58.-)

Excludes2: fracture at wrist and hand level (S62.-)

The appropriate 7th character is to be added to each code from category S52

A - initial encounter for closed fracture

B - initial encounter for open fracture type I or II

C - initial encounter for open fracture type IIIA, IIIB, or IIIC

D - subsequent encounter for closed fracture with routine healing

E - subsequent encounter for open fracture type I or II with routine healing

F - subsequent encounter for open fracture type IIIA, IIIB, or IIIC with routine healing

G - subsequent encounter for closed fracture with delayed healing

H - subsequent encounter for open fracture type I or II with delayed healing

J - subsequent encounter for open fracture type IIIA, IIIB, or IIIC with delayed healing

K - subsequent encounter for closed fracture with nonunion

M - subsequent encounter for open fracture type I or II with nonunion

N - subsequent encounter for open fracture type IIIA, IIIB, or IIIC with nonunion

P - subsequent encounter for closed fracture with malunion

Q - subsequent encounter for open fracture type I or II with malunion

R - subsequent encounter for open fracture type IIIA, IIIB, or IIIC with malunion

S - sequela

fractures. In addition, for subsequent encounters, the code extensions specify whether the fracture is undergoing routine healing (D–F) or if there is a problem such as delayed healing (G–J), nonunion (K–N), or malunion (P–R). For example:

- A patient who suffered a traumatic fracture of the shaft of the left humerus a month earlier is admitted with fever and pain secondary to diverticulitis. The fracture is healing well and is treated minimally.

Principal diagnosis:	K57.92	Diverticulitis of intestine, part unspecified, without perforation or abscess without bleeding
Additional diagnosis:	S42.302D	Unspecified fracture of shaft of humerus, left arm, subsequent encounter for fracture with routine healing

- A young man who fractured the lateral malleolus of the left fibula six weeks previously is admitted for removal of the internal pins under local anesthesia.

Principal diagnosis:	S82.62xD	Displaced fracture of lateral malleolus of left fibula, subsequent encounter for fracture with routine healing

Several different methodologies are used to classify fractures. ICD-10-CM uses the Gustilo classification in the assignment of the seventh-character extension for open fractures (see figure 30.2). However, coders should not select the fracture type without provider documentation in the medical record, even though the fracture may be described using the terminology found in the Gustilo classification (figure 30.3). For example, if the documentation reflects an open fracture with a 2-centimeter wound and soft tissue damage, it should not be coded as a Gustilo type II fracture without physician confirmation. Instead, query the provider if the documentation does not reflect the type of open fracture.

Initial Care

The seventh-character extension for initial encounter (A, B, C) for traumatic fracture is assigned while the patient is receiving active treatment for the fracture. Examples of active treatment are surgical treatment, emergency department encounter, and evaluation and treatment by a new physician.

Subsequent Care

Fractures are coded using the seventh-character extension for subsequent care for encounters after the patient has completed active treatment of the fracture and is receiving routine care for the fracture during the healing or recovery phase. Examples of fracture aftercare are cast change or removal, removal of external or internal fixation device, medication adjustment, and follow-up visits following fracture treatment.

Subsequent care for complications of fractures, such as malunion and nonunion, should be reported with the appropriate seventh-character extensions for subsequent care with nonunion (K, M, N,) or subsequent care with malunion (P, Q, R). However, if a patient delays seeking treatment for a fracture and presents for initial care for a fracture or nonunion, the appropriate seventh character for "initial encounter," rather than "subsequent encounter," should be assigned. Care for complications of surgical treatment for fracture repairs during the healing or recovery phase should be coded with the appropriate complication codes rather than the seventh-character extensions.

Malunion implies that bony healing has occurred but that the fracture fragments are in poor position. Treatment of malunion ordinarily involves surgical cutting of the bone (osteotomy), repositioning the bone, and adding some type of internal fixation device with or without bone graft. Malunion is frequently diagnosed while the fracture is still in a healing state, but sometimes no surgical intervention is used in the hope that the patient may not have any functional problems as a result of the malunion.

FIGURE 30.3   Gustilo Classification of Open Fractures

I   Low energy, wound less than 1 cm

II   Wound greater than 1 cm with moderate soft tissue damage

III   High energy wound greater than 1 cm with extensive soft tissue damage

   IIIA   Adequate soft tissue cover

   IIIB   Inadequate soft tissue cover

   IIIC   Associated with arterial injury

Nonunion, on the other hand, implies that healing has not occurred and that there is still separation of the bony structures involved in the fracture. Treatment of nonunion usually involves opening the fracture, scraping away intervening soft tissue (usually scar tissue), performing a partial debridement of the bone end, and repositioning the bone. Treating nonunion of a fracture is more complicated and difficult to perform than treating a malunion.

Skull Fractures and Intracranial Injuries

Fractures of skull and facial bones are classified to category S02. Fourth characters indicate the area of the skull (e.g., base) or face (e.g., mandible) fractured. Fifth characters provide additional specificity, such as the specific bone or the type of fracture. Any associated intracranial injury is coded separately using a code from category S06.

If an intracranial injury involves an open wound of the head (S01.-) or a fracture of the skull (S02.-), these are coded separately, as instructed by the notes in the Tabular List. Codes for intracranial injury (S06.-) have additional characters to indicate:

- Whether a loss of consciousness was associated with the injury
- How long the unconscious state lasted
- If the loss of consciousness was greater than 24 hours
  —with return to preexisting level of consciousness
  —without return to preexisting level of consciousness with patient surviving
- Whether there was loss of consciousness of any duration with death due to brain injury or due to any other cause, prior to regaining consciousness

Because the type of information above is rarely included in the diagnostic statement, it usually must be obtained through a review of the medical record, particularly the emergency department record and admitting note.

Category S06, Intracranial injury, which includes traumatic injury, is divided into the following subcategories:

S06.0	Concussion
S06.1	Traumatic cerebral edema
S06.2	Diffuse traumatic brain injury
S06.3	Focal traumatic brain injury (with further subdivisions for unspecified; contusion and laceration of right, left, or unspecified cerebrum; traumatic hemorrhage of right, left, or unspecified cerebrum; and contusion, laceration, and hemorrhage of cerebellum or brainstem)
S06.4	Epidural hemorrhage
S06.5	Traumatic subdural hemorrhage
S06.6	Traumatic subarachnoid hemorrhage
S06.8	Other intracranial injuries (including injury of right or left internal carotid artery, intracranial portion, and other intracranial injury)
S06.9	Unspecified intracranial injury

Concussion (S06.0x-) is the most common type of traumatic brain injury. It refers to cerebral bruising that sometimes leads to a transient unconsciousness, often followed by brief amnesia, vertigo, nausea, and weak pulse. The patient may experience severe headache and blurred vision after regaining consciousness. Recovery usually takes place within 24 to 48 hours. Patients with this type of head injury are often dazed, and the physician may have to rely on clinical findings alone to make a diagnosis of concussion. When there is documentation of concussion with other intracranial injuries classified in category S06, the code for the specified intracranial injury should be assigned. When the head injury is further described as a cerebral laceration or a cerebral contusion or when it is associated with subdural, subarachnoid, other intracranial hemorrhage, or other specified condition classifiable in category S06, the code for concussion is not assigned.

Postconcussional syndrome (F07.81) includes a variety of symptoms that may occur for a variable period of time following a concussion, sometimes as long as a few weeks. The symptoms most often associated with postconcussional syndrome are headache, dizziness, vertigo, fatigue, difficulty in concentrating, depression, anxiety, tinnitus, heart palpitations, and apathy. Any of these conditions may cause the patient to seek treatment. Code F07.81 is ordinarily not assigned on the initial admission for treatment of the concussion. When the patient is treated for symptoms within 24 to 48 hours of injury and the physician lists a diagnosis as postconcussional syndrome, postcontusional syndrome, or posttraumatic brain syndrome, the coder should ask the physician whether the concussion is still in the current state. If it is, it should be coded to S06.0x- rather than F07.81. Posttraumatic headache is often associated with postconcussion syndrome. Use an additional code (G44.3-) to capture any associated acute or chronic posttraumatic headache along with code F07.81.

Vertebral Fractures

Vertebral fractures are classified according to the region of the spine affected: cervical spine (S12.-), thoracic spine (S22.0-), and lumbar spine (S32.0-). Fourth characters at category S12 indicate the vertebra (e.g., first cervical vertebra), while fifth and sixth characters provide additional information on the type of fracture (e.g., stable, unstable, displaced, nondisplaced). Fifth characters at subcategories S22.0 and S32.0 indicate the vertebra (e.g., second thoracic vertebra, third lumbar vertebra, etc.), while sixth characters specify the type of fracture (e.g., wedge compression, stable burst). For example:

S12.030-	Displaced posterior arch fracture of first cervical vertebra
S22.020-	Wedge compression fracture of second thoracic vertebra
S32.031-	Stable burst fracture of third lumbar vertebra

Additional codes are used to report any associated spinal cord injuries, as follows:

S14.0, S14.1-	Cervical spinal cord injury
S24.0, S24.1-	Thoracic spinal cord injury
S34.-	Lumbar spinal cord and spinal nerve injury

If the fracture of the ribs, sternum, and thoracic spine also involve injury of intrathoracic organs, these should be coded separately using codes from subcategory S27.

Fractures of the Extremities

Category codes S42, S49, S52, S59, S62, S72, S79, S82, S89, and S92 classify fractures of the extremities. Fourth characters usually indicate a general part of the bone (e.g., upper end of ulna), fifth characters indicate a more specific part of the bone (e.g., olecranon process with intraarticular extension of ulna), and sixth characters provide information on laterality (e.g., right, left, or unspecified) as well as whether the fracture is displaced or nondisplaced. For example:

S42.142B   Displaced fracture of glenoid cavity of scapula, left shoulder, initial encounter for open fracture

S52.044C   Nondisplaced fracture of coronoid process of right ulna, initial encounter for open fracture type IIIA, IIIB, or IIIC

Physeal fractures (categories S49, S59, S79, and S89), which include growth plate fractures, refer to a disruption in the cartilaginous physis of long bones that may or may not involve epiphyseal or metaphyseal bone. These fractures account for 15–20 percent of major long-bone fractures and 34 percent of hand fractures in childhood. The large majority of these fractures heal well without any further problems. However, some lead to clinically significant shortening and angulation; others lead to disorders due to destruction of epiphyseal circulation, which inhibits development of growth plate or formation of bone bridge.

There are many different classification systems throughout the world related to physeal fractures, with the Salter-Harris (SH) classification being the preferred system in North America. ICD-10-CM provides fifth characters to capture the SH type of fracture (type I, II, III, or IV), if documented by the physician. For example:

S49.002A   Unspecified physeal fracture of upper end of humerus, left arm, initial encounter for closed fracture

S49.011D   Salter-Harris Type I physeal fracture of upper end of humerus, right arm, subsequent encounter for fracture with routine healing

Multiple fractures of the same bone(s) classified with different fourth-character or fifth-character subdivisions (bone part) within the same three-character category are coded individually by site. For example:

- Initial encounter for comminuted fracture of the shaft of the right humerus, with nondisplaced closed-fracture dislocation of right shoulder involving the greater tuberosity, is coded **S42.301A, Unspecified fracture of shaft of humerus, right arm, initial encounter for closed fracture,** and **S42.254A, Nondisplaced fracture of greater tuberosity of right humerus, initial encounter for closed fracture.**

- Initial encounter closed fractures of the olecranon process and coronoid process of the left ulna are coded **S52.022A, Displaced fracture of olecranon process without intra-articular extension of left ulna, initial encounter for closed fracture,** and **S52.042A, Displaced fracture of coronoid process of left ulna, initial encounter for closed fracture.**

EXERCISE 30.2

Code the following diagnoses. Assume these are for initial encounters unless otherwise noted. Do not assign External cause codes.

1. Comminuted fracture, upper end of left tibia — S82.102A

2. Fracture, left ischium — S32.602A
   Fracture, left second, third, fourth, fifth, and sixth ribs — S22.42xA

3. Closed fracture of vault of skull with subdural hemorrhage; three-hour loss of consciousness — S02.0xxA / S06.5x3A

4. Open Monteggia's fracture, type II — S52.279B

5. Cerebral concussion — S06.383A
   Brain stem contusion without open wound
   Patient unconscious for almost two hours

6. Trimalleolar fracture, left ankle — S82.852A

7. Closed fracture, lateral condyle, left humerus — S42.432A

8. Compound fracture, coronoid process of mandible — S02.63xB

9. Compound fracture, type II, shaft of tibia and fibula, left — S82.202B / S82.832B

10. Bilateral compound depressed skull fractures — S02.91xB
    Bilateral massive cerebral contusion and laceration — S06.310A / S06.320A

Pathological Fractures

Bones weakened by conditions such as osteoporosis or neoplastic disease often develop pathological fractures that occur with no trauma or only minor trauma that would not result in fracture in a healthy bone. This type of fracture is classified with musculoskeletal conditions rather than with injuries and is discussed in chapter 23 of this handbook.

Current pathologic fractures are reported using categories/subcategories M80, M84.4-, M84.5, and M84.6. For example:

- A patient with a chronic vertebral pathological fracture with orders for pain medication is admitted for an unrelated condition. Code **M84.48xA, Pathological fracture, other site, initial encounter for fracture,** is assigned for a chronic vertebral fracture. The seventh-character extension "D" is not appropriate because the patient has not completed active treatment.

Compression Fractures

Compression fractures may be due either to disease or to trauma. The coder should search the medical record for any recent significant trauma or for any indication of concurrent bone disease that might point to pathological fracture. If the diagnosis cannot be clarified, the physician should be asked to provide further specificity.

Fractures Due to Birth Injury

Fractures due to birth injury are not classified in the injury chapter of ICD-10-CM but instead are classified as perinatal conditions (category P13) and are discussed in chapter 27 of this handbook.

PROCEDURES RELATED TO FRACTURES

In the treatment of fractures, the primary goal is to achieve correct bone alignment and maintain alignment until healing is completed and normal function can be restored. Procedures include open and closed reduction, simple manipulation, and application of various types of fixation and traction devices. The type of treatment depends on the general condition of the patient, the presence of any associated injuries, and the type and location of the fracture.

Reduction of Fractures

The most common fracture treatment involves moving bone fragments into as nearly normal an anatomic position as possible, with stabilization to maintain the bone in this position until it is sufficiently healed to prevent displacement. ICD-10-PCS classifies reduction of a displaced fracture to the root operation "Reposition." The application of a cast or splint in conjunction with the "Reposition" procedure is not coded separately. Treatment of a nondisplaced fracture is coded to the procedure performed; for example, casting is classified to the root operation "Immobilization" in the Placement Section.

In an open reduction, the surgeon exposes the bone by extending the open wound over the fracture or making a further incision to work directly with the bone for the purpose of restoring correct alignment. Debridement is often necessary to remove debris or other material that has entered an open fracture site. In a closed reduction, alignment is achieved without incision to the fracture site. Debridement of the bone is not needed.

Internal Fixation

Internal fixation includes the use of pins, screws, staples, rods, and plates that are inserted into the bone to maintain alignment. When the fractured bone is in good alignment so that no manipulation is necessary, internal fixation may be used to stabilize the bone without any fracture reduction being performed. Internal fixation is also used without reduction when it is necessary to reinsert an internal fixation device because the original is either displaced or broken. An incision is made for the purpose of inserting the internal fixation wires or pins; a code from the root operation "Insertion" is assigned for fixation that is not associated with fracture reduction. Internal fixation can also be used with closed fracture reduction. The small incision necessary to insert the fixation device does not warrant considering the procedure to be an open reduction.

External Fixation

Unlike internal fixation, external fixation is ordinarily noninvasive and includes "Traction" or "Immobilization" by the use of casts or splints. The classification essentially recognizes four types of external fixation devices: monoplanar (seventh-character qualifier "3"), ring system (seventh-character qualifier "4"), hybrid system (seventh-character qualifier "5"), and limb-lengthening device (seventh-character qualifier "9"). When "Traction" is performed, a code from the Placement Section, root operation "Traction," is used. External fixation devices may later be removed using the root operation "Removal" in the Medical and Surgical Section. "Removal" of splints, casts, and braces are classified to the Placement Section, root operation "Removal."

Although "Traction" devices are usually applied by means of Kirschner wires or Steinmann pins, the use of these materials is not considered an internal fixation. "Traction" devices include the following:

- Skin "Traction," such as tape, foam, or felt traction devices applied directly to the skin, with longitudinal force applied to the limb
- Skeletal "Traction" into or through the bone that applies force directly to the long bones (the wires or pins are drilled transversely through the bone and exit through the skin)
- Cervical spinal "Traction," such as Baron's tongs, Crutchfield tongs, and halo skull "Traction"
- Upper-extremity "Traction," such as Dunlap's skin "Traction"
- Lower-extremity "Traction," such as Buck's extension skin "Traction," Charnley's "Traction" unit, Hamilton-Russell's "Traction," balanced suspension "Traction," and fixed skeletal "Traction"

EXERCISE 30.3

Code the following procedures; do not code diagnoses.

---

1. Traction to right lower extremity with   2W6LX0Z
   traction apparatus

---

2. Open reduction and debridement
   of Monteggia fracture, right upper
   extremity, with Rush pin (internal)
   to stabilize ulna   Reposition

                                Excision   0PSK04Z

   0PBK0ZZ

---

3. Open reduction of fracture, right tibia, with
   Knowles pins (internal) and two-inch screw
   Below-the-knee cast applied   0QSG04Z

---

4. Open reduction and Kirschner wire
   fixation (internal) of distal to main
   fragment, fracture of left humerus shaft   0PSG04Z

---

5. Open reduction of fracture, left hip,
   with Jewett nail fixation (upper femur)   0QS704Z

---

6. Reduction, displaced fracture right humerus shaft
   (external approach) with cast   0PSFXZZ

---

7. Open reduction and internal fixation,
   fracture of right mandible   0NST04Z

---

8. Open reduction, fracture of left maxilla and
   left zygomatic arch
   Closed reduction, nasal bone fracture (external approach)   0NSS0ZZ

   0NSN0ZZ

   0NSBXZZ

---

9. Bifrontal craniotomy with reposition and
   debridement of compound skull fractures
   Open reduction, right orbital fracture
   Tracheostomy (percutaneous)   0NSP0ZZ

   0NS00ZZ

   0NB10ZZ

   0NB20ZZ

   0B113Z4

ADMISSIONS OR ENCOUNTERS FOR ORTHOPEDIC AFTERCARE

Patients who have had fracture reduction usually require aftercare for removal of wires, pins, plates, or external fixation devices. In addition, patients with orthopedic injuries still in the healing stage may be seen primarily for conditions not related to the injury but with some monitoring or clinical evaluation of the injury carried out during the episode of care. Aftercare for traumatic fractures is coded to the acute fracture with the appropriate seventh character extension for subsequent care. The aftercare Z codes should not be used for aftercare of injuries. For aftercare of an injury, the acute injury code is assigned, with the appropriate seventh-character extension for subsequent encounter.

Z codes are provided for admissions or encounters for other (non-fracture related) orthopedic aftercare, as follows:

Z47.1	Aftercare following joint replacement surgery
Z47.2	Encounter for removal of internal fixation device
Z47.81	Encounter for orthopedic aftercare following surgical amputation
Z47.82	Encounter for orthopedic aftercare following scoliosis surgery
Z47.89	Encounter for other orthopedic aftercare

However, code **Z47.2, Encounter for removal of internal fixation device,** should not be used if the encounter is for removal of the internal fixation device due to infection or inflammatory reaction to an internal fixation device (T84.6-) or a mechanical complication of an internal fixation device (T84.1-). The appropriate code from T84.6- or T84.1- should be used instead.

Z codes are also provided to indicate an orthopedic status when it is significant for the episode of care. Orthopedic status codes include **Z96.6-, Presence of orthopedic joint implants; Z96.7, Presence of other bone and tendon implants; Z97.1-, Presence of artificial limb (complete) (partial);** and **Z98.1, Arthrodesis status.**

Aftercare codes should be used in conjunction with any other aftercare codes or other diagnosis codes to provide better detail on the specifics of an aftercare encounter visit, unless otherwise directed by the classification. The sequencing of multiple aftercare codes depends on the circumstances of the encounter. For example:

- A patient had a right intertrochanteric hip fracture that was repaired through a total hip joint replacement. He is now receiving aftercare at the physician's office. Codes **Z47.1, Aftercare following joint replacement surgery,** and **Z96.641, Presence of right artificial hip joint,** are assigned for the encounter. Each code represents a different piece of information regarding the aftercare and is needed to describe the encounter fully. Code **S72.141D, Displaced intertrochanteric fracture of right femur, subsequent encounter for closed fracture with routine healing,** is not appropriate because there is no longer a fracture; the hip has been replaced by a prosthetic joint.

DISLOCATIONS AND SUBLUXATIONS

Joint dislocation occurs when bones in a joint become displaced or misaligned and the ligaments are damaged. A subluxation is a partial or incomplete dislocation. Dislocation or subluxation associated with fracture is included in the fracture code, and reduction of the dislocation is included in the code for the fracture reduction. Dislocation or subluxation of a joint without associated fracture is classified in the following categories:

S03   Dislocation and sprain of joints and ligaments of head
S13   Dislocation and sprain of joints and ligaments at neck level
S23   Dislocation and sprain of joints and ligaments of thorax
S33   Dislocation and sprain of joints and ligaments of lumbar spine and pelvis
S43   Dislocation and sprain of joints and ligaments of shoulder girdle
S53   Dislocation and sprain of joints and ligaments of elbow
S63   Dislocation and sprain of joints and ligaments at wrist and hand level
S73   Dislocation and sprain of joint and ligaments of hip
S83   Dislocation and sprain of joints and ligaments of knee
S93   Dislocation and sprain of joints and ligaments at ankle, foot, and toe level

The first axis is the general site, such as wrist and hand, with the fifth character indicating a more specific site such as midcarpal dislocation of the wrist; the sixth-character axis indicates whether it is a subluxation or dislocation, and laterality. Any associated open wound or spinal cord injury is coded separately.

Reduction of dislocation not associated with fracture is coded to the Medical and Surgical Section, root operation "Reposition," with the body part being the appropriate joint (rather than the actual bone, as with procedures to reduce fractures).

INTERNAL INJURIES OF THE CHEST, ABDOMEN, AND PELVIS

Internal injuries of the chest, abdomen, and pelvis are classified to categories S24–S27 and S34–S37. Any associated open wounds are coded separately. For example:

S27.0-   Pneumothorax (traumatic) without mention of open wound
S27.1- + S21.309-   Hemothorax with open wound front wall of thorax into thoracic cavity
S36.400-   Injury of duodenum without mention of open wound into cavity
S26.91-   Contusion of heart

Codes from subcategory S37.0, Injury of kidney, are used to describe an internal injury of the kidney caused by trauma. A nontraumatic acute kidney injury is coded **N17.9, Acute kidney failure, unspecified.**

BLOOD VESSEL AND NERVE INJURIES

When a primary injury results in minor damage to peripheral nerves or blood vessels, the primary injury is sequenced first, with additional codes for injuries to nerves and spinal cord (such as category S04) and/or injury to blood vessels (such as category S15). When the primary injury is to a blood vessel or nerve, however, the code for that injury should be sequenced first.

For example, an open wound of the abdominal wall without penetration into the peritoneal cavity, but with rupture of the aorta, would be coded **S35.00-, Injury to abdominal aorta,** with S31.109- as an additional code.

OPEN WOUNDS

Open wounds such as lacerations, puncture wounds, cuts, animal bites, avulsions, and traumatic amputations that are not associated with fracture are coded separately in categories S01, S11, S21, S31, S41, S51, S61, S71, S81, and S91. Fourth characters provide more specificity regarding the body area. Fifth and sixth characters indicate the type of wound such as laceration, puncture wound, or open bite, and whether there is a foreign body. Any associated injury to internal organs or wound infection are coded separately.

Both cellulitis and osteomyelitis sometimes occur as complications of open wounds. Sequencing of codes for open wounds with these major infections depends on the circumstances of admission. It is important to determine whether it is the wound that is being addressed or only the resulting infection. For example, a patient who had an open wound of the hand six weeks ago might be seen because osteomyelitis has developed. In this situation, the osteomyelitis would ordinarily be designated as the principal diagnosis, with an additional code for the open wound. A patient who had a slight puncture wound earlier in the week might show evidence of cellulitis at the site. The wound itself did not require any attention. The reason for the encounter is cellulitis, and cellulitis is the principal diagnosis.

AMPUTATIONS

When listed as a diagnosis, traumatic amputation is classified to subcategories S08.1- through S08.8-, S28.1- through S28.2-, S38.1- through S38.2-, S48.0- through S48.9-, S58.0- through S58.9-, S68.0- through S68.7-, S78.0- through S78.9-, S88.0- through S88.9-, and S98.0- through S98.9-, rather than classified as an open wound. ICD-10-CM distinguishes between complete and partial traumatic amputations. An amputation not identified as partial or complete should be coded to complete amputation. For example:

S58.019-	Traumatic amputation of arm at elbow
S58.122-	Partial traumatic amputation of left arm below elbow
S88.011-	Complete traumatic amputation of right leg at knee

The term "amputation" is also used for an amputation procedure, which can be performed for a variety of reasons other than the treatment of trauma. Amputation is performed by either disarticulation or cutting through the bone. Amputation procedures are classified in ICD-10-PCS to the Medical and Surgical Section, root operation "Detachment." The body part value is the site of the "Detachment." If applicable, a qualifier is assigned to specify the level where the extremity was detached. "Detachment" procedures are found only in body systems "X" ("anatomical regions, upper extremities") and "Y" ("anatomical regions, lower extremities") because amputations are performed on the extremities, across overlapping body layers (e.g., skin, muscle, bone), and therefore cannot be coded to a specific musculoskeletal body system, such as bones or joints.

The root operation "Detachment" makes use of specific qualifiers that are dependent on the body part value in the "upper extremities" and "lower extremities" body systems. Definitions of the terms used with "Detachment" are shown in table 30.1. Sample codes include the following:

0X6J0Z0	Disarticulation of right wrist, complete, open
0Y6M0Z0	Complete amputation right foot
0Y6C0Z3	Amputation above right knee, distal shaft of femur
0X680Z2	Mid-shaft amputation, right humerus

TABLE 30.1   Definitions of Terms Used for Qualifiers for "Detachment" Procedures

Body Part	Qualifier Term Definition
Upper arm and upper leg	**High:** Amputation at the proximal portion of the shaft of the humerus or femur
	Mid: Amputation at the middle portion of the shaft of the humerus or femur
	Low: Amputation at the distal portion of the shaft of the humerus or femur
Hand and foot	**Complete:** Amputation through the carpometacarpal joint of the hand or through the tarsometatarsal joint of the foot
	Partial: Amputation anywhere along the shaft or head of the metacarpal bone of the hand or of the metatarsal bone of the foot
Thumb, finger, or toe	**Complete:** Amputation at the metacarpophalangeal/metatarsophalangeal joint
	High: Amputation anywhere along the proximal phalanx
	Mid: Amputation through the proximal interphalangeal joint or anywhere along the middle phalanx
	Low: Amputation through the distal interphalangeal joint or anywhere along the distal phalanx

OTHER INJURIES

Superficial injuries such as contusions, blisters, abrasions, superficial foreign bodies, and insect bites are classified to categories S00, S10, S20, S30, S40, S50, S60, S70, S80, and S90. The fourth and fifth characters indicate a more specific site or type of injury. The sixth character indicates laterality. When these injuries are associated with a major injury, such as fracture of the same site, a code for the superficial injury is usually not assigned. Note that the term "superficial" does not refer to the severity of the injury but to the superficial structures affected, that is, those pertaining to or situated near the surface.

The presence of a foreign body entering through an orifice is classified in categories T15 through T19. When the foreign body is associated with a penetrating wound, it is coded as an open wound, by site, residual foreign body in soft tissue. A splinter without open wound is classified to superficial injury by body region. A foreign body accidentally left during a procedure in an operative wound is considered to be a complication of a procedure and is coded T81.5-. Codes within T15–T19 that include the external cause do not need an additional External cause code.

EARLY COMPLICATIONS OF TRAUMA

Certain early complications of trauma that are not included in the code for the injury are classified in category T79, Certain early complications of trauma, not elsewhere classified. The fourth-character axis indicates the type of complication, such as air or fat embolism, traumatic secondary and recurrent hemorrhage and seroma, traumatic shock, traumatic anuria, traumatic ischemia of muscle, traumatic subcutaneous emphysema, or traumatic compartment syndrome. Ordinarily, codes from category T79 are assigned as secondary codes, with the code for the injury sequenced first. With today's shorter lengths of stay and increased emphasis on outpatient care, however, the complication itself may occasionally be the reason for an outpatient encounter or admission and is the principal diagnosis in such cases.

Subcategory T79.A, Traumatic compartment syndrome, classifies compartment syndrome secondary to trauma. Nontraumatic compartment syndrome is classified to M79.a-. Acute traumatic compartment syndrome is usually a sequela of a serious injury to the lower or upper extremities, abdomen, or other sites and can lead to significant motor and sensory deficits, pain, stiffness, and deformity when untreated. Acute traumatic compartment syndrome is always associated with fractures, dislocations, and/or crush injuries. Other risk factors for the development of acute traumatic compartment syndrome include vascular injuries and coagulopathy. The diagnosis is established by multiple compartment pressure readings. Traumatic compartment syndrome is coded as follows:

T79.a0	Compartment syndrome, unspecified
T79.a11	Traumatic compartment syndrome of right upper extremity
T79.a12	Traumatic compartment syndrome of left upper extremity
T79.a19	Traumatic compartment syndrome of unspecified upper extremity
T79.a21	Traumatic compartment syndrome of right lower extremity
T79.a22	Traumatic compartment syndrome of left lower extremity
T79.a29	Traumatic compartment syndrome of unspecified lower extremity
T79.a3	Traumatic compartment syndrome of abdomen
T79.a9	Traumatic compartment syndrome of other sites

EXERCISE 30.4

Code the following diagnoses. Assume these are for initial encounters unless otherwise noted. Do not assign External cause codes.

---

1. Stab wound of abdominal wall, infected — S31.119A
   L08.9

---

2. Lacerations, left foot, with foreign body — S91.322A

---

3. Traumatic amputation of left arm and hand above the elbow — S48.112A

---

4. Traumatic anuria due to injury to kidney — S37.009A
   T79.5xxA

OTHER EFFECTS OF EXTERNAL CAUSE

Categories T66 through T78 classify other and unspecified effects of external causes resulting from exposure to heat and to cold and a variety of other conditions due to external causes that are not classifiable elsewhere in ICD-10-CM. Codes from these categories are not assigned when a more specific code for the effect is available. For example, colitis due to radiation therapy is coded **K52.0, Gastroenteritis and colitis due to radiation,** because the effect is identified. A diagnosis of complication of radiation therapy not otherwise specified and with no further information documented in the medical record is coded **T66.-, Radiation sickness, unspecified.**

Code T68.- is assigned for hypothermia, with several exceptions. If it is due to anesthesia, code T88.51 is assigned. When the hypothermia is not due to low temperature, code **R68.0, Hypothermia not associated with low environmental temperature,** is assigned. An additional code is used to identify the source of exposure, such as exposure to excessive cold of man-made origin (W93) or of natural origin (X31). Three codes are provided for hypothermia of the newborn: **P80.0, Cold injury syndrome; P80.8, Other hypothermia of newborn;** and **P80.9, Hypothermia of newborn, unspecified.**

Category T78, Adverse effects not elsewhere classified, is used to classify a variety of adverse effects such as anaphylactic shock, adverse food reactions, angioneurotic edema, unspecified allergy, and Arthus phenomenon.

Anaphylaxis is an immunologic reaction that affects multiple body systems. Reactions can range from mild—with hives, itchiness, swelling of eyes and lips, and some congestion—to life threatening, with airway obstruction and cardiovascular collapse. Shock occurs when there is excessive fluid leakage from the blood vessels into the tissues. Anaphylactic shock due to an adverse food reaction is coded T78.0, with a fifth character indicating the type of food involved. For example:

- A patient with a known allergy to tree nuts presents to the emergency department with wheezing and urticaria. The patient is diagnosed with an anaphylactic reaction secondary to eating cookies containing walnuts. Assign code **T78.05xA, Anaphylactic shock due to tree nuts and seeds, initial encounter.** Codes from subcategory T78.0 are assigned for both anaphylactic reaction and anaphylactic shock due to adverse food reaction.

Anaphylactic shock due to correct medicinal substances properly administered is classified to a code from T36 through T50, with fifth or sixth character "5" to identify the drug, followed by **T88.6-, Anaphylactic shock due to adverse effect of correct drug or medicament properly administered.** When the shock is due to an incorrect use of a drug, a medicinal or biological substance, or a toxic material not chiefly medicinal, anaphylactic shock is classified as a poisoning, with the poisoning code sequenced first and an additional code of T78.2- assigned to indicate the shock.

EXERCISE 30.5

Code the following diagnoses and assign External cause codes. Assume these are for initial encounters unless otherwise noted.

1. Heat prostration due to salt and water depletion	T67.4xxA
2. Frostbite, all toes due to cold exposure	T33.831A T33.832A X31.xxxA
3. Radiation cataract	H26.8 W90.8xxA
4. Anaphylactic shock due to eating peanuts	T78.01xA

LATE EFFECTS OF INJURIES

In coding late effects of injuries, the residual condition or specific type of sequela (such as scar, deformity, or paralysis) is sequenced first, followed by the injury code with the seventh-character extension "S," sequela. A seventh character of "S" is also assigned to the External cause of injury code. A current injury code is never used with a late effect code for the same type of injury.

EXERCISE 30.6

Code the following diagnoses and assign External cause codes; sequence the codes according to the principles for coding late effects.

1. Paralysis of right wrist due to previous accidental self-inflicted laceration of right radial nerve	G56.91 S64.21xS X58.xxxS
2. Esophageal stricture due to old lye burn of esophagus	K22.2 T28.6xxS

3. Nonunion fracture of neck of left femur   S72.002K
    suffered in a bar brawl three months ago   Y04.0xxS

4. Posttraumatic scars of cheek due to old   L90.5
    accidental lacerations   S01.419S
                                                                    X58.xxxS

EXERCISE 30.7

Code the following diagnoses and procedures. Assume these are for initial encounters unless otherwise noted. Assign External cause codes where information is provided.

1. Anterior dislocation of left shoulder,   S43.015A
    patient thrown from horse she was riding   V80.010A
    while working as a horse trainer   Y93.52
                                                                    Y99.0

    Dislocation reduction, external approach   0RSKXZZ

2. Displaced fracture dislocation left humerus,   S42.212A
    surgical neck; patient caught in avalanche   X36.1xxA
    while on vacation skiing at mountain resort   Y92.838
                                                                    Y93.23
                                                                    Y99.8

    Open reduction and internal fixation   0PSD04Z
    with Rush pin and screws

3. Colles fracture, right   S52.531A
    Patient fell from chair at home   W07.xxxA
                                                                    Y92.099
                                                                    Y99.8

    Closed reduction with anterior-posterior   0PSHXZZ
    plaster splints (external approach)

4. Intracapsular fracture, neck of femur, right   S72.011A

    Patient fell from in-line skates   V00.111A

           Y93.51

           Y99.8

    Closed reduction with insertion of   0QS634Z

    Smith-Petersen nail (percutaneous approach)

---

5. Closed fractures of right upper femur and left ilium   S72.001A

    Fat emboli, posttraumatic   S32.302A

    Patient driving motorcycle on highway   T79.1xxA

    lost control and overturned   V28.4xxA

                     Loss of control

    Open reduction with plate fixation, right upper   0QS604Z

    femur, with skeletal traction   2W67X0Z

    for ilium fracture

---

6. Fracture of base of skull, with right   S02.10xA

    subdural hemorrhage without loss of consciousness;   S06.5x0A

    patient fell from parachute in a voluntary descent   V97.29

    during military training   Y99.1

---

7. Posttraumatic shortening of left radius   M21.732

    due to previous comminuted fracture of   S52.502S

    distal end of left forearm, broken in   V86.92xS

    accidental crash of snowmobile

---

8. Ruptured spleen, traumatic   S36.09xA

    Major contusion to left kidney   S37.022A

    Traumatic shock   T79.4xxA

    Patient caught in heavy farm machinery   W30.9xxA

    that he was operating on his farm   Y92.79

           Y99.0

    Excretory urography with low osmolar contrast   07TP4ZZ

    Laparoscopic splenectomy   BT141ZZ

---

9. Cerebral cortex contusion; patient died   S06.337A
    from brain injury without regaining consciousness;   W13.0xxA
    patient had fallen through balcony from skyscraper   Y92.29
    observation tower while sightseeing   Y93.89
         Y99.8

---

10. Confirmed battered wife syndrome due to severe   T74.11xA
    beating of chest wall by husband   S20.219A
    Multiple contusions over trunk   Y04.0xxA
         Y07.01

---

11. Anoxic brain damage due to previous   G93.1
    intracranial injury with loss of consciousness   S06.9x9S
    three years ago, when patient was accidentally struck by   V03.90xS
    car while walking along highway

---

12. Comminuted fracture of the right distal radius   S52.501A
    and ulna; child fell from playground equipment;   S52.601A
    initial treatment is in the physician's office   W09.8xxA
         Y93.89
         Y99.8

    Two weeks later, patient had   S52.501A
    open reduction and internal fixation   S52.601A
    (ORIF) at an acute care hospital   W09.8xxA
         0PSK04Z
         0PSH04Z

    Follow-up visit to the physician's office   S52.501D
    for X-rays and postoperative examination   S52.601D

CHAPTER 31

Burns

CHAPTER OVERVIEW

- Categories T20 through T32 are assigned for all burns and corrosions except sunburn and friction burns.

- ICD-10-CM distinguishes between burns and corrosions. Burn codes are assigned to thermal burns from a heat source. Corrosion codes are for burns due to chemicals.

- Burns are first classified by general anatomical site. A fourth character indicates the type of burn according to depth: first, second, or third degree.

- Codes are sequenced to reflect the degree of the burn. The highest degree takes precedence.

  — Multiple burns on the same site require classification of only the highest degree of burn.

  — Multiple burns at different sites require sequencing the most severe burn first and using additional codes for the burns of other sites.

- The extent of the body surface involved is estimated using the "rule of nines," a guideline that is also used to help code the burn.

- External cause codes are used to classify the place of occurrence as well as:

  — The source of the burns and corrosions, such as fire, electric current, and hot liquid

  — Situations such as accident, assault, and suicide

- Other injuries associated with burns often require additional codes.

- Certain pre-existing conditions might have an impact on the prognosis or care of the patient. These pre-existing conditions should be coded as additional diagnoses.

LEARNING OUTCOMES

After studying this chapter you should be able to:

Understand the difference between first-, second-, and third-degree burns.

Properly sequence the codes of multiple burns and related conditions.

Understand how the extent of burn is calculated using the "rule of nines."

Identify injuries and illnesses that might be coded in association with the burns.

TERM TO KNOW

Rule of nines
a tool to help physicians estimate the amount of body surface involved in a burn

REMEMBER . . .

Burns heal at different rates. It is possible to have both healed and unhealed burns for the same episode of care.

INTRODUCTION

Codes from categories T20 through T32 are assigned for burns and corrosions except sunburn and friction burns, which are classified as dermatitis and superficial injury, respectively. ICD-10-CM distinguishes between burns and corrosions. The burn codes are for thermal burns, except sunburns, that are a result of a heat source (e.g., fire, hot appliance). Burns due to chemicals are classified to corrosion. The guidelines for both burns and corrosions are the same. Nonhealing burns and necrosis of burned skin are coded as acute current burns (categories T20–T28, seventh character "A" for initial encounter or "D" for subsequent encounter). Sequelae (such as scarring or contracture) that remain after a burn has healed are classified as sequela (categories T20–T28, seventh character "S" for sequela). Because burns heal at different rates, a patient may have both healed and unhealed burns during the same episode of care. For this reason, it is possible to use current burn codes as well as late-effect burn codes on the same record (when both a current burn and sequelae of an old burn exist).

ANATOMICAL SITE OF BURN

The first axis for classifying burns is the general anatomical site, with a fifth character or sixth character to indicate a more specific site, as follows:

T20–T25   Burns and corrosions of external body surface, specified by site
T26–T28   Burns and corrosions confined to eye and internal organs
T30–T32   Burns and corrosions of multiple and unspecified body regions

When coding burns, assign separate codes for each burn site. Codes for multiple sites and category T30 should only be used if the location of the burns is not documented. Category T30, Burn and corrosion, body region unspecified, is extremely vague and should rarely be used.

FIGURE 31.1   Skin Layers

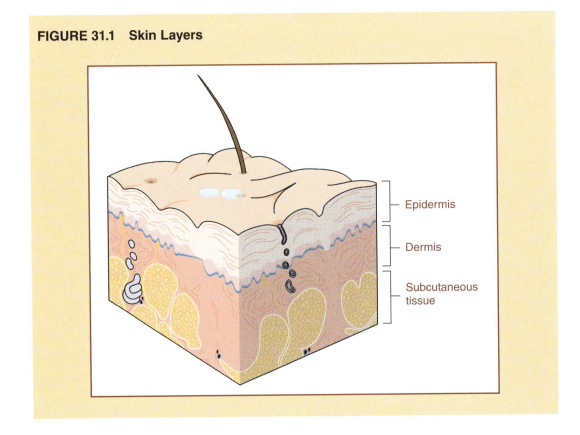

Epidermis

Dermis

Subcutaneous tissue

DEPTH OF BURN

For categories T20 through T25, the fourth-character axis indicates the type of burn or corrosion according to depth or degree, as follows:

- First degree (erythema)
- Second degree (blistering)
- Third degree (full-thickness involvement)

First Degree

Damage from first-degree burns is limited to the outer layer of the epidermis, with erythema and increased tenderness. First-degree burns have good capillary refill and do not represent significant injury in terms of fluid replacement needs.

Second Degree

Second-degree burns represent a partial-thickness injury to the dermis, which may be either superficial or deep. Deep second-degree burns heal much more slowly than first-degree burns and are prone to developing infection. The end result of second-degree burns may be hypertrophic scarring.

Third Degree

In third-degree burns, the dermal barrier is lost, and the presence of necrotic tissue creates fluid volume loss with systemic effects on capillaries well away from the burn site. In addition, the burn site establishes an ideal culture medium for infection, which may be life threatening. The critical factor in healing of third-degree burns is blood supply. Areas rich in blood supply, such as hair follicles and sweat glands, have a better chance for reepithelialization.

Deep third-degree burns are characterized by an underlying necrosis with thrombosed vessels. Codes for burns of this depth are assigned only on the basis of a specific diagnosis made by the physician.

Burns of the eye and internal organs (T26–T28) are classified by site, but not by degree. Categories T31 and T32 classify burns and corrosions by the extent of body surface involved and the extent of body surface with third-degree burn or corrosion, but not by specific sites.

SEQUENCING OF CODES FOR BURNS/CORROSIONS AND RELATED CONDITIONS

Burns and corrosions of the same local site at the three-character category level (T20–T28) but of different degrees (depth) are classified to the subcategory identifying the highest degree recorded in the diagnosis. A third-degree burn takes precedence over a second-degree burn, and a second-degree burn takes precedence over a first-degree burn. For example, first-degree and second-degree burns of the leg are classified as second-degree burn of limb (T24.209-); no code is assigned for the first-degree burn.

When coding multiple burns, sequence first the code that reflects the burn of the highest degree (most severe), with additional codes for the burns of other sites. For example, a patient is admitted with third-degree burns of the lower leg and first-degree and second-degree burns of the forearm. The following codes should be assigned:

T24.339-   Third-degree burn of leg
T22.219-   Second-degree burn of forearm

The circumstances of the admission will determine the principal diagnosis or first-listed diagnosis if a patient has both internal and external burns.

When a patient is admitted for burn injuries and other related conditions such as smoke inhalation and/or respiratory failure, the circumstances of admission govern the selection of the principal or first-listed diagnosis.

Codes for corrosion require that a code from categories T51 through T65, Toxic effects of substances chiefly nonmedicinal as to source, be assigned first to identify chemical and intent.

SEVENTH-CHARACTER EXTENSIONS

Categories T20 through T28 require the following seventh-character extensions:

A   Initial encounter
D   Subsequent encounter
S   Sequela

Extension "A" (initial encounter) is used while the patient is receiving active treatment for the injury. Examples of active treatment are surgical treatment, emergency department encounter, and evaluation and treatment by a new physician.

Extension "D" (subsequent encounter) is used for encounters after the patient has received active treatment of the injury and is receiving routine care for the injury during the healing or recovery phase. Examples of subsequent care are medication adjustment, other aftercare, and follow-up visits following injury treatment. The aftercare Z codes should not be used for aftercare for injuries. For aftercare of an injury, assign the acute injury code with the seventh character "D" (subsequent encounter).

Extension "S" (sequela) is for use for complications or conditions that arise as a direct result of an injury, such as scar formation after a burn; the scars are sequelae of the burn. When using extension "S," it is necessary to use both the injury code that precipitated the sequela and the code for the sequela itself. The "S" is added only to the burn or corrosion code, not the sequela code. The "S" extension identifies the injury responsible for the sequela. The specific type of sequela (e.g., scar) is sequenced first, followed by the injury code.

Note that using code **Z41.1, Encounter for cosmetic surgery,** is inappropriate for burn patients admitted for repair of scar tissue, skin contracture, or other sequelae. For such patients, a code should be assigned for the condition being treated.

EXTENT OF BURN

Categories T31 and T32 classify burns and corrosions according to the extent of body surface involved. The fourth character indicates the total percentage of body surface involved in all types of burns (T31) or corrosions (T32), including third-degree burns. The fifth character indicates the percentage of the body surface involved in third-degree burns only. Because the fourth character refers to total body surface, the fifth character can never be greater than the total body surface amount. For example, code T31.73 indicates that 70–79 percent of the body surface was involved in some type of burn; the fifth character indicates that third-degree burns were involved in 30–39 percent of the body surface. The fifth character zero (0) is assigned when less than 10 percent of body surface (or no body surface) is involved in a third-degree burn.

The extent of body surface involved in a burn injury is an important factor in burn mortality, and hospitals with burn centers need this information for evaluating patient care management and for preparing statistical data. In addition, third-party payment is often influenced by the extent of the burn. When more than 20 percent of the body surface is involved in third-degree burns, it is advisable to assign an additional code from category T31. Burn centers sometimes use a code from category T31 as a solo code because many of their patients present with such extensive and severe burns involving many sites that coding them individually is difficult.

Categories T31 and T32 are based on the classic "rule of nines" for estimating the amount of body surface involved in a burn. Physicians may modify the percentage assignments for head and neck in infants and small children because young children have proportionately larger heads than do adults. The percentage may also be modified for adults with large buttocks, abdomen, or thighs. The rule of nines establishes estimates of body surface involved, as follows:

Head and neck	9 percent
Each arm	9 percent
Each leg	18 percent
Anterior trunk	18 percent
Posterior trunk	18 percent
Genitalia	1 percent

For example, based on this rule a physician can calculate that first-degree burns involve 9 percent of the body surface, second-degree burns involve 18 percent, and third-degree burns involve 36 percent. Adding these together, 63 percent of the body was involved in some type of burn. Code T31.63 (burn of any degree involving 60–69 percent of body surface, with 30–39 percent involved in third-degree burn) could then be assigned. Coders are not expected to calculate the extent of a burn, but understanding the rule of nines may help the coder recognize when burns are so extensive that the physician should be asked for additional information.

SUNBURN

Sunburn and other ultraviolet radiation burns are classified in chapter 12, Diseases of Skin and Subcutaneous Tissue. Category L55, Sunburn, is assigned for first-degree (L55.0), second-degree (L55.1), and third-degree sunburns (L55.2) or for an unspecified degree (L55.9). Sunburn due to other ultraviolet radiation exposure, such as a tanning bed, is classified to category L56, Other acute skin changes due to ultraviolet radiation, or category L57, Skin changes due to chronic exposure to nonionizing radiation.

EXTERNAL CAUSES OF BURNS

External cause codes, including codes from category Y92, Place of occurrence of the external cause, are assigned for burns and corrosions, as discussed in chapter 30 of this handbook, which covers other injuries. The following External cause categories should be used to report source and intent:

X00–X08	Exposure to smoke, fire and flames
X10–X19	Contact with heat and hot substances
X75	Intentional self-harm by explosive material
X76	Intentional self-harm by smoke, fire and flames
X77	Intentional self-harm by steam, hot vapors and hot objects
X96	Assault by explosive material
X97	Assault by smoke, fire and flames
X98	Assault by steam, hot vapors and hot objects

ASSOCIATED INJURIES AND ILLNESSES

When a burn is described as infected, two codes are required. The code for the burn is sequenced first, with an additional code for the infection, for example, Initial encounter, *Staphylococcus* infection, second-degree burn of abdominal wall, is coded to T21.22xA + L08.89 + B95.8.

Other injuries frequently occur with burns, and other conditions are sometimes caused by burns. Examples of such injuries include the following:

- Smoke inhalation often occurs in cases of burns due to combustible products (category T59). Certain toxic substances from plastic products may produce hydrogen cyanide (T57.3-). Hydrogen cyanide is absorbed well by inhalation and can produce death within minutes. When a patient presents with a burn injury and another related condition, such as smoke inhalation or respiratory failure, the circumstances of admission determine the selection of the principal or first-listed diagnosis.

  For example, a child who was rescued from a burning house has no obvious burns, but soot is present about his nose and mouth. The patient is intubated and ventilated for less than 48 hours because of the risk of airway edema from the smoke. The provider diagnoses smoke inhalation. Code **T59.91xA, Toxic effect of unspecified gases, fumes and vapors, accidental (unintentional), initial encounter,** is assigned as the principal diagnosis. Assign code **X00.1xxA, Exposure to smoke in uncontrolled fire in building or structure, initial encounter,** for the external cause of the injury. The patient suffered no obvious burns but was admitted for airway management secondary to the toxic effects of smoke. In addition, assign codes **5A1945Z, Respiratory ventilation, 24-96 consecutive hours,** and **0BH17EZ, Insertion of endotracheal airway into trachea, via natural or artificial opening.**

- Electrical burns, such as those caused by high-tension wires, may cause ventricular arrhythmias (I49.-) that require immediate attention.

- Traumatic shock (T79.4-) is often present at the time of admission or may occur later.

Pre-existing conditions may also have an impact on the burn patient's prognosis and care management and therefore should be coded as additional diagnoses when they otherwise meet criteria for reportable diagnoses. Examples of potentially harmful pre-existing conditions that should be reported include the following:

- Cardiovascular disorders (such as angina, congestive heart failure, or valvular disease) may increase ischemia and precipitate myocardial infarction in a patient with extensive second-degree or third-degree burns. Pulmonary wedge monitoring may be necessary in these cases.

- Asthma, chronic bronchitis, and other chronic obstructive pulmonary diseases may require ventilation therapy.

- Peptic ulcers, either gastric or duodenal, and ulcerative colitis are pre-existing conditions that may lead to gastrointestinal bleeding and require treatment along with the burn.

- Pre-existing kidney disease increases the risk of tubular necrosis and renal failure in patients with third-degree burns or extensive second-degree burns.

- Alcoholism may pose a threat of alcohol withdrawal syndrome, requiring prophylactic treatment for delirium tremens.

- Diabetes mellitus slows the healing process, and diabetes mellitus with stated manifestations can further complicate the management of burn cases.

EXERCISE 31.1

Code the following diagnoses, including External cause codes. Assume that the incidents are for the initial encounter unless otherwise stated.

1. First-degree burn of lower left leg and second-degree burns of left foot when adding wood to bonfire at beach resort while on vacation

   T25.222A
   T24.132A
   X03.8xxA
   Y93.89
   Y99.8
   Y92.838

2. First-degree burns of face and both eyes, involving cornea, eyelids, nose, cheeks, and lips, due to accidental lye spill at home

   T54.3x1A
   T26.51xA
   T26.52xA
   T26.61xA
   T26.62XA
   T20.52XA
   T20.54XA
   T20.56XA
   Y99.8
   Y92.099

3. Burns over 38 percent of body, with 10 percent of body involved in third-degree burns and 28 percent involved in second-degree burns; firefighter burned in forest fire

   T31.31
   X01.8xxA
   Y99.0
   Y92.821

4. Acid burns to left cornea from nitric acid

   T54.2x1A
   T26.62XA

5. Subsequent encounter with nonhealing first- and second-degree burns of back that occurred five weeks ago when patient's clothing caught fire in kitchen accident in his home

   T21.23xD
   X02.0XXD

6. Food service employee sustained first-degree and second-degree burns, thumb and two fingers, right, from kitchen fire in nursing home while cooking, initial encounter

T23.241A
X02.8xxA
Y93.G3
Y99.0
Y92.120

7. Farm employee admitted with severe shock due to third-degree burns of back due to uncontrolled barn fire, initial encounter

T21.33xA
T79.4xxA
X00.0xxA
Y99.0
Y92.71

8. First-, second-, and third-degree burns of trunk; 10 percent first degree, 15 percent second degree, and 32 percent third degree; patient is crew member of steamship on which boiler exploded

T21.30xA
T31.53
W35.xxxA
Y99.0
V93.09xA

9. Severe sunburn of face, neck, and shoulders; patient spent most of the day at the beach

L55.9
X32.XXXA
Y99.8
Y92.832
Y93.89

10. Infected friction burn of left thigh due to rope burn while water skiing barefoot at Lake Berryessa

S70.312A
L08.89
V94.4xxA
Y93.17
Y99.8
Y92.828

11. First-degree burns of back of left hand due to hot tap water in home where patient was visiting

T23.162A
X11.8xxA
Y99.8
Y92.099

Poisoning, Toxic Effects, Adverse Effects, and Underdosing of Drugs

CHAPTER OVERVIEW

- A condition caused by drugs or other ingested substances can be considered as an adverse effect, a toxic effect, or a poisoning.
- Underdosing refers to taking less of a medication than is prescribed by a provider or a manufacturer's instruction.
  - Underdosing codes should never be assigned as the principal or first-listed codes.
  - If the reduction in the prescribed dose of the medication results in a relapse or an exacerbation of the medical condition for which the drug is prescribed, then the medical condition itself should be coded first.
- An adverse effect is one caused by a correctly prescribed and used drug.
  - The combination code that includes the adverse effect and the responsible substance is sequenced first.
  - A code indicating the manifestation of the adverse effect follows.
- Poisoning is a condition caused by the incorrect use of a drug or another substance.
  - A code from categories T36- through T65 is sequenced first.
  - This is followed by the code for the manifestation of the poisoning.
  - When no intent of poisoning is indicated, the code for accidental poisoning should be assigned.
- Interactions of properly used therapeutic drugs and alcohol or nonprescription drugs are considered instances of poisoning.
- Codes for poisoning, adverse effects, and underdosing are found in the ICD-10-CM Table of Drugs and Chemicals.
- No additional External cause code is required for poisoning, toxic effect, adverse effect, and underdosing codes.
- Acute conditions caused by alcohol or drug abuse are considered poisonings, but chronic conditions are not.
- The late effects of poisoning, adverse effects, and underdosing are coded with the seventh character "S" for sequela.

LEARNING OUTCOMES

After studying this chapter you should be able to:

- Differentiate between adverse effects and poisoning.
- Locate codes associated with poisoning and adverse effects.
- Code for poisoning due to substance abuse.
- Code for late effects for adverse reactions and poisoning.

TERMS TO KNOW

Adverse effect
classification of a condition caused by a drug or another substance when used correctly

Poisoning
classification of a condition caused by a drug or another substance when used incorrectly

Toxic effect
classification of a condition caused by ingestion or contact with a harmful substance

Underdosing
classification of a condition caused by taking less of a medication than is prescribed by a provider or a manufacturer's instruction

REMEMBER . . .

A condition caused by the use of a drug may be classified as either an adverse effect or a poisoning. The determination is based only on whether or not the substance was correctly prescribed and properly administered.

INTRODUCTION

CHAPTER 32

*Poisoning,
Toxic Effects,
Adverse
Effects, and
Underdosing
of Drugs*

Conditions due to drugs and medicinal and biological substances are classified to categories T36 through T50. Codes in these categories are combination codes that specify both the responsible substance and whether it is a poisoning (including the intent, e.g., accidental), an adverse effect, or an underdosing, with the fifth or sixth character used to specify the following:

1   Poisoning, accidental (unintentional)
2   Poisoning, intentional self-harm
3   Poisoning, assault
4   Poisoning, undetermined
5   Adverse effect
6   Underdosing

Toxic effects of substances chiefly nonmedicinal as to source are classified to categories T51 through T65. Similar to categories T35 through T50, codes in categories T51 through T65 are combination codes that specify the responsible substance as well as the intent (e.g., accidental). However, adverse effect and underdosing are not applicable to toxic effects. As with other categories in chapter 19 of ICD-10-CM, categories T30- through T65 require seventh-character extensions, as follows: "A" for initial encounter, "D" for subsequent encounter, and "S" for sequela. These extensions are described in more detail in chapter 30 of this handbook.

The condition is classified as an adverse effect when the correct substance was administered as prescribed. When the substance was used incorrectly, it is classified as a poisoning with the appropriate fifth or sixth character of "1" through "4," depending on the intent of the poisoning (e.g., accidental). The condition may be exactly the same and the drug may be the same; the determination of whether it is a poisoning or an adverse effect is based on the manner in which the substance was used. ICD-10-CM makes the distinction between adverse effects of drugs administered correctly and poisoning—to facilitate the collection of data on adverse effects that result from the correct use of drugs, and on the extent to which incorrect use results in patient care problems.

Note that using the prescribed medication less frequently than prescribed, using it in smaller amounts, or not using the medication as instructed by the manufacturer is not coded as poisoning, but rather as underdosing.

When the drug was correctly prescribed and properly administered, a code for the adverse effect is sequenced first (e.g., T36.0x5-), followed by additional codes for all manifestations of adverse effects. Drug adverse effect manifestations can range from minor or temporary effects to more serious and sometimes permanent damage. Examples of adverse effect manifestations include rash, tachycardia, delirium, gastrointestinal hemorrhage, vomiting, hepatitis, renal failure, and respiratory failure.

When the condition results from the interaction of two or more therapeutic drugs, each used correctly, it is classified as an adverse effect, and each drug is coded individually, unless the combination code is listed in the Table of Drugs and Chemicals.

When the condition is a poisoning, the poisoning code (e.g., T36.0x1-) is sequenced first, followed by additional codes for all manifestations. Poisoning codes have an associated intent, and code selection is based on the circumstance of the poisoning. When no intent of poisoning is indicated, the code for accidental poisoning should be assigned. The codes for undetermined poisoning (fifth or sixth character "4") are reserved for use when there is specific documentation in the record that the intent of the poisoning cannot be determined. For example, a diagnosis of coma due to codeine is coded as follows:

T40.2x1A + R40.20	Coma due to accidental poisoning due to codeine
T40.2x2A + R40.20	Coma due to codeine taken in a suicide attempt
T40.2x4A + R40.20	Coma due to overdose of codeine, cause unknown
T40.2x1A + R40.20	Coma due to poisoning due to codeine

If there is also a diagnosis of abuse of or dependence on the substance, the abuse or dependence is also coded.

CHAPTER 32

*Poisoning,
Toxic Effects,
Adverse
Effects, and
Underdosing
of Drugs*

Because codes in categories T36 through T65 include the responsible substances as well as the external cause, no additional External cause code is required for these codes. However, if the intent of the underdosing is known, External cause codes may be used to report failure in dosage during medical and surgical care (Y63.61, Y63.8–Y63.9) or patient's underdosing of medication regime (Z91.12- through Z91.13-).

The adverse effects of therapeutic substances correctly prescribed and properly administered (toxicity, synergistic reaction, side effect, and idiosyncratic reaction) may be due to (1) differences among patients, such as age, sex, disease, and genetic factors, and (2) drug-related factors, such as type of drug, route of administration, duration of therapy, dosage, and bioavailability.

Harmful substances ingested or coming into contact with a person are classified as toxic effects. These are assigned to categories T51 through T65, Toxic effects of substances chiefly non-medicinal as to source, except for contact with and (suspected) exposure to toxic substances (Z77.-). Code examples include the following:

T57.2x1-   Chronic manganese toxicity
T57.0x1-   Toxicity due to exposure to arsenical pesticide
Z77.090   Toxicity due to asbestos exposure

Toxic effect codes should be sequenced first, followed by the appropriate code(s) to identify all the associated manifestations of the toxic effect, such as respiratory conditions due to external agents (J60–J70). Similar to the codes for poisoning, toxic effect codes are combination codes that include the substance as well as the associated intent by the use of the following fifth or sixth characters:

1   accidental
2   intentional self-harm
3   assault
4   undetermined

Also similar to the codes for poisoning, when no intent is indicated, the code for accidental intent (fifth or sixth character "1") should be assigned. The codes for undetermined intent (fifth or sixth character "4") are reserved for use when there is specific documentation in the record that the intent of the toxic effect cannot be determined.

A diagnostic statement of toxic effect, toxicity, or intoxication due to a prescription drug, such as digitalis or lithium, without any further qualification usually refers to an adverse effect of a correctly administered prescription drug. The adverse effect should be coded as such unless medical record documentation indicates otherwise. The following terms in the medical record usually indicate correct usage and identify the condition as an adverse effect:

- "Allergic reaction"
- "Cumulative effect of drug" (toxicity)
- "Hypersensitivity to drug"
- "Idiosyncratic reaction"
- "Paradoxical reaction"
- "Synergistic reaction"

When the medical record documents an error in dosage or administration, the condition should be coded as a poisoning. Terms that usually identify the condition as a poisoning include the following:

- "Wrong medication given" or "wrong medication taken"
- "Error made in drug prescription"

CHAPTER 32

*Poisoning,
Toxic Effects,
Adverse
Effects, and
Underdosing
of Drugs*

- "Wrong dosage given" or "wrong dosage taken" (unless specified as underdosing, or lower dosage than prescribed)
- "Intentional drug overdose"
- "Nonprescribed drug taken with correctly prescribed and properly administered drug"

The poisoning code is sequenced first, followed by the code for the manifestation. This sequencing is based on the chapter-specific guideline providing such direction. Therefore, it applies even if the poisoning may have already been addressed.

For example, a patient is seen in the emergency department in a coma and suffering from acute respiratory failure due to a drug overdose. The patient undergoes a gastric lavage for the drug overdose. The patient is also intubated, connected to an invasive mechanical ventilator, and transferred to another hospital for continued toxicology management and treatment of the acute respiratory failure. The poisoning is still sequenced as the principal diagnosis at the receiving hospital.

When a condition is the result of the interaction of a therapeutic drug used correctly with a nonprescription drug or with alcohol, it is classified as a poisoning. Poisoning codes are also assigned for each drug. For example, a diagnosis of coma identified as an adverse reaction to Valium taken correctly but associated with the intake of two martinis is coded as follows:

T51.0x1A	Poisoning due to alcohol, accidental
T42.4x1A	Poisoning due to Valium, accidental
R40.20	Coma

Taking a larger or more frequent dosage than prescribed is classified as a poisoning. Note that taking a lower amount or discontinuing the use of a prescribed medication is not classified as either a poisoning or an adverse reaction, but rather as underdosing. Underdosing codes should never be assigned as the principal or first-listed code. If the reduction in the prescribed dose of the medication results in a relapse or an exacerbation of the medical condition for which the drug is prescribed, then the medical condition itself should be coded first.

For example, a patient was prescribed Amiodarone to control his atrial fibrillation. The patient quit taking his prescribed medication on his own one week ago, because he said the medication made him nauseous. He is now admitted for control of atrial fibrillation and medication adjustment. The atrial fibrillation is coded as the principal diagnosis and the underdosing code as an additional diagnosis, as follows:

I48.0	Atrial fibrillation
T46.2x6A	Underdosing of Amiodarone
Z91.14	Patient's noncompliance with medication

Figure 32.1 illustrates a process for coding poisoning and adverse effects of drugs.

LOCATION OF CODES ASSOCIATED WITH POISONING, ADVERSE EFFECTS, AND UNDERDOSING

Codes for poisonings, adverse effects, and underdosing are located most easily by referring to the ICD-10-CM Table of Drugs and Chemicals (see figure 32.2). Drugs and other chemicals are listed in alphabetical order at the far left of the Table, with the first column on the right listing the accidental poisoning code for that substance. The remaining columns provide codes for poisoning for the other external circumstances (intentional self-harm, assault, and undetermined), for adverse effect, and for underdosing.

If a specific drug cannot be located in the Table, it can usually be found by either the generic name or the drug class or type (e.g., antibiotic). The hospital pharmacist can also be a valuable source of information.

505

CHAPTER 32

Poisoning,
Toxic Effects,
Adverse
Effects, and
Underdosing
of Drugs

Codes should not be assigned directly from the Table without verification in the Tabular List. The Table of Drugs and Chemicals is extensive and very detailed, but it does not take into account the instructional notes in the Tabular List. For example, the Table lists codes from category T36, Poisoning by, adverse effect of and underdosing of systemic antibiotics, but the exclusion note at category T36 indicates that codes from subcategory T45.1 should be used for antineoplastic antibiotics.

FIGURE 32.1 Decision Tree for Coding Adverse Effects of Drugs or Poisoning Due to Drugs or Medicinal or Biological Substances

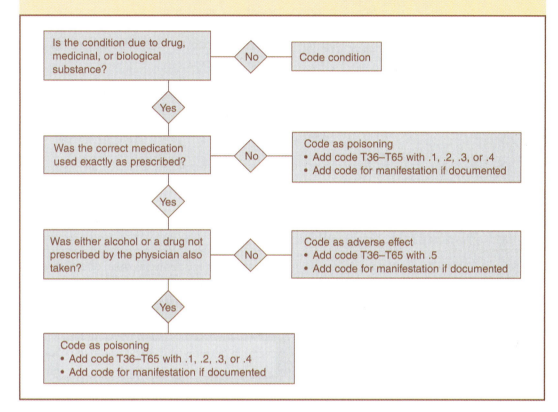

Figure 32.2 Excerpt from ICD-10-CM Table of Drugs and Chemicals

Substance	Poisoning, Accidental (Unintentional)	Poisoning, Intentional Self-Harm	Poisoning, Assault	Poisoning, Undetermined	Adverse Effect	Underdosing
Acetylphenylhydrazine	T39.8x1	T39.8x2	T39.8x3	T39.8x4	T39.8x5	T39.8x6
Acetylsalicylic acid (salts)	T39.011	T39.012	T39.013	T39.014	T39.015	T39.016
-enteric coated	T39.011	T39.012	T39.013	T39.014	T39.015	T39.016
Acetylsulfamethoxypyridazine	T37.0x1	T37.0x2	T37.0x3	T37.0x4	T37.0x5	T37.0x6
Achromycin	T36.4x1	T36.4x2	T36.4x3	T36.4x4	T36.4x5	T36.4x6
-ophthalmic preparation	T49.5x1	T49.5x2	T49.5x3	T49.5x4	T49.5x5	T49.5x6
-topical NEC	T49.0x1	T49.0x2	T49.0x3	T49.0x4	T49.0x5	T49.0x6
Aciclovir	T37.5x1	T37.5x2	T37.5x3	T37.5x4	T37.5x5	T37.5x6

CHAPTER 32

Poisoning,
Toxic Effects,
Adverse
Effects, and
Underdosing
of Drugs

GUIDELINES FOR ASSIGNMENT OF CODES FOR POISONING, ADVERSE EFFECTS, UNDERDOSING, AND TOXIC EFFECTS

When two or more drugs or medicinal or biological substances are reported as being responsible for a poisoning, an adverse effect, an underdosing, or a toxic effect, code each substance individually unless the same code would describe the causative agent for more than one adverse reaction, poisoning, toxic effect, or underdosing. In other words, assign the code only once when the same code identifies more than one responsible substance. For example:

T46.0x5A + T42.4x5A + I49.1	Supraventricular premature beats secondary to use of digitalis and Valium, both used as prescribed, initial encounter (either T46.0x5A or T42.4x5A may be the principal or first-listed code)
T50.A15A + R50.83	An infant with a high fever due to correct administration of DPT vaccine
T42.3x5A + R68.2 + L29.9	Patient suffering from dry mouth and itching as a result of taking phenobarbital as prescribed by his physician

The coder should assign as many codes as needed to completely describe all responsible substances for either an adverse effect or a poisoning.

ENVIRONMENTAL TOXINS

Subcategory T65.82, Toxic effect of harmful algae and algae toxins, describes toxic effects of exposure to harmful algae bloom, such as toxic effect of blue-green algae bloom, brown tide, cyanobacteria bloom, Florida red tide, *Pfiesteria piscicida*, and red tide. *Karennia brevis* (*K. brevis*) are microscopic, fast-growing marine algae that create blooms called red tides. *K. brevis* produces a powerful toxin called brevetoxin. When shellfish feed on *K. brevis*, brevetoxin becomes concentrated in the shellfish. Individuals who eat shellfish contaminated with brevetoxin develop neurotoxic shellfish poisoning. This type of food poisoning leads to severe gastrointestinal and neurologic symptoms. Assign code Z77.121 to describe possible contact with and exposure to harmful algae and algae toxins. This code may be assigned when the patient may have been in the vicinity of algae bloom but has not developed symptoms, or when the patient may have symptoms suspicious of exposure to algae bloom, but a definitive cause of the symptoms has not been confirmed.

Environmental exposure to brevetoxin can also affect people who swim in an ocean polluted by brevetoxins or who inhale brevetoxins in the air. Symptoms can include irritation of the eyes, nose, and throat; tingling of the lips and tongue; coughing; wheezing; and shortness of breath. For example, a patient develops severe abdominal pain, vomiting, and a tingling sensation in the fingers after eating shellfish. The patient is diagnosed with neurotoxic shellfish poisoning due to red tides. Assign code **T65.821A, Toxic effect of harmful algae and algae toxins, accidental (unintentional), initial encounter.**

CHAPTER 32

Poisoning,
Toxic Effects,
Adverse
Effects, and
Underdosing
of Drugs

EXERCISE 32.1

Code the following diagnoses, assuming that the drug involved was taken correctly unless otherwise specified. Assume these are initial encounters.

1. Coma due to acute barbiturate intoxication, attempted suicide

   T42.3x2A
   R40.20

2. Two-year-old patient ingested an unknown quantity of mother's Enovid

   T38.4x1A

3. Syncope due to hypersensitivity to antidepressant medication

   Table

   T43.205A
   R55

4. Hypokalemia resulting from reaction to Diuril given by mistake in physician's office

   T50.2x1A
   E87.6

5. Diplopia due to allergic reaction to antihistamine, taken as prescribed

   Table

   T45.0x5A
   H53.2

6. Lethargy due to unintentional overdose of sleeping pills

   T42.71xA
   R53.83

7. Electrolyte imbalance due to interaction between lithium carbonate and Diuril, both taken as prescribed

   Table

   T43.595A
   T50.2x5A
   E87.8

8. Parkinsonism, secondary to correct use of haloperidol

   Table

   T43.4x5A
   G21.11

CHAPTER 32

*Poisoning,
Toxic Effects,
Adverse
Effects, and
Underdosing
of Drugs*

9. Cerebral anoxia resulting from
   barbiturate overdose, suicide attempt

   T42.3x2A
   G93.1

---

10. Toxic encephalopathy due to
    excessive use of aspirin

    T39.011A
    G92

---

11. Ataxia due to Valium (taken as prescribed)
    consumed with three martinis

    Table, Valium
    Table, alcohol

    T42.4x1A
    T51.0x1A
    R27.0

---

12. Allergic dermatitis due to slow-acting insulin

    Table

    T38.3x5A
    L27.0

---

13. Coumadin intoxication due to accumulative
    effect resulting in gross hematuria

    Table

    T45.515A
    R31.0

---

14. Severe bradycardia due to accidental
    double dose of digoxin

    Table, digoxin

    T46.0x1A
    R00.1

---

15. Generalized convulsions due to accidental
    Darvon overdose

    T39.8x1A
    R56.9

---

16. Light-headedness resulting from interaction
    between Aldomet and peripheral
    vasodilating agent
    (both taken as prescribed)

    Table

    T46.5x5A
    T46.7x5A
    R42

---

17. Uncontrolled hypertension due to patient having
    reduced his anti-hypertensive medication
    (patient couldn't afford it)

    I10
    T46.5x6A
    Z91.120

UNSPECIFIED ADVERSE EFFECT OF DRUGS

CHAPTER 32

Poisoning,
Toxic Effects,
Adverse
Effects, and
Underdosing
of Drugs

ICD-10-CM provides code **T88.7-, Unspecified adverse effect of drug or medicament,** to identify adverse reactions when the nature of the reaction is not specified. The code from categories T36 through T50 with fifth or sixth character "5" is used first to identify the responsible drug. Code T88.7 may be used in the outpatient setting, but only when no sign or symptom of the adverse effect is documented. The use of code T88.7 for inpatient reporting is inappropriate. If the patient is exhibiting symptoms or signs, the code for that condition should be assigned. If the adverse condition cannot be identified, one of the following codes should be assigned:

R82.5   Elevated urine levels of drugs, medicaments and biological substances

R82.6   Abnormal urine levels of substances chiefly nonmedicinal as to source

R89.2   Abnormal level of other drugs, medicaments and biological substances in specimens from other organs, systems and tissues

R89.3   Abnormal level of substances chiefly nonmedicinal as to source in specimens from other organs, systems and tissues

ICD-10-CM provides subcategory T50.90-, Poisoning by, adverse effect of and underdosing of unspecified drugs, medicaments and biological substances, for instances when the drug or substance responsible for the poisoning, adverse effect, or underdosing is not specified.

POISONING DUE TO SUBSTANCE ABUSE OR DEPENDENCE

An acute condition due to a reaction resulting from the interaction of alcohol and a drug(s) or due to a drug involved in abuse or dependence is classified as a poisoning. Additional codes are assigned for both the acute manifestation of the poisoning and the dependence or abuse. For example:

T40.1x1A + J81.0 + F11.20   Acute pulmonary edema due to accidental heroin overdose in a patient who is heroin dependent

Chronic conditions related to alcohol or drug abuse or dependence are not classified as poisoning. The code for the chronic condition is sequenced first, followed by a code for the abuse or dependence. For example:

K70.30 + F10.20   Alcoholic cirrhosis of the liver; chronic alcohol dependence

K70.10 + F10.20   Alcoholic hepatitis; chronic alcohol dependence, episodic

F14.14   Drug-induced depressive state due to cocaine abuse

CHAPTER 32

Poisoning,
Toxic Effects,
Adverse
Effects, and
Underdosing
of Drugs

EXERCISE 32.2

Code the following diagnoses. Assign External cause codes where appropriate. Assume these are initial encounters.

1. Muscle cramps of leg due to occupational
   use of arsenic pesticide

   Table, arsenic

   T57.0x1A
   R25.2

2. Systemic hypocalcemia and
   hypokalemia due to use of lye in
   household chores

   Table, lye

   T54.3x1A
   E83.51
   E87.6
   Y92.099

3. Bradycardia due to ingestion of oleander
   leaves

   Table, oleander

   T62.2x1A
   R00.1

LATE EFFECTS OF POISONING, ADVERSE EFFECTS, AND UNDERDOSING

The code for the responsible drug or substance is sequenced first, with the seventh character "S" for sequela. The "S" extension identifies the substance responsible for the sequela. The code from categories T36 through T65 is sequenced first (with the seventh character "S") followed by the specific type of sequela (e.g., brain damage).

Long-term chronic effects of a prescription drug taken over a period of time—and still being taken at the time the chronic effects arise—are coded as current adverse effects. For example, steroid-induced diabetes may be caused by an adverse effect of correctly administered medications, poisoning, or late effect of poisoning. For a patient who develops steroid-induced diabetes and is currently taking steroids as prescribed, his condition is coded as an adverse effect (T38.0x5- + E09.-).

If the patient suffers delayed effects that arose or remain long after the medication was discontinued, code T38.0x5S is assigned first, to indicate that this is a sequela, followed by code E09.-. For example:

T36.0x5A + G93.9   Brain damage due to allergic reaction to penicillin (current medication)
T36.0x5S + G93.9   Brain damage due to allergic reaction to penicillin (use of medication discontinued six months ago)

CHAPTER 32

*Poisoning,
Toxic Effects,
Adverse
Effects, and
Underdosing
of Drugs*

EXERCISE 32.3

Code the following diagnoses, sequencing the codes correctly. Assign External cause code if appropriate.

1. Extrapyramidal disease resulting from previous overdose of Thorazine in an attempted suicide six months ago
   T43.3x2S
   G25.9

2. Bilateral neural deafness resulting from accidental overdose of streptomycin administered in physician's office two years ago
   T36.5x5S
   H90.3

3. Anoxic brain damage secondary to previous accidental overdose of Nembutal nine months ago
   T42.3x1S
   G93.1

4. Secondary parkinsonism due to poisoning by lithium four years ago
   T56.891S
   G21.8

5. Patient recently discharged from the hospital with diagnosis of acute systolic congestive heart failure. Discharged with a prescription for digoxin 200 mcg once daily, with instructions for a low-fat and low-sodium diet and avoidance of alcohol and caffeine. Two weeks later, patient is seen in the emergency department with shortness of breath on minimal exertion and severe edema. On questioning, patient admits to having reduced digoxin to every other day because it is too expensive. Diagnosis: Relapse of acute systolic congestive heart failure due to low dose of digoxin.
   I50.21
   T46.0x6A
   Z91.120

CHAPTER 33

Complications of Surgery and Medical Care

CHAPTER OVERVIEW

- Categories T80 through T88 in ICD-10-CM cover complications of medical and surgical care that are not already classified elsewhere.

- Not all postcare conditions are classified as complications.

  — There must be an unexpected or abnormal occurrence.

  — There must be a documented relationship between the condition and the care.

  — There must be an indication that it is a complication.

- There are several instructional notes (in particular, exclusion notes) related to complications.

- When coding, look for a subterm indicating postoperative or iatrogenic condition.

- Look to the main term **Complications** if no subterms are found in the particular entry for the condition.

- Complications involving an internal device, an implant, or a graft are classified first.

- It is important to distinguish between admission for complications and admission for routine and scheduled aftercare.

LEARNING OUTCOMES

After studying this chapter you should be able to:

Understand when and when not to code a condition or an occurrence as a complication.

Locate complication codes.

Use all of the instructional notes present in ICD-10-CM to properly classify a condition caused by a complication of medical or surgical care.

TERM TO KNOW

Iatrogenic condition
condition resulting from the treatment of another condition

REMEMBER . . .

Coders should never make assumptions with regard to complications because of the legal ramifications of these codes.

INTRODUCTION

Categories T80 through T88 are provided in ICD-10-CM for complications of medical and surgical care that are not classified elsewhere. Categories T80 through T85 and T88 require a seventh-character extension to specify initial encounter ("A"), subsequent encounter ("D"), or sequela ("S"), similar to other codes in chapter 19 of ICD-10-CM. Note that not all conditions that occur following surgery or other patient care are classified as complications. First, there must be more than a routinely expected condition or occurrence. For example, a major amount of bleeding is expected with joint replacement surgery; hemorrhage should not be considered a complication unless such bleeding is particularly excessive. In addition, there must be a documented cause-and-effect relationship between the care provided and the condition, and some indication must be present that it is a complication, not a postoperative condition in which no complication is present, such as an artificial opening status or an absence of an extremity. In some cases, this is implicit, as in a complication due to the presence of an internal device, an implant, or a graft or due to a transplant. Code assignment for postprocedural complications is based on the provider's documentation of the relationship between the complication and the procedure. The coder cannot make this determination. Note that the term "complication" as used in ICD-10-CM does not imply that improper or inadequate care is responsible for the problem.

No time limit is defined for the development of a complication. It may occur during the hospital episode in which the care was provided, shortly thereafter, or even years later. When it occurs during the episode in which the operation or other care was given, it is assigned as an additional code. When it develops later and is the reason for the hospital admission or encounter, it is designated as the principal or first-listed diagnosis. Complications of surgical and medical care are classified in ICD-10-CM as follows:

- Complications that occur only in other specified body sites are classified in that chapter of ICD-10-CM.

- Complications that affect multiple sites or body systems are generally classified in categories T80 through T88. An additional code(s) is assigned to identify the specific condition resulting from the complication.

- Intraoperative and postprocedural complication codes are found within the body system chapters, with codes specific to the organs and structures of that body system. These codes should be sequenced first, followed by a code(s) for the specific complication, if applicable.

- Complications of abortion, pregnancy, labor, or delivery are classified in chapter 15 of ICD-10-CM.

It is imperative that the coder use the Alphabetic Index carefully and follow all instructional notes. Exclusion notes are fairly extensive in this section and often direct the coder elsewhere. There are several basic exclusions that must be observed:

- Complications of medicinal agents, such as adverse effects, poisoning, and toxic effects of drugs and chemicals

- Any encounters with medical care for postoperative conditions in which no complications are present, such as artificial opening status, closure of external stoma, or fitting and adjustment of external prosthetic device

- Burns and corrosions from local applications and irradiation

- Mechanical complication of respirator or ventilator

- Postprocedural fever
- Complications of the condition for which surgery was performed
- Specified conditions classified elsewhere, such as ostomy complications, postlaminectomy syndrome, postgastric surgery syndromes, or postmastectomy lymphedema syndrome.
- Any condition classified elsewhere in the Alphabetic Index when described as being due to a procedure or medical care, such as disorders of fluid and electrolyte imbalance or functional disturbances during cardiac surgery (Note that the adjective "iatrogenic" is often used to indicate that the condition is a result of treatment.)

LOCATING COMPLICATION CODES IN THE ALPHABETIC INDEX

The coder should first refer to the main term for the condition and look for a subterm indicating a postoperative or another iatrogenic condition. For example:

> **Adhesion(s) . . .**
> -postoperative (gastrointestinal tract) . . . K66.0
> --with obstruction K91.3 . . .
> --pelvic peritoneal N99.4 . . .
> -vagina N99.2
> **Colostomy . . .**
> -malfunction K94.03

When no entry can be found under the main term for the condition, the coder should refer to the main term **Complications** and look for an appropriate subterm, such as one of the following:

- Nature of complication, such as "foreign body," "accidental puncture," or "hemorrhage"
- Type of procedure, such as "colostomy," "dialysis," or "shunt"
- Anatomical site or body system affected, such as "respiratory system"
- General terms, such as "mechanical," "infection," or "graft"

Examples include the following entries from the Alphabetic Index:

> **Complications**
> -postmastoidectomy . . . H95.19-
> **Complications**
> -cardiac . . .
> --device, implant or graft T82.9
> ---infection . . . T82.7
> ---mechanical
> ----breakdown T82.519 . . .
> ----displacement T82.529

POSTOPERATIVE CONDITIONS NOT CLASSIFIED AS COMPLICATIONS

Certain conditions resulting from medical or surgical care are residual conditions of a procedure, but no complicating factor is involved. For example, postlaminectomy syndrome often occurs following laminectomy, but it is a sequela of the procedure, not a complication. The extensive exclusion list at the beginning of the T80–T88 series is helpful in making some of these distinctions. Other examples include:

K56.5	Postoperative intestinal or peritoneal adhesions with obstruction
K94.12 + B95.4	Infection of enterostomy due to group C *Streptococcus*
N73.6	Postoperative pelvic adhesions (female)

Some conditions that occur postoperatively are not classified as complications, nor do they have special codes to indicate that they are postoperative in nature. Postoperative pain not associated with a specific postoperative complication, for example, is assigned to the appropriate postoperative pain code in category G89 (G89.18, G89.22, G89.28), but **only** if it is not routine or if postoperative pain was not expected immediately after surgery, and only if it meets the guidelines for a reportable diagnosis.

Patients are frequently admitted from outpatient surgery with pain and/or nausea and vomiting, but these are common symptoms during postoperative recovery and are not coded to categories T80 through T88 unless the physician identifies them specifically as complications of the surgery. The principal diagnosis is the symptom or other condition that occasions the postoperative admission.

Sometimes the patient is admitted because of a general concern rather than because of specific symptoms. Although physicians may state that the admission is for observation, this type of situation is ordinarily not coded to category Z03, Encounter for medical observation for suspected diseases and conditions ruled out. If no specific condition is identified, the principal diagnosis is admission for postprocedural aftercare (Z48.-).

Postoperative anemia is rarely considered to be a complication of surgery. When the physician documents postoperative anemia due to blood loss, code **D62, Acute posthemorrhagic anemia,** is assigned, but no complication code is assigned unless the physician documents excessive bleeding as a complication. The fact that blood is administered during a surgical procedure does not indicate a postoperative anemia. Transfusions are sometimes given as a prophylactic replacement to avoid postoperative anemia. Anemia is not assigned solely because the patient received a transfusion; the physician must document the condition.

A diagnosis of postoperative hypertension often means only that the patient has a pre-existing essential hypertension or an elevated blood pressure. If the physician clearly identifies it as a postoperative complication, code **I97.3, Postprocedural hypertension,** is assigned.

EXERCISE 33.1

Code the following diagnoses. Do not assign External cause codes.

1.	Postoperative fever	R50.82
2.	Postoperative esophagitis	K20.9
3.	Colostomy malfunction	K94.03
4.	Postleukotomy syndrome	F07.0
5.	Postoperative peritoneal adhesions	K66.0
6.	Postoperative blind loop syndrome	K90.2

COMPLICATIONS AFFECTING SPECIFIC BODY SYSTEMS

ICD-10-CM classifies many intraoperative and postprocedural complication codes within the body system chapters with codes specific to the organs and structures of that body system. These codes should be sequenced first, followed by a code(s) for the specific complication, if applicable. Intraoperative and postprocedural complications and disorders are classified within body system chapters to the categories listed below:

D78	Spleen
E36 and E89	Endocrine system
G97	Nervous system
H59	Eye and adnexa
H95	Ear and mastoid process
I97	Circulatory system
J95	Respiratory system
K91	Digestive system
L76	Skin and subcutaneous tissue
M96	Musculoskeletal system
N99	Genitourinary system

The above categories (except for E89 and K94) provide additional characters to specify complications such as intraoperative or postprocedural hemorrhage and hematoma, or accidental puncture and laceration (e.g., inadvertent rents, tears, or lacerations) during a procedure. In addition, codes distinguish whether the conditions resulted from a procedure on the specified organ or from complications of other procedures. For example:

- Hemorrhage after repair of spleen laceration is coded to **D78.21, Postprocedural hemorrhage and hematoma of spleen following a procedure on the spleen.**
- Accidental laceration of the spleen secondary to colectomy is coded to **D78.12, Accidental puncture and laceration of spleen during other procedure.**

Several of the categories listed above provide additional specificity for certain other procedures or other complications besides intraoperative or postprocedural hemorrhage and hematoma, accidental puncture, and laceration. Category E89, Postprocedural endocrine and metabolic complications and disorders, not elsewhere classified, is further subdivided to provide specific codes for the following types of complications:

E89.0	Postprocedural hypothyroidism
E89.1	Postprocedural hypoinsulinemia
E89.2	Postprocedural hypoparathyroidism
E89.3	Postprocedural hypopituitarism
E89.40	Asymptomatic postprocedural ovarian failure
E89.41	Symptomatic postprocedural ovarian failure
E89.5	Postprocedural testicular hypofunction
E89.6	Postprocedural adrenocortical (-medullary) hypofunction
E89.810	Postprocedural hemorrhage and hematoma of an endocrine system organ or structure following an endocrine system procedure
E89.811	Postprocedural hemorrhage and hematoma of an endocrine system organ or structure following other procedure
E89.89	Other postprocedural endocrine and metabolic complications and disorders

Category G97, Intraoperative and postprocedural complications and disorders of nervous system, not elsewhere classified, includes additional codes for problems related to spinal or lumbar puncture and ventricular shunting, such as cerebrospinal fluid leak from spinal puncture (G97.0), other reaction to spinal and lumbar puncture (G97.1), and intracranial hypotension following ventricular shunting (G97.2). Category H95, Intraoperative and postprocedural complications and disorders of ear and mastoid process, not elsewhere classified, provides additional codes for problems related to postmastoidectomy, such as chronic inflammation, granulation, mucosal cyst, and other disorders, as well as postprocedural stenosis of the external ear canal.

Category I97, Intraoperative and postprocedural complications and disorders of circulatory system, not elsewhere classified, also includes codes for conditions such as postcardiotomy syndrome (I97.0), other postprocedural cardiac functional disturbances (I97.11–I97.191), postmastectomy lymphedema syndrome (I97.2), postprocedural hypertension (I97.3), intraoperative cardiac functional disturbances (I97.71–I97.791), and other complications such as intraoperative or postprocedural cerebrovascular infarction (I97.81–I97.821).

Category J95, Intraoperative and postprocedural complications and disorders of respiratory system, not elsewhere classified, includes specific codes for several other complications, such as the following:

J95.00–J95.09	Tracheostomy complications
J95.1, J95.2	Acute pulmonary insufficiency following thoracic surgery (J95.1) and following nonthoracic surgery (J95.2)
J95.3	Chronic pulmonary insufficiency following surgery
J95.4	Chemical pneumonitis due to anesthesia
J95.5	Postprocedural subglottic stenosis
J95.81	Postprocedural pneumothorax
J95.82	Postprocedural respiratory failure
J95.84	Transfusion-related acute lung injury (TRALI)
J95.85-	Complication of respirator, which includes ventilator-associated pneumonia (see chapter 19 of this handbook for a more detailed discussion)

Category M96, Intraoperative and postprocedural complications and disorders of musculoskeletal system, not elsewhere classified, includes specific codes for the following conditions:

M96.0	Pseudarthrosis after fusion or arthrodesis
M96.1	Postlaminectomy syndrome, not elsewhere classified
M96.2, M96.3	Kyphosis post radiation (M96.2) and postlaminectomy (M96.3)
M96.4, M96.5	Lordosis postsurgical (M96.4) or postradiation scoliosis (M96.5)
M96.6-	Fracture of bone following insertion of orthopedic implant, joint prosthesis, or bone plate

ICD-10-CM differentiates between cardiac functional disturbances that occur intraoperatively during cardiac or any type of surgery (I97.7-) and postprocedural cardiac functional effects following cardiac or other surgery (I97.1-). For example:

K81.0 + I97.191 + I49.9	Acute cholecystitis; postoperative cardiac arrhythmia (same admission)
I97.130 + I50.9	Heart failure following cardiac surgery performed during previous admission; patient discharged one month ago
I97.131 + I50.21	Acute systolic heart failure on second postoperative day following cholecystectomy

EXERCISE 33.2

Code the following diagnoses. Do not assign External cause codes.

---

1. Cataract fragments in left eye following cataract surgery   H59.022

                   Complications

---

2. Headache due to lumbar puncture   G97.1

---

3. Post iridectomy plateau iris syndrome   H21.82

---

4. Seroma of transabdominal myocutaneous (TRAM) flap   N99.820
   post mastectomy of the left breast

---

5. Postprocedural hypertension   I97.3

---

6. 35-year-old female patient presents to physician's office with   E89.41
   complaints of flushing, sleeplessness, headache, and lack of
   concentration after having had uterine artery embolization for
   uterine leiomyoma a few months ago. Physician diagnoses
   patient with premature postsurgical menopause.

COMPLICATIONS FOLLOWING INFUSION, TRANSFUSION, AND THERAPEUTIC INJECTION

Category T80 includes the following complications following infusion, transfusion, and therapeutic injections:

T80.0-	Air embolism
T80.1-	Vascular complications
T80.2-	Infections
T80.3-	ABO incompatibility reaction due to transfusion
T80.4-	Rh incompatibility reaction
T80.A-	Non-ABO incompatibility reaction
T80.5-	Anaphylactic shock due to serum
T80.6-	Other serum reactions (e.g., intoxication, protein sickness, serum rash, serum sickness, serum urticaria)
T80.81-	Extravasation of vesicant agents
T80.89-	Other complications
T80.9-	Unspecified complication

Extravasation is the accidental infiltration of intravenously infused drugs into the surrounding tissue. Vesicants are chemically active substances that can produce blistering on direct contact with the skin or mucous membrane. Extravasation of antineoplastic drugs during cancer treatment can lead to serious complications. In milder cases, extravasation can cause pain, reddening, or irritation on the arm at the site of the infusion needle. In severe cases, tissue damage may involve tissue necrosis and lead to loss of the limb. The following codes are assigned to describe complications following extravasation of vesicant agent:

T80.810	Extravasation of vesicant antineoplastic chemotherapy
T80.818	Extravasation of other vesicant agent

ICD-10-CM provides codes to report transfusion reactions due to blood or blood product incompatibility, as follows:

T80.30–T80.39	ABO incompatibility reaction due to transfusion of blood or blood products
T80.40–T80.49	Rh incompatibility reaction due to transfusion of blood or blood products
T80.A0–T80.A9	Non-ABO incompatibility reaction due to transfusion of blood or blood products

These codes also provide information on the different types of hemolytic transfusion reactions, including both acute hemolytic transfusion reaction and delayed hemolytic transfusion reaction. A hemolytic transfusion reaction is a systemic response by the body to the administration of blood that is incompatible with the recipient's blood, resulting in destruction of red blood cells. This condition can lead to acute renal failure and/or disseminated intravascular coagulation.

Please note that other transfusion-related problems are coded to other chapters, such as hemochromatosis due to repeated blood cell transfusions (E83.111), transfusion-associated circulatory overload (E87.71), post-transfusion purpura (D69.51), and post-transfusion fever (R50.84).

COMPLICATIONS DUE TO PRESENCE OF INTERNAL DEVICE, IMPLANT, OR GRAFT

Categories T82 through T85 classify conditions that occur only because an internal device, implant, or graft is present. These complications are classified according to the body system, as follows:

T82	Complications of cardiac and vascular prosthetic devices, implants and grafts
T83	Complications of genitourinary prosthetic devices, implants and grafts
T84	Complications of internal orthopedic prosthetic devices, implants and grafts
T85	Complications of other internal prosthetic devices, implants and grafts

Complications of this type are classified first according to whether they are mechanical or nonmechanical in nature. A mechanical complication is one that results from a failure of the device, implant, or graft, such as breakdown, displacement, leakage, or other malfunction. These are classified by the type of mechanical complication and the type of device involved. For example:

T83.39-	Perforation of uterus by intrauterine contraceptive device
T84.195-	Protrusion of intramedullary nail in left femur
T85.621-	Displacement of peritoneal dialysis catheter
T82.49-	Obstruction of arteriovenous dialysis catheter
T82.511-	Breakdown of surgically created arteriovenous shunt
T82.111-	Defective cardiac pulse generator

Subcategory T84.0, Mechanical complications of internal joint prosthesis, classifies a range of complications involving prosthetic joint implants, with additional characters to identify the specific joint (e.g., right knee, left hip). The specific mechanical complications are indicated as follows:

T84.01	Broken internal joint prosthesis
T84.02	Dislocation of internal joint prosthesis
T84.03	Mechanical loosening of internal prosthetic joint
T84.04	Periprosthetic fracture around internal prosthetic joint
T84.05	Periprosthetic osteolysis of internal prosthetic joint
T84.06	Wear of articular bearing surface of internal prosthetic joint
T84.09	Other mechanical complication of internal joint prosthesis

Infection and inflammatory reactions due to the presence of a device, an implant, or a graft that is functioning properly are classified in the following subcategories:

T82.6-	Infection and inflammatory reaction due to cardiac valve prosthesis
T82.7-	Infection and inflammatory reaction due to other cardiac and vascular devices, implants and grafts
T83.6-	Infection and inflammatory reaction due to prosthetic device, implant and graft in genital tract
T84.5-	Infection and inflammatory reaction due to internal joint prosthesis
T84.6-	Infection and inflammatory reaction due to internal fixation device
T84.7	Infection and inflammatory reaction due to other internal orthopedic prosthetic devices, implants and grafts
T85.7-	Infection and inflammatory reaction due to other internal prosthetic devices, implants and grafts

Additional codes should be assigned to identify the infection.

Subcategory T82.7-, Infection and inflammatory reaction due to other cardiac and vascular devices, implants and grafts, is used for infections due to arterial, dialysis, or peripheral venous catheters or an infusion catheter not otherwise specified. Infections due to central venous catheters should be assigned code T80.21- rather than a code from subcategory T82.7-. Examples of central venous catheters include the Hickman catheter, peripherally inserted central catheter, portacath, umbilical venous catheter, and triple lumen catheter. Code **T83.51-, Infection and inflammatory reaction due to indwelling urinary catheter,** should have additional codes for the specific infection, such as cystitis or sepsis, and for the responsible organism, if that information is available. For example:

T82.7xxA	Infected pacemaker pocket, initial encounter
<u>T85.71xA</u> + B96.2	*Escherichia coli* infection due to peritoneal dialysis catheter, initial encounter
<u>T83.51xA</u> + N30.11	Chronic interstitial cystitis with hematuria due to indwelling catheter, initial encounter

Subcategories T82.8, T83.8, T84.8, and T85.8 classify other complications due to the presence of an internal prosthetic device, implant, or graft. This includes nonmechanical complications, with additional characters indicating embolism, fibrosis, hemorrhage, pain, stenosis, or thrombosis.

When the complication is documented as postoperative pain due to the presence of a device, an implant, or a graft left in a surgical site, an additional code from category G89 is used to identify acute (G89.18) or chronic (G89.28) pain due to presence of the device, implant, or graft.

Code T82.857- is assigned for occlusion of a coronary bypass graft unless it is identified by the physician as being due to arteriosclerosis. Arteriosclerotic occlusions of a coronary artery bypass graft are classified as codes I25.70 through I25.799, Coronary atherosclerosis. The fifth character indicates the type of graft (autologous vein, autologous artery, nonautologous biological graft, transplanted heart, bypass graft of transplanted heart, and other coronary bypass graft). Occlusion of the coronary artery when there is no history of bypass graft is classified as arteriosclerosis of native coronary arteries (I25.10–I25.119).

TRANSPLANT COMPLICATIONS

Category T86, Complications of transplanted organs and tissue, is reserved for transplant complications such as failure, infection, rejection, or malignancy associated with organ transplant, with the fourth, fifth, or sixth character indicating the organ involved. When infection is present, a code from categories B95 through B97 should be assigned as an additional code. A transplant complication code is assigned only if the complication affects the function of the transplanted organ. Additional codes are assigned to identify other transplant complications, such as graft-versus-host disease (D89.81-), malignancy associated with organ transplant (C80.2), or post-transplant lymphoproliferative disorders (D47.z1). Two codes are required to fully describe a transplant complication: the appropriate code from category T86 and a secondary code that identifies the complication. For example:

T86.09 + D89.810	Acute graft-versus-host disease resulting from complications of bone marrow transplant
T86.19 + C80.2 + C64.9	Malignant neoplasm of transplanted kidney
T86.858 + D47.z1	Lymphoproliferative disorder post intestinal transplant

Pre-existing conditions or conditions that develop after the transplant are not coded as complications unless they affect the function of the transplanted organs. Post-transplant surgical complications that do not relate to the function of the transplanted organ are classified to the specific complication. For example, a postsurgical infection is coded as a postoperative wound infection, not as a transplant complication. However, infections affecting the function of transplanted organs are classified to category T86, such as **T86.812, Lung transplant infection.** Post-transplant patients who are seen for treatment unrelated to the transplanted organ are assigned a code from category Z94, Transplanted organ and tissue status, to capture the transplant status of the patient. A code from category Z94 should never be used with a code from category T86 for the same organ.

Patients with chronic kidney disease (CKD) following a transplant should not be assumed to have transplant failure or rejection unless it is documented by the provider. Patients who have undergone kidney transplant may still have some form of CKD because the transplant may not fully restore kidney function. If documentation supports the presence of failure, infection, rejection, or another transplant complication, then it is appropriate to assign a code from subcategory T86.1, Complications of kidney transplant, followed by the appropriate CKD code (N18.-). For patients with CKD following a kidney transplant who do not have a transplant complication such as failure or rejection, code **Z94.0, Kidney transplant status,** should be assigned instead of T86.1-.

COMPLICATIONS OF REATTACHMENT AND AMPUTATION

Complications of reattached extremities and amputated stump are classified to category T87. Complications of reattached extremities are classified by whether they relate to the upper extremity (T87.0x-) or the lower extremity (T87.1x-). The sixth character indicates laterality. Complications of other reattached body parts are classified to code T87.2.

Complications of amputated stump include neuroma (T87.30–T87.34), infection (T87.40–T87.44), necrosis (T87.50–T87.54), other complication (T87.8), and unspecified (T87.9). The fifth characters for subcategories T87.3- through T87.5- specify whether the condition is of the upper or lower extremity, as well as laterality. Code **T87.8, Other complications of amputation stump,** includes amputation stump contracture, contracture of next proximal joint, flexion, edema, and hematoma.

Phantom limb syndrome is a condition relatively common in amputees whereby the patient has the perception of sensations, usually including pain, in an arm or a leg after the limb has been amputated. Phantom limb syndrome is not coded to category T87, but to codes G54.6 and G54.7, depending on whether or not there is associated pain.

EXERCISE 33.3

Code the following diagnoses. Do not assign External cause codes. Assume cases are for initial encounters unless otherwise noted.

1. Leakage of breast prosthesis — T85.43xA

2. Intrauterine contraceptive device imbedded in uterine wall — T83.39xA

   Imbedding

3. Erosion of skin by pacemaker electrodes — T821.90A

   Complication

4. Bone marrow transplant with rejection syndrome — T86.01
   Acute graft-versus-host disease — D89.810

   Complication

5. Displaced lens implant, right eye — T85.22xA

   Complication

6. Complication of transplanted intestine   T86.858
    Malignant neoplasm of colon related to   C80.2
    intestinal transplant   C18.9

7. Broken right hip joint prosthesis after fall   T84.010A

8. A 60-year-old type 2 diabetic woman had a   T87.43
    right above-the-knee amputation two months ago   B95.6
    due to severe diabetic circulatory problems in the   L02.415
    limb. The stump had developed an abscess with   E11.51
    Staphylococcus aureus cultured.

COMPLICATIONS OF PROCEDURES NOT CLASSIFIED ELSEWHERE

Category T81, Complications of procedures, not elsewhere classified, is used to classify a miscellaneous group of postoperative complications. Additional codes are not usually required because the complication code itself provides sufficient specificity. Category T81 requires a seventh character to be added to each code to specify initial encounter ("A"), subsequent encounter ("D"), or sequela ("S"). Examples of codes in category T81 include:

T81.31   Disruption of external operation (surgical) wound
T81.83   Persistent postprocedural fistula
T81.1   Postoperative shock

Wound dehiscence involves partial or total disruption of any or all layers of an operative wound site. Common causes of wound dehiscence include excess tension on the sutured edges, necrosis of the wound edges, seroma or hematoma causing pressure on the wound, and wound infection. ICD-10-CM provides codes to distinguish between disruption of internal (T81.32-) and external (T81.31-) surgical wounds as well as a disruption of a traumatic injury wound repair (T81.33-). For example:

- An eight-year-old had a lower leg traumatic laceration that was sutured several weeks ago. The patient was seen in the emergency department two weeks after the sutures were removed because of disruption of the wound repair. Code T81.33xA is assigned for this encounter.

Subcategory T81.5, Complications of foreign body accidentally left in body following procedure, is assigned for situations in which there is an unintended retention of a foreign object (e.g., sponge) in a patient after surgery or another procedure. The occurrence of unintended retention of objects at any point after the surgery ends should be captured regardless of setting or whether the object is removed. Subcategory T81.5 is further subdivided to specify the complication due to the foreign body, such as adhesions (T81.51-), obstruction (T81.52-), perforation (T81.53-), other complication (T81.59-), or unspecified complication (T81.50-). Sixth characters specify whether the foreign body was accidentally left following surgical operation ("0"); following infusion or transfusion ("1"); following kidney dialysis ("2"); following injection or immunization ("3"); following endoscopic examination ("4"); following heart catheterization ("5"); following aspiration, puncture, or other catheterization ("6"); following removal of catheter or packing ("7"); following other procedure ("8"); or following unspecified procedure ("9").

Acute reaction to foreign substance (rather than foreign body) accidentally left during a procedure is coded to subcategory T81.6, rather than subcategory T81.5. Category T81 also provides codes for complications of artery following a procedure, such as mesenteric artery (T81.710-), renal artery (T81.711-), other artery (T81.718-), or unspecified artery (T81.719-).

COMPLICATIONS OF SURGICAL AND MEDICAL CARE NOT CLASSIFIED ELSEWHERE

Category T88, Other complications of surgical and medical care, not elsewhere classified, is used to classify a number of specific conditions that may occur following almost any type of procedure. For example:

T88.0	Sepsis following immunization
T88.1	Generalized vaccinia
T88.2	Shock due to anesthesia
T88.4	Failed or difficult intubation

COMPLICATIONS VERSUS AFTERCARE

As discussed earlier, it is important to differentiate between an admission for a complication of surgery or medical care and one for aftercare. An admission for aftercare is usually planned in advance to take care of an expected residual or to carry out follow-up activity, such as removal of pins or plates placed during earlier orthopedic surgery. Aftercare is classified to categories Z42 through Z51. The aftercare Z codes should not be used for aftercare for injuries. For aftercare of an injury, the acute injury code is assigned with the appropriate seventh-character extension for subsequent encounter.

Subcategory Z48.0, Encounter for attention to dressings, sutures and drains, distinguishes between encounters for change or removal of nonsurgical wound dressing (Z48.00), for change or removal of surgical wound dressing (Z48.01), for removal of sutures (Z48.02), and for removal of drains (Z48.03).

The coder must be careful not to assign complication codes for routine aftercare encounters. For example:

Z47.2	Admitted for removal of pins from femur
Z46.89	Patient visit for removal of cast

EXERCISE 33.4

Code the following diagnoses, some of which identify complications and some of which identify aftercare. Assume initial encounter unless otherwise noted. Do not assign External cause codes or procedure codes.

1. Admitted for removal of internal fixation   T84.192A
   nail in right forearm that has extruded into surrounding
   tissue, causing severe pain

   Complication, orthopedic

2. Admitted for closure of colostomy   Z43.3

3. Admitted for adjustment of breast prosthesis   Z44.30

4. Admitted for removal of displaced breast prosthesis   T85.42xA

   Complication, surgical, internal

STATUS POST

The term "status post" used in diagnostic statements is sometimes interpreted by coders to mean that there is a postoperative complication; however, the term is rarely intended to carry this meaning. It usually indicates that the patient underwent the procedure at some time in the past. The condition ordinarily would be classified in the Z80–Z87 series but only when it is significant for the current episode of care.

SURGICAL OR MEDICAL CARE AS EXTERNAL CAUSE

As with certain other ICD-10-CM chapter 19 codes, some of the complication of care codes have the external cause included in the code. The code includes the nature of the complication as well as the type of procedure that caused the complication. No External cause code indicating the type of procedure is necessary for these codes. For example, code **M96.621, Fracture of humerus following insertion of orthopedic implant, joint prosthesis, or bone plate, right arm,** includes the nature of the complication (fracture) as well as the type of procedure that caused the complication (insertion of orthopedic implant, joint prosthesis, or bone plate).

In addition, ICD-10-CM provides three sets of External cause codes to indicate medical or surgical care as the cause of a complication:

Y62–Y69   Misadventures to patients during surgical and medical care

Y70–Y82   Medical devices associated with adverse incidents in diagnostic and therapeutic use

Y83–Y84   Surgical and other medical procedures as the cause of abnormal reaction of the patient, or of later complication, without mention of misadventure at the time of the procedure

Codes from categories Y62 through Y69 are used only when the condition is stated to be due to a misadventure of medical or surgical care. These categories include failure of sterile precautions during surgical and medical care (Y62.0–Y62.9), failure in dosage (Y63.0–Y63.9), contaminated medical or biological substances (Y64.0–Y64.9), other misadventures (Y65.0–Y65.53), other specified misadventure (Y65.8), nonadministration of surgical and medical care (Y66), and unspecified misadventure (Y69).

Code Y65.51 is assigned when the wrong operation (procedure) is performed on the correct patient and includes a wrong device implanted into a correct surgical site. Code Y65.52 is assigned for performance of an operation (procedure) on a patient not scheduled for surgery. This includes performance of procedure intended for another patient and performance of procedure on the wrong patient. Code Y65.53 is assigned for performance of the correct operation (procedure) on the wrong side/body part.

Categories Y70–Y82 are used to report breakdown or malfunction of medical devices during use, after implantation, or with ongoing use. The codes are used to report adverse incidents with the following types of devices:

Y70	Anesthesiology devices
Y71	Cardiovascular devices
Y72	Otorhinolaryngological devices
Y73	Gastroenterology and urology devices
Y74	General hospital and personal-use devices
Y75	Neurological devices
Y76	Obstetric and gynecological devices
Y77	Ophthalmic devices
Y78	Radiological devices
Y79	Orthopedic devices
Y80	Physical medicine devices
Y81	General- and plastic-surgery devices
Y82	Other and unspecified medical devices

Codes from categories Y83–Y84 are used when the condition is described as due to medical or surgical care but without mention of misadventure.

Examples include the following:

J70.0 + Y63.2	Radiation pneumonitis due to adverse reaction to overdose of radiotherapy
T81.89x- + Y65.51	Left femoral component inserted into right leg instead of right femoral component during total knee replacement

Because of the potential legal problems that may develop from reporting these codes, the facility should give careful thought to formulating policies and guidelines for their use. Coders should never make an assumption that there has been a misadventure; such codes should be assigned only when there is a clear-cut diagnostic statement to this effect by the physician.

EXERCISE 33.5

Code the following diagnoses. Do not assign External cause or Z codes. Assume initial encounters unless otherwise noted.

1. Infected injection site, left buttock — T80.29xA

   or Complications

2. Sloughing of skin graft due to rejection of pedicle graft to right arm — T86.820

3. Headache due to lumbar puncture — G97.1

4. Postoperative cardiac arrest occurring in operating room during closure of abdomen, with successful resuscitation — I97.711

5. Persistent vomiting following gastrointestinal surgery — K91.0

6. Air embolism resulting from intravenous infusion — T80.0xxA

7. Thrombophlebitis of antecubital vein of the upper arm resulting from intravenous infusion — T80.1xxA / I80.8

   Postoperative

8. Hypovolemic shock due to surgery this morning — T81.1xxA

   Postoperative

9. Persistent postoperative vesicovaginal fistula — T81.83xA / N82.0

10. Cardiac insufficiency resulting from mitral valve prosthesis, in place for three years — I97.110

11. Perforation of coronary artery by
    catheter during cardiac catheterization

    <u>Complication</u>

    I97.51

---

12. Displacement of cardiac pacemaker
    electrode

    <u>Complication, mechanical</u>

    T82.120A

---

13. <u>Phantom limb</u> with pain following surgical amputation

    G54.6

---

14. <u>Neuroma</u> of stump following surgical
    amputation of left leg

    T87.34

---

15. Methicillin-susceptible *Staphylococcus aureus*
    infection of transplanted kidney

    <u>Complication, transplant, organ</u>

    <u>T86.13</u>
    B95.6

---

16. A patient with leukemia is admitted to the hospital after
    noting feelings of palpitations and shortness of breath.
    The patient has an infusion catheter in place for the administration
    of chemotherapy. A chest X-ray shows that the tip of the infusion
    catheter had broken off and traveled to the pulmonary artery.

    <u>T82.514A</u>
    C95.90

---

17. A 13-year-old male status post open reduction internal fixation
    of a right radial shaft fracture is admitted with bowing and angulation
    (malunion) of the fracture site secondary to a bent plate
    (internal fixation device). The physician states that vigorous activity
    on the child's part caused the plate to break and plans to reinsert
    a six-hole plate for fixation of the fracture.

    <u>T84.112A</u>
    S52.301P

Final Review Exercise

Final Review Exercise

The final review exercise draws on concepts presented throughout this handbook. Read each brief summary below and assign codes for all diagnoses and procedures, including codes for external causes and locations of occurrence as needed. For purposes of this assignment, accept narrative statements (for example, conditions, procedures, or other therapy) as though listed in a diagnostic statement.

In day-to-day practice, many hospitals have opted through their internal coding policies not to collect data on noninvasive diagnostic services performed in the inpatient setting, such as X-rays, electrocardiograms (EKGs), computed tomography scans (CTs), and ultrasounds. For this reason, codes for these minor diagnostic services have been omitted from the answers. If you are using the *without Answers* version of this handbook, ask your instructor for the answers.

1. A patient was admitted with complaint of a dull ache and occasional acute pain in the right calf. Examination revealed swelling and redness of the calf as well as a slight fever. The patient gave a history of having been on Premarin therapy for the past 20 years and stated that she has always followed the doctor's instructions for its use. Venous plethysmography revealed the presence of a thrombus. The estrogen therapy dosage was modified, and the patient was discharged with a diagnosis of deep vein thrombosis and thrombophlebitis of the right femoral vein due to supplemental estrogen therapy. She will be seen in the physician's office in one week and will be followed regularly over the next several months.

T38.5x5A	Adverse effect of other estrogens and progestogens, initial encounter
I82.411	Acute embolism and thrombosis of right femoral vein
Z79.818	Long term (current) use of other agents affecting estrogen receptors and estrogen levels

Comment: Assign only the code for the thrombosis based on the excludes1 note at category I80. Because this condition is an adverse effect of estrogen use, the code for the adverse effect is sequenced first, followed by the manifestations.

2. A patient was admitted to the hospital because he was suffering acute abdominal pain. He was also found to be intoxicated, and his medical history indicated that he has been alcohol dependent for several years with episodic binging every three to four months. The current binge apparently started three days ago. The abdominal pain proved to be due to alcohol-induced acute pancreatitis, and he was treated with nasogastric suction, administration of IV fluids, and pain control. The patient was observed for possible withdrawal reaction with standby orders; multiple vitamins were given.

K85.2	Alcohol induced acute pancreatitis
F10.229	Alcohol dependence with intoxication, unspecified
HZ2ZZZZ	Alcohol detoxification

Comment: The condition responsible for the admission was the acute pancreatitis. No code is assigned for the abdominal pain because it is integral to the acute pancreatitis. The observation for withdrawal, standby orders, and administration of multiple vitamins are sufficient to code detoxification, but no withdrawal delirium occurred and so only the code for acute intoxication in alcoholism is assigned.

3. A patient with a four-year history of anorexia nervosa was seen in the physician's office because of significant weight loss over the past three months, going from 82 pounds down to 53 pounds. She was admitted to increase body weight and to be given nutritional counseling because of her severe malnutrition.

F50.00	Anorexia nervosa
E43	Severe malnutrition

Comment: Code E43, Unspecified severe protein-calorie malnutrition, should be assigned as an additional diagnosis for the severe malnutrition. For some anorexic patients, the weight loss is so severe that it leads to malnutrition. Code E43 further describes the severity of the patient's condition.

4. A patient was admitted through the emergency department following a fall from a ladder while painting the outside of his single-family house. He had contusions of the scalp and face and an open type I intertrochanteric fracture of the right femur. The fracture site was debrided, and an open reduction with internal fixation was carried out.

S72.141B	Displaced intertrochanteric fracture of right femur, initial encounter, for open fracture type I or II
S00.03xA	Contusion of scalp
S00.83xA	Contusion of other part of head
W11.xxxA	Fall from ladder
Y92.018	Other place in single-family (private) house as the place of occurrence of the external cause
Y99.8	Other external cause status
Y93.H9	Other activity involving property and land maintenance, building and construction
0QS604Z	Open reduction with internal fixation (reposition right upper femur)
0QB60ZZ	Debridement (root operation "Excision")

Comment: When several injuries are present, the most severe is designated as the principal diagnosis. When a fracture is not indicated as displaced or nondisplaced, it should be coded to displaced. The seventh-character extension for the femur fracture is "B" because initial encounters for open fracture type I are classified to "B." The fracture reduction of the intertrochanteric femur is classified to the root operation "Reposition." The intertrochanteric area is between the greater and lesser trochanter, which is classified to the upper femur.

5. A patient who underwent a modified radical mastectomy of the left breast six months earlier because of carcinoma now has metastasis to the bone. She was admitted for a transfusion of nonautologous packed red blood cells to treat aplastic anemia, probably due to her treatment by chemotherapy. She was discharged with a hemoglobin count of 11.5 and will be followed as an outpatient.

T45.1x5A	Adverse effect of antineoplastic and immunosuppressive drugs, initial encounter
D61.1	Drug-induced aplastic anemia
C79.51	Secondary malignant neoplasm of bone
Z85.3	History of malignant neoplasm of breast
30233N1	Transfusion of red blood cells
Z90.12	Acquired absence of left breast and nipple

Comment: The adverse effect of anemia is designated the principal diagnosis because of the sequencing instructions associated with the aplastic anemia, as well as the sequencing instructions in the ICD-10-CM Official Coding Guidelines, Section I.C.2.c.2 for anemia associated with an adverse effect of chemotherapy. Chemotherapy-induced aplastic anemia requires two codes, with the T45.- code sequenced first, followed by D61.1. A code is assigned for the metastasis to the bone, and a history code is assigned to indicate the previous breast malignancy.

6. A patient was admitted for cholecystectomy because of chronic cholecystitis. Before she went to the operating room the next morning, nursing personnel noted that she had apparently developed a urinary infection, and laboratory tests confirmed a diagnosis of urinary tract infection due to *E. coli*. Because of the infection, the surgery was canceled, antibiotic therapy was instituted, and the patient was discharged on the third hospital day to continue antibiotic therapy at home. She will be seen in the physician's office in three weeks, and surgery will be rescheduled.

<u>K81.1</u>	Chronic cholecystitis
N39.0	Urinary tract infection, due to
B96.2	E. coli
Z53.09	Surgery not carried out because of contraindication

Comment: The principal diagnosis does not change because the planned treatment was not carried out; therefore, the cholecystitis is the principal diagnosis. Code Z53.09 is assigned to indicate that the planned surgery was canceled because of a contraindication, which was the urinary tract infection.

7. A patient who recently underwent an oophorectomy because of adenocarcinoma of the ovary was admitted to the hospital for chemotherapy. Shortly after administration of the therapy, the patient developed a fever and chills and on the second day she had a productive cough. Chest X-rays indicated an acute pneumonia, and sputum culture was positive for *Klebsiella*. Antibiotics were administered, and the patient was discharged on the fifth hospital day after the chemotherapy was administered via peripheral vein.

<u>Z51.11</u>	Encounter for antineoplastic chemotherapy
C56.9	Malignant neoplasm of unspecified ovary
J15.0	Pneumonia due to Klebsiella pneumoniae
3E03305	Introduction of antineoplastic (chemotherapy) into peripheral vein

Comment: When a patient is receiving therapy for neoplastic disease, a code for that condition is assigned, rather than a history code, even though resection may have been performed previously. Because the patient was admitted solely for chemotherapy, Z51.11 remains the principal diagnosis even though the patient remained in the hospital because of the pneumonia. Code C56.9 is assigned as an additional code, rather than a history code, because the patient is still under treatment.

8. A patient who had noticed significant abdominal enlargement over a period of several weeks without a change in her dietary habits was admitted for exploratory laparotomy. Surgery revealed a large malignant ovarian tumor, and the left ovary was resected. The pelvic cavity was explored thoroughly for any evidence of metastatic spread, but none was noted. Chemotherapy treatments were started (via peripheral vein) on the day prior to discharge, and the patient was scheduled to continue therapy on an outpatient basis.

<u>C56.2</u>	Malignant neoplasm of left ovary
0UT10ZZ	Resection left ovary, open approach
3E03305	Introduction of antineoplastic (chemotherapy) into peripheral vein

Comment: When adjunct therapy such as radiotherapy or chemotherapy is given during an admission in which definitive surgery was performed, the code for the neoplasm is designated as the principal diagnosis and no code from category Z51 is assigned. No code is assigned for the laparotomy because it is the operative approach for the oophorectomy.

9. A female patient who had undergone surgery for carcinoma of the right breast two months earlier has since been on a program of chemotherapy. On a routine office visit yesterday, the physician noted that she had become severely dehydrated as a result of this program, and she was admitted for IV therapy for rehydration. Her regular chemotherapy session (via peripheral vein) was carried out on the third day.

T45.1x5A	Adverse effect of antineoplastic and immuno-suppressive drugs, initial encounter
E86.0	Dehydration
C50.911	Malignant neoplasm of right female breast
3E03305	Introduction of antineoplastic (chemotherapy) into peripheral vein

Comment: The adverse effect codes (e.g., T45.1x5) have tabular note instructions requiring that codes from T36 through T65 should be sequenced first, followed by the code(s) that specifies the nature of the adverse effect, poisoning, or toxic effect. According to the ICD-10-CM Official Coding Guidelines, "The instructions and conventions of the classification take precedence over guidelines." In this case, the chemotherapy was the cause of the dehydration; therefore, the dehydration is assigned as a secondary diagnosis. The guideline regarding the management of dehydration due to the malignancy does not apply because the dehydration was an adverse effect of the therapy, rather than due to the malignancy. The malignant neoplasm is assigned as a secondary diagnosis. Even though she received chemotherapy during her hospital stay, the admission was not solely for that purpose and so Z51.11 is not assigned.

10. A patient was admitted with abdominal pain and complaints of melena noted for the past two days. Examination revealed an acute diverticulitis of the colon. Laboratory studies reported a significant hypokalemia. The provider documented hypokalemia, and the patient was placed on oral potassium. Bleeding from the diverticulitis subsided within a few days on conservative treatment, and the patient was discharged to be followed on an outpatient basis.

K57.33	Diverticulitis of colon with bleeding
E87.6	Hypokalemia

Comment: The presence of melena indicates that bleeding is associated with the diverticulitis. Bleeding in a patient with diverticulitis is presumed to be due to the diverticulitis unless the physician specifies that it is due to a different cause. No code is assigned for the abdominal pain, as it is implicit in the diagnosis. The low potassium was treated and therefore is a reportable diagnosis.

11. A patient was admitted with complaints of severe joint pain affecting both hands and hips. The physician's diagnosis indicated rheumatoid arthritis with sympathetic inflammatory myopathy.

M05.49	Rheumatoid myopathy with rheumatoid arthritis of multiple sites

Comment: No code for the joint pain is assigned because it is a characteristic component of rheumatoid arthritis.

12. A patient who was two months pregnant contracted rubella. On her next prenatal visit to the doctor's office, it was decided to admit the patient for therapeutic abortion because of the probability of abnormality of the fetus. Complete abortion was carried out by D & C.

Z33.2	Encounter for elective termination of pregnancy
O35.3xx0	Maternal care for (suspected) damage to fetus from viral disease in mother
10A07ZZ	Abortion of products of conception, via natural or artificial opening

Comment: Because the fetal condition was responsible for modifying the treatment of the mother, the code for it is assigned to explain the rationale for the abortion.

13. Increasing fetal stress was noted during labor. The patient was transferred to the surgical suite, where a classical cesarean delivery was performed. A full-term normal male was delivered.

O77.9	Fetal stress
10D00Z0	Classical cesarean section
Z37.0	Single live birth

Comment: In this case, the fetal stress affected the management of the mother, leading to the decision to deliver by cesarean. Cesarean section is classified to the Obstetrics Section, root operation "Extraction."

14. A patient was admitted with systolic heart failure, acute on chronic, congestive heart failure, and unstable angina. The unstable angina was treated with nitrates, and IV Lasix was administered to manage the heart failure. Both conditions improved, and the patient was discharged to be followed on an outpatient basis.

I50.23	Acute on chronic systolic (congestive) heart failure
I20.0	Unstable angina

Comment: Because both conditions equally meet the criteria for principal diagnosis, either may be listed first. It is not necessary to assign code I50.9 because I50.23 includes the congestive heart failure.

15. A patient was admitted for observation and evaluation for possible intracranial injury following a collision with another car while he was driving to work. The patient had minor bruises on the upper back and abrasions of the skin of the left upper arm. The bruises did not appear to need any treatment; the abrasions were swabbed with disinfectant, and Neosporin was applied. Intracranial injury was ruled out.

Z04.1	Observation examination and observation following transport accident
S20.229A	Contusion of unspecified back wall of thorax
S40.812A	Abrasion of left upper arm
V43.52xA	Car driver injured in collision with other type car in traffic accident

Comment: When the patient is admitted for observation for a possible serious injury such as an intracranial injury, the Z04 code is assigned as the principal diagnosis even when minor injuries are present. In this case, the purpose of admission was to observe the patient; the minor injuries would not have required hospital admission. Additional codes are assigned for the minor injuries. Code S30.0- should not be used because it refers to the lower back rather than the upper back.

16. A patient was brought to the emergency department following a burn injury experienced in a fire at the garage where he works. He was admitted and treated for first-degree and second-degree burns of the forearm and third-degree burn of the back.

T21.34xA	Third-degree burn of back
T22.219A	Second-degree burn of forearm
X00.0xxA	Exposure to flames in uncontrolled fire in building or structure
Y92.59	Other trade areas as the place of occurrence of the external cause
Y99.0	Civilian activity done for income or pay

Comment: When several burns are present, the burn of the highest degree takes precedence; therefore, the third-degree burn of the back is designated as the principal diagnosis. When more than one degree of burn occurs at the same site, only the code for the highest degree is assigned; therefore, only the second degree of the forearm is coded.

17. A patient was admitted because of suspected carcinoma of the colon. Exploratory laparotomy was carried out, and a significant mass was discovered in the sigmoid colon. The sigmoid colon was resected and end-to-end anastomosis accomplished. Small nodules were noted on the liver, and a needle biopsy of the liver was performed during the procedure. The pathology report confirmed adenocarcinoma of the sigmoid colon with metastasis to the liver.

C18.7	Malignant neoplasm of sigmoid colon
C78.7	Secondary malignant neoplasm of liver
0DTN0ZZ	Resection of sigmoid colon, open approach
0FB03ZX	Needle biopsy of liver

Comment: No code is assigned for the exploratory laparotomy because it is the operative approach for the sigmoidectomy. End-to-end anastomosis is included in the code for the colon resection. A needle biopsy performed during open surgery is coded as a percutaneous biopsy.

18. A patient was discharged following prostate surgery with an indwelling catheter in place. He was readmitted with urinary sepsis due to methicillin-resistant *Staphylococcus aureus* (MRSA) due to the presence of the catheter. The physician confirmed the diagnosis of sepsis due to MRSA. The catheter was removed and the patient started on antibiotic therapy. The patient's condition improved over several days, and he was discharged without an indwelling catheter.

T83.51xA	Urinary sepsis due to indwelling urinary catheter
A41.0	Sepsis due to Staphylococcus aureus
Z16	Infection with drug resistant microorganism
N39.0	Urinary tract infection, site not specified
Y84.6	Urinary catheterization as the cause of abnormal reaction of the patient, or of later complication, without mention of misadventure at the time of the procedure
0TPDX0Z	Removal of drainage device from urethra, external approach

Comment: This infection was caused by the presence of the indwelling catheter and is coded as an infection of that device. The physician also confirmed the diagnosis of sepsis. Code A41.0 is assigned for *Staphylococcus aureus* sepsis instead of code A41.9, because the organism is specified. Code Z16 is assigned to specify the infection as due to a drug-resistant organism.

19. A patient six months pregnant was diagnosed as having an iron-deficiency anemia and was admitted for transfusion of nonautologous packed red blood cells.

O99.012	Anemia complicating pregnancy, second trimester
D50.9	Iron-deficiency anemia, unspecified
30233N1	Transfusion of red blood cells

Comment: Code O99.012 from chapter 15 of ICD-10-CM is assigned as the principal diagnosis because the anemia is complicating the pregnancy. Second trimester is assigned because the patient is six months pregnant. Code D50.9 is also assigned to provide greater specificity as to the type of anemia.

20. A patient was admitted with occlusion (due to plaque) of the right common carotid artery, and open carotid endarterectomy was carried out with extracorporeal circulation (continuous cardiac output) used throughout the procedure.

I65.21	Occlusion and stenosis of right carotid artery
03CH0ZZ	Extirpation of matter from right common carotid, open approach
5A1221Z	Performance of cardiac output, continuous (extracorporeal circulation)

Comment: The objective of the carotid endarterectomy was to take out or cut out the solid matter (plaque) occluding the carotid artery; therefore, the procedure is coded to the root operation "Extirpation" rather than "Excision" (cutting out or off, without replacement, a portion of a body part). The extracorporeal circulation is classified to the Extracorporeal Assistance and Performance Section, root operation "Performance," because the machine has taken over the patient's cardiac function during the procedure.

21. A patient was admitted in a coma due to acute cerebrovascular thrombosis with cerebral infarction; the coma cleared by the fourth hospital day. Aphasia and hemiparesis were also present. The aphasia had cleared by discharge, but the hemiparesis was still present.

I63.30	Cerebral thrombosis with cerebral infarction
R40.20	Coma
R47.01	Aphasia
G81.90	Hemiplegia, unspecified, affecting unspecified side

Comment: A code for coma is assigned because it is not integral to a diagnosis of cerebral thrombosis. Codes are assigned for aphasia and hemiparesis; any neurological deficits that occur, even if they have resolved by discharge, are coded because they affect the patient's care.

22. A patient was admitted with severe abdominal pain that began two days prior to admission and progressed in severity. Esophagogastro-duodenoscopy (EGD) revealed an acute gastric ulcer, but no signs of hemorrhage or malignancy were noted. The provider documented acute gastric ulcer, and the patient was put on a medical regimen, including a bland diet, and was advised not to take aspirin.

K25.3	Acute gastric ulcer without hemorrhage or perforation
0DJ08ZZ	Inspection of upper intestinal tract, via natural or artificial opening, endoscopic (esophagogastro-duodenoscopy)

Comment: No code is assigned for the abdominal pain because it is integral to gastric ulcer.

23. A patient with type 1 diabetes mellitus with hyperglycemia was admitted for regulation of insulin dosage. The patient had been in the hospital four weeks earlier for an acute ST elevation myocardial infarction of the inferoposterior wall, and an EKG was performed to check its current status.

E10.65	Diabetes mellitus, type 1 with hyperglycemia
I21.19	ST elevation (STEMI) myocardial infarction involving other coronary artery of inferior wall

Comment: A patient admitted four weeks after an acute myocardial infarction will always require clinical evaluation; in this case, a specific diagnostic study was also performed.

24. A patient who was treated seven weeks ago at Community Hospital for an acute anterolateral myocardial infarction is now admitted to University Hospital for surgical repair of an atrial septal defect resulting from the recent infarction. Following thoracotomy, the defect was repaired with a nonautologous tissue graft; cardiopulmonary bypass (extracorporeal circulation, continuous cardiac output) was used during the procedure. The patient was discharged in good condition, to be followed as an outpatient.

I51.0	Atrial septal defect, acquired
I25.2	Old myocardial infarction
02U50KZ	Supplement atrial septum with nonautologous tissue substitute, open approach
5A1221Z	Performance of cardiac output, continuous (cardiopulmonary bypass)

Comment: Because seven weeks have elapsed since the infarction, neither the acute myocardial infarction nor code I23.1, Atrial septal defect as current complication following acute myocardial infarction, should be reported. Codes from category I23 are used for certain current complications following ST elevation (STEMI) and non-ST elevation (NSTEMI) myocardial infarction, but only within the 28 days post myocardial infarction. Codes from category I21, ST elevation (STEMI) and non-ST elevation (NSTEMI) myocardial infarction, are also used within four weeks (28 days) of onset. Instead, code I25.2, Old myocardial infarction, may be assigned. No code is assigned for the thoracotomy because it is the operative approach for the repair. The objective of the atrial septal repair was to supplement the atrial septum with the graft, so the procedure is coded to the root operation "Supplement."

25. A patient with bilateral mixed conductive and sensorineural hearing loss was admitted for cochlear implantation. Bilateral multiple-channel implants were inserted, and the patient was discharged, to be followed as an outpatient.

H90.6	Mixed conductive and sensorineural hearing loss, bilateral
09HD0S3	Insertion of multiple channel cochlear prosthesis hearing device into right inner ear, open approach
09HE0S3	Insertion of multiple channel cochlear prosthesis hearing device into left inner ear, open approach

Comment: Because a combination code including both types of hearing loss is provided, only code H90.6 is assigned rather than individual codes for the hearing loss. Because the prosthetic device was inserted in both ears and a single code is not available for bilateral, two procedure codes are necessary, one for each ear.

26. A patient who underwent a right kidney transplant three months ago is admitted for biopsy because of an increased creatinine level discovered on an outpatient visit. Percutaneous biopsy revealed chronic rejection syndrome. The patient was discharged on a modified medication regimen, to be followed closely as an outpatient.

| T86.11 | Kidney transplant rejection |
| 0TB03ZX | Excision of right kidney, percutaneous approach, diagnostic |

Comment: Transplant rejection is coded as a complication of the transplanted organ. A percutaneous biopsy is coded to the root operation "Excision," with the qualifier "diagnostic."

27. A patient was admitted with a displaced fracture of the shaft of the right femur. Closed reduction was carried out and a cast was applied.

| S72.301A | Unspecified fracture of shaft of right femur |
| 0QS6XZZ | Reposition right upper femur, external approach |

Comment: When the diagnostic statement does not indicate whether the fracture is open or closed, ICD-10-CM classifies it as closed. Reduction of a dislocated fracture is classified to the root operation "Reposition." Because this was a closed reduction, no incision or skin puncture was performed and the approach is external. Cast application in conjunction with the "Reposition" procedure is not coded separately.

28. A patient who has had recurrent attacks of angina was seen in his physician's office because he felt that the anginal attacks seemed to be occurring more frequently and to be more severe and more difficult to control. He had not had a thorough evaluation previously, and bypass surgery had not been recommended in the past. He was admitted to the hospital for diagnostic studies to determine the underlying cause of this unstable angina. He underwent combined right- and left-heart catheterization, which revealed significant atherosclerotic heart disease. He was advised that coronary artery bypass surgery was indicated, but he did not want to make a decision without further discussion with his family. He was discharged on antianginal medication and will be seen in the doctor's office in one week.

| I25.110 | Atherosclerotic heart disease of native coronary artery with unstable angina pectoris |
| 4A023N8 | Measurement of cardiac sampling and pressure, bilateral, percutaneous approach |

Comment: I25.110 is a combination code that includes both the atherosclerosis and the unstable angina pectoris. Because this patient has not had a bypass surgery in the past, the arteriosclerosis is of a native coronary artery. Cardiac catheterization is classified to the Measurement and Monitoring Section, root operation "Measurement," body system "cardiac." Because the catheterization was for both the right and left sides, the qualifier "bilateral" is used.

29. The patient discussed in the preceding case returned to the hospital for bypass surgery. His angina is under control with the antianginal medications he was prescribed. Reverse right greater saphenous vein grafts were brought from the aorta to the obtuse marginal and the right coronary artery; the left internal mammary artery was loosened and brought down to the left anterior descending artery to bypass this obstruction. The gastroepiploic artery was used to bypass the circumflex. Extracorporeal circulation (continuous cardiac output) and intraoperative pacemaker were used during the procedure.

<u>I25.119</u>	Atherosclerotic heart disease of native coronary artery with unspecified angina pectoris
021109W	Bypass coronary artery, two sites to aorta with autologous venous tissue, open approach
02100Z9	Bypass coronary artery, one site to left internal mammary, open approach
02100ZF	Bypass coronary artery, one site to abdominal artery, open approach
06BP0ZZ	Excision of right greater saphenous vein, open approach
5A1221Z	Performance of cardiac output, continuous (cardiopulmonary bypass)
5A1223Z	Performance of cardiac pacing, continuous (intraoperative pacemaker)

Comment: Code I25.110 is not used because his angina is not specified to be unstable. Four coronary artery bypass grafts were placed, two of which were aortocoronary, one a left internal mammary-coronary artery, and one an abdominal-coronary bypass. A code for the "Excision" of the saphenous vein for harvesting of the graft is also assigned. Codes are assigned for the cardiopulmonary bypass and the intraoperative pacemaker.

30. A patient was brought to the hospital by ambulance after a fall from the scaffolding while working on the construction of a new bank building. He had struck his head and experienced a brief period of unconsciousness (approximately 45 minutes). On examination, he was found to have an open skull fracture with cerebral laceration and contusion. The skull fracture was reduced after debridement and the patient was transferred to the intensive care unit, where he stayed for four days. He was discharged on the tenth day in good condition and advised to avoid any strenuous activity and to see his physician in one week.

S02.91xB	Unspecified fracture of skull, initial encounter for open fracture
S06.332A	Contusion and laceration of cerebrum, unspecified, with loss of consciousness of 31 minutes to 59 minutes, initial encounter
W12.xxxA	Fall from scaffolding, initial encounter
Y92.61	Building [any] under construction as the place of occurrence of the external cause
Y99.0	Civilian activity done for income or pay
Y93.H3	Activity, building and construction
0NS00ZZ	Reposition skull, open approach

Comment: Code S02.91 requires the seventh-character extension "B" to indicate that this is an open fracture. Any intracranial injury (S06.-) associated with the skull fracture requires a separate code. In this case, code S06.332- is assigned because the patient was documented to have loss of consciousness for less than one hour. Debridement of compound (open) fracture of the skull is included in the code for fracture reduction.

31. A patient was admitted for corrective surgery for a keloid of the left hand due to a burn experienced in a brush fire one year ago. Radical excision of the scar was carried out, and the defect was covered with a full-thickness graft taken from the left upper arm. The patient was discharged in good condition, to be seen in the physician's office in two weeks.

L91.0	Keloid scar
T23.002S	Burn of unspecified degree of left hand, unspecified site, sequela
X01.0xxS	Exposure to flames in uncontrolled fire, not in building or structure, sequela
0HBGXZZ	Excision of left hand skin, external approach
0HRGX73	Replacement of left hand skin with autologous tissue substitute, full thickness, external approach
0HBCXZZ	Excision of left upper arm skin, external approach

Comment: The residual keloid is sequenced first, with code T23.002S indicating that it is a late effect of a burn of the hand. Because the condition is a late effect, the External cause of morbidity code must also be a late effect code; therefore, the seventh-character extension "S," for sequela, is assigned. A separate code is assigned for obtaining the autograft (per the ICD-10-PCS Official Coding Guidelines) because the tissue is obtained from a different body part in order to complete the objective of the procedure.

32. A patient was brought to the emergency department by ambulance at 1:00 a.m. by her husband, who stated that they had been to a dinner party at a friend's home earlier in the evening. His wife had two martinis before the meal and several glasses of wine with the meal. At bedtime she took Valium that her physician had ordered prn for nervousness and inability to sleep. Shortly thereafter, the husband noticed that she appeared to be somewhat stuporous, became worried about her condition, and brought her to the emergency department. The provider documented accidental overdose secondary to Valium taken with alcohol.

T51.0x1A	Toxic effect of ethanol, accidental (unintentional), initial encounter
T42.4x1A	Poisoning by benzodiazepines, accidental (unintentional), initial encounter (Valium)
R40.1	Stupor
Y92.099	Unspecified place in other non-institutional residence as the place of occurrence of the external cause

Comment: Although the Valium was used correctly, the fact that alcohol was also taken during the same period makes this a poisoning. Because two substances were involved, two poisoning codes are assigned. Either poisoning code can be designated as the principal diagnosis.

33. A patient was admitted to the hospital with an admitting diagnosis of acute hip pain. There was no history of trauma; she stated that she had simply stood up from her chair, immediately experienced acute pain in the left leg, and fallen back into the chair. She has had osteoporosis for several years and is also a known diabetic. An X-ray revealed a fracture of the lower third of the shaft of the femur. A routine preoperative chest X-ray showed a few strands of atelectasis and a small cloudy area that may have represented mild pleural effusion. A cast was applied to the leg to immobilize the fracture. Her blood sugars were monitored and remained normal throughout the stay. The physician documented spontaneous fracture secondary to osteoporosis.

M80.052A	Age-related osteoporosis with current pathological fracture, left femur, initial encounter
E11.9	Type 2 diabetes mellitus without complications
2W3MX2Z	Immobilization of left lower extremity using cast

Comment: Spontaneous fractures such as this are always classified as pathological. Codes in category M80 are combination codes that include the osteoporosis with current pathological fracture. ICD-10-CM classifies osteoporosis not otherwise specified to age-related osteoporosis. No codes are assigned for the atelectasis or possible pleural effusion because these represent X-ray findings only, without further evaluation or treatment. The diabetes was monitored, and so a code is assigned. Diabetes mellitus unspecified as to type is classified to type 2. Because only a cast was placed on the fracture without the need for reduction ("Reposition"), the procedure is coded to the root operation "Immobilization" in the Placement Section.

34. A patient with a five-year history of emphysema was brought to the hospital's emergency department in acute respiratory failure. Endotracheal intubation was carried out in the emergency department, and the patient was placed on mechanical ventilation. She was then admitted to the ICU, where she remained on the ventilator for three days and then was taken off the ventilator without a weaning period. She was discharged on the fifth hospital day.

J96.00	Acute respiratory failure, unspecified whether with hypoxia or hypercapnia
J43.9	Emphysema, unspecified
5A1945Z	Respiratory ventilation, 24-96 consecutive hours
0BH17EZ	Insertion of endotracheal airway into trachea, via natural or artificial opening

Comment: Acute respiratory failure associated with chronic pulmonary disease, such as emphysema, can be designated as the principal diagnosis. The patient was on mechanical ventilation only three days, a total of less than 96 hours. A code is assigned for the tube insertion because it was performed in the emergency department of the hospital with immediate admission.

35. A patient in acute respiratory failure was brought to the hospital by ambulance with ventilator in place. In the ambulance, an endotracheal tube was inserted into the patient. He had a long history of congestive heart failure, and studies confirmed that he was in congestive failure, with pleural effusion and acute pulmonary edema. The patient was treated with diuretics, and his cardiac condition was brought back into an acceptable range. He continued on ventilation for four days and was weaned on the fifth day. The physician was questioned regarding the reason for the admission, and she indicated that the patient was admitted for the acute respiratory failure.

J96.00	Acute respiratory failure, unspecified whether with hypoxia or hypercapnia
I50.9	Heart failure, unspecified
5A1955Z	Respiratory ventilation, greater than 96 consecutive hours

Comment: When a patient is admitted with respiratory failure and another acute condition (e.g., congestive heart failure), the principal diagnosis will not be the same in every situation. Selection of the principal diagnosis will depend on the circumstances of admission. In this instance, the physician had to be queried to determine whether the congestive heart failure or the respiratory failure was responsible for the admission. Pulmonary edema and pleural effusion with heart condition or heart failure is classified to heart failure; no additional codes are assigned for these conditions. Time counting for mechanical ventilation begins at time of admission when the ventilator is already in use. No code is assigned for the endotracheal tube insertion because it was done in the ambulance and cannot be reported by the hospital.

36. A five-year-old child was brought to the emergency department after the mother found the child playing with an open bottle of her prescription sedatives. She could not tell if the child had taken any pills, but she wanted the child evaluated for possible problems. The child was evaluated, and no evidence of poisoning or any other signs or symptoms were found. The mother was reassured, and the child was taken home.

Z03.6	Encounter for observation for suspected toxic effect from ingested substance ruled out

Comment: It is appropriate to use category Z03 when a patient is seen for evaluation and no diagnosis is made. If the suspected diagnosis or a related diagnosis had been established, including a significant sign or symptom, the code for that condition would be assigned rather than the code from category Z03.

37. A patient with hypertensive and diabetic end-stage renal disease who is on chronic dialysis is admitted because of disequilibrium syndrome (electrolyte imbalance) caused by the dialysis.

E87.8	Other disorders of electrolyte and fluid balance, not elsewhere classified
I12.0	Hypertensive chronic kidney disease with stage 5 chronic kidney disease or end-stage renal disease
N18.6	End-stage renal disease
E11.29	Type 2 diabetes mellitus with other diabetic kidney complication
Z99.2	Dependence on renal dialysis
Y84.1	Kidney dialysis as the cause of abnormal reaction of the patient, or of later complication, without mention of misadventure at the time of the procedure

Comment: When end-stage renal disease is the result of both hypertension and diabetes mellitus, both diabetes and hypertension are coded because they are responsible for the condition (I12.- and E11.29). Because the patient has hypertensive end-stage renal disease and is on chronic dialysis, codes I12.0 and N18.6 are assigned. Code Y84.1 is assigned to indicate the external cause.

38. A patient who has had arteriosclerotic disease of the right lower extremity with intermittent claudication for three years recently progressed to ulceration, and is now admitted with ulceration and gangrene of the toes of the right foot resulting from the arteriosclerosis. A tarsometatarsal amputation of the right foot was performed, and the patient left the operating room in good condition.

I70.261	Atherosclerosis of native arteries of extremities with gangrene, right leg
L97.519	Non-pressure chronic ulcer of other part of right foot with unspecified severity
0Y6M0Z0	Detachment at right foot, complete, open approach

Comment: Code I70.261 includes gangrene. An additional code may be assigned for the ulceration. Amputations are coded to the root operation "Detachment." Amputations through the tarsometatarsal joint of the foot are considered complete; therefore, the qualifier "complete" is selected.

39. A two-year-old child with a severe cough was admitted to the hospital with a history of having experienced malaise, loss of appetite, and cough for several days. In addition to the cough, he was experiencing some shortness of breath, and a chest X-ray showed an acute pneumonia. Sputum cultures showed *B. pertussis*. He was started on IV antibiotics and became afebrile on the fifth hospital day. A repeat chest X-ray was negative on the sixth hospital day, and the cough had partially cleared. He was discharged on the eighth day to be cared for at home and followed as an outpatient.

| A37.01 | Whooping cough due to Bordetella pertussis with pneumonia |

Comment: Whooping cough is the condition resulting from infection by *B. pertussis*. Code A37.01 identifies the pneumonia associated with whooping cough, and no separate code for the pneumonia is assigned.

40. A 10-year-old boy was admitted because of severe cellulitis of the left leg. He had gone on a hiking trip in the nearby forest with his Boy Scout troop a week earlier and now has a painful reddened area on the left leg. He stated that there was a good deal of thorny brush and that he had several minor thorn punctures of the left leg but had experienced no problem with them. The day before admission he had developed a painful swollen area that had become worse during the night. A diagnosis of cellulitis due to *Streptococcus* A was made, and antibiotics were administered. The wound itself was evaluated but did not appear to need specific treatment. The area on the leg progressively healed. The patient was discharged to continue the antibiotic series at home and will be seen in the physician's office in one week.

L03.116	Cellulitis of left lower limb
S81.832A	Puncture wound without foreign body, left lower leg
B95.0	Bacterial infection due to group A *Streptococcus*
W60.xxxA	Contact with nonvenomous plant thorns and spines and sharp leaves
Y92.821	Forest as the place of occurrence of the external cause
Y93.01	Activity, walking, marching and hiking
Y99.8	Other external cause status

Comment: In this case, the minor puncture wounds did not require treatment at the time they occurred and would not have required hospital care; therefore, the cellulitis is designated as the principal diagnosis. The wounds were evaluated, however, and so a code for the injury is assigned. Although thorn punctures were noted, there was no mention of a thorn in the wounds; therefore, no code for foreign bodies was assigned.

41. An unconscious diving instructor was admitted with concussion and a skull fracture and subdural hematoma after jumping from a high diving board and hitting the side of the pool at the gymnasium where he worked. Drainage of the subdural space was carried out by incision and the fracture reduced. The patient left the operating room in fair condition but died from his brain injury the following day without having ever regained consciousness.

S02.91xA	Unspecified fracture of skull, initial encounter for closed fracture
S06.5x7A	Traumatic subdural hemorrhage with loss of consciousness of any duration with death due to brain injury before regaining consciousness, initial encounter
W16.532A	Jumping or diving into swimming pool striking wall causing other injury, initial encounter
Y92.39	Other specified sports and athletic area as the place of occurrence of the external cause
Y93.12	Springboard and platform diving
Y99.0	Civilian activity done for income or pay
0NS00ZZ	Reposition of skull, open approach
00940ZZ	Drainage of subdural space, open approach

Comment: No code is assigned for concussion when there is skull fracture with intracranial injury. Code S06.5x7A is used because the patient was unconscious on admission, never regained consciousness, and expired the following day from the brain injury. Two procedure codes are needed, one for the fracture reduction and one for the incision and "Drainage" of the hematoma.

42. A patient was admitted because of increasing confusion and memory loss, which his family was unable to deal with. The patient was disoriented and unable to furnish any information. He was diagnosed as having senile dementia with Alzheimer's disease and was transferred to a nursing home.

| G30.9 | Alzheimer's disease, unspecified |
| F02.80 | Dementia in other diseases classified elsewhere without behavioral disturbance |

Comment: When dementia is associated with Alzheimer's disease, the code for Alzheimer's disease is sequenced first, followed by code F02.80.

43. Newborn twin girls, both living, were delivered in the hospital at 35 weeks, with extremely low birth weight of 850 grams for twin #1 and 900 grams for twin #2. Both were transferred to the neonatal intensive care nursery with a diagnosis of extreme immaturity.

Twin #1:	Z38.30	Twin liveborn infant, delivered vaginally
	P07.03	Extremely low birth weight newborn, 750-999 grams
	P07.32	Other preterm newborn, 32-36 completed weeks
Twin #2:	Z38.30	Twin liveborn infant, delivered vaginally
	P07.03	Extremely low birth weight newborn, 750-999 grams
	P07.32	Other preterm newborn, 32-36 completed weeks

Comment: A code from category Z38 is always designated as the principal diagnosis for the episode in which birth occurs. For babies born in the hospital, the fifth digit indicates whether the delivery was by cesarean; in this case, it was not. When both birth weight and gestational age of the newborn are available, both should be coded, with birth weight sequenced before gestational age.

44. A patient with a long history of angina pectoris came to the emergency department complaining of increasing anginal pain that he could not relieve with nitroglycerin and rest. The pain had occurred again about an hour ago and has been increasing in severity. Cardiac catheterization done recently showed some occlusion of the right coronary artery. It was decided to go ahead with a percutaneous transluminal coronary angioplasty, administering a thrombolytic agent to a coronary artery, in the hope of averting what appeared to be an impending myocardial infarction. The procedure was carried out without incident and the infarction was averted, but the patient did have an occlusion of the coronary artery.

I24.0	Acute coronary thrombosis not resulting in myocardial infarction
02703ZZ	Dilation of coronary artery, one site, percutaneous approach
3E07317	Introduction of other thrombolytic into coronary artery, percutaneous approach

Comment: The code for unstable angina (I20.0) is not assigned when a code from category I24 is assigned. Code 02703ZZ is assigned for the PTCA on a single site. The infusion of a thrombolytic agent is reported separately using code 3E07317.

45. A patient was admitted to the hospital with unstable angina that had been increasing in severity since the previous day. He was placed on bed rest and telemetry, and IV nitroglycerin was administered. An EKG showed some paroxysmal tachycardia as well, and so IV heparin was added to his medication program. His angina returned to its normal status, and the tachycardia was not shown on repeat studies at the end of one week. The patient was discharged to be seen by a visiting nurse over the next two weeks to supervise his medication regimen, and an appointment with his physician was made for two weeks later.

I20.0   Unstable angina

I47.9   Paroxysmal tachycardia, unspecified

Comment: In this case, no studies were done to identify the underlying pathology and no surgical intervention was undertaken. Therefore, the unstable angina is the principal diagnosis.

46. A patient who had been HIV-positive for several years was seen in his physician's office with skin lesions over his back suggestive of HIV-related Kaposi's sarcoma. He was seen for incisional biopsy, which confirmed the diagnosis.

B20   Human immunodeficiency virus (HIV) disease

C46.0   Kaposi's sarcoma of skin

0HB6XZX   Excision of back skin, external approach, diagnostic

Comment: When the patient is admitted for treatment of a condition due to HIV infection, the code for the infection is designated as the principal diagnosis, with an additional code for the related condition.

47. A patient was admitted through the emergency department with acute right flank pain and was taken to surgery for removal of a ruptured appendix. At the time of the appendectomy, generalized peritonitis was observed along with some suspicious nodules on the head of the pancreas. A needle biopsy was performed while the abdomen was open; a diagnosis of carcinoma of the pancreas head was made on the basis of the pathological examination.

K35.2   Acute appendicitis with generalized peritonitis

C25.0   Malignant neoplasm of pancreas, head of pancreas

0DTJ0ZZ   Resection of appendix, open approach

0FBG3ZX   Excision of pancreas, percutaneous approach, diagnostic

Comment: The code for the appendicitis is designated the principal diagnosis because it was clearly the condition that occasioned the admission. The code for the malignant neoplasm is also assigned, but there is no guideline that suggests that a malignancy takes any precedence in a situation of this type. A needle biopsy done in the course of an open surgical procedure is coded as a closed biopsy.

48. A patient with a long history of type 2 diabetes mellitus was admitted in hyperosmolar coma with blood sugars out of control. Modification of the insulin regimen was instituted, and the patient was monitored carefully throughout her stay. The coma cleared on the first hospital day, and the patient was brought into control over the next four days. In addition to this acute metabolic condition, she also had a diagnosis of diabetic chronic kidney disease with stage 2 chronic kidney disease. The patient was discharged on a modified insulin regimen and will be followed by a visiting nurse until the diabetes stabilizes.

E11.01   Type 2 diabetes mellitus with hyperosmolarity with coma

E11.22   Type 2 diabetes mellitus with diabetic chronic kidney disease

N18.2   Chronic kidney disease, stage 2 (mild)

Comment: The code for diabetes mellitus with hyperosmolarity includes the associated coma. Although a diagnosis of diabetic kidney disease was also established during this episode of care, it was the coma that occasioned the admission; therefore, it is designated as the principal diagnosis. Code N18.2 is assigned as an additional code to specify the stage of chronic kidney disease.

49. A patient was admitted with a severe stage 3 pressure ulcer on the left buttock, with extensive necrotic tissue and gangrene. She was taken to the operating room, where the surgeon carefully excised the necrotic tissue (skin). The ulcer site was then treated with antibiotic ointment and gauze bandage, and the patient was returned to the nursing unit, where the wound was monitored carefully and additional antibiotic treatment was administered. By the fourth day, healing was beginning to close the area, but treatment was continued until discharge on the seventh day. The family was advised to use an egg crate mattress and to turn the patient regularly. The patient was scheduled for an outpatient visit in one week.

I96   Gangrene, not elsewhere classified

L89.323   Pressure ulcer of left buttock, stage 3

0HB8XZZ   Excision of buttock skin, external approach

Comment: The code for gangrene must be sequenced first because of the instructional note at category L89 to code first any associated gangrene. Excisional debridement is classified to the root operation "Excision" of the appropriate layer, in this case, skin.

50. A patient with a diagnosis of end-stage renal disease due to type 1 diabetes mellitus was admitted for her first hemodialysis session. A right internal jugular vein catheter was placed and a single hemodialysis session carried out. The patient tolerated the procedure well and will continue receiving hemodialysis on a regular schedule.

Z49.01   Encounter for fitting and adjustment of extracorporeal dialysis catheter

E10.22   Type 1 diabetes mellitus with diabetic chronic kidney disease

N18.6   End-stage renal disease

5A1D00Z   Performance of urinary filtration, single

05HM33Z   Insertion of infusion device into right internal jugular vein, percutaneous approach

Comment: Code Z49.01 is the principal diagnosis because this admission was solely for the purpose of dialysis. Subcategory Z49.0, Preparatory care for renal dialysis, includes encounters for dialysis instruction and training. The fact that the venous catheter was inserted does not affect principal diagnosis assignment when the catheterization is followed by dialysis. Code E10.22 is assigned for the diabetes mellitus with diabetic chronic kidney disease. The end-stage renal disease is the manifestation of the diabetes and the condition for which the dialysis is performed. Procedure codes are assigned for both the catheter "Insertion" and the hemodialysis.

Appendix A

Reporting of the Present on Admission Indicator

The present on admission (POA) indicator is a data element required for Medicare claims reporting. The POA indicator provides information on whether a diagnosis was present at the time of a patient's admission. The Medicare POA requirement applies to all diagnosis codes involving inpatient admissions to general acute care hospitals (except for critical care access hospitals, Maryland waiver hospitals, long-term care hospitals, cancer hospitals, and children's inpatient facilities). Some states (e.g., Maryland) have additional regulatory requirements for POA reporting. State guidelines for public health and quality reporting may differ from the national Medicare reporting requirements. In addition, several commercial health plans require POA reporting by contractual agreement with the hospital.

It is important that the POA indicator be reported correctly because it is significant in quality-of-care reporting and analysis and potentially significant for medicolegal and reimbursement issues. Beginning October 1, 2008, a select number of hospital-acquired conditions are not recognized by the Medicare severity-adjusted diagnosis-related group (MS-DRG) system if the condition is the only complication/comorbidity (CC) or major complication/comorbidity (MCC).

The POA indicator should be reported for principal and secondary diagnosis codes and External cause of injury codes based on a review of the provider's documentation. Distinguishing between pre-existing conditions and complications enhances the use of administrative data for outcomes reporting. Secondary diagnoses may be chronic illnesses that have been in existence for some time, or they may have developed after admission. Unless the POA indicator is reported, it is not easy to determine the difference between pre-existing conditions and complications when analyzing only the ICD-10-CM codes.

DEFINITION

The term "present on admission" means "present at the time the order for inpatient admission occurs." Conditions or adverse events that occur prior to an inpatient admission are considered to be present on admission, including any conditions occurring in the emergency department, observation, clinic, or outpatient surgery prior to inpatient admission.

DOCUMENTATION

The usefulness of POA data for quality-of-care, medicolegal, and reimbursement issues is dependent on the provider's accurate and complete medical record documentation. "Provider" in this context refers to the physician or any qualified health care practitioner who is legally accountable for establishing the patient's diagnosis, similar to the definition used for code assignment. The coder should not include documentation from nurses or other allied health professionals who are not legally accountable for establishing the patient's diagnosis (except for the reporting of pressure ulcer staging and body mass index).

The provider must resolve any inconsistent, missing, conflicting, or unclear documentation before the appropriate POA indicator may be selected. Resolving inconsistencies may necessitate querying the provider for clarification.

There is no required time frame as to when a provider must identify or document a condition to be present on admission. In some clinical situations, it may not be possible for a provider to make a definitive diagnosis (or a condition may not be recognized or reported by the patient) for a period of time after admission. In some cases it may be several days before the provider arrives at a definitive diagnosis. This does not mean that the condition was not present on admission. Determination of whether the condition was present on admission is based on the applicable POA guideline or the provider's best clinical judgment.

GUIDELINES

Guidelines for the selection of POA indicators are included in the *ICD-10-CM Official Guidelines for Coding and Reporting* as appendix I effective with the 2011 update. The POA guidelines are not intended to replace any guidelines in the main body of the official guidelines, nor are they intended to provide guidance on when a condition should be coded. Rather, the POA guidelines are intended to show how to apply the POA indicator to the final set of diagnosis codes already selected.

The guidelines are not intended to be a substitute for a provider's clinical judgment as to whether a condition was or was not present on admission. Issues related to the linking of signs and symptoms, timing of test results, or findings should be referred to the provider for clarification.

REPORTING OPTIONS

There are five options for reporting all diagnoses:

Code	Definition
Y	Yes (present at the time of inpatient admission)
N	No (not present at the time of inpatient admission)
U	Unknown (documentation is insufficient to determine if condition is present on admission)
W	Clinically undetermined (provider is unable to clinically determine whether condition was present on admission or not)
Unreported/not used	Exempt from POA reporting [This option is the only circumstance in which the POA field is left blank. The condition must be on the list of ICD-10-CM codes for which this field is not applicable.]

Conditions Present on Admission

Assign "Y" as the POA reporting option for the following circumstances:

- Condition explicitly documented as being present on admission.

- Condition diagnosed prior to inpatient admission (e.g., hypertension, diabetes mellitus, asthma).

- Condition diagnosed during the admission but clearly present (but not diagnosed) before admission (e.g., a patient with a lump in her breast is admitted and has a biopsy, and the pathology report reveals carcinoma of the breast).

- Condition diagnosed as possible, probable, suspected, or rule out at the time of discharge and, based on signs, symptoms, or clinical findings, condition is suspected during admission (e.g., a patient is admitted with chest pain, transferred to another facility, and discharged as possible myocardial infarction).

- Condition that developed during an outpatient encounter prior to a written order for inpatient admission (e.g., a patient falls while in the emergency department, sustains a fracture, and is subsequently admitted as an inpatient).

- Condition diagnosed as impending or threatened, based on symptoms or clinical findings that were present on admission (e.g., a patient with a known history of coronary atherosclerosis is now admitted for treatment of impending myocardial infarction; the final diagnosis is documented as "impending" myocardial infarction).

- Condition reported with a combination code, and all parts of the combination code are present on admission (e.g., a patient with acute prostatitis is admitted with hematuria).

- Condition reported with the same ICD-10-CM code representing two or more conditions during the same encounter, and all conditions were present on admission (e.g., bilateral unspecified age-related cataracts).

- Single code that only identifies the chronic condition and not the acute exacerbation (e.g., acute exacerbation of chronic leukemia).

- Chronic condition, even if it is not diagnosed until after admission (e.g., lung cancer is diagnosed during hospitalization).

- Condition in which the final diagnosis includes comparative or contrasting diagnoses, and both are present or suspected at the time of admission (e.g., a patient is admitted with severe abdominal pain, nausea, and vomiting, with the admitting diagnosis of acute pyelonephritis versus diverticulum of the colon; the patient is discharged and sent home).

- Infection codes that include the causal organism, if the infection (or signs of the infection) is present on admission, even though the culture results may not be known until after admission (e.g., a patient is admitted with severe cough, fever, and congestion and his culture of sputum reveals staphylococcal infection; the patient is diagnosed with staphylococcal pneumonia).

- Congenital conditions and anomalies (except for codes Q00–Q99, which are exempt). Congenital conditions are always considered to be present on admission.

- Condition present at birth or that develops in utero, including conditions that occur during delivery (e.g., injury during delivery).

- External cause code representing an external cause of morbidity that occurred prior to inpatient admission (e.g., the patient fell out of bed at home).

Conditions Not Present on Admission

Assign "N" as the POA reporting option for the following circumstances:

- Condition the provider explicitly documents as not present at the time of admission (e.g., a patient develops a vascular catheter infection a few days after the insertion of the catheter).

- Condition reported as an inconclusive final diagnosis based on signs, symptoms, or clinical findings that were not present on admission (e.g., a patient develops a fever after surgery, and the final diagnosis includes "possible postoperative infection").

- Condition diagnosed as impending or threatened and based on symptoms or clinical findings that were not present on admission (e.g., a patient is admitted to the hospital for prostate surgery and postoperatively develops chest pain; the final diagnosis includes "impending myocardial infarction").

- Condition reported with a combination code, and any part of the combination code is not present on admission (e.g., obstructive chronic bronchitis with acute exacerbation, and the exacerbation is not present on admission).

- Conditions reported with the same ICD-10-CM code representing two or more conditions during the same encounter, and any one of the conditions was not present on admission (e.g., traumatic secondary and recurrent hemorrhage and seroma are assigned to a single code, T79.2, but only one of the conditions was present on admission).

- External cause code representing an external cause of morbidity that occurs during inpatient hospitalization (e.g., a patient falls out of the hospital bed during his stay, or he experiences an adverse reaction to a medication administered after inpatient admission).

Unclear Documentation

Assign "U" as the POA indicator when the medical record documentation is unclear as to whether the condition was present on admission. Coding professionals are encouraged to query the providers when the documentation is unclear. It is important to note that "U" should not be routinely assigned but should be used only under very limited circumstances, such as when the provider is not available to provide clarification.

Conditions Clinically Undetermined

Assign "W" as the POA indicator when the medical record documentation indicates that it cannot be clinically determined whether the condition was present on admission. For example, a patient is admitted in active labor, and during the stay a breast abscess is noted when she attempts to breast feed. The provider is unable to determine if the abscess was present on admission.

It is important to distinguish between the reporting options "U" and "W." For example, if the provider is queried and is not able to determine whether the condition was present on admission, report using "W." In contrast, if the documentation is not available and the provider is not queried, or the provider is not available to provide a response, report using "U." Coders should make every attempt to limit the number of "U" options reported, as this may potentially be construed as an error or treated as "N" for Medicare payment purposes.

Conditions Exempt from POA Reporting

A list of categories and codes exempt from the POA requirement may be found in the *ICD-10-CM Official Guidelines for Coding and Reporting* as part of appendix I. These codes are exempt because they indicate circumstances regarding the health care encounter or factors influencing the health status but do not represent a current disease or injury or are always present on admission. Examples include injury, poisoning, and certain other consequences of external causes with the seventh character "S," personal and family history codes, and need for vaccination Z codes.

The codes and categories on the exempt list are the only codes that are exempt from POA reporting. The list of exempt codes is updated every year based on the new codes implemented for the year.

Special Considerations

For obstetrical patients, whether or not delivery occurs during the current hospitalization does not affect assignment of the POA indicator. The determining factor for POA assignment is whether the pregnancy complication or obstetrical condition described by the code is present at the time of admission. If the obstetrical code includes information that is not a diagnosis, do not consider that information in the POA determination. If the obstetrical code includes more than one diagnosis and any one of the diagnoses identified by the code was not present on admission, assign "N" (e.g., category O11, Pre-existing hypertension with pre-eclampsia).

Newborns are not considered to be admitted until after birth; therefore, any condition that is present at birth or that develops in utero is considered to be present at admission.

EXERCISE A.1

Assign the appropriate POA indicator for the following scenarios:

1. A patient is treated in observation, falls out of bed, and breaks a hip. The patient is subsequently admitted as an inpatient to treat the hip fracture. What is the POA indicator for the fracture?   **Y**

2. A patient is admitted to the hospital for coronary artery bypass surgery. Postoperatively, he develops a pulmonary embolism. What is the POA indicator for the pulmonary embolism?   **N**

3. A patient is admitted in active labor. She is known to have a gastric ulcer under medical management. After delivering the baby, she complains of melena and is noted to have bleeding from the gastric ulcer. What is the POA indicator for bleeding from the gastric ulcer?   **N**

4. A single liveborn infant is delivered in the hospital. The physician documents neonatal tachycardia. What is the POA indicator for the neonatal tachycardia?   **Y**

5. A patient is admitted with fever, weakness, severe malaise, and coughing. She is diagnosed with pneumonia. She deteriorates rapidly and is transferred to the ICU with severe sepsis. On physician query, the physician documents that he cannot determine whether the patient had sepsis on admission because she deteriorated so quickly. What is the POA indicator for the severe sepsis?   **W**

EXERCISE A.2

Locate the POA exempt list in the *ICD-10-CM Official Guidelines for Coding and Reporting*. Write an "X" next to each code below that is exempt from POA reporting.

1. O80   Encounter for full-term uncomplicated delivery   **X**

2. O60.10   Preterm labor with preterm delivery, unspecified trimester

3. Z99.2   Dependence on renal dialysis   **X**

4. V00.311- Fall from snowboard   **X**

5. Y30.-   Falling, jumping or pushed from a high place, undetermined intent   **X**

Appendix B

APPENDIX B

Case Summary Exercises

Therese M. Jorwic, MPH, RHIA, CCS, CCS-P, FAHIMA,
and Janatha R. Ashton, MS, RHIA

CONTENTS

ABOUT THIS APPENDIX

The case summary exercises in this appendix are based on the actual health records of both inpatients and outpatients. The patients described often have multiple conditions that may or may not be related to the current episode of care. Some exercises include several episodes of care for the same patient in various settings.

How to Use This Appendix

The case summary style of the exercises requires you to consider the patient's condition as well as all relevant information provided: medical history, reason for admission or encounter, laboratory results, procedures performed, and diagnoses listed. In all exercises, you need to apply pertinent coding principles and official coding guidelines in making code assignments and designating the principal diagnosis and procedure for each episode of care.

Each exercise includes a brief summary and a diagnosis statement that should be read carefully. You may assume that all diagnoses and procedures that are mentioned and that should be coded have been approved by the patient's physician. Be sure to sequence the principal diagnosis first; however, sequencing of the procedure code(s) is discretionary.

After referring to the appropriate ICD-10-CM and ICD-10-PCS coding manuals, fill in the codes that you think should be assigned (including any appropriate codes for external causes and locations of occurrence as needed) in the space provided next to each case summary. For inpatient care and the outpatient and ambulatory care settings, assign and sequence codes according to the *ICD-10-CM Official Guidelines for Coding and Reporting.*

The sequence of this appendix corresponds to chapters 13 through 33 of the handbook and progresses from simpler to more difficult areas. It is recommended that you will have read all of the chapters (1–33) of the handbook before you begin the case summary exercises in this appendix. You may, however, complete the exercises in any order after you have learned the basic coding principles and understand how to apply official coding guidelines.

About the Answers

Answers are provided in the right-hand column of the *with Answers* version of the handbook. (Ask your instructor for the answers if you are using the *without Answers* version.) The right-hand column lists the appropriate codes for each exercise, with the codes for the principal diagnosis and principal procedure sequenced first. Explanatory comments discuss why certain codes are appropriate while others are not, and why some conditions listed in the case summaries are not coded at all. The comments also indicate how principal diagnosis and procedure codes were designated and which symptoms are inherent to certain conditions and so are not coded separately.

For outpatient encounters, ICD-10-PCS codes are typically not reported when a claim is submitted. According to the Health Insurance Portability and Accountability Act (HIPAA) Standards for Electronic Transactions (published in the *Federal Register,* vol. 65, no. 160, p. 50325, August 17, 2000), "The use of ICD-9-CM procedure codes is restricted to the reporting of inpatient procedures by hospitals." ICD-10-PCS was developed to replace ICD-9-CM procedure codes in whatever setting they are currently used. However, a hospital may choose to collect ICD-10-PCS codes for internal or non-claim-related purposes. In addition, hospitals may report procedure codes for outpatient services for specific payers under contractual agreements or as required by their state data reporting regulations.

In day-to-day practice, many hospitals have opted through their internal coding policies not to collect data on noninvasive (without contrast) diagnostic services performed in the inpatient setting, such as X-rays, electrocardiograms (EKGs), computed tomography scans (CTs), and ultrasounds. For this reason, codes for these minor diagnostic services have been omitted from the answers.

The codes and comments in the answers reflect the latest *ICD-10-CM Official Guidelines for Coding and Reporting* (2011 edition) and *ICD-10-PCS Official Coding Guidelines* (2011 edition). At press time, a revised set of guidelines was expected to be available for 2012. Please visit www. ahacentraloffice.org for guideline revisions. Specific guidelines are referenced in parentheses by section and guideline number.

APPENDIX B

Case
Summary
Exercises

1. SYMPTOMS, SIGNS, AND ILL-DEFINED CONDITIONS

1. **Inpatient admission:** The patient, an elderly man, was admitted through the emergency department for severe urinary retention. In the emergency department, it was also determined that his hypertension was accelerated (210/105). He had been hospitalized three months earlier for identical problems, and he said he had not taken any of his medications since the last hospitalization, as he could not afford the cost. The urinary retention was relieved by placement of a Foley catheter. Medications were started, and the hypertension improved rapidly. The patient was evaluated for the extent of benign prostatic hypertrophy. Transurethral resection of the prostate was recommended, but it was refused by the patient.

Discharge diagnoses: (1) Malignant hypertension, (2) acute urinary retention secondary to benign hypertrophy of the prostate, (3) noncompliance with treatment program.

N40.1	Enlarged prostate with lower urinary tract symptoms (LUTS)
R33.8	Other retention of urine
I10	Essential (primary) hypertension
T46.5x6A	Underdosing of other antihypertensive drugs, initial encounter
Z91.120	Patient's intentional underdosing of medication regimen due to financial hardship
0T9B70Z	Drainage of bladder with drainage device, via natural or artificial opening

Comments: Codes for symptoms, signs, and ill-defined conditions such as urinary retention (R33.8) are not used as a principal diagnosis when a related definitive diagnosis (prostatic hypertrophy) has been established. However, as indicated by the "use additional code" note at code N40.1, an additional code should be assigned in conjunction with the benign prostatic hypertrophy code to identify other lower urinary tract symptoms. Hypertension is not classified as malignant or benign; all cases are assigned to category I10. Underdosing of medication is coded in ICD-10-CM. Locate the main term **Anti-hypertensive drug NEC** in the Table of Drugs and Chemicals and reference the underdosing column. See the Alphabetic Index under the main term **Noncompliance,** subterms "with," "medication regimen NEC," "underdosing," "intentional," "due to financial hardship of patient." Foley catheter placement is classified to the Medical and Surgical Section, root operation "Drainage."

2. Inpatient admission: The patient was admitted for recurrent epistaxis that did not respond to nasal packing in the emergency department. He was status post myocardial infarct seven weeks earlier, with no current symptoms. An EKG was performed to evaluate the status of the MI. The patient also suffered from a deviated nasal septum. Multiple attempts were made to stop the bleeding with more packing, but none was successful for more than a few hours. Therefore, the following procedures were performed: (1) anterior and posterior nasal packing, (2) endoscopic ethmoidal artery ligation, (3) endoscopic septoplasty. He was transfused via central vein with two units of packed red cells during the operation.

Discharge diagnoses: (1) Severe and recurrent epistaxis, (2) post myocardial infarct, (3) deviated nasal septum.

R04.0	Epistaxis
J34.2	Deviated nasal septum
I25.2	Old myocardial infarction
03LR4ZZ	Occlusion of face artery, percutaneous endoscopic approach
2Y41X5Z	Packing of nasal region using packing material
09QM4ZZ	Repair nasal septum, percutaneous endoscopic approach
30233N1	Transfusion of nonautologous red blood cells into peripheral vein, percutaneous approach

Comments: Following the Uniform Hospital Discharge Data Set (UHDDS) definition of principal diagnosis, epistaxis is the condition established after study to be responsible for occasioning the admission of the patient to the hospital for care. Because no related condition was identified, the symptom code can be designated as the principal diagnosis. Deviated nasal septum is not designated as principal because epistaxis is not specified as being due to this condition. The myocardial infarction occurred more than four weeks ago without any symptoms.

The ethmoid artery originates in the ophthalmic artery, with distribution to the ethmoidal cell and the lateral wall of the nasal cavity, and is therefore classified as an artery of the face. Ligation of the ethmoid artery is classified to the root operation "Occlusion." Nasal packing is classified in the Placement Section, root operation "Packing."

3. Inpatient admission: The reason for the patient's admission was substernal chest pain with some arm involvement. A combined right and left selective low osmolar contrast coronary angiography and a bilateral low osmolar contrast pulmonary angiography were performed. No coronary artery disease or pulmonary embolus was found.

Discharge diagnosis: Chest pain without occlusive coronary artery disease.

R07.2	Precordial pain
B2061ZZ	Plain radiography of right and left heart using low osmolar contrast
B2011ZZ	Plain radiography of multiple coronary arteries using low osmolar contrast
B30S1ZZ	Plain radiography of right pulmonary artery using low osmolar contrast
B30T1ZZ	Plain radiography of left pulmonary artery using low osmolar contrast

Comments: Because no underlying etiology for the substernal chest pain was identified, the symptom is designated as the principal diagnosis. Code both the right and left pulmonary artery for the angiography.

4. Inpatient admission: The patient, a 19-year-old man, was transferred from another hospital with intractable headache. The accompanying CT scan was normal, but clinical symptomatology was suggestive of subarachnoid hemorrhage. Lumbar puncture, non-contrast bilateral internal carotid cerebral arteriogram, and contrast cerebral MRI were all normal. When the findings were discussed with the patient, he became increasingly belligerent. Although his headaches were only somewhat improved, he refused further treatment and was discharged for follow-up with his own physician.

Discharge diagnosis: Headache.

R51	Headache
009U3ZX	Drainage of spinal canal, percutaneous approach, diagnostic
B308ZZZ	Plain radiography of bilateral internal carotid arteries
B33RYZZ	Magnetic resonance imaging (MRI) of intracranial arteries using other contrast

Comments: No cause for the headache was determined because subarachnoid hemorrhage was ruled out through testing. Therefore, the symptom is the principal diagnosis.

5. Inpatient admission: The patient has a known diagnosis of prostatic cancer. He started having fevers approximately one week earlier. The fevers did not respond to outpatient antibiotics. Blood and urine cultures showed no growth. He was admitted for workup of the fevers with possible prostatic abscess formation. There were no obvious signs of infection or abscess on a transrectal ultrasound of the prostate. An iodine-123 radioisotope bone scan of the body revealed no skeletal metastases. The antibiotic therapy was changed, and he was given an IV push. He improved and was discharged.

Discharge diagnoses: (1) Fever of unknown origin, (2) cancer of the prostate.

R50.9	Fever, unspecified
C61	Malignant neoplasm of prostate
CW1MFZZ	Planar nuclear medicine imaging of upper extremity using iodine 123 (I-123)

6. Inpatient admission: The two-year-old patient had an acute onset of fever and some shaking chills at home. He was thought to have experienced a febrile seizure and was admitted for workup and treatment. There was some infiltrate in the right lung per chest X-ray. All laboratory work was within normal limits. He was observed during his stay. No problems were noticed, and he remained afebrile after the first day. He was discharged for office follow-up.

Discharge diagnosis: Rule out febrile seizure.

R56.00	Simple febrile convulsions

Comments: The "rule out" wording in the final diagnosis means that febrile seizure was suspected. Suspected conditions that have not been ruled out at the end of the stay are coded as if confirmed for inpatients. A separate code for fever is not necessary because code R56.00 includes the fever. Although infiltrate was noticed on the right lung X-ray, no further mention was made of it, and apparently it was not considered significant. (Abnormal findings are not coded and reported unless the physician indicates their clinical significance.)

7. Inpatient admission: The patient was admitted through the emergency department with possible acute cholecystitis. She had severe abdominal pain and a markedly elevated white count. A gallbladder ultrasound, cholecystogram, and contrast intravenous pyelogram were all normal. The next day her pain was almost gone, and the white blood count dropped to nearly normal. It was not felt worthwhile to continue the workup.

Discharge diagnoses: (1) Abdominal pain, (2) leukocytosis.

R10.9	Unspecified abdominal pain
D72.829	Elevated white blood cell count, unspecified
BF12YZZ	Fluoroscopy of gallbladder using other contrast
BT14YZZ	Fluoroscopy of kidneys, ureters and bladder using other contrast

Comments: The symptom, abdominal pain, is the principal diagnosis because no underlying etiology was identified. Leukocytosis should be coded as an additional diagnosis.

8. Inpatient admission: The patient, an obese male, was admitted with generalized abdominal pain suggestive of early appendicitis, although he had a normal white count and normal differential. An intravenous pyelogram and X-ray of the lower gastrointestinal tract with barium enema were negative. All laboratory studies were normal. He improved while in the hospital without a definite cause for his pain ever being identified. He was placed on a low-fat, 1,500-calorie diet prior to discharge.

Discharge diagnoses: (1) Abdominal pain of undetermined origin, generalized; (2) obesity.

R10.84	Generalized abdominal pain
E66.9	Obesity, unspecified
BT14YZZ	Fluoroscopy of kidneys, ureters and bladder using other contrast

Comments: No cause for the abdominal pain could be determined; therefore, it is designated as the principal diagnosis. Although obesity was not responsible for admission, it is coded because it was clinically evaluated and treatment was started. Although the patient was placed on a low-fat diet, code E66.01, Morbid (severe) obesity due to excess calories, is not appropriate because the obesity was not documented as such.

9. Inpatient admission: This patient with type 2 diabetes was admitted for evaluation of elevated liver function tests. An abdominal ultrasound showed cholelithiasis. The hepatitis profile was negative. Her sugars stayed within the low normal range throughout hospitalization. At discharge, the physician was unable to determine whether the abnormal liver functions were due to diabetes mellitus or cholelithiasis.

Discharge diagnosis: Abnormal liver function secondary to either diabetes mellitus or cholelithiasis.

R94.5	Abnormal results of liver function studies
E11.9	Type 2 diabetes mellitus without complications
K80.20	Calculus of gallbladder without cholecystitis without obstruction

Comments: The diagnostic statement represents a symptom followed by contrasting/comparative diagnoses. The symptom is coded and sequenced first, followed by codes for the contrasting/comparative diagnoses.

10. Inpatient admission: The patient, a woman with type 1 diabetes, was admitted because of increased swelling of the right foot that was determined to be an abscess. *Staphylococcus aureus* grew from the abscess. She underwent a percutaneous incision and drainage of the foot abscess. Her course in the hospital otherwise was essentially unremarkable. The foot gradually improved with antibiotic therapy, hyperbaric oxygen therapy, and daily whirlpool therapy.

Discharge diagnoses: (1) Abscess right foot, (2) type 1 diabetes mellitus.

L02.611	Cutaneous abscess of right foot
B95.6	Staphylococcus aureus as the cause of diseases classified elsewhere
E10.9	Type 1 diabetes mellitus without complications
0Y9M3ZZ	Drainage of right foot, percutaneous approach
F08G5BZ	Wound management treatment of integumentary system—lower back/lower extremity using physical agents
5A05121	Extracorporeal hyperbaric oxygenation, intermittent

Comments: The symptom, swelling of the foot, is not coded because the swelling was determined to be an abscess. Code L02.611 is assigned as the principal diagnosis. The abscess is not stated as due to the diabetes; therefore, code E10.9 is the appropriate code choice. Incision with drainage is the principal procedure because it was performed as treatment for the abscess. Whirlpool treatment to the wound is classified to the Physical Rehabilitation and Diagnostic Audiology Section, root operation "Activities of daily living," with the qualifier "wound management." Code 5A05121 is assigned for the oxygenation of the surgical wound.

11. Inpatient admission: The child was admitted with a fever and lethargy. The admitting diagnosis was "rule out sepsis." When admitted, he was responsive but lethargic. The physical examination was within normal limits except for the left eardrum, which was reddened. He was placed on intravenous antibiotics after the full septic workup was complete. Improvement was evident by the next day, when he was alert, active, and started on feedings. He became afebrile and was discharged on oral antibiotics for otitis media, with sepsis ruled out.

Discharge diagnoses: (1) Fever, (2) otitis media.

H66.92	Otitis media, unspecified, left ear

Comments: Fever is a symptom and should not be sequenced as the principal diagnosis because the related definitive diagnosis of otitis media has been established as the underlying etiology. Fever is an inherent part of otitis media and does not require a separate code assignment. ICD-10-CM has codes to indicate the ear affected.

12. Inpatient admission: The patient, a 10-month-old male, presented with acute stridor and respiratory distress. His mother felt that he had possibly choked on a peach. Nothing was seen on chest X-ray. A rigid bronchoscopy ruled out foreign body, but the findings were consistent with croup. He was discharged on medication to follow up with his pediatrician in one week.

Discharge diagnosis: Croup.

J05.0	Acute obstructive laryngitis [croup]
0BJ08ZZ	Inspection of tracheobronchial tree, via natural or artificial opening endoscopic

Comments: The symptoms, stridor and respiratory distress, are integral to the diagnosis of croup and are not coded separately.

2. INFECTIOUS AND PARASITIC DISEASES

1. **Inpatient admission:** This HIV-positive patient was admitted with skin lesions on the chest and back. Biopsies were taken, and the pathologic diagnosis was Kaposi's sarcoma. Leukoplakia of the lips and splenomegaly were also noted on physical examination.

   Discharge diagnoses: (1) HIV infection; (2) Kaposi's sarcoma, back and chest; (3) leukoplakia; (4) splenomegaly.

B20	Human immunodeficiency virus [HIV] disease
C46.0	Kaposi's sarcoma of skin
K13.21	Leukoplakia of oral mucosa, including tongue
R16.1	Splenomegaly, not elsewhere classified
0HB5XZX	Excision of chest skin, external approach, diagnostic
0HB6XZX	Excision of back skin, external approach, diagnostic

2. **Inpatient admission:** The patient underwent an outpatient laparoscopic-assisted cholecystectomy for cholecystitis and was admitted the next day because of a flare-up of chronic hepatitis C. The chronic hepatitis C was secondary to intravenous drug use. With medication, the chronic hepatitis C was controlled, and the woman was discharged.

   Discharge diagnoses: (1) Chronic hepatitis C, (2) IV drug dependence.

B18.2	Chronic viral hepatitis C
F19.20	Other psychoactive substance dependence, uncomplicated

   Comments: Although an outpatient procedure was performed for cholecystitis, the reason for admission, per the UHDDS definition of principal diagnosis, is chronic hepatitis C.

3. **Inpatient admission:** An elderly male patient with a history of benign hypertension became extremely febrile the day before admission. On admission he was extremely lethargic with a possible septic urinary tract infection. He was pan cultured and started on IV antibiotics and fluids. Pseudomonas showed in the urine culture. The next day, his mind was quite clear and the fever defervesced from an initial 104.6 to 99.0 degrees. However, he had gross hematuria. As the IV fluids were decreased, he resumed his usual hypertensive state. By the third hospital day, the urine had cleared and he was discharged on oral antibiotics, with septicemia ruled out.

   Discharge diagnoses: (1) Urinary tract infection due to *Pseudomonas,* (2) gross hematuria, (3) benign essential hypertension.

N39.0	Urinary tract infection, site not specified
B96.5	Pseudomonas (aeruginosa) (mallei) (pseudomallei) as the cause of diseases classified elsewhere
R31.0	Gross hematuria
I10	Essential (primary) hypertension

   Comments: The instruction with code N39.0, "Use additional code to identify organism . . ." must always be followed when the organism is known. Because hematuria is not integral to a urinary tract infection, it is coded. All hypertension is coded to I10.

4. **Inpatient admission:** The patient, with arterio-sclerotic coronary heart disease and type 2 diabetes mellitus, came to the hospital with symptoms that were felt to represent sepsis. She was placed on antibiotics, and the symptoms improved. ST- and T-wave changes were evident on an EKG. The patient's glucose showed marked elevation, thought to be secondary to the sepsis. The blood sugars were brought under control with an adjustment of her insulin therapy and an appropriate diet.

Discharge diagnoses: (1) Arteriosclerotic coronary heart disease, (2) uncontrolled type 2 diabetes mellitus, (3) questionable sepsis.

A41.9	Sepsis, unspecified
I25.10	Atherosclerotic heart disease of native coronary artery without angina pectoris
E11.65	Type 2 diabetes mellitus with hyperglycemia
Z79.4	Long term (current) use of insulin

Comments: The admission was necessitated by signs and symptoms of sepsis, which was never ruled out and, therefore, is the principal diagnosis. ICD-10-CM coding guidelines state that for a diagnosis of sepsis, the appropriate code for the underlying systemic infection is assigned. Code A41.9 is assigned if the type of infection or causal organism is not further identified.

For the diabetes code, see the main term in the Alphabetic Index **Inadequately controlled,** with the cross-reference that states "code to Diabetes, by type, with hyperglycemia. See the Index, diabetes, with hyperglycemia, E11.65."

No code is assigned for the ST- and T-wave changes on the EKG because they represent abnormal findings that were not treated or further evaluated.

Code Z79.4 is assigned because the patient is on insulin therapy.

5. **Outpatient clinic visit:** The HIV-infected patient was suffering from an acute lymphadenitis due to his HIV infection. The glands in the neck area were most affected. Antibiotics were prescribed, but the patient refused antiretroviral treatment at this time. He was of the opinion that his religion would eventually make antiretroviral medication unnecessary. Another consideration was his narcotic dependency. He was encouraged to continue participation in both the narcotic addiction and HIV support groups.

Diagnoses: (1) Acute lymphadenitis secondary to HIV infection, (2) narcotic dependence, (3) refusal of medication due to religious reasons.

B20	Human immunodeficiency virus [HIV] disease
F11.20	Opioid dependence, uncomplicated
Z53.1	Procedure and treatment not carried out because of patient's decision for reasons of belief and group pressure

Comments: Code B20 is assigned for all HIV infections and is designated as the reason for encounter when the patient was seen for HIV infection or a related condition. Code L04.0, Acute lymphadenitis of face, head and neck, should not be assigned along with code B20 because of the exclude1 note at code L04.0 excluding HIV disease resulting in generalized lymphadenopathy (B20). For the narcotic dependence code, see the main term in the Index **Dependence,** narcotic (drug) NEC, which refers the user to "see Dependence, drug, opioid." Following this instructional note, the user arrives at code F11.20. Code Z53.1 may be assigned to show the refusal of medications for religious reasons.

3. ENDOCRINE, NUTRITIONAL, AND METABOLIC DISEASES AND IMMUNE-SYSTEM DISORDERS

1. **Inpatient admission:** The patient was admitted for an evaluation of her adrenal malfunction. She had a four-year history of hypertension and hypokalemia with evidence of primary aldosteronism. A non-contrast CT scan of the abdomen also suggested a left adrenal mass. She was discharged and was to return for a left adrenalectomy the following week.

   Discharge diagnoses: (1) Probable adrenal mass, left; (2) hypertension and hypokalemia probably due to primary aldosteronism.

E27.8	Other specified disorders of adrenal gland
E26.9	Hyperaldosteronism, unspecified
E87.6	Hypokalemia
I10	Essential (primary) hypertension

   Comments: Either of the interrelated diagnoses, adrenal mass or aldosteronism, can be designated as the principal diagnosis because the patient was admitted for evaluation of adrenal malfunction. In the Alphabetic Index, reference the main term **Mass,** specified organ NEC, which directs to disease of specified organ or site. Under disease, adrenal, specified, NEC code E27.8 is located.

2. **Inpatient admission:** The patient was admitted for severe malnutrition and hematuria secondary to amyotrophic lateral sclerosis. Because of her malnutrition, a nasogastric feeding tube was placed under fluoroscopy. During her stay, the hematuria cleared spontaneously, and she was discharged to home care.

   Discharge diagnoses: (1) Malnutrition, (2) hematuria secondary to amyotrophic lateral sclerosis.

E43	Unspecified severe protein-calorie malnutrition
G12.21	Amyotrophic lateral sclerosis
R31.9	Hematuria, unspecified
3E0G36Z	Introduction of nutritional substance into upper GI, percutaneous approach

   Comments: Admission was necessitated by malnutrition, not the underlying amyotrophic lateral sclerosis. Therefore, severe malnutrition, the condition requiring placement of a feeding tube, is the principal diagnosis.

3. **Inpatient admission:** The patient fell at his single-family home and was unable to get up. Neighbors found him several hours later, and he does not remember any circumstances surrounding the event. Blood sugars were monitored, and a diagnosis of diabetes mellitus was given. It became rapidly evident to the attending physician that, even with dietary restriction, the patient would need insulin therapy to lower his blood sugar level. Insulin therapy was started. The only other positive finding was beta-*Streptococcus* group B, which grew from the urine culture and was treated with oral antibiotics.

   Discharge diagnoses: (1) New onset type 2 diabetes mellitus, out of control; (2) urinary tract infection with beta-*Streptococcus.*

E11.65	Type 2 diabetes mellitus with hyperglycemia
N39.0	Urinary tract infection, site not specified
B95.1	Streptococcus, group B, as the cause of diseases classified elsewhere
W19.xxxA	Unspecified fall, initial encounter
Y92.099	Unspecified place in other non-institutional residence as the place of occurrence of the external cause

   Comments: The condition, after study, that necessitated admission was newly diagnosed diabetes out of control. Type 2 diabetic patients often require insulin to bring blood sugar down to an acceptable level, but this does not mean that the diabetes has become insulin dependent. For the diabetes code, see the main term in the Index **Inadequately controlled,** with the cross-reference that states "code to Diabetes, by type, with hyperglycemia. See the Index, diabetes, with hyperglycemia, E11.65."

   The code for Long-term (current) use of insulin is not appropriate because the insulin therapy was just started and there is no information about long-term use. ICD-10-CM does not classify out-of-control diabetes mellitus. An activity code is not reported, as the activity is not stated.

4. Outpatient clinic visit: The patient with type 2 diabetes was status post cadaveric kidney and pancreatic transplants. He was being seen for follow-up of a recent below-the-knee amputation (BKA) and a nonhealing, gangrenous ulcer on his left foot secondary to diabetic peripheral vascular disease. The operative site was healing very nicely, and there was no evidence of infection.

Diagnoses: (1) Status post left foot amputation, (2) status post kidney and pancreas transplants, (3) diabetes mellitus.

Z09	Encounter for follow-up examination after completed treatment for conditions other than malignant neoplasm
E11.51	Type 2 diabetes mellitus with diabetic peripheral angiopathy without gangrene
Z94.0	Kidney transplant status
Z94.83	Pancreas transplant status
Z89.52	Acquired absence of left leg below knee

Comments: The reason for the encounter was for follow-up examination following surgery. Code Z89.52 indicates the status post below-the-knee amputation—the reason follow-up was necessary. For the status post BKA, a code is available to denote the left side. Diabetes and complication of peripheral vascular disease are included in one code. The gangrene is not coded as current, as the foot has been amputated and the gangrene is no longer present. Other codes represent conditions that required consideration in evaluating the patient's current status.

5. Inpatient admission: The patient, an elderly woman with type 2 diabetes mellitus, developed hypoglycemia at the nursing home and was symptomatic. In the emergency department, her decreased blood sugar was treated with intravenous D5W. A urinary tract infection was also present and was treated with antibiotics. The urine culture grew *Klebsiella*, sensitive to Cipro. She then developed mild congestive heart failure, probably secondary to the hypoglycemic reaction, which responded to oxygen and rest. Her Diabeta was restarted at a lower dosage.

Discharge diagnoses: (1) Congestive heart failure secondary to hypoglycemia, (2) type 2 diabetes mellitus, (3) urinary tract infection.

E11.649	Type 2 diabetes mellitus with hypoglycemia without coma
I50.9	Heart failure, unspecified
N39.0	Urinary tract infection, site not specified
B96.1	Klebsiella pneumoniae [K. pneumoniae] as the cause of diseases classified elsewhere

Comments: ICD-10-CM has a specific code for type 2 diabetes with hypoglycemia

6. Inpatient admission: The patient, a woman with a diagnosis of cell-mediated immune deficiency with thrombocytopenia and eczema, was admitted for incision and drainage of a foot abscess. Her course in the hospital was essentially unremarkable. The foot gradually improved with hyperbaric oxygen therapy and daily whirlpool therapy. *Staphylococcus aureus* grew from the abscess.

Discharge diagnoses: (1) Abscess right foot, (2) cell-immune deficiency with thrombo-cytopenia and eczema.

L02.611	Cutaneous abscess of right foot
D82.0	Wiskott-Aldrich syndrome
B95.6	Staphylococcus aureus as the cause of diseases classified elsewhere
0Y9M3ZZ	Drainage of right foot, percutaneous approach
F08G5BZ	Wound management treatment of integumentary system—lower back/lower extremity using physical agents
5A05121	Extracorporeal hyperbaric oxygenation, intermittent

7. Inpatient admission: The patient, a young male with type 1 diabetes, was brought in a comatose state to the emergency department by friends. He was admitted in ketoacidosis and was resuscitated with saline hydration via insulin drip. After regaining consciousness, he reported that the morning of admission he was experiencing nausea and vomiting and decided not to take his insulin because he had not eaten. He was treated with intravenous hydration and insulin drip. By the following morning, his laboratory work was within normal range and he was experiencing no symptoms.

Discharge diagnoses: (1) Diabetic ketoacidosis, (2) juvenile-type diabetes.

E10.641	Type 1 diabetes mellitus with hypoglycemia with coma
T38.3x6A	Underdosing of insulin and oral hypoglycemic [antidiabetic] drugs, initial encounter
Z91.128	Patient's intentional underdosing of medication regimen for other reason

Comments: See the main term **Diabetes,** subterms "type 1," "with," "ketoacidosis," "with coma." In ICD-10-CM there are codes for underdosing. See the Table of Drugs and Chemicals under "insulin" and consult the column for underdosing. Add the seventh-character "A," as this is the initial encounter. Also code for intentional underdosing for other reason by consulting the main term **Noncompliance,** subterms "medication regimen," "intentional NEC."

8. Inpatient admission: The patient with type 1 diabetes mellitus seriously out of control was admitted for regulation of insulin dosage. He had a recently abscessed right molar, which was determined, in part, to be responsible for the elevation of his blood sugar. The patient had been in the hospital three weeks earlier for an acute myocardial infarction of the inferoposterior wall, and an EKG was performed to check its current status.

Discharge diagnoses: (1) Myocardial infarction, (2) abscessed tooth, (3) uncontrolled type 1 diabetes mellitus.

E10.65	Type 1 diabetes mellitus with hyperglycemia
K04.7	Periapical abscess without sinus
I21.11	ST elevation (STEMI) myocardial infarction involving right coronary artery

Comments: Type 1 diabetes is classified to category E10. See the main term **Diabetes,** subterm "inadequately controlled" with the cross-reference that states "code to Diabetes, by, type, with hyperglycemia. See the Index, diabetes, Type 1 with hyperglycemia." The abscessed tooth is significant as a possible etiology of the out-of-control diabetes and was also under treatment during this admission. Code I21.11 is assigned for the myocardial infarction, which occurred less than four weeks ago and was evaluated during this admission.

4. MENTAL DISORDERS

1. Outpatient clinic visit: The patient was seen to evaluate his progress in dealing with his long-standing alcoholism. In addition, he had a passive-aggressive personality and was dependent on Librium. He was actively participating in Alcoholics Anonymous and stated he would continue to participate. He apparently now had some alcoholic liver damage and was referred to an internist for further investigation of that condition.

Diagnoses: (1) Alcohol dependence; (2) passive-aggressive personality disorder; (3) drug dependence, Librium; (4) alcoholic liver damage.

F10.20	Alcohol dependence, uncomplicated
F13.20	Sedative, hypnotic or anxiolytic dependence, uncomplicated
F60.89	Other specific personality disorders
K70.9	Alcoholic liver disease, unspecified

Comments: ICD-10-CM classifies dependence by uncomplicated, in remission, with intoxication, etc.

2. Outpatient clinic visit: The patient, a young female, was brought in by her sister. She has had periods of severe depression for many years. Her medications consisted of Lithium, Synthroid, and Midrin for depression, hypothyroidism, and migraine headaches, respectively. During the past week, however, she became manic, running all her credit cards to the limit, getting inappropriately involved in a woman's suicide attempt, quitting her job, and trying to take over the pulpit at church. On the day of the clinic visit, she threatened to strike the telephone repairman with a lead pipe. She was to be admitted for Lithium adjustment.

Diagnoses: (1) Bipolar disorder, manic type; (2) hypothyroidism; (3) migraine headaches.

F31.10	Bipolar disorder, current episode manic without psychotic features, unspecified
E03.9	Hypothyroidism, unspecified
G43.909	Migraine, unspecified, not intractable, without status migrainosus

Comments: No code assignment is necessary for depression because depression is a component of bipolar disorder. Although not psychiatric conditions, both hypothyroidism and migraine headaches are coexisting conditions under treatment and should be coded.

3. Inpatient admission: The woman was brought in by police for observation of a suspected mental condition. They found her roaming the streets, and she seemed disoriented and confused. She was treated for scabies, body lice, and cellulitis of the right foot. Her mental status cleared rapidly. The only psychiatric disorder found was moderate mental retardation.

Discharge diagnoses: (1) Moderate mental retardation; (2) scabies; (3) body lice; (4) cellulitis, right foot.

F71	Moderate mental retardation
B86	Scabies
B85.1	Pediculosis due to Pediculus humanus corporis
L03.115	Cellulitis of right lower limb

Comments: Although the scenario indicates that the patient was admitted for observation, a condition (moderate mental retardation) is identified as the etiology for the patient's disorientation and confusion. No code is assigned for observation in the presence of a confirmed condition.

All the nonpsychiatric conditions meet the UHDDS definition of additional diagnoses. They were diagnosed and treated; therefore, codes are assigned.

ICD-10-CM classifies cellulitis as either the toe or the lower limb, along with laterality. Because the foot is documented as the condition site, the lower limb code is used based on cross-reference under the main term **Cellulitis**, subterm "foot—see Cellulitis, lower limb." The code for the right side is selected.

4. Outpatient clinic visit: This 59-year-old male patient with a history of paranoid schizophrenia has had constant conflict with his family and coworkers for years. His wife reported that he was in danger of losing his job because he threatened his supervisor's life. He recently spent the night in jail after an altercation with a neighbor. Medication was prescribed, and he was to return for follow-up in one week.

Diagnosis: Schizophrenia, paranoid type, chronic with acute exacerbation.

F20.0   Paranoid schizophrenia

Comments: ICD-10-CM does not include codes for acute/chronic remission/exacerbation for schizophrenia.

5. Outpatient clinic visit: An 18-year-old teenage patient was described by his mother as recently having periods of depression, throwing temper tantrums, and stealing from neighbors. He has a history of type 1 diabetes and sometimes refuses to take his insulin or follow his diet. His speech, best described as "baby talk," had also become worse during the previous two months. A prescription was to be written for his depression.

Diagnoses: (1) Depression, (2) borderline personality disorder, (3) delayed speech development, (4) type 1 diabetes mellitus.

F32.9   Major depressive disorder, single episode, unspecified

F60.3   Borderline personality disorder

F80.9   Developmental disorder of speech or language, unspecified

E10.9   Type 1 diabetes mellitus without complications

Z79.4   Long term (current) use of insulin

Comments: Because medication was prescribed for the patient's depression, depression is sequenced first. The insulin use code is not required for type 1 diabetics because these patients require insulin. However, this code may be assigned, if desired, to provide additional information. ICD-10-CM provides a code for underdosing of medication. Although the patient is described as sometimes refusing to take his insulin, the documentation does not indicate that underdosing of insulin was a factor at the present time. Therefore, code T38.3x6A is not assigned.

6. Inpatient admission: The patient was brought to the emergency department by the police and admitted to psychiatric service. Police requested an evaluation after the man was disorderly and aggressive at the scene of an automobile accident in which he was involved. He is admitted with a diagnosis of probable dementia.

Discharge diagnoses: (1) Organic brain syndrome with presenile dementia, (2) probably Alzheimer's disease with dementia.

G30.9   Alzheimer's disease, unspecified

F02.81   Dementia in other diseases classified elsewhere, with behavioral disturbance

Comments: Alzheimer's disease is coded to G30.9 with a "use additional code" note for dementia. The dementia is coded to F02.81, Dementia in other diseases classified elsewhere with behavioral disturbances, due to the disorderly and aggressive behavior.

7. Inpatient admission: The patient, with a four-year history of anorexia nervosa, was seen in the physician's office because of significant weight loss over the past three months, going from 82 pounds down to 53 pounds. She was admitted to increase body weight and to be given nutritional counseling because of her severe malnutrition.

Discharge diagnosis: Anorexia nervosa, severe malnutrition with marasmus.

F50.00	Anorexia nervosa, unspecified
E41	Nutritional marasmus

Comments: Code E41, Nutritional marasmus, should be assigned as an additional diagnosis for the severe malnutrition. For some anorexic patients, the weight loss is so severe that it leads to malnutrition. Code E41 further describes the severity of the patient's condition.

8. Inpatient admission: The patient was admitted with possible pyelonephritis. Her complaints were bilateral flank pain and chills. A contrast intravenous pyelogram was normal. Within two days of admission, the character of her pain changed somewhat in that it became primarily in the right upper quadrant. The physician documented in the progress notes that significant features of conversion hysteria were present and accounted for the patient's symptoms. On the third hospital day, the patient's IV was discontinued, liver function tests were rechecked, and antibiotics were discontinued. Later that day, she left abruptly, saying she would not return.

Discharge diagnoses: (1) Right upper quadrant abdominal pain, (2) conversion disorder.

F44.9	Dissociative and conversion disorder, unspecified
R10.11	Right upper quadrant pain
BT14YZZ	Fluoroscopy of kidneys, ureters and bladder using other contrast

Comments: Codes for symptoms, signs, and ill-defined conditions from chapter 18 of ICD-10-CM are acceptable when a related definitive diagnosis has not been established by the provider. Although the patient was admitted with possible pyelonephritis, this condition was not confirmed and it was determined that conversion hysteria (definitive diagnosis) was the reason for the patient's symptoms and therefore the principal diagnosis.

9. Psychiatry clinic visit: The HIV-infected patient, who had a long history of cocaine addiction, started using cocaine again. Several months ago he was admitted for treatment of *Pneumocystis carinii* pneumonia. Presently, severe depression brought him to the clinic. He and the physician had an extensive discussion about returning to Narcotics Anonymous and also joining an AIDS support group. A prescription for Prozac was given for his depression.

Diagnoses: (1) Depression, (2) cocaine addiction, (3) HIV infection.

F32.9	Major depressive disorder, single episode, unspecified
B20	Human immunodeficiency virus [HIV] disease
F14.20	Cocaine dependence, uncomplicated

Comments: Depression was responsible for the clinic visit and is sequenced as the reason for the encounter. The HIV infection contributed to the patient's depression, but it was the depression that was the reason for admission.

5. DISEASES OF THE BLOOD AND BLOOD-FORMING ORGANS AND CERTAIN DISORDERS INVOLVING THE IMMUNE MECHANISM

1. Inpatient admission: The patient had a congenital aplastic anemia that had been responding well to treatment. She was admitted for observation following a full-mouth extraction for multiple dental caries with pulp exposure and pyorrhea in outpatient surgery. She had only minimal bleeding following surgery. However, it was believed to be necessary to admit her for monitoring. She was discharged the next day with her blood counts remaining at acceptable levels.

Discharge diagnosis: Aplastic anemia.

D61.01   Constitutional (pure) red blood cell aplasia

Comments: Dental caries and pyorrhea are the reasons for the outpatient encounter; however, aplastic anemia represents the reason for inpatient admission, per the UHDDS definition of principal diagnosis. See the main term **Anemia,** subterms "aplastic," "congenital."

2. Inpatient admission: The patient, who had sickle-cell anemia, presented to the emergency department with a two- to three-day history of severe right leg and arm pain. After she was admitted, parenteral narcotics were administered and the pain improved. The blood counts returned to a stable level within 24 hours.

Discharge diagnosis: Sickle-cell pain crisis.

D57.00   Hb-SS disease with crisis, unspecified

Comments: Pain is a symptom integral to sickle-cell crisis. Therefore, a separate code assignment for the pain is not necessary.

3. Inpatient admission: The patient was an elderly woman visiting her physician with complaints of heart palpitations. A routine office evaluation revealed significant anemia. She had not been eating well because she had recently moved from her home of 30 years. After admission to the hospital, a cardiology consultation suggested that the palpitations were probably due to the anemia. During the gastrointestinal workup, mild gastritis was revealed. After a transfusion of two units of packed red blood cells into the peripheral vein, her hemoglobin returned to normal range. The patient was discharged to the nursing home with a prescription for Zantac to control her gastritis.

Discharge diagnoses: (1) Nutritional anemia, (2) gastritis.

D53.9   Nutritional anemia, unspecified
K29.70   Gastritis, unspecified, without bleeding
R00.2   Palpitations
30240N1   Transfusion of nonautologous red blood cells into central vein, open approach

Comments: Although palpitations were the reason for admission, the underlying cause was determined to be anemia, so the anemia is sequenced as the principal diagnosis. In addition, a code is assigned to identify palpitations that are not inherent in anemia and were worked up by cardiology as a significant condition.

4. Inpatient admission: The patient had locally advanced bladder cancer. He had excellent response to chemotherapy treatments administered prior to admission, with only a small amount of residual disease noted in the bladder. He was admitted with increasing nausea, anorexia, fevers, and constipation. His calcium levels were found to be elevated. A slight decrease was achieved with IV hydration, and it continued to fall with IV pamidronate. Because he was asymptomatic, further workup was not indicated, and he was discharged.

Discharge diagnoses: (1) Hypercalcemia, (2) bladder cancer.

E83.52	Hypercalcemia
C67.9	Malignant neoplasm of bladder, unspecified

Comments: Although the primary site of the neoplasm had been treated in the past, residual disease was still present and under treatment; therefore, the bladder cancer code should be assigned. Nausea, anorexia, fevers, and constipation are inherent to hypercalcemia and are not coded.

5. Inpatient admission: The patient was diagnosed with Coombs' negative hemolytic anemia four years earlier. Since diagnosis, her disease course waxed and waned. During some bouts, she had 15 to 20 blood transfusions of two to three units of packed red blood cells each. This admission was for splenectomy. The plan also called for removing a kidney stone on the left side, which was identified on her preadmission workup. Both surgeries, total splenectomy and laparoscopic pyelolithotomy, were performed without incident. Her postoperative recovery also went smoothly.

Discharge diagnoses: (1) Hypersplenism secondary to acquired hemolytic anemia; (2) stone, left kidney.

D73.1	Hypersplenism
D59.9	Acquired hemolytic anemia, unspecified
N20.0	Calculus of kidney
07TP0ZZ	Resection of spleen, open approach
0TC44ZZ	Extirpation of matter from left kidney pelvis, percutaneous endoscopic approach

Comments: The spleen was removed because of hypersplenism, which is a further manifestation of hemolytic anemia. Hypersplenism is the principal diagnosis because it was the reason for admission and the condition to which the thrust of treatment was directed. No specific treatment was addressed to the anemia, but it is related to the hypersplenism and therefore is coded. Splenectomy and pyelolithotomy are both therapeutic procedures; however, splenectomy is designated as the principal procedure because it is related to the principal diagnosis. Although the diagnosis refers to stone in the left kidney, a pyelolithotomy refers to removal of stone from the renal pelvis.

6. Inpatient admission: A 50-year-old man receiving Coumadin therapy was admitted with hematemesis secondary to acute gastritis. A prolonged prothrombin time was reported, secondary to the anticoagulant effect of the Coumadin therapy.

Discharge diagnosis: Acute gastritis.

K29.01	Acute gastritis with bleeding
Z79.01	Long term (current) use of anticoagulants

Comments: Code K29.01 includes the acute gastritis with hemorrhage. No code is assigned for the prolonged bleeding time.

ICD-10-CM and ICD-10-PCS Coding Handbook, with Answers, 2012 Revised Edition

6. DISEASES OF THE NERVOUS SYSTEM AND SENSE ORGANS

1. **Ophthalmology clinic visit:** The HIV-infected patient complained of difficulty focusing while reading. His examination revealed no evidence of retinopathy. He did have early presbyopia, for which "drugstore readers" were recommended.

   Diagnoses: (1) Presbyopia, (2) HIV infection.

   H52.4   Presbyopia

   B20   Human immunodeficiency virus [HIV] disease

   Comments: Presbyopia is designated as the reason for the encounter because it was chiefly responsible for the services received. The HIV infection was not specified as causing the presbyopia and was not treated. Nevertheless, it is documented as a coexisting condition.

2. **Inpatient admission:** The patient was under medical management for long-standing, primary open-angle glaucoma, as well as age-related bilateral macular degeneration. Three days previously, an abnormally high intraocular pressure developed. The patient was treated successfully as an outpatient. The next day, another pressure spike occurred, and the patient was admitted for further management. He was treated medically for two days, and both the pressure and visual acuity improved sufficiently for discharge.

   Discharge diagnoses: (1) Acute primary open-angle glaucoma, (2) macular degeneration, (3) intraocular pressure.

   H40.11   Primary open-angle glaucoma

   H35.30   Unspecified macular degeneration (age-related)

   Comments: Glaucoma is coded and sequenced as the principal diagnosis following the UHDDS definition. High intraocular pressure is integral to glaucoma and is not coded. Macular degeneration is under current medical management and meets the UHDDS definition of additional diagnosis.

3. **Inpatient admission:** The patient previously suffered anterior dislocation of the left hip, which was reduced; however, this was followed by numbness and weakness in the left femoral nerve distribution. Evaluation indicated that she would benefit from surgery. A left femoral nerve external neurolysis was carried out successfully.

   Discharge diagnosis: Mononeuritis, femoral nerve.

   G57.22   Lesion of femoral nerve, left side

   S73.032S   Other anterior subluxation of left hip, sequela

   01ND3ZZ   Release femoral nerve, percutaneous approach

   Comments: Mononeuritis is the condition necessitating admission of the patient to the hospital for surgery. Dislocation is not coded because it is a previous condition no longer under treatment, but a code indicating that the mononeuritis is a late effect of the dislocation is assigned. The mononeuritis code allows for laterality. Late effects in ICD-10-CM are coded with the seventh character "S." The neurolysis procedure is classified to the root operation "Release."

4. Inpatient admission: The patient, a teenager, was admitted for evaluation and control of his intractable seizures. On days one, three, and four, seizures were recorded per video EEG. His video EEGs were consistent with epileptiform discharges of right temporal lobe origin. Dilantin and phenobarbital dosages were adjusted, and the patient was discharged in satisfactory condition.

Discharge diagnosis: Partial complex epilepsy localized to the right temporal lobe.

G40.219	Localization-related (focal) (partial) symptomatic epilepsy and epileptic syndromes with complex partial seizures, intractable, without status epilepticus
4A10X4Z	Monitoring of central nervous electrical activity, external approach

Comments: In the Alphabetic Index of Diseases and Injuries, the main term **Epilepsy** is searched, with subterms "localization," "symptomatic," "with complex partial seizures," "intractable." Video EEG is classified to the Measurement and Monitoring Section, root operation "Monitoring," "electrical activity" function.

5. Ambulatory surgery: The patient was brought in for surgical intervention of a mature, symptomatic cataract in the left eye and high intraocular pressures despite medical therapy. Procedures performed were an external trabeculectomy and phacoemulsification.

Diagnoses: (1) Advanced primary open-angle glaucoma; (2) cataract, left eye.

H40.11	Primary open-angle glaucoma
H26.9	Unspecified cataract
08133Z4	Bypass left anterior chamber to sclera, percutaneous approach
08DK3ZZ	Extraction of left lens, percutaneous approach

Comments: Either the glaucoma or the cataract could be designated as the first-listed diagnosis because both were present on admission and both were treated. The procedure performed for the definitive treatment of cataract is sequenced as the first procedure. The trabeculectomy is for the glaucoma and is therefore listed first as sequenced above. For the trabeculectomy, see the root operation "Bypass," body part "anterior chamber." For the procedure, in the Index see **Phacoemulsification, Lens,** without IOL implant see Extraction, Eye 08D.

6. Inpatient admission: The patient, an 18-month-old boy, was admitted with right orbital cellulitis. He was started on antibiotics and seemed to be improving. However, the day after admission a slight exophthalmos was noticed. A non-contrast CT scan of the head showed increasing edema of the eye orbit with filling of ethmoid sinuses. The medications were changed. A right endoscopic complete ethmoidectomy was performed because the ethmoid sinuses were filled on the right side. The infant improved and was discharged in satisfactory condition.

Discharge diagnoses: (1) Right orbital abscess, (2) exophthalmos, (3) orbital edema, (4) acute ethmoidal sinusitis.

H05.011	Cellulitis of right orbit
H05.20	Unspecified exophthalmos
J01.20	Acute ethmoidal sinusitis, unspecified
09BU4ZZ	Excision of right ethmoid sinus, percutaneous endoscopic approach

Comments: The principal diagnosis is orbital cellulitis/abscess because this was the condition necessitating admission. Orbital edema is integral to orbital cellulitis and should not be coded separately. However, exophthalmos is not integral to orbital cellulitis and should be coded. Ethmoidal sinusitis was qualified as acute.

7. Inpatient admission: The elderly male patient, a type 1 diabetic, developed weakness of the right arm and leg. The weakness worsened; eventually he fell and was unable to move. When brought to the emergency department, he was able to speak but unable to use his right arm or leg. A consultation after admission suggested either an acute left-sided cortical stroke or a TIA. Diagnostic radiographic procedures were scheduled; however, he completely recovered before the procedures could be completed and was able to ambulate with no neurological deficits within 24 hours of admission. He was discharged and will have a workup performed for cerebrovascular insufficiency as an outpatient.

Discharge diagnoses: (1) Probable transient ischemic attack, (2) diabetes mellitus.

G45.9	Transient cerebral ischemic attack, unspecified
E10.9	Type 1 diabetes mellitus without complications
Z79.4	Long term (current) use of insulin

Comments: Acute cerebrovascular attack was ruled out and therefore is not coded. Arm and leg paralysis were transient, focal neurological deficits that completely cleared during the hospitalization; therefore, no code assignments are required. The "probable" condition necessitating admission was TIA. Conditions described as probable on discharge are coded as though confirmed. A code is assigned for diabetes even though no specific treatment was given because it is a condition that always requires clinical evaluation when any other medical problem is present. Code Z79.4 is not required for type 1 diabetics because these patients require insulin. However, this code may be assigned, if desired, to provide additional information.

8. Inpatient admission: The patient, an elderly female nursing home resident, was under medical management for chronic senile dementia and postherpetic neuralgia. She also had a history of renal cyst. She was admitted with nausea and emesis, which cleared after several days. She also complained of increasing nasal sinus congestion and headache. She was treated with antibiotics and decongestants for sinusitis. Recovery was uneventful, and she was returned to the nursing home for further care.

Discharge diagnoses: (1) Postherpetic neuralgia, (2) sinusitis, (3) chronic senile dementia.

J32.9	Chronic sinusitis, unspecified
B02.29	Other postherpetic nervous system involvement
F03	Unspecified dementia

Comments: Although postherpetic neuralgia and chronic senile dementia were also present, the condition determined to be responsible for admission was sinusitis. No code is assigned for the renal cyst because it was qualified as "history of" and was not further evaluated or treated during the patient's stay.

9. Neurology clinic visit: The patient, a 23-month-old right-handed child, has congenital mitral stenosis. After a cardiac catheterization six months earlier, she had a large middle cerebral artery infarct. She is being followed for left arm paralysis, residuals of the cerebrovascular accident. She appeared to be making progress with weekly physical therapy. The muscle strength, tone, and stretch reflexes were improved, but she had some decrease in light touch sensation.

Diagnoses: (1) Paralysis, left arm; (2) congenital mitral stenosis.

I69.334	Monoplegia of upper limb following cerebral infarction affecting left non-dominant side
Q23.2	Congenital mitral stenosis

Comments: Monoplegia, as a sequela of the previous stroke, is coded in the I69.3 subcategory. Because the patient is right-handed, the left side is considered nondominant. In coding late effects of cerebrovascular disease, a combination code identifies both the residual and the late effect; therefore, only code I69.334 is required. Because this residual was the reason for her visit, this code is listed as the reason for the encounter.

7. DISEASES OF THE RESPIRATORY SYSTEM

1. **Inpatient admission:** The patient, a 51-year-old woman with acute respiratory failure secondary to an acute exacerbation of chronic obstructive bronchitis, was brought to the emergency department by emergency medical services. In the emergency department, she was intubated and placed on mechanical ventilation. On admission, it soon became apparent that she had suffered severe, irreversible hypoxic encephalopathy. On day 5, she was weaned from the ventilator and extubated; however, significant neurological function was never regained. In accordance with her advance directive, tube feedings were discontinued. She became febrile and dyspneic. Antibiotics were started to provide comfort and relief of her pneumonia. She expired on day 13.

   Discharge diagnoses: (1) Acute respiratory failure with hypoxia secondary to chronic obstructive bronchitis, (2) pneumonia, (3) encephalopathy.

J96.01	Acute respiratory failure with hypoxia
J44.1	Chronic obstructive pulmonary disease with (acute) exacerbation
G93.1	Anoxic brain damage, not elsewhere classified
J18.9	Pneumonia, unspecified organism
5A1955Z	Respiratory ventilation, greater than 96 consecutive hours
0BH17EZ	Insertion of endotracheal airway into trachea, via natural or artificial opening

Comments: Respiratory failure was responsible for admission and is designated as the principal diagnosis. The patient was intubated in the emergency department and maintained on mechanical ventilation until day 5, more than 96 hours.

2. **Inpatient admission:** The elderly patient came to the emergency department complaining of shortness of breath and nausea. It was apparent that she was suffering from congestive heart failure and respiratory failure, and she was admitted for immediate treatment of the acute respiratory failure. Before any diagnostic work could be accomplished, she died.

   Discharge diagnoses: (1) Acute respiratory failure, (2) congestive heart failure.

J96.00	Acute respiratory failure, unspecified whether with hypoxia or hypercapnia
I50.9	Heart failure, unspecified

Comments: When a patient is admitted with respiratory failure and another acute condition, the principal diagnosis will depend on the circumstances of admission. In this case, the patient was admitted for immediate treatment of the acute respiratory failure; therefore, it is sequenced as the principal diagnosis. Congestive heart failure is coded as an additional diagnosis.

3. **Inpatient admission:** The patient was admitted after visiting the emergency department for shortness of breath, chest pain, hypoxia, and a white cell count of 32,600. The patient had a history of chronic obstructive pulmonary disease. Interstitial infiltrate at the right middle and lower lobes of the lung was seen on chest X-ray. Sputum culture grew *Streptococcus pneumoniae*. He tolerated the antibiotics, and the symptoms improved significantly.

   Discharge diagnoses: (1) Right lower lobe pneumonia due to *Streptococcus pneumoniae,* (2) acute exacerbation of chronic obstructive lung disease.

J13	Pneumonia due to Streptococcus pneumoniae
J44.1	Chronic obstructive pulmonary disease with (acute) exacerbation
R09.02	Hypoxemia

Comments: *Streptococcus pneumoniae* is the causative organism. Because this organism is specified in the title of code J13, an additional code assignment is not necessary. Code J44.1 is assigned for exacerbated chronic obstructive pulmonary disease. Chronic obstructive pulmonary disease is one of the conditions that requires clinical evaluation even if no further treatment is given. Therefore, it is listed as an additional code. Code R09.02, Hypoxemia, is assigned as an additional diagnosis for the hypoxia because it is not inherent in pneumonia.

4. **Inpatient admission:** The patient, a young man, came to the emergency department after being ill for at least three weeks. He initially had a head cold and sore throat, followed by fever, difficulty swallowing, chills, and brown sputum. Because of severe lymphadenopathy in the neck, as well as other stated symptomatology, he was admitted. A huge left tonsil confluent with the surrounding tissues and covered with exudate was also noted on the physical examination. This appeared to represent a peritonsillar abscess and severe tonsillitis. A throat culture showed a heavy growth of beta-*Streptococcus* group C. Intravenous antibiotics were given with success, and he was discharged.

Discharge diagnoses: (1) Severe tonsillitis with beta-*Streptococcus* group C, (2) probable left peritonsillar abscess.

J36	Peritonsillar abscess
B95.4	Other streptococcus as the cause of diseases classified elsewhere

Comments: Both tonsillitis and peritonsillar abscess were present at admission. Both conditions were treated, and both meet the criteria for principal diagnosis. However, only one of them should be coded because of the excludes1 instructional note at code J36 and category J03 that precludes the coding of both conditions together. Because the abscess is the more severe condition, assign only code J36. Assign also code B95.4 to identify the infectious organism as instructed by the use additional code note at J36.

5. **Inpatient admission:** The type 1 diabetic patient was admitted with a right heel ulcer that had failed a number of outpatient therapies. Also, because the patient was hypoxic on admission with a history of COPD, he was given supplemental oxygen. He coughed up sputum, and a chest X-ray showed a mild increase in interstitial markings. Consequently, he was treated for acute bronchitis with erythromycin, which provided good results. Gradually, the foot ulcer healed. But the hypoxia persisted, and an increase in his oxygen therapy was helpful. He was to be followed by home health services.

Discharge diagnoses: (1) Diabetic foot ulcer, right heel; (2) acute bronchitis; (3) diabetes mellitus; (4) history of COPD.

E10.621	Type 1 diabetes mellitus with foot ulcer
L97.419	Non-pressure chronic ulcer of right heel and midfoot with unspecified severity
J44.0	Chronic obstructive pulmonary disease with acute lower respiratory infection
J20.9	Acute bronchitis, unspecified
R09.02	Hypoxemia
Z79.4	Long term (current) use of insulin

Comments: The diabetes code includes the ulcer, but an additional code specifies the site of the ulcer. Code J44.0, Chronic obstructive pulmonary disease with acute lower respiratory infection, has a note to use an additional code to identify the infection; code J20.9 is added. There is an excludes2 note under category J20 for acute bronchitis with chronic obstructive pulmonary disease. Because both conditions exist at the same time it is acceptable to use both codes. Code R09.02 is assigned for the hypoxia, which is not inherent in COPD. Code Z79.4 is not required for type 1 diabetics because these patients require insulin. However, this code may be assigned, if desired, to provide additional information.

6. Inpatient admission: The patient, a man in extremely poor health due to chronic obstructive pulmonary disease and chronic alcoholism, was admitted for severe shortness of breath, a PO_2 of 42, abdominal pain, and what appeared to be impending delirium tremens. He was placed on Ventolin and Solu-Medrol. Librium was also given to prevent delirium tremens. A colonoscopy was performed because of a past history of polyps, with no recurrence found. It was felt that the patient had mild colitis. On discharge, he was no longer dyspneic at rest. He was to start taking Zantac for colitis and to continue Solu-Medrol.

Discharge diagnoses: (1) Chronic lung disease with acute bronchospasm, (2) impending delirium tremens, (3) alcohol dependence, (4) colitis, (5) history of colon polyps.

J98.01	Acute bronchospasm
J44.9	Chronic obstructive pulmonary disease, unspecified
F10.231	Alcohol dependence with withdrawal delirium
K52.9	Noninfective gastroenteritis and colitis, unspecified
Z86.010	Personal history of colonic polyps
0DJD8ZZ	Inspection of lower intestinal tract, via natural or artificial opening, endoscopic

Comments: Bronchospasm represents the exacerbation of the COPD and was the reason for admission. ICD-10-CM includes the delirium tremens in alcoholism in one code, F10.231. Code Z86.010 is assigned because the history of polyps was the reason for the colonoscopy.

7. Inpatient admission: The patient, a 13-month-old girl, had two apnea alarms within the past few hours. After the last discharge from this hospital for apnea, an apnea alarm was ordered. Because of continued alarms, the mother returned the child to the hospital. She was placed on a cardiac apnea monitor with event record mode and on continuous bioximeter. There were no alarms noted during hospitalization. She was discharged home with an apnea monitor with event record mode in place.

Discharge diagnosis: Rule out apnea.

R06.81	Apnea, not elsewhere classified
4A12X9Z	Monitoring of cardiac output, external approach

Comments: Rule out apnea as a probable diagnosis. On inpatient discharge, suspected conditions are coded as though confirmed. The apnea monitor is indexed under the main term **Monitoring,** subterm "cardiac output."

8. Inpatient admission: The patient, a three-year-old male, was admitted for evaluation of fever, cough, and persistent pulmonary interstitial infiltrate. A chest tube was placed on the right side for drainage. The child's condition was consistent with pneumonia and aspiration of mucus. On the day after chest tube insertion, the chest X-ray was clear, and the chest tube was pulled. He was placed on aspiration precautions and antibiotics. He was to be followed up as an outpatient.

Discharge diagnosis: Pneumonia secondary to aspiration of mucus.

J69.0	Pneumonitis due to inhalation of food and vomit
0W9930Z	Drainage of right pleural cavity with drainage device, percutaneous approach

Comments: After study, the condition found to be chiefly responsible for the admission of the patient for care was aspiration pneumonia. Code J69.0 includes both the aspiration and the pneumonia. The chest tube insertion was performed for drainage; refer to the Index main term **Drainage,** subterms "cavity," "pleural," "right."

9. Inpatient admission: The patient, a five-year-old male, was seen as an outpatient for chronic asthmatic bronchitis with exacerbation without improvement. He was admitted for further treatment and on physical examination was also found to have bilateral suppurative otitis media. After being placed in a croup tent and treated with antibiotics, his temperature gradually returned to normal, and he improved.

Discharge diagnoses: (1) Asthmatic bronchitis, (2) acute suppurative otitis media.

10. Inpatient admission: The patient was admitted after she developed progressive dyspnea and wheezing, intractable to ambulatory care management. The provisional admitting diagnosis was status asthmaticus. Her history showed that she was status post mastectomy for breast cancer and still had some residual lymphedema in the left upper extremity. In the hospital, she received low-flow oxygen, antibiotics, bronchodilators, and IV steroids, as well as her usual medications for hypertension and hypothyroidism.

Discharge diagnoses: (1) Status asthmaticus, (2) hypertension, (3) hypothyroidism, (4) status post breast cancer with lymphedema.

11. Inpatient admission: The patient, an elderly woman, was known to have congestive heart failure, arteriosclerotic heart disease, and chronic obstructive pulmonary disease. She has no history of CABG. She developed increased shortness of breath, dyspnea on exertion, temperature elevation, and productive cough. These problems were felt to represent congestive failure and pneumonia. She was admitted for cultures, IV antibiotics, pulmonary toilet, and increased diuresis. Her initial non-contrast chest film showed congestive heart failure and bilateral lung infiltrates. In discussing this case with the pulmonary consultant, the physician felt it was wise to transfer the patient to another hospital so that both pulmonary and cardiology staff could work together with this patient.

Discharge diagnoses: (1) Arteriosclerotic heart disease, (2) congestive heart failure, (3) pneumonia, (4) chronic obstructive lung disease.

J44.1   Chronic obstructive pulmonary disease with (acute) exacerbation

J45.901   Unspecified asthma with (acute) exacerbation

H66.003   Acute suppurative otitis media without spontaneous rupture of ear drum, bilateral

Comments: Category J44 is selected for chronic asthmatic bronchitis, with the fourth character denoting the acute exacerbation. There is a "code also" note for asthma at category J44, so the J45.901 code is added. ICD-10-CM has codes for right, left, or bilateral otitis media.

J45.902   Unspecified asthma with status asthmaticus

I97.2   Postmastectomy lymphedema syndrome

I10   Essential (primary) hypertension

E03.9   Hypothyroidism, unspecified

Z85.3   Personal history of malignant neoplasm of breast

Comments: Code J45.902 is used for unspecified asthma with status asthmaticus. Status asthmaticus is usually considered to be present when the condition does not respond to treatment on an ambulatory basis. However, the provider must document status asthmaticus.

I50.9   Heart failure, unspecified

J18.9   Pneumonia, unspecified organism

J44.0   Chronic obstructive pulmonary disease with acute lower respiratory infection

I25.10   Atherosclerotic heart disease of native coronary artery without angina pectoris

Comments: Either congestive heart failure or pneumonia could be designated as the principal diagnosis because both were present on admission and attention was directed to both conditions. Code J44.0, Chronic obstructive pulmonary disease with acute lower respiratory infection, is assigned instead of J44.9 because of the presence of pneumonia. Code I25.10 for arteriosclerosis of native artery, as there is no evidence of bypass surgery in the past.

12. Inpatient admission: The patient, a 94-year-old man with known arteriosclerotic coronary artery disease, no history of bypass, and exacerbation of end-stage chronic obstructive bronchitis, was admitted with a provisional diagnosis of acute respiratory failure. He was treated with IV antibiotics and pulmonary toilet. Although his long-term prognosis was poor, he was improved upon discharge.

Discharge diagnoses: (1) Arteriosclerotic coronary artery disease, (2) end-stage chronic obstructive bronchitis, (3) angina, (4) acute respiratory failure.

J96.00	Acute respiratory failure, unspecified whether with hypoxia or hypercapnia
J44.9	Chronic obstructive pulmonary disease, unspecified
I25.119	Atherosclerotic heart disease of native coronary artery with unspecified angina pectoris

Comments: Respiratory failure is listed as the principal diagnosis because it is the reason for the admission. Code I25.119, for arteriosclerosis of native artery, is assigned because there has been no previous bypass surgery. Angina is included in this code as well.

13. Inpatient admission: The patient, a five-week-old infant, had been discharged from the hospital following her birth without any complaints. She was now admitted through the emergency department, where she was found to be febrile and lethargic and to have a weak cry. Dry mucous membranes were also noted. The admission diagnosis was "rule out sepsis." She was given STAT respiratory treatment and IV fluids, followed by intravenous antibiotics. Urine cultures grew *Enterococcus.* Blood cultures were negative. Sputum cultures grew *Mycoplasma pneumoniae.* She gradually improved and was weaned from the oxygen tent. She improved rapidly and was discharged three days following admission.

Discharge diagnoses: (1) Right lower lobe pneumonitis due to *Mycoplasma pneumoniae,* (2) fever, (3) dehydration, (4) urinary tract infection.

J15.7	Pneumonia due to Mycoplasma pneumoniae
E86.0	Dehydration
N39.0	Urinary tract infection, site not specified
B95.2	Enterococcus as the cause of diseases classified elsewhere

Comments: Any of the conditions could have been designated as the principal diagnosis according to symptoms on admission and treatment rendered. All conditions meet the criteria for additional diagnoses except for fever, which is integral to pneumonia. Code J15.7 is assigned rather than the newborn infection codes because in this case, the infant had previously been discharged in good condition and developed the pneumonitis later, which would mean that it was a community-acquired condition.

14. Inpatient admission: The patient, an 18-month-old male, was admitted with reactive airway disease versus viral pneumonia. His symptoms of wheezing and congestion had become increasingly worse over the past few days. He had been healthy since birth except for congenital pulmonary stenosis, which was evaluated during this admission. He was placed on medications and oxygen. Blood culture and viral panel were negative. He was to be followed by the pulmonary clinic.

Discharge diagnoses: (1) Acute exacerbation of reactive airway disease, (2) mild pulmonary stenosis.

J45.901	Unspecified asthma with (acute) exacerbation
Q25.6	Stenosis of pulmonary artery

Comments: Viral pneumonia was ruled out and should not be coded. The main term **Disease,** reactive airway, in the Alphabetic Index of Diseases and Injuries says, "see Asthma." Although the asthma had not reached the status asthmaticus stage, it had become exacerbated. Congenital pulmonary stenosis is coded because it probably is involved in the reactive airway disease and would have received clinical evaluation during the stay.

8. DISEASES OF THE DIGESTIVE SYSTEM

1. **Inpatient admission:** This patient underwent a gastric bypass three weeks earlier and is now admitted because of continuous vomiting and severe dehydration. Radiologic and laboratory studies provided no indication of problems with the previous surgery or other abnormalities. Rehydration was accomplished. On close observation, it appeared that she was eating too fast and too much.

Discharge diagnoses: (1) Exogenous morbid obesity with recent gastric bypass, (2) dehydration due to continuous vomiting.

K91.0	Vomiting following gastrointestinal surgery
E86.0	Dehydration
E66.01	Morbid (severe) obesity due to excess calories

Comments: Although the vomiting is not specified as due to the gastric surgery, the Tabular List and Alphabetic Index of Diseases and Injuries instruct the coder to assign K91.0 for any vomiting following gastrointestinal surgery.

2. **Inpatient admission:** The elderly nursing home patient was admitted with aspiration pneumonitis. She was unable to swallow or eat as a result of a stroke, which occurred two months earlier. She was experiencing progressive aspiration and weight loss. It was hoped that anchoring a feeding tube would alleviate the situation. Therefore, a percutaneous endoscopic gastrostomy with placement of a feeding tube was performed.

Discharge diagnoses: (1) Difficulty swallowing secondary to cerebrovascular infarction, (2) impending malnutrition, (3) aspiration pneumonia.

J69.0	Pneumonitis due to inhalation of food and vomit
I69.391	Dysphagia following cerebral infarction
R13.10	Dysphagia, unspecified
R63.4	Abnormal weight loss
0DH64UZ	Insertion of feeding device into stomach, percutaneous endoscopic approach

Comments: Aspiration pneumonia is sequenced as the principal diagnosis. Because no code exists for impending malnutrition, code R63.4 is assigned to identify loss of weight, the precursor condition.

Dysphagia is the late effect of the previous cerebrovascular accident. I69.3 is the subcategory for sequelae of stroke not otherwise specified. As indicated by the "use additional code" note at code I69.391, an additional code is assigned to identify the type of dysphagia. Because the type of dysphagia has not been further specified other than as difficulty swallowing, code R13.10 is assigned.

The percutaneous endoscopic gastrostomy is classified to the Medical and Surgical Section, root operation "Insertion," and the sixth-character value for feeding device.

3. **Inpatient admission:** The patient was transferred in from facility A, where he experienced 12 hours of hematemesis requiring transfusions with 14 units of red blood cells and six units of fresh-frozen plasma. Upon admission to facility B, a gastroscopic examination revealed a 4- by 2-centimeter gastric ulcer with visible vessels. He was taken to the operating room, where a hemigastrectomy with Billroth I anastomosis of the duodenum was performed.

Discharge diagnosis: Bleeding gastric ulcer.

K25.4	Chronic or unspecified gastric ulcer with hemorrhage
0DB60ZZ	Excision of stomach, open approach
0D160Z9	Bypass stomach to duodenum, open approach
0DJ68ZZ	Inspection of stomach, via natural or artificial opening endoscopic

Comments: The ulcer is unspecified as acute or chronic, with hemorrhage and without mention of obstruction. Code K25.4 is assigned to identify the bleeding gastric ulcer to the greatest degree of specificity available.

Two codes are required for the hemigastrectomy and Billroth I anastomosis of the stomach to the duodenum. Hemigastrectomy is coded to the root operation "Excision," as a portion of a body part is removed. The Billroth I procedure is classified to the root operation "Bypass," while the gastroscopy is coded to the root operation "Inspection."

4. **Inpatient admission:** The patient's admitting diagnosis was acute pancreatitis. Findings on a CT scan performed prior to admission were consistent with acute and chronic pancreatitis and pancreatic duct calculi. Multiple stones were noted on endoscopic retrograde cholangiopancreatography (ERCP); one of them was big enough to occlude the pancreatic duct. There was generalized stenosis of the pancreatic duct. (During ERCP, a stent was put in place to bypass the area of obstruction. The patient improved immediately.) Extracorporeal shock wave lithotripsy (ESWL) then achieved partial fragmentation of the stone. Because of abdominal pain, a second ESWL was required and, again, achieved only partial fragmentation of the stone. The patient underwent another ERCP, which identified multiple stones and pancreatic duct stenosis with occlusion of the previously placed stent. During the procedure, the obstructed area was passed through, but there was still a 2-millimeter area of pancreatic duct stenosis. A balloon was inserted to dilate this area endoscopically. There were multiple stones, and the occluded stent was removed and replaced with a new one beyond the area of obstruction. There was no puncture of the skin or mucous membrane necessary to remove or replace the occluded stent.

Discharge diagnoses: (1) Acute and chronic pancreatitis, (2) pancreatic calculi.

Procedures: (1) ERCP with pancreatic duct stent insertion, (2) ESWL (pancreatic stone) on two separate occasions, (3) ERCP with prolonged dilation of pancreatic duct and removal of occluded stent and replacement with a new, single-pigtail stent.

K85.9	Acute pancreatitis, unspecified
K86.1	Other chronic pancreatitis
K86.8	Other specified diseases of pancreas
0F7D8DZ	Dilation of pancreatic duct with intraluminal device, via natural or artificial opening endoscopic
0FPB8DZ	Removal of intraluminal device from hepatobiliary duct, via natural or artificial opening endoscopic
0FFDXZZ	Fragmentation in pancreatic duct, external approach

Comments: Because the patient had both acute and chronic pancreatitis and separate subterms exist in the Alphabetic Index, both codes are assigned, with the acute pancreatitis sequenced first.

ERCP with dilation and stent insertion is included in 0F7D8DZ, with the device value of "D" for "intraluminal device." The root operation "Dilation" is chosen, as this was the objective of the procedure. Code 0FPB8DZ is assigned to identify the removal of the occluded stent (root operation "Change"). The extracorporeal shock wave lithotripsy is coded to the root operation "Fragmentation" because the objective of the procedure was to break up the stone. The approach for the ESWL is external because the shock waves are delivered through the skin and no incisions are made.

5. **Outpatient visit:** The patient came in complaining of severe abdominal pain. Abdominal scout film showed scoliosis and some degenerative changes in the lumbar spine. However, a high osmolar contrast abdominal CT scan showed extensive diverticulosis involving the descending and sigmoid portions of the colon, with obvious evidence of diverticulitis.

Diagnosis: Diverticulitis.

K57.32	Diverticulitis of large intestine without perforation or abscess without bleeding
BW200ZZ	Computerized tomography (CT scan) of abdomen using high osmolar contrast

6. **Inpatient admission:** The 86-year-old woman was admitted with rectal bleeding. She was also massively dehydrated, with a BUN of 124. On admission, some IV fluids and transfusions of whole blood via a central vein were administered because her initial hemoglobin was 9.5 and later dropped to 7.4. On colonoscopy, multiple ulcers of the rectum, consistent with ulcerative proctitis, were found and biopsies were taken. The tissue was negative for neoplastic disease, and the patient was started on steroid enemas, with resolution.

Discharge diagnoses: (1) Rectal bleeding, (2) dehydration, (3) acute blood loss anemia, (4) ulcerative proctitis.

K51.211	Ulcerative (chronic) proctitis with rectal bleeding
E86.0	Dehydration
D62	Acute posthemorrhagic anemia
0DBE8ZX	Excision of large intestine, via natural or artificial opening endoscopic, diagnostic
30243H1	Transfusion of nonautologous whole blood into central vein, percutaneous approach

Comments: Ulcerative proctitis is sequenced as the principal diagnosis because the workup and treatment were directed at identifying and treating the cause of the bleeding. ICD-10-CM provides a combination code that includes rectal bleeding and proctitis. Acute blood loss anemia, a further manifestation of ulcerative proctitis, and dehydration are also coded because both meet criteria for additional diagnoses.

7. **Inpatient admission:** The patient, a 20-year-old female, presented to the emergency department complaining of bilateral arm and shoulder pain, "yellow eyes," and dark urine. The emergency department evaluation revealed profound jaundice with markedly elevated liver function tests. The patient was admitted for further evaluation. A non-contrast gallbladder ultrasound was negative for gallstones. Hematological studies indicated sickle-cell disease, which could be contributing to the jaundice. Because the liver function gradually improved, it was felt that she could be further evaluated as an outpatient for probable acute hepatitis B.

Discharge diagnosis: Jaundice secondary to sickle-cell disease versus acute hepatitis B.

R17	Unspecified jaundice
B16.9	Acute hepatitis B without delta-agent and without hepatic coma
D57.1	Sickle-cell disease without crisis

Comments: When a symptom is followed by contrasting or comparative diagnoses, the symptom should be sequenced first.

8. Inpatient admission: The patient was admitted for evaluation of guaiac-positive stools. All sites that could be visualized on esophagogastroduodenoscopy (EGD) were within normal limits except a small area in the gastric fundus, which was biopsied. A colonoscope was then inserted to 35 centimeters, and diverticula were noted. Because of narrowing resulting from edema due to diverticulitis, it was not possible to pass the scope farther. The tissue report showed benign acute and chronic gastritis but no ulcer.

Discharge diagnoses: (1) Occult blood in stool of undetermined origin, (2) diverticulosis with diverticulitis of colon, (3) acute and chronic gastritis.

R19.5	Other fecal abnormalities
K29.00	Acute gastritis without bleeding
K29.40	Chronic atrophic gastritis without bleeding
K57.32	Diverticulitis of large intestine without perforation or abscess without bleeding
0DB68ZX	Excision of stomach, via natural or artificial opening endoscopic, diagnostic
0DJD8ZZ	Inspection of lower intestinal tract, via natural or artificial opening endoscopic

Comments: No cause for the blood in stools was determined; therefore, the symptom is the principal diagnosis. When diverticulitis is present, it is understood that diverticulosis also exists, and an additional code for the latter condition is unnecessary. Two endoscopic procedures were performed: EGD and colonoscopy. When an endoscope is passed through more than one area of the body, the procedure is coded to the farthest site only.

9. Inpatient admission (episode 1): Because the patient had a 20-year history of severe complicated ulcerative colitis, he was admitted for surgical intervention. A total abdominal colectomy with ileostomy was performed. The postoperative recovery was without incident.

Discharge diagnosis: Ulcerative colitis.

K51.919	Ulcerative colitis, unspecified with unspecified complications
0DTE0ZZ	Resection of large intestine, open approach
0D1B0Z4	Bypass ileum to cutaneous, open approach

Comments: The condition necessitating admission and surgery was ulcerative colitis. Colectomy is the definitive treatment for colitis and is therefore designated as the principal procedure. The ileostomy is coded to the root operation "Bypass."

Inpatient admission (episode 2): Three months after surgery, the patient was again admitted for a percutaneous endoscopic endorectal pull-through with excision of the submucosal portion of the rectum with endoscopic formation of a loop ileostomy via the existing ileostomy. This procedure was further treatment for the long-standing and intractable ulcerative colitis.

Discharge diagnosis: Ulcerative colitis.

K51.919	Ulcerative colitis, unspecified with unspecified complications
0DBP4ZZ	Excision of rectum, percutaneous endoscopic approach
0D1B8Z4	Bypass ileum to cutaneous, via natural or artificial opening endoscopic

Comments: More extensive surgery was required to further control the patient's ulcerative colitis. Colitis is, again, the condition necessitating admission. Endorectal pull-through, or removal of the submucosal portion of the rectum, is the definitive treatment for ulcerative colitis and is therefore the principal procedure.

Inpatient admission (episode 3): Four months following the second surgery, the patient was admitted for ileostomy closure. He had no symptoms of ulcerative colitis. The postoperative course was uneventful.

Discharge diagnosis: Status post ileostomy closure.

Z43.2	Encounter for attention to ileostomy
0DQB0ZZ	Repair ileum, open approach

Comments: The ulcerative colitis responded to the previous surgeries and was no longer present; therefore, it is not coded. The sole purpose for the third admission is ileostomy closure. In the Alphabetic Index to Procedures (ICD-10-PCS), the main term **Closure** has a note to "see Repair." See "Repair, ileum," for the first four characters for the ileostomy closure.

10. **Inpatient admission:** The patient experienced rectal pain for several months due to a 2.5-centimeter mass on the anterior rectal wall. An open transanal excision of the mass was performed, and a frozen section revealed an inflammatory lesion without evidence of malignancy. The final pathology report showed the tissue to represent a granuloma of the rectum.

Discharge diagnosis: Rectal granuloma.

K62.89	Other specified diseases of anus and rectum
0DBP7ZZ	Excision of rectum, via natural or artificial opening

Comments: The condition, established after study, that necessitated the admission of the patient to the hospital for care was rectal granuloma. Although the lesion was not initially identified, the physician was able to further specify the condition as granuloma following "Excision" and pathologic examination.

11. **Inpatient admission:** The patient, a woman with chronic right upper-quadrant abdominal pain, was admitted for possible pancreatitis after two episodes of vomiting clear fluid. Pain medications were started and a nasogastric tube was placed for drainage, with intermittent suction. The NG tube was pulled three days after admission, and the patient was discharged to follow up with her physician one week later.

Discharge diagnosis: Pancreatitis.

Principal procedure: Insertion, nasogastric tube.

K85.9	Acute pancreatitis, unspecified
0D9670Z	Drainage of stomach with drainage device, via natural or artificial opening

Comments: Pain and vomiting are not coded because they are integral to pancreatitis. Although the pancreatitis is not qualified as acute or chronic, code K85.9 is assigned because this is the code provided in the Alphabetic Index of Diseases and Injuries for pancreatitis that is not further specified. The objective for the insertion of the NG tube is drainage. Therefore, the procedure is coded to the root operation "Drainage."

12. **Inpatient admission:** The patient, a man with a long history of alcohol dependence with resultant alcoholic cirrhosis, was admitted with red, coffee-ground hematemesis. An emergent esophagogastroduodenoscopy revealed bleeding esophageal varices, which were excised. The varices are secondary to the alcoholic cirrhosis. No problems were identified in the stomach or duodenum. He was transfused via peripheral vein in his left arm with multiple units of packed red cells and frozen plasma, and yet the bleeding continued. He was returned to surgery, and an esophagoscopy was performed to sclerose the bleeding esophageal varices a second time.

Discharge diagnoses: (1) Upper gastrointestinal bleed, (2) esophageal varices, (3) Laennec's cirrhosis, (4) alcohol dependence.

Principal procedure: Control of esophageal bleeding by excision of varices.

K70.30	Alcoholic cirrhosis of liver without ascites
I85.11	Secondary esophageal varices with bleeding
F10.20	Alcohol dependence, uncomplicated
0DB58ZZ	Excision of esophagus, via natural or artificial opening endoscopic
0DB58ZZ	Excision of esophagus, via natural or artificial opening endoscopic
30233N1	Transfusion of nonautologous red blood cells into peripheral vein, percutaneous approach
30233K1	Transfusion of nonautologous frozen plasma into peripheral vein, percutaneous approach

Comments: The esophageal varices are due to the alcoholic cirrhosis. In the Index, refer to the main term **Varix,** esophagus, in (due to) cirrhosis of the liver, bleeding, I85.11. There is a "code first" note at the I85.1 subcategory instructing that the underlying disease should be coded first. Therefore, the code for the alcoholic cirrhosis is sequenced first.

The varices were endoscopically excised, or sclerosed, two times, so the code is listed twice. Separate codes for the EGD and esophagoscopy are not assigned because these procedures were performed only as the approach to the more definitive procedure.

13. Inpatient admission: The patient, a 35-year-old male, was admitted for possible gastritis. He had undergone a cadaveric renal transplant for end-stage renal disease secondary to focal membranous glomerulonephritis two years earlier. On endoscopic examination of the lower esophagus and stomach, patchy erythemas were seen in the stomach and biopsies were taken. A linear erosion was noted at the gastroesophageal junction. The impression was mild reflux esophagitis and mild antral duodenitis. As his dietary intake improved, his physical condition improved as well.

Discharge diagnoses: (1) Reflux esophagitis, (2) duodenitis.

K21.0	Gastro-esophageal reflux disease with esophagitis
K29.80	Duodenitis without bleeding
Z94.0	Kidney transplant status
0DB68ZX	Excision of stomach, via natural or artificial opening endoscopic, diagnostic

Comments: Either esophagitis or duodenitis can be designated as the principal diagnosis because both are consistent with the reason for admission, both were identified during the hospitalization, and both were treated. The previous kidney transplant is coded because it was significant in the patient's current care and treatment.

14. Inpatient admission: The patient recently underwent an ultrasound that showed a filling defect in the gallbladder, thought to represent a cholelithiasis. It was felt that the woman's symptoms were suggestive of cholecystitis and that cholecystectomy was in order. On admission, a laparoscopic cholecystectomy with lysis of adhesions around the gallbladder was carried out, followed by a contrast intraoperative cholangiogram. A proctologist was consulted due to the presence of persistent rectal pain. A mild anal fissure was identified on flexible sigmoidoscopy. A needle biopsy of the liver was performed due to an abnormal liver function study times 3. The pathology report indicated that the liver tissue was normal.

Discharge diagnoses: (1) Chronic cholecystitis and cholelithiasis, (2) anal fissure, (3) abnormal liver function studies.

K80.10	Calculus of gallbladder with chronic cholecystitis without obstruction
K60.2	Anal fissure, unspecified
R94.5	Abnormal results of liver function studies
0FT44ZZ	Resection of gallbladder, percutaneous endoscopic approach
0FB03ZX	Excision of liver, percutaneous approach, diagnostic
BF03YZZ	Plain radiography of gallbladder and bile ducts using other contrast
0DJD8ZZ	Inspection of lower intestinal tract, via natural or artificial opening endoscopic

Comments: Code K80.10 includes both chronic cholecystitis and cholelithiasis. Adhesions and lysis of adhesions are not coded because adhesions were not listed as a discharge diagnosis. Lysis of adhesions is fairly common in cholecystectomy surgery and is not coded unless the significance was specified by the physician. Although the biopsy of the liver was normal, the physician still felt that there was an abnormality in the liver function lab studies, so this was coded.

15. Inpatient admission: The male patient came in complaining of headache, nausea, vomiting, and chest pain. The impression on admission was possible coronary artery disease and probable viral gastroenteritis. Only a small, sliding hiatal hernia was found on air contrast upper GI. No ischemia was found on cardiac evaluation. The patient gradually improved and was discharged two days later to follow up with his family physician in one week for gastroenteritis and further evaluation of the hiatal hernia.

Discharge diagnoses: (1) Probable viral gastroenteritis, (2) hiatal hernia.

A08.4	Viral intestinal infection, unspecified
BD15YZZ	Fluoroscopy of upper GI using other contrast

Comments: The reason for admission was possible coronary artery disease and probable gastroenteritis. Possible coronary artery disease was ruled out by diagnostic evaluation and is not coded. The principal diagnosis is viral gastroenteritis. Probable diagnoses at the time of discharge are coded as though confirmed. No code is assigned for the hiatal hernia because it is an incidental X-ray finding for a condition that was not treated or evaluated further during the current encounter and therefore is not reportable.

16. Inpatient admission: The patient, a woman with a long history of Crohn's disease, was admitted with abdominal cramping, vomiting, and diarrhea of sudden onset. Admitting orders included all current medications for Crohn's disease. Her amylase was 241 on admission, and she had a slightly elevated white blood count. Both returned to normal with treatment for pancreatitis, and the abdominal problems also slowed down. She was to be followed as an outpatient.

Discharge diagnoses: (1) Pancreatitis, (2) Crohn's disease.

K85.9   Acute pancreatitis, unspecified

K50.90   Crohn's disease, unspecified, without complications

Comments: Patient's symptomatology and treatment were related to pancreatitis. Sequence pancreatitis as the principal diagnosis. Crohn's disease, a coexisting condition, is coded because it was also treated.

17. Physician office visit (episode 1): The patient, an elderly woman, came in for severe epigastric abdominal pain. She had some nausea but no vomiting. She was referred for further studies to rule out cholecystitis and localized ulcer perforation.

Diagnosis: Possible cholecystitis and/or perforated gastric ulcer.

R10.13   Epigastric pain

R11.0   Nausea

Comments: Only symptoms can be coded for this visit because questionable diagnoses are coded as if established only for hospital inpatients. Conditions are coded to the highest level of certainty on physician office visits. Either abdominal pain or nausea can be sequenced as the reason for the encounter.

Inpatient admission (episode 2): An ultrasound was negative and an upper GI failed to yield a diagnosis. Therefore, the patient was admitted for further evaluation because of the continued severity of her abdominal pain. An exploratory laparotomy was performed and immediately revealed a perforated appendix lying in a subhepatic space with abscess. An appendectomy was performed. The abscess cleared postoperatively with administration of high doses of intravenous antibiotics.

Discharge diagnosis: Appendicitis with perforation and subhepatic abscess.

K35.3   Acute appendicitis with localized peritonitis

0DTJ0ZZ   Resection of appendix, open approach

Comments: The patient's symptomatology was explained by the definitive finding of appendicitis with perforation. Abdominal pain and nausea are inherent to appendicitis and should not be coded separately. Perforation and peritonitis are both included in code K35.3.

18. **Inpatient admission:** The patient was admitted with vague abdominal pain, and a workup was carried out. All laboratory findings were within normal limits, except for a slightly elevated white blood count. The patient requested transfer to another hospital close to his home for further evaluation. The patient was transferred with a working diagnosis of diverticulitis versus colon tumor.

   Discharge diagnosis: Diverticulitis versus tumor of colon.

K57.92	Diverticulitis of intestine, part unspecified, without perforation or abscess without bleeding
D49.0	Neoplasm of unspecified behavior of digestive system

   Comments: When diagnoses are stated in a comparative or contrasting manner, both conditions are coded and sequenced according to the circumstances of admission. In this instance, either condition is consistent with abdominal pain, and either can be sequenced as the principal diagnosis.

19. **Inpatient admission:** The patient, an eight-year-old boy, was brought in from school because of persistent cyclical vomiting with accompanying abdominal pain. He was admitted for observation and monitoring of vital signs. Laboratory work was within normal limits, vital signs remained stable, the abdomen remained flat and soft, and there was no muscle guarding or tenderness. He was discharged the following day in an improved condition.

   Discharge diagnoses: (1) Cyclical vomiting, (2) abdominal pain.

G43.A09	Cyclical vomiting, not intractable, without status migrainosus
R10.9	Unspecified abdominal pain

   Comments: Vomiting, not otherwise specified, is coded as a symptom. However, when the vomiting is specified as cyclical, it is classified to code G43.A09.

20. **Inpatient admission:** The patient had a history of recurrent infections in the perianal area. He was seen two days earlier in the physician's office for a perianal abscess and anal fistula. The prescribed medication and enemas did not alleviate the situation, so he was admitted for surgical intervention. In surgery, an anal fistulotomy was performed on the skin of the perineum with drainage of the perianal abscess. The patient responded to further treatments of antibiotics and diet and was to be followed in the office.

   Discharge diagnoses: (1) Perianal abscess, (2) anal fistula.

K61.0	Anal abscess
K60.3	Anal fistula
0D9QXZZ	Drainage of anus, external approach
0H89XZZ	Division of perineum skin, external approach

21. Inpatient admission: The patient is status post heart transplantation six months earlier. Since then, he had been admitted numerous times for fever and diarrhea, presumably due to cytomegalovirus. On this occasion, he was admitted for further evaluation of fever and diarrhea. Stool and blood cultures were negative. A single, shallow erosion in the colon was viewed and biopsied on colonoscopy. Internal, bleeding hemorrhoids were also visualized. The pathology report showed moderate, nonspecific, chronic colitis with no diagnostic evidence of cytomegalovirus. Chronic colitis was determined to be the cause of the patient's symptomatology. The patient was also followed by endocrinology for his diabetes, and no changes were recommended in his medication. His diarrhea improved, medication and diet were prescribed for bleeding hemorrhoids and chronic colitis, and he was released.

Discharge diagnoses: (1) Chronic colitis; (2) bleeding internal hemorrhoids; (3) diabetes mellitus, type 1; (4) status post heart transplant.

K52.9	Noninfective gastroenteritis and colitis, unspecified
I84.111	Internal bleeding hemorrhoids
E10.9	Type 1 diabetes mellitus without complications
Z94.1	Heart transplant status
Z79.4	Long term (current) use of insulin
0DBE8ZX	Excision of large intestine, via natural or artificial opening endoscopic, diagnostic

Comments: Chronic colitis is designated as the principal diagnosis because it is the condition, established after study, that necessitated admission. A previous heart transplant is significant to the current care and treatment of the patient. A code for long-term insulin use is not required for type 1 diabetics because these patients require insulin. However, this code may be assigned, if desired, to provide additional information.

The biopsy was performed during the colonoscopy; therefore, the root operation is "Excision," with a qualifier for "diagnostic."

22. Inpatient admission: The patient had undergone cardiac transplantation about three years earlier. On this occasion, he came to the emergency department with a three-day history of right lower quadrant pain. The white blood count was elevated, and a small-bowel X-ray examination showed some dilated small bowel loops but no free air. He was admitted, and an abdominal gastrointestinal ultrasound showed a mass measuring about 5 by 5 by 4 centimeters, which was presumed to be an appendiceal cyst. He underwent an ultrasound-directed percutaneous right lower quadrant aspiration; only a few drops of material were collected for diagnostic examination. Blood cultures were sterile, leukocytosis improved, and he remained afebrile with gradually decreasing pain. He was discharged on antibiotics and was to return in a few weeks for an interval appendectomy.

Discharge diagnoses: (1) Probable appendiceal cyst, (2) status post cardiac transplantation.

Procedure performed: Ultrasound-directed aspiration of appendiceal mass.

K38.8	Other specified diseases of appendix
Z94.1	Heart transplant status
0D9J3ZX	Drainage of appendix, percutaneous approach, diagnostic

Comments: Probable appendiceal cyst is coded as though confirmed. The fact that the patient had a transplanted heart is important during all subsequent medical care. Aspiration of appendiceal mass for diagnostic examination is coded to the root operation "Drainage," percutaneous approach, with a qualifier for "diagnostic."

9. DISEASES OF THE GENITOURINARY SYSTEM

1. Inpatient admission: The patient, an 83-year-old woman, came in through the emergency department complaining of fever, confusion, and lethargy. Urine and blood cultures were positive for *E. coli*. Sepsis and urinary tract infection were diagnosed. The patient slowly responded to IV antibiotic therapy, but she began to experience vomiting episodes with abdominal pain. These episodes were probably related to her hiatal hernia with reflux esophagitis. The vomiting seemed to improve with medications and diet. The patient was discharged one week following admission on oral Keflex and Zantac to follow up as an outpatient.

Discharge diagnoses: (1) Urinary tract infection, (2) gram-negative sepsis secondary to diagnosis 1, (3) hiatal hernia with reflux esophagitis.

A41.51	Sepsis due to Escherichia coli [E. coli]
N39.0	Urinary tract infection, site not specified
B96.2	Escherichia coli [E. coli] as the cause of diseases classified elsewhere
K44.9	Diaphragmatic hernia without obstruction or gangrene
K21.0	Gastro-esophageal reflux disease with esophagitis

Comments: Although sepsis and urinary tract infection (UTI) were both present on admission, sepsis is sequenced as the principal diagnosis as guided by the ICD-10-CM Official Coding Guidelines (Section I.C.1.d.4, Sepsis and severe sepsis with a localized infection). That guideline provides direction to sequence first the code for the underlying systemic infection when the reason for the admission is both sepsis and a localized infection. ICD-10-CM codes both the sepsis and the causative agent in one code. However, because *E. coli* grew in both the urine and blood cultures, code B96.2 is assigned to identify the infectious agent responsible for the UTI. The hiatal hernia is coded because it was treated.

2. Inpatient admission: The patient was admitted for abnormal uterine bleeding. An ultrasound performed prior to admission suggested a possible bicornuate uterus. Because of her morbid obesity, a hysteroscopy with dilation and curettage was performed. Findings indicated a single cavity without any septum, polyps, or submucous fibroids. The patient was seen by the dietitian and discharged on a 1,500-calorie diet to reduce her weight.

Discharge diagnoses: (1) Morbid obesity, (2) abnormal uterine bleeding unrelated to menstruation.

N93.9	Abnormal uterine and vaginal bleeding, unspecified
E66.01	Morbid (severe) obesity due to excess calories
0UDB8ZZ	Extraction of endometrium, via natural or artificial opening endoscopic

3. Inpatient admission: The patient, a young man with hypertensive heart disease and end-stage renal disease, was admitted for placement of an arteriovenous fistula in his left arm to prepare for hemodialysis. The AV fistula was accomplished between the left radial artery and cephalic antebrachial vein in the lower arm. Hemodialysis was provided to treat the end-stage chronic kidney disease.

Discharge diagnoses: (1) Hypertensive heart disease and nephrosclerosis, (2) end-stage chronic kidney disease.

I13.11	Hypertensive heart and chronic kidney disease without heart failure, with stage 5 chronic kidney disease, or end stage renal disease
N18.6	End stage renal disease
031C0ZF	Bypass left radial artery to lower arm vein, open approach

Comments: When a patient is admitted for placement of a fistula for future dialysis, the condition necessitating the dialysis is coded as the principal diagnosis. Hypertensive heart disease, kidney disease, and chronic kidney disease are classified to the combination code I13.11. Code N18.6 is assigned as an additional code to identify the specific end-stage renal disease. The creation of the AV fistula is classified to the root operation "Bypass."

4. Inpatient admission: The patient had a history of frequent episodes of severe chronic interstitial cystitis. Despite previous treatment, she has had no resolution of her symptoms. She was admitted for and received an open partial cystectomy and bilateral ileoureterostomy.

Discharge diagnosis: Severe, chronic interstitial cystitis.

N30.10	Interstitial cystitis (chronic) without hematuria
0TBB0ZZ	Excision of bladder, open approach
0T180ZC	Bypass bilateral ureters to ileocutaneous, open approach

Comments: Because only part of the bladder was removed, the root operation is "Excision." The ileoureterostomy involves both ureters being diverted via the ileum to the outside of the body and is classified to the root operation "Bypass."

5. Inpatient admission: The patient had chronic kidney disease secondary to malignant hypertension and was status post insertion of a left arteriovenous fistula six months earlier. He presented with exacerbation of his renal condition and was admitted for evaluation and hemodialysis. His medications were adjusted, and he received several hemodialysis sessions during this admission. His condition stabilized, and he was discharged in an improved state.

Discharge diagnoses: (1) End-stage renal disease associated with malignant hypertension, (2) exacerbation of kidney disease.

I12.0	Hypertensive chronic kidney disease with stage 5 chronic kidney disease or end stage renal disease
N18.6	End stage renal disease
Z99.2	Dependence on renal dialysis
5A1D60Z	Performance of urinary filtration, multiple

Comments: Code I12.0 is a combination code that encompasses the hypertension and the patient's chronic kidney disease. ICD-10-CM does not distinguish between malignant and benign forms of hypertension. There is no additional code available to indicate the exacerbation of the renal failure. Acute renal failure is not an exacerbation of chronic kidney disease; it is essentially a different condition. An additional code, N18.6, is assigned to identify the end-stage renal disease. Assign code Z99.2 to identify that the patient is a dialysis patient.

6. Inpatient admission: The patient had end-stage renal disease and chronic kidney disease secondary to hypertension. He was admitted for a cadaveric renal transplant. He underwent a single renal hemodialysis session prior to transplant. The left donor kidney was placed in the right iliac fossa. Postoperative recovery was uneventful.

Discharge diagnosis: End-stage renal disease resulting from hypertension.

I12.0	Hypertensive chronic kidney disease with stage 5 chronic kidney disease or end stage renal disease
N18.6	End stage renal disease
0TY10Z0	Transplantation of left kidney, allogeneic, open approach
5A1D00Z	Performance of urinary filtration, single

Comments: Code I12.0 is a combination code that encompasses the hypertension and the patient's chronic kidney disease. The fact that the kidney transplant is from a cadaver is indicated via the qualifier for allogeneic.

7. Inpatient admission: The patient became ill the day before admission with nausea, vomiting, dysuria, and hematuria. Initial laboratory work included a urinalysis report of RBCs too numerous to count, and a repeat urinalysis the following day reported the same results. On contrast retrograde pyelogram of both kidneys, the ureters, and the bladder, hydronephrosis of the right kidney and possibly some secondary hydronephrosis with obstruction of the ureteropelvic junction were seen. Spontaneously, the hematuria and other symptoms cleared. The patient was to be referred to a urologist for follow-up.

Discharge diagnosis: Hematuria and hydronephrosis possibly due to idiopathic ureteropelvic obstruction.

N13.1	Hydronephrosis with ureteral stricture, not elsewhere classified
R31.9	Hematuria, unspecified
BT14YZZ	Fluoroscopy of kidneys, ureters and bladder using other contrast

Comments: ICD-10-CM has a combination code that identifies both the ureteral obstruction and the hydronephrosis.

8. Physician office visit (episode 1): The patient, an elderly man, has had carcinoma of the bladder with numerous recurrences since 2007. On his annual bladder checkup, an obstructive prostate with urinary retention was present, but no evidence of a recurrence of the carcinoma was found. He was to be admitted for further evaluation of the prostatic obstruction.

Diagnoses: (1) Prostatic obstruction with urinary retention, (2) no evidence of recurrence of bladder carcinoma.

N40.1	Enlarged prostate with lower urinary tract symptoms (LUTS)
R33.8	Other retention of urine
Z85.51	Personal history of malignant neoplasm of bladder

Comments: The patient had not had any recurrence of carcinoma of the bladder. Therefore, code Z85.51 is assigned for history of bladder cancer. Code R33.8 is assigned as an additional code as indicated by the "use additional code" note at code N40.1.

Inpatient admission (episode 2): On cystoscopy, a mild urethral stricture and an obstructive prostate with urinary retention were found. The urethra was dilated, and the patient underwent transurethral prostatectomy (TURP) without complication. The pathology report showed benign prostatic hypertrophy.

Discharge diagnoses: (1) Urethral stricture secondary to benign prostatic hypertrophy (BPH), (2) urinary retention, (3) history of carcinoma of the bladder.

N40.1	Enlarged prostate with lower urinary tract symptoms (LUTS)
N35.8	Other urethral stricture
R33.8	Other retention of urine
Z85.51	Personal history of malignant neoplasm of bladder
0VB08ZZ	Excision of prostate, via natural or artificial opening endoscopic
0T7D8ZZ	Dilation of urethra, via natural or artificial opening endoscopic

Comments: Code N40.1 includes the BPH and LUTS, but additional codes are needed for the urethral stricture and the urinary retention. Only a part of the prostate is removed in a TURP, so the root operation "Excision" is used.

9. Inpatient admission: The nursing home patient had frequent urinary tract infections and numerous courses of antibiotics. The most recent urine culture grew *Pseudomonas aeruginosa*, resistant to all oral antibiotics. The patient was admitted for IV antibiotic therapy. Significant in her history was the placement about three years earlier of a cardiac pacemaker for conduction defects. It was working satisfactorily during her hospitalization. Because the cultures continued to show *Pseudomonas* after IV antibiotics were given, a cystoscopy was performed. The patient still had a bladder infection with erythema of the bladder wall. Urine cultures were obtained at that time, and the report showed a high colony count of *Pseudomonas* that was then susceptible to oral antibiotics. She was discharged on oral Cipro.

Discharge diagnoses: (1) Bladder infection, resistant to oral antibiotics; (2) pacemaker in situ.

N30.90	Cystitis, unspecified without hematuria
B96.5	Pseudomonas (aeruginosa) (mallei) (pseudomallei) as the cause of diseases classified elsewhere
Z16	Infection with drug resistant microorganisms
Z95.0	Presence of cardiac pacemaker
0TJB8ZZ	Inspection of bladder, via natural or artificial opening endoscopic

Comments: The cystoscopy specified the urinary tract infection to be of the bladder; therefore, the more specific code of N30.90 is used. Code Z16 shows that the *Pseudomonas* was drug resistant.

10. Inpatient admission: The patient was experiencing heavy, abnormal uterine bleeding and abdominal pain. On vaginal examination, there was bright red blood in the vagina and the left adnexa was enlarged. The woman was admitted and taken to surgery, where an exploratory laparotomy revealed a left follicular ovarian cyst. While the surgeon was examining the left ovary, the cyst spontaneously ruptured. An ovarian cystectomy was performed without complication. The postoperative course was uneventful, and the patient was discharged.

Discharge diagnosis: Ruptured left follicular ovarian cyst.

N83.0	Follicular cyst of ovary
0UB10ZZ	Excision of left ovary, open approach

Comments: The laparotomy is the approach to the "Excision" of the cyst.

11. **Inpatient admission:** The male patient was admitted with severe colic secondary to a left ureteral calculus. A cystoscopy was performed, and a stone extracted. On retrograde pyelography, no stone was seen in the ureter or kidney. However, the pathology report indicated that only a small fragment of the stone was retrieved. Postoperatively, the patient did well at first but then began having severe colic again. He was returned to surgery for another cystoscopy. The remainder of the stone was located in the distal left ureter and extracted. The postoperative course was uncomplicated.

   Discharge diagnosis: Left ureteral calculus.

N20.1	Calculus of ureter
0TC78ZZ	Extirpation of matter from left ureter, via natural or artificial opening endoscopic
0TC78ZZ	Extirpation of matter from left ureter, via natural or artificial opening endoscopic
BT14YZZ	Fluoroscopy of kidneys, ureters and bladder using other contrast

Comments: Because the cystoscopic calculus extraction was repeated, the code is assigned twice to identify two separate surgical procedures. The procedure for extraction of ureteral calculus is classified to the root operation "Extirpation," taking or cutting out solid matter from a body part.

12. **Inpatient admission:** The patient, a woman with insignificant past medical and surgical history, was the sister of a patient with end-stage renal disease secondary to hypertension. She was to be a living related kidney donor for her brother. She was prepared for surgery the day of admission, but due to her brother's active hepatitis C infection, the surgery was canceled.

   Discharge diagnoses: (1) Kidney donor, (2) procedure canceled.

Z52.4	Kidney donor
Z53.8	Procedure and treatment not carried out for other reasons

Comments: Code Z52.4 is indexed in the Alphabetic Index of Diseases and Injuries under the main term **Donor,** subterm "kidney." Code Z53.8 is indexed under **Procedure** (surgical), "not done," "specified reason NEC." Because it is the brother's condition and not the donor's that necessitated the decision to cancel the procedure, code Z53.8, not Z53.09, is assigned.

13. **Inpatient admission:** The patient was previously evaluated and found to be a suitable kidney donor for his eight-year-old son. A total unilateral left donor nephrectomy was performed without complication, and the patient was discharged.

   Discharge diagnosis: Donor nephrectomy.

Z52.4	Kidney donor
0TT10ZZ	Resection of left kidney, open approach

Comments: Code Z52.4 is indexed in the Alphabetic Index under the main entry **Donor,** subterm "kidney."

14. **Inpatient admission:** The patient, a young woman, was admitted with a two-day history of dysuria, frequency, and urgency, with onset of severe flank pain on the evening prior to admission. A laboratory workup confirmed pyelonephritis, and she was immediately started on intravenous medications and fluid. Urine cultures grew *Enterobacter aerogenes,* which was sensitive to several antibiotics.

   Discharge diagnoses: (1) Acute pyelonephritis, (2) abdominal and flank pain.

N10	Acute tubulo-interstitial nephritis
B96.89	Other specified bacterial agents as the cause of diseases classified elsewhere

Comments: All symptoms are integral to pyelonephritis and are not coded. Because the organism is not identified in the title of code N10, code B96.89 is added to provide further specificity.

15. **Inpatient admission:** The patient was admitted for a hysterectomy. Prior to admission, a diagnostic workup showed extensive endometriosis involving the uterus, ovaries, and fallopian tubes. Because the patient had asthma, she was seen by the pulmonary consult service and cleared for surgery. A total abdominal hysterectomy and a bilateral salpingo-oophorectomy were performed without complication. Postoperatively, the patient did well and was discharged.

Discharge diagnoses: (1) Endometriosis of uterus, ovaries, and fallopian tubes; (2) asthma.

N80.0	Endometriosis of uterus
N80.1	Endometriosis of ovary
N80.2	Endometriosis of fallopian tube
J45.909	Unspecified asthma, uncomplicated
0UT90ZZ	Resection of uterus, open approach
0UTC0ZZ	Resection of cervix, open approach
0UT20ZZ	Resection of bilateral ovaries, open approach
0UT70ZZ	Resection of bilateral fallopian tubes, open approach

Comments: Any of the category endometriosis codes can be designated as the principal diagnosis.

The total abdominal hysterectomy (0UT90ZZ) is designated as the principal procedure code because it is most consistent with endometriosis of the uterus. However, if code N80.1 or N80.2 were sequenced as the principal diagnosis, the bilateral removal of either the ovaries or fallopian tubes would have been sequenced as the principal procedure. Separate codes are assigned to reflect the "Resection" of the uterus, cervix, ovaries, and fallopian tubes.

16. **Inpatient admission:** The patient, a young woman, was admitted for treatment of a persistent, symptomatic right adnexal mass. The cystic mass was about 5 centimeters and presumed to be ovarian in origin. An exploratory laparotomy was performed, with right ovarian cystectomy. Pathologic findings confirmed a follicular cyst. The patient's postoperative course was unremarkable, and she was discharged.

Discharge diagnosis: Follicular cyst, right ovary.

N83.0	Follicular cyst of ovary
0UB00ZZ	Excision of right ovary, open approach

Comments: The laparotomy is the approach to the "Excision" of the cyst.

10. DISEASES OF THE SKIN AND SUBCUTANEOUS TISSUE

1. Inpatient admission: The female patient was admitted for treatment of an open wound of the scalp with cellulitis of the scalp and left ear. The wound was the result of a cut two days before admission. Excisional debridement of both the scalp and the left ear was carried out in the operating room. The patient was treated with antibiotics during her two-day stay. She was discharged on oral antibiotics in an improved condition.

Discharge diagnosis: Cellulitis of scalp and ear secondary to laceration.

S01.01xA	Laceration without foreign body of scalp, initial encounter
L03.811	Cellulitis of head [any part, except face]
H60.12	Cellulitis of left external ear
0HB0XZZ	Excision of scalp skin, external approach
0HB3XZZ	Excision of left ear skin, external approach

Comments: The open wound is sequenced as the principal diagnosis based on the circumstances of admission. Also, treatment was directed primarily toward the open wound (excisional debridement).

2. Inpatient admission: The patient, a young man with spina bifida of the lumbar region, was admitted for excision of a sacral pressure ulcer. He had a ventriculoperitoneal shunt in place on the right side for hydrocephalus. The lesion was successfully fulgurated without complication.

Discharge diagnoses: (1) Stage III pressure ulcer, sacrum; (2) lumbar spina bifida; (3) status post placement of a ventriculoperitoneal shunt for hydrocephalus.

L89.153	Pressure ulcer of sacral region, stage 3
Q05.2	Lumbar spina bifida with hydrocephalus
Z98.2	Presence of cerebrospinal fluid drainage device
0H56XZZ	Destruction of back skin, external approach

Comments: The site and the stage of the pressure ulcer are captured in one code. Hydrocephalus and lumbar region spina bifida are included in code Q05.2. The ventriculoperitoneal shunt is present but did not require attention (Z98.2). Fulguration of skin is classified to the root operation "Destruction."

3. Inpatient admission: The female patient was admitted from the nursing home with a large stage III sacral pressure ulcer, which was treated with excisional debridement and a flap-graft closure of the back. She had chronic lymphocytic B-cell leukemia, which required peripheral vein transfusions with three units of whole blood. She was stabilized and returned to the nursing home.

Discharge diagnoses: (1) Pressure ulcer, sacrum; (2) chronic lymphocytic leukemia.

L89.153	Pressure ulcer of sacral region, stage 3
C91.10	Chronic lymphocytic leukemia of B-cell type not having achieved remission
0HB6XZZ	Destruction of back skin, external approach
0HX6XZZ	Transfer back skin, external approach
30233H1	Transfusion of nonautologous whole blood into peripheral vein, percutaneous approach

Comments: The site and the stage of the pressure ulcer are captured in one code. After the excisional debridement, closure was accomplished by flap graft, which is synonymous with pedicle graft of skin. This is classified to the root operation "Transfer."

4. Inpatient admission: The patient, an elderly man, had an acute onset of swelling, erythema, and tenderness in the left anterior neck. He was admitted for evaluation and IV antibiotic therapy, with provisional diagnoses of thyroiditis and cellulitis. Radiological findings showed a large, mixed-density, soft-tissue mass in the left lower neck compatible with cellulitis. The mass appeared to involve the soft tissue of the neck but not the thyroid gland. Abscess formation could not be excluded, although none was directly visualized. His symptomatology responded well to antibiotic therapy.

Discharge diagnoses: (1) Cellulitis, (2) possible abscess.

L03.221   Cellulitis of neck

Comments: The thyroiditis is not coded because it was ruled out.

5. Inpatient admission: The patient's admitting diagnoses were abdominal pain and ventral wall hernia. The woman presented for hernia repair. At the time of surgery, she was noted to have numerous mid-abdominal adhesions of the peritoneum, mostly in the area of a previous midline scar. Sharp lysis of the extensive adhesions was undertaken, and then the hernia was repaired. Postoperatively, the patient did very well.

Discharge diagnoses: (1) Ventral wall hernia, (2) abdominal adhesions.

K43.90   Ventral hernia, unspecified, without obstruction or gangrene

K66.0   Peritoneal adhesions (postprocedural) (postinfection)

0WQF0ZZ   Repair abdominal wall, open approach

0DNW0ZZ   Release peritoneum, open approach

Comments: The express reason for admission was hernia repair; therefore, the hernia is sequenced as the principal diagnosis. Abdominal adhesions are coded because they required extensive lysis before attention could be directed to the hernia repair and were documented as a discharge diagnosis. The lysis of adhesions is coded to the root operation "Release."

6. Inpatient admission: The patient was admitted for intravenous antibiotic treatment of cellulitis of the left leg secondary to a minor scratch. By the third hospital day, the erythema was much improved. During the entire hospitalization, the patient, a known opioid drug abuser, exhibited considerable drug-seeking behavior and requested narcotics, especially IV morphine. All narcotics were discontinued on the third hospital day, and he exhibited no withdrawal symptoms. He was discharged for follow-up in the physician's office.

Discharge diagnoses: (1) Cellulitis, left leg; (2) drug abuse; (3) scratch, left leg.

L03.116   Cellulitis of left lower limb

F11.10   Opioid abuse, uncomplicated

Comments: No code is assigned for the minor injury (scratch on leg) because it had progressed to cellulitis, and the cellulitis is coded instead.

11. DISEASES OF THE MUSCULOSKELETAL SYSTEM AND CONNECTIVE TISSUE

1. Inpatient admission: The patient had experienced increasingly severe pain in his left arm, left shoulder, and neck for two months. A magnetic resonance imaging performed prior to admission showed evidence of a C7-T1 disc herniation. His only other health problem was benign hypertension, controlled with medications. He was admitted for a cervical laminotomy and complete cervical discectomy of the cervical thoracic disc, which was performed by oblique, muscle-splitting incision. His postoperative course was unremarkable, and he was discharged after two days.

Discharge diagnoses: (1) Cervical disc herniation, C7-T1; (2) benign essential hypertension.

M50.23	Other cervical disc displacement, cervicothoracic region
I10	Essential (primary) hypertension
0RT50ZZ	Resection of cervicothoracic vertebral disc, open approach

Comments: The cervical disc herniation is at C7-T1 (between the last cervical disc and the first thoracic disc); therefore, the code for the cervical thoracic region is selected. Hypertension, although under control, is coded because it is a coexisting chronic, systemic condition that meets the UHDDS definition of additional diagnosis. Because the entire disc is removed, "Resection" is the root operation.

2. Outpatient encounter (episode 1): The patient's complaints were neck pain that radiated into both arms, hand pain with numbness and clumsiness, and electric shock–type pains down her body when she bent down. A magnetic resonance imaging scan showed marked spinal stenosis at C3-C4 and C5-C6. She was to be admitted for repair of the spinal stenosis.

Diagnosis: Spinal stenosis.

| M48.02 | Spinal stenosis, cervical region |
| BR30ZZZ | Magnetic resonance imaging (MRI) of cervical spine |

Comments: The symptoms (pain, numbness, and clumsiness) are integral to the diagnosis of spinal stenosis and therefore are not coded. Code BR30ZZZ is assigned for the magnetic imaging of the spine.

Inpatient admission (episode 2): The patient was admitted for repair of spinal stenosis. A laminectomy with fusion of C3-C4 and C5-C6 was carried out using an anterior approach with a graft of bone excised from the right iliac crest.

Discharge diagnosis: Severe cervical spine stenosis.

M48.02	Spinal stenosis, cervical region
0RG2070	Fusion of 2 or more cervical vertebral joints with autologous tissue substitute, anterior approach, anterior column, open approach
0SB40ZZ	Excision of lumbosacral disc, open approach

Comments: The procedure code 0RG2070 includes the number of vertebral joints fused: two or more. An anterior approach is used and is indicated in the qualifier character. The bone graft harvesting is classified to the root operation "Excision."

3. Inpatient admission: The patient, a 33-year-old woman, had a history of low back pain. She recently developed intractable left sciatic pain and paresthesia. Lumbar magnetic resonance imaging procedures, performed prior to admission, showed progressive lumbosacral disc herniation on the left. She was also receiving medications for gastric ulcers and asthma, and these were continued during the hospital stay. A lumbosacral microdiscectomy was performed for a protruded lumbosacral disc herniation, which also had a subligamentous extrusion. The patient recovered with resolution of symptoms and was discharged to follow up with her physician in one week.

Discharge diagnoses: (1) Lumbosacral disc extrusion, (2) gastric ulcers, (3) asthma.

M51.27	Other intervertebral disc displacement, lumbar region
K25.9	Gastric ulcer, unspecified as acute or chronic, without hemorrhage or perforation
J45.909	Unspecified asthma, uncomplicated
0RBB0ZZ	Excision of thoracolumbar vertebral disc, open approach

Comments: The term **Extrusion** leads to the note "see Displacement, intervertebral disc" in the Alphabetic Index. Because asthma and ulcers are under current treatment and meet the UHDDS definition of additional diagnoses, they are assigned codes as coexisting conditions. In a microdiscectomy, only a portion of the disc is removed, so the root operation "Excision" is used.

4. Inpatient admission: The teenage patient had complained of left hip pain for the past three weeks. The pain started after a fall that occurred while he was playing basketball in a gym. X-rays revealed a grade I, slipped capital femoral epiphysis of the left hip. The hip was pinned percutaneously, and the postoperative course was uneventful.

Discharge diagnosis: Slipped femoral epiphysis, left hip.

S72.022A	Displaced fracture of epiphysis (separation) (upper) of left femur, initial encounter
W18.30xA	Fall on same level, unspecified, initial encounter
Y92.39	Other specified sports and athletic area as the place of occurrence of the external cause
Y93.67	Activity, basketball
Y99.8	Other external cause status
0QH734Z	Insertion of internal fixation device into left upper femur, percutaneous approach

Comments: For the slipped epiphysis, refer to the term "slipped" in the Index. See the note for subterm "current traumatic," which says to code as fracture by site. ICD-10-CM guidelines for fractures state that a fracture not specified as displaced or not displaced is coded as displaced. Activity and status codes are included for playing basketball as a recreational activity.

There was no reduction of the slipped epiphysis, but an "internal fixation device" was inserted.

5. Inpatient admission: An emergency open repair of a right rotator cuff tear was performed on this patient after she was crushed between a sliding patio door and its frame at her apartment. Exploration revealed a torn right rotator cuff and ruptured deltoid muscle, right shoulder. Open repair of the rotator cuff tendon and repair of the ruptured deltoid muscle were accomplished. The patient recovered and was discharged to follow-up in one week.

Discharge diagnoses: (1) Tear, right rotator cuff; (2) rupture, deltoid muscle.

S43.421A	Sprain of right rotator cuff capsule, initial encounter
S46.811A	Strain of other muscles, fascia and tendons at shoulder and upper arm level, right arm, initial encounter
W23.0xxA	Caught, crushed, jammed, or pinched between moving objects, initial encounter
Y92.099	Unspecified place in other non-institutional residence as the place of occurrence of the external cause
0LQ10ZZ	Repair right shoulder tendon, open approach
0KQ50ZZ	Repair right shoulder muscle, open approach

Comments: Either condition (rotator cuff tear or ruptured deltoid muscle) can be sequenced as the principal diagnosis because both were present on admission, both were surgically corrected, and both meet the UHDDS definition of principal diagnosis. The seventh character to indicate initial encounter is assigned. For the ruptured deltoid muscle, refer to the Index for the main term **Rupture,** subterm "muscle (traumatic)"; see also the main term **Strain.** Under the main term **Strain,** subterm "muscle," the coder is directed to see **Injury,** muscle, by site, strain. Because a specific entry for the deltoid muscle is not available and the deltoid is in the shoulder area, see **Injury,** muscle, shoulder, strain. The code referenced in the Index is for unspecified muscle. Code S46.811A is selected for strain of other muscle of the shoulder.

The type of home is not specified, so code Y92.099 is selected. Activity is not stated, so no code is assigned.

6. Inpatient admission: The patient, status post cadaveric renal and pancreas transplants with type 2 diabetes and diabetic peripheral angiopathy, had a nonhealing ulcer on his left heel with muscle necrosis that had been debrided three weeks earlier. He came to the emergency department complaining of a three-day history of left foot pain, fever, and foul-smelling discharge from the ulcer. He was admitted, and a left below-the-knee amputation at the distal portion of the femur was performed.

Discharge diagnosis: Diabetic gangrene of the left foot.

E11.52	Type 2 diabetes mellitus with diabetic peripheral angiopathy with gangrene
L97.423	Non-pressure chronic ulcer of left heel and midfoot with necrosis
Z94.0	Kidney transplant status
Z94.83	Pancreas transplant status
0Y6J0Z3	Detachment at left lower leg, low, open approach

Comments: ICD-10-CM allows for the classification of the diabetes along with the manifestations in one code: E11.52 includes type 2 diabetes, peripheral angiopathy, and gangrene. Codes identifying the patient as status post renal and pancreas transplants are significant to the current episode of care and should be included.

For the procedure code, amputation is coded to the root operation "Detachment." The qualifier "low" in the seventh character is defined as amputation at the distal portion of the shaft of the femur.

7. Inpatient admission: The patient, an elderly man with chest pain, was admitted to rule out acute myocardial infarct. Two weeks prior to admission, he had a respiratory infection that caused excessive coughing. On evaluation, there was no evidence of cardiac problems, and his chest pain was believed to be due to costochondritis secondary to excessive coughing.

Discharge diagnosis: Costochondritis.

M94.0	Chondrocostal junction syndrome [Tietze]
R05	Cough

Comments: Costochondritis is assigned as the principal diagnosis because suspected conditions are coded as confirmed diagnoses for inpatients. Code R05 is assigned for the excessive coughing, which is the underlying cause of the costochondritis. No code is assigned for the chest pain, which is integral to the costochondritis.

8. Inpatient admission: The patient, an elderly woman, had severe pain in her left hip. The pain started after a hip fracture five years ago, when she was injured in an automobile accident. Her admission diagnoses were traumatic arthritis and ankylosis of the left hip. She also had a pacemaker and was a type 2 diabetic. A total hip replacement was performed without complication.

Discharge diagnoses: (1) Arthritis and ankylosis secondary to old hip fracture, left side; (2) diabetes mellitus.

M12.552	Traumatic arthropathy, left hip
M24.652	Ankylosis, left hip
S72.002S	Fracture of unspecified part of neck of left femur, subsequent encounter
E11.9	Type 2 diabetes mellitus without complications
Z95.0	Presence of cardiac pacemaker
V49.9xxS	Car occupant (driver) (passenger) injured in unspecified traffic accident
0SRB0JZ	Replacement of left hip joint with synthetic substitute, open approach

Comments: ICD-10-CM allows for laterality; in this case, codes M12.552 and M24.652 include the designation of the left hip in the sixth character. In ICD-10-CM late effects of a fracture are coded as fracture, with the seventh-character extension "S" to indicate sequelae. The Alphabetic Index instructs that fracture of the hip is coded as neck of the femur, so code S72.002S is selected for the late effect of the left hip fracture. The External cause code with the seventh-character extension "S" indicates sequelae.

For the procedure code, the type of prosthesis used for the hip replacement is not specified, so the qualifier "Z" is selected.

9. Inpatient admission: The patient's right knee had bothered him for several months. He had a very painful chronic, indolent, septic prepatellar bursa. It was treated with many antibiotics, cleared up, and then recurred. He was currently admitted for surgical intervention. The site was incised and drained, and then the prepatellar bursa was partially excised. He was referred for physical therapy on discharge.

Discharge diagnosis: Septic joint, right knee.

M00.861	Arthritis due to other bacteria, right knee
0MBN0ZZ	Excision of right knee bursa and ligament, open approach

Comments: A separate code is not assigned to identify the incision and drainage of the knee because it is integral to the procedural process for the bursectomy.

10. **Inpatient admission:** For two weeks, the patient had been complaining of left sciatica and had failed outpatient management with bed rest and pain medications. A magnetic resonance imaging procedure confirmed L5-S1 disc herniation on the left. She was hospitalized at complete bed rest with conservative management and pain medications as needed. She received good pain relief with IV pain medication and an epidural steroid injection. She was discharged for physical therapy follow-up.

Discharge diagnosis: Intractable pain secondary to herniation of the L5-S1 disc, with S1 radiculopathy.

M51.27	Other intervertebral disc displacement, lumbosacral region
3E0S33Z	Introduction of anti-inflammatory into epidural space, percutaneous approach

Comments: Intractable pain and radiculopathy are integral to the underlying disease and are therefore not coded. The epidural injection of the steroid is covered in code 3E0S33Z. Steroid is an anti-inflammatory; therefore, the sixth character value "3" is selected.

11. **Inpatient admission:** The patient was admitted with traumatic arthritis and ankylosis of the left hip due to an old fracture of the femoral neck suffered in a car accident. She was in good health except for suffering mild arteriosclerotic heart disease. X-rays were taken before surgery to evaluate the extent of this problem, but it was felt that it did not contradict the planned surgery. Both the femoral head and acetabulum of the left hip were replaced with a prosthesis. The surgery and postoperative course were without complication. She was transferred to a nursing home for rehabilitation therapy.

Discharge diagnoses: (1) Arthritis and ankylosis, left hip; (2) arteriosclerotic cardiovascular disease.

M24.652	Ankylosis, left hip
M12.552	Traumatic arthropathy, left hip
S72.002S	Fracture of unspecified part of neck of left femur
I25.10	Atherosclerotic heart disease of native coronary artery without angina pectoris
V49.9xxS	Car occupant (driver) (passenger) injured in unspecified traffic accident, subsequent encounter
0SRB0JZ	Replacement of left hip joint with synthetic substitute, open approach

Comments: Either ankylosis or arthritis could be designated as the principal diagnosis because both were equally responsible for the admission. Ankylosis and arthritis are late effects of the previous hip fracture, which is reflected in the S72.002S code as a sequela. Replacement of both the femoral head and the acetabulum is classified as a total hip replacement, 0SRB0JZ. The type of bearing surface for the hip replacement is not known, so the qualifier is listed as "Z."

12. Inpatient admission: The patient, a 12-year-old female, had a history of scoliosis secondary to neurofibromatosis, type 1, and had been treated with a brace for four years. She was now admitted for surgical repair of the progressive scoliosis. A posterior lumbar fusion of T2-L3 using Isola instrumentation interbody fusion device and right iliac crest bone grafting was performed. Her postoperative course was uneventful.

Discharge diagnosis: Thoracolumbar scoliosis secondary to neurofibromatosis, type 1.

M41.55	Other secondary scoliosis, thoracolumbar region
Q85.00	Neurofibromatosis, unspecified
0RG8031	Fusion of 8 or more thoracic vertebral joints with interbody internal fixation device, posterior approach, posterior column, open approach
0RGA031	Fusion of thoracolumbar vertebral joint with interbody internal fixation device, posterior approach, posterior column, open approach
0QB20ZZ	Excision of right pelvic bone, open approach

Comments: In the Index, scoliosis secondary NEC is coded to M41.50. See the Tabular List to select the more specific code for the site. Q85.00 is listed for the neurofibromatosis.

The T2-L3 vertebrae were fused, meaning that 11 of the 12 thoracic vertebrae were fused in this area. In addition, three lumbar vertebrae were fused. Therefore, two procedure codes are necessary for the fusion procedure, one for the thoracic and one for the thoracolumbar vertebral joints. The ICD-10-PCS Official Coding Guidelines (B3.10.C) state that if an "interbody fusion device" is used to render the joint immobile (alone or containing other material like bone graft), the procedure is coded with the device value "interbody fixation device." The harvesting of the iliac crest bone for grafting is coded separately to the root operation "Excision."

12. COMPLICATIONS OF PREGNANCY, CHILDBIRTH, AND THE PUERPERIUM

1. **Inpatient admission (episode 1):** The patient was admitted with pregnancy at term. A repeat low transverse cervical cesarean section and elective laparoscopic bilateral tubal ligation were performed. A 3,300-gram male infant was delivered, with Apgar scores of 9 and 10. The postoperative course was unremarkable. On day 3, the mother's staples were removed, and both the mother and the baby were discharged.

Discharge diagnoses: (1) Term pregnancy delivered, (2) elective tubal ligation.

O34.21	Maternal care for scar from previous cesarean delivery
Z37.0	Single live birth
Z30.2	Encounter for sterilization
10D00Z1	Extraction of products of conception, low cervical, open approach
0UL74ZZ	Occlusion of bilateral fallopian tubes, percutaneous endoscopic approach

Comments: The *ICD-10-CM Official Guidelines for Coding and Reporting* provide guidance on the selection of the principal or first-listed diagnosis in obstetrical encounters. In cases of cesarean delivery, the principal diagnosis should be the reason for the cesarean—unless the reason for the admission/encounter was unrelated to the condition necessitating the cesarean delivery. The fact that the patient had a previous cesarean delivery (O34.21) is therefore assigned first. The summary does not indicate any other condition requiring cesarean delivery. Code Z30.2 is assigned to indicate that a tubal ligation was performed for elective sterilization. To indicate the outcome of delivery (e.g., single birth, multiple birth), code Z37.0 is assigned.

The C-section delivery is classified to the Obstetrics Section, root operation "Extraction." The tubal ligation procedure is classified to the root operation "Occlusion."

Inpatient admission (episode 2): The patient underwent a cesarean section seven days earlier. She had an infection in the operative wound at the time she was admitted through the emergency department with a temperature of 101 degrees and minimal drainage of the incision. IV Kefzol was started, but she continued to spike up to a temperature of 101.8 degrees. The antibiotic therapy was changed, and the patient defervesced.

Discharge diagnosis: Postoperative wound infection.

O86.0	Infection of obstetric surgical wound

Comments: The postoperative wound infection is classified to the pregnancy chapters of ICD-10-CM because it represents a complication of the postpartum period and is related to an obstetrical wound.

2. **Inpatient admission:** This type 1 diabetic patient was status post a low transverse cesarean delivery 12 days earlier. The day before admission, she noticed a large amount of bloody discharge from her wound. She was taken to the operating room, where the wound was opened and a very large hematoma was evacuated. The wound was drained and packed. Three days later, a secondary wound closure was accomplished.

Discharge diagnoses: (1) Postpartum hematoma, (2) diabetes mellitus.

O90.2	Hematoma of obstetric wound
O24.03	Pre-existing diabetes mellitus, type 1, in the puerperium
Z79.4	Long term (current) use of insulin
0JCB0ZZ	Extirpation of matter from perineum subcutaneous tissue and fascia, open approach
0WQFXZZ	Repair abdominal wall, external approach

Comments: The ICD-10-CM code for diabetes in pregnancy includes the type of diabetes. Because there are no manifestations, an additional diabetes code is not necessary. The code for long-term insulin use is optional.

3. **Inpatient admission:** The patient, a 39-year-old female, gravida II, para 1, was admitted in active labor at 39 weeks gestation. She was dilated to 5 centimeters approximately six hours following admission. Pitocin augmentation was started, and she progressed to complete dilation. Outlet forceps were used. There was no episiotomy, but there was a second-degree perineal laceration that was repaired with 3-0 Dexon. A male infant was delivered weighing 2,835 grams, with Apgar scores of 9 and 9. The patient had indicated before delivery that she desired a sterilization procedure. Following delivery, a laparoscopic bilateral tubal ligation was accomplished.

Discharge diagnoses: (1) Delivery at term, (2) perineal laceration, (3) elective sterilization.

O66.5	Attempted application of vacuum extractor and forceps
O70.1	Second degree perineal laceration during delivery
Z37.0	Single live birth
Z30.2	Encounter for sterilization
10D07Z3	Extraction of products of conception, low forceps, via natural or artificial opening
0WQNXZZ	Repair female perineum, external approach
0UL74ZZ	Occlusion of bilateral fallopian tubes, percutaneous endoscopic approach

Comments: The forceps delivery code is located in the Index under the main term **Delivery,** subterm "forceps." Code Z30.2 shows that the tubal ligation was performed for the purpose of voluntary sterilization.

4. Inpatient admission: The admitting diagnoses were intrauterine pregnancy at 29 weeks gestation, premature labor, premature rupture of membranes times 12 days, and chorioamnionitis. Radiological findings revealed a vertex right occiput transverse presentation with a compound presentation of a fetal hand. Because the patient had a temperature of 101.4 degrees, chorioamnionitis was presumed and antibiotics were started. On a subsequent examination, the fetus was found to be presenting vertex left occiput anterior with right hand compound presentation. The right hand was reducible and was pushed up toward the left side of the fetal body. Following a prolonged second stage, a female infant with Apgar scores of 5 and 7 was delivered spontaneously over an intact perineum. A prior cesarean section scar was found to be intact with no lacerations.

Discharge diagnoses: (1) Delayed delivery following premature rupture of membrane, (2) chorioamnionitis.

O60.13x0	Preterm labor second trimester with preterm delivery third trimester
O42.113	Preterm premature rupture of membranes, onset of labor more than 24 hours following rupture, third trimester
O34.21	Maternal care for scar from previous cesarean delivery
O41.1230	Chorioamnionitis, third trimester
O32.8xx0	Maternal care for other malpresentation of fetus
Z37.0	Single live birth
10E0XZZ	Delivery of products of conception, external approach

Comments: Premature labor is designated as the principal diagnosis because it necessitated admission. The third trimester is from 28 weeks 0 days until delivery. Ruptured membranes did not necessitate admission because they had been ruptured for 12 days. Code O42.113 indicates a delayed delivery. Although there was malpresentation of the fetus, it was reducible and did not result in obstructed labor, so a code is not assigned for obstructed labor. The seventh character for obstetrics codes, when required, is 0 for single gestations or multiple gestations when the fetus is not specified.

5. Inpatient admission: The patient, gravida II, para 1, was admitted in labor with a 27-week pregnancy. The fetus was in a complete breech position. Labor ceased within a few hours after admission, but the patient was observed closely because she had a history of recurrent pregnancy loss. By the second day, contractions recurred and she rapidly progressed to complete dilation. Because the breech presentation resulted in obstruction, an emergent low cervical cesarean section was performed, and a living female infant was delivered. The postpartum course was uneventful, and the patient was discharged in good condition on the third postoperative day.

Discharge diagnosis: Preterm delivery, complicated by breech presentation.

O60.12x0	Preterm labor second trimester with preterm delivery second trimester
O64.1xx0	Obstructed labor due to breech presentation
O26.22	Pregnancy care for patient with recurrent pregnancy loss, second trimester
Z37.0	Single live birth
10D00Z1	Extraction of products of conception, low cervical, open approach

Comments: In this case the breech position resulted in the need for a cesarean delivery. Although the code resulting in a cesarean delivery is ordinarily listed as the principal diagnosis, the threatened early delivery was the reason for admission and therefore is listed first. The seventh character for obstetrics codes, when required, is 0 for single gestations or multiple gestations when the fetus is not specified. The second trimester ends at 28 weeks. ICD-10-CM provides a combination code that combines obstructed labor and the reason for the obstruction into a single code. Subcategory O26.2- is assigned for a patient with a history of recurrent pregnancy loss who is currently pregnant.

6. Inpatient admission: The patient, gravida II, para 1, was admitted at 37 weeks gestation with spontaneous rupture of membranes and contractions every two to three minutes. She had a history of congenital heart block with pacemaker. Because there was no descent, even though she was pushing adequately, three attempts at forceps delivery were made with no success due to cephalopelvic disproportion. Because of failure of forceps due to bony pelvic obstruction, a primary low transverse cesarean section was performed. A live single male was delivered. The postoperative course was uneventful.

Discharge diagnosis: Cesarean delivery of term, live infant, complicated by bony pelvis and cephalopelvic disproportion and failed forceps.

O65.4	Obstructed labor due to fetopelvic disproportion, unspecified
O66.5	Attempted application of vacuum extractor and forceps
Z37.0	Single live birth
Z95.0	Presence of cardiac pacemaker
10D00Z1	Extraction of products of conception, low cervical, open approach

Comments: The condition that required the cesarean delivery was the obstruction due to the cephalopelvic disproportion. ICD-10-CM has a combination code for these conditions. The congenital heart block was under control by the pacemaker and so no code is assigned for the condition, but a status code indicating that the patient had a pacemaker is assigned. Diagnosis code O66.5 is assigned to indicate the failed forceps prior to the cesarean delivery.

7. Inpatient admission: The patient was admitted with an intrauterine pregnancy at 34 weeks gestation in preterm labor. The labor ceased spontaneously, and she was discharged the next day.

Discharge diagnosis: Preterm labor.

O47.03	False labor before 37 completed weeks of gestation, third trimester

Comments: The code for the preterm labor includes the fact that the patient is in the third trimester.

8. Inpatient admission: The patient, at 10 weeks gestation, was admitted for severe dehydration due to hyperemesis gravidarum. The patient had glaucoma, and treatment with eye drops was continued during the patient's stay. She responded well to IV fluid hydration and antiemetics.

Discharge diagnoses: (1) Hyperemesis gravidarum with dehydration, (2) glaucoma.

O21.1	Hyperemesis gravidarum with metabolic disturbance
E86.0	Dehydration
H40.9	Unspecified glaucoma

Comments: Code O21.1 covers the fact that the patient is less than 20 weeks gestation and has a metabolic disturbance (dehydration). Code E86.0 is assigned to add specific information on the nature of the metabolic disturbance. A code is assigned for the glaucoma because it was treated, but there is no evidence that it complicated the pregnancy. Every condition that may coexist with pregnancy is not necessarily a complication of the pregnancy or affected adversely by the pregnancy.

9. **Inpatient admission:** The patient was admitted for Prostin termination of a nonviable fetus at 27 1/2 weeks gestation. An ultrasound prior to admission showed severe renal malformations in the dysmorphic fetus. A pediatric urology consult concluded fetal nonviability secondary to severe oligohydramnios, enlarged kidneys, and a nonoperable candidate. A Prostin capsule was placed intravaginally, and the patient went on to have a spontaneous vaginal delivery of a stillborn female. The patient was discharged the following day.

Discharge diagnoses: (1) Spontaneous vaginal delivery of stillborn fetus with multiple congenital anomalies (pregnancy), (2) oligohydramnios.

O36.4xx0	Maternal care for intrauterine death
O35.8xx0	Maternal care for other (suspected) fetal abnormality and damage
O41.02x0	Oligohydramnios, second trimester
Z37.1	Single stillbirth
10A07ZX	Abortion of products of conception, abortifacient, via natural or artificial opening

Comments: The seventh character is for the fetus, unspecified or not applicable. The code for oligohydramnios includes specification of the trimester; 27 weeks is the second trimester.

10. **Inpatient admission:** When admitted, this woman, with triplet gestation at 28 weeks, was thought to have had premature rupture of membranes. She was placed on magnesium sulfate after rupture of membranes was ruled out. Tocolysis and fetal monitoring were continued until she underwent spontaneous rupture of membranes one week later. She had a rapid vaginal delivery with liveborn triplets.

Discharge diagnosis: Spontaneous vaginal delivery of liveborn triplets.

O60.14x0	Preterm labor third trimester with preterm delivery third trimester
O30.103	Triplet pregnancy, unspecified number of placenta and unspecified number of amniotic sacs, third trimester
Z37.51	Triplets, all liveborn
10E0XZZ	Delivery of products of conception, external approach
10H073Z	Insertion of monitoring electrode into products of conception, via natural or artificial opening

Comments: This patient is at 28 weeks pregnancy, which is the beginning point of the third trimester. Because rupture of membranes was ruled out, a code for this condition cannot be assigned. However, she went into labor and delivered one week after admission; code O60.14x0 should be assigned. Code O30.103 is assigned to indicate that this was a triplet gestation, with the number of placenta and amniotic sacs unspecified. Code 10E0XZZ can be assigned for the uncomplicated obstetrics delivery.

11. Inpatient admission: The patient, a 44-year-old female, gravida I, para 0, was admitted for termination of an intrauterine fetal death. On a routine office visit 10 days earlier, no fetal heartbeat was heard. An ultrasound confirmed the suspicions. She chose termination of the pregnancy rather than waiting for a spontaneous delivery and was admitted. A Pitocin drip was started and some contractions were obtained, but the cervix remained unchanged. Dilation and curettage were performed, and she was discharged that afternoon.

Discharge diagnoses: (1) Intrauterine fetal death at 23 weeks, (2) macerated fetus, (3) elderly primigravida.

O36.4xx0	Maternal care for intrauterine death
O09.512	Supervision of elderly primigravida, second trimester
10A07ZZ	Abortion of products of conception, via natural or artificial opening

Comments: The principal diagnosis and reason for admission are intrauterine fetal death. Weeks of gestation were 23 weeks, so second trimester is selected. Code O09.512, for elderly primigravida, is assigned, which includes women who will be 35 years of age or older at the expected date of delivery. The macerated fetus is not a complication of pregnancy, labor, or delivery and is not coded.

12. Inpatient admission: The 14-year-old patient (gravida I, para 0) is pregnant at 25 weeks gestation. She was admitted with abdominal pain and questionable labor. On examination she was 50 percent effaced and tight fingertip dilated with cephalic presentation. She was placed on Terbutaline. By the next day, she was without discomfort or contractions and was discharged.

Discharge diagnosis: Premature labor.

| O60.02 | Preterm labor without delivery, second trimester |
| O09.612 | Supervision of young primigravida, second trimester |

Comments: Code O60.02 for premature labor without delivery in the second trimester is assigned as the patient is at 25 weeks gestation. Premature labor was documented, but the labor was arrested and delivery did not occur. Code O09.612 is assigned for a primigravida in the second trimester, less than 16 years of age at expected date of delivery, as the patient is 14 years old.

13. Inpatient admission: The young patient, gravida I, para 0, ab 0, at 43 weeks gestation, presented in labor and labored poorly but succeeded in reaching 4 to 5 centimeters. Augmentation with Pitocin resulted in no change after several hours, and a primary lower uterine segmental cesarean section was performed due to prolonged labor, with birth of a 7-pound, 5-ounce female. The patient did well after delivery and was discharged on the fourth postoperative day.

Discharge diagnoses: (1) Postterm, intrauterine pregnancy; (2) failure to progress in labor, with prolonged first stage.

O63.0	Prolonged first stage (of labor)
O48.1	Prolonged pregnancy
Z37.0	Single live birth
10D00Z1	Extraction of products of conception, low cervical, open approach

Comments: Code O63.0 is assigned for prolonged first stage of labor. Code O48.1 indicates the postterm pregnancy, which is a pregnancy that has advanced beyond 42 completed weeks gestation and is assigned because the patient is at 43 weeks.

14. Inpatient admission: The patient, gravida II, para 1, was admitted at approximately 25 1/2 weeks gestation with a history of contractions for 24 hours. She was contracting every four to six minutes. Radiological findings showed an intrauterine fetal death of fetus 1 of the triplet pregnancy but that the other two were progressing normally. The contractions stopped and then started again. The patient was given magnesium sulfate for tocolysis but contracted through the magnesium and was placed on Ritadrine. Because she then developed a fever with suspected chorioamnionitis and was in active labor, a primary low cervical cesarean section delivered three male infants, two liveborn and one fetal death. Postoperatively, she did well on antibiotics.

Discharge diagnoses: (1) Cesarean delivery of triplets (two liveborn and one fetal death) at 25 1/2 weeks, (2) chorioamnionitis.

O60.12x0	Preterm labor second trimester with preterm delivery second trimester
O36.4xx1	Maternal care for intrauterine death
O30.112	Triplet pregnancy with two or more monochorionic fetuses, second trimester
O41.1220	Chorioamnionitis, second trimester
Z37.61	Triplets, some liveborn
10D00Z1	Extraction of products of conception, low cervical, open approach

Comments: The patient was admitted in early labor with a 25-completed-week gestation with subsequent delivery; 25 weeks is in the second trimester. It was noted that one of the triplets, identified as fetus 1, was dead. Code O36.4xx1 is assigned for maternal care for intrauterine death, with the seventh character "1" to indicate the code applies to fetus 1. Code O30.112 is assigned for triplet pregnancy with two or more monochorionic fetuses, second trimester. She developed suspected chorioamnionitis, and suspected conditions on inpatient admissions should be coded as though confirmed. The outcome of delivery was triplets, two liveborn and one fetal death; therefore, code Z37.61 is assigned.

15. Inpatient admission: The young patient in the 37th week of gestation was admitted with contractions occurring every few minutes. The cervix was 25 percent effaced with a 6-centimeter dilation. Although she had undergone a previous cesarean section, she wished a trial at vaginal delivery. The membranes were artificially ruptured. Six hours later, she was tried on Pitocin augmentation and within the hour progressed to complete dilation and began pushing. She pushed for two hours and was unable to progress satisfactorily. She was taken to surgery, where a repeat low cervical cesarean section was performed for obstructed labor due to cephalo-pelvic disproportion. A healthy, single, liveborn female was delivered. The postpartum course was uneventful.

Discharge diagnoses: (1) Intrauterine pregnancy at term, (2) previous cesarean section, (3) cephalopelvic disproportion (CPD).

O65.4xx0	Obstructed labor due to fetopelvic disproportion, unspecified
O34.21	Maternal care for scar from previous cesarean delivery
Z37.0	Single live birth
10D00Z1	Extraction of products of conception, low cervical, open approach
10907ZC	Drainage of amniotic fluid, therapeutic from products of conception, via natural or artificial opening

Comments: The obstructed labor due to cephalopelvic disproportion is designated as the principal diagnosis because it necessitated the performance of a cesarean section for delivery. Only one code is needed to reflect the obstruction and the CPD. Code O34.21 is assigned for maternal care for a scar from previous cesarean delivery because the patient had undergone a previous cesarean section. The artificial rupture of membranes is coded to the Obstetrics Section, root operation "Drainage," and the qualifier "amniotic fluid, therapeutic."

16. **Inpatient admission:** The patient, in her 25th week of gestation, was transferred from another hospital with complete effacement, complete dilation, and occasional contractions. She underwent a primary low cervical cesarean section with preoperative diagnoses of preterm labor, advanced cervical dilation, and failed magnesium tocolysis. Findings included a live male infant weighing 880 grams. The patient's postoperative course was uneventful except for the occurrence of hemorrhoids, which were successfully treated with suppositories.

Discharge diagnoses: (1) Intrauterine pregnancy at 25 weeks, (2) preterm labor.

O60.12x0	Preterm labor second trimester with preterm delivery second trimester
O87.2	Hemorrhoids in the puerperium
Z37.0	Single live birth
10D00Z1	Extraction of products of conception, low cervical, open approach

Comments: Preterm labor with delivery in the second trimester is coded because the patient is in the 25th week. ICD-10-CM has a specific code for hemorrhoids in the puerperium, so only code O87.2 is required.

17. **Inpatient admission:** The patient was admitted in active labor at term. She had multiple sclerosis, which had been exacerbated by the pregnancy. In the delivery room, she spontaneously delivered a liveborn female infant over a midline episiotomy without complication.

Discharge diagnoses: (1) Spontaneous vaginal delivery of term, live female; (2) multiple sclerosis.

O99.353	Diseases of the nervous system complicating pregnancy, third trimester
G35	Multiple sclerosis
Z37.0	Single live birth
10E0XZZ	Delivery of products of conception, external approach
0W8NXZZ	Division of female perineum, external approach

Comments: Multiple sclerosis represents a nonobstetrical condition of the nervous system complicating the pregnancy. An additional code of G35 is assigned to further specify the complication. Both the episiotomy and the delivery require codes in the ICD-10-PCS. The episiotomy is coded in the Medical and Surgical (rather than the Obstetrics) Section, as it is performed on the patient rather than the fetus. The episiotomy is coded to the root operation "Division," body part "female perineum."

18. **Physician office visit:** The patient came in for her routine prenatal checkup. She was a primigravida in her first trimester. There were no complications.

Diagnosis: Normal pregnancy at 10 weeks.

Z34.01	Encounter for supervision of normal first pregnancy, first trimester

Comments: This is the only code assignment necessary because no complications are present.

19. **Physician office visit:** The patient came in for her routine prenatal checkup. She was a primigravida in her first trimester. She complained of hyperemesis. She had been unable to eat and had lost 2 pounds since her last visit. Medication was prescribed. She was to call the office immediately if there was no improvement within 12 hours. She was to be rescheduled for a return visit the following week.

Diagnosis: First trimester pregnancy complicated by mild hyperemesis gravidarum.

O21.0   Mild hyperemesis gravidarum

Comments: The hyperemesis gravidarum is before 20 weeks and stated to be mild.

20. **Inpatient admission:** The patient was admitted in labor with an estimated 39-week gestation. When she was approximately 7 to 8 centimeters dilated, an amniotomy was performed that revealed meconium-stained liquor. She rapidly progressed to complete cervical dilation. Fetal distress necessitated delivery. The infant's head was visible and in the occiput anterior position. Low forceps were applied, a midline episiotomy was performed, and the infant was successfully delivered. The midline episiotomy was repaired.

Discharge diagnoses: (1) Term delivery of liveborn infant, (2) meconium-stained liquor, (3) fetal stress.

O77.9   Labor and delivery complicated by fetal stress, unspecified

O77.0   Labor and delivery complicated by meconium in amniotic fluid

Z37.0   Single live birth

10D07Z3   Extraction of products of conception, low forceps, via natural or artificial opening

0W8NXZZ   Division of female perineum, external approach

10D07Z3   Extraction of products of conception, low forceps, via natural or artificial opening

Comments: Two codes, one for fetal stress and one for meconium, are assigned. The forceps delivery and the episiotomy require separate codes in ICD-10-PCS. The low forceps delivery is coded to the root operation "Extraction," with the seventh-character qualifier "low forceps."

21. **Inpatient admission:** The patient, a young woman with estimated gestation of 29 weeks, was admitted for gestational diabetes. It was felt that close monitoring of her blood sugars was in order and the possibility of starting insulin should receive consideration. Throughout her stay, she had no problems or complications. She was maintained on an 1,800-calorie diet. Her blood sugars were borderline abnormal, and a trial at diet control was to be instituted before further consideration was given to the use of insulin.

Discharge diagnoses: (1) Gestational diabetes; (2) intrauterine pregnancy, 29 weeks.

O24.410   Gestational diabetes mellitus in pregnancy, diet controlled

Comments: The gestational diabetes in pregnancy is diet controlled at this point and therefore is coded to O24.410.

22. **Inpatient admission:** The patient, with an estimated 37-week gestation, was admitted in labor. Her prenatal course was uncomplicated, except for mild pre-existing hypertension. The labor was also uneventful, and the membranes spontaneously ruptured. A 7-pound, 3-ounce viable male was delivered. The delivery was spontaneous and vaginal, with a midline episiotomy, which extended into a third-degree laceration. The laceration was sutured. Following delivery, the mother was stable, with no apparent complications.

Discharge diagnoses: (1) Spontaneous vaginal delivery of term male infant, (2) third-degree perineal laceration.

O70.2	Third degree perineal laceration during delivery
O10.013	Pre-existing essential hypertension complicating pregnancy, third trimester
Z37.0	Single live birth
10E0XZZ	Delivery of products of conception, external approach
0W8NXZZ	Division of female perineum, external approach
0WQNXZZ	Repair female perineum, external approach

Comments: Either the pre-existing hypertension or the perineal laceration can be assigned as the principal diagnosis. ICD-10-PCS requires a code for the delivery, the episiotomy, and the "Repair" of the perineal laceration.

23. **Inpatient admission:** The patient, with an estimated gestation of 39.5 weeks, presented with spontaneous rupture of the membranes and irregular contractions. Her previous pregnancy was delivered by cesarean section. At first, labor failed to progress despite irregular contractions, and she was started on Pitocin. She then moved ahead with labor and pushed for approximately 45 minutes. The baby was delivered spontaneously, with the help of a midline episiotomy. A third-degree laceration was sutured and the episiotomy was closed.

Discharge diagnoses: (1) Term pregnancy delivered of liveborn male infant, (2) previous cesarean section, (3) third-degree laceration.

O34.21	Maternal care for scar from previous cesarean delivery
O70.2	Third degree perineal laceration during delivery
Z37.0	Single live birth
10E0XZZ	Delivery of products of conception, external approach
0W8NXZZ	Division of female perineum, external approach
0WQNXZZ	Repair female perineum, external approach

Comments: Previous cesarean and third-degree perineal laceration occurring during delivery are coded. ICD-10-PCS requires a code for the delivery, the episiotomy, and the "Repair" of the perineal laceration.

13. ABORTION AND ECTOPIC PREGNANCY

1. **Inpatient admission:** The 22-year-old patient was at 10 weeks gestation with an intrauterine pregnancy. She believed this pregnancy to be the result of a rape and did not wish to carry it to term. A complete abortion was accomplished with a dilation and curettage. There were no complications.

   Discharge diagnoses: (1) Elective abortion, (2) history of rape.

Z33.2	Encounter for elective termination of pregnancy
Z64.0	Problems related to unwanted pregnancy
T74.21xA	Adult sexual abuse, confirmed, initial encounter
10A07ZZ	Abortion of products of conception, via natural or artificial opening

   Comments: An elective abortion is classified in ICD-10-CM to the Factors Influencing Health Status and Contact with Health Services chapter, rather than the Pregnancy chapter. Because this patient confirmed that she was raped, the code for confirmed rape is used rather than the code for suspected rape. Procedure code 10A07ZZ is assigned for the abortion.

2. **Inpatient admission:** The patient, at 12 weeks gestation, wished to have the pregnancy terminated following studies showing the fetus to be anencephalic. An intrauterine saline injection produced an incomplete abortion. This procedure was followed by a dilation and curettage.

   Discharge diagnosis: Therapeutic abortion secondary to fetal abnormality.

Z33.2	Encounter for elective termination of pregnancy
O35.0xx0	Maternal care for (suspected) central nervous system malformation in fetus, not applicable or unspecified
10A07ZX	Abortion of products of conception, abortifacient, via natural or artificial opening
10D17ZZ	Extraction of products of conception, retained, via natural or artificial opening

   Comments: An elective abortion is classified in ICD-10-CM to the Factors Influencing Health Status and Contact with Health Services chapter, rather than the Pregnancy chapter. The first procedure was the abortion using saline, classified as an abortifacient. It was followed by a dilation and curettage for extraction of the retained products of conception.

3. **Inpatient admission:** The patient was admitted following a spontaneous abortion, which she experienced earlier in the day. On examination, it appeared that the abortion was incomplete, and she was bleeding heavily. A dilation and curettage was performed.

   Discharge diagnosis: Incomplete spontaneous abortion.

O03.1	Delayed or excessive hemorrhage following incomplete spontaneous abortion
10D17ZZ	Extraction of products of conception, retained, via natural or artificial opening

   Comments: The abortion was spontaneous, complicated by excessive bleeding, and incomplete, and is coded to O03.1. Code 10D17ZZ is assigned for completion of the spontaneous abortion. The root operation is "Extraction."

4. **Obstetrics clinic visit:** The patient had an elective abortion performed at another facility two days earlier. She visited the clinic because of pelvic pain, fever, and a nonbloody discharge. She was given antibiotics.

   Diagnosis: Acute endometritis following abortion.

O04.5	Genital tract and pelvic infection following (induced) termination of pregnancy
N71.0	Acute inflammatory disease of uterus

   Comments: Category O04 is for complications following an induced abortion, with a fourth character indicating that this is an infection of the genital tract. Code N71.0 is assigned as an additional code to provide more specificity regarding the complication.

5. Obstetrics clinic visit: The 35-year-old patient wished to electively terminate a pregnancy because of her hyperthyroidism, which has been difficult to control. She was at 10 weeks gestation. A complete abortion resulted from the vacuum aspiration curettage.

Diagnoses: (1) Therapeutic abortion, complete; (2) hyperthyroidism.

Z33.2	Encounter for elective termination of pregnancy
O99.281	Endocrine, nutritional and metabolic diseases complicating pregnancy, first trimester
E05.90	Thyrotoxicosis, unspecified without thyrotoxic crisis or storm
10A07Z6	Abortion of products of conception, vacuum, via natural or artificial opening

Comments: An elective abortion is classified in ICD-10-CM to the Factors Influencing Health Status and Contact with Health Services chapter, rather than the Pregnancy chapter. The reason for the abortion was thyroid dysfunction, coded to O99.281, with an additional code, E05.90, to specify the hyperthyroidism. The therapeutic abortion was completed via vacuum aspiration. The root operation is "Abortion," with the vacuum identified through the seventh-character qualifier.

6. Inpatient admission: The young patient was transferred in from another hospital, where she had been treated for a cerebrovascular accident. She was making a good recovery at the other hospital until yesterday, when she became agitated and aggressive and complained of abdominal pain without significant findings on examination. Her husband suggested the possibility of pregnancy, and an HCG assay confirmed the condition, with pregnancy estimated at 6 weeks. After a series of discussions with the patient and family, it was decided to proceed with an abortion. She was admitted here for the abortion. A complete abortion was accomplished with vacuum aspiration curettage. Her mental status improved, and she was discharged.

Discharge diagnosis: Elective abortion, complete, secondary to cerebrovascular accident.

Z33.2	Encounter for elective termination of pregnancy
O99.411	Diseases of the circulatory system complicating pregnancy, first trimester
I63.9	Cerebral infarction, unspecified
10A07Z6	Abortion of products of conception, vacuum, via natural or artificial opening

Comments: An elective abortion is classified in ICD-10-CM to the Factors Influencing Health Status and Contact with Health Services chapter, rather than the Pregnancy chapter. The reason for the abortion was an acute cerebrovascular accident, reflected by code O99.411, with the addition of code I63.9 to specify the stroke. Note that subcategory O99.4 is for diseases of the circulatory system complicating pregnancy, childbirth, or the puerperium and includes conditions in categories I00 through I99. The therapeutic abortion was completed via vacuum aspiration.

7. Inpatient admission: The patient, known to be in early pregnancy, was admitted with acute abdominal pain. Ultrasound revealed a tubal pregnancy. The tubal pregnancy was removed laparoscopically via a small incision in the abdomen. The patient was discharged the next day in good condition. She was to be seen in the doctor's office in two weeks.

Discharge diagnosis: Ectopic pregnancy.

O00.1	Tubal pregnancy
10T24ZZ	Resection of products of conception, ectopic, percutaneous endoscopic approach

Comments: Ectopic pregnancies are classified by site. The removal of the tubal pregnancy is classified to the Obstetrics Section, root operation "Resection." The procedure involved a small incision and a laparoscope, so the approach is percutaneous endoscopic.

14. CONGENITAL ANOMALIES

1. **Inpatient admission:** The 27-year-old patient was admitted for a pacemaker implant for her atrioventricular heart block, presumably congenital. A skin incision was made and a dual-chamber synchronous pacemaker was inserted into a subcutaneous pocket. The right atrioventricular transvenous leads were inserted percutaneously. She was kept on bed rest until she was stable and then discharged.

   Discharge diagnosis: Atrioventricular heart block, probably congenital in origin.

Q24.6	Congenital heart block
0JH60P2	Insertion of pacemaker, dual chamber into chest subcutaneous tissue and fascia, open approach
02HK3MA	Insertion of pacemaker lead into right ventricle, percutaneous approach
02H63MA	Insertion of pacemaker lead into right atrium, percutaneous approach

Comments: Congenital anomaly codes apply to both pediatric and adult patients; the patient's age does not preclude the use of these codes. The heart block is suspected to be congenital in origin and is coded as confirmed.

The insertion of the pacemaker requires three codes: one for the insertion of the pacemaker, one for the right atrium lead, and one for the right ventricular lead.

2. **Inpatient admission:** The patient, an infant, was admitted for repair of bilateral undescended testes. In the operating room, he underwent bilateral orchiopexies. On the second post-operative day, a diffuse paralytic ileus was visualized on a KUB. The infant began vomiting secondary to the obstruction caused by the ileus. A nasogastric tube was placed, and he was maintained on nasogastric suction and IV hydration for the following two days. On postoperative day 4, the tube was manually removed, and the patient was discharged. The postoperative ileus extended this admission by two days.

   Discharge diagnoses: (1) Undescended testes; (2) postoperative ileus, secondary to bilateral orchiopexies.

Q53.20	Undescended testicle, unspecified, bilateral
K91.3	Postprocedural intestinal obstruction
Y83.8	Other surgical procedures as the cause of abnormal reaction of the patient, or of later complication, without mention of misadventure at the time of the procedure
0VQC0ZZ	Repair bilateral testes, open approach
0D9670Z	Drainage of stomach with drainage device, via natural or artificial opening
0DP6X0Z	Removal of drainage device from stomach, external approach

Comments: Code Q53.20 includes the bilateral undescended testes. Code K91.3 provides information on the obstruction. Code K56.0 is excluded in cases of postoperative intestinal obstruction, coded to K91.3. The operation on the testes was a repair, not a reconstruction, so code Y83.8 is selected for other surgical procedures as the cause of abnormal reaction.

The objective of the orchiopexy was to repair the testes and restore the testes to their correct anatomical position; therefore, the root operation "Repair" was selected. There is a body part value for "bilateral testes," so only one procedure code is required for the procedure. The NG tube was inserted for drainage. Therefore, the root operation "Drainage" was selected and the approach is "via natural or artificial opening" because the tube is inserted through the nose. For the removal of the NG tube, the procedure is coded to the root operation "Removal," and the approach is "external." According to the ICD-10-PCS Official Coding Guidelines, "procedures performed within an orifice on structures that are visible without the aid of any instrumentation are coded to the approach External." In this instance, the tube is clearly visible.

3. Inpatient admission: The patient, a six-week-old infant, was admitted for evaluation of a fever. She was placed on IV antibiotics, and blood cultures grew out coagulase-negative *Staphylococcus*. Because a murmur was noticed on physical examination, an echocardiogram was done. This revealed physiologic peripheral branch pulmonary artery stenosis and a small left-to-right atrial shunt, most likely a patent foramen ovale.

Discharge diagnoses: (1) Coagulase-negative, community-acquired staphylococcal sepsis; (2) peripheral pulmonary artery stenosis; (3) patent foramen ovale.

A41.1	Sepsis due to other specified staphylococcus
Q21.1	Atrial septal defect
Q25.6	Stenosis of pulmonary artery

Comments: The causative bacteria for the sepsis, coagulase-negative *Staphylococcus,* is specified as an inclusion term under code A41.1. Because severe sepsis or associated acute organ failure is not documented, a code from subcategory R65.2 is not assigned. Pulmonary artery stenosis is assumed to be congenital unless specified as acquired. Foramen ovale is always congenital in nature.

4. Inpatient admission: The patient, a two-month-old infant, was referred for evaluation of a faulty airway. The mother reported that he had had noisy breathing since birth and that it had worsened recently. Severe to moderate laryngomalacia was identified on a flexible bronchoscopy. A supraglottostomy with repair of the larynx was performed without complication during the procedure or afterward. The patient received antibiotics postoperatively and was discharged in good condition.

Discharge diagnosis: Laryngomalacia.

Q31.5	Congenital laryngomalacia
0CQS0ZZ	Repair larynx, open approach
0BJ08ZZ	Inspection of tracheobronchial tree, via natural or artificial opening endoscopic

Comments: Laryngomalacia is considered to be a congenital condition whether specified as such or not. The supraglottostomy is not coded because it is only the opening of the operative site. The supraglottis is part of the larynx.

5. Inpatient admission: The patient, a 14-year-old male, had congenital honeycomb lung and type 1 diabetes. On admission, congestive heart failure was present. His breathing was labored, and lower extremity edema was evident. Recently, his oxygen requirements increased dramatically, he ran intermittent fevers, and he consumed large amounts of liquids. With diuretics, significant reduction of the pitting edema was achieved. Antidepressants were added to his medications to help his agitation and anxiety. Humidified oxygen mask, alternating percussion, and postural drainage helped his breathing. The insulin dosage and type were adjusted. He was discharged on a diabetic diet in stable condition.

Discharge diagnoses: (1) Heart failure, (2) honeycomb lung, (3) type 1 diabetes mellitus, (4) depression.

I50.9	Heart failure, unspecified
Q33.0	Congenital cystic lung
E10.9	Type 1 diabetes mellitus without complications
F32.9	Major depressive disorder, single episode, unspecified

Comments: Honeycomb lung can be acquired or congenital. Documentation must specify congenital to appropriately assign code Q33.0. Honeycomb lung is significant to the care of a patient under treatment for congestive heart failure. The symptoms mentioned (i.e., edema, labored breathing) are integral to the diagnosed conditions. ICD-10-CM guidelines state that code Z79.4 should be assigned for type 2 patients who use insulin on a long-term basis. This patient is type 1, so the code is not assigned.

6. Inpatient admission: This four-year-old patient has a diverticulum of the left ventricle. She had a pulmonary artery band inserted four years ago for another congenital defect. Shortly after the surgery, she suffered a stroke and now has a residual paralysis of the right arm. She required feeding by nursing staff as the right side is dominant. Currently, she was admitted with labored breathing and shortness of breath. Her lungs showed infiltrates on chest X-ray, and sputum culture showed presence of *Klebsiella*. She was placed on antibiotics and continuous supersaturated oxygen therapy for pneumonia, and she slowly improved. During this admission, her congenital problem was reevaluated by diagnostic testing. She was discharged in satisfactory condition.

Discharge diagnoses: (1) *Klebsiella* pneumonia; (2) monoplegia; (3) diverticulum, left ventricle.

J15.0	Pneumonia due to Klebsiella pneumoniae
Q24.8	Other specified congenital malformations of heart
I69.331	Monoplegia of upper limb following cerebral infarction affecting right dominant side
5A0522C	Extracorporeal supersaturated oxygenation, continuous

Comments: Diverticulum of the left ventricle is always a congenital defect and should be assigned to code Q24.8. Code I69.331 identifies the monoplegia as a late effect of the earlier stroke affecting the right dominant side.

7. Inpatient admission: The patient, a two-year-old male, had congenital bilateral clubfoot and atretic spinal cord at level T11-L4. He needed a walker to ambulate, using mostly the upper extremities to get around. He was admitted for repair of a left tibial torsion. A tibial rotational osteotomy was performed, with insertion of pins. He was placed in a splint postoperatively and was changed to a long leg cast the next day. The patient was discharged subsequently to follow up with the orthopedic surgeon in one week.

Discharge diagnosis: Atretic spinal cord at T11-L4 with left tibial torsion.

M21.862	Other specified acquired deformities of left lower leg
Q66.8	Other congenital deformities of feet
Q06.8	Other specified congenital malformations of spinal cord
0Q8H0ZZ	Division of left tibia, open approach
0QHH04Z	Insertion of internal fixation device into left tibia, open approach
2W3RX1Z	Immobilization of left lower leg using splint
2W3RX2Z	Immobilization of left lower leg using cast

Comments: The left tibial torsion is not stated to be congenital and is coded as other specified acquired deformity of the left lower leg. The club foot is assumed to be congenital. The most specific code for the atretic spinal cord is Q06.8, Other specified congenital malformations of the spinal cord. The osteotomy is for "Division" rather than "Drainage," so "Division" is used as the root operation. The cast and splint applications are classified under the Placement Section, root operation "Immobilization."

8. **Inpatient admission:** The patient, a 20-month-old girl, was admitted for correction of a left talipes equinovarus clubfoot. Shortly after admission, she started running a fever and it became apparent that she had acute otitis media. She was placed on antibiotics and discharged. Surgery was to be rescheduled at a later date.

Discharge diagnoses: (1) Talipes equinovarus, left; (2) bilateral otitis media.

Q66.0	Congenital talipes equinovarus
H66.93	Otitis media, unspecified, bilateral
Z53.09	Procedure and treatment not carried out because of other contraindication

Comments: The clubfoot is documented as the reason for the admission and is therefore listed as the principal diagnosis. Clubfoot can be classified as either congenital or acquired, but ICD-10-CM presumes it to be congenital unless specified otherwise. Surgery was canceled because of other contra-indication (Z53.09), namely, the otitis media. ICD-10-CM has a code that denotes the bilateral presentation of the otitis media.

9. **Inpatient admission:** The patient, a teenage male, was referred by his orthodontist for surgical correction of multiple congenital deformities. Examination revealed maxillary hypoplasia and maxillary asymmetry. He was found to have an excessive crossbite, with the maxillary midline several millimeters to the right. Surgical correction was indicated, and the plan was to perform both maxillary and mandibular osteotomies to achieve the amount of movement needed. During surgery, it was possible to move the left maxilla into its desired position without a mandibular osteotomy being performed. Postoperatively, he did very well, and the occlusion was good.

Discharge diagnoses: (1) Maxillary hypoplasia, (2) maxillary asymmetry, (3) excessive crossbite.

Procedure performed: Segmental maxillary osteotomy.

M26.24	Reverse articulation
M26.02	Maxillary hypoplasia
M26.11	Maxillary asymmetry
0NQS0ZZ	Repair left maxilla, open approach

Comments: Any of the conditions can be listed as the principal diagnosis in accordance with the guidelines. Although the surgeon did not perform an osteotomy on the mandible, a code for cancelled surgery is not assigned. The mandibular surgery was found to be unnecessary but was not a canceled procedure. The maxillary hypoplasia and asymmetry are located in the Diseases of the Digestive System chapter of ICD-10-CM rather than in the Congenital Anomalies chapter. The objective of the osteotomy was to repair the maxilla, restoring, to the extent possible, a body part to its normal anatomic structure and function.

10. **Inpatient admission:** The patient, a 10-month-old infant, had congenital extrahepatic biliary atresia. She was admitted for a liver transplant workup and at admission was in chronic liver failure. The workup included a chest X-ray, KUB, Doppler ultrasound of liver, and EKG, as well as an upper GI endoscopy of the esophagus, stomach, and duodenum.

Discharge diagnoses: (1) Extrahepatic biliary atresia; (2) placed on liver transplant list, stage II.

Q44.2	Atresia of bile ducts
K72.10	Chronic hepatic failure without coma
0DJ08ZZ	Inspection of upper intestinal tract, via natural or artificial opening endoscopic

Comments: Both conditions were present on admission and both necessitated the workup for liver transplant. Either condition can be sequenced as the principal diagnosis in accordance with the ICD-10-CM Official Coding Guidelines. The biliary atresia is presumed to be congenital unless specified otherwise.

15. PERINATAL CONDITIONS

1. Inpatient admission: The patient, a preterm, newborn male triplet (1,720 grams), was delivered by cesarean section, as were the other two liveborn mates. He initially required supplemental oxygen and a nasal prong CPAP for transient tachypnea. He was weaned five hours after birth. The one-minute Apgar score was 6, and the five-minute score was 8. He was also treated for diaper dermatitis. A circumcision was performed prior to discharge.

Discharge diagnoses: (1) Premature male triplet, (2) transient tachypnea, (3) diaper dermatitis.

Z38.69	Other multiple liveborn infant, delivered by cesarean
P07.16	Other low birth weight newborn, 1500-1749 grams
P07.30	Other preterm newborn, unspecified weeks
P22.1	Transient tachypnea of newborn
L22	Diaper dermatitis
0VTTXZZ	Resection of prepuce, external approach
5A09357	Assistance with respiratory ventilation, less than 24 consecutive hours, continuous positive airway pressure

Comments: Z38.69 is the principal diagnosis because the liveborn triplet was born on this admission by cesarean section. A code for both the preterm infant in terms of weight and weeks of gestation is assigned. Because the weeks are not specified, P07.30 is assigned. In circumcision, the foreskin, or prepuce, is removed. Because this has its own body part and it is completely removed, the root operation "Resection" is selected.

2. Inpatient admission: The patient, a one-day-old, 2,200-gram infant, was born prematurely at 34 weeks gestation. She was transferred from another hospital for evaluation of a congenital diaphragmatic hernia. Just before transfer, intubation was necessitated by some respiratory distress. The ventilatory support was continued for three days. When she was stabilized, the diaphragmatic hernia was repaired with an abdominal approach, and the hernia sac was excised. The infant progressed rapidly and was discharged on the second postoperative day.

Discharge diagnoses: (1) Prematurity, (2) diaphragmatic hernia, (3) respiratory distress.

Q79.0	Congenital diaphragmatic hernia
P07.18	Other low birth weight newborn, 2000-2499 grams
P07.32	Other preterm newborn, 32-36 completed weeks
P22.9	Respiratory distress of newborn, unspecified
0WQF0ZZ	Repair abdominal wall, open approach
5A1945Z	Respiratory ventilation, 24-96 consecutive hours

Comments: Because the patient was admitted at one day old, no code from the Z38 category is assigned. The principal diagnosis is the reason for admission, congenital diaphragmatic hernia. Code P07.18 is assigned for the prematurity and birth weight. Code P07.32 is assigned because of the additional note to identify the number of weeks of gestation, 34 weeks in this case. Intubation is not coded because it was performed at the other hospital. The objective of the hernia procedure is "Repair," and the site is the "abdominal wall." Mechanical ventilation was continued for three days, or 72 hours, so code 5A1945Z is assigned.

3. Inpatient admission: The patient, a newborn female infant, was delivered spontaneously at term. She was noticed to be jaundiced on the initial screening labs. The total bilirubin was increased, and she was started on a single session of phototherapy under bilirubin lights. She progressed rapidly and was discharged to home with the mother.

Discharge diagnoses: (1) Term female newborn, (2) neonatal jaundice.

Z38.00	Single liveborn infant, delivered vaginally
P59.9	Neonatal jaundice, unspecified
6A600ZZ	Phototherapy of skin, single

Comments: Z38.00 is the principal diagnosis because the infant was born by spontaneous vaginal delivery during this admission. An additional code is assigned for the jaundice because it was identified as a problem and required treatment.

4. Inpatient admission: The patient, a preterm male infant, was delivered vaginally at approximately 29 weeks gestation. He weighed 1,855 grams at birth. Initially he did well; but on the evening of birth, he was noted to have dusky spells when feeding. During that night, he developed tachypnea. Due to abnormal heart sounds, tachypnea, and dusky spells, an echocardiogram was performed. It showed a patent foramen ovale. The next day, the patient did well and was released to follow up with a pediatric cardiologist on an outpatient basis.

Discharge diagnoses: (1) Premature, single, male newborn; (2) patent foramen ovale.

Z38.00	Single liveborn infant, delivered vaginally
P07.17	Other low birth weight newborn, 1750-1999 grams
P07.31	Other preterm newborn, 28-31 completed weeks
Q21.1	Atrial septal defect

Comments: Z38.00 is the principal diagnosis because the infant was delivered vaginally on this admission. The birth weight and prematurity are identified by the use of codes P07.17 and P07.31, respectively. A separate code is not assigned to identify tachypnea because this is integral to patent foramen ovale.

5. Inpatient admission: The patient, a newborn preterm male infant delivered by cesarean section, weighed 2,300 grams at birth and had Apgar scores of 8 and 9. Shortly after birth, an increased respiratory rate, effort, and grunting required that he be placed on oxygen. A classical hyaline membrane disease then developed, consistent with his 32- to 33-week gestational age and size. An umbilical artery catheter on the right side was percutaneously placed immediately to allow ease in administration of IV fluids and medication. A right pneumothorax, identified on chest X-ray, was immediately needle aspirated, and a chest tube was placed. Subsequently, he was transferred to the newborn intensive care nursery at another hospital.

Discharge diagnoses: (1) Prematurity, (2) hyaline membrane disease, (3) spontaneous right pneumothorax.

Procedures performed: (1) Umbilical artery catheter placement, (2) right chest tube placement, (3) right lung aspiration.

Z38.01	Single liveborn infant, delivered by cesarean
P07.18	Other low birth weight newborn, 2000-2499 grams
P07.32	Other preterm newborn, 32-36 completed weeks
P22.0	Respiratory distress syndrome of newborn
P25.1	Pneumothorax originating in the perinatal period
0B9K30Z	Drainage of right lung with drainage device, percutaneous approach
04HE33Z	Insertion of infusion device into right internal iliac artery, percutaneous approach

Comments: Z38.01 is the principal diagnosis because the infant was born by cesarean section on this particular admission. The birth weight and prematurity are identified by the use of codes P07.18 and P07.32, respectively. Hyaline membrane disease is always a congenital condition and should be classified only to code P22.0. Pneumothorax is classified to code P25.1 only when it occurs during the perinatal period.

The pneumothorax was relieved by needle aspiration, and the chest tube was placed during the same session, so this activity is reflected as a "drainage device" in the sixth-character level. A catheter was inserted into the umbilical artery for the purpose of administering medications and infusions. There is not a specific code for this artery, but the umbilical artery is located in the Alphabetic Index, and the user is referred to the internal iliac artery. The approach was percutaneous, and the catheter serves as an "infusion device."

626

6.

Inpatient admission: The patient was delivered prematurely by cesarean section and weighed 1,750 grams. She had multiple problems, including microcephaly and congenital heart disease. This newborn was transferred to another hospital for further evaluation and intensive pediatric care.

Discharge diagnoses: (1) Prematurity, (2) microcephaly, (3) congenital heart disease.

Z38.01	Single liveborn infant, delivered by cesarean
P07.17	Other low birth weight newborn, 1750-1999 grams
P07.30	Other preterm newborn, unspecified weeks
Q24.9	Congenital malformation of heart, unspecified
Q02	Microcephaly

Comments: Z38.01 is the principal diagnosis because the infant was born by cesarean section on this admission. Congenital malformation of the heart, not otherwise specified, is assigned to code Q24.9.

7.

Inpatient admission: The patient, a six-day-old female, was admitted with respiratory distress, wheezes, and a heart murmur. She was intubated on admission and improved on the ventilator. She was extubated 48 hours later. Respiratory syncytial viral bronchiolitis was diagnosed. Other treatment included antibiotics and aerosols. An echocardiogram indicated a ventricular septal defect. She was to return at a later date for further evaluation.

Discharge diagnoses: (1) Respiratory syncytial viral bronchiolitis, (2) ventricular septal defect.

P39.8	Other specified infections specific to the perinatal period
J21.0	Acute bronchiolitis due to respiratory syncytial virus
Q21.0	Ventricular septal defect
0BH17EZ	Insertion of endotracheal airway into trachea, via natural or artificial opening
5A1945Z	Respiratory ventilation, 24-96 consecutive hours

Comments: The P39.8 code indicates that this is a newborn infection, and the J21.0 code specifies the type of infection. The patient was intubated and placed on a ventilator for 48 hours. This is a form of extracorporeal performance in which the respiratory system is taken over by the ventilator.

8.

Inpatient admission: The patient, an 11-month-old male infant, had congenital cytomegalovirus infection. Because of distorted, loud, and rattling breathing, he was admitted for evaluation of his hypertrophied tonsils and adenoids. Treatment for congenital cytomegaloviral infection was continued throughout the admission. In surgery, a microrigid laryngoscopy, a microrigid bronchoscopy, and an external adenotonsillectomy were performed. No abnormalities were noted on laryngoscopy or bronchoscopy. The patient's postoperative course was uncomplicated.

Discharge diagnoses: (1) Hypertrophied adenoids and tonsils, (2) congenital cytomegalovirus infection.

J35.3	Hypertrophy of tonsils with hypertrophy of adenoids
P35.1	Congenital cytomegalovirus infection
0CTPXZZ	Resection of tonsils, external approach
0CTQXZZ	Resection of adenoids, external approach
0BJ08ZZ	Inspection of tracheobronchial tree, via natural or artificial opening endoscopic
0CJS8ZZ	Inspection of larynx, via natural or artificial opening endoscopic

Comments: The condition that occasioned admission is hypertrophy of the tonsils and adenoids. The code for congenital cytomegalovirus infection is assigned because treatment was continued during the hospital stay. The symptoms (i.e., distorted, loud, and rattling breathing) are integral to hypertrophied tonsils and adenoids and should not be coded separately.

Two procedure codes are required for the removal of the tonsils and adenoids, as they each have a unique body part.

9. **Inpatient admission:** The patient, an 11-month-old male, was found to have a dysplastic kidney on the right side. Because the kidney was not functioning, he was admitted to have it removed. A right, simple nephrectomy was performed. The procedure was uncomplicated, as was the postoperative course. The pathology report showed the kidney to be both dysplastic and multicystic.

Discharge diagnosis: Right multicystic dysplastic kidney.

Q61.4	Renal dysplasia
0TT00ZZ	Resection of right kidney, open approach

Comments: Both dysplastic kidney and multicystic kidney are congenital conditions always classified to chapter 17 of ICD-10-CM regardless of the age of the patient. Both conditions are covered in code Q61.4. ICD-10-PCS allows for coding the removal of the right kidney.

10. **Inpatient admission:** The patient, a 7-pound, 6-ounce male infant, was delivered to a 31-year-old woman (gravida II, para 0-1) at 43 weeks gestation. The mother's pregnancy was uncomplicated, labor lasted 24 hours, and the delivery was spontaneous. Apgar scores were 5 and 7. Due to transient tachypnea and a continued oxygen requirement, the infant was taken to the special care nursery. His overall condition improved rapidly with oxygen and adjustments in body fluids.

Discharge diagnoses: (1) Postterm newborn male, (2) transient tachypnea of the newborn.

Z38.00	Single liveborn infant, delivered vaginally
P08.22	Prolonged gestation of newborn
P22.1	Transient tachypnea of newborn
5A0522C	Extracorporeal supersaturated oxygenation, continuous

Comments: Z38.00 is the principal diagnosis because the infant was born vaginally on this admission. Codes are not assigned for the Apgar scores. Prolonged gestation is more than 42 weeks.

11. **Inpatient admission:** The patient, a three-week-old male, was admitted through the emergency department with a three-day history of upper respiratory tract infection (URI). Following admission, he was observed not breathing for short periods during sleep. Antibiotics were started for the URI, and he was observed closely. He had been followed in the outpatient clinic for failure to thrive. All evaluative workups were negative, and no active disease other than the respiratory infection was found. The upper respiratory infection cleared, but the apneic episodes continued. He was to be transferred to the children's hospital for more detailed studies of his apneic episodes and failure to thrive.

Discharge diagnoses: (1) Failure to thrive, (2) upper respiratory tract infection, (3) apnea.

P39.8	Other specified infections specific to the perinatal period
J06.9	Acute upper respiratory infection, unspecified
R62.51	Failure to thrive (child)
P28.3	Primary sleep apnea of newborn

Comments: Upper respiratory infection was the reason for admission and should be sequenced as the principal diagnosis: Code P39.8 indicates that this is a newborn infection, and code J06.9 specifies that this is an upper respiratory infection.

12. **Inpatient admission:** The infant patient was born in the hospital to a 36-year-old primigravida woman at an estimated 34 weeks gestation. The mother's pregnancy was complicated by maternal hypertension and gestational diabetes. The infant was delivered by a primary cesarean section due to fetal distress and metabolic acidemia resulting from the mother's failure to progress. The infant was placed on oxygen by nasal prong following birth in response to fetal distress. The oxygen was removed when heart rate, breathing, and blood gases returned to normal. The infant's blood sugars were low following birth, and an infusion of intravenous glucose was initiated until the blood sugars stabilized.

Discharge diagnoses: (1) Premature newborn male with birth weight of 1,880 grams, (2) transient hypoglycemia.

Z38.01	Single liveborn infant, delivered by cesarean
P07.17	Other low birth weight newborn, 1750-1999 grams
P07.32	Other preterm newborn, 32-36 completed weeks
P70.0	Syndrome of infant of mother with gestational diabetes
P19.1	Metabolic acidemia in newborn first noted during labor
5A0522C	Extracorporeal supersaturated oxygenation, continuous

Comments: Code P70.0 is used to denote hypoglycemia in an infant with a mother experiencing gestational diabetes. The mother's hypertension, diabetes, and failure to progress at labor were complications of her delivery and are not coded on the newborn record unless there is an adverse effect to the newborn. The fetal distress and metabolic acidemia were first noted in labor and were treated with oxygen and further monitoring following birth, so code P19.1 is assigned as an additional diagnosis code. It is doubtful that the oxygen therapy would be coded.

13. **Inpatient admission:** The patient, a preterm male infant, was born the day before admission in another hospital. He weighed 2,608 grams and had Apgar scores of 7 and 9. He was noted to have elevated temperature. WBCs were also elevated. He was transferred here for investigative studies. A urinary tract infection was confirmed with a urine culture that was positive for *E. coli*, and the infection was treated with intravenous antibiotics. Left hydronephrosis was confirmed by bilateral renal ultrasound. Suspected septicemia was ruled out when all blood cultures were negative prior to institution of antibiotic therapy.

Discharge diagnoses: (1) Urinary tract infection, (2) congenital hydronephrosis, (3) prematurity.

P39.3	Neonatal urinary tract infection
B96.2	Escherichia coli [E. coli] as the cause of diseases classified elsewhere
P07.30	Other preterm newborn, unspecified weeks
Q62.0	Congenital hydronephrosis

Comments: Code P39.3 is referenced in the Alphabetic Index of Diseases and Injuries under **Infection,** urinary, newborn. Code B96.2 is added to show *E. coli* as the causative organism. ICD-10-CM does not classify a birth weight over 2,500 grams as low birth weight. Congenital hydronephrosis was noted. No code from the Z38 category is assigned because the infant was born in another hospital.

16. DISEASES OF THE CIRCULATORY SYSTEM

1. **Inpatient admission (episode 1):** The reason for this woman's admission was repair of a 4.7-centimeter infrarenal abdominal aortic aneurysm. She also had arterial hypertension. Because of her strong family history of aneurysms, she wished to have her aneurysm removed on an elective basis rather than waiting for it to follow its natural course. An infrarenal excision of the aortic aneurysm, open approach, was performed using a 16-millimeter Dacron graft replacement. The procedure was successful, and the patient was discharged on the fifth postoperative day.

Discharge diagnoses: (1) Infrarenal abdominal aortic aneurysm, (2) arterial hypertension.

I71.4	Abdominal aortic aneurysm, without rupture
I10	Essential (primary) hypertension
Z82.49	Family history of ischemic heart disease and other diseases of the circulatory system
04R00JZ	Replacement of abdominal aorta with synthetic substitute, open approach

Comments: The Z82.49 code identifies the family history of aneurysms and explains why the repair was performed on an elective basis. The objective of the procedure was "Replacement" of the portion of the aorta that the aneurysm was located within, that is, putting in or on biological or synthetic material that physically takes the place and/or function of all or a portion of a body part.

Physician office visit (episode 2): The patient presented for routine follow-up examination of an abdominal aortic aneurysm repair with graft replacement. She was doing well, with only mild discomfort. The midline incision was well healed. Femoral and distal pulses were palpable bilaterally. She was to return again in three months.

Diagnosis: Status post aortic aneurysm.

Z09	Encounter for follow-up examination after completed treatment for conditions other than malignant neoplasm

Comments: Z09 is assigned because the patient was seen, after the initial care was completed, for the purpose of determining whether there were any problems related to the surgery.

2. **Inpatient admission:** The patient was admitted for workup of right carotid artery stenosis. A carotid duplex performed as an outpatient procedure at another facility showed 80 percent stenosis on the right side and 40 percent on the left. A nonselective low osmolar carotid arteriography, conducted the day after admission, showed only a 50 percent stenosis of the right common carotid artery. The external carotids were found to be small, but there was no significant internal carotid disease on either side. Therefore, because the patient was asymptomatic, it was felt that surgery would present a higher risk of stroke than treating her medically.

Discharge diagnosis: Carotid artery disease.

I65.23	Occlusion and stenosis of bilateral carotid arteries
B3051ZZ	Plain radiography of bilateral common carotid arteries using low osmolar contrast
B30C1ZZ	Plain radiography of bilateral external carotid arteries using low osmolar contrast

Comments: Although only carotid artery disease was documented on discharge, arteriography indicated the specific condition to be stenosis. Code I65.23 indicates that this condition affects both the right and left arteries. Two ICD-10-PCS codes are required to reflect the bilateral common and external carotid arteriography.

3. Inpatient admission: This patient was admitted for repair of a left common carotid stenosis. Two months earlier, an endarterectomy of a right carotid stenosis had been performed. Six months earlier, she had suffered a cerebral hemorrhage that resulted in apraxia and difficulty in swallowing, both of which required additional nursing assistance. The open left endarterectomy was successfully accomplished, and the patient was discharged on the fourth hospital day.

Discharge diagnoses: (1) Left carotid stenosis, (2) residuals of old cerebrovascular accident.

I65.23	Occlusion and stenosis of bilateral carotid arteries
I69.390	Apraxia following cerebral infarction
I69.391	Dysphagia following cerebral infarction
R13.10	Dysphagia, unspecified
03CJ0ZZ	Extirpation of matter from left common carotid artery, open approach

Comments: The residual apraxia and difficulty in swallowing represent late effects of the previous cerebrovascular accident. They are reportable, as they required additional nursing care. Subcategory I69.3 is for stroke not otherwise specified (NOS). As indicated by the "use additional code" note at code I69.391, code R13.10 is assigned to show the type of dysphagia, which in this case is difficulty in swallowing, NOS. Endarterectomy refers to the removal of diseased material from the inside of an artery; therefore, this procedure is coded to the root operation "Extirpation": taking or cutting out solid matter from a body part. The procedure does not require excision of the artery.

4. Inpatient admission: The patient was admitted with recurrent unstable angina that could not be controlled with sublingual nitroglycerin. There was no history of bypass or angioplasty in the past. On left cardiac catheterization with coronary arteriography, a narrowing in the left anterior descending coronary artery and a stenotic area in an intermediate branch were identified. A successful percutaneous transluminal coronary angioplasty (PTCA) of both vessels was carried out.

Discharge diagnosis: (1) Unstable angina secondary to coronary arteriosclerosis, (2) chronic total occlusion of coronary artery.

I25.110	Atherosclerotic heart disease of native coronary artery with unstable angina pectoris
I25.82	Chronic total occlusion of coronary artery
02713ZZ	Dilation of coronary artery, two sites, percutaneous approach
4A023N7	Measurement of cardiac sampling and pressure, left heart, percutaneous approach
B201YZZ	Plain radiography of multiple coronary arteries using other contrast

Comments: In ICD-10-CM the unstable angina and the arteriosclerosis are included in one code. Because there was no mention of previous bypass surgery, the native artery is selected. In the Index, see the main term **Arteriosclerosis,** subterms "coronary," "native vessel," "with," "angina pectoris," "unstable." ICD-10-PCS includes the angioplasty of two vessels without a device in one code; the root operation is "Dilation."

5. **Inpatient admission:** The patient received his first pacing system 15 years earlier because of congenital complete heart block and severe bradycardia. At the time of admission, he was experiencing these conditions again, plus fatigue secondary to pacemaker pulse generator malfunction. He was admitted for insertion of a new generator and atrial lead. He was prepped for surgery, and, via an incision into the subcutaneous pocket, the old pacemaker and leads were removed, new leads were inserted into the right atrium and ventricle, and a new dual-chamber pacing device was inserted as a replacement. The postoperative period was uncomplicated.

   Discharge diagnosis: Malfunctioning pacemaker.

T82.111A	Breakdown (mechanical) of cardiac pulse generator (battery), initial encounter
Q24.6	Congenital heart block
R00.1	Bradycardia, unspecified
0JPT0PZ	Removal of cardiac rhythm related device from trunk subcutaneous tissue and fascia, open approach
0JH60P2	Insertion of pacemaker, dual chamber into chest subcutaneous tissue and fascia, open approach
02PA0MZ	Removal of cardiac lead from heart, open approach
02H60MA	Insertion of pacemaker lead into right atrium, open approach
02HK0MA	Insertion of pacemaker lead into right ventricle, open approach

Comments: The reason the patient had a pacemaker is to compensate for a heart block and bradycardia. These conditions are also the reasons why he had a new pacemaker inserted. Therefore, both conditions are coded as secondary diagnoses. Fatigue is not coded because it is integral to severe bradycardia. To reflect the pacemaker replacement procedure, the removal of both the leads and the pacemaker and the insertion of the new device and leads are coded.

6. **Inpatient admission:** The patient came to the emergency department because she was unable to speak well. She was admitted because she appeared to be somewhat aphasic. Following admission, she was found to be in atrial fibrillation. A CT scan of the head showed only some probable old defects, and the aphasia was thought to probably be due to a recent cerebral embolus. By the fifth day, she was stable and able to go home. The aphasia had cleared, and the fibrillation was controlled with medication.

   Discharge diagnoses: (1) Cerebral embolism, (2) atrial fibrillation.

| I66.9 | Occlusion and stenosis of unspecified cerebral artery |
| I48.0 | Atrial fibrillation |

Comments: The reason for admission was aphasia, which after study was found to be due to a cerebral embolus. Therefore, the embolus is the principal diagnosis. Aphasia is not coded because it was no longer present at the time of discharge.

7. **Inpatient admission:** The patient was admitted for severe aortic valve stenosis and left ventricular hypertrophy. The aortic valve was replaced with a prosthesis. The patient was successfully weaned from the cardiopulmonary bypass (extracorporeal cardiac) machine. An intraoperative echocardiogram revealed appropriate functioning of the prosthesis.

   Discharge diagnoses: (1) Aortic stenosis and calcification, (2) left ventricular hypertrophy.

I35.0	Nonrheumatic aortic (valve) stenosis
I51.7	Cardiomegaly
02RF0JZ	Replacement of aortic valve with synthetic substitute, open approach
5A1221Z	Performance of cardiac output, continuous

Comments: The cardiopulmonary bypass is coded in the Extracorporeal Assistance and Performance Section.

8. **Inpatient admission:** The admission diagnoses were aortic and mitral insufficiency. The patient also had HIV infection. A bacterial endocarditis, involving the aortic and mitral valves, had developed five months before admission and was treated and resolved with antibiotics. Procedures performed were mitral and aortic valve replacement with prosthesis and cardiopulmonary bypass (extracorporeal cardiac) during the procedure. The patient improved considerably during the next two days with medications and was transferred to the rehabilitation hospital.

   Discharge diagnoses: (1) Aortic and mitral insufficiency, (2) HIV infection.

I08.0	Rheumatic disorders of both mitral and aortic valves
B20	Human immunodeficiency virus [HIV] disease
02RG0JZ	Replacement of mitral valve with synthetic substitute, open approach
02RF0JZ	Replacement of aortic valve with synthetic substitute, open approach
5A1221Z	Performance of cardiac output, continuous

Comments: The HIV was not the reason for admission; therefore, it is not the principal diagnosis. The cardiopulmonary bypass is coded in the Extracorporeal Assistance and Performance Section.

9. **Inpatient admission:** The patient was admitted with atypical chest pain and aching of the left upper extremity. Following admission, she had episodic visual blurring and dizziness. A myocardial infarction was ruled out. Neurological checks were unremarkable, except for a questionable small infarct in the left occipital lobe. Her aspirin therapy was increased, and within two days she was fully ambulatory and asymptomatic.

   Discharge diagnoses: (1) Atypical chest pain of unclear etiology, (2) transient ischemic attacks.

R07.89	Chest pain, unspecified
G45.9	Transient cerebral ischemic attack, unspecified

Comments: Transient ischemic attacks should not be confused with "transient residuals" of an acute cerebrovascular accident. The neurological symptoms did not appear until after admission; therefore, chest pain is sequenced as the principal diagnosis.

10. **Inpatient admission:** The patient, a young woman, was admitted with pain and edema in the left leg, which had started two days earlier when she drove home from Florida without stopping. Findings on a CT scan of the pelvic region were consistent with thrombosis. She was discharged on Coumadin.

    Discharge diagnosis: Iliac vein thrombosis on the left, acute.

I82.422	Acute embolism and thrombosis of left iliac vein

Comments: The symptoms of pain and edema in the leg are integral to the iliac vein thrombosis and should not be coded separately.

11. **Inpatient admission:** The patient was brought to the hospital emergency department with burning, low sternal, epigastric pain. While in the ED, she developed respiratory distress and subsequent acute myocardial infarction with cardiopulmonary arrest. She was resuscitated, and maneuvers involved in this activity included intubation and defibrillation. Chest X-rays confirmed pulmonary edema and congestive heart failure. EKGs confirmed acute subendocardial myocardial infarction in progress. The patient was then admitted and remained on the ventilator for approximately 24 hours, with gradual improvement. She was transferred to another hospital for further workup and treatment.

Discharge diagnoses: (1) Acute myocardial infarction, (2) pulmonary edema, (3) congestive heart failure, (4) cardiopulmonary arrest.

I21.4	Non-ST elevation (NSTEMI) myocardial infarction
I50.9	Heart failure, unspecified
I46.2	Cardiac arrest due to underlying cardiac condition
5A2204Z	Restoration of cardiac rhythm, single
0BH17EZ	Insertion of endotracheal airway into trachea, via natural or artificial opening
5A1945Z	Respiratory ventilation, 24-96 consecutive hours

Comments: Cardiac arrest due to underlying cardiac condition is coded to I46.2, with the cardiac condition coded first; therefore, in this case, the myocardial infarction is coded first.

12. **Inpatient admission:** The patient was admitted for evaluation of a three-month history of fever, fatigue, and headaches. She received consultation from the rheumatology service, which recommended biopsy of the temporal arteries. The left temporal artery was negative for inflammation. The right temporal artery, however, showed inflammation of the intima. The histologic picture was compatible with arteritis. Prednisone was given, and the headaches subsided.

Discharge diagnoses: (1) Right temporal arteritis; (2) open biopsy, right and left temporal arteries.

M31.6	Other giant cell arteritis
03BS0ZX	Excision of right temporal artery, open approach, diagnostic
03BT0ZX	Excision of left temporal artery, open approach, diagnostic

Comments: Headaches are integral to inflammation of the temporal artery and are not coded separately. The procedure is classified as "Excision," with the qualifier for "diagnostic" to indicate that this was a biopsy. A code for both the right and left temporal arteries is added.

ICD-10-CM and ICD-10-PCS Coding Handbook, with Answers, 2012 Revised Edition

13. Inpatient admission: The patient was admitted for treatment of a stroke. She has a history of type 2 diabetes. The major manifestations were ptosis on the right; moderate expressive aphasia; right-to-left disorientation; and a slow, shuffling gait. On a CT scan of the head, a low-density area at the posterior limb of the left internal capsule and the left posterior parietal subcortical white matter was seen. No hemorrhage was viewed. Gradually, the manifestations improved and then resolved. The patient also had a right midfoot ulcer that required bedside debridement (using a Versajet) by the physician. She was discharged to be followed up by a home health nurse.

Discharge diagnoses: (1) Cerebrovascular infarction of a thromboembolic source, left posterior artery; (2) type 2 diabetes; (3) diabetic foot ulcer.

I63.432	Cerebral infarction due to embolism of left posterior cerebral artery
E11.621	Type 2 diabetes mellitus with foot ulcer
L97.419	Non-pressure chronic ulcer of right heel and midfoot with unspecified severity
0HDMXZZ	Extraction of right foot skin, external approach

Comments: The CT scan showed the left posterior artery as affected. The symptoms had resolved at discharge, so they are not coded. Refer to the Alphabetic Index, **Infarction,** due to embolism, cerebral arteries, which provides code I63.4-. The foot ulcer and the diabetes are reflected in the E11.621 code, with a "use additional code" note for the site of the ulcer. The Versajet debridement has as its objective "Extraction," pulling or stripping away or off all or a portion of a body part by the use of force.

14. Inpatient admission: The patient had a three-month history of progressive cyanosis of the fingers and toes. Due to sudden and dramatic progression of symptoms, she was admitted. A right upper-extremity arteriogram revealed complete absence of arterial flow to all proximal phalanges. The findings were thought to be consistent with vasculitis. A percutaneous vascular biopsy of the artery of the right hand was performed to confirm this diagnosis. The report indicated changes consistent with chronic inflammation and necrotizing vasculitis. On vascular surgery consultation, it was felt that her gangrene would demarcate without surgical intervention. There was gradual improvement in pain, and she was switched to oral medications.

Discharge diagnoses: (1) Necrotizing vasculitis, (2) digital gangrene.

I77.6	Arteritis, unspecified
I96	Gangrene, not elsewhere classified
03BD3ZX	Excision of right hand artery, percutaneous approach, diagnostic
B30HZZZ	Plain radiography of right upper extremity arteries

Comments: Gangrene represents a further manifestation of vasculitis and is coded separately. The biopsy of the artery of the right hand is classified as "Excision," with the qualifier "diagnostic" to indicate that this was a biopsy.

15. Inpatient admission: The patient was transferred from another hospital for evaluation of a possible recurrent pulmonary embolism and left lower-extremity pain and swelling determined to be DVT (prior to transfer). A pulmonary arteriogram confirmed a left pulmonary embolus, and heparin was started. Bilateral mammograms were taken to evaluate a right breast lump with discharge, which was found on physical examination. The finding was a suspicious density of her right breast. The patient was to be referred to the gynecology clinic for follow-up of this problem after discharge. All medications were adjusted, and she showed much improvement.

Discharge diagnoses: (1) Deep venous thrombosis, right leg; (2) recurrent pulmonary embolism; (3) lump, right breast.

I82.401	Acute embolism and thrombosis of unspecified deep veins of right lower extremity
I26.99	Other pulmonary embolism without acute cor pulmonale
N63	Unspecified lump in breast
B30TZZZ	Plain radiography of left pulmonary artery
BH02ZZZ	Plain radiography of bilateral breasts

Comments: Either pulmonary embolism or DVT could be sequenced as the principal diagnosis. The patient was admitted for further evaluation and treatment of both. The right breast lump is not considered an incidental finding. Although it was not treated, it was identified and workup begun, with the patient being referred for further follow-up.

16. Inpatient admission: The patient, who had peripheral vascular disease, came in for a second opinion about possible reconstruction of right femorotibial occlusive disease. An angiogram demonstrated a peroneal vessel that would allow reconstruction. Following an evaluation, he was scheduled to undergo the procedure. However, because he had no other significant diseases or active cardiac ischemia, he was felt to be at low risk for a distal reconstruction. The patient was discharged prior to the procedure due to the development of an upper respiratory infection. The procedure was to be rescheduled in two weeks.

Discharge diagnoses: (1) Right femorotibial occlusion, (2) URI.

I74.3	Embolism and thrombosis of arteries of the lower extremities
J06.9	Acute upper respiratory infection, unspecified
Z53.09	Procedure and treatment not carried out because of other contraindication
B40FYZZ	Plain radiography of right lower extremity arteries using other contrast

Comments: In the Index, under **Occlusion,** artery, the cross-reference is to "see also **Embolism,** artery." See **Embolism,** limb, lower, to find code I74.3.

17. Inpatient admission: The patient was admitted with probable acute myocardial infarction. He was admitted to the critical care unit and also found to be in atrial fibrillation. He was given several medications. A cardiology consultation confirmed an acute inferolateral myocardial infarction on echocardiogram, and the patient was transferred to another hospital for cardiac catheterization.

Discharge diagnoses: (1) Acute myocardial infarction, (2) atrial fibrillation.

I21.19	ST elevation (STEMI) myocardial infarction involving other coronary artery of inferior wall
I48.0	Atrial fibrillation

Comments: Although the patient had both acute myocardial infarction and atrial fibrillation, the reason for admission was acute myocardial infarction, which is sequenced first.

18. Inpatient admission: The patient, an elderly man, was transferred from a nursing home. He had had nondominant left-sided hemiplegia since suffering a cerebral thrombosis about three months earlier. He was doing well until the day of admission. A CT scan of the head showed an acute cerebral hemorrhage. He was treated and improved somewhat but then had increased problems secondary to extension of the bleeding. Another CT scan showed a large hematoma in the right basal ganglia. With consultation, it was decided that only supportive care was needed, and the patient was returned to the nursing home.

Discharge diagnoses: (1) Acute cerebral hemorrhage, (2) right basal ganglia hematoma, (3) previous cerebral thrombosis with residual left-sided hemiplegia.

I61.9	Nontraumatic intracerebral hemorrhage, unspecified
I69.354	Hemiplegia and hemiparesis following cerebral infarction affecting left non-dominant side
B020ZZZ	Computerized tomography (CT scan) of brain
B020ZZZ	Computerized tomography (CT scan) of brain

Comments: The reason for admission was acute cerebral hemorrhage. There was an extension of the cerebral hemorrhage, and a hematoma developed in the right basal ganglia, which is also covered by code I61.9. There is a left-sided nondominant residual hemiplegia, which is a late effect (sequela) of a previous cerebral thrombosis. In reporting, the CT scan of the head is coded twice, with different dates indicated.

19. Inpatient admission: The patient, a female resident of a nursing home, was transferred because of nausea and vomiting. She also suffered from type 1 diabetes mellitus and arteriosclerotic cardiovascular disease. An upper GI X-ray showed esophageal obstruction. She was then admitted with provisional diagnoses of esophageal obstruction versus hiatal hernia versus esophagitis. A gastroscopy was performed, and a partial obstruction due to stricture to the level of the distal esophagus was viewed and dilated. The patient improved without further symptoms. Her blood sugar levels rose to 500 on the third day of admission, and the diabetes was diagnosed as out of control. Her insulin was increased twice in an attempt to lower her blood sugar to baseline. The long-term outlook was not good inasmuch as the patient was not a candidate for definitive surgery. The esophageal stricture was thought to have resulted from a previous cerebrovascular accident.

Discharge diagnoses: (1) Esophageal stricture; (2) arteriosclerotic cardiovascular disease; (3) uncontrolled diabetes mellitus, type 1.

I69.998	Other sequelae following unspecified cerebrovascular disease
K22.2	Esophageal obstruction
I25.10	Atherosclerotic heart disease of native coronary artery without angina pectoris
E10.65	Type 1 diabetes mellitus with hyperglycemia
0D758ZZ	Dilation of esophagus, via natural or artificial opening endoscopic
0DJ68ZZ	Inspection of stomach, via natural or artificial opening endoscopic

Comments: The stricture is a late effect of a previous CVA (cerebrovascular accident). Code K22.2 is also assigned to provide greater specificity. No code is assigned for the nausea and vomiting because these symptoms are a common finding with esophageal stricture. For diabetes out of control, see the main term **Diabetes,** subterm "inadequately controlled," with the cross-reference that states "code to **Diabetes,** by, type, with hyperglycemia." See the Index entry "**Diabetes,** type 1 with hyperglycemia." A code for long-term use of insulin is optional for type 1 diabetics because these patients require insulin.

20. Inpatient admission: The patient was admitted through the emergency department with substernal chest pain, thought to represent unstable angina. He got pain relief with nitroglycerin. The next morning he asked to be discharged because he had no insurance and could not afford to be in the hospital. Because his physician did not agree with his decision, the patient signed himself out against medical advice. He promised to see the cardiologist immediately and take his medications.

Discharge diagnosis: Angina, probably unstable.

I20.0	Unstable angina
Z91.19	Patient's noncompliance with other medical treatment and regimen

Comments: Because angina is documented at discharge as probably unstable, code I20.0 should be assigned. The patient signed himself out against medical advice (AMA). Code Z91.19 indicates noncompliance with other medical treatment and regimen.

21. Inpatient admission: The patient, who had no history of bypass or angioplasty, was admitted with recurrent chest pain, which could not be controlled with medications and ultimately resulted in an anterior AMI. On combined right and left cardiac catheterization with coronary cineangiography, a narrowing in the left anterior descending coronary artery and stenoses in the left circumflex and distal right coronary artery were found. A successful three-vessel coronary artery bypass graft was carried out. The left internal mammary was used to bypass the left anterior descending, and a reverse segment of the left saphenous vein graft was used to bypass the left circumflex and distal right coronary arteries. The saphenous vein was harvested via a percutaneous endoscopic procedure.

Discharge diagnoses: (1) Anterior acute myocardial infarction, (2) coronary arteriosclerosis.

Procedure: Three-vessel coronary artery bypass graft.

I21.09	ST elevation (STEMI) myocardial infarction involving other coronary artery of anterior wall
I25.10	Atherosclerotic heart disease of native coronary artery without angina pectoris
021109W	Bypass coronary artery, two sites to aorta with autologous venous tissue, open approach
02100Z9	Bypass coronary artery, one site to left internal mammary, open approach
06BQ4ZZ	Excision of left greater saphenous vein, percutaneous endoscopic approach
4A023N8	Measurement of cardiac sampling and pressure, bilateral, percutaneous approach
B206YZZ	Plain radiography of right and left heart using other contrast

Comments: The left internal mammary was used to bypass the left anterior descending, equaling one bypass. A segment of the left saphenous vein graft was used to bypass the left circumflex and distal right coronary arteries, equaling two aortocoronary bypasses. Coding the bypasses separately is consistent with Official Coding Guideline B3.6c, which states that "if multiple coronary artery sites are bypassed, a separate procedure is coded for each coronary artery site that uses a different device and/or qualifier." A code is added for the harvest of the saphenous vein. The cardiac catheterization and angiography were combined right and left procedures.

22. Inpatient admission: The patient was admitted for a planned exploratory laparotomy and a possible excision of a cystic mass in the pelvis. Shortly after admission, however, she developed bigeminal pulse. The anesthesiologist believed that she should not have surgery. The surgery was canceled, and she was referred back to her internist.

Discharge diagnoses: (1) Bigeminal pulse, (2) pelvic mass.

R19.00	Intra-abdominal and pelvic swelling, mass and lump, unspecified site
R00.8	Other abnormalities of heart beat
Z53.09	Procedure and treatment not carried out because of other contraindication

Comments: The reason for admission was pelvic mass. Even though the treatment plan was not carried out, it should still be sequenced as the principal diagnosis. The complication bigeminal pulse developed after admission and is sequenced as a secondary diagnosis. Code Z53.09 shows that the planned procedure was canceled due to a contraindication.

23. Inpatient admission: The patient, an elderly woman, had a rather sudden onset of severe pleuritic chest discomfort that brought her to the emergency department. She had been undergoing a series of radiation therapy treatments for history of endometrial carcinoma. She was admitted for further evaluation. A right pulmonary angiogram confirmed the diagnosis of pulmonary embolism in the right lower lobe. She was treated with heparin and later Coumadin. Coumadin was to be continued on discharge. The patient was to return for her regular radiation therapy treatment as scheduled.

Discharge diagnoses: (1) Pulmonary embolism, (2) history of endometrial carcinoma of the uterus.

I26.99	Other pulmonary embolism without acute cor pulmonale
C54.3	Malignant neoplasm of fundus uteri
B30SZZZ	Plain radiography of right pulmonary artery

Comments: Endometrial carcinoma of the uterus is no longer present; however, the site is still under active treatment. Therefore, code C54.3 is assigned rather than a code from personal history of carcinoma.

24. Inpatient admission: The patient was transferred from another hospital for treatment of an acute inferior myocardial infarction. She also suffered from hypercholesterolemia and benign hypertension; treatment of these conditions was continued during the hospital stay. A left cardiac catheterization with coronary angiogram and arteriography was performed and revealed coronary arteriosclerosis. It was determined that she would benefit from a percutaneous transluminal coronary angioplasty. The angioplasty was performed on the left coronary artery. She tolerated the procedure well and was to continue her medical treatment after discharge.

Discharge diagnoses: (1) Acute inferior myocardial infarction, (2) coronary arteriosclerosis, (3) hypercholesterolemia, (4) benign essential hypertension.

I21.19	ST elevation (STEMI) myocardial infarction involving other coronary artery of inferior wall
I25.10	Atherosclerotic heart disease of native coronary artery without angina pectoris
E78.0	Pure hypercholesterolemia
I10	Essential (primary) hypertension
02703ZZ	Dilation of coronary artery, one site, percutaneous approach
4A023N7	Measurement of cardiac sampling and pressure, left heart, percutaneous approach
B201YZZ	Plain radiography of multiple coronary arteries using other contrast

Comments: Both the transferring hospital and this facility will assign I21.19 for the acute myocardial infarct. ICD-10-PCS codes the angioplasty to the root operation "Dilation."

17. NEOPLASMS

1. Inpatient admission: The elderly woman's admitting diagnosis was carcinoma of the stomach with metastasis to the ovaries. An exploratory laparotomy was performed for the purpose of excising the gastric tumor, but it was so densely attached to other structures that it could not be resected. However, a total abdominal hysterectomy and bilateral salpingo-oophorectomy were accomplished and the patient returned to her room in fair condition. Palliative systemic chemotherapy infusions were given. On the third postoperative day, a large right pleural effusion developed, and a chest tube was percutaneously placed in the right pleural cavity for drainage. Cytology for malignant cells in the pleural effusion was negative. The patient remained stable and wanted to return to her home. The chest tube was removed before discharge.

Discharge diagnoses: (1) Carcinoma of the stomach metastatic to the ovaries, (2) pleural effusion.

C16.9	Malignant neoplasm of stomach, unspecified
C79.60	Secondary malignant neoplasm of unspecified ovary
J90	Pleural effusion, not elsewhere classified
0UT90ZZ	Resection of uterus, open approach
0UTC0ZZ	Resection of cervix, open approach
0UT20ZZ	Resection of bilateral ovaries, open approach
0UT70ZZ	Resection of bilateral fallopian tubes, open approach
0W9930Z	Drainage of right pleural cavity with drainage device, percutaneous approach
3E04305	Introduction of other antineoplastic into central vein, percutaneous approach
0WP9X0Z	Removal of drainage device from right pleural cavity, external approach

Comments: Even though pleural effusion developed following surgery, the physician did not identify it as a complication of the surgery and the cytology for the effusion was negative. The code for the exploratory laparotomy is not assigned because it was the approach for the total abdominal hysterectomy and bilateral salpingo-oophorectomy. Separate ICD-10-PCS codes are necessary for the removal of the uterus, cervix, ovaries, and fallopian tubes to represent a total hysterectomy.

2. Inpatient admission: The patient underwent a hemicolectomy and splenectomy a year earlier for excision of a primary adenocarcinoma of the colon. Recently, he developed abdominal pain. He was admitted with a questionable liver lesion. An ultrasound of the liver, a CT scan of the abdomen, and an exploratory laparotomy with needle biopsy of the liver were performed. The findings indicated inoperable adenocarcinoma of the liver.

Discharge diagnosis: Adenocarcinoma of the colon metastatic to the liver, unresectable.

C78.7	Secondary malignant neoplasm of liver and intrahepatic bile duct
Z85.030	Personal history of malignant carcinoid tumor of large intestine
0FB03ZX	Excision of liver, percutaneous approach, diagnostic
0WJG0ZZ	Inspection of peritoneal cavity, open approach

Comments: A "history of" code is assigned for the adenocarcinoma of the colon because it had previously been excised. The liver is specified as the secondary site because the neoplasm spread to it from the colon. The patient was admitted with a questionable liver lesion, which after study was diagnosed as a liver metastasis and therefore assigned as the principal diagnosis. The exploratory laparotomy is coded because it was not followed by definitive surgery. Even though the biopsy was performed during the laparotomy, a needle biopsy of the liver is considered a closed biopsy, and therefore the percutaneous approach is used.

3. **Inpatient admission:** The patient was admitted through the emergency department with severe shortness of breath. She had a history of left upper lobe, non–small cell carcinoma, which had been treated with radiation. Recently, a recurrence in the left supraclavicular area of the lung was found, and she received palliative radiation therapy. She also had a history of severe chronic obstructive bronchitis and had used home oxygen for several years. Her medications were increased for the chronic obstructive pulmonary disease, and she improved sufficiently for discharge.

Discharge diagnoses: (1) Chronic obstructive pulmonary disease with acute exacerbation, (2) recurrent non–small cell lung cancer.

J44.1	Chronic obstructive pulmonary disease with (acute) exacerbation
C34.12	Malignant neoplasm of upper lobe, left bronchus or lung

Comments: The thrust of treatment was toward the chronic obstructive pulmonary disease, and it is therefore designated as the principal diagnosis. Because the chronic obstructive pulmonary disease is described more specifically in the body of the record as chronic obstructive bronchitis with acute exacerbation, code J44.1 is assigned. Recurrence of a neoplasm is coded as a primary neoplasm of that site. ICD-10-CM allows for specifying the left lung.

4. **Inpatient admission:** On a previous admission, the patient was diagnosed with poorly differentiated papillary serous cystadenocarcinoma of the right ovary. She was admitted for, and received, her fifth chemotherapy treatment (into central vein) with Taxol and Cisplatin.

Discharge diagnosis: Papillary serous cystadenocarcinoma, stage III.

Z51.11	Encounter for antineoplastic chemotherapy
C56.1	Malignant neoplasm of right ovary
3E04305	Introduction of other antineoplastic into central vein, percutaneous approach

Comments: The sole reason for admission was to receive chemotherapy; therefore, code Z51.11 is designated as the principal diagnosis. A code is also assigned for the neoplasm under treatment.

5. **Inpatient admission:** The patient was seen in the outpatient clinic, where an X-ray revealed compression fractures of T6 and T8. He gave no history of trauma. He was admitted for further evaluation to determine the etiology of the pathologic fractures. Bone marrow aspirate from the vertebrae and biopsies revealed multiple myeloma. During the stay, he went into fluid overload and developed some chest heaviness with runs of ventricular tachycardia. The tachycardia necessitated his transfer to cardiac level II to rule out myocardial infarction. Myocardial infarct was ruled out, and he was discharged after stabilization. He was to be followed up by the oncology clinic.

Discharge diagnoses: (1) Multiple myeloma; (2) compression fractures, T6 and T8; (3) fluid overload; (4) tachycardia.

C90.00	Multiple myeloma not having achieved remission
M84.58xA	Pathological fracture in neoplastic disease, vertebrae, initial encounter for fracture
E87.70	Fluid overload, unspecified
I47.2	Ventricular tachycardia
07DS3ZX	Extraction of vertebral bone marrow, percutaneous approach, diagnostic

Comments: Although the compression fractures might appear to be the reason for admission, the purpose was clearly to determine the cause of these apparently spontaneous fractures. Diagnostic studies revealed that the underlying problem was the multiple myeloma. ICD-10-CM provides subcategory M84.5 for pathological fracture in neoplastic disease, with code M84.58 specifying vertebrae. The placeholder character "x" and the seventh-character extension "A" are added to indicate that this is the initial encounter for the fracture.

6. **Physician office visit:** The 63-year-old patient made her annual visit to her gynecologist. She had no complaints. Examination revealed a 6- to 7-centimeter mass at the vaginal apex. She was to be scheduled for an exploratory laparotomy.

   Diagnosis: Vaginal mass.

N89.9	Noninflammatory disorder of vagina, unspecified

Comments: A mass is not classified to the Neoplasm chapter of ICD-10-CM unless it has been evaluated and determined to be neoplastic. There is no Alphabetic Index entry for the specific site under **Mass.** The Index provides direction to "see Disease of specified organ or site for **Mass,** specified organ NEC," which leads to code N89.9.

7. **Inpatient admission:** The patient was admitted for workup of an abdominal mass. An esophago-gastroduodenoscopy with ultrasound of the abdomen demonstrated a complex cystic solid mass in the pancreas, which had invaded the portal vein. The mass was most consistent with carcinoma of the pancreas. The patient refused colonoscopy, biopsy, and surgery. Therefore, she was discharged with medication and was to follow up with her local physician for palliative treatment of carcinoma.

   Discharge diagnosis: Probable carcinoma of the pancreas with extension to the portal vein.

C25.9	Malignant neoplasm of pancreas, unspecified
C79.89	Secondary malignant neoplasm of other specified sites
0DJ08ZZ	Inspection of upper intestinal tract, via natural or artificial opening endoscopic

Comments: Suspected carcinoma that is under treatment as if proven is coded as confirmed. Once a primary neoplasm spreads/extends beyond the boundary of the organ where it originated into an adjacent structure, it is coded as a secondary neoplasm. Metastatic neoplasms of veins are coded to neoplasms of connective tissue as directed in the Alphabetic Index of Diseases and Injuries.

8. **Inpatient admission (episode 1):** The patient had a rapidly progressing, drug-resistant, primitive melanotic neuroectodermal tumor (PNET) metastatic to the left femur. He was admitted for fixation of a pathologic fracture of the left femur. An open reduction with internal fixation of the left proximal femur with intramedullary nail insertion was performed.

   Discharge diagnoses: (1) PNET metastatic to the femur; (2) pathologic fracture, neck of the left femur.

M84.552A	Pathological fracture in neoplastic disease, left femur, initial encounter for fracture
C79.51	Secondary malignant neoplasm of bone
C80.1	Malignant (primary) neoplasm, unspecified
0QS706Z	Reposition left upper femur with intramedullary fixation device, open approach

Comments: Because the focus of the encounter is for the pathological fracture due to the neoplasm, the M84.552A code is sequenced first. Although the Alphabetic Index under **Tumor,** melanotic, neuroectodermal, directs the coder to "see **Neoplasm,** by site, benign," this neoplasm is obviously a malignant form because it has metastasized. The primary site is not identified, nor is guidance provided by the Alphabetic Index. Therefore, code C80.1, for an unknown primary site, is assigned.

ICD-10-PCS classifies fracture reduction to the root operation "Reposition."

Inpatient admission (episode 2): The patient was readmitted for management of a right-sided pleural effusion. A right-sided thoracentesis was accomplished, and he had some relief of his breathing. Cytology confirmed the pleural effusion as malignant. A closed biopsy of the right lung confirmed metastasis to the lung. The patient improved and was discharged to follow up in his physician's office.

Discharge diagnoses: (1) Malignant pleural effusion, (2) PNET metastatic to the left femur and right lung.

C78.01	Secondary malignant neoplasm of right lung
C79.51	Secondary malignant neoplasm of bone
C80.1	Malignant (primary) neoplasm, unspecified
J91.0	Malignant pleural effusion
0W993ZZ	Drainage of right pleural cavity, percutaneous approach
0BBK3ZX	Excision of right lung, percutaneous approach, diagnostic

Comments: The malignant pleural effusion is assigned to code J91.0. In addition, when coding malignant pleural effusion, code first the malignant neoplasm, if known. Code C80.1 is assigned to indicate that the primary malignancy has not been identified. The objective of the thoracentesis was drainage of the pleural effusion to assist in breathing.

Inpatient admission (episode 3): The patient was again admitted, this time for terminal care. The admission diagnosis was severe hypoxemia. He had massive bilateral pulmonary metastases. It was hoped that he could be relieved by chest tube drainage; however, it was obvious from his chest X-ray that removing a small amount of lung fluid would not affect the overall clinical situation. He had significant hemoptysis the second day of hospitalization and was in a comatose state until his death that evening.

Discharge diagnoses: (1) Hypoxemia and hemoptysis secondary to malignant pleural effusion, (2) coma, (3) primitive melanotic neuroectodermal tumor metastatic to the left femur and lungs. Primary unknown.

C78.01	Secondary malignant neoplasm of right lung
C79.51	Secondary malignant neoplasm of bone
C80.1	Malignant (primary) neoplasm, unspecified
J91.0	Malignant pleural effusion
R04.2	Hemoptysis
R40.20	Unspecified coma
R09.02	Hypoxemia
Z51.5	Encounter for palliative care

Comments: Although hypoxemia and hemoptysis are related to the pleural effusion, neither is routinely present with this condition, nor is coma integral to the diagnosed conditions. Therefore, symptom codes are assigned as additional diagnoses. Z51.5, Encounter for palliative care, is assigned as a secondary code because this patient was admitted for terminal care. Palliative care is an alternative to aggressive treatment for patients who are in the terminal phase of their illness. Palliative care is focused toward management of pain and symptoms.

9. **Inpatient admission:** The patient was admitted for chemotherapy. She had ovarian papillary serous cystadenocarcinoma, stage III. Three months earlier, diaphragmatic and omental masses were positive as well. She received Taxol and Cisplatin percutaneously via central vein IV without difficulty. She was to return in three weeks for her next treatment.

Discharge diagnosis: Stage III papillary serous cystadenocarcinoma with metastases to the diaphragm and omentum.

Z51.11	Encounter for antineoplastic chemotherapy
C56.9	Malignant neoplasm of unspecified ovary
C79.89	Secondary malignant neoplasm of other specified sites
C78.6	Secondary malignant neoplasm of retroperitoneum and peritoneum
3E04305	Introduction of other antineoplastic into central vein, percutaneous approach

Comments: The sole reason for admission is for administration of chemotherapy; therefore, Z51.11 is the principal diagnosis. Additional codes are assigned for the neoplastic disease under treatment; personal history of malignant neoplasm codes are not assigned when treatment is still in progress.

10. **Inpatient admission:** The patient was admitted for removal of an abdominal aortic aneurysm. When the abdomen was opened, carcinoma of the esophagus was found. Because the patient was elderly and the aneurysm was small, the surgeon decided not to repair it or to excise the neoplasm. Prior to discharge, a percutaneous endoscopic gastrostomy tube was inserted to ensure adequate caloric intake. The patient recovered without difficulty and was discharged to home with family.

Discharge diagnoses: (1) Aortic aneurysm, (2) carcinoma of esophagus.

I71.4	Abdominal aortic aneurysm, without rupture
C15.9	Malignant neoplasm of esophagus, unspecified
0DH63UZ	Insertion of feeding device into stomach, percutaneous approach
0WJG0ZZ	Inspection of peritoneal cavity, open approach

Comments: Even though the initial treatment plan was not carried out, the principal diagnosis remains code I71.4 because the abdominal aneurysm was the condition that occasioned the admission. When only one site for a neoplasm is mentioned, it is assumed to be primary in the absence of any other information to the contrary.

11. **Outpatient visit:** The patient complained of dyspnea on exertion, moderate night sweats, and intermittent fevers. On routine chest X-ray, a mass was visualized in the mediastinum. He was to be scheduled for a CT scan.

Diagnosis: Probable neoplastic disease.

R22.2	Localized swelling, mass and lump, trunk
R06.00	Dyspnea, unspecified
R50.9	Fever, unspecified
R61	Generalized hyperhidrosis

Comments: Suspected conditions are not coded in the ambulatory care setting; therefore, only codes for the presenting symptoms and the mass identified on X-ray are assigned.

12. **Inpatient admission (episode 1):** The patient was admitted for evaluation of a mediastinal mass. On CT scan of the thorax, a large mass was identified in the anterior superior portion. Multiple pulmonary nodules were also seen. Needle biopsies of nodules in the lungs, obtained during an exploratory thoracotomy, were positive for yolk sac tumor. The first of a series of five chemotherapy treatments was administered percutaneously via central vein IV prior to discharge.

Discharge diagnosis: Yolk sac tumor of mediastinum with metastases to both lungs.

C38.1	Malignant neoplasm of anterior mediastinum
C78.01	Secondary malignant neoplasm of right lung
C78.02	Secondary malignant neoplasm of left lung
0BBM3ZX	Excision of bilateral lungs, percutaneous approach, diagnostic
0WJ90ZZ	Inspection of right pleural cavity, open approach
0WJB0ZZ	Inspection of left pleural cavity, open approach
3E04305	Introduction of other antineoplastic into central vein, percutaneous approach
BP2WYZZ	Computerized tomography (CT scan) of thorax using other contrast

Comments: Even though chemotherapy was administered, the admission was not solely for this purpose; therefore, the procedure code shows that chemotherapy was administered. The code for yolk sac tumor is located by referring to **Tumor,** yolk sac, in the Alphabetic Index, then referring to the Neoplasm Table. Because the metastasis is to both lungs, and ICD-10-CM does not provide a single combination code for both lungs, separate codes are assigned. A code is assigned for the exploratory thoracotomy because no definitive surgery was associated with it. Because this was for both the left and right side, two codes are assigned.

Inpatient admission (episode 2): This admission was for a second cycle of chemotherapy (into central vein) for the yolk sac tumor of the mediastinum. The patient had minimal nausea and vomiting and was discharged following his treatment.

Discharge diagnosis: Yolk sac tumor of mediastinum with metastases to both lungs.

Z51.11	Encounter for antineoplastic chemotherapy
C38.1	Malignant neoplasm of anterior mediastinum
C78.01	Secondary malignant neoplasm of right lung
C78.02	Secondary malignant neoplasm of left lung
3E04305	Introduction of other antineoplastic into central vein, percutaneous approach

Comments: This admission was for the sole purpose of providing chemotherapy; therefore, code Z51.11 is the appropriate principal diagnosis code. The addition of the neoplasm codes indicates the conditions requiring the therapy.

13. **Inpatient admission:** The female patient had suffered from melanoma for a number of years. She had undergone a primary resection 10 years ago without recurrence, but one year ago, melanoma was discovered in her axilla. She underwent axillary dissection but, a few months later, presented with sacral pain, which bone scan revealed to be left femoral neck and right midfemur sites of metastasis. She had hepatic and adrenal metastases as well. She was admitted for the fifth course of chemotherapy, which was given percutaneously into central vein IV.

Discharge diagnosis: Metastatic melanoma left and right femur, liver, and adrenal gland.

Z51.11	Encounter for antineoplastic chemotherapy
C79.51	Secondary malignant neoplasm of bone
C78.7	Secondary malignant neoplasm of liver and intrahepatic bile duct
C79.70	Secondary malignant neoplasm of unspecified adrenal gland
3E04305	Introduction of other antineoplastic into central vein, percutaneous approach

Comments: The sole reason for this admission was to provide chemotherapy. Codes are assigned for the current metastatic neoplasms; the history code is not assigned because the recurrent secondary neoplasms are the same type of neoplasm as the earlier neoplasms.

14. **Outpatient clinic visit:** The patient, an elderly woman, returned to the clinic for follow-up of her right malignant extramedullary ileal plasmacytoma. On a recent MRI, it was evident that the neoplasm, which was previously irradiated, had grown. Although she had failed current radiotherapy, there was no evidence that the neoplasm had spread outside its original location. She was started on medication and was to be scheduled for pelvic MRI.

Diagnosis: Malignant ileal plasmacytoma.

C90.20	Extramedullary plasmacytoma not having achieved remission

Comments: **Plasmacytoma** is referenced in the Alphabetic Index, with the subterm "extramedullary." It is necessary to go to the Tabular List to complete the code.

15. **Inpatient admission:** The female patient had had abdominal pain for several months and infertility for three years. On hysterosalpingo-gram taken before admission, a right tubal occlusion and questionable uterine myoma were visualized. She was admitted for a myomectomy. During the procedure, multiple adhesions were noted from the tubes to a previous myomectomy site, and lysis was carried out. It was felt that the constriction of the tubes by the adhesions might be the cause of the infertility. On the third postoperative day, the staples were removed and the patient went home.

Discharge diagnoses: (1) Symptomatic leiomyoma, (2) infertility, (3) adhesions.

D25.9	Leiomyoma of uterus, unspecified
N73.6	Female pelvic peritoneal adhesions (postinfective)
N97.1	Female infertility of tubal origin
0UB90ZZ	Excision of uterus, open approach
0UN70ZZ	Release bilateral fallopian tubes, open approach

Comments: The myoma of the uterus is the principal diagnosis because it was the reason for admission; the lysis of the adhesions was secondary to the excision of the myoma and was required in order to remove the leiomyoma. Dual coding is required for the infertility associated with peritubal adhesions. Lysis of adhesions is classified to the root operation "Release."

16. **Inpatient admission:** The patient was admitted for treatment of a moderately differentiated adenocarcinoma of the endometrium and myometrium. The diagnosis was made after a diagnostic D & C performed a month earlier. She was taken to surgery, where a laparotomy was performed through a midline incision. Exploration revealed no palpable nodes. A total abdominal hysterectomy and bilateral salpingo-oophorectomy were performed without incident or complication. Frozen section of the myometrium showed only minimal invasion at less than one-third of the depth. The postoperative course was benign, and the patient was discharged.

Discharge diagnosis: Adenocarcinoma of the endometrium, moderately well differentiated, with minimal myometrial involvement.

C54.1	Malignant neoplasm of endometrium
C54.2	Malignant neoplasm of endometrium
0UT90ZZ	Resection of uterus, open approach
0UTC0ZZ	Resection of cervix, open approach
0UT20ZZ	Resection of bilateral ovaries, open approach
0UT70ZZ	Resection of bilateral fallopian tubes, open approach

Comments: The endometrium and myometrium are both parts of the uterus and are coded separately (C54.1 and C54.2). No additional code for secondary neoplasm is assigned. The exploratory laparotomy is the operative approach for the hysterectomy and salpingo-oophorectomy; therefore, a separate code for exploratory laparotomy (root operation "Inspection") is not assigned. Separate ICD-10-PCS codes are necessary for the removal of the uterus, cervix, ovaries, and fallopian tubes to represent a total hysterectomy.

17. **Outpatient surgery (episode 1):** The patient had a persistent left lung infiltrate on X-ray and subsequently had left pleural effusion. Thoracentesis and bronchoscopy with brush biopsy of the left lung were performed. Tissue studies yielded no diagnosis. The patient was to be admitted for further evaluation.

Diagnosis: Left pleural infiltrate on X-ray, pleural effusion.

J90	Pleural effusion, not elsewhere classified
R91	Abnormal findings on diagnostic imaging of lung
0W9B3ZZ	Drainage of left pleural cavity, percutaneous approach
0BBL8ZX	Excision of left lung, via natural or artificial opening endoscopic, diagnostic

Comments: The pleural effusion was the reason for the encounter. A code is assigned for the abnormal X-ray finding because the physician felt it to be significant and listed it as a diagnosis. The objective of the thoracentesis is to drain fluid from the pleural cavity.

Inpatient admission (episode 2): The patient was taken to surgery, where a thoracoscopy with decortication and left pleural biopsy were performed. The final specimen report showed moderately differentiated epidermoid carcinoma of the left lung. The patient's first course of electron beam radiation therapy was given prior to discharge.

Discharge diagnosis: Primary carcinoma of lung.

C34.92	Malignant neoplasm of unspecified part of left bronchus or lung
0BDP4ZZ	Extraction of left pleura, percutaneous endoscopic approach
0BBP4ZX	Excision of left pleura, percutaneous endoscopic approach, diagnostic
DB023ZZ	Beam radiation of lung using electrons

Comments: This admission was for further evaluation of the patient's condition, and surgery for the malignancy was performed. Although radiation therapy was begun during the hospital stay, it was not the purpose for this admission.

18. **Inpatient admission:** The patient developed right-sided tinnitus two years earlier, followed by a precipitous loss of hearing on the right side. A preadmission MRI scan identified a large acoustic neuroma. Because hearing on the right was totally lost, it was decided to excise the neuroma using an open radiosurgical destruction technique. The tumor was dissected completely. There were no postoperative complications, and the patient was discharged in satisfactory condition.

Discharge diagnosis: Acoustic neuroma on the right.

D33.3	Benign neoplasm of cranial nerves
005N0ZZ	Destruction of acoustic nerve, open approach

Comments: The hearing loss is integral to the neuroma, and so no additional code is assigned. The neuroma was destroyed using radiosurgical technique and therefore coded to the root operation "Destruction."

19. Inpatient admission: The patient, an elderly right-handed woman, was transferred from a nursing home with left hemiparesis and a diagnosis of suspected brain tumor. She underwent a CT-guided stereotactic biopsy without complications. The frozen-section diagnosis was glioblastoma. She was to come back for radiation therapy the following week, and in the meantime she was to be transferred back to the nursing home for further management. She had continued left hemiparesis, which prevents her from being managed at home.

Discharge diagnoses: (1) Primary glioblastoma, right temporal lobe; (2) left hemiparesis.

C71.2	Malignant neoplasm of temporal lobe
G81.94	Hemiplegia, unspecified affecting left nondominant side
0W914ZX	Drainage of cranial cavity, percutaneous endoscopic approach, diagnostic

Comments: The hemiparesis is not considered a late effect of the glioblastoma because glioblastoma is a current condition under treatment. Late effect is defined as "the residual effect that remains after the termination of the acute phase of an illness or injury."

20. Inpatient admission: The patient, an elderly woman, entered the hospital with a history of weight loss, anorexia, dysphagia, and rectal bleeding. She had also fallen many times at home. A fecal impaction was diagnosed from an abdominal CT scan following admission. Preparation for colonoscopy took about three days, and when the colonoscopy was finally accomplished, the impaction had cleared and no abnormalities were seen. A hiatal hernia was found on esophagogastroduodenoscopy, and two meningiomas were identified on magnetic resonance imaging of the head. She was started on Zantac for the hiatal hernia. It seemed that most of her generalized symptoms were secondary to the fecal impaction. The falling episodes are most likely related to the meningiomas, although they showed no mass effect. Neurological consultation was to be obtained as an outpatient. The patient was discharged on stool softeners for prevention of fecal impaction and Zantac for hiatal hernia.

Discharge diagnoses: (1) Meningiomas, (2) fecal impaction, (3) hiatal hernia.

K56.4	Fecal impaction
D32.9	Benign neoplasm of meninges, unspecified
K44.9	Diaphragmatic hernia without obstruction or gangrene
Z91.81	History of falling
0DJD8ZZ	Inspection of lower intestinal tract, via natural or artificial opening endoscopic
0DJ08ZZ	Inspection of upper intestinal tract, via natural or artificial opening endoscopic
BW20ZZZ	Computerized tomography (CT scan) of abdomen
B030ZZZ	Magnetic resonance imaging (MRI) of brain

Comments: Fecal impaction is designated as the principal diagnosis because it was felt to account for most of the admitting symptoms. Both the hiatal hernia and the meningiomas were diagnosed as the result of further evaluation of the patient's symptoms, with both conditions further evaluated and/or treated during this admission. Code Z91.81, History of falling, is assigned because of the patient's history of having fallen at home many times. This code is for patients who have fallen in the past and may be more susceptible to falling in the future. It also includes the concept of a person at risk for falling.

21. Inpatient admission: The patient was admitted with severe back pain. He had prostate cancer excised in 2006. An MRI performed prior to admission showed metastasis to the S1, S2, and S3 areas of the spine. A fine-needle aspiration biopsy of the sacrum was performed, and the report confirmed that metastatic adenocarcinoma, consistent with a prostatic primary, was strongly positive. A bilateral open scrotal orchiectomy was performed without complication. Megavoltage beam radiation treatments (photons 9 MeV) to the operative site were started, and the pain came under control with intravenous morphine. The patient was discharged with pain well controlled on oral medications.

Discharge diagnosis: Metastatic prostate cancer.

C79.51	Secondary malignant neoplasm of bone
G89.3	Neoplasm related pain (acute) (chronic)
Z85.46	Personal history of malignant neoplasm of prostate
0VTC0ZZ	Resection of bilateral testes, open approach
0QB13ZX	Excision of sacrum, percutaneous approach, diagnostic
DV010ZZ	Beam radiation of testis using photons <1 MeV

Comments: The narrative indicates that there are secondary sites of neoplasm in the spine. The primary site (prostate) was removed in 2006, and because there is no mention of any recurrence, history code Z85.46 is assigned. Radiotherapy was begun on this admission, but it was not the sole purpose of the admission. Code G89.3 is assigned as an additional diagnosis because the admission was for management of the neoplasm, and the pain associated with the neoplasm is also documented.

22. Inpatient admission: This 14-year-old patient was admitted to the hospital with a diagnosis of glioblastoma multiforme. The patient is now admitted to undergo a blood brain barrier disruption and percutaneous intra-arterial chemotherapy via the right internal carotid artery and, two days later, via the right basilar artery.

Discharge diagnosis: Glioblastoma multiforme, admit for chemotherapy.

Z51.11	Encounter for antineoplastic chemotherapy
C71.9	Malignant neoplasm of brain, unspecified
3E053GN	Introduction of blood brain barrier disruption substance into peripheral artery, percutaneous approach
3E06305	Introduction of other antineoplastic into central artery, percutaneous approach

Comments: Code Z51.11 is assigned as the principal diagnosis because the patient was admitted for chemotherapy, which was administered through the blood brain barrier for quicker absorption. Both the blood brain barrier disruption and the administration of chemotherapy should be assigned for the procedures.

18. INJURIES

1. **Inpatient admission:** The patient was struck in the face with a softball during a recreational ball game with no loss of consciousness. The result was severe compound fractures of the left ethmoid sinus and frontal sinus bones. The fractures were debrided, and open reduction was carried out. Initially, the postoperative course was uneventful, and the nasal packs, sutures, and nasal splint were removed. However, on the eighth day, the patient became confused and combative. A lumbar puncture was grossly positive for submeningitis. Again, improvement was rapid with antibiotics and intravenous steroids.

Discharge diagnoses: (1) Compound nasal, ethmoid, and frontal sinus fractures; (2) post-operative meningitis.

Procedures: Open reduction of compound fractures of the ethmoid and frontal sinus bones.

S02.19xB	Other fracture of base of skull, initial encounter for open fracture
G03.9	Meningitis, unspecified
W21.07xA	Struck by softball, initial encounter
Y92.838	Other recreation area as the place of occurrence of the external cause
Y93.64	Baseball
Y99.8	Other external cause status
0NSG0ZZ	Reposition left ethmoid bone, open approach
0NS20ZZ	Reposition left frontal bone, open approach
009U3ZX	Drainage of spinal canal, percutaneous approach, diagnostic

Comments: Compound fractures are open by definition. In ICD-10-CM the fracture code has a seventh-character qualifier. In this case the fractures are open and this is the initial encounter for the fracture. A placeholder "x" is used to allow for the seventh-character qualifier to be applied. When each of the fractured bones is referenced under the main term **Fracture,** there is an instruction to "see **Fracture,** skull, base."

The External cause code W21.07xA shows that the patient was struck by a softball. These codes require a seventh-character qualifier to indicate that this is the initial or subsequent encounter or a sequela. The placeholder "x" is used so that the qualifier character can be applied. The Y92.838 code indicates that the accident occurred in a place for recreation. ICD-10-CM has activity codes and activity status codes that are assigned for the initial encounter. Codes Y93.64 for playing softball and Y99.8 for recreational activity are assigned.

Fracture reduction is coded to the root operation "Reposition" in ICD-10-PCS, for moving to its normal location or other suitable location all or a portion of a body part. Separate codes exist for each bone, and laterality is required. The lumbar puncture is a drainage procedure for diagnostic purposes, so the qualifier character is X.

650

2. **Inpatient admission:** The patient, an elderly woman, was cleaning the bathroom and fell backward into the bathtub at her home. She was admitted with possible compression fractures of the lumbar spine. She had had several similar falls in the past due to frequent transient ischemic attacks. She lives alone in a single-family residence. X-rays of the spine showed some degenerative disk disease of L4 and L5, but there were no fractures. She was treated for pain and released after two days.

Discharge diagnoses: (1) Lumbar sprain injury to back, (2) probable transient ischemic attack.

S33.5xxA	Sprain of ligaments of lumbar spine, initial encounter
G45.9	Transient cerebral ischemic attack, unspecified
W18.12xA	Fall from or off toilet with subsequent striking against object, initial encounter
Y92.012	Bathroom of single-family (private) house as the place of occurrence of the external cause
Z91.81	History of falling
Y93.E5	Floor mopping and cleaning
Y99.8	Other external cause status

Comments: The compression fractures were ruled out; therefore, no codes are assigned. In ICD-10-CM the injury code has a seventh-character extension to indicate the status of the encounter. This is the initial encounter for the injury, so placeholder "x" is used as needed to allow the seventh-character extension to be applied. For the External cause of injury code, again the placeholder "x" is used before the seventh character for initial encounter.

The "probable" transient ischemic attack is coded as an established diagnosis because it is listed as a final diagnosis for an inpatient admission, and the summary strongly implies that the fall was probably due to another such attack. The radiology report contained incidental findings of degenerative disk disease that was not treated or further evaluated; therefore, no code is assigned for this condition. Code Z91.81, History of falling, is added because the patient has had several similar falls in the past. An activity code and activity status are added for the case.

Although the fractures were located in the lumbar area, the summary does not specify the area included in the X-ray.

3. Inpatient admission: The patient was carrying a bicycle up an outside stairway at his house when he fell from the stairway into the alley. An X-ray of the lumbosacral spine taken in the emergency department showed an L4 fracture, and X-ray of the upper arm revealed a nondisplaced comminuted fracture of the shaft of the right humerus. An L4-L5 bilateral posterior foraminotomy with fusion and a bone graft (obtained from the iliac crest) to the posterior column L4-L5 facet joints were performed. The fracture of the humerus was treated with application of a sling and immobilization for five days.

Discharge diagnoses: (1) Fracture, L4; (2) nondisplaced fracture, humerus.

S32.049A	Unspecified fracture of fourth lumbar vertebra, initial encounter for closed fracture
S42.354A	Nondisplaced comminuted fracture of shaft of humerus, right arm, initial encounter for closed fracture
W10.9xxA	Fall (on) (from) unspecified stairs and steps, initial encounter
Y92.018	Other place in single-family (private) house as the place of occurrence of the external cause
0SG1071	Fusion of 2 or more lumbar vertebral joints with autologous tissue substitute, posterior approach, posterior column, open approach
0QB20ZZ	Excision of right pelvic bone, open approach
2W38XYZ	Immobilization of right upper extremity using other device

Comments: The vertebral fracture is the more serious injury and received the major thrust of treatment; therefore, it is designated as the principal diagnosis. The ICD-10-CM code is specific for the L4 site, but the type of fracture is not specified. The closed nature of the fracture is reflected in the seventh-character qualifier. The S42.354A code includes the side of the body, nondisplaced, and the specific type of fracture as well as the fact that this is the initial encounter for a closed fracture. The patient was carrying a bicycle and not bicycling at the time of the accident, so no activity code is assigned.

Code 0SG1071 includes the open posterior approach to the posterior column, fusion, and use of bone graft, autologous tissue substitute. Code 0QB20ZZ is assigned to identify the harvesting of bone from the right iliac crest for use as a bone graft. The sling is placed on the entire arm, so the body part "upper extremity, right," is used.

4. Inpatient admission: The patient was admitted following a fall from a ladder at home while watering flowerboxes in the garden, in which she sustained numerous injuries. X-rays showed a nondisplaced fracture of the right humeral neck. A splint was applied, but no other treatment was required. There were contusions on her forehead, thighs, and knees, as well as small abrasions of her forehead and right thigh. The patient received pain medications because of the contusions. The abrasions were superficial and healed without treatment and without evidence of infection.

Discharge diagnoses: (1) Nondisplaced fracture, right humerus; (2) contusions of forehead, thighs, and knees; (3) abrasions on forehead and right thigh.

S42.214A	Unspecified nondisplaced fracture of surgical neck of right humerus, initial encounter for closed fracture
S00.83xA	Contusion of other part of head, initial encounter
S70.11xA	Contusion of right thigh, initial encounter
S70.12xA	Contusion of left thigh, initial encounter
S80.01xA	Contusion of right knee, initial encounter
S80.02xA	Contusion of left knee, initial encounter
W11.xxxA	Fall on and from ladder, initial encounter
Y92.017	Garden or yard in single-family (private) house as the place of occurrence of the external cause
Y93.H2	Activity, gardening and landscaping
Y99.8	Other external cause status
2W3CX1Z	Immobilization of right lower arm using splint

Comments: The fracture is the most severe injury and is therefore designated as the principal diagnosis. Because the fracture was not displaced, no "Reduction" was required. The code is located by referencing the main term **Fracture,** subterms "anatomic neck," "see fracture humerus," "upper end." At this entry subterm "upper end anatomical neck," see "fracture, humerus, upper end, specified NEC, non-displaced" to get to the code S42.21-. Complete the code by checking the Tabular List.

Codes are listed for the contusions of the forehead and for both the left and right thighs and knee, as pain killers were administered for these injuries. No codes are assigned for the abrasions because they required no further evaluation, and no definitive treatment was directed to them.

5. Inpatient admission: The patient was admitted with diagnoses of probable rib fractures and pneumonia. She slipped and fell in the bathtub of her single-family home while taking a shower about four days before admission and had experienced increasingly severe upper back and neck pain. Just prior to admission, she began running a fever, felt short of breath, and developed inspiratory chest wall pain. No rib fractures were identified on chest X-ray, but right upper lobe pneumonia was evident. Sputum culture grew *Klebsiella*. The patient was started on antibiotics and the pneumonia improved. Back pain was relieved by pain medication and bed rest.

Discharge diagnoses: (1) Right upper lobe pneumonia, (2) cervical and thoracic back strain.

J15.0	Pneumonia due to Klebsiella pneumoniae
S13.4xxA	Sprain of ligaments of cervical spine, initial encounter
S23.8xxA	Sprain of other specified parts of thorax, initial encounter
W18.2xxA	Fall in (into) shower or empty bathtub, initial encounter
Y92.012	Bathroom of single-family (private) house as the place of occurrence of the external cause
Y93.E1	Activity, personal bathing and showering
Y99.8	Other external cause status

Comments: The condition responsible for admission, after study, was found to be pneumonia. The back strain occurred four days prior to admission and probably would not have required hospital admission if it had been the only problem. Although this injury happened four days ago, this is still the initial encounter while the patient is receiving active treatment for the condition. The pneumonia was described in the narrative as being due to *Klebsiella*; pneumonia of a lobe of the lung is not "lobar" pneumonia. In addition, the activity and activity status codes for bathing are also assigned.

6. **Emergency department visit:** The patient and her husband had been drinking heavily, became intoxicated, and had an argument when they got home to their second-floor apartment. During the argument, he shoved her and she fell in the bedroom against the corner of the water bed, striking her left upper back and chest. She came to the emergency department complaining of severe pain and difficulty breathing. She was found to have subcutaneous emphysema due to the fractures of the ninth and tenth ribs. The ribs were strapped, and she was given a prescription for pain medication. She was released to be followed up as an outpatient.

Diagnoses: (1) Fractured left ribs, ninth and tenth posteriorly; (2) subcutaneous emphysema; (3) alcohol abuse with intoxication.

S22.42xA	Multiple fractures of ribs, left side, initial encounter for closed fracture
T79.7xxA	Traumatic subcutaneous emphysema, initial encounter
F10.129	Alcohol abuse with intoxication, unspecified
W18.09	Striking against other object with subsequent fall, initial encounter
Y92.032	Bedroom in apartment as the place of occurrence of the external cause
Y04.0xxA	Assault by unarmed brawl or fight, initial encounter

Comments: The fractured ribs were the reason for the emergency department encounter. Although the alcohol abuse was not further evaluated or treated, it was closely related to the trauma and should be coded.

7. **Inpatient admission:** The patient, an elderly woman, was admitted following a fall off her porch at her single-family home while sweeping leaves off the porch. A femoral intertrochanteric fracture was diagnosed in the emergency department, and she was admitted. An open reduction with internal fixation was carried out. As anticipated, postoperative transfusions of whole blood via central vein for blood loss were required during surgery. The blood loss resulted in a drop in hemoglobin and hematocrit, which were monitored daily. Her postoperative recovery went smoothly, and she was transferred to the skilled nursing unit for rehabilitation.

Discharge diagnoses: (1) Closed fracture, right femur; (2) acute blood loss anemia.

S72.141A	Displaced intertrochanteric fracture of right femur, initial encounter for closed fracture
D62	Acute posthemorrhagic anemia
W13.9xxA	Fall from, out of or through building, not otherwise specified, initial encounter
Y92.018	Other place in single-family (private) house as the place of occurrence of the external cause
Y93.H9	Activity, other involving exterior property and land maintenance, building and construction
Y99.8	Other external cause status
0QS604Z	Reposition right upper femur with internal fixation device, open approach
30243H1	Transfusion of nonautologous whole blood into central vein, percutaneous approach

Comments: The fracture is described as intertrochanteric in the narrative and so the more specific code is assigned. Fractures not specified as open or closed are coded as closed. Fractures not specified as displaced or nondisplaced are coded as displaced. The surgery resulted in only an expected amount of blood loss. However, treatment was rendered (transfusions) and monitoring continued (hemoglobin and hematocrit).

8. Inpatient admission: Three weeks before admission, the patient, a construction worker, sustained a perilunate dislocation along with closed fractures of the third metacarpal and proximal middle phalanx bones of the left hand in an accident. The accident occurred when he went to sleep at the wheel and the dump truck he was driving overturned in the median of the interstate; no other vehicles were involved. Immediately after the accident, the patient was seen in a local emergency department, where the metacarpal fracture was reduced and casted and the proximal phalanx was reduced and splinted. The perilunate dislocation was not reduced at that time. He was now admitted to this hospital, where a closed reduction of the perilunate dislocation was carried out after X-rays confirmed there was no fracture and the phalangeal and metacarpal fractures remained in good alignment. A short arm cast was applied, and he was discharged.

Discharge diagnoses: (1) Closed right perilunate dislocation, (2) healing fractures of the metacarpal shaft and proximal phalanx on the right.

S63.092A	Other subluxation of left wrist and hand, initial encounter
S62.323A	Displaced fracture of shaft of third metacarpal bone, left hand, initial encounter for closed fracture
S62.613A	Displaced fracture of proximal phalanx of left middle finger, initial encounter for closed fracture
V85.5xxA	Driver of special construction vehicle injured in nontraffic accident, initial encounter
Y92.411	Interstate highway as the place of occurrence of the external cause
Y93.H9	Activity, other involving exterior property and land maintenance, building and construction
Y99.0	Civilian activity done for income or pay
0RSPXZZ	Reposition left wrist joint, external approach

Comments: The lunate bone is in the wrist. Fractures that are not specified as open or closed are coded as closed; those not specified as nondisplaced or displaced are coded as displaced. Although three weeks old, the fractures have not healed and are current injuries, and the patient is receiving active treatment for the fracture. This qualifies as an initial encounter as the patient is still involved in active treatment of the injury with a new physician. Code V85.5xxA is referenced in the Index to External Causes of Injury under the entry **Accident,** dump truck,—see **Accident,** transport, construction vehicle occupant. Refer to the Tabular List to complete the code. Activity codes are assigned as this is the initial encounter for treatment of this particular injury.

9. Inpatient admission: The patient fell from a tree that he was pruning on his farm. He was able to drive himself to the hospital, but it was apparent on admission that his left arm was fractured. He underwent an open reduction and internal fixation of a fracture of the proximal humerus and an open reduction and internal fixation of the comminuted fractures of the radial and ulnar shafts. He recovered without incident and was discharged to follow up in one week.

Discharge diagnoses: (1) Comminuted left radius and ulnar shaft fractures, (2) displaced left proximal humerus fracture.

S42.202A	Unspecified fracture of upper end of left humerus, initial encounter for closed fracture
S52.252A	Displaced comminuted fracture of shaft of ulna, left arm, initial encounter for closed fracture
S52.352A	Displaced comminuted fracture of shaft of radius, left arm, initial encounter for closed fracture
W14.xxxA	Fall from tree, initial encounter
Y92.79	Other farm location as the place of occurrence of the external cause
Y93.H2	Activity, gardening and landscaping
Y99.0	Civilian activity done for income or pay
0PSG04Z	Reposition left humeral shaft with internal fixation device, open approach
0PSJ04Z	Reposition left radius with internal fixation device, open approach
0PSL04Z	Reposition left ulna with internal fixation device, open approach

Comments: ICD-10-CM requires separate codes for the fractures of the radius and ulna. The narrative provides more specificity as to the location of the fractures, and so the more specific codes are assigned. Either fracture could have been designated as the principal diagnosis because both are essentially equal in severity. ICD-10-PCS codes are assigned for each site repositioned.

10. **Inpatient admission:** The patient fell in her apartment after tripping over her cat while carrying a laundry basket to the washer. She was brought in by ambulance and admitted with a fracture of the shaft of right femur. An open reduction with internal fixation was performed. A postoperative fever developed, and a chest X-ray showed severe atelectasis as the cause of the fever. Respiratory therapy gave instructions on incentive spirometry, antibiotics were initiated, and the patient was discharged to a nursing home.

    Discharge diagnoses: (1) Closed fracture, femur; (2) postoperative fever and atelectasis.

S72.301A	Unspecified fracture of shaft of right femur, initial encounter for closed fracture
J98.11	Atelectasis
J95.89	Other postprocedural complications and disorders of respiratory system, not elsewhere classified
W01.0xxA	Fall on same level from slipping, tripping and stumbling without subsequent striking against object, initial encounter
Y92.039	Unspecified place in apartment as the place of occurrence of the external cause
Y93.E2	Activity, laundry
Y99.8	Other external cause status
0QS804Z	Reposition right femoral shaft with internal fixation device, open approach

Comments: The information in the narrative is used to assign a more specific code for the fracture. Assign codes J98.11 and J95.89 because the fever and atelectasis were specified as postoperative. The fever is a symptom of the atelectasis. Postoperative atelectasis is often an incidental radiographic or physical finding that is frequently a self-limiting condition, in which case it would not be coded or reported. In this case, it was associated with fever and required further diagnostic (e.g., chest X-ray) and therapeutic (e.g., incentive spirometry) workup.

11. **Inpatient admission:** The patient was admitted after a box fell on his head at the service garage where he works. A CT scan of the head was negative for any abnormalities, but hourly neurological checks were made to rule out an intracranial injury. No injury was found. A small abrasion on his upper right arm, where the box scraped the skin, was cleansed and Neosporin applied.

    Discharge diagnosis: Observation for possible intracranial injury.

Z04.2	Encounter for examination and observation following work accident
S40.811A	Abrasion of right upper arm, initial encounter
W20.8xxA	Other cause of strike by thrown, projected or falling object, initial encounter
Y92.524	Gas station as the place of occurrence of the external cause
Y93.89	Activity, other specified
Y99.0	Civilian activity done for income or pay

Comments: The purpose of the admission was to determine whether the patient had suffered any kind of intracranial injury; this was ruled out. Even though there was a minor injury that did not require hospital admission, the observation code is still assigned as the principal diagnosis. This situation is consistent with the inclusion note with category Z04, "when a person without a diagnosis is suspected of having an abnormal condition, without signs or symptoms, which requires study, but after examination and observation, is ruled out."

12. **Inpatient admission:** The patient, a seven-year-old male, sustained a high-velocity gunshot wound in a drive-by shooting. He was riding his bike in his neighborhood street. He was brought to the emergency department with a massive hemorrhage from the left groin due to the gunshot wound. He also sustained major lacerations of the femoral artery and femoral vein at the hip level, in addition to a bullet lodged in the femur. The patient was immediately taken to surgery. The following procedures were performed via incision: (1) left internal iliac to femoral artery bypass graft with reverse saphenous vein graft; (2) left popliteal to femoral vein bypass graft with greater saphenous vein graft; (3) removal of bullet from the femur; (4) insertion of pins in fracture, left femur.

Discharge diagnoses: (1) Lacerations of left common femoral artery and femoral vein, with massive hemorrhage; (2) gunshot wound to left groin with high-velocity rifle; (3) bullet lodged in femur; (4) open, nondisplaced, type III C nondisplaced subtrochanteric fracture of left femur.

S75.022A	Major laceration of femoral artery, left leg, initial encounter
S75.122A	Major laceration of femoral vein at hip and thigh level, left leg, initial encounter
S31.124A	Laceration of abdominal wall with foreign body, left lower quadrant without penetration into peritoneal cavity, initial encounter
S72.25xC	Nondisplaced subtrochanteric fracture of left femur, initial encounter for open fracture type IIIA, IIIB, or IIIC
X95.8xxA	Assault by other firearm discharge, initial encounter
Y92.414	Local residential or business street as the place of occurrence of the external cause
Y93.55	Activity, bike riding
Y99.8	Other external cause status
041F09J	Bypass left internal iliac artery to left femoral artery with autologous venous tissue, open approach
0QH704Z	Insertion of internal fixation device into left upper femur, open approach
0QC70ZZ	Extirpation of matter from left upper femur, open approach
06BQ0ZZ	Excision of left greater saphenous vein, open approach

Comments: Because the hemorrhage was life threatening, either blood vessel laceration could represent the principal diagnosis. The injury was not incidental to the fracture (did not occur secondary to the fracture) but occurred in addition to the fracture as a result of the gunshot wound. The fracture was stated to be a type IIIC, so the seventh character "C" is used. There were two bypass procedures performed. In ICD-10-PCS the body part value identifies the origin of the bypass and the qualifier identifies the destination. The harvesting of the greater saphenous vein used for the bypass graft is coded separately to the root operation "Excision." Putting a pin into a nondisplaced fracture is coded to the root operation "Insertion." The removal of the bullet from the femur meets the definition of the root procedure "Extirpation": taking or cutting out solid matter from a body part.

13. **Inpatient admission:** The patient, a 10-year-old boy, was admitted through the emergency department after being struck by an automobile while riding his bicycle in the street in front of his home. His injuries were fractures of the left tibia and fibula, a 4-centimeter laceration and superficial abrasions on the left side of head, and a 1-centimeter-deep laceration on the right earlobe. The fractures were reduced via incision, and an intramedullary Rush rod was placed in the left tibia. The earlobe and head lacerations were sutured.

Discharge diagnoses: (1) Simple fractures, left tibia and fibula; (2) right ear laceration; (3) left parietooccipital laceration.

S82.202A	Unspecified fracture of shaft of left tibia, initial encounter for closed fracture
S82.402A	Unspecified fracture of shaft of left fibula, initial encounter for closed fracture
S01.01xA	Laceration without foreign body of scalp, initial encounter
S01.311A	Laceration without foreign body of right ear, initial encounter
V13.4	Pedal cycle driver injured in collision with car, pick-up truck or van in traffic accident
Y92.414	Local residential or business street as the place of occurrence of the external cause
Y93.55	Activity, bike riding
Y99.8	Other external cause status
0QSH06Z	Reposition left tibia with intramedullary fixation device, open approach
0QSK0ZZ	Reposition left fibula, open approach
0HQ2XZZ	Repair right ear skin, external approach
0HQ0XZZ	Repair scalp skin, external approach

Comments: No code is assigned for the superficial abrasions because they are associated with a more severe injury at the same site. Fractures not specified as open or closed are coded as closed. ICD-10-CM has separate codes for fractures of the tibia and fibula, and ICD-10-PCS has separate codes for the reductions, which qualify as the root procedure "Reposition." A Rush rod is an "intramedullary fixation device."

14. **Emergency department visit (episode 1):** The patient had been drinking heavily in recent weeks. While visiting the area, he reduced his alcohol intake during the past 24 hours and suffered a seizure. In the emergency department, he seemed to be normal. No neurological or physical abnormalities were noted, and he was released after receiving Dilantin.

Diagnosis: Seizure, probably due to decrease in alcohol consumption.

R56.9	Unspecified convulsions

Comments: Code R56.9 is the appropriate code assignment for this encounter. "Probable" conditions are not coded in the outpatient setting.

Inpatient admission (episode 2): The patient returned to his room at a local motel, had another seizure, and then fell in the bathroom. He was again brought to the emergency department and found to have a dislocated shoulder. Several attempts were made to replace the shoulder to its proper position. Because this reduction was not successful, he was admitted. With medications to control alcohol withdrawal and seizures along with IV fluids, he became mentally clear. A closed reduction of the dislocated shoulder was performed. The injury became a difficult management problem because the patient would not leave the orthopedic appliance on, and the next day a heavy plaster cast was placed on the shoulder to ensure correct positioning and activity reduction.

Discharge diagnoses: (1) Alcohol withdrawal seizure, (2) left shoulder dislocation.

S43.005A	Unspecified dislocation of left shoulder joint, initial encounter
F10.239	Alcohol dependence with withdrawal, unspecified
R56.9	Unspecified convulsions
W18.00XA	Striking against unspecified object with subsequent fall, initial encounter
Y92.59	Other trade areas as the place of occurrence of the external cause
0RSJXZZ	Reposition right shoulder joint, external approach
2W39X2Z	Immobilization of left upper extremity using cast

Comments: Because attempts to reduce the dislocation were unsuccessful in the emergency department, the patient was admitted. Therefore, shoulder dislocation is the principal diagnosis.

15. **Emergency department visit (episode 1):** The 14-year-old patient was brought to the emergency department with severe pain and swelling of his left ankle. He sustained the injury when he fell off his skateboard on the grade school playground. An X-ray showed a simple trimalleolar fracture of his left ankle. The fracture was reduced, and he was placed in a long leg cast.

Diagnosis: Severe pain and swelling, left ankle, associated with trimalleolar fracture.

S82.852A	Displaced trimalleolar fracture of left lower leg, initial encounter for closed fracture
V00.131A	Fall from skateboard, initial encounter
Y92.211	Elementary school as the place of occurrence of the external cause
Y93.51	Activity, roller skating (inline) and skateboarding
Y99.8	Other external cause status
0QSH3ZZ	Reposition left tibia, percutaneous approach

Comments: A trimalleolar fracture involves the medial, lateral, and posterior malleoli of the tibia. A simple fracture is closed. Fractures that are not specified as nondisplaced or displaced are coded as displaced. Reduction of a displaced fracture is coded to the root operation "Reposition," and the application of a cast or splint in conjunction with the "Reposition" procedure is not coded separately.

Orthopedic clinic visit (episode 2): The patient was status post trimalleolar fracture of the left ankle. He had been in the cast since sustaining the injury three weeks earlier. He had no complaints regarding the fracture, but he had worn down the cast. The cast breakdown extended the length of the sole of the foot. The long leg cast was removed, and the skin was intact. X-rays showed a healing fracture with no change in the reduction. Therefore, he was placed back into a short leg walking cast.

Diagnosis: Aftercare, healing left trimalleolar fracture.

S82.852D	Displaced trimalleolar fracture of left lower leg, subsequent encounter for closed fracture with routine healing
V00.131D	Fall from skateboard, subsequent encounter
2W0RX2Z	Change cast on left lower leg

Comments: The fracture is healing, and the patient was seen solely for cast change. In ICD-10-CM, aftercare for fractures is indicated by using the fracture code with a seventh-character extension for subsequent encounter. In this case "D" is used, as this is routine healing for a closed fracture. The External cause code is used for each encounter for which the injury or condition is being treated. This code also has the seventh-character extension "D," showing that this is a subsequent encounter.

Orthopedic clinic visit (episode 3): The patient is status post trimalleolar fracture of the left ankle. The fracture now appears to be well healed. The cast was removed. There is no swelling or redness. No additional follow-up is anticipated.

Diagnosis: Aftercare, status post left trimalleolar fracture.

S82.852D	Displaced trimalleolar fracture of left lower leg, subsequent encounter for closed fracture with routine healing
V00.131D	Fall from skateboard, subsequent encounter
2W5RX2Z	Removal of cast on left lower leg

Comments: The fracture has healed, and the patient is seen solely for removal of cast. This episode of care qualifies as a subsequent encounter, after the patient has received active treatment of the injury and is receiving routine care during the healing or recovery phase. The External cause code is used for each encounter for which the injury or condition is being treated. Both codes have the qualifier "D," showing that this is a subsequent encounter.

16. **Inpatient admission:** The patient fractured her left knee several years earlier when she was thrown off a horse. Since then she had undergone realignment and debridement procedures of the undersurface of the patella. At the time of admission, she was severely disabled with multiple effusions, pain, crepitation, and inability to bear weight on the leg. She was taken to surgery and underwent an uneventful total patellectomy. The knee was immobilized with a cast, and she was discharged.

Discharge diagnosis: Left patellofemoral arthritis.

M12.562	Traumatic arthropathy, left knee
S82.002S	Unspecified fracture of left patella, sequela
Z87.81	Personal history of (healed) traumatic fracture
V80.010S	Animal-rider injured by fall from or being thrown from horse in noncollision accident, sequela
0QTF0ZZ	Resection of left patella, open approach

Comments: The current arthritis is a late effect of the previous fracture and is therefore coded as traumatic arthritis. ICD-10-CM has the qualifier character "S," which is added to the fracture code to indicate a late effect of a fracture. Code Z87.81 is assigned to show a history of traumatic fracture. The External cause code is used for each encounter for which the injury or condition is being treated. The seventh-character extension "S" is added to indicate that this is a sequela of the injury.

17. **Inpatient admission:** The woman suffered a displaced fracture dislocation of her right ankle. The injury happened when she jumped off her single-family home front porch in an attempt to catch her fleeing dog, who was being given a bath. She underwent an open reduction and internal fixation of the fracture and was treated with elevation, bed rest, analgesics, and antibiotics. She was released in stable condition.

Discharge diagnosis: Trimalleolar fracture dislocation, right ankle.

S82.851A	Displaced trimalleolar fracture of right lower leg, initial encounter for closed fracture
W13.8xxA	Fall from, out of or through other building or structure, initial encounter
Y92.018	Other place in single-family (private) house as the place of occurrence of the external cause
Y93.K9	Activity, other involving animal care
Y99.8	Other external cause status
0QSG04Z	Reposition right tibia with internal fixation device, open approach

Comments: A trimalleolar fracture involves the medial, lateral, and posterior malleoli of the tibia. A fracture dislocation is coded to fracture. A displaced fracture is a closed fracture.

18. Inpatient admission: The patient was shopping at a retail food warehouse when a gallon can of tomatoes fell on his head from a shelf about 15 feet overhead. He was briefly unconscious and disoriented. X-rays of his skull showed a depressed parasagittal skull fracture with considerable parasagittal depression. He was admitted and taken to surgery, where a craniectomy was performed, with elevation of the depressed skull fracture.

Discharge diagnosis: Depressed skull fracture.

S02.0xxA	Fracture of vault of skull, initial encounter for closed fracture
S06.9x1A	Unspecified intracranial injury with loss of consciousness of 30 minutes or less, initial encounter
W20.8xxA	Other cause of strike by thrown, projected or falling object, initial encounter
Y92.512	Supermarket, store or market as the place of occurrence of the external cause
0NS00ZZ	Reposition skull, open approach

Comments: The parasagittal area is where the two parietal bones come together in the vault of the skull. The patient was briefly unconscious following the injury. In the Alphabetic Index under **Loss,** consciousness, the cross-reference is to **Injury,** intracranial. S06.9x1A indicates head injury NOS with a loss of consciousness for 30 minutes or less. The accident occurred in a retail store. The procedure had as its objective to "Reposition," moving to its normal location or other suitable location all or a portion of a body part.

19. Inpatient admission: The patient fractured her left patella when she suffered a fall into a hole while golfing on the public golf course. She was taken to surgery, where an open reduction and internal fixation were performed without complication. By the second postoperative day, she was ambulatory on crutches and ready for discharge.

Discharge diagnosis: Closed fracture, left patella.

S82.002A	Unspecified fracture of left patella, initial encounter for closed fracture
W17.2xxA	Fall into hole, initial encounter
Y92.39	Other specified sports and athletic area as the place of occurrence of the external cause
Y93.53	Activity, golf
Y99.8	Other external cause status
0QSF04Z	Reposition left patella with internal fixation device, open approach

Comments: Although the fracture was closed, an open reduction procedure with internal fixation was performed.

20. Physician office visit: The patient went to see his physician after falling off a moving motorcycle. He complained of leg pain, and the physician noted swelling in the right lower extremity. The physician felt that a fracture of the tibia was probable and referred the patient for X-ray to confirm or rule out. For reasons unknown, the patient did not report to the hospital radiology department and did not return to see the physician as instructed.

Diagnosis: Suspected fracture, right tibia.

M79.604	Pain in right leg
M79.89	Other specified soft tissue disorders
V28.4xxA	Motorcycle driver injured in noncollision transport accident in traffic accident, initial encounter

Comments: Conditions are coded only to the highest level of certainty in the physician office setting. Therefore, codes are assigned only for the symptoms of leg pain and swelling. No code is assigned for the possible tibial fracture.

19. BURNS

1. Inpatient admission: The patient sustained flash burns when his clothing caught fire. Someone had thrown gasoline onto the park cooking grill by which he was cooking. He suffered second-degree burns to the face, neck, and upper chest, with some first- and second-degree burns on the left forearm. All in all, 12 percent of the total body surface area was burned. The wounds were treated with antibiotics and pain medications. Physical therapists debrided the burned areas and provided hydrotherapy. The wounds continued to heal, and the patient was discharged.

Discharge diagnoses: (1) Second-degree burns, face, neck, and upper chest; (2) first- and second-degree burns, left forearm; (3) 12 percent of body surface affected by burns.

T22.212A	Burn of second degree of left forearm, initial encounter
T20.20xA	Burn of second degree of head, face, and neck, unspecified site, initial encounter
T21.21xA	Burn of second degree of chest wall, initial encounter
T31.10	Burns involving 10-19% of body surface with 0% to 9% third degree burns
X04.xxxA	Exposure to ignition of highly flammable material, initial encounter
Y92.830	Public park as the place of occurrence of the external cause
Y93.G2	Activity, grilling and smoking food
Y99.8	Other external cause status
F08D5BZ	Wound management treatment of integumentary system—head and neck using physical agents
F08F5BZ	Wound management treatment of integumentary system—upper back / upper extremity using physical agents
0HD1XZZ	Extraction of face skin, external approach
0HD4XZZ	Extraction of neck skin, external approach
0HDEXZZ	Extraction of left lower arm skin, external approach
0HD5XZZ	Extraction of chest skin, external approach

Comments: The patient had first- and second-degree burns on the forearm, but only the highest degree is coded. Code T31.10 is assigned to identify 12 percent of the total body surface that was affected by first- and second-degree burns, with no third-degree burns. Code X04.xxxA indicates that the cause was the ignition of highly flammable material, and code Y92.830 indicates that the injury took place in a park. The activity code is assigned for grilling. Hydrotherapy codes are assigned for the two areas treated. See the Alphabetic Index under the main term **Debridement,** subterm "nonexcisional"; the root operation is "Extraction." One code for each site debrided is assigned.

2. **Inpatient admission:** The patient was brought to the emergency department after being burned. He had been clearing and burning brush in a field at his farm when a gust of wind moved the fire to his tractor. There was an explosion because of the gasoline fumes, and he caught fire. He was treated with IV fluids, antibiotics, and pain medications. All in all, 14 percent of the total body surface was affected by the burns, of which 4 percent was third degree. He was transferred to a burn treatment center for surgical debridement and skin grafting.

Discharge diagnoses: (1) First- and second-degree burns of the face, right ear, right forearm, and right thumb; (2) third-degree burns of the left hand.

T23.302A	Burn of third degree of left hand, unspecified site, initial encounter
T20.20xA	Burn of second degree of head, face, and neck, unspecified site, initial encounter
T20.211A	Burn of second degree of right ear [any part, except ear drum], initial encounter
T22.211A	Burn of second degree of right forearm, initial encounter
T23.211A	Burn of second degree of right thumb (nail), initial encounter
T31.10	Burns involving 10-19% of body surface with 0% to 9% third degree burns
W30.89xA	Contact with other specified agricultural machinery, initial encounter
W40.1xxA	Explosion of explosive gases, initial encounter
Y92.73	Farm field as the place of occurrence of the external cause
Y93.H9	Activity, other involving exterior property and land maintenance, building and construction
Y99.8	Other external cause status

Comments: The first- and second-degree burns are coded to second degree only. The third-degree burns to the left hand are coded T23.302A. The third degree is sequenced first because it reflects the highest degree of burns. Fourteen percent of the body was affected by burns, of which 4 percent was affected by third degree. The fourth character "0" is assigned because there was less than 10 percent third-degree burn. W30.89xA indicates that the accident was caused by farm machinery; W40.1xxA indicates explosion.

3. **Inpatient admission (episode 1):** The patient was admitted with burns of her right hand and fingers up to the wrist. She had reached into hot water, not realizing the temperature, while canning on her farm. She was taken to surgery, where an excisional debridement of the burns was carried out. A split thickness skin graft was applied over the dorsum and volar aspects of the hand. The postoperative recovery was without infection or other complication.

Discharge diagnosis: Second- and third-degree burns, right hand and fingers (3 percent of total body surface burned, 2 percent affected by third degree).

T23.391A	Burn of third degree of multiple sites of right wrist and hand, initial encounter
X12.xxxA	Contact with other hot fluids, initial encounter
Y92.79	Other farm location as the place of occurrence of the external cause
Y93.G3	Activity, cooking and baking
Y99.8	Other external cause status
0HRFX74	Replacement of right hand skin with autologous tissue substitute, partial thickness, external approach
0HBFXZZ	Excision of right hand skin, external approach

Comments: For burns of more than one degree of the same site, code to the most severe degree. To identify multiple sites of wrist and hands, assign code T23.391A. The skin graft meets the objective of the root operation "Replacement," putting in or on biological or synthetic material that physically takes the place and/or function of all or a portion of a body part.

Physician office visit (episode 2): Both the burns and the surgical site on this woman's hand seem to be healing nicely. There was no evidence of infection. The area was rebandaged. Antibiotics were continued, and she was to return the following week.

Diagnosis: Second- and third-degree burns, right hand and fingers.

T23.391D	Burn of third degree of multiple sites of right wrist and hand, subsequent encounter
X12.xxxD	Contact with other hot fluids, subsequent encounter

Comments: This episode of care qualifies as a subsequent encounter, after the patient has received active treatment of the injury and is receiving routine care during the healing or recovery phase. The External cause code is used for each encounter for which the injury or condition is being treated. Both codes have the qualifier "D," showing that this is a subsequent encounter.

20. POISONING, TOXIC EFFECTS, ADVERSE EFFECTS, AND UNDERDOSING OF DRUGS

1. Inpatient admission: The patient, a 33-year-old male, was admitted through the emergency department after an overdose of Dilantin. His gait was ataxic and he had nausea, vomiting, and blurry vision. His Dilantin level was 48. He had AIDS-related complex (ARC), well documented from previous hospitalizations. He also had posttraumatic seizure disorder, which resulted from an intracranial injury received in a 1987 motor vehicle accident. On questioning, he admitted to taking an additional 400 milligrams of Dilantin accidentally on the day of admission. Over the next four days, the Dilantin level gradually decreased to 16.1, and the regular dosage was restarted. It was clear that the current dosage was adequate in preventing seizures without significant side effects.

Discharge diagnoses: (1) Dilantin toxicity, (2) HIV positive, (3) posttraumatic seizure disorder.

T42.0x1A	Poisoning by hydantoin derivatives, accidental (unintentional), initial encounter
R26.0	Ataxic gait
R11.2	Nausea with vomiting, unspecified
H53.8	Other visual disturbances
B20	Human immunodeficiency virus [HIV] disease
G40.909	Epilepsy, unspecified, not intractable, without status epilepticus
S06.9x9S	Unspecified intracranial injury with loss of consciousness of unspecified duration, sequela
V89.2xxS	Person injured in unspecified motor-vehicle accident, traffic, sequela

Comments: In ICD-10-CM the poisoning code includes information on the cause (e.g., the responsible substance) as well as the intent (e.g., accidental), and no additional External cause code is required for the poisoning. The late effect of the intracranial Injury is indicated by the code for the injury with the qualifier character "S" for sequelae. The External cause code is used for each encounter for which the injury is being treated. In this case, the "S" for sequelae is used as the seventh-character extension.

2. Outpatient clinic visit: The patient came in because of a new rash on his trunk. The thrush, previously diagnosed and being treated with Dapsone, is improving.

Diagnoses: (1) Skin rash due to an allergic reaction to Dapsone taken internally as prescribed, (2) thrush.

T37.1x5A	Adverse effect of antimycobacterial drugs, initial encounter
L27.0	Generalized skin eruption due to drugs and medicaments taken internally
B37.0	Candidal stomatitis

Comments: The reason for this outpatient encounter is the skin rash, which is an adverse reaction to the therapeutic use of Dapsone. In ICD-10-CM the code from categories T30 through T50 that indicates adverse effect is used and sequenced first, with an additional code for any manifestations of adverse effects.

3. **Inpatient admission:** The patient underwent an autologous bone marrow transplantation for choriocarcinoma 13 days earlier. He was readmitted four hours after discharge with a rash, which changed character to an urticarial type of eruption. A skin biopsy of the right lower arm revealed superficial perivascular infiltrate consistent with urticaria. The patient had been started on vancomycin the morning prior to admission. Vancomycin was discontinued, and the urticaria cleared spontaneously.

Discharge diagnoses: (1) Vancomycin allergy with an urticarial reaction, (2) choriocarcinoma.

T36.8x5A	Adverse effect of other systemic antibiotics, initial encounter
L40.0	Psoriasis vulgaris
C62.90	Malignant neoplasm of unspecified testis, unspecified whether descended or undescended
0HBDXZX	Excision of right lower arm skin, external approach, diagnostic

Comments: The manifestation of the adverse reaction (urticaria) was responsible for admission. In ICD-10-CM, the code from categories T30 through T50 that indicates adverse effect is used and sequenced first, with an additional code for any manifestations of adverse effects.

Choriocarcinoma is referenced under its name, as a main entry, in the Alphabetic Index of Diseases and Injuries. The code for an unspecified site, male patient, is C62.90.

The skin biopsy is coded as "Excision," with a qualifier for diagnostic.

4. **Inpatient admission:** The patient, a 73-year-old male, was admitted for upper and lower gastrointestinal endoscopy for gastrointestinal bleeding. The preoperative evaluation showed a heart rate on three occasions of 35, 36, and 37. The patient normally had a heart rate in the upper 40s and had never had one in the 30s. The procedure was canceled due to his bradycardia, and a cardiac evaluation was to be obtained prior to rescheduling. The slow heart rate may have been a reaction to atropine because it occurred shortly after administration of the drug.

Discharge diagnoses: (1) Gastrointestinal bleed, (2) slow heart rate due to atropine correctly administered.

K92.2	Gastrointestinal hemorrhage, unspecified
T44.4x5A	Adverse effect of predominantly alpha-adrenoreceptor agonists, initial encounter
R00.1	Bradycardia, unspecified
Z53.09	Procedure and treatment not carried out because of other contraindication

Comments: The gastrointestinal bleed remains the principal diagnosis even though the planned treatment was not carried out because of the adverse reaction to the atropine. Slow heart rate is bradycardia. T44.4x5A indicates that this is an adverse effect and initial encounter. Code Z53.09 is assigned to indicate that the planned treatment was not carried out because of a contraindication due to the bradycardia.

5. Inpatient admission: The patient, a 46-year-old with AIDS, was recently discharged after workups for fever and weight loss, which were negative. He was readmitted because of histoplasmosis. Amphotericin B was started, and he tolerated the treatment well. Because the patient needed to continue treatment with this medication at home over a fairly long period of time, a Hickman catheter was inserted as a vascular access device to facilitate administration. He also had severe granulocytopenia, thought to be due to AZT, which was discontinued.

Discharge diagnoses: (1) Acquired immuno-deficiency syndrome; (2) disseminated histoplasmosis; (3) granulocytopenia, possibly due to AZT.

B20	Human immunodeficiency virus [HIV] disease
B39.9	Histoplasmosis, unspecified
D70.9	Neutropenia, unspecified
T37.5x5A	Adverse effect of antiviral drugs, initial encounter
0JH63XZ	Insertion of vascular access device into chest subcutaneous tissue and fascia, percutaneous approach

Comments: Even though histoplasmosis is stated as the current problem, it is related to the patient's AIDS, which is appropriately designated as the principal diagnosis. In the Index under the main term **Granulocytopenia,** see also "agranulocytosis." In this reference, see also **Neutropenia.** Adverse reaction to AZT is referenced in the Table of Drugs and Chemicals. The Hickman catheter is a "vascular access device" that is tunneled percutaneously through the jugular or subclavian vein to the chest.

6. Inpatient admission: The patient was admitted in an altered mental state, showing some confusion as well as ataxia, jaundice, and dizziness. Her husband reported that he felt that the problem related to a massive overusage of an herbal tea given to her by a "healer." She was told to use about a tablespoon per day in a cup of tea but instead had been drinking about a gallon a day. She had a fibroid mass diagnosed about one year earlier but refused conventional treatment. Instead, she was trying to cure it with the tea. After checking with the Poison Control Center, it was determined that the phenylbutazone in this particular brand of tea was probably what was causing her problems. Her mental status returned to its baseline state within 48 hours, and the other problems related to herbal tea consumption disappeared in the same time frame. The presence of a huge uterine mass was confirmed on CT scan, and surgery was offered but refused.

Discharge diagnoses: (1) Central nervous and digestive system problems secondary to herbal tea intoxication, (2) uterine mass.

T39.2x1A	Poisoning by pyrazolone derivatives, accidental (unintentional), initial encounter
R41.82	Altered mental status, unspecified
R27.0	Ataxia, unspecified
R17	Unspecified jaundice
R42	Dizziness and giddiness
N94.89	Other specified conditions associated with female genital organs and menstrual cycle

Comments: The poisoning code is sequenced as the principal diagnosis, with additional codes for each of the individual manifestations. Phenylbutazone is referenced in the Table of Drugs and Chemicals under **Phenyl,** butazone, poisoning, accidental. The T39.2x1A code includes the accidental intent. The uterine mass is not further identified as to type and so code N94.89 is assigned.

7. **Inpatient admission:** The patient, a young man, collapsed on the street after leaving a bar. An ambulance brought him to the emergency department in severe respiratory distress, which escalated to respiratory failure. He was endoscopically intubated, ventilatory support was initiated, and he was admitted. Respiratory arrest ensued. He died within three hours of admission. Autopsy findings indicated lethal levels of Valium, cocaine, marijuana, and ephedrine.

Discharge diagnosis: Respiratory failure secondary to overdoses of multiple substances.

T42.4x1A	Poisoning by benzodiazepines, accidental (unintentional), initial encounter
T40.5x1A	Poisoning by cocaine, accidental (unintentional), initial encounter
T40.7x1A	Poisoning by cannabis (derivatives), accidental (unintentional), initial encounter
T44.991A	Poisoning by other drug primarily affecting the autonomic nervous system, accidental (unintentional), initial encounter
J96.00	Acute respiratory failure, unspecified whether with hypoxia or hypercapnia
5A1935Z	Respiratory ventilation, less than 24 consecutive hours
0BH18EZ	Insertion of endotracheal airway into trachea, via natural or artificial opening endoscopic

Comments: When multiple drugs are responsible for a poisoning, each is assigned a separate code. Any one of the poisoning codes could have been designated as the principal diagnosis. The accidental intent is included in the poisoning code. Respiratory distress has evolved to acute respiratory failure as the manifestation of the poisoning, but the poisoning codes must be sequenced first. The patient was intubated and remained on ventilatory support, which qualifies as "Performance" for the root operation. This was for less than 24 hours, and so the code is 5A1935Z.

8. **Inpatient admission:** The patient was admitted for a transurethral resection of the prostate (TURP) for benign prostatic hypertrophy. He was taken to the operating room, but immediately following the induction with general anesthesia, atrial fibrillation developed. The procedure was canceled and the atrial fibrillation treated. It was determined that the arrhythmia was due to the anesthetic.

Discharge diagnoses: (1) Benign prostatic hypertrophy, (2) atrial fibrillation secondary to anesthesia.

N40.0	Enlarged prostate without lower urinary tract symptoms (LUTS)
I48.0	Atrial fibrillation
T41.45xA	Adverse effect of unspecified anesthetic, initial encounter
Z53.09	Procedure and treatment not carried out because of other contraindication

Comments: The development of a complication, atrial fibrillation, an adverse reaction to anesthesia, does not change the principal diagnosis. Even though the planned TURP was not carried out, the benign hypertrophy of the prostate was the condition responsible for the admission.

9. Inpatient admission: The patient was admitted with nausea and vomiting for the past 24 hours. He was found to have an elevated digoxin level, and after adjustment of dosage, the level came down and the nausea and vomiting ceased. On questioning, he seemed to be taking the digoxin correctly. A new prescription was written, and the patient's digoxin level was to be monitored.

Discharge diagnosis: Digoxin toxicity.

T46.0x5A	Adverse effect of cardiac-stimulant glycosides and drugs of similar action, initial encounter
R11.2	Nausea with vomiting, unspecified

Comments: ICD-10-CM includes the adverse effect in the T46 code, and this is listed first, followed by the manifestation of the adverse effect.

10. Inpatient admission: The patient was admitted with moderate persistent asthma, which had become intractable to management on an ambulatory care basis. The medications consisted of antibiotics, bronchodilators, and IV steroids. Unfortunately, her stay was prolonged because of an allergic reaction to two of the medications. Celestone and prednisone caused jitteriness and anxiety to the extent that Lorazepam was necessary.

Discharge diagnoses: (1) Severe asthma, (2) medication allergy.

J45.42	Moderate persistent asthma with status asthmaticus
T38.0x5A	Adverse effect of glucocorticoids and synthetic analogues, initial encounter
F41.9	Anxiety disorder, unspecified

Comments: Asthma is assigned to J45.42 to indicate moderate persistent asthma that is intractable, or with status asthmaticus. The allergy to Celestone and prednisone resulted in an anxiety state that represents an adverse reaction to drugs that were administered correctly. "Celestone" and "prednisone" are located in the Table of Drugs and Chemicals and carry the same T code, so it is reported only once.

11. Inpatient admission: The patient came to the outpatient area with swelling and discoloration of the right arm. She was admitted with a provisional diagnosis of axillary vein thrombosis. A venogram of the right arm showed nearly complete obstruction of the axillary vein with an intraluminal clot. She gave a history of having started on birth control pills recently, and it was felt that the drug (Orval) was the cause of the thrombosis. She was taken off the birth control pills and started on IV anticoagulation. When discharged, her prothrombin time was in the therapeutic range, and the arm pain and edema were better.

Discharge diagnosis: Right axillary vein thrombosis.

T38.4x5A	Adverse effect of oral contraceptives, initial encounter
I82.A11	Acute embolism and thrombosis of right axillary vein
B50MYZZ	Plain radiography of right upper extremity veins using other contrast

Comments: In ICD-10-CM the adverse effect code comes first. The axillary vein thrombosis is an adverse reaction to Orval. The adverse effect code for Orval can be located in the Table of Drugs and Chemicals by referencing **Contraceptives,** oral.

12. **Inpatient admission:** The patient, an elderly woman, was admitted with shortness of breath, dyspnea on exertion, fever, and productive cough. These problems were felt to represent lobar pneumonia. She was admitted for cultures and intravenous antibiotics. A chest film showed bilateral lung infiltrates. Erythromycin and Bactrim (also known as sulfamethoxazole and trimethoprim) were given intravenously. However, diarrhea resulted. These drugs were discontinued; when she was switched to Ceftin, her condition showed rapid improvement.

Discharge diagnoses: (1) Lobar pneumonia, (2) diarrhea.

J18.1	Lobar pneumonia, unspecified organism
T36.8x5A	Adverse effect of other systemic antibiotics, initial encounter
T36.3x5A	Adverse effect of macrolides, initial encounter
R19.7	Diarrhea, unspecified

Comments: The admitting symptoms are all integral to a diagnosis of lobar pneumonia. Diarrhea represents an adverse reaction to erythromycin and Bactrim. Separate adverse effect codes are assigned for each drug. Bactrim is not listed in the Table of Drugs and Chemicals, so the generic name, sulfamethoxazole and trimethoprim, is referenced in the Table of Drugs and Chemicals.

13. **Inpatient admission:** The patient, a young woman, was brought to the emergency department via ambulance. She was suffering from acute alcohol intoxication. She admitted, however, that she had also ingested a handful of Compazine and Advil (an ibuprofen), thinking they were vitamins and aspirin. In the emergency department, she was treated with charcoal and Narcan and admitted for observation. A psychiatric consultation was obtained, and the psychiatrist deemed the patient stable and not dangerous to herself or others. The patient agreed to obtain drug and alcohol treatment and was discharged.

Discharge diagnoses: (1) Acute alcohol intoxication; (2) multiple substance overdose, Compazine, Advil, and alcohol.

T43.3x1A	Poisoning by phenothiazine antipsychotics and neuroleptics, accidental (unintentional), initial encounter
T39.311A	Poisoning by propionic acid derivatives, accidental (unintentional), initial encounter
T51.91xA	Toxic effect of unspecified alcohol, accidental (unintentional), initial encounter
F10.129	Alcohol abuse with intoxication, unspecified

Comments: A poisoning code should be sequenced as the principal diagnosis because it is unlikely that alcohol intoxication alone would have required inpatient attention. This represents an accidental poisoning by Compazine and Advil because the patient thought she was taking vitamins and aspirin. The accidental intent is included in the T code. There is no entry for Advil in the Table of Drugs and Chemicals, but there is one for ibuprofen. Code F10.129 is assigned for acute alcohol abuse with intoxication without a diagnosis of alcoholism.

14. Inpatient admission: The patient was admitted with subdural hematoma that appeared to be related to the anticoagulation she had been on for some time. She underwent an initial CT scan of the brain, which confirmed the subdural hematoma. She had been on chronic Coumadin therapy and had also been taking aspirin as prescribed by her physician for a left lower-extremity deep venous thrombosis. Her Coumadin and aspirin were held, and the prothrombin time was measured on a daily basis. The Coumadin was adjusted, and the aspirin was discontinued. Her condition at discharge was good.

Discharge diagnoses: (1) Subdural hematoma secondary to medications; (2) chronic deep venous thrombosis, left leg.

T45.515A	Adverse effect of anticoagulants, initial encounter
T39.015A	Adverse effect of aspirin, initial encounter
I62.01	Nontraumatic acute subdural hemorrhage
I82.502	Chronic embolism and thrombosis of unspecified deep veins of left lower extremity
Z79.01	Long term (current) use of anticoagulants

Comments: The subdural hematoma is an adverse reaction involving both Coumadin and aspirin. Therefore, adverse effect codes are assigned for each drug from the Table of Drugs and Chemicals. Code Z79.01 is assigned for the long-term use of Coumadin (anticoagulant).

15. Inpatient admission: The patient fractured her left patella when she fell down the basement steps in her single-family home. An open reduction was performed with internal fixation yesterday. During recovery, she had problems with nausea, vomiting, and urinary retention secondary to morphine administration. The pain medication was changed to Demerol, and the symptoms subsided by the second day. The patient was discharged in satisfactory condition the same day.

Discharge diagnoses: (1) Closed fracture, left patella; (2) allergic reaction to morphine.

Procedure: Open reduction of patellar fracture with internal fixation.

S82.002	Unspecified fracture of left patella, initial encounter for closed fracture
W10.8xxA	Fall (on) (from) other stairs and steps, initial encounter
Y92.018	Other place in single-family (private) house as the place of occurrence of the external cause
R11.2	Nausea with vomiting, unspecified
R33.9	Retention of urine, unspecified
T40.2x5A	Adverse effect of other opioids, initial encounter
0QSF04Z	Reposition left patella with internal fixation device, open approach

Comments: Nausea and vomiting and urinary retention represent adverse reactions to morphine. These symptoms developed after admission, and the fracture of the patella remains the principal diagnosis.

21. COMPLICATIONS OF SURGERY AND MEDICAL CARE

1. Inpatient admission: The patient was suffering an acute rejection episode involving her left cadaveric renal transplant. She had undergone the transplant three months earlier for end-stage renal disease (ESRD) due to focal glomerulonephritis. An endoscopic-guided percutaneous biopsy of the transplanted kidney was performed, and it was deemed suitable for her to go home after a pulse of steroids.

Discharge diagnosis: Kidney transplant rejection.

T86.11	Kidney transplant rejection
0TB14ZX	Excision of left kidney, percutaneous endoscopic approach, diagnostic

Comments: Although a patient who has undergone kidney transplant may still have some form of chronic kidney disease (the kidney transplant may not fully restore kidney function), ESRD and focal glomerulonephritis should not be coded because there is no mention of these conditions being present during the current admission. The biopsy is a diagnostic "Excision," performed using a percutaneous approach, endoscopically guided.

2. Inpatient admission: The admitting diagnosis was revision of hip arthroplasty. The patient had undergone a total left hip arthroplasty five weeks earlier for osteoarthritis. The prosthesis worked well until the previous week, when she heard a pop. X-rays taken on admission showed a superior displacement of the left acetabular cup, which continued to migrate proximally despite bed rest. The left acetabular component of the prosthesis was revised by insertion of a 60-Ganz plate. Three days after surgery, the patient had a hemoglobin of 10.9 and was transfused with two units of packed red blood cells. Hemoglobin count improved, and the patient was discharged on the fifth postoperative day.

Discharge diagnoses: (1) Superior displacement, left acetabular cup prosthesis; (2) acute blood loss anemia.

T84.021A	Dislocation of internal left hip prosthesis, initial encounter
D62	Acute posthemorrhagic anemia
0SRE0KZ	Replacement of left hip joint, acetabular surface with nonautologous tissue substitute, open approach
30233N1	Transfusion of nonautologous red blood cells into peripheral vein, percutaneous approach

Comments: Displacement of an orthopedic device is classified as a mechanical complication. In the Alphabetic Index under the main term **Displacement**, the coder is directed to "see **Complications**, joint prosthesis mechanical" under the subterm "joint prosthesis." Code 0SRE0KZ is assigned for the revision of the hip replacement acetabular component, by replacing a portion of the acetabular component.

3. Inpatient admission: The patient was admitted for removal of a left knee prosthesis, which had caused persistent pain since it was placed three years earlier. A recurrent thrombophlebitis was also present in the right lower extremity and was currently being treated with Coumadin. The left knee prosthesis was examined via incision, and there was necrotic tissue of the bone ends (tibia and fibula), which was debrided. Components of the prosthesis were noted to be loosened, and the prosthesis was removed and replaced. Physical therapy was started, and the patient was discharged on antibiotics.

Discharge diagnoses: (1) Necrosis, bone; (2) malfunctioning left knee prosthesis; (3) thrombophlebitis, right leg.

T84.54xA	Infection and inflammatory reaction due to internal left knee prosthesis, initial encounter
T84.033A	Mechanical loosening of internal left knee prosthetic joint, initial encounter
Z79.01	Long term (current) use of anticoagulants
0SPD0JZ	Removal of synthetic substitute from left knee joint, open approach
0SRD0JZ	Replacement of left knee joint with synthetic substitute, open approach
0QBH0ZZ	Excision of left tibia, open approach
0QBK0ZZ	Excision of left fibula, open approach
F07L7ZZ	Manual therapy techniques treatment of musculo-skeletal system—lower back / lower extremity

Comments: In the left leg, there was a mechanical complication (loose components) of the prosthesis (T84.033A) as well as a nonmechanical complication, necrosis (T84.54xA). Either could be designated as the principal diagnosis. Code Z96.652, Presence of left artificial knee joint, is not assigned in accordance with instructions from the ICD-10-CM Official Coding Guidelines that a status code should not be used with a diagnosis code from one of the body system chapters, if the diagnosis code includes the information provided by the status code. In this case, the complication codes from category T84 indicate the presence of a left knee prosthetic joint, and therefore the status code does not provide additional information. Code Z79.01 is assigned to show the long-term use of Coumadin.

ICD-10-PCS codes are assigned for the "Removal" of the original prosthesis and "Replacement" with a new prosthesis. The debridement of the bone requires two codes, one for each site. Physical therapy is coded in the Physical Rehabilitation and Diagnostic Audiology Section.

4. Inpatient admission: Two months before admission, the patient completed 37 X-ray therapy treatments following resection of his tongue for removal of primary squamous cell carcinoma. He was admitted for evaluation and therapy of spontaneous extraoral drainage from an exposed bone plate of the left mandible. After debridement of the affected site via incision, he was discharged for follow-up care at the referring hospital.

Discharge diagnosis: Osteoradionecrosis of left mandible.

M27.2	Inflammatory conditions of jaws
Z85.810	Personal history of malignant neoplasm of tongue
Y84.2	Radiological procedure and radiotherapy as the cause of abnormal reaction of the patient, or of later complication, without mention of misadventure at the time of the procedure
0NBV0ZZ	Excision of left mandible, open approach

Comments: See the Alphabetic Index under the main term **Osteoradionecrosis,** subterm "jaw." Because the primary site of the neoplasm is no longer present or under active treatment, code Z85.810 is assigned. Code Y84.2 is assigned to identify the adverse effects of radiation therapy. For the procedure code, in the Index under the main term **Debridement,** excisional, see "Excision."

5. Inpatient admission: The patient underwent a laryngoscopy with biopsy in the ambulatory surgery area, and a primary neoplasm of the false vocal cords was confirmed. In the recovery room, she developed acute respiratory insufficiency and was placed on oxygen. Because of the severity of the respiratory insufficiency, she was admitted. By the third hospital day, her blood gases returned to normal, and she was discharged.

Discharge diagnoses: (1) Carcinoma of vocal cords, (2) postoperative respiratory insufficiency.

J95.2	Acute pulmonary insufficiency following nonthoracic surgery
C32.1	Malignant neoplasm of supraglottis
0CBS8ZX	Excision of larynx, via natural or artificial opening endoscopic, diagnostic

Comments: Postoperative respiratory insufficiency is an example of an intraoperative and postprocedural complication of the respiratory system not elsewhere classified, in category J95. The principal diagnosis is the condition necessitating admission as an inpatient, postoperative respiratory insufficiency. Codes for the ambulatory surgery and the condition for which it was performed are generally assigned when patients are admitted from the outpatient surgery unit.

6. Inpatient admission: The patient was admitted because of a displaced T tube, which was partially out of the common bile duct. The T tube was blocked by a malignant tumor of the pancreas, which caused the tube to buckle and leak. The patient was transferred to another hospital for care.

Discharge diagnoses: (1) Bile in peritoneum due to T tube partially out of common duct; (2) tumor, head of pancreas.

| T85.520A | Displacement of bile duct prosthesis, initial encounter |
| C25.0 | Malignant neoplasm of head of pancreas |

Comments: Code T85.520A is assigned by referencing the main term **Complication** in the Index, subterm "bile duct implant, mechanical, displacement." "Displacement" of a device is a mechanical complication.

7. Inpatient admission: The admission diagnoses were possible uterine septum and adnexal mass. A left ovarian cystic mass, which was thought to be an endometrioma and a uterine septum, was confirmed on hysteroscopy and laparoscopy. In the course of evaluation, a perforation of the left uterine horn occurred. Laparotomy was performed, and the cystic mass was excised from the ovary. The abdominal cavity was copiously irrigated and the uterine perforation repaired. Pathologic findings identified the cystic mass as a dermoid cyst of the ovary.

Discharge diagnoses: (1) Dermoid cyst, left ovary; (2) uterine septum; (3) inadvertent puncture, left uterine horn.

D27.1	Benign neoplasm of left ovary
Q51.2	Other doubling of uterus
N99.71	Accidental puncture and laceration of a genitourinary system organ or structure during a genitourinary system procedure
0UB10ZZ	Excision of left ovary, open approach
0UQ90ZZ	Repair uterus, open approach
0UJD8ZZ	Inspection of uterus and cervix, via natural or artificial opening endoscopic
0WJJ4ZZ	Inspection of pelvic cavity, percutaneous endoscopic approach

Comments: A dermoid cyst is benign per instructions in the Alphabetic Index under the main term **Cyst,** subterm "dermoid." ICD-10-CM has a code for the left and right ovary. The code for uterine septum is located by following the Index, main term **Septum,** subterm "uterus," see **Double,** uterus. For the accidental puncture code, see the Index under the main term **Complication,** subterms "accidental puncture" or "laceration." Follow the cross-reference to **Complications,** intraoperative, puncture or laceration, and then locate the subterm "specified NEC, genitourinary."

Therapeutic procedures are sequenced before diagnostic procedures. The hysteroscopy and laparoscopy were performed first, and then a laparotomy was necessary to remove the cyst and repair the uterine perforation.

8. **Inpatient admission:** The patient underwent a cystoscopy, with endoscopic passage of a stone basket up the left ureter and a contrast retrograde pyelogram of the kidneys, ureters, and bladder the day before admission. After release, she experienced terrible pain in the ureteral area and had to be readmitted for pain control. A repeat intravenous pyelogram was normal, and laboratory studies were all within normal limits. By the end of the second day, her pain was controlled with oral medications, and she was discharged.

Discharge diagnosis: Postoperative pain of undetermined cause.

G89.18	Other acute postprocedural pain
N23	Unspecified renal colic
0TC78ZZ	Extirpation of matter from left ureter, via natural or artificial opening endoscopic
BT14YZZ	Fluoroscopy of kidneys, ureters and bladder using other contrast

Comments: Assign code G89.18 as the principal diagnosis because the stated reason for the admission is documented as postoperative pain control. The narrative indicates that the pain was in the ureteral area; therefore, code N23 is assigned to provide greater specificity regarding the location of the postoperative pain. Because the surgery was performed the preceding day at the same facility, the diagnosis and procedure codes for the outpatient encounter are added.

9. **Inpatient admission:** The patient underwent a cold conization of the cervix and fractional dilatation and curettage for postmenopausal bleeding in the outpatient surgery center. The surgery was uncomplicated, and the operative site was dry at the conclusion of the procedure. An examination of tissue rendered a pathologic diagnosis of severe cervical dysplasia, CIN-III. Within two hours postoperatively, there was excessive bleeding and a vaginal pack was placed. She bled through the pack and was then admitted for suture repair of site of the previous cervical biopsy. Postoperatively, she remained dry with no further problems and was discharged in good condition.

Discharge diagnoses: (1) Severe cervical dysplasia, CIN-III; (2) postoperative bleeding.

N99.820	Postprocedural hemorrhage and hematoma of a genitourinary system organ or structure following a genitourinary system procedure
D06.9	Carcinoma in situ of cervix, unspecified
N95.0	Postmenopausal bleeding
0UQC3ZZ	Repair cervix, percutaneous approach
0UBC7ZZ	Excision of cervix, via natural or artificial opening
0UDB7ZZ	Extraction of endometrium, via natural or artificial opening

Comments: The principal diagnosis is postoperative bleeding, the reason for inpatient admission. No additional code is required to describe postoperative bleeding. A diagnosis of CIN-III with severe dysplasia of the cervix is coded to D06.9. An additional code is assigned for the postmenopausal bleeding, which was the reason for the original outpatient surgery, and for the dilatation and curettage as well as the suture of the cervix because they were performed within a brief period of time before admission.

10. Inpatient admission: The patient had a subtrochanteric stress fracture of the left femur, which had been repaired with pin insertion three weeks earlier. She returned with an infection of the operative wound site and delayed healing of the fracture. A wide excisional debridement of the infection site of the soft tissue was carried out via incision. No definite infection could be demonstrated within the bone. Cultures of the operative wound grew *Staphylococcus aureus*, sensitive to everything, and the patient was maintained on IV antibiotics until discharge.

Discharge diagnosis: Deep soft tissue infection, left thigh.

T81.4xxA	Infection following a procedure, initial encounter
M84.352G	Stress fracture, left femur, subsequent encounter for fracture with delayed healing
B95.6	Staphylococcus aureus as the cause of diseases classified elsewhere
0JBM0ZZ	Excision of left upper leg subcutaneous tissue and fascia, open approach

Comments: The postoperative wound infection was of the soft tissue incision site only, not of the site of pin insertion into the bone. The wound infection code, T81.4xxA, represents an initial encounter, as this is the first encounter for the infection. The stress fracture code has the seventh-character qualifier to indicate that this is a subsequent encounter for a fracture with delayed healing. Code 0JBM0ZZ is assigned for the wide excisional debridement of the postoperative wound infection of the soft tissue.

11. Inpatient admission: The patient underwent a cervical diskectomy and fusion last year. The pain improved for a few months but has recurred. He was readmitted for further surgery. A left C3-C4, C5-C6, and C6-C7 posterior cervical decompressive laminectomy with foraminotomy was performed. There was considerable postoperative pain, well out of proportion to what would be expected for this surgery. He remained in the hospital the week following surgery, primarily to receive intramuscular pain medications.

Discharge diagnoses: (1) Cervical spondylosis, (2) severe postoperative back pain.

M47.812	Spondylosis without myelopathy or radiculopathy, cervical region
M54.9	Dorsalgia, unspecified
G89.18	Other acute postprocedural pain
0RB30ZZ	Excision of cervical vertebral disc, open approach

Comments: Code G89.18, Other acute postprocedural pain, is assigned to identify an unusual amount of postoperative pain. This is not coded as a postoperative complication. Code M54.9 is coded for additional specificity to identify the site of the pain.

12. **Inpatient admission:** A month earlier, the patient had undergone open reduction and internal fixation of a traumatic fracture of the left femur. She came to the emergency department with a severe and deep infection of the left thigh. She was admitted and taken to surgery immediately, where a wide excisional debridement of the subcutaneous tissue of the infection was carried out and hardware was removed from the upper portion of the femur. Cultures of fixation pins grew *Staphylococcus aureus*, and she was maintained on IV Oxacillin. She was to continue antibiotics at home after discharge.

Discharge diagnosis: Staphylococcal infection due to orthopedic fixation device.

T84.621A	Infection and inflammatory reaction due to internal fixation device of left femur, initial encounter
B95.6	Staphylococcus aureus as the cause of diseases classified elsewhere
Z87.81	Personal history of (healed) traumatic fracture
0JBM0ZZ	Excision of left upper leg subcutaneous tissue and fascia, open approach
0QP704Z	Removal of internal fixation device from left upper femur, open approach

Comments: Because the infection resulted from the presence of an orthopedic device, code T84.621A is used. Z87.81 indicates a history of traumatic fracture.

13. **Inpatient admission:** This acutely ill patient was admitted with fever, weakness, and chills. He had undergone a bilateral herniorrhaphy four days before admission. He is now experiencing some urgency on urination and dysuria. On admission to the hospital, the operative incisions were slightly red and tender and the abdomen somewhat distended. Blood cultures and wound cultures revealed a heavy growth of *Staphylococcus aureus*, which also grew on a urine culture. *Enterococcus faecalis* also grew on the urine culture. The chills and fever receded with IV antibiotics. It was believed that the patient's problems represented postoperative complications of the herniorrhaphy.

Discharge diagnoses: (1) Postoperative sepsis and urinary tract infection, (2) postoperative wound infection.

T81.4xxA	Infection following a procedure, initial encounter
N99.89	Other postprocedural complications and disorders of genitourinary system
N39.0	Urinary tract infection, site not specified
B95.6	Staphylococcus aureus as the cause of diseases classified elsewhere
B95.2	Enterococcus as the cause of diseases classified elsewhere
A41.0	Sepsis due to Staphylococcus aureus
Y83.8	Other surgical procedures as the cause of abnormal reaction of the patient, or of later complication, without mention of misadventure at the time of the procedure

Comments: The reason for the admission is the postoperative infection. The T81.4xxA code shows the postoperative infection. Code N99.89 indicates that this is a postprocedural complication of the genitourinary system, and code N39.0 indicates that this is a UTI. The causative agents are also coded. ICD-10-CM includes the sepsis and causative agent in one code, A41.0.

Index

---

*Page numbers in color refer to tables, figures, or illustrations.